Audi A4
Service and Repair Manual

A K Legg LAE MIMI & Spencer Drayton

Models covered

Audi A4 Saloon & Estate (Avant)

1595 & 1781cc 4-cylinder petrol and 1896cc 4-cylinder diesel (including turbo versions)

Does not include S4, V6 (petrol/diesel), or Quattro (4x4) models

(3575 - 312 - 1AP3)

© J H Haynes & Co. Ltd. 2010

A book in the **Haynes Service and Repair Manual Series**

ISBN **978 1 78521 379 3**

British Library Cataloguing in Publication Data
A catalogue record for this book is available from the British Library.

J H Haynes & Co. Ltd.
Haynes North America, Inc

www.haynes.com

Disclaimer

There are risks associated with automotive repairs. The ability to make repairs depends on the individual's skill, experience and proper tools. Individuals should act with due care and acknowledge and assume the risk of performing automotive repairs.

The purpose of this manual is to provide comprehensive, useful and accessible automotive repair information, to help you get the best value from your vehicle. However, this manual is not a substitute for a professional certified technician or mechanic.

This repair manual is produced by a third party and is not associated with an individual vehicle manufacturer. If there is any doubt or discrepancy between this manual and the owner's manual or the factory service manual, please refer to the factory service manual or seek assistance from a professional certified technician or mechanic.

Even though we have prepared this manual with extreme care and every attempt is made to ensure that the information in this manual is correct, neither the publisher nor the author can accept responsibility for loss, damage or injury caused by any errors in, or omissions from, the information given.

Contents

LIVING WITH YOUR AUDI A4

Roadside Repairs

Weekly Checks

MAINTENANCE

Routine maintenance and servicing

Contents

REPAIRS AND OVERHAUL

Engine and Associated Systems

Transmission

Brakes and Suspension

Body Equipment

REFERENCE

Index

The Audi A4 models covered by this manual were first introduced to the UK in February 1995. Mechanically there is a fundamental similarity to the VW Passat, but with the engines fitted 'in-line' instead of transverse. Saloon and Estate (Avant) models are available, equipped with a variety of engine sizes. This manual covers the 4-cylinder petrol and diesel engine models, including both normally-aspirated and turbocharged versions. The smallest engine is the petrol 1600 SOHC, and in addition there are 1781 cc DOHC petrol engines. All diesel engines are SOHC turbocharged.

Fully-independent front suspension is fitted, with the components attached to a subframe assembly; the rear suspension is semi-independent, with a torsion beam and trailing arms.

A five-speed manual gearbox is fitted as standard to all models.

A wide range of standard and optional equipment is available within the model range to suit most tastes, including an anti-lock braking system and air conditioning.

For the home mechanic, the A4 is quite straightforward to maintain, and most of the items requiring frequent attention are easily accessible.

Your Audi A4 Manual

The aim of this manual is to help you get the best value from your vehicle. It can do so in several ways. It can help you decide what work must be done (even should you choose to get it done by a garage). It will also provide information on routine maintenance and servicing, and give a logical course of action and diagnosis when random faults occur. However, it is hoped that you will use the manual by tackling the work yourself. On simpler jobs it may even be quicker than booking the car into a garage and going there twice, to leave and collect it. Perhaps most important, a lot of money can be saved by avoiding the costs a garage must charge to cover its labour and overheads.

Audi A4 petrol Saloon

Audi A4 diesel Estate (Avant)

The manual has drawings and descriptions to show the function of the various components so that their layout can be understood. Tasks are described and photographed in a clear step-by-step sequence. The illustrations are numbered by the Section number and paragraph number to which they relate - if there is more than one illustration per paragraph, the sequence is denoted alphabetically.

References to the 'left' or 'right' of the vehicle are in the sense of a person in the driver's seat, facing forwards.

Acknowledgements

Thanks are due to Duckhams Oils, who provided lubrication data. Thanks are also due to Draper Tools Limited, who provided some of the workshop tools, and to all those people at Sparkford who helped in the production of this manual.

This manual is not a direct reproduction of the vehicle manufacturer's data, and its publication should not be taken as implying any technical approval by the vehicle manufacturers or importers.

We take great pride in the accuracy of information given in this manual, but vehicle manufacturers make alterations and design changes during the production run of a particular vehicle of which they do not inform us. No liability can be accepted by the authors or publishers for loss, damage or injury caused by any errors in, or omissions from, the information given.

Project vehicles

The main vehicle used in the preparation of this manual, and which appears in many of the photographic sequences, was a 1997 Audi A4 1.8 litre petrol Saloon. Also included was a 1998 1.9 litre turbo-diesel Estate.

The Audi A4 Team

Haynes manuals are produced by dedicated and enthusiastic people working in close co-operation. The team responsible for the creation of this book included:

Authors	A.K. Legg LAE MIMI
	Spencer Drayton
Page Make-up	Steve Churchill
Workshop manager	Paul Buckland
Photo Scans	John Martin
Cover illustration & Line Art	Roger Healing
Wiring diagrams	Matthew Marke

We hope the book will help you to get the maximum enjoyment from your car. By carrying out routine maintenance as described you will ensure your car's reliability and preserve its resale value.

Working on your car can be dangerous. This page shows just some of the potential risks and hazards, with the aim of creating a safety-conscious attitude.

General hazards

Scalding

• Don't remove the radiator or expansion tank cap while the engine is hot.
• Engine oil, automatic transmission fluid or power steering fluid may also be dangerously hot if the engine has recently been running.

Burning

• Beware of burns from the exhaust system and from any part of the engine. Brake discs and drums can also be extremely hot immediately after use.

Crushing

• When working under or near a raised vehicle, always supplement the jack with axle stands, or use drive-on ramps. *Never venture under a car which is only supported by a jack.*
• Take care if loosening or tightening high-torque nuts when the vehicle is on stands. Initial loosening and final tightening should be done with the wheels on the ground.

Fire

• Fuel is highly flammable; fuel vapour is explosive.
• Don't let fuel spill onto a hot engine.
• Do not smoke or allow naked lights (including pilot lights) anywhere near a vehicle being worked on. Also beware of creating sparks (electrically or by use of tools).
• Fuel vapour is heavier than air, so don't work on the fuel system with the vehicle over an inspection pit.
• Another cause of fire is an electrical overload or short-circuit. Take care when repairing or modifying the vehicle wiring.
• Keep a fire extinguisher handy, of a type suitable for use on fuel and electrical fires.

Electric shock

• Ignition HT voltage can be dangerous, especially to people with heart problems or a pacemaker. Don't work on or near the ignition system with the engine running or the ignition switched on.

• Mains voltage is also dangerous. Make sure that any mains-operated equipment is correctly earthed. Mains power points should be protected by a residual current device (RCD) circuit breaker.

Fume or gas intoxication

• Exhaust fumes are poisonous; they often contain carbon monoxide, which is rapidly fatal if inhaled. Never run the engine in a confined space such as a garage with the doors shut.
• Fuel vapour is also poisonous, as are the vapours from some cleaning solvents and paint thinners.

Poisonous or irritant substances

• Avoid skin contact with battery acid and with any fuel, fluid or lubricant, especially antifreeze, brake hydraulic fluid and Diesel fuel. Don't syphon them by mouth. If such a substance is swallowed or gets into the eyes, seek medical advice.
• Prolonged contact with used engine oil can cause skin cancer. Wear gloves or use a barrier cream if necessary. Change out of oil-soaked clothes and do not keep oily rags in your pocket.
• Air conditioning refrigerant forms a poisonous gas if exposed to a naked flame (including a cigarette). It can also cause skin burns on contact.

Asbestos

• Asbestos dust can cause cancer if inhaled or swallowed. Asbestos may be found in gaskets and in brake and clutch linings. When dealing with such components it is safest to assume that they contain asbestos.

Special hazards

Hydrofluoric acid

• This extremely corrosive acid is formed when certain types of synthetic rubber, found in some O-rings, oil seals, fuel hoses etc, are exposed to temperatures above 400°C. The rubber changes into a charred or sticky substance containing the acid. *Once formed, the acid remains dangerous for years. If it gets onto the skin, it may be necessary to amputate the limb concerned.*
• When dealing with a vehicle which has suffered a fire, or with components salvaged from such a vehicle, wear protective gloves and discard them after use.

The battery

• Batteries contain sulphuric acid, which attacks clothing, eyes and skin. Take care when topping-up or carrying the battery.
• The hydrogen gas given off by the battery is highly explosive. Never cause a spark or allow a naked light nearby. Be careful when connecting and disconnecting battery chargers or jump leads.

Air bags

• Air bags can cause injury if they go off accidentally. Take care when removing the steering wheel and/or facia. Special storage instructions may apply.

Diesel injection equipment

• Diesel injection pumps supply fuel at very high pressure. Take care when working on the fuel injectors and fuel pipes.

⚠ *Warning: Never expose the hands, face or any other part of the body to injector spray; the fuel can penetrate the skin with potentially fatal results.*

Remember...

DO

• Do use eye protection when using power tools, and when working under the vehicle.

• Do wear gloves or use barrier cream to protect your hands when necessary.

• Do get someone to check periodically that all is well when working alone on the vehicle.

• Do keep loose clothing and long hair well out of the way of moving mechanical parts.

• Do remove rings, wristwatch etc, before working on the vehicle – especially the electrical system.

• Do ensure that any lifting or jacking equipment has a safe working load rating adequate for the job.

DON'T

• Don't attempt to lift a heavy component which may be beyond your capability – get assistance.

• Don't rush to finish a job, or take unverified short cuts.

• Don't use ill-fitting tools which may slip and cause injury.

• Don't leave tools or parts lying around where someone can trip over them. Mop up oil and fuel spills at once.

• Don't allow children or pets to play in or near a vehicle being worked on.

The following pages are intended to help in dealing with common roadside emergencies and breakdowns. You will find more detailed fault finding information at the back of the manual, and repair information in the main chapters.

If your car won't start and the starter motor doesn't turn

☐ If it's a model with automatic transmission, make sure the selector is in 'P' or 'N'.
☐ Open the bonnet and make sure that the battery terminals are clean and tight.
☐ Switch on the headlights and try to start the engine. If the headlights go very dim when you're trying to start, the battery is probably flat. Get out of trouble by jump starting (see next page) using a friend's car.

If your car won't start even though the starter motor turns as normal

☐ Is there fuel in the tank?
☐ Is there moisture on electrical components under the bonnet? Switch off the ignition, then wipe off any obvious dampness with a dry cloth. Spray a water-repellent aerosol product (WD-40 or equivalent) on ignition and fuel system electrical connectors like those shown in the photos. Pay special attention to the ignition coil wiring connector and HT leads. (Note that Diesel engines don't normally suffer from damp.)

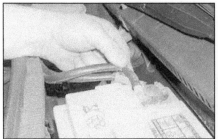

A Check the condition and security of the battery connections

B Check the fuel injection system airflow meter wiring is secure

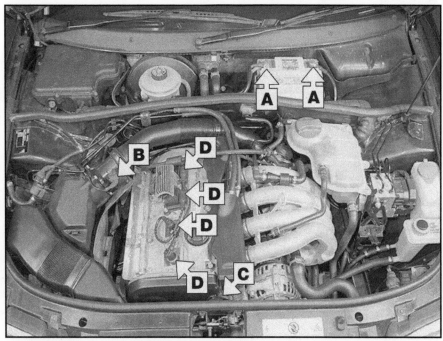

Check that electrical connections are secure (with the ignition switched off) and spray them with a water dispersant spray like WD-40 if you suspect a problem due to damp

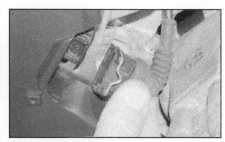

C Check the ignition system Hall sender wiring is secure

D Check that the HT leads are securely connected to the spark plugs on petrol engines. To do this, remove the engine top cover first

Jump starting

Jump starting will get you out of trouble, but you must correct whatever made the battery go flat in the first place. There are three possibilities:

1 *The battery has been drained by repeated attempts to start, or by leaving the lights on.*

2 *The charging system is not working properly (alternator drivebelt slack or broken, alternator wiring fault or alternator itself faulty).*

3 *The battery itself is at fault (electrolyte low, or battery worn out).*

When jump-starting a car using a booster battery, observe the following precautions:

✔ Before connecting the booster battery, make sure that the ignition is switched off.

✔ Ensure that all electrical equipment (lights, heater, wipers, etc) is switched off.

✔ Take note of any special precautions printed on the battery case.

✔ Make sure that the booster battery is the same voltage as the discharged one in the vehicle.

✔ If the battery is being jump-started from the battery in another vehicle, the two vehicles MUST NOT TOUCH each other.

✔ Make sure that the transmission is in neutral (or PARK, in the case of automatic transmission).

1 Connect one end of the red jump lead to the positive (+) terminal of the flat battery

2 Connect the other end of the red lead to the positive (+) terminal of the booster battery.

3 Connect one end of the black jump lead to the negative (-) terminal of the booster battery

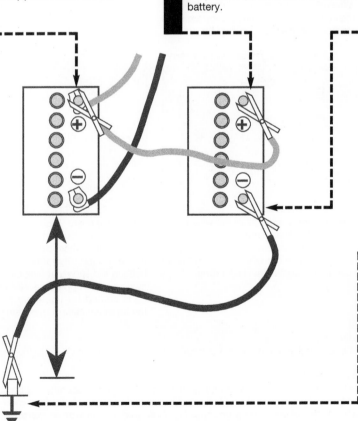

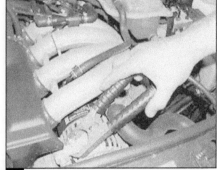

4 Connect the other end of the black jump lead to a bolt or bracket on the engine block, well away from the battery, on the vehicle to be started.

5 Make sure that the jump leads will not come into contact with the fan, drive-belts or other moving parts of the engine.

6 Start the engine using the booster battery and run it at idle speed. Switch on the lights, rear window demister and heater blower motor, then disconnect the jump leads in the reverse order of connection. Turn off the lights etc.

Wheel changing

Some of the details shown here will vary according to model. For instance, the location of the spare wheel and jack is not the same on all cars. However, the basic principles apply to all vehicles.

Warning: Do not change a wheel in a situation where you risk being hit by another vehicle. On busy roads, try to stop in a lay-by or a gateway. Be wary of passing traffic while changing the wheel - it is easy to become distracted by the job in hand.

Preparation

- ☐ When a puncture occurs, stop as soon as it is safe to do so.
- ☐ Park on firm level ground, if possible, and well out of the way of other traffic.
- ☐ Use hazard warning lights if necessary.
- ☐ If you have one, use a warning triangle to alert other drivers of your presence.
- ☐ Apply the handbrake and engage first or reverse gear (or Park on models with automatic transmission).
- ☐ Chock the wheel diagonally opposite the one being removed – a couple of large stones will do for this.
- ☐ If the ground is soft, use a flat piece of wood to spread the load under the jack.

Changing the wheel

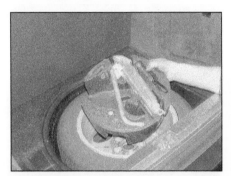

1 The spare is stored beneath the luggage compartment floor covering. The jack and tool kit are located in the spare wheel. Unscrew the bolt and remove the tool kit. Lift the spare wheel from the well in the floor.

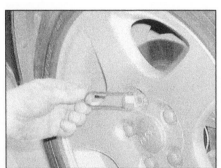

2 Where fitted, insert a screwdriver into the slot and lever the cap from the wheel. Where fitted, use the hook in the tool kit to pull the cover from the wheel. If caps are fitted to each bolt, use the tool to pull off the covers.

3 Loosen each wheel bolt by half a turn. Use the special adapter where a locking wheel bolt is fitted.

4 Locate the jack head below the reinforced jacking point nearest the wheel to be changed. The jacking point is indicated by a diamond pressed into the sill. Turn the handle to raise the wheel clear of the ground.

5 Remove the bolts and lift the wheel from the vehicle. After removing the first bolt, screw in the guide as an aid to fitting the spare wheel. Place the wheel beneath the sill as a precaution against the jack failing.

6 Fit the spare wheel and remove the guide pin, then tighten the bolts moderately with the wheel brace. Lower the vehicle to the ground, then finally tighten the wheel bolts in a diagonal sequence. Refit the wheel cover/cap as applicable. Note that the wheel bolts should be tightened to the specified torque at the earliest opportunity.

Finally...

- ☐ Remove the wheel chocks.
- ☐ Stow the jack and tools in the correct locations in the car.
- ☐ Check the tyre pressure on the wheel just fitted. If it is low, or if you don't have a pressure gauge with you, drive slowly to the nearest garage and inflate the tyre to the right pressure.
- ☐ Have the damaged tyre or wheel repaired as soon as possible.

Note: *If a temporary 'space-saver' spare wheel has been fitted, special conditions apply to its use. This type of spare wheel is only intended for use in an emergency, and should not remain fitted any longer than it takes to get the punctured wheel repaired. While the temporary wheel is in use, do not exceed 50 mph (80 km/h), and avoid harsh acceleration, braking or cornering. Note that, besides being narrower than a normal roadwheel, the temporary spare wheel is of smaller diameter; therefore, since ground clearance will be slightly reduced with the temporary spare in use, take care when travelling over rough ground.*

Identifying leaks

Puddles on the garage floor or drive, or obvious wetness under the bonnet or underneath the car, suggest a leak that needs investigating. It can sometimes be difficult to decide where the leak is coming from, especially if the engine bay is very dirty already. Leaking oil or fluid can also be blown rearwards by the passage of air under the car, giving a false impression of where the problem lies.

 Warning: Most automotive oils and fluids are poisonous. Wash them off skin, and change out of contaminated clothing, without delay.

 HAYNES HiNT *The smell of a fluid leaking from the car may provide a clue to what's leaking. Some fluids are distinctively coloured. It may help to clean the car carefully and to park it over some clean paper overnight as an aid to locating the source of the leak.*
Remember that some leaks may only occur while the engine is running.

Sump oil

Engine oil may leak from the drain plug...

Oil from filter

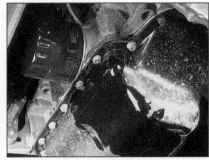

...or from the base of the oil filter.

Gearbox oil

Gearbox oil can leak from the seals at the inboard ends of the driveshafts.

Antifreeze

Leaking antifreeze often leaves a crystalline deposit like this.

Brake fluid

A leak occurring at a wheel is almost certainly brake fluid.

Power steering fluid

Power steering fluid may leak from the pipe connectors on the steering rack.

Towing

When all else fails, you may find yourself having to get a tow home – or of course you may be helping somebody else. Long-distance recovery should only be done by a garage or breakdown service. For shorter distances, DIY towing using another car is easy enough, but observe the following points:
☐ Use a proper tow-rope – they are not expensive. The vehicle being towed must display an ON TOW sign in its rear window.
☐ Always turn the ignition key to the 'on' position when the vehicle is being towed, so that the steering lock is released, and that the direction indicator and brake lights will work.
☐ A rear towing eye is provided below the right-hand side of the bumper. The front towing eye is provided behind the cover on the right-hand side of the front bumper -

carefully pull on the plastic tab provided on the cover **(see illustration)**.
☐ Before being towed, release the handbrake and select neutral on the transmission.
☐ Note that greater-than-usual pedal pressure will be required to operate the brakes, since the vacuum servo unit is only operational with the engine running.
☐ On models with power steering, greater-than-usual steering effort will also be required.
☐ The driver of the car being towed must keep the tow-rope taut at all times to avoid snatching.
☐ Make sure that both drivers know the route before setting off.
☐ Only drive at moderate speeds and keep the distance towed to a minimum. Drive smoothly and allow plenty of time for slowing down at junctions.

☐ On models with automatic transmission, special precautions apply. If in doubt, do not tow, or transmission damage may result.

⚠ *Warning: To prevent damage to the catalytic converter on petrol models, do not tow or push-start a vehicle more than 50 metres. Where possible, use jump leads (see Jump starting).*

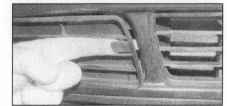

Pull on the tab to release the cover

Introduction

There are some very simple checks which need only take a few minutes to carry out, but which could save you a lot of inconvenience and expense.

These *Weekly checks* require no great skill or special tools, and the small amount of time they take to perform could prove to be very well spent, for example;

☐ Keeping an eye on tyre condition and pressures, will not only help to stop them wearing out prematurely, but could also save your life.

☐ Many breakdowns are caused by electrical problems. Battery-related faults are particularly common, and a quick check on a regular basis will often prevent the majority of these.

☐ If your car develops a brake fluid leak, the first time you might know about it is when your brakes don't work properly. Checking the level regularly will give advance warning of this kind of problem.

☐ If the oil or coolant levels run low, the cost of repairing any engine damage will be far greater than fixing the leak, for example.

Underbonnet check points

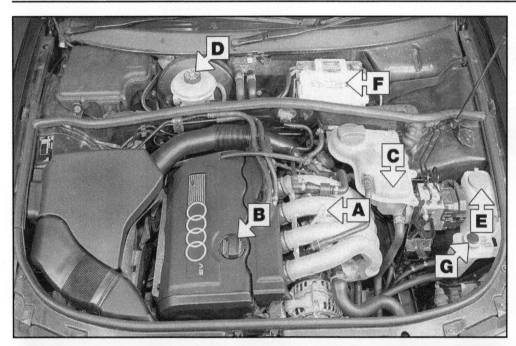

◀ 1.8 litre petrol

A *Engine oil level dipstick*

B *Engine oil filler cap*

C *Coolant expansion tank*

D *Brake fluid reservoir*

E *Screen washer fluid reservoir*

F *Battery*

G *Power steering fluid reservoir*

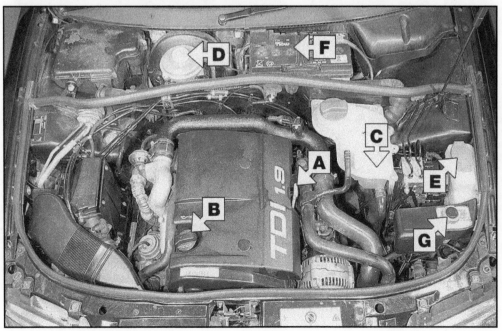

◀ 1.9 litre diesel

A *Engine oil level dipstick*

B *Engine oil filler cap*

C *Coolant expansion tank*

D *Brake fluid reservoir*

E *Screen washer fluid reservoir*

F *Battery*

G *Power steering fluid reservoir*

Engine oil level

Before you start

✔ Make sure that your car is on level ground.
✔ Check the oil level before the car is driven, or at least 5 minutes after the engine has been switched off.

 If the oil is checked immediately after driving the vehicle, some of the oil will remain in the upper engine components, resulting in an inaccurate reading on the dipstick!

The correct oil

Modern engines place great demands on their oil. It is very important that the correct oil for your car is used (see Lubricants and fluids).

Car Care

● If you have to add oil frequently, you should check whether you have any oil leaks. Place some clean paper under the car overnight, and check for stains in the morning. If there are no leaks, the engine may be burning oil.

● Always maintain the level between the upper and lower dipstick marks (see photo 3). If the level is too low severe engine damage may occur. Oil seal failure may result if the engine is overfilled by adding too much oil.

1 The dipstick is located on the left-hand side of the engine (see *Underbonnet check points* for exact location). Withdraw the dipstick.

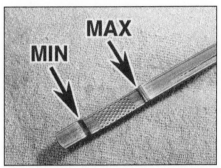

3 Note the oil level on the end of the dipstick, which should be between the upper and lower mark. Approximately 1.0 litre of oil will raise the level from the lower mark to the upper mark.

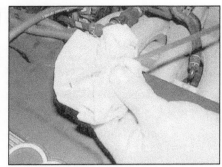

2 Using a clean rag or paper towel, wipe all oil from the dipstick. Insert the clean dipstick into the tube as far as it will go, then withdraw it again.

4 Oil is added through the filler cap on top of the engine. Turn the cap through a quarter-turn anticlockwise and withdraw it. Top-up the level. A funnel may help to reduce spillage. Add the oil slowly, checking the level on the dipstick often. Do not overfill.

Coolant level

 Warning: DO NOT attempt to remove the expansion tank pressure cap when the engine is hot, as there is a very great risk of scalding. Do not leave open containers of coolant about, as it is poisonous.

Car Care

● With a sealed-type cooling system, adding coolant should not be necessary on a regular basis. If frequent topping-up is required, it is likely there is a leak. Check the radiator, all hoses and joint faces for signs of staining or wetness, and rectify as necessary.

● It is important that antifreeze is used in the cooling system all year round, not just during the winter months. Don't top-up with water alone, as the antifreeze will become too diluted.

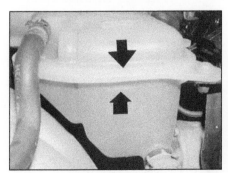

1 The coolant level varies with the temperature of the engine. When the engine is cold, the coolant level should be between the MIN and MAX marks.

2 If topping-up is necessary, wait until the engine is cold. Slowly unscrew the cap to release any pressure present in the cooling system, and remove the cap.

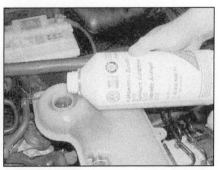

3 Add a mixture of water and antifreeze to the expansion tank until the coolant level is on the MAX mark.

Brake (and clutch) fluid level

Warning:
● *Brake fluid can harm your eyes and damage painted surfaces, so use extreme caution when handling and pouring it.*
● *Do not use fluid that has been standing open for some time, as it absorbs moisture from the air, which can cause a dangerous loss of braking effectiveness.*

● *Make sure that your car is on level ground.*
● *The fluid level in the reservoir will drop slightly as the brake pads wear down, but the fluid level must never be allowed to drop below the "MIN" mark.*

Safety First!
● If the reservoir requires repeated topping-up this is an indication of a fluid leak somewhere in the system, which should be investigated immediately.

● If a leak is suspected, the car should not be driven until the braking system has been checked. Never take any risks where brakes are concerned.

1 The MIN and MAX marks are indicated on the reservoir. The fluid level must be kept between the marks at all times.

2 If topping-up is necessary, first wipe clean the area around the filler cap to prevent dirt entering the hydraulic system. Unscrew the reservoir cap.

3 Carefully add fluid, taking care not to spill it onto the surrounding components. Use only the specified fluid; mixing different types can cause damage to the system. On completion, securely refit the cap and wipe away any spilt fluid. With the ignition switched on, check the operation of the brake fluid low level warning lamp by having an assistant depress the button on the top of the reservoir cap.

Power steering fluid level

Before you start:
✔ Park the vehicle on level ground.
✔ With the engine idling, turn the steering wheel slowly from lock to lock 2 or 3 times and set the front wheels at the straight-ahead position, then stop the engine.

✔ For the check to be accurate, the engine must be at operating temperature, and the steering must not be turned once the engine has been stopped.

Safety First!
● The need for frequent topping-up indicates a leak, which should be investigated immediately.

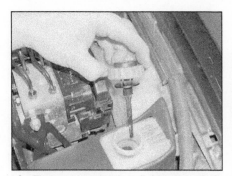

1 The power steering fluid reservoir is located on the left-hand side of the engine compartment. Slowly unscrew and remove the filler cap, which incorporates a fluid level dipstick.

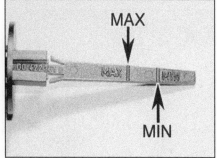

2 Check that the fluid level is between the MIN and MAX marks on the dipstick, preferably near the MAX mark. If necessary, wipe the dipstick with a clean cloth, then place it on the filler neck base and remove again.

3 Where topping-up is required, add the specified type of fluid until the level reaches the MAX mark. On completion refit and tighten the cap.

Battery

Caution: Before carrying out any work on the vehicle battery, read the precautions given in Safety first at the start of this manual.

✔ Make sure that the battery tray is in good condition, and that the clamp is tight. Corrosion on the tray, retaining clamp and the battery itself can be removed with a solution of water and baking soda. Thoroughly rinse all cleaned areas with water. Any metal parts damaged by corrosion should be covered with a zinc-based primer, then painted.

✔ Periodically (approximately every three months), check the charge condition of the battery as described in Chapter 5A.

✔ If the battery is flat, and you need to jump start your vehicle, see **Roadside Repairs**.

1 The battery is located on the bulkhead at the rear of the engine compartment.

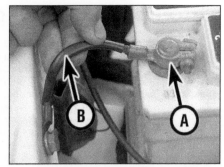

2 Check the tightness of battery clamps (A) to ensure good electrical connections. You should not be able to move them. Also check each cable (B) for cracks and frayed conductors.

HAYNES HiNT

Battery corrosion can be kept to a minimum by applying a layer of petroleum jelly to the clamps and terminals after they are reconnected.

3 If corrosion (white, fluffy deposits) is evident, remove the cables from the battery terminals, clean them with a small wire brush, then refit them. Automotive stores sell a tool for cleaning the battery post . . .

4 . . . as well as the battery cable clamps

Electrical systems

✔ Check all external lights and the horn. Refer to the appropriate Sections of Chapter 12 for details if any of the circuits are found to be inoperative.

✔ Visually check all accessible wiring connectors, harnesses and retaining clips for security, and for signs of chafing or damage.

HAYNES HiNT *If you need to check your brake lights and indicators unaided, back up to a wall or garage door and operate the lights. The reflected light should show if they are working properly.*

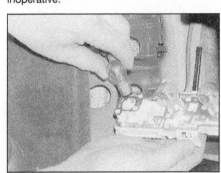

1 If a single indicator light, brake light or headlight has failed, it is likely that a bulb has blown and will need to be replaced. Refer to Chapter 12 for details. If both brake lights have failed, it is possible that the brake light switch operated by the brake pedal has failed. Refer to Chapter 9 for details.

2 If more than one indicator light or headlight has failed, it is likely that either a fuse has blown or that there is a fault in the circuit (see Chapter 12). The main fusebox is located beneath a cover on the driver's end of the facia panel; further fuses are located in the engine compartment. On diesel models, the glow plug fuse is located in the plenum chamber at the rear of the engine compartment.

3 To replace a blown fuse, pull it from its location in the fusebox. Fit a new fuse of the same rating, available from car accessory shops.

Tyre condition and pressure

It is very important that tyres are in good condition, and at the correct pressure - having a tyre failure at any speed is highly dangerous. Tyre wear is influenced by driving style - harsh braking and acceleration, or fast cornering, will all produce more rapid tyre wear. As a general rule, the front tyres wear out faster than the rears. Interchanging the tyres from front to rear ("rotating" the tyres) may result in more even wear. However, if this is completely effective, you may have the expense of replacing all four tyres at once! Remove any nails or stones embedded in the tread before they penetrate the tyre to cause deflation. If removal of a nail does reveal that

the tyre has been punctured, refit the nail so that its point of penetration is marked. Then immediately change the wheel, and have the tyre repaired by a tyre dealer.

Regularly check the tyres for damage in the form of cuts or bulges, especially in the sidewalls. Periodically remove the wheels, and clean any dirt or mud from the inside and outside surfaces. Examine the wheel rims for signs of rusting, corrosion or other damage. Light alloy wheels are easily damaged by "kerbing" whilst parking; steel wheels may also become dented or buckled. A new wheel is very often the only way to overcome severe damage.

New tyres should be balanced when they are fitted, but it may become necessary to re-balance them as they wear, or if the balance weights fitted to the wheel rim should fall off. Unbalanced tyres will wear more quickly, as will the steering and suspension components. Wheel imbalance is normally signified by vibration, particularly at a certain speed (typically around 50 mph). If this vibration is felt only through the steering, then it is likely that just the front wheels need balancing. If, however, the vibration is felt through the whole car, the rear wheels could be out of balance. Wheel balancing should be carried out by a tyre dealer or garage.

1 Tread Depth - visual check
The original tyres have tread wear safety bands (B), which will appear when the tread depth reaches approximately 1.6 mm. The band positions are indicated by a triangular mark on the tyre sidewall (A).

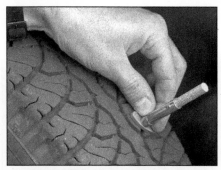

2 Tread Depth - manual check
Alternatively, tread wear can be monitored with a simple, inexpensive device known as a tread depth indicator gauge.

3 Tyre Pressure Check
Check the tyre pressures regularly with the tyres cold. Do not adjust the tyre pressures immediately after the vehicle has been used, or an inaccurate setting will result.

Tyre tread wear patterns

Shoulder Wear

Underinflation (wear on both sides)
Under-inflation will cause overheating of the tyre, because the tyre will flex too much, and the tread will not sit correctly on the road surface. This will cause a loss of grip and excessive wear, not to mention the danger of sudden tyre failure due to heat build-up.
Check and adjust pressures
Incorrect wheel camber (wear on one side)
Repair or renew suspension parts
Hard cornering
Reduce speed!

Centre Wear

Overinflation
Over-inflation will cause rapid wear of the centre part of the tyre tread, coupled with reduced grip, harsher ride, and the danger of shock damage occurring in the tyre casing.
Check and adjust pressures

If you sometimes have to inflate your car's tyres to the higher pressures specified for maximum load or sustained high speed, don't forget to reduce the pressures to normal afterwards.

Uneven Wear

Front tyres may wear unevenly as a result of wheel misalignment. Most tyre dealers and garages can check and adjust the wheel alignment (or "tracking") for a modest charge.
Incorrect camber or castor
Repair or renew suspension parts
Malfunctioning suspension
Repair or renew suspension parts
Unbalanced wheel
Balance tyres
Incorrect toe setting
Adjust front wheel alignment
Note: *The feathered edge of the tread which typifies toe wear is best checked by feel.*

Washer fluid level

Screenwash additives not only keep the windscreen clean during foul weather, they also prevent the washer system freezing in cold weather - which is when you are likely to need it most. Don't top up using plain water as the screenwash will become too diluted, and will freeze during cold weather. *On no account use coolant antifreeze in the washer system - this could discolour or damage paintwork.*

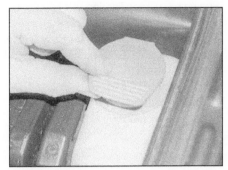

1 The reservoir for the windscreen and headlight washer systems is on the left-hand side of the engine compartment.

2 A screenwash additive should be added in the quantities recommended on the bottle.

Wiper blades

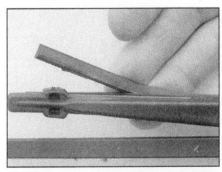

1 Check the condition of the wiper blades. If they are cracked or show any signs of deterioration, or if the glass swept area is smeared, renew them. For maximum clarity of vision, wiper blades should be renewed annually, as a matter of course.

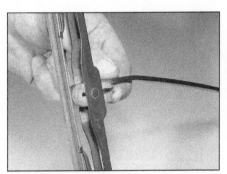

2 To remove a windscreen wiper blade, pull the arm fully away from the screen until it locks. Swivel the blade through 90°, then depress the locking tab with a screwdriver or your fingers.

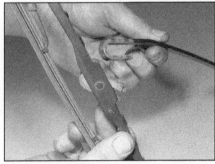

3 Slide the wiper blade out of the hooked end of the arm, then feed the arm through the hole in the blade. When fitting the new blade, make sure that the blade locks securely into the arm, and that the blade is orientated correctly.

Lubricants and fluids

Engine

Petrol . . . . Engine oil to specification VW 500 00, or VW 501 01, viscosity SAE 10W-30 to 15W-50

Diesel . . . . Engine oil to specification VW 500 00, or VW 505 00, viscosity SAE 10W-30 to 15W-50

Cooling system . . . . Antifreeze VW G 011 V8C, or to specification TL-VW 774 C

Manual transmission . . . . Synthetic gear oil G50, viscosity SAE 75W-90

Automatic transmission . . . . Dexron II type ATF

Final drive (automatic transmission) . . . . Synthetic gear oil G50, viscosity SAE 75W-90

Braking system . . . . Hydraulic fluid to DOT 4

Power steering system . . . . Audi/VAG hydraulic oil G 002 000

Tyre pressures

Note: *The recommended tyre pressures for each vehicle are given on a sticker attached to the inside of the fuel filler flap. The pressures given are for the original equipment tyres - the recommended pressures may vary if any other make or type of tyre is fitted; check with the tyre manufacturer or supplier for latest recommendations.*

Chapter 1 Part A:
Routine maintenance and servicing - petrol models

Contents

Degrees of difficulty

Easy, suitable for novice with little experience	**Fairly easy,** suitable for beginner with some experience	**Fairly difficult,** suitable for competent DIY mechanic	**Difficult,** suitable for experienced DIY mechanic	**Very difficult,** suitable for expert DIY or professional

Lubricants and fluids .... Refer to end of *Weekly checks*

Capacities

Engine oil (including filter)
1595 cc engines (ADP, AHL) .... 3.3 litres
All other engines .... 3.9 litres

Cooling system
Petrol models .... 6.0 litres approx.

Transmission
Manual transmission .... 2.25 litres
Automatic transmission fluid:
   Initial filling .... 5.5 litres
   Fluid change .... 3.5 litres
Automatic transmission final drive .... 1.0 litre

Power-assisted steering
All models .... 1.5 litres (approx.)

Fuel tank
All models (approximate) .... 62 litres

Cooling system
Antifreeze mixture:
   40% antifreeze .... Protection down to -25°C
   50% antifreeze .... Protection down to -35°C

Ignition system
Ignition timing .... Refer to Chapter 5B

Spark plugs:	Type	Gap
Non-turbocharged engines	Bosch FR 7 LD+	0.9 mm
	or Bosch F 7 LTCR	1.0 mm
Turbocharged engines	Bosch FR 78	Not adjustable
	or Bosch F 7 DPP 222 T	0.8 mm

Brakes
Front brake pad minimum thickness (including backing) .... 7.0 mm
Rear brake pad minimum thickness (including backing) .... 7.0 mm

Auxiliary drivebelt
Tension adjustment:
   Main drivebelt .... Automatically adjusted
   Coolant pump drivebelt .... Not adjustable
   Air conditioning compressor drivebelt .... Apply a torque of 25 Nm to the hexagon on the tensioner body

Torque wrench settings

	Nm	lbf ft
Automatic transmission final drive oil filler/level plug	25	18
Automatic transmission inspection plug (01N)	15	11
Automatic transmission overflow pipe (01N)	2	1
Coolant pump drain plug	30	22
Manual transmission filler/level plug	25	18
Power steering pump mounting	25	18
Roadwheel bolts	120	89
Spark plugs	30	22
Sump drain plug:		
Engine codes ADP, AHL	30	22
All other engines	50	37

The maintenance intervals in this manual are provided with the assumption that you, not the dealer, will be carrying out the work. These are the minimum intervals recommended by us for vehicles driven daily. If you wish to keep your vehicle in peak condition at all times, you may wish to perform some of these procedures more often. We encourage frequent maintenance, since it enhances the efficiency, performance and resale value of your vehicle. **Note**: *The mileage conversions from kilometres are approximate.*

All Audi A4 models are equipped with a service interval display indicator in the instrument panel. Every time the engine is started the panel will illuminate for a few seconds, displaying one of the following:

Models up to 1997
OIL - 15 000 km service required
In 1 - 12 month, 30 000 km or 60 000 km inspection service required, according to mileage completed
In 2 - 24 month service required

Models from 1997
Service OIL - 15 000 km service required
Service INSP - 12 month, 30 000 km or 60 000 km 120 000 km or 24 month service required, according to mileage completed

This is basically a reminder that a service is due, eg: when the Audi technician completes an oil change service, the display indicator is re-programmed to show OEL when another 15 000 km have been covered. When a service is due, the display will begin indicating it 1000 km or 10 days beforehand. The indicator is programmed in km, even if the vehicle has mileage indication.

Note: *A 'long-life' service schedule was introduced towards the end of 1999, applicable only to vehicles built from model-year 2000 onwards. Full details of the service schedule were not available at the time of writing - refer to your VAG dealer for further information.*

Every 250 miles (400 km) or weekly

☐ Refer to *Weekly checks*

Every 10 000 miles (15 000 km) - 'OEL' or 'service OIL' on interval display

☐ Renew the engine oil and filter (Section 3)

Note: *Frequent oil and filter changes are good for the engine. We recommend changing the oil more frequently than the mileage specified here, or at least twice a year.*

☐ Check the front brake pad thickness (Section 4)
☐ Check condition of the auxiliary drivebelt (Section5)
☐ Check the condition of the timing belt (Section 6)
☐ Reset the service interval display (Section 7)

Every 12 months - 'In 1' or 'service INSP' on interval display

☐ Check the operation of the windscreen/tailgate/headlight washer system(s) (Section 8)
☐ Check the tyre wear (Section 9)
☐ Lubricate all hinges and locks (Section 10)
☐ Check the battery electrolyte level (Section 11)
☐ Check the engine management ECU memory for faults (Section 12)
☐ Check all underbonnet components and hoses for fluid leaks (Section 13)
☐ Check the cooling system for anti-freeze content (Section 14)
☐ Check all brake flexible hoses and rigid pipes for condition (Section 15)
☐ Check the rear brake pad/shoe lining thickness (Section 16)
☐ Check the condition of the exhaust system and its mountings (Section 17)
☐ Check the steering and suspension components for condition and security (Section 18)
☐ Carry out a road test (Section 19)

Every 20 000 miles (30 000 km) - 'In 1' or 'service INSP' on interval display

Note: *Carry out the following work in addition to that described for the 12 months interval.*

☐ Renew the fuel filter (Section 20)
☐ Renew the pollen filter (Section 21)
☐ Check the underbody sealant (Section 22)
☐ Check manual transmission oil level (Section 23)
☐ Check the headlight beam adjustment (Section 24)

Every 40 000 miles (60 000 km) - 'In 1' or 'service INSP' on interval display

Note: *Carry out the following work in addition to that described for the 12 month and 20 000 mile intervals.*

☐ Renew the air filter element (Section 25)
☐ Renew the spark plugs. Note: Every 3 years if less than 40 000 miles (Section 26)
☐ Check the final drive oil level and top up if necessary (automatic transmission) (Section 27)
☐ Renew the automatic transmission fluid. Note: Every 4 years if less than 40 000 miles (Section 28)
☐ Renew the timing belt (Section 29)*

***Note:** The manufacturer's recommendation is to renew the timing belt at 80 000 miles (120 000 km) however we recommend it is renewed at 40 000 miles (60 000 km) especially if the vehicle is used mainly for short journeys or a lot of stop-start driving. The actual belt renewal interval is very much up to the individual owner but, bearing in mind that severe engine damage will result if the belt breaks in use, we recommend you err on the side of caution.*

Every 80 000 miles (120 000 km) - 'In 1' or 'service INSP' on interval display

☐ Renew the auxiliary drivebelt(s) (Section 30)

Every 2 years (regardless of mileage) - 'In 2' or 'service INSP' on interval display

☐ Renew the brake fluid (Section 31)
☐ Renew the coolant (Section 32)
☐ Carry out an exhaust emissions check (Section 33)

Underbonnet view of a 1.8 litre DOHC 20-valve petrol engine model (code ADR)

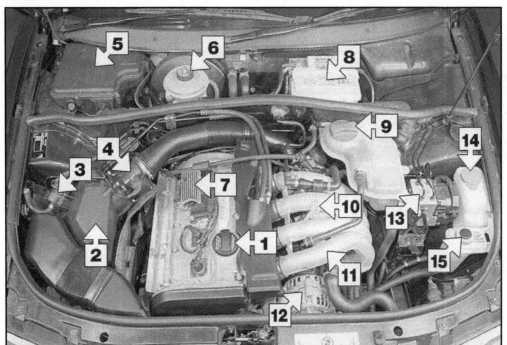

1 Engine oil filler cap
2 Air cleaner
3 Carbon canister solenoid valve
4 Airflow meter
5 Engine management ECU
6 Brake fluid reservoir
7 Ignition coil unit
8 Battery
9 Cooling system expansion tank
10 Engine oil level dipstick
11 Inlet manifold
12 Alternator
13 ABS unit
14 Washer fluid reservoir
15 Power steering fluid reservoir

Front underbody view of a 1.8 litre DOHC 20-valve petrol engine model (code ADR)

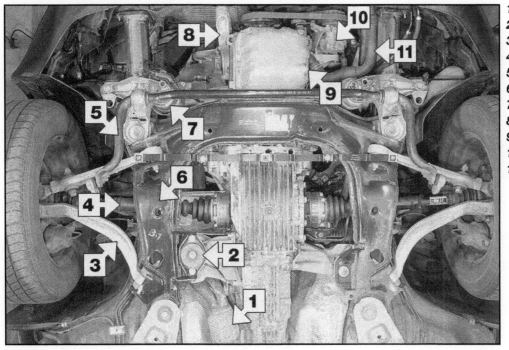

1 Exhaust front downpipe
2 Transmission mounting
3 Front suspension arm
4 Driveshaft
5 Front anti-roll bar
6 Front subframe
7 Engine mounting
8 Engine front torque arm
9 Engine sump oil drain plug
10 Power steering pump
11 Radiator bottom hose

Rear underbody view of a petrol engine model

1   Intermediate exhaust pipe
2   Rear suspension anti-roll
    bar
3   Rear axle beam
4   Tail pipe and silencer
5   Fuel tank
6   Handbrake cables
7   Fuel filter

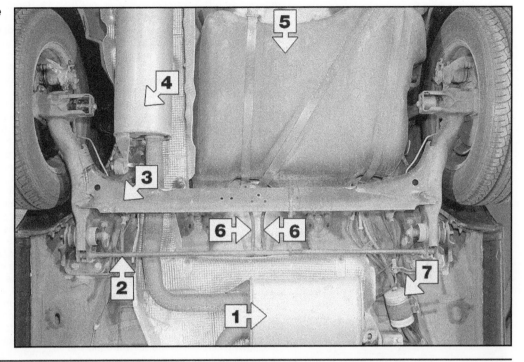

1   Introduction

This Chapter is designed to help the home mechanic maintain his/her vehicle for safety, economy, long life and peak performance.

The Chapter contains a master maintenance schedule, followed by Sections dealing specifically with each task in the schedule. Visual checks, adjustments, component renewal and other helpful items are included. Refer to the accompanying illustrations of the engine compartment and the underside of the vehicle for the locations of the various components.

Servicing your vehicle in accordance with the mileage/time maintenance schedule and the following Sections will provide a planned maintenance programme, which should result in a long and reliable service life. This is a comprehensive plan, so maintaining some items but not others at the specified service intervals, will not produce the same results.

As you service your vehicle, you will discover that many of the procedures can - and should - be grouped together, because of the particular procedure being performed, or because of the proximity of two otherwise unrelated components to one another. For example, if the vehicle is raised for any reason, the exhaust can be inspected at the same time as the suspension and steering components.

The first step in this maintenance pro-gramme is to prepare yourself before the actual work begins. Read through all the Sections relevant to the work to be carried out, then make a list and gather all the parts and tools required. If a problem is encountered, seek advice from a parts specialist, or a dealer service department.

2   Regular maintenance

1 If, from the time the vehicle is new, the routine maintenance schedule is followed closely, and frequent checks are made of fluid levels and high-wear items, as suggested throughout this manual, the engine will be kept in relatively good running condition, and the need for additional work will be minimised.
2 It is possible that there will be times when the engine is running poorly due to the lack of regular maintenance. This is even more likely if a used vehicle, which has not received regular and frequent maintenance checks, is purchased. In such cases, additional work may need to be carried out, outside of the regular maintenance intervals.
3 If engine wear is suspected, a compression test (refer to the relevant Part of Chapter 2) will provide valuable information regarding the overall performance of the main internal components. Such a test can be used as a basis to decide on the extent of the work to be carried out. If, for example, a compression test indicates serious internal engine wear,

conventional maintenance as described in this Chapter will not greatly improve the per-formance of the engine, and may prove a waste of time and money, unless extensive overhaul work is carried out first.
4 The following series of operations are those most often required to improve the per-formance of a generally poor-running engine:

Primary operations

a) Clean, inspect and test the battery (See Weekly checks).
b) Check all the engine-related fluids (See Weekly checks).
c) Check the condition of the auxiliary drivebelts (Sections 5 and 30).
d) Renew the spark plugs (Section 26).
e) Inspect the ignition system components (Chapter 5B).
f) Check the condition of the air filter, and renew if necessary (Section 25).
g) Check the fuel filter (Section 20).
h) Check the condition of all hoses, and check for fluid leaks (Section 13).

5 If the above operations do not prove fully effective, carry out the following secondary operations:

Secondary operations

All items listed under Primary operations, plus the following:
a) Check the charging system (Chapter 5A).
b) Check the ignition system (Chapter 5B).
c) Check the fuel system (Chapter 4A).
d) Renew the ignition HT leads (Chapter 5B)

Every 10 000 miles (15 000 km)

3 Engine oil and filter renewal

1 Frequent oil and filter changes are the most important maintenance procedures which can be undertaken by the DIY owner. As engine oil ages, it becomes diluted and contaminated, which leads to premature engine wear.
2 Before starting this procedure, gather all the necessary tools and materials. Also make sure that you have plenty of clean rags and newspapers handy, to mop up any spills. Ideally, the engine oil should be warm, as it will drain better, and more built-up sludge will be

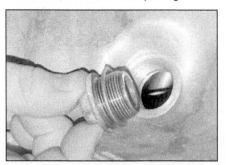

3.3 Removing the drain plug from the sump

As the drain plug releases from the threads, move it away quickly so that the stream of oil running out of the sump goes into the drain pan and not up your sleeve

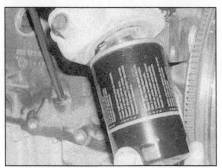

3.7 Removing the oil filter on the ADR engine (shown with engine on bench)

removed with it. Take care, however, not to touch the exhaust or any other hot parts of the engine when working under the vehicle. To avoid any possibility of scalding, and to protect yourself from possible skin irritants and other harmful contaminants in used engine oils, it is advisable to wear gloves when carrying out this work. Access to the underside of the vehicle is possible if it can be raised on a lift, driven onto ramps, or jacked up and supported on axle stands (see *Jacking and vehicle support*). Whichever method is chosen, make sure that the vehicle remains level, or if it is at an angle, that the drain plug is at the lowest point. With the vehicle raised, remove the engine compartment undershield (where applicable).
3 Using a socket and wrench or a ring spanner, slacken the drain plug about half a turn. Position the draining container under the drain plug, then remove the plug completely **(see Haynes Hint)**. Recover the sealing ring from the drain plug **(see illustration)**.
4 Allow some time for the old oil to drain, noting that it may be necessary to reposition the container as the oil flow slows to a trickle.
5 After all the oil has drained, wipe off the drain plug with a clean rag, and fit a new sealing washer. Clean the area around the drain plug opening, and refit the plug. Tighten the plug securely.
6 If the filter is also to be renewed, move the container into position under the oil filter, which is located on the left-hand rear side of the cylinder block.
7 Using an oil filter removal tool if necessary, slacken the filter initially, then unscrew it by hand the rest of the way **(see illustration)**. Empty the oil in the filter into the container.
8 Use a clean rag to remove all oil, dirt and sludge from the filter sealing area on the engine. Check the old filter to make sure that the rubber sealing ring has not stuck to the engine. If it has, carefully remove it.
9 Apply a light coating of clean engine oil to the sealing ring on the new filter, then screw it into position on the engine. Tighten the filter firmly by hand only - **do not** use any tools.
10 Remove the old oil and all tools from under the car then refit the undershield and lower the car to the ground.

3.11 Removing the oil filler cap from the cylinder head cover (ADR engine)

11 Remove the dipstick, then unscrew the oil filler cap from the cylinder head cover **(see illustration)**. Fill the engine, using the correct grade and type of oil (see *Lubricants and fluids*). An oil can spout or funnel may help to reduce spillage. Pour in half the specified quantity of oil first, then wait a few minutes for the oil to settle in the sump. Continue adding oil a small quantity at a time until the level is up to the lower mark on the dipstick. Adding around 1.0 litre will bring the level up to the upper mark on the dipstick. Refit the filler cap.
12 Start the engine and run it at idle speed for a few minutes; check for leaks around the oil filter seal and the sump drain plug. Note that there may be a few seconds delay before the oil pressure warning light goes out when the engine is started, as the oil circulates through the engine oil galleries and the new oil filter before the pressure builds up.
Caution: On models with a turbocharger, leave the engine idling until the oil pressure light goes out. Increasing the engine speed with the warning light on will damage the turbocharger!
13 Switch off the engine, and wait a few minutes for the oil to settle in the sump once more. With the new oil circulated and the filter completely full, recheck the level on the dipstick, and add more oil as necessary.
14 Dispose of the used engine oil safely, with reference to *General repair procedures* in the *Reference* section of this manual.

4 Front brake pad thickness check

1 Firmly apply the handbrake, loosen the front roadwheel bolts, then jack up the front of the car and support it securely on axle stands (see *Jacking and vehicle support*). Remove the front roadwheels.
2 For a comprehensive check, the brake pads should be removed and cleaned. The operation of the caliper can then also be checked, and the condition of the brake disc itself can be fully examined on both sides. Refer to Chapter 9 **(see Haynes Hint)**.

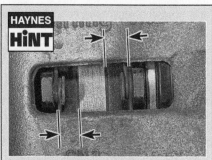

The thickness of the brake pads can be viewed through the inspection aperture in the caliper body

3 If any pad's friction material is worn to the specified thickness or less, *all four pads must be renewed as a set.*

5 Auxiliary drivebelt condition and tension check

1 Depending on the vehicle specification and engine type, one, two or three auxiliary drivebelts may be fitted. The main drivebelt drives the alternator, viscous coupling fan, and the power steering pump. Where air conditioning is fitted, a secondary drivebelt from the crankshaft pulley drives the air conditioning compressor. On all engines except AHL, a third drivebelt from an additional pulley on the power steering pump drives the coolant pump.
2 For access to the drivebelts, apply the handbrake, then jack up the front of the vehicle and support it on axle stands (see *Jacking and vehicle support*). Remove the splash guard from under the engine, and where applicable remove the engine top cover as well.
3 Examine the auxiliary drivebelts along their entire length for damage and wear in the form of cuts and abrasions, fraying and cracking. The use of a mirror and possibly a torch will help, and the engine may be turned with a spanner on the crankshaft pulley in order to observe all areas of the belt.
4 If a drivebelt requires renewal, refer to Chapter 2A for the removal, refitting and adjustment procedure.

6 Timing belt condition check

1 Release the spring clips and remove the upper timing cover from the front of the engine (refer to Chapter 2A, Section 4).
2 Inspect the timing belt for signs of excessive wear, fraying, cracking and damage. Also check for traces of oil which may have come from a faulty oil seal. The full length of the timing belt should be checked by turning the engine with a spanner on the crankshaft pulley bolt.
3 On completion of the check, refit the upper timing cover.

7 Reset the service interval display

1 With the ignition switched off, press and hold the display's right-hand (trip meter) button.
2 Switch the ignition on, and 'OIL' will be displayed. Release the button. If the 'INSP' service is to be reset, press the right-hand button again, until 'INSP' is shown.
3 To reset either 'OIL' or 'INSP', pull out the left-hand (clock adjuster) button for about 2 seconds.
4 On completion, switch off the ignition.

Every 12 months

8 Operation of the windscreen/tailgate/headlight washer system(s)

1 Check that each of the washer jet nozzles are clear and that each nozzle provides a strong jet of washer fluid. The jets should be aimed to spray at a point slightly above the centre of the screen/headlight. On the windscreen washer nozzles where there are two jets, aim one of the jets slightly above then centre of the screen and aim the other just below to ensure complete coverage of the screen. If necessary, adjust the jets using a pin.
2 Carry out a check of all wiper blades. Look for splits or cracks on the wiping surface and renew as necessary. Check that the wipers clean efficiently across their entire sweep; any gaps in the swept area may be caused by defective wiper blade hinges, preventing the blade from following the contours of the screen/lens surface. Check that the wiper blades do not overshoot the edge of the screen/lens at the end of their sweep and that the blades park in the correct position when switched off. If this is not the case, or if the blades overlap each other at the midpoint of their stroke, the wiper arms may be incorrectly fitted (see Chapter 12).

9 Tyre wear check

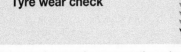

1 Raise and securely support the relevant side of the car in turn to allow a thorough check of each tyre to be performed; refer to *Jacking and vehicle support* for reference.
2 Turn the tyre slowly by hand and carry out an inspection as described in *Weekly checks - Tyre condition and pressure check.*

10 Lubricate all hinges and locks

1 Lubricate the hinges of the bonnet, doors and tailgate with a light general-purpose oil. Similarly, lubricate all latches, locks and lock strikers. At the same time, check the security and operation of all the locks, adjusting them if necessary (see Chapter 11).
2 Lightly lubricate the bonnet release mechanism and cable with a suitable grease.

11 Battery electrolyte level check

1 Where a standard battery is fitted, the level of the electrolyte may be checked and if necessary topped up. On some batteries, MIN and MAX marks are printed on the side of the battery and the level may be checked without removing the cell covers. Where there are no exterior marks, remove the cover(s) from the top of the cells and check that the level of the electrolyte is approximately 2 or 3 mm above the internal plates. Some batteries may have a plastic internal level indicator.
2 If necessary, top up the cells using distilled or de-ionised water.
3 Refit the cell cover(s).

12 Engine management ECU memory fault code check

This check can only be carried out by an Audi/VAG dealer or garage having the necessary equipment. If a fault code is evident, the problem must be corrected to ensure efficient operation of the engine.

13 Underbonnet/underbody components and hoses fluid leak check

1 For access to the top and bottom of the engine, remove the engine top cover, then jack up the front of the vehicle and support it on axle stands (see *Jacking and vehicle support*) and remove the undershield. Visually inspect the engine joint faces, gaskets and seals for any signs of water or oil leaks. Pay particular attention to the areas around the camshaft cover, cylinder head, oil filter and sump joint faces. Bear in mind that, over a period of time, some very slight seepage from these areas is to be expected - what you are really looking for is any indication of a serious leak **(see Haynes Hint)**. Should a leak be found, renew the offending gasket or oil seal by referring to the appropriate Chapters in this manual.
2 Also check the security and condition of all the engine-related pipes and hoses. Ensure that all cable-ties or securing clips are in place and in good condition. Clips which are broken or missing can lead to chafing of the hoses, pipes or wiring, which could cause more serious problems in the future.

A leak in the cooling system will usually show up as white- or rust- coloured crusty deposits on the area surrounding the leak

3 Carefully check the radiator hoses and heater hoses along their entire length. Renew any hose which is cracked, swollen or deteriorated. Cracks will show up better if the hose is squeezed. Pay close attention to the hose clips that secure the hoses to the cooling system components. Hose clips can pinch and puncture hoses, resulting in cooling system leaks.

4 Inspect all the cooling system components (hoses, joint faces etc.) for leaks. A leak in the cooling system will usually show up as white- or rust-coloured deposits on the area adjoining the leak. Where any problems of this nature are found on system components, renew the component or gasket with reference to Chapter 3.

5 Where applicable, inspect the automatic transmission fluid cooler hoses for leaks or deterioration.

6 With the vehicle raised at the rear, inspect the petrol tank and filler neck for punctures, cracks and other damage. The connection between the filler neck and tank is especially critical. Sometimes a rubber filler neck or connecting hose will leak due to loose retaining clamps or deteriorated rubber.

7 Carefully check all rubber hoses and metal fuel lines leading away from the petrol tank. Check for loose connections, deteriorated hoses, crimped lines, and other damage. Pay particular attention to the vent pipes and hoses, which often loop up around the filler neck and can become blocked or crimped. Follow the lines to the front of the vehicle, carefully inspecting them all the way. Renew damaged sections as necessary.

8 From within the engine compartment, check the security of all fuel hose attachments and pipe unions, and inspect the fuel hoses and vacuum hoses for kinks, chafing and deterioration.

9 Where applicable, check the condition of the power steering fluid hoses and pipes.

10 On completion, refit the undershield and engine top cover, and lower the vehicle to the ground.

14 Cooling system anti-freeze concentration check

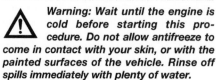

⚠ *Warning: Wait until the engine is cold before starting this procedure. Do not allow antifreeze to come in contact with your skin, or with the painted surfaces of the vehicle. Rinse off spills immediately with plenty of water.*

1 Note that a tester will be required to check the coolant strength; these can be obtained relatively cheaply from most motor accessory shops.

2 With the engine completely cold, unscrew and remove the filler cap from the coolant expansion tank. Follow the instructions supplied with the tester and check the coolant mixture is sufficient to give protection down to temperatures well below freezing. If the coolant has been renewed regularly this shouldn't be a problem. However, if the coolant mixture is not strong enough to provide sufficient protection it will be necessary to drain the cooling system and renew the coolant (see Section 32).

3 Once the test is complete, check the coolant level is correct (see *Weekly checks*) then securely refit the expansion tank cap.

15 Brake flexible hoses and rigid pipes condition check

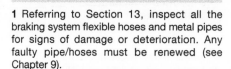

1 Referring to Section 13, inspect all the braking system flexible hoses and metal pipes for signs of damage or deterioration. Any faulty pipe/hoses must be renewed (see Chapter 9).

16 Rear brake pad lining thickness check

1 Firmly chock the front wheels and select first gear or PARK, then jack up the rear of the vehicle and support it securely on axle stands (see *Jacking and vehicle support*). Remove the rear roadwheels.

2 For a quick check, the pad thickness can be carried out via the inspection hole on the rear of the caliper. Using a steel rule, measure the thickness of the pad lining including the backing plate. This must not be less than that indicated in the Specifications.

3 The view through the caliper inspection hole gives a rough indication of the state of the brake pads. For a comprehensive check, the brake pads should be removed and cleaned. The operation of the caliper can then also be checked, and the condition of the brake disc itself can be fully examined on both sides. Chapter 9 contains a detailed description of how the brake disc should be checked for wear and/or damage.

4 If any pad's friction material is worn to the specified thickness or less, *all four pads must be renewed as a set*. Refer to Chapter 9 for details.

5 On completion, refit the roadwheels and lower the vehicle to the ground.

17 Exhaust system and mountings condition check

1 With the engine cold, check the complete exhaust system from the engine to the end of the tailpipe. The exhaust system is most easily checked with the vehicle raised on a hoist, or suitably supported on axle stands, so that the exhaust components are readily visible and accessible.

2 Check the exhaust pipes and connections for evidence of leaks, severe corrosion and damage. Make sure that all brackets and mountings are in good condition, and that all relevant nuts and bolts are tight. Leakage at any of the joints or in other parts of the system will usually show up as a black sooty stain in the vicinity of the leak.

3 Rattles and other noises can often be traced to the exhaust system, especially the brackets and mountings. If the components are able to come into contact with the body or suspension parts, secure the system with new mountings. Otherwise separate the joints (if possible) and twist the pipes as necessary to provide additional clearance.

18 Steering and suspension components condition/ security check

Front suspension and steering check

1 Raise the front of the vehicle, and securely support it on axle stands.

2 Visually inspect the balljoint dust covers and the steering rack gaiters for splits, chafing or deterioration. Any wear of these components will cause loss of lubricant, together with dirt and water entry, resulting in rapid deterioration of the balljoints or steering gear.

3 On vehicles with power steering, check the fluid hoses for chafing or deterioration, and the pipe and hose unions for fluid leaks. Also check for signs of fluid leakage under pressure from the steering gear rubber gaiters, which would indicate failed fluid seals within the steering gear.

4 Grasp the roadwheel at the 12 o'clock and 6 o'clock positions, and try to rock it **(see illustration)**. Very slight free play may be felt, but if the movement is appreciable, further investigation is necessary to determine the source. Continue rocking the wheel while an assistant depresses the footbrake. If the movement is now eliminated or significantly reduced, it is likely that the hub bearings are

18.4 Check for signs of wear in the hub bearings by grasping the roadwheel at the 12 o'clock and 6 o'clock positions, and trying to rock it

at fault. If the free play is still evident with the footbrake depressed, then there is wear in the suspension joints or mountings.

5 Now grasp the wheel at the 9 o'clock and 3 o'clock positions, and try to rock it as before. Any movement felt now may again be caused by wear in the hub bearings or the steering track-rod balljoints. If the inner or outer balljoint is worn, the visual movement will be obvious.

6 Using a large screwdriver or flat bar, check for wear in the suspension mounting bushes by levering between the relevant suspension component and its attachment point. Some movement is to be expected as the mountings are made of rubber, but excessive wear should be obvious. Also check the condition of any visible rubber bushes, looking for splits, cracks or contamination of the rubber.

7 With the car standing on its wheels, have an assistant turn the steering wheel back and forth about an eighth of a turn each way. There should be very little, if any, lost movement between the steering wheel and roadwheels. If this is not the case, closely observe the joints and mountings previously described, but in addition, check the steering column universal joints for wear, and the rack-and-pinion steering gear itself.

Suspension strut/shock absorber check

8 Check for any signs of fluid leakage around the suspension strut/shock absorber body, or from the rubber gaiter around the piston rod. Should any fluid be noticed, the suspension strut/shock absorber is defective internally, and should be renewed. **Note:** *Suspension struts/shock absorbers should always be renewed in pairs on the same axle.*

9 The efficiency of the suspension strut/ shock absorber may be checked by bouncing the vehicle at each corner. Generally speaking, the body will return to its normal position and stop after being depressed. If it rises and returns on a rebound, the suspension strut/shock absorber is probably suspect. Examine also the suspension strut/shock absorber upper and lower mountings for any signs of wear.

Driveshafts

10 With the vehicle raised and securely supported on stands, turn the steering onto full lock then slowly rotate the roadwheel. Inspect the condition of the outer constant velocity (CV) joint rubber gaiters while squeezing the gaiters to open out the folds. Check for signs of cracking, splits or deterioration of the rubber which may allow the grease to escape and lead to water and grit entry into the joint. Also check the security and condition of the retaining clips. Repeat these checks on the inner CV joints. If any damage or deterioration is found, the gaiters should be renewed as described in Chapter 8, Section 3.

11 At the same time check the general condition of the CV joints themselves by first holding the driveshaft and attempting to rotate the wheel. Repeat this check by holding the inner joint and attempting to rotate the driveshaft. Any appreciable movement indicates wear in the joints, wear in the driveshaft splines or loose driveshaft retaining nut.

19 Road test

Instruments and electrical equipment

1 Check the operation of all instruments and electrical equipment.

2 Make sure that all instruments read correctly, and switch on all electrical equipment in turn, to check that it functions properly.

Steering and suspension

3 Check for any abnormalities in the steering, suspension, handling or road feel.

4 Drive the vehicle, and check that there are no unusual vibrations or noises.

5 Check that the steering feels positive, with no excessive sloppiness, or roughness, and check for any suspension noises when cornering and driving over bumps.

Drivetrain

6 Check the performance of the engine, clutch (where applicable), gearbox/ transmission and driveshafts.

7 Listen for any unusual noises from the engine, clutch and gearbox/transmission.

8 Make sure that the engine runs smoothly when idling, and that there is no hesitation when accelerating.

9 Check that, where applicable, the clutch action is smooth and progressive, that the drive is taken up smoothly, and that the pedal travel is not excessive. Also listen for any noises when the clutch pedal is depressed.

10 On manual gearbox models, check that all gears can be engaged smoothly without noise, and that the gear lever action is not abnormally vague or notchy.

11 On automatic transmission models, make sure that all gearchanges occur smoothly, without snatching, and without an increase in engine speed between changes. Check that all the gear positions can be selected with the vehicle at rest. If any problems are found, they should be referred to a Audi/VAG dealer.

Check the operation and performance of the braking system

12 Make sure that the vehicle does not pull to one side when braking, and that the wheels do not lock prematurely when braking hard.

13 Check that there is no vibration through the steering when braking.

14 Check that the handbrake operates correctly without excessive movement of the lever, and that it holds the vehicle stationary on a slope.

15 Test the operation of the brake servo unit as follows. With the engine off, depress the footbrake four or five times to exhaust the vacuum. Hold the brake pedal depressed, then start the engine. As the engine starts, there should be a noticeable give in the brake pedal as vacuum builds up. Allow the engine to run for at least two minutes, and then switch it off. If the brake pedal is depressed now, it should be possible to detect a hiss from the servo as the pedal is depressed. After about four or five applications, no further hissing should be heard, and the pedal should feel considerably harder.

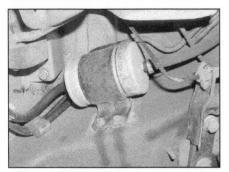

20.1 Fuel filter location on the right-hand side of the fuel tank

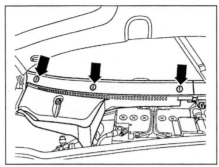

21.3 Release the scuttle cover panel fasteners (arrowed)

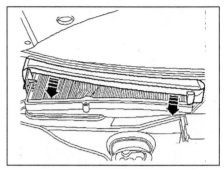

21.4 Detach the seal from the top of the engine compartment bulkhead

Every 20 000 miles (30 000 km)

20 Fuel filter renewal

1 The fuel filter is located beneath the rear of the car on the right-hand side of the fuel tank **(see illustration)**.
2 Note the fitted position of the filter, then loosen the clips and disconnect the fuel pipes from each end.
3 Press the filter forwards and remove it from the mounting clamp. If it is tight, unbolt and remove the clamp and filter.
4 Where removed, refit the clamp and tighten the bolts.
5 Locate the new filter in position and re-connect the fuel pipes. Tighten the clips. Make sure the filter is located the correct way round, with the flow direction arrow pointing towards the engine.

21 Pollen filter renewal

1 The pollen filter (where fitted) is located beneath the windscreen cowl panels; it is located on the left side on right-hand-drive models, and the right side on left-hand drive models.
2 Switch on the windscreen wipers, then switch off the ignition when the wipers are

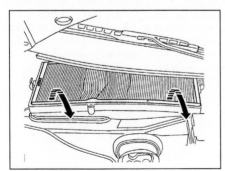

21.5 Lift the pollen filter from its housing

mid-sweep, so that they park vertically on the windscreen.
3 Release the scuttle cover panel fasteners by turning them as necessary **(see illustration)**.
4 Peel back the rubber seal from the relevant end of the top of the engine compartment bulkhead **(see illustration)**.
5 Lift the pollen filter from its housing **(see illustration)**.
6 Wipe clean the filter housing, then fit the new filter. Clip the filter securely in position and refit the cover. Ensure that the OBEN marking on the new filter element faces upwards.
7 The remainder of the refitting procedure is a reversal of removal.

22 Underbody sealant check

Raise and support the vehicle on axle stands (see Jacking and vehicle support). Using an electric torch or lead light, inspect the entire underside of the vehicle, paying particular attention to the wheel arches. Look for any damage to the flexible underbody coating, which may crack or flake off with age, leading to corrosion. Also check that the wheel arch liners (where fitted) are securely attached with any clips provided - if they come loose, dirt may get in behind the liners and defeat their purpose. If there is any damage to the underseal, or any corrosion, it should be repaired before the damage gets too serious.

23 Manual transmission oil level check

1 The oil filler/level plug is located on the left-hand side of the manual transmission, below the speedometer sender, and on some models it may be concealed by a heatshield **(see illustration)**. The plug may be either of 17 mm Allen key type, or alternatively of multi-splined type.

2 Apply the handbrake, then jack up the front and rear of the vehicle and support it on axle stands (see *Jacking and vehicle support*). To ensure an accurate check, make sure that the vehicle is level.
3 Unscrew and remove the filler/level plug.
4 Check that the oil level is 7.0 mm below the bottom lip of the filler hole. To do this, use a piece of angled metal such as welding rod.
5 If necessary, add the specified oil through the filler/level hole. If the level requires constant topping up, check for leaks and repair.
6 Refit the plug and tighten to the specified torque, then lower the vehicle to the ground.

24 Headlight beam adjustment

Halogen headlamps

1 Accurate adjustment of the headlight beam is only possible using optical beam setting equipment, and this work should therefore be carried out by a VAG dealer or suitably equipped workshop.
2 For reference, the headlights can be adjusted using the adjuster screws, accessible via the top of each light unit (see the illustrations given in Chapter 12, Section 9).
3 Some models are equipped with an

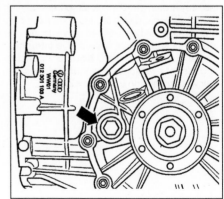

23.1 Oil filler/level plug location on the 012 manual transmission

electrically operated headlight beam adjustment system which is controlled through the switch in the facia. On these models, ensure that the switch is set to the basic 0 position before adjusting the headlight aim.

Electrical discharge headlights

4 The headlamp range is controlled dynamically by an electronic control unit which monitors the ride height of the vehicle via sensors fitted to the front and rear suspension. Beam adjustment can only be carried out using VAG test equipment.

Every 40 000 miles (60 000 km)

25 Air filter element renewal

1 Remove the air cleaner cover and air duct, then prise open the retaining clips and lift the upper cover from the air cleaner body. If necessary, temporarily remove the carbon canister solenoid valve from the cover **(see illustrations)**. Note that the airflow meter is attached to the upper cover.
2 Remove the air cleaner filter element, noting which way round it is fitted **(see illustration)**.
3 Wipe clean the main body, then fit the new air filter, making sure it is the correct way round.
4 Refit the upper cover and secure with the retaining clips.

26 Spark plug renewal

1 The correct functioning of the spark plugs is vital for the correct running and efficiency of the engine. It is essential that the plugs fitted are appropriate for the engine (a suitable type is specified at the beginning of this Chapter). If this type is used and the engine is in good condition, the spark plugs should not need attention between scheduled replacement intervals. Spark plug cleaning is rarely necessary, and should not be attempted unless specialised equipment is available, as damage can easily be caused to the firing ends.
2 First remove the engine top cover, and on engine codes ADR, AFY, APT, AEB, APU, AJL remove the ignition coil(s) as described in

Chapter 5B. If the marks on the original-equipment spark plug (HT) leads cannot be seen, mark the leads 1 to 4, to correspond to the cylinder the lead serves (No 1 cylinder is at the timing belt end of the engine). Pull the leads from the plugs by gripping the end fitting, not the lead, otherwise the lead connection may be fractured.
3 It is advisable to remove the dirt from the spark plug recesses using a clean brush, vacuum cleaner or compressed air before removing the plugs, to prevent dirt dropping into the cylinders.
4 Unscrew the plugs using a spark plug spanner, suitable box spanner or a deep socket and extension bar **(see illustration)**. Keep the socket aligned with the spark plug - if it is forcibly moved to one side, the ceramic insulator may be broken off. As each plug is removed, examine it as follows.

25.1a Remove the air cleaner cover . . .

25.1b . . . and air duct . . .

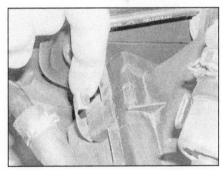

25.1c . . . then prise open the cover clips

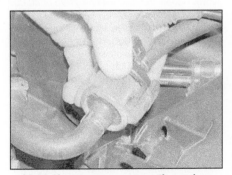

25.1d If necessary, remove the carbon canister solenoid valve from the cover

25.2 Removing the air cleaner element

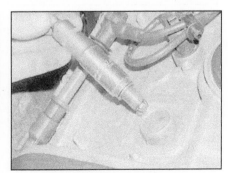

26.4 Removing the spark plugs (engine code ADR)

26.9a If single electrode plugs are being fitted, check the electrode gap using a feeler gauge . . .

26.9b . . . or a wire gauge . . .

26.10 . . . and if necessary adjust the gap by bending the electrode

5 Examination of the spark plugs will give a good indication of the condition of the engine. If the insulator nose of the spark plug is clean and white, with no deposits, this is indicative of a weak mixture or too hot a plug (a hot plug transfers heat away from the electrode slowly, a cold plug transfers heat away quickly).
6 If the tip and insulator nose are covered with hard black-looking deposits, then this is indicative that the mixture is too rich. Should the plug be black and oily, then it is likely that

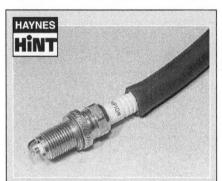

HAYNES
HiNT

It is very often difficult to insert spark plugs into their holes without cross-threading them. To avoid this possibility, fit a short length of rubber hose over the end of the spark plug. The flexible hose acts as a universal joint to help align the plug with the plug hole. Should the plug begin to cross-thread, the hose will slip on the spark plug, preventing thread damage to the aluminium cylinder head

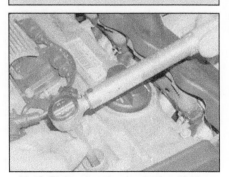

26.12 Tightening the spark plugs with a torque wrench

the engine is fairly worn, as well as the mixture being too rich.
7 If the insulator nose is covered with light tan to greyish-brown deposits, then the mixture is correct and it is likely that the engine is in good condition.
8 The spark plug electrode gap is of considerable importance as, if it is too large or too small, the size of the spark and its efficiency will be seriously impaired. On engines fitted with multi-electrode spark plugs, it is recommended that the plugs are renewed rather attempting to adjust the gaps. With other spark plugs, the gap should be set to the value given by the manufacturer.
9 To set the gap, measure it with a feeler blade and then bend open, or closed, the outer plug electrode until the correct gap is achieved. The centre electrode should never be bent, as this may crack the insulator and cause plug failure, if nothing worse. If using feeler blades, the gap is correct when the appropriate-size blade is a firm sliding fit **(see illustrations)**.
10 Special spark plug electrode gap adjusting tools are available from most motor accessory shops, or from some spark plug manufacturers **(see illustration)**.
11 Before fitting the spark plugs, check that the threaded connector sleeves are tight, and that the plug exterior surfaces and threads are clean. It's often difficult to screw in new spark plugs without cross-threading them - this can be avoided using a piece of rubber hose **(see Haynes Hint)**.
12 Remove the rubber hose (if used), and tighten the plug to the specified torque using

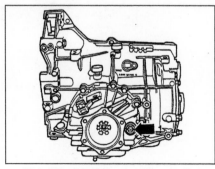

27.1 Filler/level plug location on the automatic transmission

the spark plug socket and a torque wrench **(see illustration)**. Refit the remaining spark plugs in the same manner.
13 Reconnect the HT leads and where necessary refit the ignition coil(s) with reference to Chapter 5B.
14 Refit the engine top cover.

27 Final drive oil level check and top up (automatic transmission)

1 The final drive oil filler/level plug is located on the left-hand side of the automatic transmission, behind the left-hand driveshaft inner joint **(see illustration)**. Apply the handbrake, then jack up the front of the vehicle and support it on axle stands (see *Jacking and vehicle support*). Remove the engine undershield. To ensure an accurate check, make sure that the vehicle is level.
2 Unscrew and remove the filler/level plug and check that the oil level is on the bottom lip of the filler hole. If necessary, add the specified oil through the filler/level hole. If the level requires constant topping up, check for leaks and repair.
3 Refit the plug and tighten to the specified torque, then lower the vehicle to the ground.

28 Automatic transmission fluid renewal

Note: *Renew the fluid every 4 years or 40 000 miles/60 000 km, whichever comes first.*
1 Apply the handbrake, then jack up the front of the vehicle and support it on axle stands (see *Jacking and vehicle support*). Remove the engine undershield.
Note: *For an accurate fluid level, Audi technicians use an electronic tester which is plugged into the transmission electronic system, and which determines that the temperature of the fluid is between 35°C and 40°C. In view of this, it is recommended that the vehicle is taken to an Audi dealer to have the work done. The following procedure is given on the understanding that the level is checked by an Audi dealer on completion.*

2 Note that the transmission must be refilled from below the vehicle, so make sure that the vehicle is supported in a level position.

3 Position a suitable container beneath the transmission. Wipe clean the oil pan, then unscrew the inspection plug, followed by the overflow pipe, from the bottom of the oil pan **(see illustration)**. Allow the fluid to drain into the container.

4 Refit the overflow pipe and tighten to the specified torque.

5 Remove the sealing cap and plug from the filling tube attached to the side of the oil pan. **Note:** *The later sealing cap and plug should be renewed whenever removed.*

6 Add fluid to the oil pan until it runs out of the overflow pipe.

7 With P selected, run the engine at idling speed until it reaches normal temperature. If necessary add more fluid until it runs out of the overflow pipe.

8 Apply the footbrake pedal, then select each position with the selector lever, pausing for about 3 seconds in each position. Return the selector to position P.

9 At this stage, the Audi technician connects the tester to confirm that the fluid temperature is between 35°C and 40°C. **Note:** *If the fluid level is checked when the temperature is too low, overfilling will occur. If the fluid level is*

checked when the temperature is too high, underfilling will occur.

10 With the engine still running at idle speed, allow any excess fluid to run out of the overflow pipe.

11 Switch off the engine, then refit the inspection plug together with a new seal, and tighten to the specified torque.

12 Fit a new sealing cap and plug to the filling tube.

13 Lower the vehicle to the ground.

29 Timing belt renewal

Refer to Chapter 2A, Section 4.
Note: *The manufacturer's recommendation is to renew the timing belt at 80 000 miles (120 000 km) however we recommend it is renewed at 40 000 miles (60 000 km) especially if the vehicle is used mainly for short journeys or a lot of stop-start driving. The actual belt renewal interval is very much up to the individual owner but, bearing in mind that severe engine damage will result if the belt breaks in use, we recommend you err on the side of caution.*

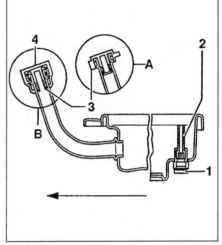

28.3 Oil pan components on the 01N automatic transmission

1 Inspection plug
2 Overflow pipe
3 Sealing cap and plug
4 Sealing cap B must be renewed after removal
A Early sealing cap
B Later sealing cap

Every 80 000 miles (120 000 km)

30 Auxiliary drivebelt renewal

Refer to Chapter 2A, Section 6.

Every 2 years (regardless of mileage)

31 Brake fluid renewal

⚠️ *Warning: Brake hydraulic fluid can harm your eyes and damage painted surfaces, so use extreme caution when handling and pouring it. Do not use fluid that has been standing open for some time, as it absorbs moisture from the air. Excess moisture can cause a dangerous loss of braking effectiveness.*

1 The procedure is similar to that for the bleeding of the hydraulic system as described in Chapter 9. The brake fluid reservoir should be emptied by siphoning, using a clean poultry baster or similar before starting, and allowance should be made for the old fluid to be expelled when bleeding a section of the circuit.

2 Working as described in Chapter 9, open the first bleed screw in the sequence, and pump the brake pedal gently until nearly all the old fluid has been emptied from the master cylinder reservoir.

3 Top-up to the MAX level with new fluid, and continue pumping until only the new fluid remains in the reservoir, and new fluid can be seen emerging from the bleed screw. Tighten the screw, and top the reservoir level up to the MAX level line.

> **HAYNES HiNT** *Old hydraulic fluid is often much darker in colour than the new, making it easy to distinguish the two.*

4 Work through all the remaining bleed screws in the sequence until new fluid can be seen at all of them. Be careful to keep the master cylinder reservoir topped-up to above the MIN level at all times, or air may enter the system and greatly increase the length of the task.

5 When the operation is complete, check that all bleed screws are securely tightened, and that their dust caps are refitted. Wash off all traces of spilt fluid, and recheck the fluid level.

6 Check the operation of the brakes before taking the car on the road.

32 Coolant renewal

Cooling system draining

⚠️ *Warning: Wait until the engine is cold before starting this procedure. Do not allow antifreeze to come in contact with your skin, or with the painted surfaces of the vehicle. Rinse off spills immediately with plenty of water. Never leave antifreeze lying around in an open container, or in a puddle in the driveway or on the garage floor. Children and pets are attracted by its sweet smell, but antifreeze can be fatal if ingested.*

1 With the engine completely cold, cover the expansion tank cap with a wad of rag, and slowly turn the cap anti-clockwise to relieve the pressure in the cooling system (a hissing sound will normally be heard). Wait until any pressure remaining in the system is released, then continue to turn the cap until it can be removed.

2 Where necessary, release the fasteners and remove the engine lower splash shield. Position a suitable container beneath the radiator bottom hose connection, then release the retaining clip and ease the hose from the radiator stub. If the hose joint has not been disturbed for some time, it will be necessary to gently manipulate the hose to break the joint. Do not use excessive force, or the radiator stub could be damaged. Allow the coolant to drain into the container. Note that the radiator is equipped with a drain tap, but this can only be accessed with the front bumper removed.

3 Where applicable, unscrew the drain plug from the underside of the coolant pump. Remove the old seal from the plug and fit a new one.

4 If the coolant has been drained for a reason other than renewal, then provided it is clean and less than two years old, it can be re-used if there is no alternative, but this is not recommended.

5 Once all the coolant has drained, reconnect the hose to the radiator and secure it in position with the retaining clip. Where applicable, refit the coolant pump drain plug (with the new seal fitted) and tighten it to the specified torque.

Cooling system flushing

6 If coolant renewal has been neglected, or if the antifreeze mixture has become diluted, then in time, the cooling system may gradually lose efficiency, as the coolant passages become restricted due to rust, scale deposits, and other sediment. Flushing the system clean can restore the cooling system efficiency.

7 The radiator should be flushed independently of the engine, to avoid unnecessary contamination.

Radiator flushing

8 To flush the radiator, disconnect the top and bottom hoses and any other relevant hoses from the radiator, with reference to Chapter 3.

9 Insert a garden hose into the radiator top inlet. Direct a flow of clean water through the radiator, and continue flushing until clean water emerges from the radiator bottom outlet.

10 If after a reasonable period, the water still does not run clear, the radiator can be flushed with a good proprietary cooling system cleaning agent. It is important that their manufacturer's instructions are followed carefully. If the contamination is particularly bad, insert the hose in the radiator bottom outlet, and reverse-flush the radiator.

Engine flushing

11 To flush the engine, remove the thermostat as described in Chapter 3, then temporarily refit the thermostat cover.

12 With the top and bottom hoses disconnected from the radiator, insert a garden hose into the radiator top hose. Direct a clean flow of water through the engine, and continue flushing until clean water emerges from the radiator bottom hose.

13 On completion of flushing, refit the thermostat and reconnect the hoses with reference to Chapter 3.

Cooling system filling

14 Before attempting to fill the cooling system, make sure that all hoses and clips are in good condition, and that the clips are tight. Note that an antifreeze mixture must be used all year round, to prevent corrosion of the engine components (see following sub-Section).

15 Slacken the clip and withdraw the heater unit supply hose from its bulkhead stub (see Chapter 3) until the bleed hole at the top of the hose is clear of the surface of the stub; do not disconnect the hose from the stub completely.

16 Remove the securing screws and detach the expansion tank from the engine compartment. Raise it approximately 100 mm above the engine compartment and support it there on a block of wood or using a length of wire.

17 Remove the expansion tank filler cap, and fill the system by slowly pouring the coolant into the expansion tank to prevent airlocks from forming.

18 If the coolant is being renewed, begin by pouring in a couple of litres of water, followed by the correct quantity of antifreeze, then top-up with more water.

19 Continue filling until coolant starts to run from the bleed hole in the heater hose. When this happens, refit the hose and tighten the clip securely.

20 Once the level in the expansion tank starts to rise, squeeze the radiator top and bottom hoses to help expel any trapped air in the system. Once all the air is expelled, top-up the coolant level to the MAX mark, refit the expansion tank cap, then refit the expansion tank to the bodywork.

21 Start the engine and run it at a fast idle for about three minutes. After this, allow the engine to idle normally until the bottom hose becomes hot.

22 Check for leaks, particularly around disturbed components. Check the coolant level in the expansion tank, and top-up if necessary. Note that the system must be cold before an accurate level is indicated in the expansion tank. If the expansion tank cap is removed while the engine is still warm, cover the cap with a thick cloth, and unscrew the cap slowly to gradually relieve the system pressure (a hissing sound will normally be heard). Wait until any pressure remaining in the system is released, then continue to turn the cap until it can be removed. Never remove the cap when the engine is still hot.

Antifreeze mixture

Caution: Models built up to June 1996 were filled with coolant containing antifreeze VAG part number G011A8C (green in colour). Models built from July 1996 were filled with coolant containing antifreeze VAG part number G012A8D (red in colour). DO NOT mix these two different types of antifreeze together in any proportion, as severe engine damage may result. If the coolant visible in the expansion tank is brown in colour, then the cooling system may have been topped up with coolant containing the wrong type of antifreeze. If you are unsure of the type of antifreeze used, or if you suspect that mixing may have occurred, the best course of action is to drain, flush and refill the cooling system.

23 The antifreeze should always be renewed at the specified intervals. This is necessary not only to maintain the antifreeze properties, but also to prevent corrosion which would otherwise occur as the corrosion inhibitors become progressively less effective.

24 Always use ethylene-glycol-based antifreeze suitable for use in mixed-metal cooling systems. The quantity of antifreeze and levels of protection are indicated in the Specifications.

25 Before adding antifreeze, the cooling system should be completely drained, preferably flushed, and all hoses checked for condition and security.

26 After filling with antifreeze, a label should be attached to the expansion tank, stating the type and concentration of antifreeze used, and the date installed. Any subsequent topping-up should be made with the same type and concentration of antifreeze.

27 Do not use engine antifreeze in the windscreen/tailgate/headlight washer system, as it will cause damage to the vehicle paintwork.

33 Exhaust emissions check

This check is part of the manufacturer's maintenance schedule, and involves testing the exhaust emissions using an exhaust gas analyser. Unless a fault is suspected, this test is not essential, although it should be noted that it is recommended by the manufacturers. Exhaust emissions testing is included as part of the MOT test.

Chapter 1 Part B:
Routine maintenance and servicing - diesel models

Contents

Degrees of difficulty

Easy, suitable for novice with little experience

Fairly easy, suitable for beginner with some experience

Fairly difficult, suitable for competent DIY mechanic

Difficult, suitable for experienced DIY mechanic

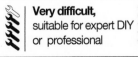
Very difficult, suitable for expert DIY or professional

Lubricants and fluids . . . . Refer to end of *Weekly checks*

Capacities

Engine oil (including filter)
All models . . . . 3.5 litres

Cooling system
All models . . . . 7.5 litres (approx.)

Transmission
Manual transmission . . . . 2.25 litres
Automatic transmission fluid:
    Initial filling . . . . 5.5 litres
    Fluid change . . . . 3.5 litres
Automatic transmission final drive . . . . 1.0 litre

Power-assisted steering
All models . . . . 1.5 litres (approx.)

Fuel tank
All models (approximate) . . . . 62 litres

Cooling system

Antifreeze mixture:
    40% antifreeze . . . . Protection down to -25°C
    50% antifreeze . . . . Protection down to -35°C
Note: *Refer to antifreeze manufacturer for latest recommendations.*

Fuel system

Glow plugs . . . . Bosch 0 250 202 022

Brakes

Front/rear brake pad minimum thickness (including backing plate) . . . . 7.0 mm

Auxiliary drivebelt

Tension adjustment:
    Main drivebelt . . . . Automatically adjusted
    Air conditioning compressor drivebelt . . . . Apply a torque of 25 Nm to the hexagon on the tensioner body

Torque wrench settings

	Nm	lbf ft
Automatic transmission final drive oil filler/level plug	25	18
Automatic transmission inspection plug (01N)	15	11
Automatic transmission overflow pipe (01N)	2	1
Coolant pump drain plug	30	22
Manual transmission filler/level plug	25	18
Power steering pump mounting	25	18
Roadwheel bolts	120	89
Sump drain plug	30	22

The maintenance intervals in this manual are provided with the assumption that you, not the dealer, will be carrying out the work. These are the minimum intervals recommended by us for vehicles driven daily. If you wish to keep your vehicle in peak condition at all times, you may wish to perform some of these procedures more often. We encourage frequent maintenance, since it enhances the efficiency, performance and resale value of your vehicle. **Note**: *The mileage conversions from kilometres are approximate.*

All Audi A4 models are equipped with a service interval display indicator in the instrument panel. Every time the engine is started the panel will illuminate for a few seconds, displaying one of the following.

Models up to 1997:
OEL - 15 000 km service required
In 1 - 12 month, 30 000 km or 60 000 km inspection service required, according to mileage completed
In 2 - 24 month service required

Models from 1997:
Service OIL - 15 000 km service required
Service INSP - 12 month, 30 000 km or 60 000 km 120 000 km or 24 month service required, according to mileage completed
This is basically a reminder that a service is due, eg: when the Audi technician completes an oil change service, the display indicator is re-programmed to show OEL when another 15 000 km have been covered. When a service is due, the display will begin indicating it 1000 km or 10 days beforehand. The indicator is programmed in km, even if the vehicle has mileage indication.

Note: *A 'long-life' service schedule was introduced towards the end of 1999, applicable only to vehicles built from model-year 2000 onwards. Full details of the service schedule were not available at the time of writing - refer to your VAG dealer for further information.*

Every 250 miles (400 km) or weekly

☐ Refer to *Weekly checks*

Every 10 000 miles (15 000 km) - 'OEL' or 'service OIL' on interval display

☐ Renew the engine oil and filter (Section 3)
Note: *Frequent oil and filter changes are good for the engine. We recommend changing the oil more frequently than the mileage specified here, or at least twice a year*
☐ Check the front brake pad thickness (Section 4)
☐ Check the condition of the auxiliary drivebelt (Section 5)
☐ Check the condition of the timing belt (Section 6)
☐ Reset the service interval display (Section 7)
☐ Drain the water from the fuel filter (Section 8)

Every 12 months - 'In 1' or 'service INSP' on interval display

☐ Check the operation of the windscreen/tailgate/headlight washer system(s) (Section 9)
☐ Check the tyre wear (Section 10)
☐ Lubricate all hinges and locks (Section 11)
☐ Check the battery electrolyte level (Section 12)
☐ Check the engine management ECU memory for faults (Section 13)
☐ Check all underbonnet components and hoses for fluid leaks (Section 14)
☐ Check the cooling system for anti-freeze content (Section 15)
☐ Check all brake flexible hoses and rigid pipes for condition (Section 16)
☐ Check the rear brake pad/shoe lining thickness (Section 17)
☐ Check the condition of the exhaust system and its mountings (Section 18)
☐ Check the steering and suspension components for condition and security (Section 19)
☐ Carry out a road test (Section 20)

Every 20 000 miles (30 000 km) - 'In 1' or 'service INSP' on interval display

Note: *Carry out the following work in addition to that described for the 12 months interval.*
☐ Renew the fuel filter (Section 21)
☐ Renew the pollen filter (Section 22)
☐ Check the underbody sealant (Section 23)
☐ Check manual transmission oil level (Section 24)
☐ Check the headlight beam adjustment (Section 25)

Every 40 000 miles (60 000 km) - 'In 1' or 'service INSP' on interval display

Note: *Carry out the following work in addition to that described for the 12 month and 20 000 mile intervals.*
☐ Renew the air filter element (Section 26)
☐ Check the final drive oil level and top up if necessary (automatic transmission) (Section 27)
☐ Renew the automatic transmission fluid. **Note:** *Every 4 years if less than 40 000 miles* (Section 28)
☐ Renew the timing belt and tensioner roller (Section 29)*
*Note: *The manufacturer's recommendation is to renew the timing belt at 60 000 miles (80 000 km) however we recommend it is renewed at 40 000 miles (60 000 km) especially if the vehicle is used mainly for short journeys or a lot of stop-start driving. The actual belt renewal interval is very much up to the individual owner but, bearing in mind that severe engine damage will result if the belt breaks in use, we recommend you err on the side of caution.*

Every 80 000 miles (120 000 km) - 'In 1' or 'service INSP' on interval display

☐ Renew the auxiliary drivebelt(s) (Section 30)

Every 2 years (regardless of mileage) - 'In 2' or 'service INSP' on interval display

☐ Renew the brake fluid (Section 31)
☐ Renew the coolant (Section 32)
☐ Carry out an exhaust emissions check (Section 33)

Underbonnet view of a 1.9 litre turbo diesel engine model (code AFN)

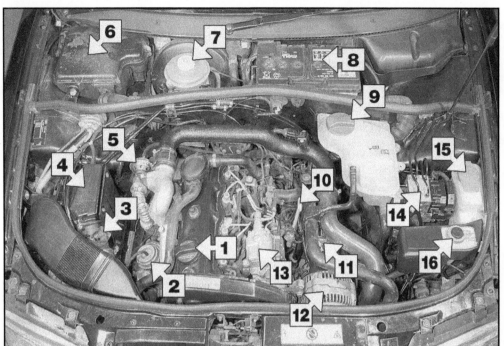

1 Engine oil filler cap
2 Turbocharger wastegate
3 Airflow meter
4 Air cleaner
5 EGR valve
6 Engine management ECU
7 Brake fluid reservoir
8 Battery
9 Cooling system expansion tank
10 Engine oil level dipstick
11 Fuel filter
12 Alternator
13 Fuel injection pump
14 ABS unit
15 Washer fluid reservoir
16 Power steering fluid reservoir

Front underbody view of a 1.9 litre turbo diesel engine model (code AFN)

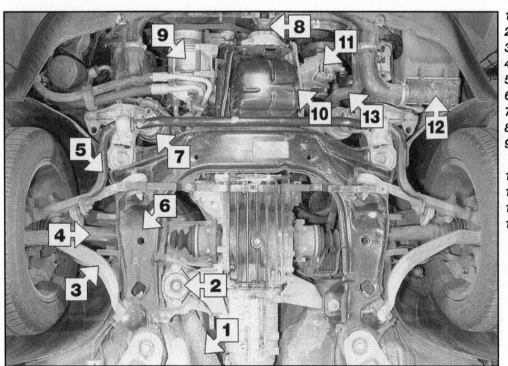

1 Exhaust front downpipe
2 Transmission mounting
3 Front suspension arm
4 Driveshaft
5 Front anti-roll bar
6 Front subframe
7 Engine mounting
8 Engine front torque arm
9 Air conditioning compressor
10 Engine sump oil drain plug
11 Power steering pump
12 Intercooler
13 Radiator bottom hose

Rear underbody view of a diesel engine model

1 Rear suspension anti-roll bar
2 Rear axle beam
3 Tail pipe and silencer
4 Fuel tank
5 Handbrake cables
6 Brake hydraulic line

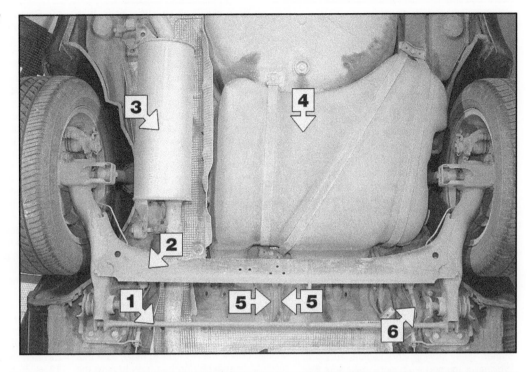

1 Introduction

This Chapter is designed to help the home mechanic maintain his/her vehicle for safety, economy, long life and peak performance.

The Chapter contains a master maintenance schedule, followed by Sections dealing specifically with each task in the schedule. Visual checks, adjustments, component renewal and other helpful items are included. Refer to the accompanying illustrations of the engine compartment and the underside of the vehicle for the locations of the various components.

Servicing your vehicle in accordance with the mileage/time maintenance schedule and the following Sections will provide a planned maintenance programme, which should result in a long and reliable service life. This is a comprehensive plan, so maintaining some items but not others at the specified service intervals, will not produce the same results.

As you service your vehicle, you will discover that many of the procedures can - and should - be grouped together, because of the particular procedure being performed, or because of the proximity of two otherwise unrelated components to one another. For example, if the vehicle is raised for any reason, the exhaust can be inspected at the same time as the suspension and steering components.

The first step in this maintenance programme is to prepare yourself before the actual work begins. Read through all the Sections relevant to the work to be carried out, then make a list and gather all the parts and tools required. If a problem is encountered, seek advice from a parts specialist, or a dealer service department.

2 Regular maintenance

1 If, from the time the vehicle is new, the routine maintenance schedule is followed closely, and frequent checks are made of fluid levels and high-wear items, as suggested throughout this manual, the engine will be kept in relatively good running condition, and the need for additional work will be minimised.
2 It is possible that there will be times when the engine is running poorly due to the lack of regular maintenance. This is even more likely if a used vehicle, which has not received regular and frequent maintenance checks, is purchased. In such cases, additional work may need to be carried out, outside of the regular maintenance intervals.
3 If engine wear is suspected, a compression test (refer to the relevant Part of Chapter 2) will provide valuable information regarding the overall performance of the main internal components. Such a test can be used as a basis to decide on the extent of the work to be carried out. If, for example, a compression test indicates serious internal engine wear, conventional maintenance as described in this Chapter will not greatly improve the performance of the engine, and may prove a waste of time and money, unless extensive overhaul work is carried out first.
4 The following series of operations are those most often required to improve the performance of a generally poor-running engine:

Primary operations

a) Clean, inspect and test the battery (See Weekly checks).
b) Check all the engine-related fluids (See Weekly checks).
c) Check the condition of the auxiliary drivebelts (Sections 5 or 30).
d) Check the condition of the air filter, and renew if necessary (Section 26).
e) Renew the fuel filter (Section 21).
f) Check the condition of all hoses, and check for fluid leaks (Section 14).

5 If the above operations do not prove fully effective, carry out the following secondary operations:

Secondary operations

All items listed under *Primary operations*, plus the following:

a) Check the charging system (refer to Chapter 5A).
b) Check the pre-heating system (refer to Chapter 5C).
c) Check the fuel system (refer to Chapter 4B).

Every 10 000 miles (15 000 km)

3 Engine oil and filter renewal

1 Frequent oil and filter changes are the most important maintenance procedures which can be undertaken by the DIY owner. As engine oil ages, it becomes diluted and contaminated, which leads to premature engine wear.
2 Before starting this procedure, gather all the necessary tools and materials. Also make sure that you have plenty of clean rags and newspapers handy, to mop up any spills. Ideally, the engine oil should be warm, as it will drain better, and more built-up sludge will be removed with it. Take care, however, not to touch the exhaust or any other hot parts of the engine when working under the vehicle. To avoid any possibility of scalding, and to protect yourself from possible skin irritants and other harmful contaminants in used engine oils, it is advisable to wear gloves when carrying out this work. Access to the underside of the vehicle is possible if it can be raised on a lift, driven onto ramps, or jacked up and supported on axle stands (see *Jacking and vehicle support*). Whichever method is chosen, make sure that the vehicle remains level, or if it is at an angle,

As the drain plug releases from the threads, move it away quickly so that the stream of oil running out of the sump goes into the drain pan and not up your sleeve

that the drain plug is at the lowest point. With the vehicle raised, remove the engine compartment undershield (where applicable).
3 Using a socket and wrench or a ring spanner, slacken the drain plug about half a turn. Position the draining container under the drain plug, then remove the plug completely **(see Haynes Hint)**. Recover the sealing ring from the drain plug **(see illustration)**.
4 Allow some time for the old oil to drain, noting that it may be necessary to reposition the container as the oil flow slows to a trickle.
5 After all the oil has drained, wipe off the drain plug with a clean rag, and fit a new sealing washer. Clean the area around the drain plug opening, and refit the plug. Tighten the plug securely.
6 If the filter is also to be renewed, move the container into position under the oil filter, which is located on the left-hand rear side of the cylinder block.
7 Using an oil filter removal tool if necessary, slacken the filter initially, then unscrew it by hand the rest of the way **(see illustration)**. Empty the oil in the filter into the container.
8 Use a clean rag to remove all oil, dirt and sludge from the filter sealing area on the engine. Check the old filter to make sure that the rubber sealing ring has not stuck to the engine. If it has, carefully remove it.
9 Apply a light coating of clean engine oil to the sealing ring on the new filter, then screw it into position on the engine. Tighten the filter firmly by hand only - **do not** use any tools.

3.3 Removing the drain plug and draining the engine oil

10 Remove the old oil and all tools from under the car then refit the undershield and lower the car to the ground.
11 Remove the dipstick, then unscrew the oil filler cap from the cylinder head cover. Fill the engine, using the correct grade and type of oil (see *Lubricants and fluids*). An oil can spout or funnel may help to reduce spillage **(see illustrations)**. Pour in half the specified quantity of oil first, then wait a few minutes for the oil to settle in the sump. Continue adding oil a small quantity at a time until the level is up to the lower mark on the dipstick. Adding around 1.0 litre will bring the level up to the upper mark on the dipstick. Refit the filler cap.
12 Start the engine and run it at idle speed for a few minutes; check for leaks around the oil filter seal and the sump drain plug. Note that there may be a few seconds delay before the oil pressure warning light goes out when the engine is started, as the oil circulates through the engine oil galleries and the new oil filter before the pressure builds up.
Caution: As a turbocharger is fitted, leave the engine idling until the oil pressure light goes out. Increasing the engine speed with the warning light on will damage the turbocharger!
13 Switch off the engine, and wait a few minutes for the oil to settle in the sump once more. With the new oil circulated and the filter completely full, recheck the level on the dipstick, and add more oil as necessary.
14 Dispose of the used engine oil safely, with reference to *General repair procedures* in the *Reference* section of this manual.

4 Front brake pad thickness check

1 Firmly apply the handbrake, loosen the front roadwheel bolts, then jack up the front of the car and support it securely on axle stands (see *Jacking and vehicle support*). Remove the front roadwheels.
2 For a comprehensive check, the brake pads should be removed and cleaned. The operation of the caliper can then also be checked, and

3.7 Removing the oil filter

3.11a Unscrewing the oil filler cap

3.11b Use a funnel when adding oil to the engine

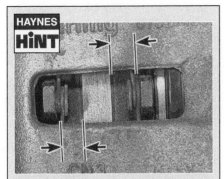

The thickness of the brake pads can be viewed through the inspection aperture in the caliper body

8.1 The fuel filter is located on the left-hand side of the engine

8.4 Water drain tap on the bottom of the fuel filter

the condition of the brake disc itself can be fully examined on both sides. Refer to Chapter 9 **(see Haynes Hint)**.

3 If any pad's friction material is worn to the specified thickness or less, *all four pads must be renewed as a set.*

5 Auxiliary drivebelt condition check

1 One main auxiliary drivebelt is fitted to drive the alternator, viscous fan, power steering pump, and coolant pump. On models with air conditioning, a separate drivebelt drives the A/C compressor. Both drivebelts are driven from pulleys mounted on the front of the crankshaft, and both drivebelts are of ribbed type.

2 For access to the drivebelts, apply the handbrake, then jack up the front of the vehicle and support it on axle stands (see *Jacking and vehicle support*). Remove the splash guard from under the engine, and where applicable remove the engine top cover as well.

3 Examine the auxiliary drivebelts along their entire length for damage and wear in the form of cuts and abrasions, fraying and cracking. The use of a mirror and possibly a torch will help, and the engine may be turned with a spanner on the crankshaft pulley in order to observe all areas of the belt.

4 If a drivebelt requires renewal, refer to Chapter 2B for the removal, refitting and adjustment procedure.

6 Timing belt condition check

1 Release the spring clips and remove the upper timing cover from the front of the engine (refer to Chapter 2B, Section 4, if necessary).

2 Inspect the timing belt for signs of excessive wear, fraying, cracking and damage. Also check for traces of oil which may have come from a faulty oil seal. The full length of the timing belt should be checked by turning the engine with a spanner on the crankshaft pulley bolt.

3 Using a steel rule or vernier calipers, measure the width of the timing belt in several places. If it is less than 22.0 mm at any point, the timing belt must be renewed with reference to Chapter 2B .

4 On completion of the check, refit the upper timing cover.

7 Reset the service interval display

1 With the ignition switched off, press and hold the display's right-hand (trip meter) button.

2 Switch the ignition on, and 'OIL' will be displayed. Release the button. If the 'INSP' service is to be reset, press the right-hand button again, until 'INSP' is shown.

3 To reset either 'OIL' or 'INSP', pull out the left-hand (clock adjuster) button for about 2 seconds.

4 On completion, switch off the ignition.

8 Drain the water from the fuel filter

1 The fuel filter is located on the left-hand side of the engine, behind the alternator **(see illustration)**. First wipe clean the filter exterior to prevent any contamination entering the fuel system.

2 Position a suitable container beneath the fuel filter. For improved access, remove the pressure air duct from the intercooler by loosening the clips and unscrewing the mounting bolt.

3 Loosen the bleed screw located on top of the filter, and attach a rubber tube to the drain tap on the bottom of the filter. Direct the tube into the container.

4 Loosen the drain tap, and drain off approximately 0.1 litre of water and fuel **(see illustration)**. Tighten the drain plug, and remove the rubber tube. Remove the container.

5 Tighten the bleed screw on top of the filter.

6 Start the engine and check for leaks.

Every 12 months

9 Operation of the windscreen/tailgate/ headlight washer system(s)

1 Check that each of the washer jet nozzles are clear and that each nozzle provides a strong jet of washer fluid. The jets should be aimed to spray at a point slightly above the centre of the screen/headlight. On the

windscreen washer nozzles where there are two jets, aim one of the jets slightly above then centre of the screen and aim the other just below to ensure complete coverage of the screen. If necessary, adjust the jets using a pin.

2 Carry out a check of all wiper blades. Look for splits or cracks on the wiping surface and renew as necessary. Check that the wipers clean efficiently across their entire sweep; any gaps in the swept area may be caused by

defective wiper blade hinges, preventing the blade from following the contours of the screen/lens surface. Check that the wiper blades do not overshoot the edge of the screen/lens at the end of their sweep and that the blades park in the correct position when switched off. If this is not the case, or if the blades overlap each other at the midpoint of their stroke, the wiper arms may be incorrectly fitted (see Chapter 12).

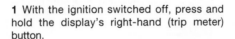

10 Tyre wear check

1 Raise and securely support the relevant side of the car in turn to allow a thorough check of each tyre to be performed; refer to *Jacking and vehicle support* for reference.
2 Turn the tyre slowly by hand and carry out an inspection as described in *Weekly checks - Tyre condition and pressure check*.

11 Lubricate all hinges and locks

1 Lubricate the hinges of the bonnet, doors and tailgate with a light general-purpose oil. Similarly, lubricate all latches, locks and lock strikers. At the same time, check the security and operation of all the locks, adjusting them if necessary (see Chapter 11).
2 Lightly lubricate the bonnet release mechanism and cable with a suitable grease.

12 Battery electrolyte level check

1 Where a standard battery is fitted, the level of the electrolyte may be checked and if necessary topped up. On some batteries, MIN and MAX marks are printed on the side of the battery and the level may be checked without removing the cell covers. Where there are no exterior marks, remove the cover(s) from the top of the cells and check that the level of the electrolyte is approximately 2 or 3 mm above the internal plates. Some batteries may have a plastic internal level indicator.
2 If necessary, top up the cells using distilled or de-ionised water.
3 Refit the cell cover(s).

13 Engine management ECU memory fault code check

This check can only be carried out by an Audi/VAG dealer or garage having the necessary equipment. If a fault code is evident, the problem must be corrected to ensure efficient operation of the engine.

14 Underbonnet components and hoses fluid leak check

1 For access to the top and bottom of the engine, remove the engine top cover, then jack up the front of the vehicle and support it on axle stands (see *Jacking and vehicle support*) and remove the undershield. Visually inspect the engine joint faces, gaskets and seals for any signs of water or oil leaks. Pay particular attention to the areas around the camshaft cover, cylinder head, oil filter and sump joint faces. Bear in mind that, over a period of time, some very slight seepage from these areas is to be expected - what you are really looking for is any indication of a serious leak (see Haynes Hint). Should a leak be found, renew the offending gasket or oil seal by referring to the appropriate Chapters in this manual.
2 Also check the security and condition of all the engine-related pipes and hoses. Ensure that all cable-ties or securing clips are in place and in good condition. Clips which are broken or missing can lead to chafing of the hoses, pipes or wiring, which could cause more serious problems in the future.
3 Carefully check the radiator hoses and heater hoses along their entire length. Renew any hose which is cracked, swollen or deteriorated. Cracks will show up better if the hose is squeezed. Pay close attention to the hose clips that secure the hoses to the cooling system components. Hose clips can pinch and puncture hoses, resulting in cooling system leaks.
4 Inspect all the cooling system components (hoses, joint faces etc.) for leaks. A leak in the cooling system will usually show up as white- or rust-coloured deposits on the area adjoining the leak. Where any problems of this nature are found on system components, renew the component or gasket with reference to Chapter 3.
5 Where applicable, inspect the automatic transmission fluid cooler hoses for leaks or deterioration.
6 With the vehicle raised at the rear, inspect the petrol tank and filler neck for punctures, cracks and other damage. The connection between the filler neck and tank is especially critical. Sometimes a rubber filler neck or connecting hose will leak due to loose retaining clamps or deteriorated rubber.
7 Carefully check all rubber hoses and metal fuel lines leading away from the petrol tank. Check for loose connections, deteriorated hoses, crimped lines, and other damage. Pay

HAYNES HINT

A leak in the cooling system will usually show up as white- or rust- coloured crusty deposits on the area surrounding the leak

particular attention to the vent pipes and hoses, which often loop up around the filler neck and can become blocked or crimped. Follow the lines to the front of the vehicle, carefully inspecting them all the way. Renew damaged sections as necessary.
8 From within the engine compartment, check the security of all fuel hose attachments and pipe unions, and inspect the fuel hoses and vacuum hoses for kinks, chafing and deterioration.
9 Where applicable, check the condition of the power steering fluid hoses and pipes.
10 On completion, refit the undershield and engine top cover, and lower the vehicle to the ground.

15 Cooling system anti-freeze content check

⚠ *Warning: Wait until the engine is cold before starting this procedure. Do not allow antifreeze to come in contact with your skin, or with the painted surfaces of the vehicle. Rinse off spills immediately with plenty of water.*

1 Note that a tester will be required to check the coolant strength; these can be obtained relatively cheaply from most motor accessory shops.
2 With the engine completely cold, unscrew and remove the filler cap from the coolant expansion tank. Follow the instructions supplied with the tester and check the coolant mixture is sufficient to give protection down to temperatures well below freezing. If the coolant has been renewed regularly this shouldn't be a problem. However, if the coolant mixture is not strong enough to provide sufficient protection it will be necessary to drain the cooling system and renew the coolant (see Section 32).
3 Once the test is complete, check the coolant level is correct (see *Weekly checks*) then securely refit the expansion tank cap.

16 Brake flexible hoses and rigid pipes condition check

1 Referring to Section 14, inspect all the braking system flexible hoses and metal pipes for signs of damage or deterioration. Any faulty pipe/hoses must be renewed (see Chapter 9).

17 Rear brake pad lining thickness check

1 Firmly chock the front wheels and select first gear or PARK, then jack up the rear of the vehicle and support it securely on axle stands (see *Jacking and vehicle support*). Remove the rear roadwheels.

2 For a quick check, the pad thickness can be carried out via the inspection hole on the rear of the caliper. Using a steel rule, measure the thickness of the pad lining including the backing plate. This must not be less than that indicated in the Specifications.

3 The view through the caliper inspection hole gives a rough indication of the state of the brake pads. For a comprehensive check, the brake pads should be removed and cleaned. The operation of the caliper can then also be checked, and the condition of the brake disc itself can be fully examined on both sides. Chapter 9 contains a detailed description of how the brake disc should be checked for wear and/or damage.

4 If any pad's friction material is worn to the specified thickness or less, *all four pads must be renewed as a set*. Refer to Chapter 9 for details.

5 On completion, refit the roadwheels and lower the vehicle to the ground.

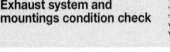

18 Exhaust system and mountings condition check

1 With the engine cold, check the complete exhaust system from the engine to the end of the tailpipe. The exhaust system is most easily checked with the vehicle raised on a hoist, or suitably supported on axle stands, so that the exhaust components are readily visible and accessible.

2 Check the exhaust pipes and connections for evidence of leaks, severe corrosion and damage. Make sure that all brackets and mountings are in good condition, and that all relevant nuts and bolts are tight. Leakage at any of the joints or in other parts of the system will usually show up as a black sooty stain in the vicinity of the leak.

3 Rattles and other noises can often be traced to the exhaust system, especially the brackets and mountings. If the components are able to come into contact with the body or suspension parts, secure the system with new mountings. Otherwise separate the joints (if possible) and twist the pipes as necessary to provide additional clearance.

19 Steering and suspension components condition and security check

Front suspension and steering check

1 Raise the front of the vehicle, and securely support it on axle stands.

2 Visually inspect the balljoint dust covers and the steering rack gaiters for splits, chafing or deterioration. Any wear of these components will cause loss of lubricant, together with dirt and water entry, resulting in rapid deterioration of the balljoints or steering gear.

19.4 Check for signs of wear in the hub bearings by grasping the roadwheel at the 12 o'clock and 6 o'clock positions, and trying to rock it

3 On vehicles with power steering, check the fluid hoses for chafing or deterioration, and the pipe and hose unions for fluid leaks. Also check for signs of fluid leakage under pressure from the steering gear rubber gaiters, which would indicate failed fluid seals within the steering gear.

4 Grasp the roadwheel at the 12 o'clock and 6 o'clock positions, and try to rock it **(see illustration)**. Very slight free play may be felt, but if the movement is appreciable, further investigation is necessary to determine the source. Continue rocking the wheel while an assistant depresses the footbrake. If the movement is now eliminated or significantly reduced, it is likely that the hub bearings are at fault. If the free play is still evident with the footbrake depressed, then there is wear in the suspension joints or mountings.

5 Now grasp the wheel at the 9 o'clock and 3 o'clock positions, and try to rock it as before. Any movement felt now may again be caused by wear in the hub bearings or the steering track-rod balljoints. If the inner or outer balljoint is worn, the visual movement will be obvious.

6 Using a large screwdriver or flat bar, check for wear in the suspension mounting bushes by levering between the relevant suspension component and its attachment point. Some movement is to be expected as the mountings are made of rubber, but excessive wear should be obvious. Also check the condition of any visible rubber bushes, looking for splits, cracks or contamination of the rubber.

7 With the car standing on its wheels, have an assistant turn the steering wheel back and forth about an eighth of a turn each way. There should be very little, if any, lost movement between the steering wheel and roadwheels. If this is not the case, closely observe the joints and mountings previously described, but in addition, check the steering column universal joints for wear, and the rack-and-pinion steering gear itself.

Suspension strut/shock absorber check

8 Check for any signs of fluid leakage around the suspension strut/shock absorber body, or

from the rubber gaiter around the piston rod. Should any fluid be noticed, the suspension strut/shock absorber is defective internally, and should be renewed. **Note:** *Suspension struts/shock absorbers should always be renewed in pairs on the same axle.*

9 The efficiency of the suspension strut/shock absorber may be checked by bouncing the vehicle at each corner. Generally speaking, the body will return to its normal position and stop after being depressed. If it rises and returns on a rebound, the suspension strut/shock absorber is probably suspect. Examine also the suspension strut/shock absorber upper and lower mountings for any signs of wear.

Driveshafts

10 With the vehicle raised and securely supported on stands, turn the steering onto full lock then slowly rotate the roadwheel. Inspect the condition of the outer constant velocity (CV) joint rubber gaiters while squeezing the gaiters to open out the folds. Check for signs of cracking, splits or deterioration of the rubber which may allow the grease to escape and lead to water and grit entry into the joint. Also check the security and condition of the retaining clips. Repeat these checks on the inner CV joints. If any damage or deterioration is found, the gaiters should be renewed as described in Chapter 8, Section 3.

11 At the same time check the general condition of the CV joints themselves by first holding the driveshaft and attempting to rotate the wheel. Repeat this check by holding the inner joint and attempting to rotate the driveshaft. Any appreciable movement indicates wear in the joints, wear in the driveshaft splines or loose driveshaft retaining nut.

20 Road test

Instruments and electrical equipment

1 Check the operation of all instruments and electrical equipment.

2 Make sure that all instruments read correctly, and switch on all electrical equipment in turn, to check that it functions properly.

Steering and suspension

3 Check for any abnormalities in the steering, suspension, handling or road feel.

4 Drive the vehicle, and check that there are no unusual vibrations or noises.

5 Check that the steering feels positive, with no excessive sloppiness, or roughness, and check for any suspension noises when cornering and driving over bumps.

Drivetrain

6 Check the performance of the engine, clutch (where applicable), gearbox/ transmission and driveshafts.

7 Listen for any unusual noises from the engine, clutch and gearbox/transmission.

8 Make sure that the engine runs smoothly when idling, and that there is no hesitation when accelerating.

9 Check that, where applicable, the clutch action is smooth and progressive, that the drive is taken up smoothly, and that the pedal travel is not excessive. Also listen for any noises when the clutch pedal is depressed.

10 On manual gearbox models, check that all gears can be engaged smoothly without noise, and that the gear lever action is not abnormally vague or notchy.

11 On automatic transmission models, make sure that all gearchanges occur smoothly, without snatching, and without an increase in engine speed between changes. Check that all the gear positions can be selected with the vehicle at rest. If any problems are found, they should be referred to a Audi/VAG dealer.

Check the operation and performance of the braking system

12 Make sure that the vehicle does not pull to one side when braking, and that the wheels do not lock prematurely when braking hard.

13 Check that there is no vibration through the steering when braking.

14 Check that the handbrake operates correctly without excessive movement of the lever, and that it holds the vehicle stationary on a slope.

15 Test the operation of the brake servo unit as follows. With the engine off, depress the footbrake four or five times to exhaust the vacuum. Hold the brake pedal depressed, then start the engine. As the engine starts, there should be a noticeable give in the brake pedal as vacuum builds up. Allow the engine to run for at least two minutes, and then switch it off. If the brake pedal is depressed now, it should be possible to detect a hiss from the servo as the pedal is depressed. After about four or five applications, no further hissing should be heard, and the pedal should feel considerably harder.

Every 20 000 miles

21 Fuel filter renewal

1 The fuel filter is located on the left-hand side of the engine, behind the alternator. First wipe clean the filter exterior to prevent any contamination entering the fuel system.

2 Position a suitable container beneath the filter. For improved access, remove the pressure air duct from the intercooler by loosening the clips and unscrewing the mounting bolt.

3 Unscrew the clamp nut and lift the fuel filter from the mounting bracket together with the hoses.

4 Attach a strap wrench to the fuel filter, then counterhold the filter head using a 17 mm spanner on the hexagon on the base of the bleeder screw. Unscrew the filter from the head. **Note:** *Do not use grips or pliers to hold the head as damage may occur resulting in leakage.*

5 Slide the plastic insert from the old filter, then slide it onto the new filter.

6 Smear a little diesel fuel on the new filter rubber seal, then fill the filter with diesel fuel. This will enable the engine to start more quickly.

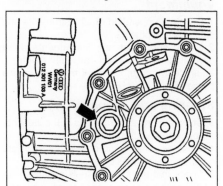

24.1 Oil filler/level plug location on the 012 manual transmission

7 Screw on the filter while counterholding the head, and tighten by hand only.

8 Insert the filter into the mounting bracket, and secure by tightening the clamp nut.

9 Start the engine and check for leaks.

22 Pollen filter renewal

Refer to the information given in Chapter 1A, Section 21.

23 Underbody sealant check

Raise and support the vehicle on axle stands (see *Jacking and vehicle support*). Using an electric torch or lead light, inspect the entire underside of the vehicle, paying particular attention to the wheel arches. Look for any damage to the flexible underbody coating, which may crack or flake off with age, leading to corrosion. Also check that the wheel arch liners (where fitted) are securely attached with any clips provided - if they come loose, dirt may get in behind the liners and defeat their purpose. If there is any damage to the underseal, or any corrosion, it should be repaired before the damage gets too serious.

24 Manual transmission oil level check

1 The oil filler/level plug is located on the left-hand side of the manual transmission, below the speedometer sender, and on some models it may be concealed by a heatshield **(see illustration)**. The plug may be either of 17 mm Allen key type, or alternatively of multi-splined type.

2 Apply the handbrake, then jack up the front and rear of the vehicle and support it on axle stands (see *Jacking and vehicle support*). To ensure an accurate check, make sure that the vehicle is level.

3 Unscrew and remove the filler/level plug.

4 Check that the oil level is 7.0 mm below the bottom lip of the filler hole. To do this, use a piece of angled metal such as welding rod.

5 If necessary, add the specified oil through the filler/level hole. If the level requires constant topping up, check for leaks and repair.

6 Refit the plug and tighten to the specified torque, then lower the vehicle to the ground.

25 Headlight beam adjustment

Halogen headlamps

1 Accurate adjustment of the headlight beam is only possible using optical beam setting equipment, and this work should therefore be carried out by a VAG dealer or suitably equipped workshop.

2 For reference, the headlights can be adjusted using the adjuster screws, accessible via the top of each light unit (see the illustrations given in Chapter 12, Section 9).

3 Some models are equipped with an electrically operated headlight beam adjustment system which is controlled through the switch in the facia. On these models, ensure that the switch is set to the basic 0 position before adjusting the headlight aim.

Electrical discharge headlights

4 The headlamp range is controlled dynamically by an electronic control unit which monitors the ride height of the vehicle via sensors fitted to the front and rear suspension. Beam adjustment can only be carried out using VAG test equipment.

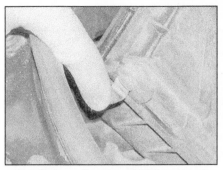

26.1 Release the clips and lift up the air cleaner cover

26.2 Removing the air cleaner element

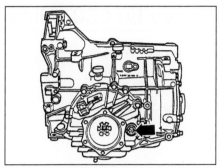

27.1 Filler/level plug location on the automatic transmission

Every 40 000 miles (60 000 km)

26 Air filter element renewal

1 Remove the air cleaner cover and air duct (if fitted), then prise open the retaining clips and lift the upper cover from the air cleaner body **(see illustration)**. Note that the airflow meter is attached to the upper cover.
2 Remove the air cleaner filter element, noting which way round it is fitted **(see illustration)**.
3 Wipe clean the main body, then fit the new air filter, making sure it is the correct way round.
4 Refit the upper cover and secure with the retaining clips.

27 Final drive oil level check and top up (automatic transmission)

1 The final drive oil filler/level plug is located on the left-hand side of the automatic transmission, behind the left-hand driveshaft inner joint **(see illustration)**. Apply the handbrake, then jack up the front of the vehicle and support it on axle stands (see *Jacking and vehicle support*). Remove the engine undershield. To ensure an accurate check, make sure that the vehicle is level.
2 Unscrew and remove the filler/level plug and check that the oil level is on the bottom lip of the filler hole. If necessary, add the specified oil through the filler/level hole. If the level requires constant topping up, check for leaks and repair.
3 Refit the plug and tighten to the specified torque, then lower the vehicle to the ground.

28 Automatic transmission fluid renewal

Note: *Renew the fluid every 4 years or 40 000 miles/60 000 km, whichever comes first.*

1 Apply the handbrake, then jack up the front of the vehicle and support it on axle stands (see *Jacking and vehicle support*). Remove the engine undershield.
Note: *For an accurate fluid level, Audi technicians use an electronic tester which is plugged into the transmission electronic system, and which determines that the temperature of the fluid is between 35°C and 40°C. In view of this, it is recommended that the vehicle is taken to an Audi dealer to have the work done. The following procedure is given on the understanding that the level is checked by an Audi dealer on completion.*
2 Note that the transmission must be refilled from below the vehicle, so make sure that the vehicle is supported in a level position.
3 Position a suitable container beneath the transmission. Wipe clean the oil pan, then unscrew the inspection plug, followed by the overflow pipe, from the bottom of the oil pan **(see illustration)**. Allow the fluid to drain into the container.
4 Refit the overflow pipe and tighten to the specified torque.
5 Remove the sealing cap and plug from the filling tube attached to the side of the oil pan.
Note: *The later sealing cap and plug should be renewed whenever removed.*
6 Add fluid to the oil pan until it runs out of the overflow pipe.
7 With P selected, run the engine at idling speed until it reaches normal temperature. If necessary add more fluid until it runs out of the overflow pipe.
8 Apply the footbrake pedal, then select each position with the selector lever, pausing for about 3 seconds in each position. Return the selector to position P.
9 At this stage, the Audi technician connects the tester to confirm that the fluid temperature is between 35°C and 40°C. **Note:** *If the fluid level is checked when the temperature is too low, overfilling will occur. If the fluid level is checked when the temperature is too high, underfilling will occur.*
10 With the engine still running at idle speed, allow any excess fluid to run out of the overflow pipe.
11 Switch off the engine, then refit the

inspection plug together with a new seal, and tighten to the specified torque.
12 Fit a new sealing cap and plug to the filling tube.
13 Lower the vehicle to the ground.

29 Timing belt and tensioner roller renewal

Refer to Chapter 2B, Sections 4 (timing belt) and 5 (tensioner roller).
Note: *The manufacturer's recommendation is to renew the timing belt at 80 000 miles (120 000 km) however we recommend it is renewed at 40 000 miles (60 000 km) especially if the vehicle is used mainly for short journeys or a lot of stop-start driving. The actual belt renewal interval is very much up to the individual owner but, bearing in mind that severe engine damage will result if the belt breaks in use, we recommend you err on the side of caution.*

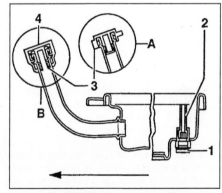

28.3 Oil pan draining components on the 01N automatic transmission

1 Inspection plug
2 Overflow pipe
3 Sealing cap and plug
4 Sealing cap B must be renewed after removal
A Early sealing cap
B Later sealing cap

Every 80 000 miles (120 000 km)

30 Auxiliary drivebelt renewal

Refer to Chapter 2B, Section 6.

Every 2 years (regardless of mileage)

31 Brake fluid renewal

⚠️ *Warning: Brake hydraulic fluid can harm your eyes and damage painted surfaces, so use extreme caution when handling and pouring it. Do not use fluid that has been standing open for some time, as it absorbs moisture from the air. Excess moisture can cause a dangerous loss of braking effectiveness.*

1 The procedure is similar to that for the bleeding of the hydraulic system as described in Chapter 9. The brake fluid reservoir should be emptied by siphoning, using a clean poultry baster or similar before starting, and allowance should be made for the old fluid to be expelled when bleeding a section of the circuit.

2 Working as described in Chapter 9, open the first bleed screw in the sequence, and pump the brake pedal gently until nearly all the old fluid has been emptied from the master cylinder reservoir.

3 Top-up to the MAX level with new fluid, and continue pumping until only the new fluid remains in the reservoir, and new fluid can be seen emerging from the bleed screw. Tighten the screw, and top the reservoir level up to the MAX level line.

 Old hydraulic fluid is often much darker in colour than the new, making it easy to distinguish the two.

4 Work through all the remaining bleed screws in the sequence until new fluid can be seen at all of them. Be careful to keep the master cylinder reservoir topped-up to above the MIN level at all times, or air may enter the system and greatly increase the length of the task.

5 When the operation is complete, check that all bleed screws are securely tightened, and that their dust caps are refitted. Wash off all traces of spilt fluid, and recheck the fluid level.

6 Check the operation of the brakes before taking the car on the road.

32 Coolant renewal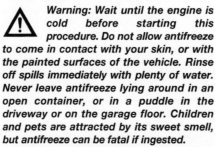

Cooling system draining

⚠️ *Warning: Wait until the engine is cold before starting this procedure. Do not allow antifreeze to come in contact with your skin, or with the painted surfaces of the vehicle. Rinse off spills immediately with plenty of water. Never leave antifreeze lying around in an open container, or in a puddle in the driveway or on the garage floor. Children and pets are attracted by its sweet smell, but antifreeze can be fatal if ingested.*

1 With the engine completely cold, cover the expansion tank cap with a wad of rag, and slowly turn the cap anti-clockwise to relieve the pressure in the cooling system (a hissing sound will normally be heard). Wait until any pressure remaining in the system is released, then continue to turn the cap until it can be removed.

2 Where necessary, release the fasteners and remove the engine lower splash shield. Position a suitable container beneath the radiator bottom hose connection, then release the retaining clip and ease the hose from the radiator stub. If the hose joint has not been disturbed for some time, it will be necessary to gently manipulate the hose to break the joint. Do not use excessive force, or the radiator stub could be damaged. Allow the coolant to drain into the container. Note that the radiator is equipped with a drain tap, but this can only be accessed with the front bumper removed.

3 Where applicable, unscrew the drain plug from the underside of the coolant pump. Remove the old seal from the plug and fit a new one.

4 If the coolant has been drained for a reason other than renewal, then provided it is clean and less than two years old, it can be re-used if there is no alternative, but this is not recommended.

5 Once all the coolant has drained, reconnect the hose to the radiator and secure it in position with the retaining clip. Where applicable, refit the coolant pump drain plug (with the new seal fitted) and tighten it to the specified torque.

Cooling system flushing

6 If coolant renewal has been neglected, or if the antifreeze mixture has become diluted, then in time, the cooling system may gradually lose efficiency, as the coolant passages become restricted due to rust, scale deposits, and other sediment. Flushing the system clean can restore the cooling system efficiency.

7 The radiator should be flushed independently of the engine, to avoid unnecessary contamination.

Radiator flushing

8 To flush the radiator, disconnect the top and bottom hoses and any other relevant hoses from the radiator, with reference to Chapter 3.

9 Insert a garden hose into the radiator top inlet. Direct a flow of clean water through the radiator, and continue flushing until clean water emerges from the radiator bottom outlet.

10 If after a reasonable period, the water still does not run clear, the radiator can be flushed with a good proprietary cooling system cleaning agent. It is important that their manufacturer's instructions are followed carefully. If the contamination is particularly bad, insert the hose in the radiator bottom outlet, and reverse-flush the radiator.

Engine flushing

11 To flush the engine, remove the thermostat as described in Chapter 3, then temporarily refit the thermostat cover.

12 With the top and bottom hoses disconnected from the radiator, insert a garden hose into the radiator top hose. Direct a clean flow of water through the engine, and continue flushing until clean water emerges from the radiator bottom hose.

13 On completion of flushing, refit the thermostat and reconnect the hoses with reference to Chapter 3.

Cooling system filling

14 Before attempting to fill the cooling

system, make sure that all hoses and clips are in good condition, and that the clips are tight. Note that an antifreeze mixture must be used all year round, to prevent corrosion of the engine components (see following sub-Section).

15 Slacken the clip and withdraw the heater unit supply hose from its bulkhead stub (see Chapter 3) until the bleed hole at the top of the hose is clear of the surface of the stub; do not disconnect the hose from the stub completely.

16 Remove the securing screws and detach the expansion tank from the engine compartment. Raise it approximately 100 mm above the engine compartment and support it there on a block of wood or using a length of wire.

17 Remove the expansion tank filler cap, and fill the system by slowly pouring the coolant into the expansion tank to prevent airlocks from forming.

18 If the coolant is being renewed, begin by pouring in a couple of litres of water, followed by the correct quantity of antifreeze, then top-up with more water.

19 Continue filling until coolant starts to run from the bleed hole in the heater hose. When this happens, refit the hose and tighten the clip securely.

20 Once the level in the expansion tank starts to rise, squeeze the radiator top and bottom hoses to help expel any trapped air in the system. Once all the air is expelled, top-up the coolant level to the MAX mark, refit the expansion tank cap, then refit the expansion tank to the bodywork.

21 Start the engine and run it at a fast idle for about three minutes. After this, allow the engine to idle normally until the bottom hose becomes hot.

22 Check for leaks, particularly around disturbed components. Check the coolant level in the expansion tank, and top-up if necessary. Note that the system must be cold before an accurate level is indicated in the expansion tank. If the expansion tank cap is removed while the engine is still warm, cover the cap with a thick cloth, and unscrew the cap slowly to gradually relieve the system pressure (a hissing sound will normally be heard). Wait until any pressure remaining in the system is released, then continue to turn the cap until it can be removed. Never remove the cap when the engine is still hot.

Antifreeze mixture

Caution: Models built up to June 1996 were filled with coolant containing antifreeze VAG part number G011A8C (green in colour) from new. Models built from July 1996 were filled with coolant containing antifreeze VAG part number G012A8D (red in colour) from new. DO NOT mix these two different types of antifreeze together in any proportion, as severe engine damage may result. If the coolant visible in the expansion tank is brown in colour, then the cooling system may have been topped up with coolant containing the wrong type of antifreeze. If you are unsure of the type of antifreeze used, or if you suspect that mixing may have occurred, the best course of action is to drain, flush and refill the cooling system.

23 The antifreeze should always be renewed at the specified intervals. This is necessary not only to maintain the antifreeze properties, but also to prevent corrosion which would otherwise occur as the corrosion inhibitors become progressively less effective.

24 Always use ethylene-glycol-based antifreeze suitable for use in mixed-metal cooling systems. The quantity of antifreeze and levels of protection are indicated in the Specifications.

25 Before adding antifreeze, the cooling system should be completely drained, preferably flushed, and all hoses checked for condition and security.

26 After filling with antifreeze, a label should be attached to the expansion tank, stating the type and concentration of antifreeze used, and the date installed. Any subsequent topping-up should be made with the same type and concentration of antifreeze.

27 Do not use engine antifreeze in the windscreen/tailgate/headlight washer system, as it will cause damage to the vehicle paintwork.

33 Exhaust emissions check

This check is part of the manufacturer's maintenance schedule, and involves testing the exhaust emissions using a diesel exhaust gas analyser. Unless a fault is suspected, this test is not essential, although it should be noted that it is recommended by the manufacturers. Exhaust emissions testing is included as part of the MOT test.

Chapter 2 Part A:
Petrol engine in-car repair procedures

Contents

Degrees of difficulty

Easy, suitable for novice with little experience	**Fairly easy,** suitable for beginner with some experience 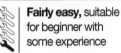	**Fairly difficult,** suitable for competent DIY mechanic 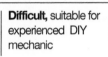	**Difficult,** suitable for experienced DIY mechanic	**Very difficult,** suitable for expert DIY or professional

Specifications

General

Engine code*
  1595 cc, Bosch Motronic 3.2 injection, 74 kW (100 bhp) . . . . ADP
  1595 cc, Simos, 74 kW (100 bhp) . . . . AHL
  1781 cc, Bosch Motronic injection, 92 kW (124 bhp) . . . . ADR
  1781 cc, Bosch Motronic injection, 88 kW (119 bhp) . . . . AFY
  1781 cc, Bosch Motronic injection, 92 kW (124 bhp) . . . . APT
  1781 cc, Bosch Motronic injection . . . . APW
  1781 cc, Bosch Motronic injection, 110 kW (149 bhp) . . . . AEB, APU
  1781 cc, Bosch Motronic injection, 132 kW (178 bhp) . . . . AJL
* **Note:** See 'Vehicle identification' at the end of this manual for the location of code marking on the engine.
Bore:
  All models . . . . 81.0 mm
Stroke:
  1.6 litre models . . . . 77.4 mm
  1.8 litre models . . . . 86.4 mm
Compression ratio:
  ADP . . . . 10.3 : 1
  AHL . . . . 10.2 : 1
  ADR . . . . 10.3 : 1
  APT . . . . 10.3 : 1
  APW . . . . 10.3 : 1
  AFY . . . . 9.2 : 1
  AEB, APU . . . . 9.5 : 1
  AJL . . . . 9.5 : 1
Compression pressures (wear limit):
  ADP, AHL, ADR, AFY . . . . 7.5 bar
  AEB, APU, AJL, APT, APW . . . . 7.0 bar
  Maximum difference between cylinders . . . . 3.0 bar
Firing order . . . . 1 - 3 - 4 - 2
No 1 cylinder location . . . . Timing belt end

Lubrication system

Oil pump type:
All except engine code AHL .... Sump-mounted, driven indirectly from intermediate shaft
AHL .... Sump-mounted, chain-driven from crankshaft
Oil pressure (oil temperature 80°C):
All except engine code AHL:
At idling .... 1.0 to 3.5 bar
At 3000 rpm .... 5.0 to 7.0 bar
AHL:
At idling .... 2.0 bar minimum
At 2000 rpm .... 3.0 to 4.5 bar
Oil pump backlash .... 0.2 mm (wear limit)
Oil pump axial clearance .... 0.15 mm (wear limit)

Torque wrench settings

	Nm	lbf ft
Air conditioning compressor drivebelt tensioner	20	15
Automatic camshaft adjuster bolt (DOHC engines)	10	7
Big-end bearing caps bolts/nuts:		
Stage 1	30	22
Stage 2	Angle-tighten a further 90°	
Camshaft bearing cap:		
Except engine code AHL, ADP	10	7
Engine code AHL, ADP	20	15
Camshaft cover	10	7
Camshaft sprocket:		
Except engine code AHL, ADP	65	48
Engine code AHL, ADP	100	74
Coolant pump pulley halves	25	19
Crankshaft front oil seal housing:		
M6 bolts	10	7
M8 bolts	25	18
Crankshaft rear oil seal housing:		
M6 bolts	10	7
M8 bolts	20	15
Crankshaft sprocket:		
Stage 1	90	66
Stage 2	Angle-tighten 90°	
Cylinder head bolts:		
Except engine code AHL:		
Stage 1	60	44
Stage 2	Angle-tighten 180° (or 2 x 90°)	
Engine code AHL:		
Stage 1	40	30
Stage 2	Angle-tighten 180° (or 2 x 90°)	
Driveplate mounting bolts:		
Stage 1	60	44
Stage 2	Angle-tighten 90°	
Engine mounting to subframe	25	18
Engine-to-transmission bolts:		
M10	45	33
M12	65	48
Exhaust pipe to manifold	30	22
Flywheel mounting bolts:		
Stage 1	60	44
Stage 2	Angle-tighten 180° (or 2 x 90°)	
Hall sender rotor to inlet camshaft (engine codes ADR, AFY, AEB, APU, AJL)	25	18
Hall sender to cylinder head	10	7
Ignition coil (engine codes AEB, APU, AJL)	10	7
Inlet manifold support bracket	20	15
Inlet manifold:		
Except engine codes AHL, ADP	10	7
Engine codes AHL, ADP	20	15
Intermediate shaft flange	25	18
Intermediate shaft sprocket:		
Except engine code ADP	65	48
Engine code ADP	80	59

Torque wrench settings (continued)

	Nm	lbf ft
Main bearing cap bolts:		
Except engine code AHL:		
Stage 1	65	48
Stage 2	Angle-tighten a further 90°	
Engine code AHL:		
Stage 1	40	30
Stage 2	Angle-tighten a further 90°	
Oil jets	27	20
Oil pump cover (engine codes ADP, ADR, AFY, AEB, APU, AJL)	10	7
Oil pump:		
Engine codes ADP, ADR, AFY, AEB, APU, AJL	25	18
Engine code AHL	15	11
Oil retention valve	8	6
Sump:		
Engine codes ADP:		
Short bolts in two stages to	20	15
Long bolts (at flywheel/driveplate end)	45	33
Engine codes ADR, AFY, AEB, APU, AJL:		
Short sump-to-block bolts in two stages to	15	11
Long sump-to-block bolts	45	33
Sump-to-transmission bolts:		
M8	25	18
M10	45	33
Engine code AHL:		
Short bolts in two stages to	15	11
Long bolts (at flywheel/driveplate end)	45	33
Timing belt rear guard	20	15
Timing belt tensioner (engine code ADP)	25	18
Timing belt tensioner nut (engine code AHL)	15	11
Viscous fan unit	45	33

1 General information

Using this Chapter

Chapter 2 is divided into three Parts; A, B and C. Repair operations that can be carried out with the engine in the vehicle are described in Part A (petrol engines) and Part B (diesel engines). Part C covers the removal of the engine/transmission as a unit, and describes the engine dismantling and overhaul procedures.

In Parts A and B, the assumption is made that the engine is installed in the vehicle, with all ancillaries connected. If the engine has been removed for overhaul, the preliminary dismantling information which precedes each operation may be ignored.

Access to the engine compartment can be improved by removing the bonnet as described in Chapter 11.

Engine description

Throughout this Chapter, engines are identified and referred to by the manufacturer's code letters, rather than capacity. A listing of all engines covered, together with their code letters, is given in the Specifications.

The engines are water-cooled, single or double overhead camshaft, in-line four-cylinder units, with cast-iron cylinder blocks and aluminium-alloy cylinder heads. All are

mounted longitudinally at the front of the vehicle, with the transmission bolted to the rear of the engine.

The crankshaft is of five-bearing type, and thrust washers are fitted to the centre main bearing to control crankshaft endfloat.

The camshaft is driven by a toothed timing belt from the crankshaft sprocket. On ADR, APT, APW, AFY, AEB, APU and AJL double overhead camshaft engines, the timing belt drives the exhaust camshaft, and the inlet camshaft is driven from the exhaust camshaft by chain at the rear of the camshafts. A hydraulic tensioner is fitted to the chain, and on ADR, AFY and APT engines this takes the form of a mechanical camshaft adjuster to automatically vary the inlet camshaft valve timing.

On ADP, ADR, AFY, APT and APW engines, the timing belt also drives the intermediate shaft, which is used to drive the oil pump and, on some engines, the distributor. The valves are operated from the camshaft through hydraulic bucket type tappets, and the valve clearances are adjusted automatically.

The cylinder head carries the single or double camshafts which are driven by a toothed timing belt. It also houses the inlet and exhaust valves, which are closed by single or double coil springs, and which run in guides pressed into the cylinder head. The camshaft actuates the valves directly via hydraulic tappets, mounted in the cylinder head. The cylinder head contains integral oilways which supply and lubricate the tappets.

On all engines except AHL, engine coolant is circulated by a pump, driven by an auxiliary drivebelt from the crankshaft pulley. On some models the pump may be driven indirectly from the power steering pump pulley. On AHL engines the coolant pump is driven by the timing belt. For details of the cooling system, refer to Chapter 3.

Lubricant is circulated under pressure by a pump, driven either by a chain from the crankshaft (AHL) or by the intermediate shaft (all other engines). Oil is drawn from the sump through a strainer, and then forced through an externally-mounted, replaceable screw-on filter. From there, it is distributed to the cylinder head, where it lubricates the camshaft journals and hydraulic tappets, and also to the crankcase, where it lubricates the main bearings, connecting rod big-ends, gudgeon pins and cylinder bores. An oil pressure switch is located on the oil filter housing, operating at 1.4 bars. On all except ADP engines, an oil cooler mounted above the oil filter is supplied with coolant from the cooling system to reduce the temperature of the oil before it re-enters the engine.

Repairs possible with the engine installed in the vehicle:

The following operations can be performed without removing the engine:

a) Auxiliary drivebelts - removal and refitting.
b) Camshaft(s) - removal and refitting.*
c) Camshaft oil seal - renewal.
d) Camshaft sprocket - removal and refitting.

2.4 TDC marks on the lower timing belt cover

e) *Coolant pump - removal and refitting (refer to Chapter 3).*
f) *Crankshaft oil seals - renewal.*
g) *Crankshaft sprocket - removal and refitting.*
h) *Cylinder head - removal and refitting.**
i) *Engine mountings - inspection and renewal.*
j) *Intermediate shaft oil seal (except engine AHL) - renewal.*
k) *Oil pump and pickup assembly - removal and refitting.*
l) *Sump - removal and refitting.*
m) *Timing belt, sprockets and cover - removal, inspection and refitting.*

*Cylinder head dismantling procedures are detailed in Chapter 2C, with details of camshaft and hydraulic tappet removal.

Note: *It is possible to remove the pistons and connecting rods (after removing the cylinder head and sump) without removing the engine. However, this is not recommended. Work of this nature is more easily and thoroughly completed with the engine on the bench, as described in Chapter 2C.*

2 Engine valve timing marks - general information and usage

General information

1 The crankshaft, camshaft and, except on engine AHL, the intermediate shaft sprockets are driven by the timing belt, and rotate in phase with each other. When the timing belt is

2.5 TDC marks on the camshaft sprocket and timing inner cover

removed during servicing or repair, it is possible for the shafts to rotate independently of each other, and the correct phasing is then lost.
2 The design of the engines covered in this Chapter is such that piston-to-valve contact will occur if the crankshaft is turned with the timing belt removed. For this reason, it is important that the correct phasing between the camshaft, crankshaft and intermediate shaft (where applicable) is preserved whilst the timing belt is off the engine. This is achieved by setting the engine in a reference condition (known as Top Dead Centre or TDC) before the timing belt is removed, and then preventing the shafts from rotating until the belt is refitted. Similarly, if the engine has been dismantled for overhaul, the engine can be set to TDC during reassembly to ensure that the correct shaft phasing is restored.
Note: *On engine code AHL, the coolant pump is also driven by the timing belt, but the pump alignment is not critical. On engine codes ADR, APT, APW, AFY, AEB, APU, AJL the intermediate shaft drives only the oil pump, so its alignment with the crankshaft and camshaft is not critical.*
3 TDC is the highest position a piston reaches within its respective cylinder - in a four-stroke engine, each piston reaches TDC twice per cycle; once on the compression stroke, and once on the exhaust stroke. In general, TDC normally refers to No 1 cylinder on the compression stroke. Note that the cylinders are numbered one to four, starting from the timing belt end of the engine.
4 The crankshaft pulley has a marking which, when aligned with a reference marking on the timing belt cover, indicates that No 1 cylinder (and hence also No 4 cylinder) is at TDC **(see illustration)**.
5 The camshaft sprocket (exhaust camshaft on DOHC engines) is also equipped with a timing mark **(see illustration)** - when this is aligned with a mark on the small upper timing belt cover or camshaft cover, No 1 cylinder is at TDC compression.
6 In addition, the flywheel/driveplate has TDC markings which can be observed by removing a protective cover from the transmission bellhousing. Note however that the markings cannot be used if the transmission has been removed from the engine for repair or overhaul.

Setting TDC on No 1 cylinder

7 Before starting work, make sure that the ignition is switched off.
8 Where applicable, remove the engine top cover.
9 On engine code ADP, note the location of No 1 HT lead on the distributor cap, then remove the cap and make a mark on the distributor body corresponding to No 1 segment position in the cap. This will help you determine when No 1 piston is at TDC.
10 Remove all of the spark plugs as described in Chapter 1A.

11 Turn the engine clockwise with a spanner on the crankshaft pulley and use a suitable rubber plug over No 1 spark plug hole to determine when No 1 piston is on its compression stroke (pressure will be felt through the spark plug hole). On engines with a distributor, the rotor arm will be approaching the mark made in paragraph 9.
12 Continue turning the engine in a clockwise direction until the TDC mark on the crankshaft pulley or flywheel/driveplate is aligned with the corresponding mark on the timing cover or transmission casing. For an additional check, remove the upper timing belt outer cover to expose the camshaft timing belt sprocket TDC marks.

3 Cylinder compression test

1 When engine performance is down, or if misfiring occurs which cannot be attributed to the ignition or fuel systems, a compression test can provide diagnostic clues as to the engine's condition. If the test is performed regularly, it can give warning of trouble before any other symptoms become apparent.
2 The engine must be fully warmed-up to normal operating temperature, the battery must be fully charged, and all the spark plugs must be removed (refer to Chapter 1A). The aid of an assistant will also be required. Where applicable, remove the engine top cover.
3 Disable the ignition system on engines with a distributor by disconnecting the ignition HT lead from the distributor cap and earthing it on the cylinder block. Use a jumper lead or similar wire to make a good connection. On engines without a distributor, disconnect the wiring from the ignition coil unit (see Chapter 5B).
4 Disable the injectors by disconnecting the wiring from each of them.
5 Fit a compression tester to the No 1 cylinder spark plug hole - the type of tester which screws into the plug thread is preferable.
6 Have an assistant hold the throttle wide open. **Note:** *Some later models are fitted with an accelerator pedal sender instead of a cable. The throttle will not operate until the ignition is switched on.* Crank the engine on the starter motor several seconds. After one or two revolutions, the compression pressure should build up to a maximum figure, and then stabilise. Record the highest reading obtained.
7 Repeat the test on the remaining cylinders, recording the pressure in each. Keep the throttle wide open.
8 All cylinders should produce very similar pressures; a difference of more than 3 bars between any two cylinders indicates a fault. Note that the compression should build up quickly in a healthy engine. Low compression on the first stroke, followed by gradually-increasing pressure on successive strokes,

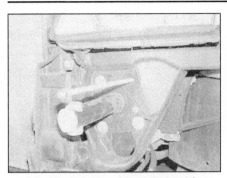

4.4a Use lengths of threaded rod for supporting the lock carrier

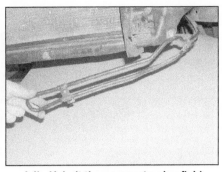

4.4b Unbolt the power steering fluid cooler . . .

4.4c . . . then unscrew the mounting bolts . . .

indicates worn piston rings. A low compression reading on the first stroke, which does not build up during successive strokes, indicates leaking valves or a blown head gasket (a cracked head could also be the cause).

9 Refer to the Specifications section of this Chapter, and compare the recorded compression figures with those stated by the manufacturer.

10 If the pressure in any cylinder is low, carry out the following test to isolate the cause. Introduce a teaspoonful of clean oil into that cylinder through its spark plug hole, and repeat the test.

11 If the addition of oil temporarily improves the compression pressure, this indicates that bore or piston wear is responsible for the pressure loss. No improvement suggests that leaking or burnt valves, or a blown head gasket, may be to blame.

12 A low reading from two adjacent cylinders is almost certainly due to the head gasket having blown between them.

13 If one cylinder is about 20 percent lower than the others and the engine has a slightly rough idle, a worn camshaft lobe could be the cause.

14 On completion of the test, refit the spark plugs, HT leads, injector wiring and top cover.

4 Timing belt -
removal, inspection
and refitting

General information

1 The primary function of the toothed timing belt is to drive the camshaft(s). Should the belt slip or break in service, the valve timing will be disturbed and piston-to-valve contact will occur, resulting in serious engine damage. For this reason, it is important that the timing belt is tensioned correctly, and inspected regularly for signs of wear or deterioration.

Removal

2 Before starting work, disconnect the battery negative (earth) lead (see Chapter 5A).

3 Apply the handbrake, then jack up the front of the vehicle and support it on axle stands (see *Jacking and vehicle support*). Where applicable, remove the splash guard from under the engine compartment.

4 Access to the timing belt is achieved by moving the complete front panel (the lock carrier assembly) away from the front of the car as far as possible, but without disconnecting the radiator hoses or electrical wiring. To do this, first remove the front bumper as described in Chapter 11, then unscrew the three quick-release clips from the noise insulation panel and unbolt the air duct from between the lock carrier and the air cleaner. Unbolt the power steering oil cooler from the bottom of the radiator. On the left-hand side of the radiator, release the wiring from the clips. Unscrew the bolts securing the lock carrier assembly to the underbody channels, then unscrew the upper side bolts located behind the headlight units. With the help of an assistant, pull the complete assembly away from the front of the car as far as possible. Audi technicians use special tools to hold the assembly, however support bars may be made out of threaded metal rod and screwed into the underbody channels **(see illustrations)**.

5 Remove the auxiliary drivebelt(s) with reference to Section 6. Also unbolt the tensioner from the front of the engine, using an Allen key **(see illustrations)**.

6 Remove the viscous fan unit with reference to Chapter 3, Section 5. Briefly, it is removed using an Allen key from behind, while holding the unit stationary with a temporary bolt inserted from behind, resting on the engine cylinder block **(see illustrations)**.

4.4d . . . and withdraw the lock carrier from the front of the car

4.5a Unscrew the bolts . . .

4.5b . . . and remove the tensioner

4.6a Unscrew the bolt . . .

4.6b . . . and remove the viscous fan unit

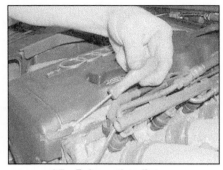

4.7a Release the clips . . .

4.7b . . . and remove the timing belt upper, outer cover

7 Unclip and remove the timing belt upper, outer cover **(see illustrations)**.

8 If the timing belt is to be refitted, mark its normal direction of travel with chalk or a marker pen.

9 Set the engine at TDC with reference to Section 2. **Note:** *Check that **all** the TDC markings align exactly, as it is not unknown for the mark on the camshaft cover to be slightly out which may lead to confusion on refitting the timing belt. If there is a slight misalignment, make a temporary second mark to use during refitting.*

10 While holding the crankshaft stationary with a socket on the centre pulley bolt, unscrew and remove the bolts securing the pulley (or vibration damper) to the sprocket. Withdraw the pulley/vibration damper **(see illustrations)**.

11 Unscrew the bolts and remove the timing belt lower outer cover from the cylinder block **(see illustrations)**.

Engine codes ADP, ADR/AFY (to 07/97), AEB, APU, AJL, APT, APW

12 Using a Torx wrench, loosen the bolt securing the tensioner roller hub to the tensioner arm. Push the tensioner hub clockwise to release the tension on the timing belt **(see illustration)**.

Engine codes ADR (08/97 on) and AFY (08/97 on)

13 Insert a 8.0 mm Allen key in the hole in the tensioner hub, and slowly turn the tensioner anticlockwise to compress the tensioner spring. Align the small holes in the top of the tensioner and the internal piston, and insert a 2.0 mm diameter twist drill to hold the tensioner spring compressed **(see illustration)**. **Do not** loosen any of the tensioner bolts.

Engine code AHL

14 Unscrew the centre nut of the semi-automatic tensioner, so that it releases all tension from the timing belt.

All engines

15 Slip the timing belt off of the crankshaft, camshaft, and the intermediate shaft or coolant sprockets, and remove it from the engine **(see illustration)**. **Do not** bend the timing belt sharply if it is to be re-used.

Inspection

16 Examine the belt for evidence of contamination by coolant or lubricant. If this is the case, find the source of the contamination before progressing any further. Check the belt for signs of wear or damage, particularly around the leading edges of the belt teeth. Renew the belt if its condition is in doubt; the cost of belt renewal is negligible compared

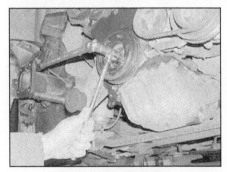

4.10a Unscrew the bolts . . .

4.10b . . . and withdraw the pulley/vibration damper

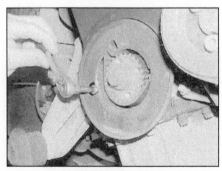

4.11a Unscrew the bolts . . .

4.11b . . . and remove the timing belt lower outer cover

4.12 Use a Torx key to loosen the timing belt tensioner roller hub bolt

4.13 Using an Allen key, turn the tensioner wheel anticlockwise, then insert the drill bit to hold it (ADR engine)

with potential cost of the engine repairs, should the belt fail in service. The belt must be renewed if it has covered the mileage stated by the manufacturer (see Chapter 1A), however, even if it has covered less, it is prudent to renew it regardless of condition as a precautionary measure. **Note:** *If the timing belt is not going to be refitted for some time, it is a wise precaution to hang a warning label on the steering wheel, to remind yourself (and others) not to turn the engine.*

Refitting

Engine codes ADP, ADR/AFY (to 07/97), AEB, APU, AJL, APT, APW

17 Ensure that the timing mark on the camshaft sprocket is correctly aligned with the corresponding TDC reference mark on the camshaft cover; refer to Section 2 for details.

18 Temporarily refit the lower timing cover, then locate the pulley for the ribbed auxiliary drivebelt on the crankshaft sprocket, using two of the retaining screws - note that the offset mounting holes allow only one fitting position. **Note:** *There is a certain amount of slack in the pulley bolt holes, so it is recommended that the pulley is set mid-way.* Make sure that the TDC marks are correctly aligned, then remove the pulley and timing cover.

19 Loop the timing belt under the crankshaft sprocket loosely, observing the direction of rotation markings if the old timing belt is being refitted.

20 On engine code ADP, temporarily refit the pulley on the crankshaft sprocket, then verify that the timing marks on the crankshaft pulley and intermediate shaft sprocket are correctly aligned. The line on the crankshaft pulley must be aligned with the **dot** on the intermediate shaft sprocket. Note however that the **OT** mark on the intermediate shaft sprocket has no significance. Check that the distributor rotor arm is aligned with the mark for No 1 cylinder on the distributor body. After making the check remove the pulley.

21 Engage the timing belt teeth with the crankshaft sprocket, then manoeuvre it into position over the intermediate shaft and camshaft sprockets **(see illustration)**. Observe the direction of rotation markings on the belt.

22 Pass the flat side of the belt over the tensioner roller - avoid bending the belt back on itself or twisting it excessively as you do this. Ensure that the front run of the belt is taut - ie all the slack should be in the section of the belt that passes over the tensioner roller.

23 Tension the belt by turning the tensioner hub anticlockwise and the spring-tensioned arm clockwise; a hole and a raised lug are provided for this purpose, and a pair of sturdy right-angled circlip pliers may be used as a suitable substitute for the correct AUDI/VAG tool. Turn the tensioner until the spring-tensioned inner piston is fully extended and the outer piston lifts approximately 1.0 mm, then tighten the lock bolt. Check that the

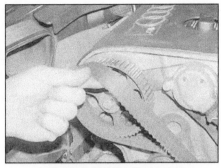

4.15 Removing the timing belt (ADR engine)

notched area A coincides with the upper end of the outer piston **(see illustrations)**. If necessary, loosen the lock bolt and re-adjust the tensioner. The distance from the top of the outer piston to the top of the inner piston eye, must be between 25.0 and 29.0 mm. **Note:** *After fitting a new timing belt, the eccentric hub will gradually rotate anticlockwise over a period of time due to the timing belt stretching. This will cause the upper end of the outer piston to rest in the area B. If the outer piston should rest in area C, it is likely that either the timing belt or tensioner components are worn excessively.*

24 On engine code ADP, temporarily refit the crankshaft pulley and check that the intermediate shaft TDC marks align correctly with the mark on the pulley. Remove the pulley.

Engine codes ADR (08/97 on) and AFY (08/97 on)

25 Ensure that the timing mark on the camshaft sprocket is correctly aligned with the corresponding TDC reference mark on the timing belt inner cover; refer to Section 2 for details. Loop the timing belt under the crankshaft sprocket loosely, observing direction of rotation markings if the old timing belt is being refitted.

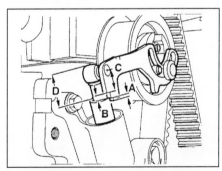

4.23a Timing belt tensioner setting

Engine codes:
ADP, ADR up to 07/97
AFY up to 07/97
AEB, APU, AJL, APT, APW
A Setting area
B Wear zone
C Adjustment required, or tensioner worn
D 25.0 to 29.0 mm

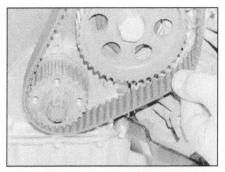

4.21 Fitting the new timing belt to the intermediate shaft sprocket

26 Temporarily refit the lower timing cover and the pulley for the ribbed auxiliary drivebelt to the crankshaft sprocket (using two of the retaining screws), noting that the offset mounting holes allow only one fitting position.

27 Check that the timing marks on the crankshaft pulley and lower timing cover are aligned with each other. The relationship of the intermediate shaft to the crankshaft is immaterial since the intermediate shaft only drives the oil pump.

28 Engage the timing belt teeth with the crankshaft sprocket, then manoeuvre it into position over the intermediate shaft and camshaft sprockets. Observe the direction of rotation markings on the belt.

29 Pass the flat side of the belt over the tensioner roller - avoid bending the belt back on itself or twisting it excessively as you do this. Ensure that the front run of the belt is taut - ie all the slack should be in the section of the belt that passes over the tensioner roller.

30 Using the 8.0 mm Allen key, turn the tensioner roller anticlockwise then remove the drill bit and release the roller to tension the timing belt.

Engine code AHL

31 Ensure that the timing mark on the camshaft sprocket is correctly aligned with the corresponding TDC reference mark on the timing belt inner cover; refer to Section 2 for details.

32 Loop the timing belt under the crankshaft sprocket loosely, observing the direction of rotation markings if the old timing belt is being refitted.

4.23b Setting the timing belt tension (ADR engine up to 07/97)

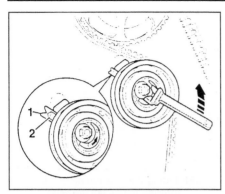

4.37 Timing belt tensioner setting (engine code AHL)

1 Notch   2 Pointer

33 Temporarily refit the lower timing cover and the pulley for the ribbed auxiliary drivebelt to the crankshaft sprocket (using two of the retaining screws), noting that the offset mounting holes allow only one fitting position.
34 Check that the timing marks on the crankshaft pulley and lower timing cover are aligned with each other.
35 Engage the timing belt teeth with the crankshaft sprocket, then manoeuvre it into position over the coolant pump and camshaft sprockets. Observe the direction of rotation markings on the belt.
36 Pass the flat side of the belt over the tensioner roller - avoid bending the belt back on itself or twisting it excessively as you do this. Ensure that the front run of the belt is taut - ie all the slack should be in the section of the belt that passes over the tensioner roller. Check that the tag on the tensioner backplate is engaged with the recess in the cylinder head.
37 Audi technicians use a special tool which engages the two holes in the tensioner wheel, however 90° circlip pliers or two close-fitting drill bits and a lever can be used. Turn the tensioner anticlockwise as far as possible, then turn it slowly clockwise until the pointer is approximately 10.0 mm below the stationary notch. Continue to turn the tensioner until the two pointers are exactly opposite each other, then tighten the nut to the specified torque **(see illustration)**.

All engines

38 Using a spanner or wrench and socket on the crankshaft pulley centre bolt, rotate the crankshaft through two complete revolutions. Reset the engine to TDC on No 1 cylinder with reference to Section 2, and check that the crankshaft pulley, intermediate shaft and camshaft sprocket timing marks are correctly aligned. Re-check the timing belt tension and adjust it, if necessary.
39 Refit the lower section of the outer timing belt cover, then refit the pulley. Finally, insert and tighten the retaining bolts.
40 Refit the timing belt upper, outer cover.
41 Refit the viscous fan unit with reference to Chapter 3, then refit the auxiliary drivebelt tensioner and tighten the bolts. Refit the auxiliary drivebelt(s) with reference to Section 6.
42 Refit the lock carrier assembly using a reversal of the removal procedure.

43 Refit the splash guard under the engine compartment, then lower the vehicle to the ground.
44 Reconnect the battery negative (earth) lead (see Chapter 5A).

5 Timing belt tensioner and sprockets - removal, inspection and refitting

Removal

1 Remove the timing belt as described in Section 4. If necessary, unbolt the inner cover from the cylinder block **(see illustration)**.

Tensioner/roller

2 To remove the tensioner spring assembly on engine codes ADP, ADR (up to 07/97), AFY (up to 07/97), AEB, APU, AJL, APT, APW, unscrew the bottom mounting bolt and the bolt securing the assembly to the roller hub **(see illustrations)**. The roller hub can then be removed from the set bolt by unscrewing the retaining nut, and the set bolt can be unscrewed from the cylinder head. On engine codes ADR and AFY, unscrew the bolt and remove the idler roller from the tensioner body.
3 To remove the tensioner roller and spring assembly on engine codes ADR (08/97 on) and AFY (08/97 on) make sure that the spring is safely retained with the drill bit (see Section 4), then unscrew the bolt from the eccentric hub. Unscrew the tensioner mounting bolts including the one on the hub, and withdraw the spring assembly and roller from the front of the engine **(see illustration)**. Recover the bearing sleeve.
4 To remove the semi-automatic tensioner on engine code AHL, unscrew the retaining nut and withdraw the tensioner and plate from the location pin. Note that the tensioner plate engages in a hole in the cylinder head.

Camshaft sprocket

5 Unscrew the camshaft sprocket bolt, while holding the sprocket stationary using a tool as shown. Remove the bolt, washer (where fitted), sprocket, and (where applicable) the key **(see illustrations)**.

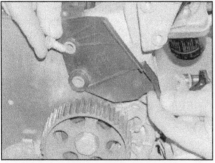

5.1 Removing the inner timing belt cover (engine code ADR)

5.2a Removing the timing belt tensioner/roller (engine code ADR up to 07/97)

5.2b Timing belt tensioner removed (engine code ADR up to 07/97)

5.3 Timing belt tensioner (engine code ADR 08/97-on)

5.5a Using a home-made tool to hold the camshaft sprocket

5.5b Removing the camshaft sprocket bolt

5.5c Removing the Woodruff key

5.6a Remove the bolt . . .

Intermediate shaft sprocket (except engine code AHL)

6 Unscrew the intermediate shaft sprocket bolt while holding the sprocket using the tool shown in paragraph 5. Remove the bolt, sprocket, and (where applicable) the key **(see illustrations)**. Note that the sprocket is fitted with the TDC marking and smaller web facing forwards.

Crankshaft sprocket

7 Unscrew the crankshaft sprocket bolt, and remove the sprocket **(see illustrations)**. The bolt is very tight, and the crankshaft must be held stationary. On manual gearbox models, engage top gear and apply the footbrake pedal firmly. On automatic transmission models, unbolt the transmission front cover and use a wide-bladed screwdriver in the ring gear to hold the crankshaft stationary.

Inspection

8 Clean all the sprockets and examine them for wear and damage. Spin the tensioner roller, and check that it runs smoothly.
9 Check the tensioner for signs of wear and/or damage and renew if necessary.

Refitting

Crankshaft sprocket

10 Locate the sprocket on the crankshaft, then tighten the bolt to the specified torque while holding the crankshaft stationary using the method employed on removal. **Note:** *Do not turn the crankshaft as the pistons may contact the valves.*

11 Refit the timing belt as described in Section 4.

Intermediate shaft sprocket (except engine code AHL)

12 Locate the key on the intermediate shaft and refit the sprocket and bolt. Tighten the bolt to the specified torque while holding the sprocket using the method employed on removal.
13 Refit the timing belt as described in Section 4.

Camshaft sprocket

14 Locate the key on the camshaft and refit the sprocket, washer (where fitted) and bolt. Tighten the bolt to the specified torque while holding the sprocket using the method employed on removal. Note on the ADR and AFY engines the sprocket must be refitted with the narrow web facing forwards.
15 Refit the timing belt as described in Section 4.

Tensioner/roller

16 Refit the tensioner roller and spring assembly using a reversal of the removal procedure.
17 Refit the timing belt as described in Section 4.

6 Auxiliary drivebelts - removal and refitting

1 Depending on the vehicle specification and engine type, one, two or three auxiliary

drivebelts may be fitted. The main drivebelt drives the alternator, viscous coupling fan, and the power steering pump. Where air conditioning is fitted, a secondary drivebelt from the crankshaft pulley drives the air conditioning compressor. On all engines except AHL, a third drivebelt from an additional pulley on the power steering pump drives the coolant pump.
2 The main drivebelt and air conditioning drivebelt are of ribbed type, however the coolant pump drivebelt fitted to non-AHL engines is of vee-type.
3 On all engines, the main drivebelt tension is adjusted automatically by a spring-tensioned idler. Where fitted, the air conditioning compressor drivebelt is adjusted using a torque wrench on the idler. On non-AHL engines, there is no adjustment for the coolant pump drivebelt.
4 To remove the drivebelts first apply the handbrake, then jack up the front of the vehicle and support it on axle stands (see *Jacking and vehicle support*). Remove the undershield from under the engine compartment.

Removal

5 If the drivebelt is to be re-used, mark it for clockwise direction to ensure it is refitted the same way round.
6 Although not essential, access to the drivebelt is best achieved by moving the complete front panel (the lock carrier assembly) away from the front of the car as far as possible, but without disconnecting the radiator hoses or electrical wiring. To do this,

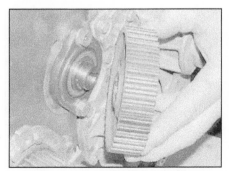

5.6b . . . and intermediate sprocket

5.7a Unscrew the bolt . . .

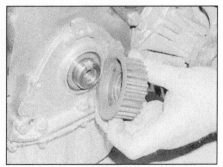

5.7b . . . and remove the crankshaft sprocket

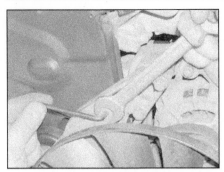

6.8a Move the tensioner clockwise with a spanner, then insert the metal rod to hold

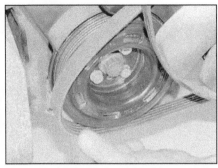

6.8b Removing the main drivebelt from the crankshaft pulley

7 Camshaft cover - removal and refitting

ADP, AHL engines (SOHC)

Removal

1 Remove the engine top cover.
2 Remove the clip and disconnect the crankcase ventilation hose from the camshaft cover. Recover the O-ring seal.
3 Unclip and remove the upper timing cover with reference to Section 4.
4 Unscrew the nuts securing the camshaft cover to the cylinder head. Note the location of the timing belt inner guard and the small support bracket, then remove the reinforcement strips.
5 Lift the camshaft cover from the cylinder head and recover the gasket.
6 Remove the oil deflector from the camshaft cover.

Refitting

7 Clean the surfaces of the camshaft cover and cylinder head, then refit the oil deflector.
8 At the rear of the cylinder head apply suitable sealant to the top edges of the semi-circular cut out in the cylinder head.
9 At the front of the cylinder head, apply suitable sealant to the two points where the camshaft bearing cap contacts the cylinder head.
10 Carefully lay the gasket on the cylinder head, then refit the camshaft cover together with the reinforcement strips, timing belt inner guard and small support bracket. Tighten the nuts progressively to the specified torque.
11 Refit the upper timing cover and secure with the clips.
12 Reconnect the crankcase ventilation hose together with a new O-ring seal, and secure with the clip.
13 Refit the engine top cover.

ADR, AFY, APT, APW engines (DOHC)

Removal

14 Remove the engine top cover.
15 Check that the ignition is switched off, then

---

first remove the front bumper as described in Chapter 11, then unscrew the three quick-release clips from the noise insulation panel and unbolt the air duct from between the lock carrier and the air cleaner. On the left-hand side of the radiator, release the wiring from the clips. Unscrew the bolts securing the lock carrier assembly to the underbody channels, then unscrew the upper side bolts located behind the headlight units. With the help of an assistant, pull the complete assembly away from the front of the car as far as possible. Audi technicians use special tools to hold the assembly, however support bars may be made out of threaded metal rod and screwed into the underbody channels.

7 On models with air conditioning, loosen the pivot and tension bolts and move the tensioner roller upwards to release the tension on the drivebelt. Slip the drivebelt from the crankshaft, compressor and tensioner pulleys.
8 To remove the main drivebelt, the automatic tensioner must be released and held with a suitable pin or tool. Using a spanner on the flats, move the tensioner clockwise until the pin holes are aligned then insert a metal rod, bolt or drill bit to hold the tensioner in its released position. Remove the drivebelt from the crankshaft, alternator, viscous fan, and power steering pump pulleys **(see illustrations)**.
9 To remove the coolant pump drivebelt (fitted to non-AHL engines), first hold the power steering pump pulley stationary using a screwdriver inserted from the rear of the pump, then unscrew the bolts securing the

pulley to the coolant pump. Remove the drivebelt and the two halves of the pulley **(see illustration)**. **Note:** *Before removing the drivebelt, check if it has stretched to the point where there is excessive slack. If necessary, renew the belt as there is no adjustment possible on refitting.*

Refitting

10 On non-AHL engines, locate the coolant pump drivebelt on the power steering pump pulley, then loosely assemble the two halves of the pulley and the drivebelt on the coolant pump and insert the retaining bolts loosely. Press the two halves of the pulley together while turning the pulleys and progressively tighten the retaining bolts. The belt must not be allowed to become trapped between the two halves of the pulley. Finally, tighten the bolts to the specified torque.
11 Locate the main drivebelt on the pulleys, then initially turn the tensioner clockwise and remove the retaining pin. Release the tensioner to tension the drivebelt, making sure that it is correctly located in all the pulley grooves.
12 On models with air conditioning, locate the drivebelt on the compressor and crankshaft pulleys, making sure that it is correctly located in all the pulley grooves. Move the tensioner pulley downwards and engage the drivebelt with the pulley grooves. Tension the drivebelt by applying a torque of 25 Nm to the hexagon on the tensioner body. Hold this torque then tighten the adjustment and pivot bolts.

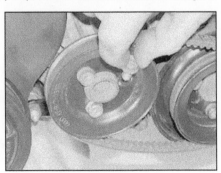

6.9a Unscrew the bolts . . .

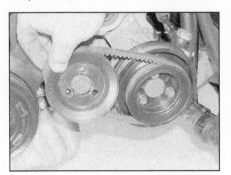

6.9b . . . remove the coolant pump drivebelt and outer pulley half . . .

6.9c . . . then remove the inner pulley half

7.19a Unscrew the nuts and bolts . . .

7.19b . . . remove the camshaft cover . . .

7.19c . . . then remove the spark plug tube gasket

disconnect the HT leads from Nos 1 and 2 spark plugs. Also disconnect the wiring from the ignition coil located on the camshaft cover.

16 Unscrew the nut and disconnect the earth wire from the ignition coil.

17 Unscrew the retaining nuts and remove the ignition coil together with the spark plug leads. Recover the gasket.

18 Unclip and remove the upper timing cover.

19 Unscrew the nuts and bolts from the camshaft cover and heat shield supports, then lift the camshaft cover from the cylinder head. Recover the main gasket, the central spark plug tube gasket and the oil deflector **(see illustrations)**.

Refitting

20 Clean the surfaces of the camshaft cover and cylinder head, then refit the oil deflector.

21 At the rear of the cylinder head apply suitable sealant to the two points where the hydraulic tensioner/camshaft adjuster contacts the cylinder head **(see illustration)**. Similarly, at the front of the cylinder head, apply the sealant to the two points where the camshaft double bearing cap contacts the cylinder head.

22 Carefully lay the main and spark plug tube gaskets on the cylinder head. Refit the oil baffle, then refit the camshaft cover **(see illustration)**. Progressively tighten the retaining nuts and bolts to the specified torque.

23 Refit the upper timing cover and secure with the clips.

24 Refit the ignition coil together with a new gasket, making sure that the HT leads are pushed fully onto the spark plugs. Tighten the retaining nuts to the specified torque.

25 Refit the engine top cover.

AEB, APU, AJL engines (Turbo)

Removal

26 Remove the engine top cover(s).

27 Loosen the clip securing the crankcase ventilation hose to the breather pipe on the front of the engine. Unscrew the mounting bolts (located on the camshaft cover and cylinder head) and disconnect the breather pipe from the hose. Move the pipe to one side.

28 Unclip and remove the upper timing cover.

29 Disconnect the wiring from the ignition coils on top of the camshaft cover.

30 On the front of the camshaft cover, unscrew the bolt and disconnect the earth wire.

31 Unscrew the retaining bolts and remove the ignition coils from the camshaft cover, at the same time disconnecting them from the spark plugs. Recover the O-ring seals, and if necessary renew them.

32 Unscrew the nuts, then lift the camshaft cover from the cylinder head. Recover the main gasket, the central spark plug tube gasket and the oil deflector.

Refitting

33 Clean the surfaces of the camshaft cover and cylinder head, then refit the oil deflector.

34 At the rear of the cylinder head apply suitable sealant to the two points where the hydraulic tensioner contacts the cylinder head. Similarly, at the front of the cylinder head, apply the sealant to the two points where the camshaft double bearing cap contacts the cylinder head.

35 Carefully lay the main and spark plug tube gaskets on the cylinder head, then refit the camshaft cover. Progressively tighten the retaining nuts and bolts to the specified torque.

36 Refit each ignition coil together with their O-ring seals, making sure that they are located on the HT leads correctly. Tighten the retaining bolts to the specified torque.

37 Reconnect the wiring to the ignition coils.

38 Refit the earth wire and tighten the bolt.

39 Refit the upper timing cover.

40 Reconnect the crankcase breather pipe to the ventilation hose, then attach the breather pipe to the camshaft cover and tighten the bolts.

41 Refit the engine top cover.

8 Camshaft oil seal - renewal

ADP, AHL engines (SOHC)

1 Remove the camshaft sprocket as described in Section 5.

2 Drill two small holes into the existing oil seal, diagonally opposite each other. Thread two self-tapping screws into the holes, and using two pairs of pliers, pull on the heads of the screws to extract the oil seal. Take great care to avoid drilling through into the seal housing or camshaft sealing surface.

3 Clean out the seal housing and sealing surface of the camshaft by wiping it with a lint-free cloth. Remove any swarf or burrs that may cause the seal to leak.

4 Lubricate the lip and outer edge of the new oil seal with clean engine oil, and push it over the camshaft until it is positioned above its housing.

5 Using a hammer and a socket of suitable diameter, drive the seal squarely into its housing. **Note:** *Select a socket that bears only on the hard outer surface of the seal, not the inner lip which can easily be damaged.*

6 Refit the camshaft sprocket with reference to Section 5.

7.21 Applying sealant to the joints on the cylinder head

7.22 Refitting the camshaft cover

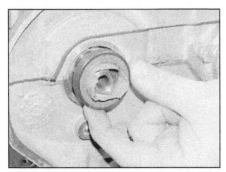

8.15 Fitting the new camshaft oil seal

8.16 Driving the new camshaft oil seal into the housing

ADR, AFY, AEB, APU, AJL engines (DOHC)

7 To remove the exhaust camshaft oil seal proceed as described in paragraphs 1 to 6. The following paragraphs describe removing the inlet camshaft oil seal.

8 Remove the auxiliary drivebelt(s) as described in Section 6. Also unbolt the tensioner from the front of the engine, using an Allen key.

9 Disconnect the wiring from the Hall sender located on the front of the inlet camshaft.

10 Unclip and remove the upper timing cover.

11 Unscrew the retaining bolt and withdraw the Hall sender assembly from the cylinder head.

12 Note the location of the Hall sender rotor and convex washer. Unscrew the central bolt and remove the washer and rotor. The rotor engages with the slot in the end of the inlet camshaft.

13 Drill two small holes into the existing oil seal, diagonally opposite each other. Thread two self-tapping screws into the holes, and using two pairs of pliers, pull on the heads of the screws to extract the oil seal. Take great care to avoid drilling through into the seal housing or camshaft sealing surface.

14 Clean out the seal housing and sealing surface of the camshaft by wiping it with a lint-free cloth. Remove any swarf or burrs that may cause the seal to leak.

15 Lubricate the lip and outer edge of the new oil seal with clean engine oil, and push it over the camshaft until it is positioned above

its housing. To prevent damage to the sealing lips, wrap some adhesive tape around the end of the camshaft (**see illustration**).

16 Using a hammer and a socket of suitable diameter, drive the seal squarely into its housing (**see illustration**). Note: *Select a socket that bears only on the hard outer surface of the seal, not the inner lip which can easily be damaged.*

17 Locate the Hall sender rotor on the end of the inlet camshaft making sure that it engages the slot. Fit the convex washer and bolt, and tighten to the specified torque.

18 Locate the Hall sender assembly on the cylinder head, and retain with the bolt tightened to the specified torque.

19 Refit the upper timing cover, making sure that it engages the bottom cover correctly, and retain with the clips.

20 Reconnect the Hall sender wiring.

21 Refit the tensioner to the front of the engine and tighten the bolts to the specified torque.

22 Refit the auxiliary drivebelt(s) with reference to Section 6.

9 Intermediate shaft oil seal - renewal

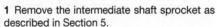

1 Remove the intermediate shaft sprocket as described in Section 5.

2 Drill two small holes into the existing oil seal, diagonally opposite each other. Thread two self-tapping screws into the holes, and using two pairs of pliers, pull on the heads of

the screws to extract the oil seal. Take great care to avoid drilling through into the seal flange. An alternative method is to unbolt the flange, remove the inner O-ring from the inner groove, and press out the seal.

3 Clean out the seal flange and sealing surface of the camshaft by wiping it with a lint-free cloth. Remove any swarf or burrs that may cause the seal to leak.

4 Lubricate the lip and outer edge of the new oil seal with clean engine oil, and start it in its housing by hand initially making sure that the closed end of the seal is facing outwards.

5 Using a hammer and a socket of suitable diameter, drive the seal squarely into its housing. **Note:** *Select a socket that bears only on the hard outer surface of the seal, not the inner lip which can easily be damaged.*

6 Where the flange has been removed, renew the O-ring, then refit the flange and tighten the bolts to the specified torque.

7 Refit the intermediate shaft sprocket with reference to Section 5.

10 Crankshaft oil seals - renewal

Crankshaft front oil seal

1 Remove the timing belt and crankshaft sprocket, with reference to Section 5.

2 The seal may be renewed without removing the housing by drilling two small holes diagonally opposite each other, inserting self-tapping screws, and pulling on the heads of the screws with pliers (**see illustration**). Alternatively, unbolt and remove the housing (including the relevant sump bolts) and remove the gasket then lever out the oil seal on the bench (**see illustration**). If necessary on engine codes ADP, ADR, AFY, AEB, APU, AJL, remove the intermediate shaft sprocket as well for improved access. If the sump gasket is damaged while removing the housing, it will be necessary to remove the sump and fit a new gasket. However, refit the sump *after* fitting the housing.

3 Dip the new seal in engine oil and drive it into the housing with a block of wood or a socket until flush (**see illustration**). Make sure that the closed end of the seal is facing outwards.

10.2a Removing the crankshaft front oil seal

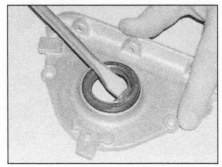

10.2b Using a screwdriver to lever out the crankshaft front oil seal from its housing

10.3 Using a socket and mallet to drive the crankshaft front oil seal into the housing

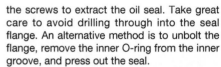

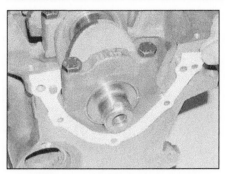

10.4a Locate a new gasket on the block . . .

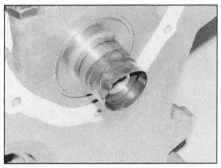

10.4b . . . then wrap some tape around the end of the crankshaft . . .

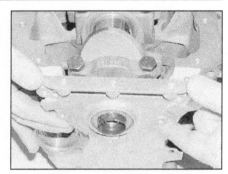

10.4c . . . refit the housing . . .

4 Fit the housing, together with a new gasket, and tighten the bolts evenly in diagonal sequence. To prevent damage to the seal as it is being fitted, wrap some tape around the end of the crankshaft first **(see illustrations)**.
5 Refit the timing belt and crankshaft sprocket, with reference to Section 5.

Crankshaft rear oil seal (flywheel/driveplate end)

Note: *Before starting work, check if the oil seal is available separate to the housing. On later engines, the oil seal is incorporated in the housing and cannot be obtained separately.*
6 Remove the flywheel/driveplate, with reference to Section 13.
7 Where the oil seal is obtainable separate to the housing, it may be renewed without removing the housing by drilling two small holes diagonally opposite each other, inserting self-tapping screws, and pulling on

the heads of the screws with pliers **(see illustration)**. Alternatively, unbolt and remove the housing (including the relevant sump bolts) and remove the gasket then drive out the oil seal on the bench. If the sump gasket is damaged while removing the housing, it will be necessary to remove the sump and fit a new gasket. However, refit the sump *after* fitting the housing. With the old seal removed from the housing, dip the new seal in engine oil and drive it into the housing with a block of wood or a socket until flush. Make sure that the closed end of the seal is facing outwards.
8 Where the oil seal is only obtainable integral with the housing, unbolt and remove the housing (including the relevant sump bolts) and remove the gasket. If the sump gasket is damaged while removing the housing, it will be necessary to remove the sump and fit a new gasket. However, refit the sump *after* fitting the housing.

9 New oil seals are provided with a fitting tool to prevent damage to the oil seal as it is being fitted. First fit the new gasket, then located the tool on the end of the crankshaft **(see illustrations)**.
10 Fit the housing and oil seal, and tighten the bolts evenly in diagonal sequence to the specified torque, then remove the tool **(see illustration)**.
11 Refit the flywheel/driveplate, with reference to Section 13.

11 Cylinder head - removal and refitting

Note: *Cylinder head dismantling and overhaul is covered in Chapter 2C.*

Removal

1 Before starting work, disconnect the battery negative (earth) lead (see Chapter 5A).
2 Apply the handbrake, then jack up the front of the vehicle and support it on axle stands (see *Jacking and vehicle support*).
3 Remove the engine top cover(s) as applicable.
4 Remove the timing belt as described in Section 4. This procedure includes removing the front bumper and positioning the front lock carrier away from the front of the car.
5 Drain the cooling system as described in Chapter 1A.
6 Detach the exhaust downpipe from the exhaust manifold with reference to Chapter 4C.

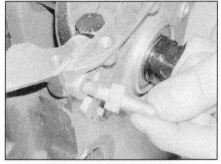

10.4d . . . and refit the bolts

10.7 Removing the crankshaft rear oil seal

10.9a Fit the new gasket . . .

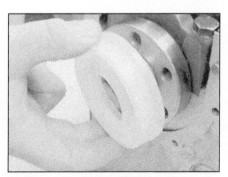

10.9b . . . then locate the fitting tool on the crankshaft . . .

10.10 Fitting the housing and oil seal over the fitting tool

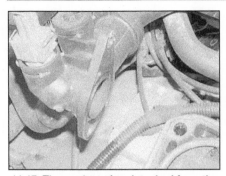

11.17 The coolant pipe detached from the rear of the cylinder head

11.19 Removing the oil splash guard (ADR engine)

11.20a Unscrewing the cylinder head bolts

Push the downpipe to the rear and recover the gasket/ring. On AEB, APU and AJL (turbocharged) engines, disconnect the breather hose located over the turbocharger, then unscrew the two bolts securing the oil supply pipe to the cylinder head. Remove the heatshield, then unbolt the turbocharger from the exhaust manifold.

7 Remove the air cleaner assembly together with the airflow meter as described in Chapter 4A. Also remove the air duct leading from the air cleaner to the throttle housing.

Engine codes ADP, ADR, AFY, AEB, APU, AJL

Note: *On engine codes ADP, ADR, AFY, AEB, APU, AJL, the cylinder head is removed together with the exhaust manifold, but without the inlet manifold.*

8 Remove the inlet manifold as described in Chapter 4A.

9 Where applicable, disconnect the wiring from the automatic camshaft adjuster.

Engine code AHL

Note: *On engine code AHL, the cylinder head is removed together with both the inlet and exhaust manifolds.*

10 Loosen the clips and disconnect the radiator bottom hose from both the radiator and engine, then remove the coolant expansion tank. Also disconnect the top hose from the coolant pipe.

11 Loosen the unions and disconnect the fuel supply and return lines. Note: *Place a cloth rag over the line before loosening the union as the fuel may be under pressure.*

12 Disconnect the accelerator cable from the throttle housing (see Chapter 4A), then disconnect the vacuum hoses from the ACF valve and brake vacuum servo.

13 Disconnect the wiring from the injectors, throttle valve sensor (on throttle housing), and camshaft position sensor (front left-hand of engine), then disconnect the wiring from the inlet air temperature sender located on the inlet manifold. Also disconnect the wiring from the oil temperature sender on the rear of the cylinder head.

14 Unbolt the inlet manifold support brackets from the manifold and left-hand side of the engine.

All engines

15 On the bulkhead at the rear of the engine, release the oxygen sensor wiring connector from the retainer then disconnect the wiring.

16 Disconnect the heater hose from the coolant elbow on the rear of the cylinder head, then disconnect the wiring from the coolant temperature sender on the elbow. On ADR, AFY, AEB, APU and AJL engines also disconnect the wiring from the second coolant sensor on the rear of the cylinder head.

17 On ADR and AFY engines, disconnect the hoses from the top coolant pipe located on the left-hand side of the cylinder head. Unscrew and remove the rear mounting bolts, then loosen only the front mounting bolt (the pipe bracket is slotted). Move the pipe to the rear and remove from the engine (see illustration).

18 On engine codes ADP and AHL, disconnect the HT leads from the spark plugs and position the leads to one side.

19 Remove the camshaft cover with reference to Section 7. This includes the removal of the ignition coil and HT leads on all engines except ADP and AHL. On engine code ADR, remove the oil splash guard (see illustration).

20 Using a splined socket, unscrew the cylinder head bolts a turn at a time, in reverse order to the tightening sequence (see illustration 11.28a or 11.28b) and remove them together with their washers (see illustrations). Note: *The cylinder head bolt heads were modified from multi-spline to Ribe, therefore two types of key may be necessary, one to remove the old bolts and another to fit the new bolts.*

21 With all the bolts removed, lift the cylinder head from the block together with the exhaust manifold (see illustration). If it is stuck, tap it free with a wooden mallet. Do not insert a lever into the gasket joint.

22 Remove the cylinder head gasket from the block (see illustration).

23 If required, remove the exhaust manifold from the cylinder head with reference to Chapter 4C. On the AHL engine, also remove the inlet manifold with reference to Chapter 4A.

Refitting

24 Thoroughly clean the contact faces of the cylinder head and block. Also clean any oil or coolant from the bolt holes in the block - if this precaution is not taken, not only will the

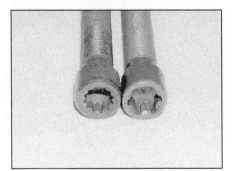

11.20b The two types of cylinder head bolt fitted

11.21 Lifting the cylinder head from the block (ADR engine)

11.22 Removing the cylinder head gasket

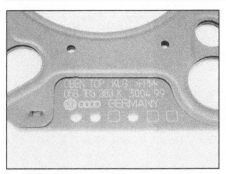

11.26 Cylinder head gasket markings

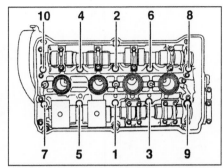

11.28a Cylinder head tightening sequence (ADR, AFY, AEB, APU, AJL engines)

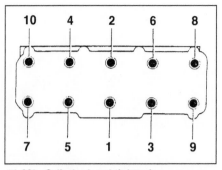

11.28b Cylinder head tightening sequence (ADP, AHL engines)

tightening torque be incorrect but there is the possibility of damaging the block. The cylinder head bolts must be renewed whenever removed (refer to the note in paragraph 19).

25 Refit the exhaust manifold to the cylinder head together with a new gasket with reference to Chapter 4C. On the AHL engine, refit the inlet manifold with reference to Chapter 4A.

26 Locate a new gasket on the block, with the part number or words OBEN TOP facing upwards **(see illustration)**. Make sure that the location dowels are in position. Audi recommend that the gasket is removed from its packaging just prior to fitting it.

27 Carefully lower the head onto the block, making sure that it engages the location dowels correctly. Do not use any jointing compound on the cylinder head joint. Insert the new cylinder head bolts, together with their washers, and initially hand-tighten them using a splined socket.

28 Using the sequence shown **(see illustrations)** tighten all the bolts to the Stage 1 torque given in the Specifications.

29 Angle-tighten the bolts in the same sequence to the Stage 2 angle given in the Specifications **(see illustration)**.

30 Refit the camshaft cover with reference to Section 7.

31 On engine codes ADP and AHL, reconnect the HT leads to the spark plugs.

32 On ADR and AFY engines, refit the top coolant pipe to the left-hand side of the cylinder head, tighten the mounting bolts and reconnect the hoses.

33 Reconnect the heater hose to the coolant elbow on the rear of the cylinder head, then reconnect the wiring to the coolant temperature sender on the elbow. On ADR, AFY, AEB, APU and AJL engines, reconnect the wiring to the second coolant sensor on the rear of the cylinder head.

34 Reconnect the oxygen sensor wiring then locate it in the retainer.

Engine code AHL

35 Refit the inlet manifold support brackets and tighten the bolts.

36 Reconnect the wiring to the injectors, throttle valve sensor (on throttle housing), and

camshaft position sensor (front left-hand of engine), also reconnect the wiring to the inlet air temperature sender located on the inlet manifold. Reconnect the wiring to the oil temperature sender on the rear of the cylinder head.

37 Reconnect the accelerator cable to the throttle housing (see Chapter 4A), then reconnect the vacuum hoses to the ACF valve and brake vacuum servo.

38 Reconnect the fuel supply and return lines and tighten the unions.

39 Refit the coolant expansion tank, reconnect the top hose to the coolant pipe, then refit the radiator bottom hose and tighten the clips.

Engine codes ADP, ADR, AFY, AEB, APU, AJL

40 Where applicable, reconnect the wiring to the automatic camshaft adjuster.

41 Refit the inlet manifold with reference to Chapter 4A.

All engines

42 Refit the air cleaner assembly together with the airflow meter with reference to Chapter 4A, then refit the air duct leading from the air cleaner to the throttle housing.

43 Reconnect the exhaust downpipe together with a new gasket with reference to Chapter 4C. On AEB, APU and AJL (turbocharged) engines, refit the turbocharger to the exhaust manifold together with the heatshield. Secure the oil supply pipe with the two bolts, then reconnect the breather hose located over the turbocharger.

11.29 Angle-tightening the cylinder head bolts

44 Refit the timing belt with reference to Section 4.

45 Refill the cooling system with reference to Chapter 1A.

46 Refit the engine top cover(s) as applicable.

47 Lower the car to the ground, then reconnect the battery (see Chapter 5A).

12 Hydraulic tappets - operational check

⚠ **Warning: After fitting hydraulic tappets, wait a minimum of 30 minutes (or preferably, leave overnight) before starting the engine, to allow the tappets time to settle, otherwise the valve heads will strike the pistons.**

1 The hydraulic tappets are self-adjusting, and require no attention whilst in service.

2 If the hydraulic tappets become excessively noisy, their operation can be checked as described below.

3 Run the engine until it reaches its normal operating temperature. Switch off the engine, then refer to Section 7 and remove the camshaft cover.

4 Rotate the camshaft by turning the crankshaft with a socket and wrench, until the first cam lobe over No 1 cylinder is pointing upwards.

5 Using a non-metallic tool, press the tappet downwards then use a feeler blade to check the free travel. If this is more than 0.2 mm before the valve starts to open, the tappet should be renewed.

6 Hydraulic tappet removal and refitting is described as part of the cylinder head overhaul sequence - see Chapter 2C for details.

7 If hydraulic tappet noise occurs repeatedly when travelling short distances, renew the oil retention valve located in the rear of the oil filter mounting housing. It will be necessary to remove the oil filter, then unbolt the housing from the cylinder block and recover the gasket. Use a suitable key to unscrew the valve, and tighten the new valve to the specified torque. Refit the housing together with a new gasket.

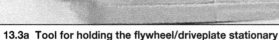

13.3a Tool for holding the flywheel/driveplate stationary

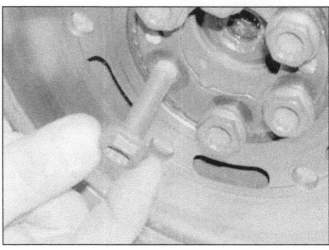

13.3b Removing a flywheel bolt

13 Flywheel/driveplate - removal, inspection and refitting

Removal

1 On manual gearbox models, remove the gearbox (see Chapter 7A) and clutch (see Chapter 6).

2 On automatic transmission models, remove the automatic transmission as described in Chapter 7B.

3 The flywheel/driveplate bolts are offset to ensure correct fitment. Unscrew the bolts while holding the flywheel/driveplate stationary. Temporarily insert a bolt in the cylinder block, and use a screwdriver to hold the flywheel/driveplate, or make up a holding tool as shown (see illustrations).

4 Lift the flywheel/driveplate from the crankshaft (see illustration). If removing a driveplate, note the location of the shim (next to the crankshaft) and the spacer.

Inspection

5 Check the flywheel/driveplate for wear and damage. Examine the starter ring gear for excessive wear to the teeth. If the driveplate or its ring gear are damaged, the complete driveplate must be renewed. The flywheel ring

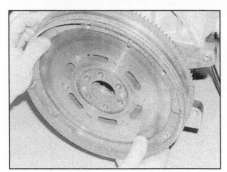

13.4 Removing the flywheel

gear, however, may be renewed separately from the flywheel, but the work should be entrusted to an Audi/VAG dealer. If the clutch friction face is discoloured or scored excessively, it may be possible to regrind it, but this work should also be entrusted to an Audi/VAG dealer.

6 With the flywheel removed, check the spigot needle bearing in the end of the crankshaft for wear by turning it with a finger. If there is any evidence of excessive wear or if the bearing has been running dry, it must be renewed. To do this, use a bearing removal puller which engages the rear end of the bearing. Drive the new bearing into position until its outer end is 1.5 mm below the end of the crankshaft. Note: A spigot needle bearing must not be fitted to the crankshaft on automatic transmission models.

Refitting

7 Refitting is a reversal of removal, however on automatic transmission models temporarily refit the driveplate using the old bolts tightened to 30 Nm, and check that the distance from the rear face of the block to the torque converter mounting face on the driveplate is 27 mm ± 1 mm. If necessary, remove the driveplate, and fit a spacer behind it to achieve the correct dimension. The raised pip on the outer shim must face the torque converter. Use new bolts when refitting the flywheel or driveplate, and coat the threads of the bolts with locking fluid before inserting them. Tighten them to the specified torque.

14 Engine mountings - inspection and renewal

Inspection

1 If improved access is required, raise the front of the car and support it securely on axle stands and remove the undershield where applicable.

2 Check the mounting rubbers to see if they are cracked, hardened or separated from the metal at any point; renew the mounting if any such damage or deterioration is evident.

3 Check that all the mounting's fasteners are securely tightened; use a torque wrench to check if possible.

4 Using a large screwdriver or a crowbar, check for wear in the mounting by carefully levering against it to check for free play. Where this is not possible, enlist the aid of an assistant to move the engine/transmission back and forth, or from side to side, while you watch the mounting. While some free play is to be expected even from new components, excessive wear should be obvious. If excessive free play is found, check first that the fasteners are correctly secured, then renew any worn components as described below.

Renewal

Front torque arm (models without air conditioning)

5 Apply the handbrake then jack up the front of the vehicle and support it on axle stands (see Jacking and vehicle support). Remove the undershield where applicable.

6 Unscrew the bolts and remove the torque arm and rubber mounting from the front of the cylinder block (see illustration). The rubber stop is available separately if required.

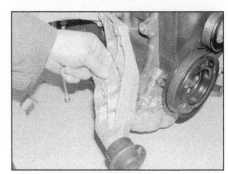

14.6 Removing the front torque arm from the engine

7 Unbolt the bracket from the front valance.
8 Fit the new torque arm and bracket using a reversal of the removal procedure.

Front torque bracket (models with air conditioning)

9 Apply the handbrake then jack up the front of the vehicle and support it on axle stands (see *Jacking and vehicle support*). Remove the undershield where applicable.
10 Unscrew the bolts and remove the stop from the bracket on the front of the engine. Move the bracket over the rubber, then prise the rubber from the cross-tube and remove the bracket.
11 If necessary, the stop plate can be unbolted from the front of the engine, and the side supports also removed.
12 Fit the new rubber and bracket using a reversal of the removal procedure.

Right- or left-hand engine mounting

13 Apply the handbrake, then jack up the front of the vehicle and support it on axle stands (see *Jacking and vehicle support*).
14 Support the weight of the engine with a hoist. Alternatively, use a trolley jack and piece of wood beneath the sump.
15 Unscrew the mounting nuts, then raise the engine and withdraw the mounting from the engine bracket and subframe **(see illustrations)**. Note that the mounting has an integral hydro action, to absorb movement of the engine and prevent engine noise transmission inside the car.
16 If necessary, unbolt the mounting bracket from the side of the cylinder block **(see illustration)**.
17 Fit the new mounting using a reversal of the removal procedure.

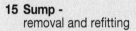

15 Sump - removal and refitting

Removal

1 Apply the handbrake, then jack up the front of the vehicle and support it on axle stands (see *Jacking and vehicle support*).
2 Unbolt and remove the undershield from under the front of the engine.
3 Position a container beneath the sump, then unscrew the drain plug and drain the engine oil. Clean the plug and if necessary renew the washer, then refit and tighten the plug after all the oil has drained **(see illustration)**. Remove the dipstick from the engine.

Engine code ADP

4 On air conditioning models, mark the compressor drivebelt for normal rotational direction, then unbolt the tensioner roller and remove the drivebelt.
5 Unbolt the engine front torque support from the engine (A/C models) or front valance (non-A/C models).
6 On air conditioning models, unbolt the

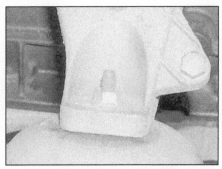

14.15a Upper mounting nut

longitudinal strut, then unbolt the torque reaction support and bracket from the engine.
7 Detach the starter motor cables from under the engine mounting by cutting the plastic cable ties.
8 Unscrew and remove the nuts from the bottom of each engine mounting.
9 Unscrew the bolts securing the coolant expansion tank to the left-hand side of the engine compartment, then disconnect the wiring from the low coolant warning switch, and place the tank to one side of the engine compartment. Leave all the hoses connected to the tank.
10 Remove the engine top cover, then remove the crankcase breather hose and air inlet duct from the rear of the engine.
11 Release the oxygen sensor wiring from the clip on the bulkhead
12 Connect a suitable hoist to the engine, then raise it as far as possible without damaging or stretching the coolant hoses and wiring. Make sure that the viscous fan does not contact the radiator; if necessary remove the fan unit with reference to Chapter 3, Section 5, and place it in the radiator cowl.
13 Unbolt the inlet manifold support bracket from the engine and transmission.
14 Unscrew the mounting bolts and remove the engine-to-transmission support bracket.
15 Unscrew and remove the sump bolts.
16 Remove the sump and gasket. If it is stuck, tap it gently with a mallet to free it.

Engine code ADR, AFY, AEB, APU, AJL

17 On air conditioning models, mark the

14.16 Engine mounting bracket on the side of the cylinder block

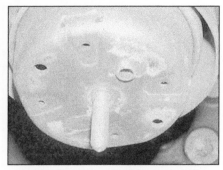

14.15b Removing the left-hand engine mounting

compressor drivebelt for normal rotational direction, then unbolt the tensioner roller and remove the drivebelt.
18 Unbolt the engine front torque support from the engine (A/C models) or front valance (non-A/C models).
19 On air conditioning models, unbolt the longitudinal strut, then unbolt the torque reaction support and bracket from the engine.
20 Detach the starter motor cables from under the engine mounting by cutting the plastic cable ties.
21 On AEB, APU and AJL engines, loosen the clip and disconnect the turbocharger hose at the air pipe in the lock carrier.
22 Unscrew and remove the nuts from the bottom of each engine mounting.
23 Remove the engine top covers.
24 Connect a suitable hoist to the engine, then raise it as far as possible without damaging or stretching the coolant hoses and wiring. Make sure that the viscous fan does not contact the radiator; if necessary remove the fan unit with reference to Chapter 3, Section 5, and place it in the radiator cowl.
25 Support the left- and right-hand front subframes with a trolley jack and length of wood. Mark the position of the subframes to ensure correct refitting and wheel alignment, then unscrew and remove the subframe mounting bolts. The front two bolts must be unscrewed first, then the rear bolts. Lower the subframes together with the anti-roll bar to the ground.
26 On manual transmission models, unscrew the left-hand transmission mounting nut until

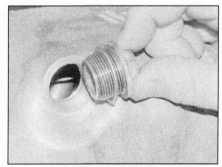

15.3 Refitting the sump drain plug (ADR engine)

15.30a Removing the rear sump bolts (flywheel removed)

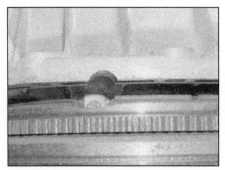

15.30b Align the cut-outs in the flywheel with the sump for access to the rear sump bolts

it is flush with the end of the bolt (approximately four turns).

27 On automatic transmission models, loosen a few turns the rear bolt on the left-hand transmission mounting, then unscrew and remove the front bolt.

28 On manual and automatic transmission models, loosen a few turns the rear bolt on the right-hand transmission mounting, then unscrew and remove the front bolt.

29 On AEB, APU and AJL engines, unscrew the flange bolts and disconnect the turbocharger oil return line from the sump. Recover the gasket.

30 Unscrew and remove the sump bolts. Note that on manual transmission models, the two rear sump bolts are accessed through a cut-out in the flywheel - turn the flywheel as necessary to align the cut-out **(see illustrations)**.

31 Remove the sump and gasket. If it is stuck, tap it gently with a mallet to free it **(see illustrations)**.

Engine code AHL

32 Access to the front of the engine is achieved by moving the complete front panel (the lock carrier assembly) away from the front of the car as far as possible, but without disconnecting the radiator hoses or electrical wiring. To do this, first remove the front bumper as described in Chapter 11, then unscrew the three quick-release clips from the noise insulation panel and unbolt the air duct from between the lock carrier and the air cleaner. On the left-hand side of the radiator,

release the wiring from the clips. Unscrew the bolts securing the lock carrier assembly to the underbody channels, then unscrew the upper side bolts located behind the headlight units. With the help of an assistant, pull the complete assembly away from the front of the car as far as possible. Audi technicians use special tools to hold the assembly, however support bars may be made out of threaded metal rod and screwed into the underbody channels.

33 On air conditioning models, mark the compressor drivebelt for normal rotational direction, then unbolt the tensioner roller and remove the drivebelt.

34 Remove the auxiliary drivebelt as described in Section 6.

35 Remove the viscous fan unit with reference to Chapter 3, Section 5. Briefly, it is removed by inserting an Allen key from behind, while holding the unit stationary with a temporary bolt inserted from behind, resting on the engine cylinder block.

36 Unbolt the torque arm bracket from the front of the engine.

37 Detach the starter motor cables from under the engine mounting by cutting the plastic cable ties.

38 Unbolt the inlet manifold support bracket from the inlet manifold and sump.

39 Unscrew the nut from the top of the left-hand engine mounting.

40 Note the location of the engine mountings on each side, then unscrew and remove the bottom nuts.

41 Connect a suitable hoist to the engine,

then raise it until the rear air duct contacts the bulkhead at the rear of the engine compartment.

42 Remove the left-hand engine mounting completely.

43 Support the left- and right-hand front subframes with a trolley jack and length of wood. Mark the position of the subframes to ensure correct refitting and wheel alignment, then unscrew and remove the subframe mounting bolts. The front two bolts must be unscrewed first, then the rear bolts. Lower the subframes together with the anti-roll bar to the ground.

44 Unscrew the left-hand transmission mounting nut until it is flush with the end of the bolt (approximately four turns).

45 Unscrew and remove the sump bolts, then remove the sump. If it is stuck, tap it gently with a mallet to free it. There is no gasket fitted, as sealant is used instead.

Refitting

46 Thoroughly clean the contact faces of the sump and block. On the AHL engine, it is recommended that a rotary wire brush is used to clean away the sealant.

Engine code AHL

Caution: Take care not to apply excessive amounts of sealant, in the hope of obtaining a better seal - if too much is applied, the excess may enter the sump and then block the oil pump strainer, causing oil starvation.

47 Apply a 2 to 3 mm bead of suitable silicone sealant to the sump mating surface. Run the bead of sealant around the inside of the bolt holes, and take particular care at the rear of the sump to keep the bead near the inner edge of the sump. The sump should be offered into position immediately, and the retaining bolts tightened hand-tight initially. If the engine is out of the car, make sure that the rear edge of the sump is flush with the rear edge of the cylinder block. Progressively tighten the sump bolts to the specified torque. Refer to the sealant manufacturer's advice on the length of time required for the sealant to set. Typically, it is advisable to wait at least 30 minutes before filling the engine with oil. If the car is to be left for some time with no oil in the sump, ensure that the battery remains disconnected, so that no attempt is made to start the engine.

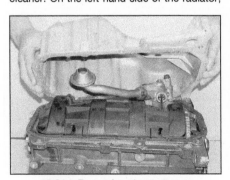

15.31a Removing the sump . . .

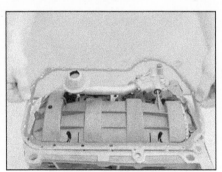

15.31b . . . and gasket

> **HAYNES HINT** *To make aligning the sump easier, obtain two or three M6 studs, and screw them by a few threads into opposite sides of the cylinder block/crankcase mating surface. The sump can be offered into position and fitted over the studs, then the remaining sump bolts can be fitted and hand-tightened. Remove the studs, and fit the rest of the sump bolts.*

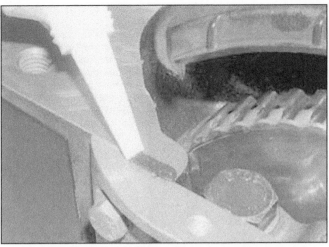

15.48 Apply sealant to the crankshaft front and rear housing joints

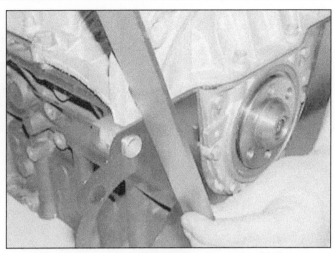

15.50 Using a straight-edge to align the sump with the rear of the engine

All engine codes except AHL

48 Apply a little sealant to the joint areas where the front and rear crankshaft oil seal housings contact the cylinder block (see illustration).

49 Locate a new gasket on the sump, then offer it up to the block and fit the bolts. Do not use any jointing compound. Tighten the bolts to the specified torque in diagonal sequence.

50 Refit the engine-to-transmission support bracket and tighten the bolts. Note: *If the sump is being fitted with the engine removed from the car and the transmission removed, make sure that the end face of the support bracket is flush with that of the intermediate plate. If the intermediate plate is removed, allow 0.8 mm for its thickness, and position the face of the bracket 0.8 mm protruding from the rear face of the cylinder block (see illustration).*

All engine codes

51 The remaining refitting procedure is a reversal removal, but tighten the nuts and bolts to the specified torque where given in the Specifications. On completion, fill the engine with the correct quantity of oil as described in Chapter 1A.

16 Oil pump and pickup - removal, inspection and refitting

Removal

1 Remove the sump as described in Section 15.

Engine codes ADP, ADR, AFY, AEB, APU, AJL

2 On engine codes ADP, ADR, AFY, AEB, APU, AJL, the oil pump is driven from the intermediate shaft

3 On models with engine code ADP, support the left- and right-hand front subframes with a trolley jack and length of wood. Mark the position of the subframes to ensure correct refitting and wheel alignment, then unscrew and remove the subframe mounting bolts. The front two bolts must be unscrewed first, then the rear bolts. Lower the subframes together with the anti-roll bar to the ground.

4 Release and remove the baffle plate from the bottom of the crankcase.

5 Using an Allen key, unscrew the bolts and remove the suction pipe from the oil pump. Remove the O-ring seal.

6 Unscrew and remove the large oil pump mounting bolts, then withdraw the pump from the block. If necessary, press the subframe downwards to provide sufficient room to remove the oil pump.

7 Unscrew the two bolts, and lift off the cover. Note that the cover incorporates the pressure relief valve.

Engine code AHL

8 On engine code AHL, the oil pump is driven by chain from the front of the crankshaft.

9 Release and remove the baffle plate from the bottom of the crankcase.

10 Unscrew and remove the three mounting bolts, and release the oil pump from the dowels in the crankcase. Unhook the oil pump drive sprocket from the chain and withdraw the oil pump and suction pipe from the engine. Note that the tensioner will attempt to tighten the chain, and it may be necessary to use a screwdriver to hold it in its released position before releasing the oil pump sprocket from the chain.

11 Unscrew the flange bolts and remove the suction pipe from the oil pump. Recover the O-ring seal. Unscrew the bolts and remove the cover from the oil pump.

12 Examine the drive chain for wear and damage. To remove the chain, the timing belt must first be removed (see Section 4), then the crankshaft front oil seal housing unbolted from the cylinder block. With the housing removed, unbolt and remove the chain tensioner, then unhook the chain from the sprocket on the front of the crankshaft.

Inspection

13 On engine codes ADP, ADR, AFY, AEB, APU, AJL, clean the components and check them for wear and damage. Using a feeler blade, check the backlash between the gears, and compare with that given in the Specifications. Similarly check the endfloat of the gears, using a straight edge across the end face of the pump. If outside the specified limits, the pump should be renewed, otherwise refit the cover and tighten the bolts.

14 On engine code AHL, clean the pump thoroughly, and inspect the gear teeth for signs of damage or wear. A suitable puller will be required to remove the sprocket from the front of the crankshaft, however note that it must be heated to 220° C for 15 minutes when refitting. Note that the broad collar of the sprocket faces the engine. To remove the sprocket from the oil pump, unscrew the retaining bolt and slide off the sprocket. Note that it can only be fitted in one position. Examine the pump gears for signs of excessive wear and damage. If evident, renew the oil pump.

Refitting

15 Prime the pump with oil by pouring oil into the suction pipe aperture while turning the driveshaft.

Engine codes ADP, ADR, AFY, AEB, APU, AJL

16 Clean the contact faces, then refit the cover to the oil pump and tighten the bolts to the specified torque.

17 Clean the oil pump and block, then refit the oil pump, insert the mounting bolts, and tighten them to the specified torque.

18 Locate a new O-ring seal on the end of the suction tube. Fit the tube to the oil pump, insert the bolts and tighten them.

19 On models with engine code ADP, refit the subframes and tighten the mounting bolts to the specified torque (see Chapter 10).

20 Refit the sump with reference to Section 15.

Engine code AHL

21 Refit the cover to the oil pump and tighten the bolts securely.

22 If the drive chain, crankshaft sprocket and tensioner have been removed, delay refitting them until after the oil pump has been mounted on the cylinder block. If they have not been removed, use a screwdriver to press the tensioner against its spring to provide sufficient slack in the chain to refit the oil pump.

23 Locate the oil pump on the dowels, then insert and tighten the three mounting bolts to the specified torque. Where applicable, engage the oil pump sprocket with the chain at this stage.

24 Where applicable, refit the drive chain, crankshaft sprocket and tensioner using a reversal of the removal procedure.

25 Refit the crankshaft front oil seal housing and timing belt where applicable. Apply suitable sealant to the front oil seal housing before fitting it.

26 Refit the baffle plate followed by the sump with reference to Section 15.

Chapter 2 Part B:
Diesel engine in-car repair procedures

Contents

Degrees of difficulty

Easy, suitable for novice with little experience	**Fairly easy,** suitable for beginner with some experience	**Fairly difficult,** suitable for competent DIY mechanic	**Difficult,** suitable for experienced DIY mechanic	**Very difficult,** suitable for expert DIY or professional

Specifications

General

Engine code: *
Electronic direct fuel injection, turbocharged, 66 kW (90 bhp)	1Z
Electronic direct fuel injection, turbocharged, 81 kW (110 bhp)	AFN
Electronic direct fuel injection, turbocharged, 55 kW (75 bhp)	AFF
Electronic direct fuel injection, turbocharged, 66 kW (90 bhp)	AHU
Electronic direct fuel injection, turbocharged, 66 kW (90 bhp)	AHH

* Note: See 'Vehicle Identification' for the location of the code marking on the engine.

Bore	79.5 mm
Stroke	95.5 mm
Compression ratio	19.5 : 1
Compression pressures (wear limit)	19.0 bar
Firing order	1 - 3 - 4 - 2
Cylinder No 1 location	Timing belt end

Lubrication system

Oil pump type	Sump-mounted, driven indirectly from intermediate shaft
Normal operating oil pressure (oil temperature 80°C):	
At 3000 rpm	3.0 to 5.0 bar
At 2000 rpm	At least 2.0 bar
Oil pump gear backlash	0.2 mm (wear limit)
Oil pump gear axial clearance	0.15 mm (wear limit)

Auxiliary drivebelt tension

Alternator/viscous fan/power steering pump/coolant pump	Automatically adjusted by tensioner
A/C compressor	Apply 25 Nm to tensioner body

Torque wrench settings

	Nm	lbf ft
A/C compressor drivebelt bracket	45	33
Alternator bracket to cylinder block	25	18
Alternator	25	18
Auxiliary drivebelt tensioner	45	33
Big-end bearing caps bolts/nuts:		
Stage 1	30	22
Stage 2	Angle-tighten a further 90°	

Torque wrench settings (continued)

	Nm	lbf ft
Brake vacuum exhauster clamp	20	15
Camshaft bearing cap	20	15
Camshaft cover	10	7
Camshaft sprocket bolt	45	33
Coolant pump pulley	25	18
Crankshaft front oil seal housing:		
M6 bolts	10	7
M8 bolts	25	18
Crankshaft pulley/vibration damper to sprocket:		
With strength rating 8.8	25	18
With strength rating 10.9	35	26
Crankshaft rear oil seal housing:		
M6 bolts	10	7
M8 bolts	20	15
Crankshaft sprocket bolt:		
Stage 1	90	66
Stage 2	Angle-tighten a further 90°	
Cylinder head bolts*:		
Stage 1	40	30
Stage 2	60	44
Stage 3	Angle-tighten a further 90°	
Stage 4	Angle-tighten a further 90°	
Driveplate (automatic transmission):		
Stage 1	60	44
Stage 2	Angle-tighten a further 90°	
Engine mounting to subframe	25	18
Engine-to-transmission bolts:		
M10	45	33
M12	65	48
Flywheel (manual transmission):		
Stage 1	60	44
Stage 2	Angle-tighten a further 180°	
Injection pump sprocket to hub (engine code AHH):		
Stage 1	20	15
Stage 2	Angle-tighten 90°	
Intermediate shaft flange bolts	25	18
Intermediate shaft sprocket bolt	45	33
Longitudinal strut:		
To bracket	25	18
To engine support	20	15
Lower timing cover	10	7
Main bearing cap bolts:		
Stage 1	65	48
Stage 2	Angle-tighten a further 90°	
Oil filter housing to block	25	18
Oil jets:		
Engines up to 06/96	7	5
Engines from 07/96	27	20
Oil pump cover	10	7
Oil pump mounting bolt	25	18
Oil return pipe to cylinder block	30	22
Oil supply pipe to turbocharger	25	18
Power steering pump pulley	25	18
Speed sender to crankshaft:		
Stage 1	10	7
Stage 2	Angle-tighten a further 90°	
Suction tube to oil pump	10	7
Sump	18	13
Timing belt small upper idler roller	25	18
Timing belt tensioner	20	15
Timing cover	10	7
Torque reaction bracket and stop	25	18
Viscous fan	45	33

Use new nuts/bolt(s)

1 General information

Using this Chapter

Chapter 2 is divided into three Parts; A, B and C. Repair operations that can be carried out with the engine in the vehicle are described in Part A (petrol engines) and Part B (diesel engines). Part C covers the removal of the engine/transmission as a unit, and describes the engine dismantling and overhaul procedures.

In Parts A and B, the assumption is made that the engine is installed in the vehicle, with all ancillaries connected. If the engine has been removed for overhaul, the preliminary dismantling information which precedes each operation may be ignored.

Access to the engine bay can be improved by removing the bonnet as described in Chapter 11 and the lock carrier (front panel) as described in Section 4.

Engine description

Throughout this Chapter, the engines are identified and referred to by manufacturer's code letters, rather than capacity. A listing of the engines covered, together with their code letters, is given in the Specifications at the start of this Chapter.

The engines are water-cooled, single overhead camshaft, in-line four cylinder units with cast-iron cylinder blocks and aluminium-alloy cylinder heads. All are mounted longitudinally at the front of the vehicle, with the transmission bolted to the rear of the engine.

The cylinder head carries the camshaft, which is driven by a toothed timing belt. It also houses the inlet and exhaust valves, which are closed by double coil springs, and which run in guides pressed into the cylinder head. The camshaft actuates the valves directly via hydraulic tappets, mounted in the cylinder head. The cylinder head contains integral oilways which supply and lubricate the tappets.

The engines are of direct injection design. Unlike indirect injection engines where the cylinder head incorporates swirl chambers, the piston crowns are shaped to form combustion chambers.

The crankshaft is supported by five main bearings, and endfloat is controlled by thrust washers fitted each side of the centre (No 3) main bearing.

The engines are fitted with a timing belt-driven intermediate shaft, which provides drive for the brake servo vacuum pump and the oil pump.

Engine coolant is circulated by a pump, driven by the auxiliary drivebelt. For details of the cooling system, refer to Chapter 3.

Lubricant is circulated under pressure by a pump, driven by the intermediate shaft. Oil is drawn from the sump through a strainer, and then forced through an externally-mounted,

replaceable screw-on filter. From there, it is distributed to the cylinder head, where it lubricates the camshaft journals and hydraulic tappets, and also to the crankcase, where it lubricates the main bearings, connecting rod big- and small-ends, gudgeon pins and cylinder bores. Oil jets are fitted to the base of each cylinder - these spray oil onto the underside of the pistons, to improve cooling. An oil cooler, supplied with engine coolant and mounted on the oil filter housing, reduces the temperature of the oil before it re-enters the engine.

Repairs possible with the engine installed in the vehicle

The following operations can be performed without removing the engine:

a) Auxiliary drivebelts - removal and refitting.
b) Camshaft - removal and refitting.*
c) Camshaft oil seal - renewal.
d) Camshaft sprocket - removal and refitting.
e) Coolant pump - removal and refitting (refer to Chapter 3).
f) Crankshaft oil seals - renewal.
g) Crankshaft sprocket - removal and refitting.
h) Cylinder head - removal and refitting.*
i) Engine mountings - inspection and renewal.
j) Intermediate shaft oil seal - renewal.
k) Oil pump and pickup assembly - removal and refitting.
l) Sump - removal and refitting.
m) Timing belt, sprockets and cover - removal, inspection and refitting.

*Cylinder head dismantling procedures are in Chapter 2C, and also contain details of camshaft and hydraulic tappet removal.
Note: It is possible to remove the pistons and connecting rods (after removing the cylinder head and sump) without removing the engine from the vehicle. However, this procedure is not recommended. Work of this nature is more easily and thoroughly completed with the engine on the bench - refer to Chapter 2C.

2 Engine valve timing marks - locating TDC on No 1 cylinder

General information

1 The crankshaft, camshaft, intermediate shaft and injection pump sprockets are driven by the timing belt. The crankshaft and camshaft sprockets move in phase with each other to ensure correct valve timing.
2 The design of the engines covered in this Chapter is such that piston-to-valve contact will occur if the crankshaft is turned with the timing belt removed. For this reason, it is important that the correct phasing between the camshaft and crankshaft is preserved whilst the timing belt is off the engine. This is achieved by setting the engine in a reference condition (known as Top Dead Centre or TDC) before the timing belt is removed, and then

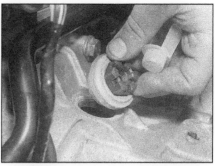

2.5a Using a large nut to unscrew the bung from the transmission bellhousing

preventing the shafts from rotating until the belt is refitted. Similarly, if the engine has been dismantled for overhaul, the engine can be set to TDC during reassembly to ensure that the correct shaft phasing is restored.
3 TDC is the highest position a piston reaches within its respective cylinder - in a four-stroke engine, each piston reaches TDC twice per cycle; once on the compression stroke, and once on the exhaust stroke. In general, TDC normally refers to No 1 cylinder on the compression stroke. Note that the cylinders are numbered one to four, starting from the timing belt end of the engine.

Setting TDC on No 1 cylinder

4 Remove the camshaft cover and auxiliary drivebelts as described in Sections 7 and 6 respectively. Also remove the timing belt upper outer cover with reference to Section 4. Remove the glowplugs as described in Chapter 5C, as an aid to turning the engine.
5 Where fitted, remove the inspection bung from the transmission bellhousing, if necessary using a large nut to unscrew it **(see illustrations)**. Rotate the crankshaft clockwise with a wrench and socket, or a spanner, until the timing mark machined onto the edge of the flywheel/driveplate lines up with the pointer on the bellhousing casting **and** the timing hole in the fuel injection sprocket lines up with the hole in the support bracket. **Note:** *On engine code AHH a cut-out on the inner section of the sprocket must be aligned with a hole in the support bracket.*

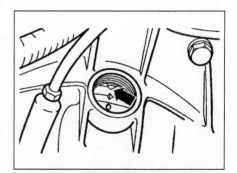

2.5b Timing mark on the edge of the flywheel (arrowed) lined up with the pointer on the bellhousing casing (manual transmission)

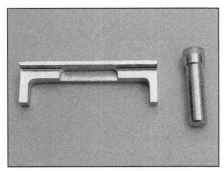

2.6 Engine locking tools

2.7 Engage the locking bar with the slot in the camshaft

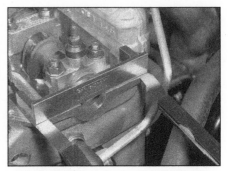

2.9 Camshaft centred and locked using the locking bar and feeler blades

6 To lock the engine in the TDC position, the camshaft (not the sprocket) and fuel injection pump sprocket must be secured in a reference position, using special locking tools. Improvised tools may be fabricated, but due to the exact measurements and machining involved, it is strongly recommended that a kit of locking tools is either borrowed or hired from a Audi/VAG dealer, or purchased from a reputable tool manufacturer **(see illustration)**.

7 Engage the edge of the locking bar with the slot in the end of the camshaft **(see illustration)**.

8 With the locking bar still inserted, turn the camshaft slightly (by turning the crankshaft clockwise, as before), so that the locking bar rocks to one side, allowing one end of the bar to contact the cylinder head surface. At the other side of the locking bar, measure the gap between the end of the bar and the cylinder head using a feeler blade.

9 Turn the camshaft back slightly, then pull out the feeler blade. The idea now is to level the locking bar by inserting two feeler blades, each with a thickness equal to *half* the originally measured gap, on either side of the camshaft between each end of the locking bar and the cylinder head. This centres the camshaft, and sets the valve timing in reference condition **(see illustration)**.

10 Insert the locking pin through the fuel injection pump sprocket alignment hole (or cut-out), and into the support bracket behind the sprocket. This locks the fuel injection pump in the TDC reference condition **(see illustrations)**.

11 The engine is now set to TDC on No 1 cylinder.

3 Cylinder compression test

Compression test

Note: *A compression tester specifically designed for diesel engines must be used for this test.*

1 When engine performance is down, or if misfiring occurs, a compression test can provide diagnostic clues as to the engine's condition. If the test is performed regularly, it can give warning of trouble before any other symptoms become apparent.

2 A compression tester specifically intended for diesel engines must be used, because of the higher pressures involved. The tester is connected to an adapter which screws into the glow plug or injector hole. It is unlikely to be worthwhile buying such a tester for occasional use, but it may be possible to borrow or hire one - if not, have the test performed by a garage.

3 Unless specific instructions to the contrary are supplied with the tester, observe the following points:

a) *The battery must be in a good state of charge, the air filter must be clean, and the engine should be at normal operating temperature.*

b) *All the injectors or glow plugs should be removed before starting the test. If removing the injectors, also remove the flame shield washers, otherwise they may be blown out.*

c) *The stop solenoid and fuel metering control wiring must be disconnected, to prevent the engine from running or fuel from being discharged.* **Note:** *As a result of the wiring being disconnected, faults will be stored in the ECU memory. These must be erased after the compression test.*

4 There is no need to hold the accelerator pedal down during the test, because the diesel engine air inlet is not throttled.

5 The manufacturers specify a wear limit for compression pressure - refer to the Specifications. Seek the advice of a Audi/VAG dealer or other diesel specialist if in doubt as to whether a particular pressure reading is acceptable.

6 The cause of poor compression is less easy to establish on a diesel engine than on a petrol one. The effect of introducing oil into the cylinders (wet testing) is not conclusive, because there is a risk that the oil will sit in the recess on the piston crown, instead of passing to the rings. However, the following can be used as a rough guide to diagnosis.

2.10a Injection pump sprocket locked using the locking pin (1Z, AHU, AFN, AFF engines)

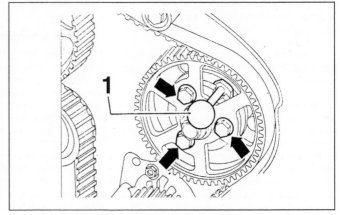

2.10b Tool (1) for locking the injection pump sprocket (AHH engine)

7 All cylinders should produce very similar pressures; a difference of more than 5.0 bars between any two cylinders indicates the existence of a fault. Note that the compression should build up quickly in a healthy engine; low compression on the first stroke, followed by gradually-increasing pressure on successive strokes, indicates worn piston rings. A low compression reading on the first stroke, which does not build up during successive strokes, indicates leaking valves or a blown head gasket (a cracked head could also be the cause).

8 A low reading from two adjacent cylinders is almost certainly due to the head gasket having blown between them; the presence of coolant in the engine oil will confirm this.

Leakdown test

9 A leakdown test measures the rate at which compressed air fed into the cylinder is lost. It is an alternative to a compression test, and in many ways it is better, since the escaping air provides easy identification of where pressure loss is occurring (piston rings, valves or head gasket).

10 The equipment needed for leakdown testing is unlikely to be available to the home mechanic. If poor compression is suspected, have the test performed by a suitably-equipped garage.

---

4 Timing belt -
removal, inspection
and refitting

Removal

1 The primary function of the toothed timing belt is to drive the camshaft, but it also drives the fuel injection pump and intermediate shaft. Should the belt slip or break in service, the valve timing will be disturbed and piston-to-valve contact may occur, resulting in serious engine damage. For this reason, it is important that the timing belt is tensioned correctly, and inspected regularly for signs of wear or deterioration.

2 Note that the removal of the *inner* section of the timing belt cover is described as part of the cylinder head removal procedure; see Section 11 later in this Chapter.

4.10 Removing the crankshaft auxiliary belt pulleys

3 Disconnect the battery (see Chapter 5A), then remove the engine top cover.

4 Apply the handbrake, then jack up the front of the vehicle and support it on axle stands (see *Jacking and vehicle support*). Where applicable, remove the splash guard from under the engine compartment.

5 Access to the timing belt is achieved by moving the complete front panel (the lock carrier assembly) away from the front of the car as far as possible, but without disconnecting the radiator hoses or electrical wiring. To do this, first remove the front bumper as described in Chapter 11, then unscrew the three quick-release clips from the noise insulation panel and unbolt the air duct from between the lock carrier and the air cleaner. On the left-hand side of the radiator, release the wiring from the clips. Unscrew the bolts securing the lock carrier assembly to the underbody channels, then unscrew the upper side bolts located behind the headlight units. With the help of an assistant, pull the complete assembly away from the front of the car as far as possible. Audi technicians use special tools to hold the assembly, however support bars may be made out of threaded metal rod and screwed into the underbody channels.

6 Remove the auxiliary drivebelt(s) with reference to Section 6. Also, unbolt the tensioner from the front of the engine using an Allen key.

7 Remove the viscous fan unit with reference to Chapter 3, Section 5. Briefly, it is removed by inserting an Allen key from behind, while holding the unit stationary using a scissor-

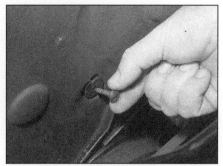

4.11a Undo the screws . . .

type tool engaged with two of the holes in the pulley - if the Audi tool cannot be obtained, make up a similar tool out of two lengths of metal with bolts to engage the holes.

8 Unbolt the small cover from the right-hand side of the timing cover, then move the charge pressure control solenoid valve to one side, leaving the hoses connected.

9 Refer to Section 2, and using the engine alignment markings, set the engine to TDC on No 1 cylinder. This procedure includes removing the camshaft cover, and locking the fuel injection pump sprocket.

10 Unscrew and remove the retaining screws, then remove the pulley for the ribbed auxiliary belt (together with the A/C compressor pulley, where fitted) from the crankshaft sprocket **(see illustration)**. On completion, check that the engine is still set to TDC.

> **HAYNES HINT** *To prevent the auxiliary belt pulley from rotating whilst the mounting screws are being slackened, select top gear (manual transmission models only) and get an assistant to apply the footbrake firmly. Alternatively, hold the pulley with an oil filter wrench or similar tool.*

11 Release the uppermost part of the timing belt outer cover by prising open the metal spring clips and where applicable, removing the screws and press-stud fixings **(see illustrations)**. Lift the cover away from the engine

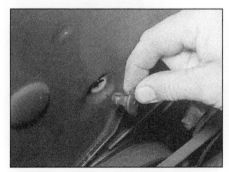

4.11b . . . and remove the inserts . . .

4.11c . . . then release the spring clips . . .

4.11d . . . and lift the timing cover from the engine

4.12 Timing belt lower cover

12 Remove the retaining screws and clips or nuts as applicable, and lift off the timing belt lower cover **(see illustration)**.

13 With reference to Section 5, relieve the tension on the timing belt by slackening the tensioner mounting nut slightly, allowing it to pivot away from the belt.

14 Examine the timing belt for manufacturer's markings that indicate the direction of rotation. If none are present, make your own using typist's correction fluid or a dab of paint - do not cut or score the belt in any way.

Caution: If the belt appears to be in good condition and can be re-used, it is essential that it is refitted the same way around, otherwise accelerated wear will result, leading to premature failure.

15 Slide the belt off the sprockets, taking care to avoid twisting or kinking it excessively if it is to be re-used.

Inspection

16 Examine the belt for evidence of contamination by coolant or lubricant. If this is the case, find the source of the contamination before progressing any further. Check the belt for signs of wear or damage, particularly around the leading edges of the belt teeth. Renew the belt if its condition is in doubt; the cost of belt renewal is negligible compared with potential cost of the engine repairs, should the belt fail in service. The belt must be renewed if it has covered 60 000 miles, however if it has covered less it is prudent to renew it regardless of condition, as a precautionary measure.

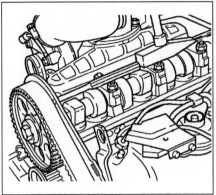

4.20 Releasing the camshaft sprocket from the taper using a pin punch

17 If the timing belt is not going to be refitted for some time, it is a wise precaution to hang a warning label on the steering wheel, to remind yourself (and others) not to attempt to start the engine.

18 On engine code AHH, the bolts securing the injection pump sprocket to the hub must be renewed every time they are loosened, so obtain three new bolts before commencing the refitting procedure. The bolts are of stretch-type requiring angle-tightening, and it is for this reason that they cannot be re-used once loosened. Audi state that the pump sprocket **must** be reset each time the timing belt is removed - it is not acceptable to simply refit the belt to the sprocket without carrying out the re-setting procedure.

Refitting

19 Ensure that the crankshaft and camshaft are still set to TDC on No 1 cylinder, as described in Section 2.

20 Refer to Section 5 and slacken the camshaft sprocket bolt by half a turn. **Do not** use the timing locking bar to hold the camshaft stationary; it must be temporarily removed while loosening the sprocket bolt. Release the sprocket from the camshaft taper mounting by carefully tapping it with a soft metal drift inserted through the hole provided in the timing belt inner cover **(see illustration)**.

21 On engine code AHH, unscrew the three bolts from the injection pump sprocket and fit the new ones (see paragraph 18), hand-tight at

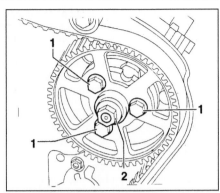

4.21 On the AHH engine, unscrew the injection pump hub bolts (1). Do not unscrew the centre nut (2)

this stage **(see illustration)**. Position the outer sprocket centrally in the elongated holes.

Caution: Do not loosen the central nut, otherwise the basic setting of the injection pump will be upset, and it will require resetting by an Audi/VW dealer or fuel injection specialist.

22 Loop the timing belt loosely under the crankshaft sprocket. **Note:** *Observe the direction of rotation markings on the belt.*

23 Engage the timing belt teeth with the crankshaft sprocket, then manoeuvre it into position around the intermediate shaft pulley, then over the injection pump and camshaft sprockets and around the tensioner pulley. Make sure that the belt teeth seat correctly on the sprockets. The upper run of the belt must be located beneath the small upper roller. **Note:** *Slight adjustment to the position of the camshaft sprocket may be necessary to achieve this.* Avoid bending the belt back on itself or twisting it excessively as you do this **(see illustrations)**.

24 Ensure that any slack in the belt is in the section of belt that passes over the tensioner roller.

25 Using a suitable tool engaged with the two holes in the tensioner hub, turn the tensioner pulley clockwise until the notch and the raised tab on the pulley and hub are aligned with each other **(see illustration)**. The tensioner is of semi-automatic type, and will

4.23a Timing belt located over the tensioner roller . . .

4.23b . . . and under the upper roller

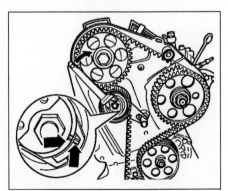

4.25 Alignment marks on the pulley and hub on the automatic tensioner

correctly tension the timing belt when the notch and tab are aligned with each other. **Note:** *If the tensioner is turned too far clockwise, it must be completely slackened off before re-tensioning.*

26 With the tensioner marks aligned, tighten the tensioner locknut to the specified torque. Check the operation of the tensioner by pressing firmly on the timing belt with the thumb while checking that the pointers move away from each other - after releasing the belt the pointers must be aligned again.

27 Remove the locking pin from the fuel injection pump sprocket (see Section 2).

28 Remove the camshaft locking bar (see Section 2).

29 On engine code AHH, tighten the new injection pump sprocket bolts to an initial 20 Nm while holding the outer sprocket stationary with a suitable tool. Take care not to disturb the setting between the inner and outer sections of the sprocket. Final tightening of the bolts is made after checking the dynamic timing of the injection pump.

30 At this stage, check the crankshaft and injection pump are still set to TDC on No 1 cylinder (see Section 2). On engine code AHH, if the locking pin cannot be inserted, temporarily loosen the three sprocket bolts, reposition the hub as necessary, then tighten the bolts to 20 Nm.

31 Refer to Section 5 and tighten the camshaft sprocket bolt to the specified torque while holding it stationary with the special tool.

32 Using a spanner or wrench and socket on the crankshaft pulley centre bolt, rotate the crankshaft through two complete revolutions. Reset the engine to TDC on No 1 cylinder, with reference to Section 2 and check that the fuel injection pump sprocket locking pin and camshaft locking bar can still be inserted.

33 Refit the camshaft cover together with a new gasket with reference to Section 7.

34 Refit the timing belt lower cover and secure with the clips and screws. Also refit the upper cover and secure it with the clips and press-stud fixings.

35 Refit the crankshaft auxiliary belt pulley and tighten the retaining screws to the specified torque, using the method employed during removal. Note that the offset of the pulley mounting holes allows only one fitting position.

36 Refit the charge pressure control solenoid valve and the small cover to the right-hand side of the timing cover, and tighten the bolts.

37 Refit the viscous fan unit with reference to Chapter 3.

38 Refit the tensioner to the front of the engine, then refit the auxiliary drivebelts with reference to Section 6.

39 Refit the lock carrier assembly using a reversal of the removal procedure.

40 Refit the splash guard under the engine compartment, then lower the vehicle to the ground. Also refit the engine top cover.

41 Reconnect the battery negative (earth) lead (see Chapter 5A).

42 On completion, refer to Chapter 4B and check the fuel injection pump timing.

43 On engine code AHH remove the upper timing cover, then angle-tighten the injection pump sprocket bolts by the specified amount. Refit the upper timing cover on completion.

5 Timing belt tensioner and sprockets - removal and refitting

1 Disconnect the battery (see Chapter 5A).

2 To gain access to the components detailed in this Section, first refer to Section 6 and remove the auxiliary drivebelts.

Timing belt tensioner

Removal

3 With reference to the relevant paragraphs of Sections 2 and 4, set the engine to TDC on No 1 cylinder, then remove the upper section of the timing belt outer cover.

4 Slacken the retaining nut at the hub of the tensioner pulley and allow the assembly to rotate anti-clockwise, relieving the tension on the timing belt. Remove the nut and recover the washer.

5 Slide the tensioner off its mounting stud.

6 Wipe the tensioner clean, but do not use solvents that may contaminate the bearings. Spin the tensioner pulley on its hub by hand. Stiff movement or excessive freeplay indicates that the tensioner is not serviceable and should be renewed.

Refitting

7 Slide the tensioner onto the mounting stud.

8 Refit the tensioner washer and retaining nut - do not fully tighten the nut at this stage.

9 With reference to Section 4, refit and tension the timing belt.

10 Refer to Section 4 and refit the timing belt covers.

11 Refit the auxiliary drivebelts (Section 6) and reconnect the battery (Chapter 5A).

Camshaft sprocket

Removal

12 Refer to Section 2 and 4, set the engine to TDC on No 1 cylinder, then remove the upper section of the timing belt outer cover.

13 Remove the camshaft cover as described in Section 7.

14 Slacken the retaining nut at the hub of the tensioner pulley and allow the assembly to rotate anti-clockwise, relieving the tension on the timing belt. Slide the timing belt off the camshaft sprocket.

15 The camshaft sprocket must be held stationary whilst its retaining bolt is slackened; if access to the correct Audi/VAG special tool is not possible, a simple home-made tool using basic materials may be fabricated **(see Tool Tip). Do not** use the timing locking bar to hold the camshaft stationary; it should be removed before loosening the sprocket bolt.

To make a camshaft sprocket holding tool, obtain two lengths of steel strip about 6 mm thick by 30 mm wide, one 600 mm long, the other 200 mm long (all dimensions approximate). Bolt the two strips together to form a forked end, leaving the bolt slack so that the shorter strip can pivot freely. At the end of each 'prong' of the fork, secure a bolt with a nut and a locknut, to act as the fulcrums; these will engage with the cut-outs in the sprocket, and should protrude by about 30 mm

16 Using the home-made tool, brace the camshaft sprocket and slacken the retaining bolt half a turn. Release the sprocket from the camshaft taper mounting by carefully tapping it with a soft metal drift inserted through the hole provided in the timing belt inner cover

17 Remove the bolt then remove the camshaft sprocket from the end of the camshaft **(see illustration)**.

18 With the sprocket removed, examine the camshaft oil seal for signs of leaking. If necessary, refer to Section 8 and renew it.

19 Wipe the sprocket and camshaft mating surfaces clean.

Refitting

20 Locate the sprocket on the camshaft, then insert the retaining bolt hand-tight at this stage.

21 With reference to Sections 2 and 4, check that the engine is still set to TDC on No 1 cylinder, then refit and tension the timing belt.

22 Refit the timing belt upper cover and the camshaft cover, then refit the auxiliary drivebelt(s) (Section 6) and reconnect the battery (Chapter 5A).

5.17 Removing the camshaft sprocket

5.28a Insert the crankshaft sprocket bolt . . .

5.28b . . . tighten it to the Stage 1 torque . . .

5.28c . . . then through the Stage 2 angle

Crankshaft sprocket

Removal

23 Remove the timing belt and the upper and lower outer covers as described in Section 4. If the timing belt is to be re-used, make sure it is marked for direction of rotation.

24 The crankshaft sprocket must be held stationary whilst its retaining bolt is slackened. If access to the Audi/VAG flywheel/driveplate locking tool is not available, lock the crankshaft in position by removing the starter motor, as described in Chapter 5A, to expose the ring gear. Get an assistant to insert a wide-bladed screwdriver between the ring gear teeth and the transmission bellhousing whilst the sprocket retaining bolt is slackened.

25 Withdraw the bolt, recover the washer and lift off the sprocket.

26 With the sprocket removed, examine the crankshaft oil seal for signs of leaking. If necessary, refer to Section 10 and renew it.

27 Wipe the sprocket and crankshaft mating surfaces clean.

Refitting

28 Offer up the sprocket to the crankshaft, engaging the lug on the inside of the sprocket with the recess in the end of the crankshaft. Insert the retaining bolt and tighten it to the specified stage 1 torque while holding the crankshaft stationary as described for removal. Then angle-tighten the bolt by the specified angle (see illustrations).

29 Working from Sections 2 and 4, check that the engine is still set to TDC on No 1 cylinder, then refit and tension the timing belt. Refit the timing belt outer covers, then refit the auxiliary drivebelts (Section 6) and reconnect the battery (Chapter 5A).

Intermediate shaft sprocket

Removal

30 Remove the timing belt and the upper and lower outer covers as described in Section 4. If the timing belt is to be re-used, make sure it is marked for direction of rotation.

31 The intermediate shaft sprocket must be held stationary whilst its retaining bolt is slackened; if access to the Audi/VAG special

tool is not possible, a simple home-made tool may be fabricated as described in the camshaft sprocket removal sub-Section. Alternatively, insert a metal dowel rod or socket wrench through one of the holes in the sprocket to hold it stationary (see illustration).

32 Slacken and remove the retaining bolt, then slide the sprocket from the end of the intermediate shaft. Recover the Woodruff key from the keyway.

33 With the sprocket removed, examine the intermediate shaft oil seal for signs of leaking. If necessary, refer to Section 9 and renew it.

34 Wipe the sprocket and shaft mating surfaces clean.

Refitting

35 Fit the Woodruff key into the keyway with the plain surface facing upwards. Offer up the sprocket to the intermediate shaft, engaging the slot in the sprocket with the Woodruff key.

36 Insert and tighten the sprocket retaining bolt to the specified torque; hold the sprocket using the method employed during removal.

37 Working from Sections 2 and 4, check that the engine is still set to TDC on No 1 cylinder, then refit and tension the timing belt. Refit the timing belt outer covers, then refit the auxiliary drivebelts (Section 6) and reconnect the battery (Chapter 5A).

Fuel injection pump sprocket

38 Refer to Chapter 4B.

5.31 Using a socket wrench to hold the intermediate shaft sprocket stationary while loosening the bolt

6 Auxiliary drivebelts -
removal, refitting and tensioning

General information

1 One main auxiliary drivebelt is fitted to drive the alternator, viscous fan, power steering pump, and coolant pump. On models with air conditioning, a separate drivebelt drives the A/C compressor. Both drivebelts are driven from pulleys mounted on the front of the crankshaft, and both drivebelts are of ribbed type (see illustration opposite).

2 The main drivebelt tension is adjusted automatically by a spring-tensioned idler. Where fitted, the air conditioning compressor drivebelt is adjusted using a torque wrench on the idler.

3 To remove the drivebelts first apply the handbrake, then jack up the front of the vehicle and support it on axle stands (see Jacking and vehicle support). Remove the undershield from under the engine compartment.

Removal

4 If any drivebelt is to be re-used, mark it for clockwise direction to ensure it is refitted the same way round.

5 Access to the drivebelt is best achieved by moving the complete front panel (the lock carrier assembly) away from the front of the car as far as possible, but without disconnecting the radiator hoses or electrical wiring. To do this, first remove the front bumper as described in Chapter 11, then unscrew the three quick-release clips from the noise insulation panel and unbolt the air duct from between the lock carrier and the air cleaner. On the left-hand side of the radiator, release the wiring from the clips. Unscrew the bolts securing the lock carrier assembly to the underbody channels, then unscrew the upper side bolts located behind the headlight units. With the help of an assistant, pull the complete assembly away from the front of the car as far as possible. Audi technicians use special tools to hold the assembly, however support bars may be made out of threaded metal rod and screwed into the underbody channels.

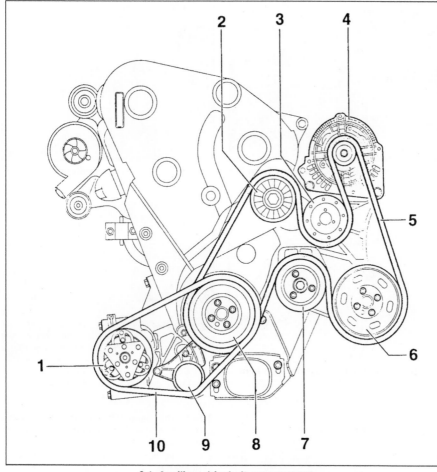

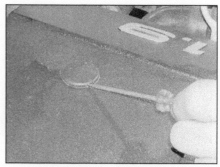

7.1a Prise out the caps . . .

7.1b . . . then unscrew the nuts . . .

6.1 Auxiliary drivebelt arrangement

1 Air conditioning compressor
2 Main auxiliary drivebelt tensioner
3 Viscous fan pulley
4 Alternator
5 Main auxiliary drivebelt
6 Power steering pump
7 Coolant pump
8 Crankshaft pulley/vibration damper
9 A/C compressor tensioner
10 A/C compressor drivebelt

downwards and engage the drivebelt with the pulley grooves. Tension the drivebelt by applying a torque of 25 Nm to the hexagon on the tensioner body. Hold this torque then tighten the adjustment and pivot bolts.

7 Camshaft cover - removal and refitting

Removal

1 Unbolt and remove the engine top cover, then disconnect the crankcase breather hose and regulator valve from the camshaft cover and recover the grommet **(see illustrations)**.
2 Remove the caps, then unscrew and remove the three camshaft cover retaining nuts - recover the washers and seals noting the order of removal **(see illustration)**.

6 On models with air conditioning, loosen the pivot and tension bolts and move the tensioner roller upwards to release the tension on the drivebelt. Slip the drivebelt from the crankshaft, compressor and tensioner pulleys.
7 To remove the main drivebelt, first note how it is fitted to each pulley to ensure correct refitting. In particular note that the flat outer surface of the drivebelt is located on the viscous fan pulley. The automatic tensioner must be released using a 15 mm ring spanner on the centre bolt. Turn the bolt anticlockwise to release the tension, then remove the drivebelt from the tensioner, alternator, viscous coupling fan, power steering pump and crankshaft pulleys. **Note:** The bolt has a left-hand thread, so it will not be loosened when turning it anticlockwise. Release the tensioner after removing the drivebelt.

Refitting

8 Locate the drivebelt on the alternator, viscous coupling fan, power steering pump and crankshaft pulleys, making sure that each

rib is correctly located in a groove. Turn the automatic tensioner anticlockwise and locate the drivebelt on the pulley, then release the tensioner to tension the drivebelt.
9 On models with air conditioning, locate the drivebelt on the compressor and crankshaft pulleys, making sure that each rib is correctly located in a groove. Move the tensioner pulley

7.1c . . . and remove the engine top cover

7.1d Crankcase breather regulator valve and hoses

7.2 Camshaft cover retaining nut

7.3 Removing the camshaft cover from the cylinder head

7.4 Removing the camshaft cover gasket

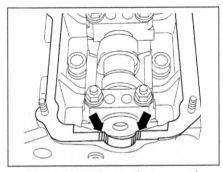

7.6a Apply sealant to the rear semi-circular cut-out . . .

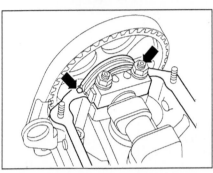

7.6b . . . and the front bearing cap joint

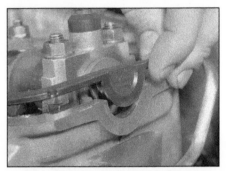

7.6c Ensure that the camshaft cover gasket is correctly seated on the cylinder head

3 Lift the cover away from the cylinder head **(see illustration)**; if it sticks, do not attempt to lever it off - instead free it by working around the cover and tapping it lightly with a soft-faced mallet.
4 Recover the camshaft cover gasket **(see illustration)**. Inspect the gasket carefully, and renew it if damage or deterioration is evident.
5 Clean the mating surfaces of the cylinder head and camshaft cover thoroughly, removing all traces of oil and old gasket - take care to avoid damaging the surfaces as you do this.

Refitting

6 Refit the camshaft cover by following the removal procedure in reverse, noting the following points:
   a) *Before refitting the camshaft cover, at the rear of the cylinder head apply suitable sealant to the top edges of the semi-circular cut- out in the cylinder head. At the front of the cylinder head, apply suitable sealant to the two points where the camshaft bearing cap contacts the cylinder head (see illustrations).*
   b) *Ensure that the gasket is correctly seated on the cylinder head, and take care to avoid displacing it as the camshaft cover is lowered into position (see illustration). Note that on early models the gasket has four location pips which engage holes in the cylinder head.*
   c) *Tighten the camshaft cover retaining nuts to the specified torque.*

8 Camshaft oil seal - renewal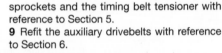

1 Refer to Section 6 and remove the auxiliary drivebelts.
2 Refer to Section 5 and remove the timing belt tensioner, and the camshaft and injection pump sprockets.
3 Unbolt and remove the timing belt inner cover.
4 Remove the camshaft cover as described in Section 7.
5 Working from the relevant Section of Chapter 2C, carry out the following:
   a) *Unscrew the nuts and remove camshaft No 1 bearing cap, then slide off the old camshaft oil seal.*
   b) *Lubricate the surface of the new camshaft oil seal with clean engine oil, and fit it over the end of the camshaft.*
   c) *Apply a thin film of suitable sealant to the mating surface of the bearing cap, then refit it making sure that the oil seal is located fully against the seating in the head and cap (see illustration). Tighten the mounting nuts progressively to the specified torque.*

6 Refer to Section 7 and refit the camshaft cover.
7 Refit the timing belt inner cover and tighten the bolts.

8 Refit the camshaft and injection pump sprockets and the timing belt tensioner with reference to Section 5.
9 Refit the auxiliary drivebelts with reference to Section 6.

9 Intermediate shaft oil seal - renewal

1 Remove the intermediate shaft sprocket with reference to Section 5.
2 With reference to Chapter 2C, remove the intermediate shaft flange and renew the shaft and flange oil seals.
3 Refit the intermediate shaft sprocket with reference to Section 5.

8.5 Refitting the camshaft bearing cap

10.2 Removing the crankshaft front oil seal using self-tapping screws

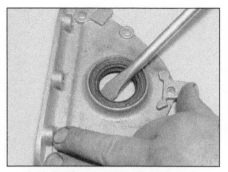

10.13 Prising the old oil seal from the crankshaft front oil seal housing

10.15 Locating the new crankshaft front oil seal housing gasket in position

10 Crankshaft oil seals - renewal

Crankshaft front oil seal

1 Remove the crankshaft sprocket with reference to Section 5.
2 Drill two small holes into the existing oil seal, diagonally opposite each other. Thread two self-tapping screws into the holes and using two pairs of pliers, pull on the heads of the screws to extract the oil seal **(see illustration)**. Take great care to avoid drilling through into the seal housing or crankshaft sealing surface.
3 Clean out the seal housing and sealing surface of the crankshaft by wiping it with a lint-free cloth - avoid using solvents that may enter the crankcase and affect component lubrication. Remove any swarf or burrs that could cause the seal to leak.
4 Smear the lip of the new oil seal with clean engine oil, and position it over the housing.
5 Using a hammer and a socket of suitable diameter, drive the seal squarely into its housing. **Note:** *Select a socket that bears only on the hard outer surface of the seal, not the inner lip, which can easily be damaged.*
6 Refit the crankshaft sprocket with reference to Section 5.

Crankshaft front oil seal housing - gasket renewal

7 Remove the crankshaft sprocket with reference to Section 5.

8 Unbolt the torque reaction bracket from the front of the engine.
9 Remove the sump as described in Section 15.
10 Progressively slacken and then remove the oil seal housing retaining bolts.
11 Lift the housing away from the cylinder block, together with the crankshaft oil seal, using a twisting motion to ease the seal along the shaft.
12 Recover the old gasket from the seal housing on the cylinder block. Clean the housing and block surfaces.
13 If necessary, prise the old oil seal from the housing using a screwdriver **(see illustration)**.
14 Wipe the oil seal housing clean, and check it visually for signs of distortion or cracking. Lay the housing on a work surface, with the mating surface face down. If removed, press in a new oil seal, using a block of wood as a press to ensure that the seal enters the housing squarely.
15 Smear the crankcase mating surface with multi-purpose grease, and lay the new gasket in position **(see illustration)**.
16 Wrap the end of the crankshaft with tape to protect the oil seal as the housing is being refitted.
17 Lubricate the inner lip of the crankshaft oil seal with clean engine oil, then offer up the seal and its housing to the end of the crankshaft. Ease the seal along the shaft using a twisting motion, until the housing is flush with the crankcase **(see illustration)**.
18 Insert the bolts and tighten them progressively to the specified torque.
19 Refer to Section 15 and refit the sump.

20 Refit the torque reaction bracket to the front of the engine and tighten the bolts.
21 Refit the crankshaft sprocket with reference to Section 5.

Crankshaft rear oil seal and housing (flywheel/driveplate end)

Note: *The oil seal is integral with the housing and must be renewed as one complete assembly.*
22 Remove the transmission as described in Chapter 7A or 7B.
23 Refer to Section 13 of this Chapter and remove the flywheel (manual transmission) or driveplate (automatic transmission).
24 Remove the intermediate plate from the dowels on the cylinder block.
25 Remove the sump as described in Section 15.
26 Progressively slacken then remove the oil seal housing retaining bolts.
27 Lift the housing away from the cylinder block, together with the crankshaft oil seal, using a twisting motion to ease the seal off the shaft.
28 Recover the old gasket from the cylinder block, then wipe clean the block before fitting the new oil seal and housing.
29 Smear the block mating surface with multi-purpose grease, and lay the new gasket in position **(see illustration)**.
30 A protective plastic cap is supplied with genuine Audi/VAG crankshaft oil seals; when fitted over the end of the crankshaft, the cap prevents damage to the inner lip of the oil seal as it is being fitted **(see illustration)**.

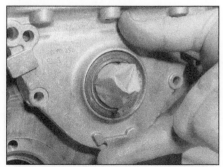

10.17 Offer up the seal and its housing to the end of the crankshaft

10.29 Locating the new crankshaft rear oil seal housing gasket in position

10.30 A protective plastic cap is supplied with genuine Audi/VAG crankshaft oil seals

10.31 Locating the crankshaft rear oil seal housing over the protective plastic cap

10.32 Tightening the crankshaft rear oil seal housing retaining bolts

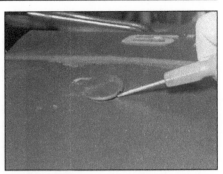

11.17a Prise out the plastic covers . . .

Use adhesive tape wrapped around the end of the crankshaft if a cap is not available.

31 Lubricate the inner lip of the crankshaft oil seal with clean engine oil, then offer up the seal and its housing to the end of the crankshaft. Ease the seal along the shaft using a twisting motion, until the housing is flush with the crankcase **(see illustration)**.

32 Insert the retaining bolts and tighten them progressively to the specified torque **(see illustration)**.

33 Refit the sump with reference to Section 15.

34 Refit the intermediate plate to the cylinder block, then insert and tighten the retaining bolts.

35 Refit the flywheel (manual transmission) or driveplate (automatic transmission) with reference to Section 13 of this Chapter.

36 Refit the transmission with reference to Chapter 7A or 7B.

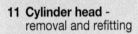

11 Cylinder head -
removal and refitting

Note: *Cylinder head dismantling and overhaul is covered in Chapter 2C.*

Removal

1 Disconnect the battery negative (earth) lead (see Chapter 5A).

2 Drain the engine oil with reference to Chapter 1B.

3 Drain the cooling system with reference to Chapter 1B.

4 Refer to Section 6 and remove the auxiliary drivebelts. This procedure includes moving the complete front panel (the lock carrier assembly) away from the front of the car sufficient to work on the front of the engine.

5 On models with air conditioning, loosen the pivot and tension bolts and move the tensioner roller upwards to release the tension on the drivebelt. Slip the drivebelt from the crankshaft, compressor and tensioner pulleys. Unbolt the A/C compressor from its mounting bracket and suspend it to one side without disconnecting the refrigerant circuit.

6 Remove the viscous fan unit with reference to Chapter 3, Section 5. Briefly, it is removed by inserting an Allen key from behind, while holding the unit stationary using a scissor-type tool engaged with two of the holes in the pulley - if the Audi tool cannot be obtained, make up a similar tool out of two lengths of metal with bolts to engage the holes.

7 Remove the air cleaner assembly as described in Chapter 4B.

8 Disconnect the hose from the turbocharger pressure/vacuum unit located on the right-hand side of the engine.

9 Unscrew the bolts/nuts securing the turbocharger to the catalytic converter. Release the front exhaust clamp and push the clamp to the rear, then disconnect the exhaust pipe and catalytic converter from the turbocharger. **Note:** *Take care not to damage the flexible joint in the exhaust pipe.*

10 Loosen the clips and remove the right-hand air intake duct leading from the air cleaner to the turbocharger.

11 Where fitted, unbolt and remove the turbocharger support bracket.

12 Unscrew the union bolt and disconnect the turbocharger oil return pipe from the cylinder block.

13 Loosen the clip and disconnect the top hose from the left-hand side of the cylinder head. Also disconnect the small purge hose from the top of the coolant expansion tank. Move the hose to one side.

14 Loosen the union nuts and remove the injector pipes complete.

15 Disconnect the wiring from the glow plugs.

16 Loosen the clip and disconnect the coolant hose from the bottom left-hand side of the cylinder head.

17 Remove the engine top cover, then refer to Section 7 and remove the camshaft cover **(see illustrations)**.

18 With reference to Section 2, set the engine to TDC on No 1 cylinder.

19 Remove the timing belt as described in Section 4.

20 Refer to Section 5 and remove the timing belt tensioner, and the camshaft and injection pump sprockets.

21 Unbolt and remove the timing belt inner cover from the engine block **(see illustrations)**.

22 Remove the air intake pipe from the rear of the engine. To do this, loosen the clips and disconnect the short hoses from the turbocharger and inlet manifold, then disconnect the EGR hoses and wiring and withdraw the pipe.

11.17b . . . then remove the nuts . . .

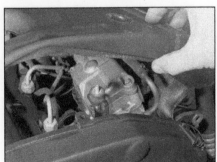

11.17c . . . and remove the engine top cover

11.21a Undo the retaining bolts . . .

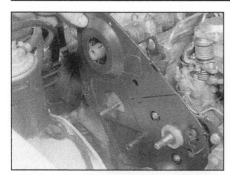

11.21b ... and lift off the timing belt inner cover

11.24 Heater outlet hose on the rear of the cylinder head

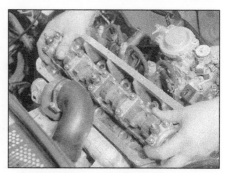

11.29 Lifting the cylinder head from the block

23 Loosen the union nut and disconnect the oil supply pipe from the turbocharger.

24 Loosen the clip and disconnect the heater outlet hose from the elbow on the rear of the cylinder head **(see illustration)**.

25 Where applicable, disconnect the wiring from the three heater elements on the elbow on the rear of the cylinder head

26 Disconnect the return fuel hose from the injectors.

27 On the front of the cylinder head, disconnect the wiring located on the top cover bracket.

28 Following the reverse of the tightening sequence **(see illustration 11.57a)**, progressively slacken the cylinder head bolts, by half a turn at a time, until all bolts can be unscrewed by hand. Discard the bolts - new ones must be fitted on reassembly.

29 Check that nothing remains connected to the cylinder head, then lift the head away from

the cylinder block; seek assistance if possible, as it is a heavy assembly, especially as it is being removed complete with the manifolds **(see illustration)**.

30 Remove the gasket from the top of the block, noting the locating dowels. If the dowels are a loose fit, remove them and store them with the head for safe-keeping. Do not discard the gasket yet - it will be needed for identification purposes.

31 If the cylinder head is to be dismantled for overhaul, refer to Chapter 2C.

Manifold separation and reassembly

32 With the cylinder head on a workbench, remove the turbocharger with reference to Chapter 4B.

33 Remove the EGR valve with reference to Chapter 4C.

34 On engine codes AZ, AFF and AHU,

unscrew the nuts and remove the small heatshield from the front of the exhaust manifold **(see illustration)**.

35 Progressively unscrew the mounting bolts and remove the inlet manifold from the cylinder head. Remove the gasket and discard it.

36 If necessary, unbolt the oil supply pipe and bracket from the exhaust manifold.

37 Progressively unscrew the mounting nuts and remove the exhaust manifold from the cylinder head. Remove the gaskets and discard. Discard the self-locking mounting nuts and obtain new ones.

38 Ensure that the inlet and exhaust manifold mating surfaces are completely clean. Refit the exhaust manifold, using new gaskets and nuts. Ensure that the gaskets are fitted the correct way around, otherwise they will obstruct the inlet manifold gasket. Tighten the exhaust manifold retaining nuts to the specified torque (see Chapter 4C) **(see illustrations)**.

39 Where necessary, refit the oil supply pipe and bracket to the exhaust manifold and tighten the bolt.

40 Fit a new inlet manifold gasket to the cylinder head, then lift the inlet manifold into position. Insert the retaining bolts and tighten them to the specified torque (see Chapter 4B) **(see illustrations)**.

41 Refit the heat shield to the studs on the exhaust manifold, then fit and tighten the retaining nuts.

42 Refit the EGR valve with reference to Chapter 4C.

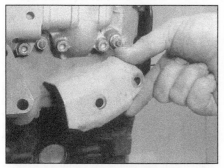

11.34 Removing the heat shield from the exhaust manifold

11.38a Fit the new exhaust manifold gaskets ...

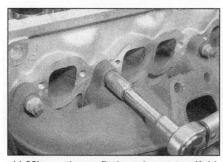

11.38b ... then refit the exhaust manifold and tighten the nuts to the specified torque

11.40a Fit the new inlet manifold gasket to the cylinder head ...

11.40b ... then lift the inlet manifold into position

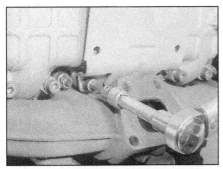

11.40c Tightening the inlet manifold retaining bolts

43 Refit the turbocharger to the inlet and exhaust manifolds with reference to Chapter 4B.

Preparation for refitting

44 The mating faces of the cylinder head and cylinder block must be perfectly clean before refitting the head. Use a hard plastic or wood scraper to remove all traces of gasket and carbon; also clean the piston crowns. Take particular care during the cleaning operations, as aluminium alloy is easily damaged. Also, make sure that the carbon is not allowed to enter the oil and water passages - this is particularly important for the lubrication system, as carbon could block the oil supply to the engine's components. Using adhesive tape and paper, seal the water, oil and bolt holes in the cylinder block/crankcase.

45 Check the mating surfaces of the cylinder block/crankcase and the cylinder head for

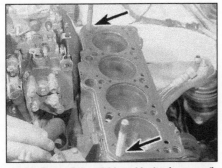

11.52 Two of the old head bolts (arrowed) used as cylinder head alignment dowels

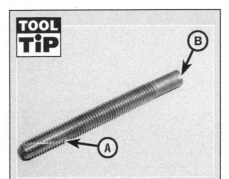

If a tap is not available, make a home-made substitute by cutting a slot (A) down the threads of one of the old cylinder head bolts. After use, the bolt head can be cut off, and the shank can then be used as an alignment dowel to assist cylinder head refitting. Cut a screwdriver slot (B) in the top of the bolt, to allow it to be unscrewed

nicks, deep scratches and other damage. If slight, they may be removed carefully with abrasive paper, but note that head machining will not be possible - refer to Chapter 2C.

46 If warpage of the cylinder head gasket surface is suspected, use a straight-edge to check it for distortion. Refer to Part C of this Chapter if necessary.

47 Clean out the cylinder head bolt drillings using a suitable tap. If a tap is not available, make a home-made substitute **(see Tool Tip)**.

48 On the engines covered in this Chapter, it is possible for the piston crowns to strike the valve heads, if the camshaft is rotated with the timing belt removed and the crankshaft set to TDC. For this reason, the camshaft must be locked at its TDC position using the locking bar engaged with the slot in the end of the camshaft while the cylinder head is being refitted. The crankshaft must also be positioned with No 1 piston at TDC before refitting the cylinder head.

Refitting

49 Examine the old cylinder head gasket for manufacturer's identification markings. These will either be in the form of notches or holes, and a part number, on the edge of the gasket.

Unless new pistons have been fitted, the new cylinder head gasket must be the same type as the old one.

50 If new piston assemblies have been fitted as part of an engine overhaul, before purchasing the new cylinder head gasket, refer to Chapter 2C and measure the piston projection. Purchase a new gasket according to the results of the measurement (see Chapter 2C Specifications).

51 Lay the new head gasket on the cylinder block, engaging it with the locating dowels. Ensure that the manufacturer's TOP and part number markings are facing upwards.

52 Cut the heads from two of the old cylinder head bolts. Cut a slot, big enough for a screwdriver blade, in the end of each bolt. These can be used as alignment dowels to assist in cylinder head refitting **(see illustration)**.

53 With the help of an assistant, place the cylinder head and manifolds centrally on the cylinder block, ensuring that the locating dowels engage with the recesses in the cylinder head.

54 Unscrew the home-made alignment dowels using a screwdriver and remove them.

55 Apply a smear of grease to the threads, and to the underside of the heads, of the new cylinder head bolts.

56 Oil the bolt threads, then carefully enter each bolt into its relevant hole (*do not drop them in*) and screw in, by hand only, until finger-tight **(see illustration)**.

57 Working progressively and in the sequence shown, tighten the cylinder head bolts to their Stage 1 torque setting, using a torque wrench and socket **(see illustrations)**. Repeat the exercise in the same sequence for the Stage 2 torque setting.

58 Once all the bolts have been tightened to their Stage 2 settings, working again in the given sequence, angle-tighten the bolts through the specified Stage 3 angle, using a socket and extension bar. It is recommended that an angle-measuring gauge is used during this stage of the tightening, to ensure accuracy. If a gauge is not available, use white paint to make alignment marks between the bolt head and cylinder head prior to tightening; the marks can then be used to check the bolt has been rotated through the correct angle during tightening. Repeat for the

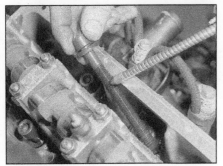

11.56 Oil the cylinder head bolt threads, then place each bolt into its relevant hole

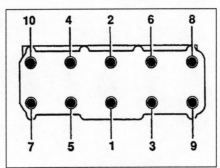

11.57a Cylinder head bolt tightening sequence

11.57b Tightening the cylinder head bolts using a torque wrench

Stage 4 setting **(see illustration)**. **Note:** *No further tightening of the cylinder head bolts is required after the engine has been started.*

59 Check that the TDC timing marks are still aligned with reference to Section 2.

60 The remainder of refitting is a reversal of the removal procedure, but on completion carry out the following:
a) *Refill the cooling system with the correct quantity of new coolant with reference to Chapter 1B.*
b) *Refill the engine with the correct grade and quantity of oil with reference to Chapter 1B.*

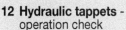
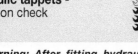

12 Hydraulic tappets - operation check

> ⚠️ *Warning: After fitting hydraulic tappets, wait a minimum of 30 minutes (or preferably, leave overnight) before starting the engine, to allow the tappets time to settle, otherwise the valve heads will strike the pistons.*

1 The hydraulic tappets are self-adjusting, and require no attention whilst in service.

2 If the hydraulic tappets become excessively noisy, their operation can be checked as described below.

3 Run the engine until it reaches its normal operating temperature, then increase the engine speed to approximately 2500 rpm for 2 minutes.

4 If irregular noisy tappets occur mainly when driving the car on short distances, but disappear after running the engine as described in paragraph 3, renew the oil retention valve located in the oil filter housing.

5 In the case of a regular noisy tappet, the faulty tappet must be renewed. To determine which one is faulty, switch off the engine, then refer to Section 7 and remove the camshaft cover.

6 Rotate the camshaft by turning the crankshaft with a socket and wrench, until the first cam lobe over No 1 cylinder is pointing upwards.

7 Using a non-metallic tool, press the tappet downwards then use a feeler blade to check the free travel. If this is more than 0.2 mm, the tappet should be renewed.

8 Hydraulic tappet removal and refitting is described as part of the cylinder head overhaul sequence - see Chapter 2C for details.

13 Flywheel/driveplate - removal, inspection and refitting

Removal

1 On manual gearbox models, remove the gearbox (see Chapter 7A) and clutch (see Chapter 6).

11.58 Angle-tightening the cylinder head bolts

2 On automatic transmission models, remove the automatic transmission as described in Chapter 7B.

3 The flywheel/driveplate bolts are offset to ensure correct fitment. Unscrew the bolts while holding the flywheel/driveplate stationary. Temporarily insert a bolt in the cylinder block, and use a screwdriver to hold the flywheel/driveplate, or make up a holding tool.

4 Lift the flywheel/driveplate from the crankshaft. If removing a driveplate, note the location of the shim and spacer.

Inspection

5 Check the flywheel/driveplate for wear and damage. Examine the starter ring gear for excessive wear to the teeth. If the driveplate or its ring gear are damaged, the complete driveplate must be renewed. The flywheel ring gear, however, may be renewed separately from the flywheel, but the work should be entrusted to an Audi/VAG dealer. If the clutch friction face is discoloured or scored excessively, it may be possible to regrind it, but this work should also be entrusted to an Audi/VAG dealer. Always renew the flywheel/driveplate bolts.

Refitting

6 Refitting is a reversal of removal, but coat the threads of the (new) bolts with locking fluid before inserting them and tightening them to the specified torque. If a replacement

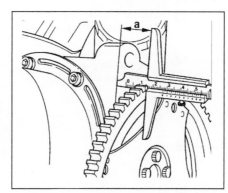

13.6 On automatic transmission models, dimension 'a' must be 27 mm ± 1 mm

driveplate is to be fitted, its position must be checked and adjusted if necessary. The distance from the rear face of the block to the torque converter *mounting face* on the driveplate must be 27 mm ± 1 mm. If necessary, remove the driveplate, and fit a spacer behind it to achieve the correct dimension **(see illustration)**. The raised pip on the outer shim must face the torque converter.

14 Engine mountings - inspection and renewal

Inspection

1 If improved access is required, raise the front of the car and support it securely on axle stands then remove the undershield.

2 Check the mounting rubbers to see if they are cracked, hardened or separated from the metal at any point; renew the mounting if any such damage or deterioration is evident.

3 Check that all the mounting's fasteners are securely tightened; use a torque wrench to check if possible.

4 Using a large screwdriver or a crowbar, check for wear in the mounting by carefully levering against it to check for free play. Where this is not possible, enlist the aid of an assistant to move the engine/transmission back and forth, or from side to side, while you watch the mounting. While some free play is to be expected even from new components, excessive wear should be obvious. If excessive free play is found, check first that the fasteners are correctly secured, then renew any worn components as described below.

Renewal

Front torque arm

5 For improved access, apply the handbrake then jack up the front of the vehicle and support it on axle stands (see *Jacking and vehicle support*).

6 Unscrew the bolts and remove the torque arm and rubber mounting from the front of the cylinder block.

7 Unbolt the bracket from the front valance.

8 Fit the new torque arm and bracket using a reversal of the removal procedure.

Right- or left-hand engine mounting

9 Apply the handbrake, then jack up the front of the vehicle and support it on axle stands (see *Jacking and vehicle support*).

10 Support the weight of the engine with a hoist.

11 Unscrew the upper mounting nut, then raise the engine and unbolt the mounting from the bracket.

12 Fit the new mounting using a reversal of the removal procedure.

15 Sump -
removal, inspection
and refitting

Removal

1 Apply the handbrake, then jack up the front of the vehicle and support it on axle stands (see *Jacking and vehicle support*). Also remove the undershield from under the engine and radiator.

2 Unscrew the nuts and remove the engine top cover.

3 Disconnect and remove the air inlet pipe leading to the air cleaner from the front panel (lock carrier).

4 At the front of the engine, unbolt and remove the small cover and solenoid valve from the right-hand side of the timing cover, and position to one side.

5 Support the weight of the engine using a suitable hoist.

6 Position a container beneath the sump, then unscrew the drain plug (refer to Chapter 1B) and drain the engine oil. Clean, refit, and tighten the plug after all the oil has drained. Remove the dipstick from the engine.

7 On models with air conditioning, mark the A/C compressor drivebelt for direction of rotation to ensure correct refitting. Loosen the pivot and tension bolts and move the tensioner roller upwards to release the tension on the drivebelt. Slip the drivebelt from the crankshaft, compressor and tensioner pulleys.

Unscrew and remove the pivot and tension bolts and remove the tensioner.

8 Unbolt the torque reaction stop from the front of the engine, then unscrew the bolts from the longitudinal struts. Also unbolt the torque reaction bracket from the front of the engine.

9 Cut the cable ties from the bottom of the right-hand engine mounting and release the starter motor wiring.

10 Unscrew the engine mounting nuts from the bottom of both engine mountings.

11 Make sure the engine is adequately supported on the hoist. Support the left- and right-hand front subframes with a trolley jack and length of wood. Mark the position of the subframes to ensure correct refitting and wheel alignment, then unscrew and remove the subframe mounting bolts. The front two bolts must be unscrewed first, then the rear bolts. Lower the subframes together with the anti-roll bar to the ground.

12 Unscrew and remove the bolts and remove the engine-to-transmission support bracket.

13 Unscrew and remove the sump bolts. Note that on manual transmission models, the two rear sump bolts are accessed through a cut-out in the flywheel - turn the flywheel as necessary to align the cut-out.

14 Remove the sump and gasket. If it is stuck, tap it gently with a mallet to free it.

Refitting

15 Clean the contact faces of the sump and block. Apply a little suitable sealant to the joint areas where the front and rear crankshaft oil seal housings contact the cylinder block.

16 Locate a new gasket on the sump, then offer it up to the block and fit the bolts. Tighten the bolts to the specified torque in diagonal sequence.

17 Refit the engine-to-transmission support bracket and tighten the bolts. **Note:** *If the sump is being fitted with the engine removed from the car and the transmission removed, make sure that the end face of the support bracket is flush with that of the intermediate plate. If the intermediate plate is removed, allow 0.8 mm for its thickness, and position the face of the bracket 0.8 mm protruding from the rear face of the cylinder block.*

18 The remaining refitting procedure is a reversal removal, but tighten the nuts and bolts to the specified torque where given in the Specifications. On models with air conditioning, refit and tension the compressor drivebelt with reference to Section 6. On completion, fill the engine with the correct quantity of oil as described in Chapter 1B.

16 Oil pump and pickup -
removal, inspection
and refitting

Removal

1 Remove the sump as described in Section 15.

2 Unscrew and remove the large oil pump mounting bolts, then withdraw the pump from the block **(see illustration)**. Note that it may be necessary to press the subframe down to provide sufficient room to remove the pump.

3 With the pump on the bench, unscrew the bolts and remove the suction tube from the oil pump. Recover the O-ring.

4 Unscrew the two bolts, and lift off the cover.

Inspection

5 Clean the components, and check them for wear and damage.

6 Using a feeler blade, check the backlash between the gears, and compare with that given in the Specifications. Similarly check the endfloat of the gears, using a straight edge across the end face of the pump. If outside the specified limits, the pump should be renewed, otherwise refit the cover and tighten the bolts.

Refitting

7 Prime the pump with oil by immersing it in oil and turning the driveshaft.

8 Clean the contact faces, then fit the oil pump to the block, insert the mounting bolts, and tighten them to the specified torque.

9 Locate a new O-ring seal on the end of the suction tube. Fit the tube to the oil pump, insert the bolts and tighten them to the specified torque.

10 Refit the sump with reference to Section 15.

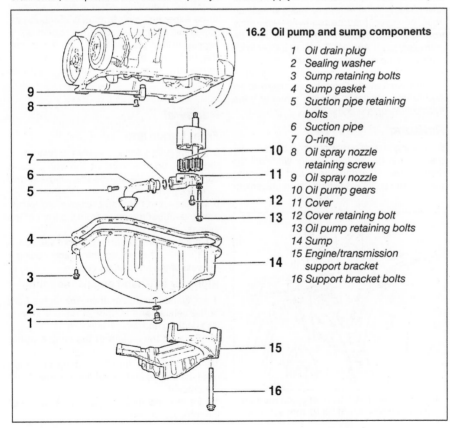

16.2 Oil pump and sump components

1 Oil drain plug
2 Sealing washer
3 Sump retaining bolts
4 Sump gasket
5 Suction pipe retaining bolts
6 Suction pipe
7 O-ring
8 Oil spray nozzle retaining screw
9 Oil spray nozzle
10 Oil pump gears
11 Cover
12 Cover retaining bolt
13 Oil pump retaining bolts
14 Sump
15 Engine/transmission support bracket
16 Support bracket bolts

Chapter 2 Part C:
Engine removal and overhaul procedures

Contents

Degrees of difficulty

Easy, suitable for novice with little experience		Fairly easy, suitable for beginner with some experience		Fairly difficult, suitable for competent DIY mechanic		Difficult, suitable for experienced DIY mechanic		Very difficult, suitable for expert DIY or professional	

Specifications

Engine codes*

Petrol engines:

1595 cc, Bosch Motronic 3.2 injection, 74 kW (100 bhp)	ADP
1595 cc, Simos, 74 kW (100 bhp)	AHL
1781 cc, Bosch Motronic injection, 92 kW (124 bhp)	ADR
1781 cc, Bosch Motronic injection, 88 kW (119 bhp)	AFY
1781 cc, Bosch Motronic injection, 92 kW (124 bhp)	APT
1781 cc, Bosch Motronic injection	APW
1781 cc, Bosch Motronic injection, 110 kW (149 bhp)	AEB, APU
1781 cc, Bosch Motronic injection, 132 kW (178 bhp)	AJL

Diesel engines:

Electronic direct fuel injection, turbocharged, 66 kW (90 bhp)	1Z
Electronic direct fuel injection, turbocharged, 81 kW (110 bhp)	AFN
Electronic direct fuel injection, turbocharged, 55 kW (75 bhp)	AFF
Electronic direct fuel injection, turbocharged, 66 kW (90 bhp)	AHU
Electronic direct fuel injection, turbocharged, 66 kW (90 bhp)	AHH

* **Note:** *See 'Vehicle Identification' for the location of the code marking on the engine.*

Cylinder head

Cylinder head gasket surface, maximum distortion:

All engines	0.1 mm

Minimum cylinder head height:

Petrol engine codes ADP, AHL	132.6 mm
Petrol engine code ADR, AFY, AEB, APU, AJL	139.25 mm
Diesel engines	Head reworking not possible

Cylinder head gasket selection (1Z, AFF, AFN, AHH, AHU diesel engines):

Piston projection 0.91 to 1.00 mm	1 hole/notch*
Piston projection 1.01 to 1.10 mm	2 holes/notches*
Piston projection 1.11 to 1.20 mm	3 holes/notches*

Disregard single oval hole

Valve stem (centre) to cylinder head top face minimum dimension:	Inlet valve	Exhaust valve
Petrol engine codes ADP, AHL	33.8 mm	34.1 mm
Petrol engine codes ADR, AFY, AEB, APU, AJL	34.0 mm (outer) 33.7 mm (centre)	34.4 mm
Diesel engine codes 1Z, AHU, AHH, AFN, AFF	35.8 mm	36.1 mm

Pistons and piston rings

Piston diameter:
  Petrol engine code ADP, ADR, AFY, AEB, APU, AJL:
    Standard .... 80.975 mm
    1st oversize .... 81.475 mm
    Maximum deviation .... 0.04 mm
  Petrol engine code AHL:
    Standard .... 80.965 mm
    1st oversize .... 81.465 mm
    Maximum deviation .... 0.04 mm
  Diesel engine codes 1Z, AHU, AHH, AFN, AFF:
    Standard .... 79.470 mm
    1st oversize .... 79.720 mm
    2nd oversize .... 79.970 mm
    Maximum deviation .... 0.04 mm
Groove-to-ring clearance:
  4-cylinder petrol engine codes ADP, AHL, ADR, AFY, AEB, APU, AJL:
    1st compression ring .... 0.06 to 0.09 mm
    2nd compression ring .... 0.05 to 0.08 mm
    Oil control ring .... 0.03 to 0.06 mm
    Wear limit:
      Compression rings .... 0.20 mm
      Oil control ring .... 0.15 mm
  4-cylinder diesel engine codes 1Z, AHU, AHH, AFN, AFF:
    1st compression ring .... 0.06 to 0.09 mm
    2nd compression ring .... 0.05 to 0.08 mm
    Oil control ring .... 0.03 to 0.06 mm
    Wear limit:
      Compression rings .... 0.25 mm
      Oil control ring .... 0.15 mm
Piston ring end gap clearance (ring 15 mm from bottom of bore):
  4-cylinder petrol engine codes ADP, AHL, ADR, AFY, AEB, APU, AJL:
    New:
      Compression rings .... 0.20 to 0.40 mm
      Oil scraper ring .... 0.25 to 0.50 mm
    Wear limit .... 0.8 mm
  4-cylinder diesel engine codes 1Z, AHU, AHH, AFN, AFF:
    New:
      Compression rings .... 0.20 to 0.40 mm
      Oil scraper ring .... 0.25 to 0.50 mm
    Wear limit .... 1.0 mm

Valves

Valve stem diameter:	Inlet	Exhaust
ADP, AHL	6.918 to 6.922 mm	6.918 to 6.922 mm
ADR, AFY, AEB, APU, AJL	5.950 to 5.970 mm	5.940 to 5.950 mm
1Z, AHU, AHH, AFN, AFF to 3/1998	7.970 mm	7.950 mm
1Z, AHU, AHH, AFN, AFF from 4/1998	6.963 mm	6.943 mm
Maximum valve head deflection (end of stem flush with top of guide):		
ADP, AHL	1.0 mm	1.3 mm
ADR, AFY, AEB, APU, AJL	0.80 mm	0.80 mm
1Z, AHU, AHH, AFN, AFF	1.3 mm	1.3 mm

Camshaft

Maximum endfloat:
  ADP, AHL, 1Z, AHU, AHH, AFN, AFF .... 0.15 mm
  ADR, AFY, AEB, APU, AJL .... 0.20 mm
Maximum runout, all engine codes .... 0.01 mm
Maximum running clearance:
  ADP, AHL, ADR, AFY, AEB, APU, AJL .... 0.10 mm
  1Z, AHU, AHH, AFN, AFF .... 0.11 mm

Intermediate shaft

Maximum endfloat:
  ADP, ADR, AFY, AEB, APU, AJL, 1Z, AHU, AHH, AFN, AFF .... 0.25 mm

Cylinder block

Bore diameter:
  Engine codes ADP, AHL, ADR, AFY, AEB, APU, AJL:
    Standard . . . . 81.01 mm
    Oversize . . . . 81.51 mm
    Maximum bore wear . . . . 0.08 mm
  Engine codes 1Z, AHU, AHH, AFN, AFF:
    Standard . . . . 79.51 mm
    1st oversize . . . . 79.76 mm
    2nd oversize . . . . 80.01 mm
    Maximum bore wear . . . . 0.10 mm

Connecting rods

Big-end side clearance (maximum):
  ADP, AHL, ADR, AFY, AEB, APU, AJL . . . . 0.40 mm
  1Z, AHU, AHH, AFN, AFF . . . . 0.37 mm

Crankshaft

Spigot needle bearing depth . . . . 1.5 mm
Endfloat:
  New:
    Petrol engine codes ADP, ADR, AFY, AEB, APU, AJL . . . . 0.07 to 0.23 mm
    Petrol engine codes AHL . . . . 0.07 to 0.21 mm
    Diesel engine codes 1Z, AHU, AHH, AFN, AFF . . . . 0.07 to 017 mm
  Wear limit:
    Petrol engine codes ADP, AHL, ADR, AFY, AEB, APU, AJL . . . . . . 0.30 mm
    Diesel engine codes 1Z, AHU, AHH, AFN, AFF . . . . 0.37 mm
Main bearing running clearance:
  New:
    Petrol engine codes ADP, ADR, AFY, AEB, APU, AJL . . . . 0.02 to 0.04 mm
    Petrol engine codes AHL . . . . 0.01 to 0.04 mm
    Diesel engine codes 1Z, AHU, AHH, AFN, AFF . . . . 0.03 to 0.08 mm
  Wear limit:
    Petrol engine codes ADP, AHL, ADR, AFY, AEB, APU, AJL . . . . . . 0.15 mm
    Diesel engine codes 1Z, AHU, AHH, AFN, AFF . . . . 0.17 mm
Main bearing journal diameter:
  Petrol engine codes ADP, ADR, AFY, AEB, APU, AJL:
    Standard size . . . . 54.00 mm -0.017-0.037
    1st undersize . . . . 53.75 mm -0.017-0.037
    2nd undersize . . . . 53.50 mm -0.017-0.037
    3rd undersize . . . . 53.25 mm -0.017-0.037
  Petrol engine codes AHL:
    Standard size . . . . 54.00 mm -0.022-0.042
    1st undersize . . . . 53.75 mm -0.022-0.042
    2nd undersize . . . . 53.50 mm -0.022-0.042
    3rd undersize . . . . 53.25 mm -0.022-0.042
  Diesel engine codes 1Z, AHU, AHH, AFN, AFF:
    Standard size . . . . 54.00 mm -0.022-0.042
    1st undersize . . . . 53.75 mm -0.022-0.042
    2nd undersize . . . . 53.50 mm -0.022-0.042
    3rd undersize . . . . 53.25 mm -0.022-0.042
Big-end bearing journal diameter:
  All engines, petrol and diesel:
    Standard size . . . . 47.80 mm -0.022-0.042
    1st undersize . . . . 47.55 mm -0.022-0.042
    2nd undersize . . . . 47.30 mm -0.022-0.042
    3rd undersize . . . . 47.05 mm -0.022-0.042
Big-end bearing running clearance:
  New:
    Petrol engine codes ADP, AHL, ADR, AFY, AEB, APU, AJL . . . . . . 0.01 to 0.05 mm
    Diesel engine codes 1Z, AHU, AHH, AFN, AFF . . . . 0.03 to 0.08 mm
  Wear limit:
    Petrol engine codes ADP, AHL, ADR, AFY, AEB, APU, AJL . . . . . . 0.12 mm
    Diesel engine codes 1Z, AHU, AHH, AFN, AFF . . . . 0.08 mm
Maximum journal out-of-round (typical) . . . . 0.03 mm

Torque wrench settings

Refer to Chapters 2A or 2B.

1 General information

1 Included in this Part of Chapter 2 are details of removing the engine from the car and general overhaul procedures for the cylinder head, cylinder block and all other engine internal components.

2 The information given ranges from advice concerning preparation for an overhaul and the purchase of replacement parts, to detailed step-by-step procedures covering removal, inspection, renovation and refitting of engine internal components.

3 After Section 5, all instructions are based on the assumption that the engine has been removed from the car. For information concerning in-car engine repair, as well as the removal and refitting of those external components necessary for full overhaul, refer to the relevant in-car repair procedure section (Chapters 2A or 2B) and to Section 5 of this Chapter. Ignore any preliminary dismantling operations described in the relevant in-car repair sections that are no longer relevant once the engine has been removed from the car.

4 Apart from torque wrench settings, which are given at the beginning of the relevant in-car repair procedure in Chapters 2A or 2B, all specifications relating to engine overhaul are at the beginning of this Part of Chapter 2.

2 Engine overhaul - general information

1 It is not always easy to determine when, or if, an engine should be completely overhauled, as a number of factors must be considered.

2 High mileage is not necessarily an indication that an overhaul is needed, while low mileage does not preclude the need for an overhaul. Frequency of servicing is probably the most important consideration. An engine which has had regular and frequent oil and filter changes, as well as other required maintenance, should give many thousands of miles of reliable service. Conversely, a neglected engine may require an overhaul very early in its life.

3 Excessive oil consumption is an indication that piston rings, valve seals and/or valve guides are in need of attention. Make sure that oil leaks are not responsible before deciding that the rings and/or guides are worn. Perform a compression test, as described in the relevant Part A or B of this Chapter, to determine the likely cause of the problem.

4 Check the oil pressure with a gauge fitted in place of the oil pressure switch, and compare it with that specified (see Chapter 2A or 2B). If it is extremely low, the main and big-end bearings, and/or the oil pump, are probably worn out.

5 Loss of power, rough running, knocking or metallic engine noises, excessive valve gear noise, and high fuel consumption may also point to the need for an overhaul, especially if they are all present at the same time. If a complete service does not remedy the situation, major mechanical work is the only solution.

6 An engine overhaul involves restoring all internal parts to the specification of a new engine. During an overhaul, the pistons and the piston rings are renewed. New main and big-end bearings are generally fitted; if necessary, the crankshaft may be renewed, to restore the journals. The valves are also serviced as well, since they are usually in less-than-perfect condition at this point. While the engine is being overhauled, other components, such as the starter and alternator, can be overhauled as well. The end result should be an as-new engine that will give many trouble-free miles. **Note:** *Critical cooling system components such as the hoses, thermostat and coolant pump should be renewed when an engine is overhauled. The radiator should be checked carefully, to ensure that it is not clogged or leaking. Also, it is a good idea to renew the oil pump whenever the engine is overhauled.*

7 Before beginning the engine overhaul, read through the entire procedure, to familiarise yourself with the scope and requirements of the job. Overhauling an engine is not difficult if you follow carefully all of the instructions, have the necessary tools and equipment, and pay close attention to all specifications. It can, however, be time-consuming. Plan on the car being off the road for a minimum of two weeks, especially if parts must be taken to an engineering works for repair or reconditioning. Check on the availability of parts and make sure that any necessary special tools and equipment are obtained in advance. Most work can be done with typical hand tools, although a number of precision measuring tools are required for inspecting parts to determine if they must be renewed. Often the engineering works will handle the inspection of parts and offer advice concerning reconditioning and renewal. **Note:** *Always wait until the engine has been completely dismantled, and until all components (especially the cylinder block and the crankshaft) have been inspected, before deciding what service and repair operations must be performed by an engineering works. The condition of these components will be the major factor to consider when determining whether to overhaul the original engine, or to buy a reconditioned unit. Do not, therefore, purchase parts or have overhaul work done on other components until they have been thoroughly inspected. As a general rule, time is the primary cost of an overhaul, so it does not pay to fit worn or sub-standard parts.*

8 As a final note, to ensure maximum life and minimum trouble from a reconditioned engine, everything must be assembled with care, in a spotlessly-clean environment.

3 Engine removal - preparation and precautions

If you have decided that the engine must be removed for overhaul or major repair work, several preliminary steps should be taken.

Locating a suitable place to work is extremely important. Adequate work space, along with storage space for the vehicle, will be needed. If a workshop or garage is not available, at the very least a solid, level, clean work surface is required.

If possible, clear some shelving close to the work area and use it to store the engine components and ancillaries as they are removed and dismantled. In this manner, the components stand a better chance of staying clean and undamaged during the overhaul. Laying out components in groups together with their fixings bolts, screws, etc will save time and avoid confusion when the engine is refitted.

Clean the engine compartment and engine before beginning the removal procedure; this will help visibility and help to keep tools clean.

The help of an assistant is essential; there are certain instances when one person cannot safely perform all of the operations required to remove the engine from the vehicle. Safety is of primary importance, considering the potential hazards involved in this kind of operation. A second person should always be in attendance to offer help in an emergency. If this is the first time you have removed an engine, advice and aid from someone more experienced would also be beneficial.

Plan the operation ahead of time. Before starting work, obtain (or arrange for the hire of) all of the tools and equipment you will need. Access to the following items will allow the task of removing and refitting the engine to be completed safely and with relative ease: a heavy-duty trolley jack - rated in excess of the weight of the engine, complete sets of spanners and sockets as described in the front of this manual, wooden blocks, and plenty of rags and cleaning solvent for mopping up spilled oil, coolant and fuel. A selection of different sized plastic storage bins will also prove useful for keeping dismantled components grouped together. If any of the equipment must be hired, make sure that you arrange for it in advance, and perform all of the operations possible without it beforehand; this may save you time and money.

Plan on the vehicle being out of use for quite a while, especially if you intend to carry out an engine overhaul. Read through the whole of this Section and work out a strategy based on your own experience and the tools, time and workspace available to you. Some of the overhaul processes may have to be carried out by an Audi dealer or an engineering works - these establishments often have busy schedules, so it would be prudent to consult them before removing or dismantling the engine, to get an idea of the amount of time required to carry out the work.

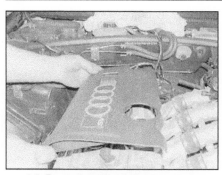

4.5 Removing the engine top cover (ADR engine)

4.6a Release the wheel arch liners . . .

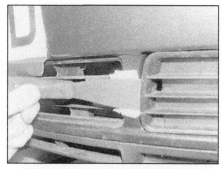

4.6b . . . then remove the side plastic covers . . .

4.6c . . . undo the screws . . .

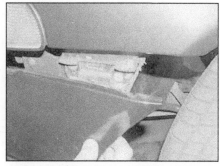

4.6d . . . and withdraw the front bumper

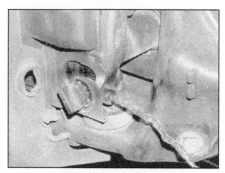

4.7 Draining the cooling system

When removing the engine from the vehicle, be methodical about the disconnection of external components. Labelling cables and hoses as they are removed will greatly assist the refitting process.

Always be extremely careful when lifting the engine from the engine bay. Serious injury can result from careless actions. If help is required, it is better to wait until it is available rather than risk personal injury and/or damage to components by continuing alone. By planning ahead and taking your time, a job of this nature, although major, can be accomplished successfully and without incident.

On all models described in this manual, the engine is lifted from the engine compartment leaving the gearbox in the car. Note that the engine should ideally be removed with the vehicle standing on all four roadwheels, but access to the exhaust system downpipe and lower bolts will be improved if the vehicle can be temporarily raised onto axle stands.

4 Engine - removal and refitting

Petrol engines

Removal

1 Select a solid, level surface to park the vehicle on. Give yourself enough space to move around it easily.
2 Disconnect the battery negative (earth) lead (see Chapter 5A).
3 Apply the handbrake, then jack up the front of the vehicle and support it on axle stands (see *Jacking and vehicle support*).
4 Remove the engine compartment under-shield after undoing the screws.
5 Where applicable, remove the cover from the top of the engine (see illustration).
6 Remove the front bumper with reference to Chapter 11 (see illustrations).

7 With reference to Chapter 1A, carry out the following:
 a) *Drain the cooling system. The drain plug is located on the front left-hand side of the radiator (see illustration), and on some engines a further plug is located on the coolant pump bearing housing.*
 b) *Drain the engine oil.*
8 Unscrew and remove the two bolts securing the power steering fluid cooling pipe to the front of the radiator, and position it to one side. Tie the outside temperature sensor in its original position.
9 Loosen the clips and disconnect the hoses from the top and bottom of the radiator, and from the thermostat housing. On engine code ADR, it may be easier to disconnect the top hose from the engine (see illustration). On engine code AHL, disconnect the hoses from the engine oil cooler and drain off the remaining coolant.
10 Unbolt the air duct leading to the air cleaner from the lock carrier (see illustrations).

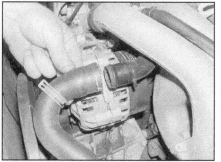

4.9 Disconnecting the top hose from the engine (ADR engine)

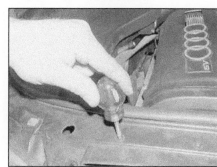

4.10a Undo the screws . . .

4.10b . . . and remove the air duct leading to the air cleaner

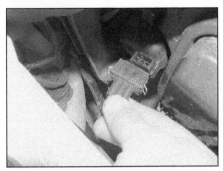

4.11 Disconnecting the wiring from the headlight range control unit

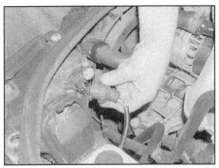

4.12 Disconnect the bulb holders from the front indicator units

4.18 Removing the cover from the power steering fluid reservoir

11 Disconnect the wiring from the headlights and headlight range control unit (see illustration).
12 Disconnect the bulb holders from the front indicator units (see illustration).
13 Disconnect the bonnet lock cable from the lock carrier.
14 On models fitted with an electric cooling fan, disconnect the wiring from the thermostat located on the bottom left-hand side of the radiator. Position the wiring to one side.
15 Disconnect the wiring from the horns, and move the wiring to one side.
16 On models equipped with air conditioning, unscrew the bolts and remove the air cowls from each side of the radiator, then remove the condenser mounting bolts. Disconnect the wiring from the low pressure switch, and also disconnect the A/C magnetic clutch wiring from the bottom of the lock carrier. Lift the condenser from its bracket,

rotate it to the side and tie it on the front wheel to secure it away from the engine compartment. Protect the condenser with card or cloth sheets to prevent damage to it when removing the engine.

 Warning: Do not disconnect the air conditioning refrigerant circuit.

17 On models with automatic transmission, position a suitable container beneath the radiator, then loosen the union nuts and disconnect the fluid pipes from the bottom of the radiator. Plug the pipes and radiator apertures to prevent entry of dust and dirt. Also unbolt the fluid pipe bracket from the engine.
18 Remove the cover from the power steering fluid reservoir (see illustration).
19 Disconnect the wiring from the ABS units located on the left-hand side of the engine compartment and from the anti-theft switch at

the front of the engine compartment (see illustration).
20 On the top left-hand side of the lock carrier, disconnect the wiring for the anti-theft alarm system at the connectors.
21 Unscrew the lock carrier mounting bolts, then with the help of an assistant, withdraw the complete lock carrier from the front of the car and place it in a safe position (see illustrations).
22 Remove the air cleaner assembly complete with air duct with reference to Chapter 4A.
23 Disconnect the main ignition lead, disconnect the wiring and position the wiring on the engine. Also where necessary, disconnect the oxygen sensor wiring.
24 Refer to Chapter 4A, and depressurise the fuel system, then disconnect the fuel supply and return lines at the fuel rail.
25 Loosen the clips and disconnect the small hoses from the coolant expansion tank on the left-hand side of the engine compartment. Disconnect the wiring from the low coolant warning switch, then unbolt the expansion tank and remove it (see illustrations).
26 On models equipped with cruise control, disconnect the actuator rod at the throttle valve control, and pull the vacuum hose from the vacuum unit.
27 Disconnect the accelerator cable from the throttle housing and support bracket and position it to one side.
28 Disconnect the vacuum hoses from the ACF valve and brake vacuum servo (see illustrations).
29 On automatic transmission models,

4.19 Disconnecting the wiring from the anti-theft switch at the front of the engine compartment

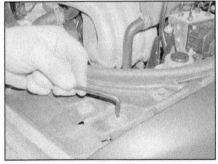

4.21a Unscrew the mounting bolts . . .

4.21b . . . and withdraw the lock carrier from the front of the car

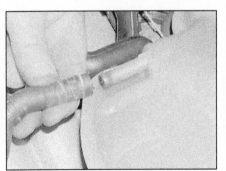

4.25a Disconnect the hoses from the coolant expansion tank . . .

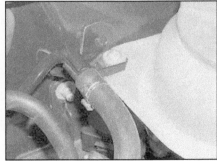

4.25b . . . then unscrew the mounting screws . . .

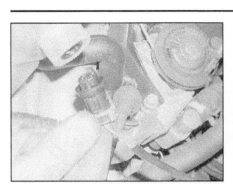

4.25c ... and disconnect the low coolant warning switch

4.28a Disconnect the ACF valve vacuum hose ...

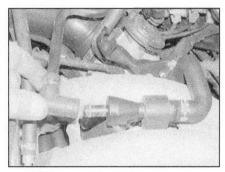

4.28b ... and brake vacuum servo

disconnect the wiring from the kick-down switch.
30 On left-hand drive models, remove the engine management ECU from the left-hand side of the bulkhead (see Chapter 4A). To do this, unbolt the cover from the electronics box first, then release the retainers and disconnect the wiring. On all models, release the engine wiring harness as required, and undo the earth cable screw, then position the wiring on the engine.
31 Remove the intake pipe and crankcase ventilation hoses from the throttle housing and engine valve cover **(see illustration)**.
32 Loosen the clips and disconnect the heater hoses from the bottom hose coolant pipe and the outlet elbow on the rear of the cylinder head.
33 Disconnect the wiring from the speedometer sender on the left-hand side of the transmission.

34 On models with a manual transmission, disconnect the wiring from the reversing light switch on the left-hand side of the transmission.
35 Remove the auxiliary drivebelts with reference to Chapter 2A.
36 Refer to Chapter 3, and unbolt the air conditioning compressor from the engine. Tie the compressor to one side away from the engine compartment.

 Warning: Do not disconnect the air conditioning refrigerant circuit.

37 Unbolt the pulley from the power steering pump, then unbolt the pump from its mounting bracket and tie it to one side **(see illustrations)**. Do not disconnect the hydraulic lines from the pump.
38 Disconnect the exhaust downpipe from the exhaust manifold with reference to Chapter 4C. Take care not to bend

excessively the flexible section of the downpipe.
39 Unbolt the heatshield from the right-hand engine mounting and lift it up. Unscrew the nuts from the tops of the right- and left-hand engine mountings. Also undo the screw and remove the earth cable from the right-hand engine mounting.
40 Remove the starter motor from the transmission with reference to Chapter 5A.
41 On automatic transmission models, unscrew and remove the three torque converter nuts accessible through the starter motor aperture. It will be necessary to turn the engine for access to each nut. To prevent the driveplate from turning while loosening the nuts, either counterhold the crankshaft pulley bolt, or place a screwdriver in the teeth of the starter ring gear.
42 Mark the positions of the engine mountings in the subframe to ensure they are refitted correctly, then unscrew the lower nuts several turns.
43 Attach a suitable hoist to the engine, and lift the engine and transmission slightly. Make sure that the engine is adequately supported.
44 Unscrew and remove the bolts securing the transmission to the rear of the engine, then lower the engine to its original position. At this stage leave one of the bolts loosely fitted.
45 Using a trolley jack and piece of wood, support the front of the transmission. Alternatively, a support bar for the transmission can be placed over the rear of the engine compartment.

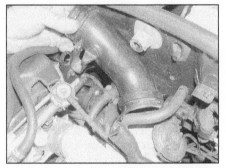

4.31 Removing the intake pipe from the throttle housing

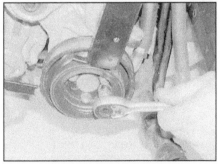

4.37a Unscrew the bolts ...

4.37b ... and remove the pulleys from the power steering pump ...

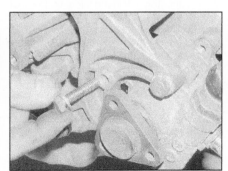

4.37c ... then unscrew the bolts ...

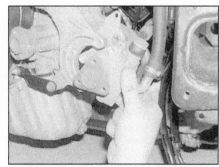

4.37d ... move the power steering pump from its mounting, and tie it to one side

4.46 Removing the engine from the engine compartment

46 Remove the last bolt, then check that all wiring and hoses have been disconnected, and lift the engine from the engine compartment **(see illustration)**. On automatic transmission models, make sure that the torque converter remains firmly in the transmission as the engine is being removed, and to prevent it falling out fit a metal bar across the bellhousing, secured with two bolts.

47 If they are loose, recover the location dowels from the rear of the cylinder block. Where necessary, remove the intermediate plate from the rear of the engine.

48 On manual transmission models, remove the clutch as described in Chapter 6.

Refitting

49 Refitting is a reversal of removal, but on manual transmission models first smear the splines of the input shaft with a little high melting point grease. Lightly grease the contact surface of the release bearing, but **do not** grease the guide sleeve for the release bearing. On automatic transmission models, check that the torque converter is fully entered on the input shaft by checking that the distance between the bellhousing mounting flange and the torque converter is approximately 23.0 mm. If it is only 13.0 mm, the torque converter is not fully entered. Ensure that all engine and transmission mountings are fitted free of strain, and tighten all nuts and bolts to the specified torque. Refit, and where applicable adjust, all engine related components and systems with reference to the Chapters concerned. Ensure that the engine is filled with oil and that the cooling system is refilled as described in Chapter 1A before starting the engine.

Diesel engines

Removal

50 Select a solid, level surface to park the vehicle on. Give yourself enough space to move around it easily.

51 Disconnect the battery negative (earth) lead (see Chapter 5A).

52 Apply the handbrake, then jack up the front of the vehicle and support it on axle stands (see *Jacking and vehicle support*).

53 Remove the engine compartment under-shield after undoing the screws.

54 Where applicable, remove the cover from the top of the engine.

55 Remove the front bumper with reference to Chapter 11.

56 With reference to Chapter 1B, carry out the following:
 a) *Drain the cooling system. A drain plug is located on the front left-hand side of the radiator, and any remaining coolant can be drained from the engine by unbolting the thermostat cover and removing the O-ring and thermostat.*
 b) *If the engine is to be dismantled, drain the engine oil.*

57 Lever up the retaining clip, and disconnect the bottom hose from the radiator.

58 On models with an electric cooling fan, disconnect the wiring from the thermoswitch located on the bottom left-hand side of the radiator.

59 On automatic transmission models, position a suitable container beneath the engine compartment, then disconnect the automatic transmission fluid pipes at the lock carrier. Plug the ends of the pipes.

60 Loosen the clip and disconnect the air inlet duct from the intercooler at the bottom left of the lock carrier.

61 Loosen the clip and disconnect the turbocharger air hose at the bottom right-hand side of the lock carrier.

62 Unscrew the bolts and remove the air pipe to air cleaner duct from the lock carrier.

63 Remove the air cleaner assembly as described in Chapter 4B.

64 Disconnect the wiring from the headlights and headlight range control unit.

65 Disconnect the bulb holders from the front indicator units.

66 Release the clip and disconnect the top hose from the radiator.

67 On models manufactured from 07/97 on, remove the air pipe and hose from the left-hand side of the engine. To do this, unscrew the retaining bolt, and loosen the clips.

68 Disconnect the bonnet lock cable from the lock carrier.

69 Remove the cover from the power steering fluid reservoir.

70 Disconnect the wiring from the ABS units located on the left-hand side of the engine compartment.

71 On the top left-hand side of the lock carrier, disconnect the wiring for the anti-theft alarm system at the connectors.

72 Disconnect the wiring from the two horns and release the wiring from the support.

73 On models equipped with air conditioning, unscrew the bolts and remove the air cowls from each side of the radiator, then remove the condenser mounting bolts. Disconnect the wiring from the low pressure switch, and also disconnect the A/C magnetic clutch wiring from the bottom of the lock carrier. Lift the condenser from its bracket, rotate it to the side and tie it on the front wheel to secure it away from the engine compartment. Protect the condenser with

card or cloth sheets to prevent damage to it when removing the engine.

 Warning: Do not disconnect the air conditioning refrigerant circuit.

74 Unscrew the lock carrier mounting bolts, then with the help of an assistant, withdraw the complete lock carrier from the front of the car and place it in a safe position.

75 Loosen the clips and remove the rear air intake duct from the rear of the engine. Disconnect the wiring from the sensors as applicable. On models manufactured from 07/97 on, unscrew the mounting nut.

76 Disconnect the hoses and wiring from the charge pressure control valve. Where necessary, unscrew the bolts and remove the valve from the front of the engine.

77 Loosen the clips and disconnect the hoses from the coolant expansion tank, then unbolt the tank and disconnect the low coolant level switch wiring.

78 Disconnect the fuel supply and return lines from the filter cover on the left-hand side of the engine.

79 On the engine compartment rear bulkhead, unbolt and remove the cover from over the engine management ECU, then use a screwdriver to lever off the retaining bar. Release the catch, and disconnect the wiring plug from the ECU. Also where fitted, disconnect the vacuum hose from the ECU.

80 Using a screwdriver, release the retainer and lift up the auxiliary relay carrier. Release the two fuse holder retainers and plug contact. If possible obtain Audi tool VAS 1978/8 to do this, alternatively use a screwdriver.

81 Unbolt the earth cables from the plenum chamber, and release the wiring from the plastic cable ties.

82 Loosen the clips and disconnect the heater hoses from the rear of the engine.

83 Disconnect the brake vacuum hose from the vacuum pump.

84 On the left-hand side of the transmission, disconnect the wiring from the speedometer sender.

85 On the manual transmission, disconnect the wiring from the reversing light switch.

86 Remove the auxiliary drivebelts with reference to Chapter 2B. Also remove the viscous fan with reference to Chapter 3.

87 Refer to Chapter 3, and unbolt the air conditioning compressor from the engine. Tie the compressor to one side away from the engine compartment.

 Warning: Do not disconnect the air conditioning refrigerant circuit.

88 Unbolt the pulley from the power steering pump, then unbolt the pump from its mounting bracket and tie it to one side. Do not disconnect the hydraulic lines from the pump.

89 Unscrew the nut and disconnect the positive cable from the starter motor located beneath the exhaust manifold on the right-hand side of the engine.

90 Unscrew the nuts securing the turbocharger to the catalytic converter. Loosen the exhaust front clamp and push it towards the rear to detach the exhaust pipes. Disconnect the exhaust front pipe and catalytic converter from the turbocharger. Take care not to bend excessively the flexible section of the downpipe.

91 Unbolt the earth wire from the right-hand engine mounting.

92 Where fitted, unbolt the turbocharger support bracket from the right-hand engine mounting.

93 Remove the starter motor from the transmission with reference to Chapter 5A.

94 On automatic transmission models, unscrew and remove the three torque converter nuts accessible through the starter motor aperture. It will be necessary to turn the engine for access to each nut. To prevent the driveplate from turning while loosening the nuts, either counterhold the crankshaft pulley bolt, or place a screwdriver in the teeth of the starter ring gear.

95 On automatic transmission models, unbolt the hydraulic fluid pipe bracket from the left-hand side of the engine.

96 Loosen the nuts on the top of each engine mounting several turns. Mark the positions of the engine mountings in the subframe to ensure they are refitted correctly, then unscrew the lower nuts several turns.

97 Attach a suitable hoist to the engine, and lift the engine and transmission slightly. Make sure that the engine is adequately supported.

98 Unscrew and remove the bolts securing the transmission to the rear of the engine, then lower the engine to its original position. At this stage leave one of the bolts loosely fitted.

99 Using a trolley jack and piece of wood, support the front of the transmission. Alternatively, a support bar for the transmission can be placed over the rear of the engine compartment.

100 Remove the last bolt, then check that all wiring and hoses have been disconnected, and lift the engine from the engine compartment. On automatic transmission models, make sure that the torque converter remains firmly in the transmission as the engine is being removed, and to prevent it falling out fit a metal bar across the bellhousing, secured with two bolts.

101 If they are loose, recover the location dowels from the rear of the cylinder block. Where necessary, remove the intermediate plate from the rear of the engine.

102 On manual transmission models, remove the clutch as described in Chapter 6.

Refitting

103 Refitting is a reversal of removal, but on manual transmission models first smear the splines of the input shaft with a little high melting point grease. Lightly grease the contact surface of the release bearing, but **do not** grease the guide sleeve for the release

bearing. On automatic transmission models, check that the torque converter is fully entered on the input shaft by checking that the distance between the bellhousing mounting flange and the torque converter is approximately 23.0 mm. If it is only 13.0 mm, the torque converter is not fully entered. Ensure that all engine and transmission mountings are fitted free of strain, and tighten all nuts and bolts to the specified torque. Refit, and where applicable adjust, all engine related components and systems with reference to the Chapters concerned. Ensure that the engine is filled with oil and that the cooling system is refilled as described in Chapter 1B before starting the engine.

5 Engine overhaul - preliminary information

It is much easier to dismantle and work on the engine if it is mounted on a portable engine stand. These stands can often be hired from a tool hire shop. Before the engine is mounted on a stand, the flywheel should be removed, so that the stand bolts can be tightened into the end of the cylinder block/crankcase. **Note:** *Do not measure cylinder bore dimensions with the engine mounted on this type of stand.*

If a stand is not available, it is possible to dismantle the engine with it blocked up on a sturdy workbench, or on the floor. Be very careful not to tip or drop the engine when working without a stand.

If you intend to obtain a reconditioned engine, all ancillaries must be removed first, to be transferred to the replacement engine (just as they will if you are doing a complete engine overhaul yourself). These components include the following:

Petrol engines

a) *Alternator (including mounting brackets) and starter motor (Chapter 5A).*
b) *The ignition system and HT components including all sensors, distributor, HT leads and spark plugs (Chapters 1A and 5B).*
c) *The fuel injection system components (Chapter 4A).*
d) *All electrical switches, actuators and sensors, and the engine wiring harness (Chapters 4A and 5B).*
e) *Inlet and exhaust manifolds (Chapters 4A and 4C).*
f) *Engine oil dipstick and tube (Chapter 2A).*
g) *Engine mountings (Chapter 2A).*
h) *Flywheel/driveplate (Chapter 2A).*
i) *Clutch components (Chapter 6).*

Diesel engines

a) *Alternator (including mounting brackets) and starter motor (Chapter 5A).*
b) *The glow plug/pre-heating system components (Chapter 5C)*
c) *All fuel system components, including the*

fuel injection pump, all sensors and actuators (Chapter 4C)
d) *The vacuum pump (Chapter 9)*
e) *All electrical switches, actuators and sensors, and the engine wiring harness (Chapter 4B, Chapter 5C).*
f) *Inlet and exhaust manifolds, and turbocharger (Chapter 4B and 4C).*
g) *The engine oil level dipstick and its tube (Chapter 2B).*
h) *Engine mountings (Chapter 2B).*
i) *Flywheel/driveplate (Chapter 2B).*
j) *Clutch components (Chapter 6).*

All engines

Note: *When removing the external components from the engine, pay close attention to details that may be helpful or important during refitting. Note the fitted position of gaskets, seals, spacers, pins, washers, bolts, and other small components.*

If you are obtaining a short engine (the engine cylinder block/crankcase, crankshaft, pistons and connecting rods, all fully assembled), then the cylinder head, sump, oil pump, timing belt (together with its tensioner and covers), auxiliary belt (together with its tensioner), coolant pump, thermostat housing, coolant outlet elbows, oil filter housing and where applicable oil cooler will also have to be removed.

If you are planning a full overhaul, the engine can be dismantled in the order given below:

a) *Inlet and exhaust manifolds (see the relevant part of Chapter 4).*
b) *Timing belt, sprockets and tensioner (see Chapter 2A or 2B).*
c) *Cylinder head (see Chapter 2A or 2B).*
d) *Flywheel/driveplate (see Chapter 2A or 2B).*
e) *Sump (see Chapter 2A or 2B).*
f) *Oil pump (see Chapter 2A or 2B).*
g) *Piston/connecting rod assemblies (see Section 7).*
h) *Crankshaft (see Section 8).*

6 Cylinder head - dismantling, cleaning, inspection and reassembly

Note: *New and reconditioned cylinder heads are available from Audi, and from engine specialists. Specialist tools are required for the dismantling and inspection procedures, and new components may not be readily available. It may, therefore, be more practical for the home mechanic to buy a reconditioned head, rather than to dismantle, inspect and recondition the original head.*

Dismantling

1 Remove the cylinder head from the engine block as described in Part A or B of this Chapter. Also remove the camshaft sprocket as described in Part A or B of this Chapter.

2 On diesel models, remove the injectors and glow plugs (see Chapters 4B and 5C).

3 Where applicable, remove the coolant outlet elbow together with its gasket/O-ring.
4 On engine code AHL, unscrew the coolant temperature sensor from the cylinder head.
5 It is important that groups of components are kept together when they are removed and, if still serviceable, refitted in the same groups.

6.5 Keep groups of components together in labelled bags or boxes

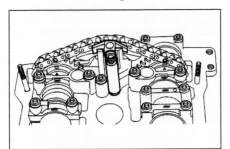

6.9a Using special tool 3366 to lock the automatic camshaft adjuster

6.9b Home-made tool for holding the automatic camshaft adjuster in its compressed state

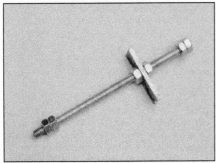

6.9c Home-made tool

If they are refitted randomly, accelerated wear leading to early failure will occur. Stowing groups of components in plastic bags or storage bins will help to keep everything in the right order - label them according to their fitted location, eg No 1 exhaust, No 2 inlet, etc **(see illustration)**. Note that No 1 cylinder is nearest the timing belt end of the engine.
6 Check that the manufacturer's orientation markings are visible on camshaft bearing caps; if none can be found, make your own using a scriber or centre-punch.
7 The camshaft bearing caps must now be removed as follows.

Engine codes ADR, AFY, AEB, APU, AJL

8 At the front of the inlet camshaft, unbolt the Hall sender then unscrew the bolt from the camshaft and remove the tapered washer and Hall sender plate.
9 The automatic camshaft adjuster must now be locked before removing it. Audi technicians use special tool 3366 to do this **(see illustration)**. Alternatively, it is possible to make up a similar tool using a threaded rod, nuts and a small metal plate to keep the adjuster compressed. As a safety precaution, use a plastic cable tie to keep the home-made tool in position **(see illustrations)**.

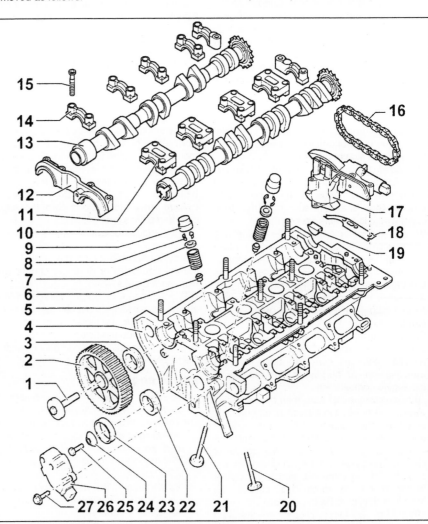

6.11 Cylinder head components (ADR, AFY, AEB, APU, AJL engines)

1 Camshaft sprocket bolt	11 Bearing cap, inlet camshaft	18 Rubber seal
2 Camshaft sprocket	12 Front combined bearing cap	19 Half round rubber grommet
3 Oil seal	13 Exhaust camshaft	20 Exhaust valve
4 Cylinder head	14 Bearing cap, exhaust camshaft	21 Inlet valve
5 Valve stem oil seal	15 Camshaft bearing bolt	22 Oil seal
6 Valve spring	16 Drive chain	23 Hall sender ring
7 Upper valve spring seat	17 Automatic camshaft adjuster	24 Tapered washer
8 Split collets		25 Ring retaining bolt
9 Hydraulic tappet		26 Hall sender
10 Inlet camshaft		27 Hall sender retaining bolt

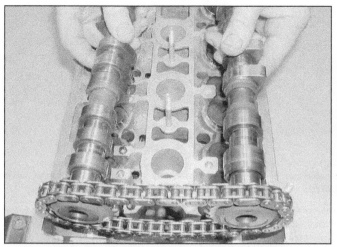

6.13 Lifting the camshafts and chain from the cylinder head

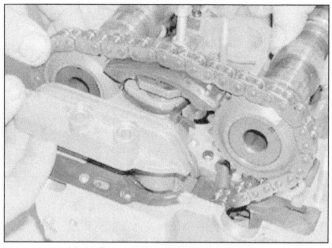

6.14 Removing the camshaft adjuster

10 Clean the chain and the camshaft sprockets in line with the arrows on the top of the camshaft rear bearing caps, then mark the sprockets and chain in relation to each other. Note that the distance between the two marks must be 16 rollers on the chain, but also note that the mark on the exhaust camshaft is slightly offset towards the centre of the cylinder head.

11 Progressively slacken the bolts from bearing caps 3 and 5 then 1 and 6 on both the inlet and exhaust camshafts **(see illustration)**. **Note:** *The caps are numbered from the rear of the cylinder head, number 6 being the combined cap that straddles the front of both camshafts.*

12 Unscrew the automatic camshaft adjuster mounting bolts.

13 Progressively slacken the bolts from bearing caps 4 and 2 on both the inlet and exhaust camshafts, then lift both camshafts from the cylinder head together with the automatic adjuster and chain **(see illustration)**.

14 Release the adjuster from the chain and remove the chain from the camshaft sprockets. Remove the oil seals from the front of each camshaft **(see illustration)**.

Engine codes ADP, AHL, 1Z, AFF, AFN, AHH, AHU

15 Slacken the nuts from bearing caps Nos 5, 1 and 3 first, then from bearing caps 2 and 4 **(see illustration)**. Slacken the nuts alternately and diagonally half a turn at a time until they can be removed then remove the bearing caps. Keep the caps in order and note their fitted positions. **Note:** *The camshaft bearing caps are numbered 1 to 5 from the timing belt end.*

16 Slide the oil seal from the front of the camshaft and discard it; a new one must be used on reassembly **(see illustration)**.

17 Carefully lift the camshaft from the cylinder head, keeping it level and supported at both ends as it is removed so that the journals and lobes are not damaged. Remove the oil seal from the front of the camshaft.

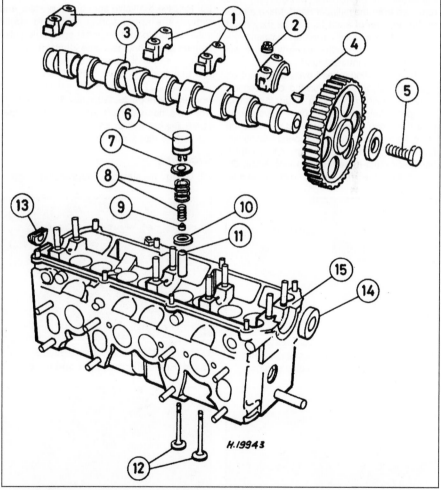

H.19943

6.15 Cylinder head components (ADP, AHL, 1Z, AFF, AFN, AHH and AHU engines)

1 Camshaft bearing cap	6 Hydraulic tappet	11 Valve guides
2 Nut	7 Upper valve spring seat	12 Valves
3 Camshaft	8 Valve springs	13 Plug
4 Woodruff key	9 Valve stem seals	14 Camshaft oil seal
5 Camshaft sprocket bolt	10 Lower valve spring seat	15 Cylinder head casting

6.16 Removing the camshaft oil seal
(ADP, AHL, 1Z, AFF, AFN, AHH and
AHU engines)

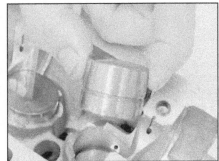

6.18 Lifting the hydraulic tappets from
their bores

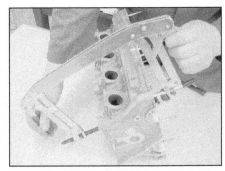

6.19a Compressing the valve springs with
a compressor tool

All engine codes

18 Lift the hydraulic tappets from their bores and store them with the valve contact surface facing downwards, to prevent the oil from draining out **(see illustration)**. It is recommended that the tappets are kept immersed in oil for the period they are removed from the cylinder head. Make a note of the position of each tappet, as they must be fitted to the same valves on reassembly - accelerated wear leading to early failure will result if they are interchanged.

19 Turn the cylinder head over, and rest it on one side. Using a valve spring compressor, compress each valve spring in turn, extracting the split collets when the upper valve spring seat has been pushed far enough down the valve stem to free them. If the spring seat sticks, tap the upper jaw of the compressor with a hammer to free it **(see illustration)**. **Note:** *On 20-valve engines, the access holes to the inlet*

valves are considerably smaller in diameter than those to the exhaust valves, and the standard size valve spring compressor may be too large. If a tool cannot be obtained from an Audi/VAG dealer, a home-made tool will have to be fabricated out of a suitable nut, washer and metal bar welded together (see illustration).

20 Release the valve spring compressor and remove the upper spring seat, and single valve spring (petrol engines) or double valve springs (diesel engines) **(see illustrations)**.

21 Use a pair of pliers or a special removal tool to extract the valve stem oil seal, then on diesel engines remove the lower spring seat from the valve guide. Withdraw the valve itself from the head gasket side of the cylinder head. Repeat this process for the remaining valves **(see illustrations)**.

Cleaning

22 Using a suitable degreasing agent,

remove all traces of oil deposits from the cylinder head, paying particular attention to the journal bearings, hydraulic tappet bores, valve guides and oilways. Scrape off any traces of old gasket from the mating surfaces, taking care not to score or gouge them. If using emery paper, do not use a grade of less than 100. Turn the head over and using a blunt blade, scrape any carbon deposits from the combustion chambers and ports. Finally, wash the entire head casting with a suitable solvent to remove the remaining debris.

23 Clean the valve heads and stems using a fine wire brush. If the valve is heavily coked, scrape off the majority of the deposits with a blunt blade first, then use the wire brush.

24 Thoroughly clean the remainder of the components using solvent and allow them to dry completely. Discard the oil seals, as new ones must be fitted when the cylinder head is reassembled.

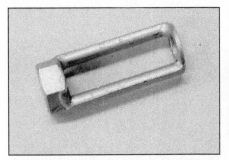

6.19b Home-made tool to access holes to
the inlet valves on 20-valve engines

6.20a Removing the upper spring seat . . .

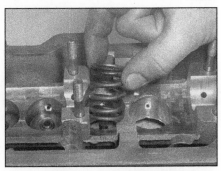

6.20b . . . and valve spring

6.21a Using a removal tool . . .

6.21b . . . to remove the valve stem oil
seals

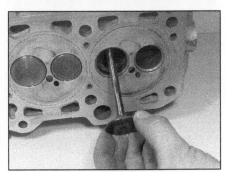

6.21c Removing the valves

Inspection

Cylinder head

Note: *On diesel engines the cylinder heads and valves cannot be reworked (although valves may be lapped in); new or exchange units must be obtained.*

25 Examine the head casting closely to identify any damage or cracks that may have developed. Pay particular attention to the areas around the valve seats and spark plug holes. If cracking is discovered in this area, Audi/VAG state that the cylinder head may be re-used, provided the cracks are no larger than 0.5 mm wide. More serious damage will mean the renewal of the cylinder head casting.

26 Moderately pitted and scorched valve seats can be repaired by lapping the valves in during reassembly, as described later in this Chapter. Badly worn or damaged valve seats may be restored by recutting, however this work should be entrusted to an engineering works.

27 Measure any distortion of the gasket surfaces using a straight edge and a set of feeler blades. Take one measurement longitudinally on both the inlet and exhaust manifold mating surfaces. Take several measurements across the head gasket surface, to assess the level of distortion in all planes **(see illustration)**. Compare the measurements with the figures in the Specifications. On petrol engines, if the head is distorted out of specification, it may be possible to have it machined by an engineering works.

28 Minimum cylinder head heights (measured between the cylinder head gasket surface and the cylinder head cover gasket surface), where quoted by the manufacturer, are listed in Specifications.

Camshaft

29 Visually inspect the camshaft for evidence of wear on the surfaces of the lobes and journals. Normally their surfaces should be smooth and have a dull shine; look for scoring, erosion or pitting and areas that appear highly polished, indicating excessive wear. Accelerated wear will occur once the hardened exterior of the camshaft has been damaged, so always renew worn items. **Note:** *If these symptoms are visible on the tips of the camshaft lobes, check the corresponding tappet, as it will probably be worn as well.*

30 Where applicable, examine the distributor drive gear for signs of wear or damage. Excessive slack in the drive caused by worn gear teeth will affect ignition timing.

31 If the machined surfaces of the camshaft appear discoloured or blued, it is likely that it has been overheated at some point, probably due to inadequate lubrication. This may have distorted the shaft, so check the runout as follows: place the camshaft between two V-blocks and using a DTI gauge, measure the runout at the centre journal. If it exceeds the figure quoted in the Specifications at the start of this Chapter, renew the camshaft.

32 To measure the camshaft endfloat,

6.27 Measuring the distortion of the cylinder head

temporarily refit the camshaft to the cylinder head, then fit the first and last bearing caps and tighten the retaining nuts to the specified first stage torque setting. Anchor a DTI gauge to the timing belt end of the cylinder head and align the gauge probe with the camshaft axis. Push the camshaft to one end of the cylinder head as far as it will travel, then rest the DTI gauge probe on the end of the camshaft, and zero the gauge display. Push the camshaft as far as it will go to the other end of the cylinder head, and record the gauge reading. Verify the reading by pushing the camshaft back to its original position and checking that the gauge indicates zero again **(see illustration)**. **Note:** *The hydraulic tappets must not be fitted whilst this measurement is being taken.*

33 Check that the camshaft endfloat measurement is within the limit listed in the Specifications. Wear outside of this limit is unlikely to be confined to any one component, so renewal of the camshaft, cylinder head and bearing caps must be considered.

34 The camshaft bearing running clearance must now be measured. One method (which will be difficult to achieve without a range of micrometers or internal/external expanding calipers) is to measure the outside diameters of the camshaft bearing surfaces and the internal diameters formed by the bearing caps and the cylinder head. The difference between these two measurements is the running clearance.

35 Another, more accurate, method of measuring the running clearance involves the use of Plastigauge. This consists of a fine thread of perfectly round plastic which is compressed between the bearing cap and the

journal. When the cap is removed, the plastic is deformed and can be measured with a special card gauge supplied with the kit. The running clearance is determined from this gauge. Plastigauge is sometimes difficult to obtain but enquiries at one of the larger specialist quality motor factors should produce the name of a stockist in your area. The procedure for using Plastigauge is as follows.

36 Ensure that the cylinder head, bearing cap and camshaft bearing surfaces are completely clean and dry. Lay the camshaft in position in the cylinder head.

37 Lay a length of Plastigauge on top of each of the camshaft bearing journals.

38 Place the bearing caps in position over the camshaft and progressively tighten the retaining nuts down to the specified torque. **Note:** *Where the torque setting is expressed in several stages, tighten the cap fixings to the first stage only. Do not rotate the camshaft whilst the bearing caps are in place, as the measurements will be affected.*

39 Unscrew the nuts and carefully remove the bearing caps again, lifting them vertically away from the camshaft to avoid disturbing the Plastigauge. The Plastigauge should remain on the camshaft bearing surface.

40 Hold the scale card supplied with the kit against each bearing journal, and match the width of the crushed Plastigauge with the graduated markings on the card. Use this to determine the running clearances.

41 Compare the camshaft running clearance measurements with those listed in the Specifications; if any are outside the specified tolerance, the camshaft and cylinder head should be renewed.

42 On DOHC engines, running clearance measurements must be carried out on both camshafts.

43 On completion, remove the bearing caps and camshaft, and clean off all remaining traces of Plastigauge.

Valves and associated components

Note: *On all engines, the valve heads cannot be re-cut, although they may be lapped in.*

44 Examine each valve closely for signs of wear. Inspect the valve stems for wear ridges, scoring or variations in diameter; measure their diameters at several points along their lengths with a micrometer **(see illustration)**.

6.32 Checking camshaft endfloat using a DTI gauge

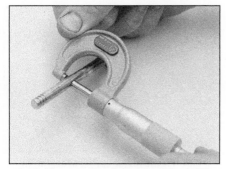

6.44 Measure the diameter of the valve stems with a micrometer

6.47 Measure the maximum deflection of the valve in its guide, using a DTI gauge

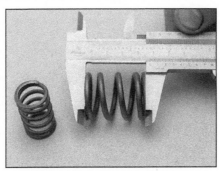

6.49 Measure the free length of each of the valve springs

6.50 Checking the squareness of a valve spring

45 The valve heads should not be cracked, badly pitted or charred. Note that light pitting of the valve head can be rectified by grinding-in the valves during reassembly, as described later in this Section.

46 Check that the valve stem end face is free from excessive pitting or indentation; this would be caused by defective hydraulic tappets.

47 Insert each valve into its respective guide in the cylinder head and set up a DTI gauge against the edge of the valve head. With the valve end face flush with the top of the valve guide, measure the maximum side to side deflection of the valve in its guide **(see illustration)**.

48 If the measurement exceeds that given in the Specifications, the valve and valve guide should be renewed as a pair. **Note:** *Valve guides are an interference fit in the cylinder head and their removal requires access to a*

hydraulic press. For this reason, it would be wise to entrust the job to an engineering workshop.

49 Using vernier calipers, measure the free length of each of the valve springs. As a manufacturer's figure is not quoted, the only way to check the length of the springs is by comparison with a new component. Note that valve springs are usually renewed during a major engine overhaul **(see illustration)**.

50 Stand each spring on its end on a flat surface, against an engineers square **(see illustration)**. Check the squareness of the spring visually, and renew it if it appears distorted.

Reassembly

51 To achieve a gas-tight seal between the valves and their seats, it will be necessary to grind-in (or lap-in) the valves. To complete this process you will need a quantity of fine/coarse grinding paste and a grinding tool - this can either be of the rubber sucker type, or the automatic type which is driven by a rotary power tool.

52 Smear a small quantity of *fine* grinding paste on the sealing face of the valve head. Turn the cylinder head over so that the combustion chambers are facing upwards and insert the valve into the correct guide. Attach the grinding tool to the valve head and using a backward/forward rotary action, grind the valve head into its seat. Periodically lift the valve and rotate it to redistribute the grinding paste **(see illustration)**.

53 Continue this process until the contact between valve and seat produces an

unbroken, matt grey ring of uniform width, on both faces. Repeat the operation on the remaining valves.

54 If the valves and seats are so badly pitted that coarse grinding paste must be used, bear in mind that there is a maximum protrusion of the end of the valve stem from the valve guide. Refer to the Specifications at the beginning of this Chapter for the minimum dimension from the end of the valve stem to the top face of the cylinder head. If this dimension is outside the limit due to excessive grinding-in, the hydraulic tappets may not operate correctly.

55 Assuming the repair is feasible, work as described previously but use coarse grinding paste initially, to achieve a dull finish on the valve face and seat. Wash off the coarse paste with solvent and repeat the process using fine grinding paste to obtain the correct finish.

56 When all the valves have been ground in, remove all traces of grinding paste from the cylinder head and valves with solvent, and allow them to dry completely.

57 Turn the head on its side. On diesel engines, fit the first lower spring seat into place, with the convex side facing the cylinder head **(see illustration)**.

58 Working on one valve at a time, lubricate the valve stem with clean engine oil, and insert it into the guide. Fit one of the protective plastic sleeves supplied with the new valve stem oil seals over the valve end face - this will protect the oil seal whilst it is being fitted **(see illustrations)**.

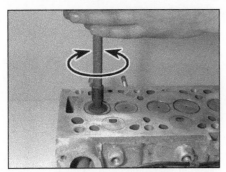

6.52 Grinding-in a valve

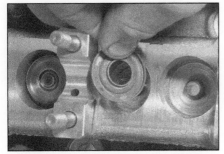

6.57 Fit the lower spring seat with the convex face facing the cylinder head (diesel engines)

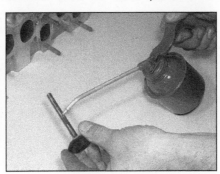

6.58a Lubricate the valve stem with clean engine oil before fitting it

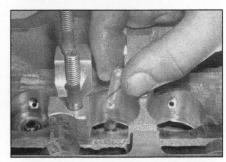

6.58b Fitting a protective plastic sleeve over the valve stem before fitting the stem seal

6.59a Fit a new valve stem seal over the valve

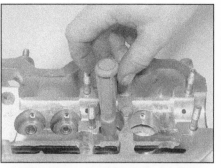

6.59b Using a special installer to fit the valve stem seals

6.60 Fitting a valve spring

59 Dip a new valve stem seal in clean engine oil, and carefully push it over the valve and onto the top of the valve guide - take care not to damage the stem seal as it passes over the valve end face. Use a suitable long reach socket or special installer to press it firmly into position **(see illustrations)**. Remove the protective sleeve.

60 Locate the valve spring(s) over the valve stem **(see illustration)**. On diesel engines, ensure that the springs locate correctly on the lower seat.

61 Fit the upper seat over the top of the springs, then using a valve spring compressor, compress the springs until the upper seat is pushed beyond the collet grooves in the valve stem. Refit the split collet, using a dab of grease to hold the two halves in the grooves **(see illustrations)**. Gradually release the spring compressor, checking that the collet remains correctly

seated as the spring extends. When correctly seated, the upper seat should force the two halves of the collet together, and hold them securely in the grooves in the end of the valve.

62 Repeat this process for the remaining sets of valve components. To settle the components after installation, strike the end of each valve stem with a mallet, using a block of wood to protect the stem from damage. Check before progressing any further that the spilt collets remain firmly held in the end of the valve stem by the upper spring seat.

63 Smear some clean engine oil onto the sides of the hydraulic tappets, and fit them into position in their bores in the cylinder head. Push them down until they contact the valves, then lubricate the camshaft lobe contact surfaces **(see illustration)**.

Engine codes ADR, AFY, AEB, APU, AJL

64 Locate the rubber/metal gasket for the

automatic camshaft adjuster, together with the half round seal **(see illustration)**, on the front of the cylinder head. If the gasket does not have any sealant compound already on it, smear a little in the area shown **(see illustration)**.

65 Lubricate the camshafts and cylinder head bearing journals with clean engine oil.

66 Engage the chain with the camshaft sprockets making sure that the distance between the marks on the sprockets is 16 rollers **(see illustration)**. Locate the adjuster between the chain runs, then carefully lower the camshafts into position on the cylinder head. Support the ends of the shafts as they are fitted, to avoid damaging the lobes and journals. Alternatively, it is possible to fit the camshafts together with the chain in the cylinder head, then slightly raise the sprocket ends of the camshafts in order to fit the adjuster.

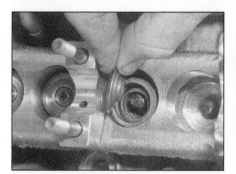

6.61a Fit the upper seat over the top of the valve spring

6.61b Use grease to hold the two halves of the split collet in the groove

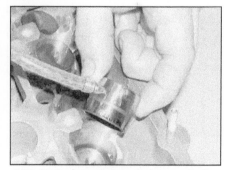

6.63 Fit the tappets into their bores in the cylinder head

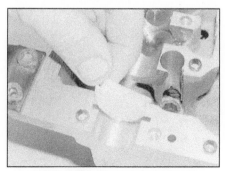

6.64a Fitting the half-round seal

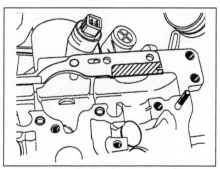

6.64b Apply sealant compound in the area shown

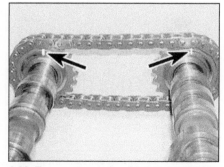

6.66 Engage the chain with the sprockets - note marks indicating distance of 16 rollers

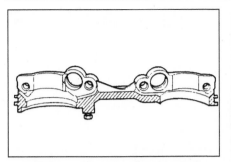

6.72 Apply a thin film of sealant to the contact face of the combined front bearing cap in the area shown on ADR engines

6.76 Lubricate the camshaft bearings with clean engine oil . . .

6.77 . . . then lower the camshaft into position on the cylinder head (ADP, AHL, 1Z, AFF, AFN, AHH and AHU engines)

67 The oil seals may be fitted at this stage, or alternatively fitted later. Dip the new oil seals in engine oil, then locate them on the front of each camshaft. Make sure the closed ends of the seals face outwards from the camshafts and take care not to damage the seal lips. Locate the seals against the seats in the cylinder head.

68 Insert the automatic camshaft adjuster mounting bolts and tighten to the specified torque.

69 Oil the upper surfaces of the camshaft bearing journals, then fit Nos 2 and 4 bearing caps to both camshafts. Ensure that they are fitted the right way around and in the correct locations, then progressively tighten the retaining bolts to the specified torque. **Note:** *The bearing caps are numbered from the rear of the engine.*

70 Fit the No 1 bearing caps to each

camshaft and progressively tighten the retaining bolts to the specified torque.

71 Remove the locking tool from the automatic camshaft adjuster.

72 Apply a thin film of sealant to the contact face of the combined front bearing cap, then fit the cap making sure that the oil seals locate against their seatings **(see illustration)**. Progressively tighten the retaining bolts to the specified torque.

73 Fit Nos 3 and 5 bearing caps and progressively tighten the retaining bolts to the specified torque.

74 Refit the Hall sender plate and tapered washer to the front of the inlet camshaft and tighten the bolt to the specified torque.

75 Refit the Hall sender and tighten the retaining bolt.

Engine codes ADP, AHL, 1Z, AFF, AFN, AHH, AHU

76 Lubricate the camshaft and cylinder head bearing journals with clean engine oil **(see illustration)**.

77 Carefully lower the camshaft into position in the cylinder head making sure that the cam lobes for No 1 cylinder are pointing upwards. Support the ends of the shaft as it is fitted, to avoid damaging the lobes and journals **(see illustration)**.

78 Dip the new oil seal in engine oil, then locate it on the front of the camshaft. Make sure the closed end of the seal faces

outwards from the camshaft and take care not to damage the seal lip. Locate the seal against the seat in the cylinder head.

79 The bearing caps have their respective cylinder numbers stamped onto them, and have an elongated lug on one side. When correctly fitted, the numbers should be readable from the exhaust side of the cylinder head, and the lugs should face the inlet side of the cylinder head. Oil the upper surfaces of the camshaft bearing journals, then fit Nos 2 and 4 bearing caps. Ensure that they are fitted the right way around and in the correct locations, then progressively tighten the retaining bolts to the specified torque **(see illustrations)**.

80 Smear the mating surfaces of bearing cap No 1 with sealant then fit caps 1, 3 and 5 over the camshaft and progressively tighten the nuts to the specified torque **(see illustration)**.

All engine codes

81 Where applicable, refit the coolant sensor and oil pressure switch to the cylinder head.

82 Where applicable, refit the coolant outlet elbow together with a new gasket/O-ring **(see illustration)**.

83 On diesel models, refit the injectors and glow plugs (see Chapters 4B and 5C).

84 Refit the cylinder head with reference to Parts A or B of this Chapter. Also refit the camshaft sprocket as described in Part A or B of this Chapter.

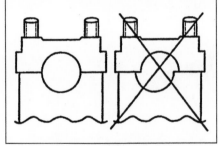

6.79a The camshaft bearing caps are drilled off-centre (ADP, AHL, 1Z, AFF, AFN, AHH and AHU engines)

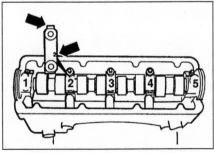

6.79b The bearing caps are fitted as shown (ADP, AHL, 1Z, AFF, AFN, AHH and AHU engines)

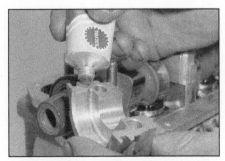

6.80 Smear the mating surfaces of cap No 1 with sealant (ADP, AHL, 1Z, AFF, AFN, AHH and AHU engines)

6.82 Fit the coolant elbow, using a new O-ring or gasket

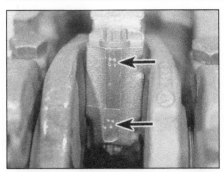

7.4 Mark the big-end caps and connecting rods with their piston numbers (arrowed)

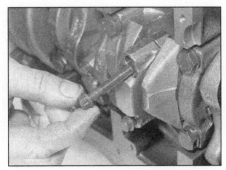

7.5a Unscrew the big-end cap bolts . . .

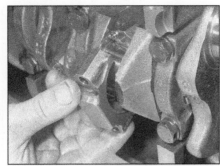

7.5b . . . and remove the cap

7 Piston/connecting rod assemblies -
removal and inspection

Removal

1 Refer to Part A or B of this Chapter (as applicable) and remove the cylinder head, flywheel, sump and baffle plate, oil pump and pickup.

7.6 Wrap the stud threads with tape

2 Inspect the tops of the cylinder bores for ridges at the point where the pistons reach top dead centre. These must be removed otherwise the pistons may be damaged when they are pushed out of their bores. Use a scraper or ridge reamer to remove the ridges.

3 Using a set of feeler blades, measure the big-end to crankpin web thrust clearance at each connecting rod, and record the measurements for later reference.

4 Rotate the crankshaft until piston No 1 is at bottom dead centre; piston No 4 will also be at bottom dead centre. Unless they are already identified, mark the big-end bearing caps and connecting rods with their respective piston numbers, using a centre-punch or a scribe (see illustration). Note the orientation of the bearing caps in relation to the connecting rod; it may be difficult to see the manufacturer's markings at this stage, so scribe alignment arrows on them both to ensure correct reassembly.

5 Unscrew the bearing cap bolts/nuts, half a turn at a time, until they can be removed and the cap withdrawn (see illustrations). Recover the bottom shell bearing, and tape it

to the cap for safe keeping. Note that if the shell bearings are to be re-used, they must be refitted to the same connecting rod.

6 Where the bearing caps are secured with nuts, wrap the threaded ends of the bolts with insulating tape to prevent them scratching the crankpins and bores when the pistons are removed (see illustration).

7 Drive the piston out of the top of the bore using a piece of wooden dowel or a hammer handle. As the piston and connecting rod emerge, recover the top shell bearing and tape it to the connecting rod for safekeeping. On engines fitted with piston cooling jets at the bottom of the cylinders, take care not to allow the connecting rod to damage the jet as the piston is being removed.

8 Remove No 4 piston and connecting rod in the same manner, then turn the crankshaft through half a turn and remove No 2 and 3 pistons and connecting rods. Remember to maintain the components in their cylinder groups, whilst they are in a dismantled state.

9 If applicable, remove the retaining screws and withdraw the piston cooling jets from the bottom of the cylinder (see illustrations).

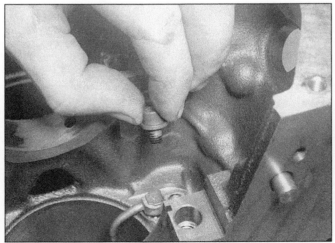

7.9a Remove the piston cooling jet retaining screws . . .

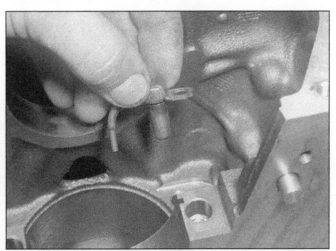

7.9b . . . and withdraw the jets from their mounting holes

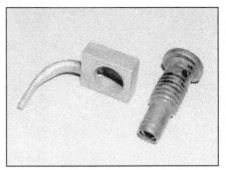

7.9c Piston cooling jet and retainer

7.10a Insert a small screwdriver into the slot and prise off the gudgeon pin circlips

7.10b Push out the gudgeon pin and separate the piston and connecting rod

Inspection

10 Insert a small flat-bladed screwdriver into the removal slot and prise the gudgeon pin circlips from each piston. Push out the gudgeon pin, and separate the piston and connecting rod **(see illustrations)**. Discard the circlips as new items must be fitted on reassembly. If the pin proves difficult to remove, heat the piston to 60°C with hot water - the resulting expansion will then allow the two components to be separated.

11 Before an inspection of the pistons can be carried out, the existing piston rings must be removed, using a removal/installation tool, or an old feeler blade if such a tool is not available. Always remove the upper piston rings first, expanding them to clear the piston crown. The rings are very brittle and will snap if they are stretched too much - sharp edges are produced when this happens, so protect

7.11 Piston rings can be removed using an old feeler blade

your eyes and hands. Discard the rings on removal, as new items must be fitted when the engine is reassembled **(see illustration)**.

12 Use a section of old piston ring to scrape the carbon deposits out of the ring grooves, taking care not to score or gouge the edges of the groove.

13 Carefully scrape away all traces of carbon from the tops of the pistons **(see illustration)**. A hand-held wire brush (or a piece of fine emery cloth) can be used, once the majority of the deposits have been scraped away. Be careful not to remove any metal from the piston, as it is relatively soft. **Note:** *Make sure each piston is kept identified for position during cleaning.*

14 Once the deposits have been removed, clean the pistons and connecting rods with paraffin or a suitable solvent, and dry thoroughly. Make sure that the oil return holes in the ring grooves are clear.

15 Examine the pistons for signs of excessive wear or damage. Some normal wear will be apparent, in the form of a vertical 'grain' on the piston thrust surfaces and a slight looseness of the top compression ring in its groove. Abnormal wear should be carefully examined, to assess whether the component is still serviceable and what the cause of the wear might be.

16 Scuffing or scoring of the piston skirt may indicate that the engine has been overheating, through inadequate cooling or lubrication. Scorch marks on the skirt indicate that blow-by has occurred, perhaps caused by worn bores or piston rings. Burnt areas on the piston crown are usually an indication of pre-

ignition, pinking or detonation. In extreme cases, the piston crown may be melted by operating under these conditions. Corrosion pit marks in the piston crown indicate that coolant has seeped into the combustion chamber. The faults causing these symptoms must be corrected before the engine is brought back into service, or the same damage will recur.

17 Check the pistons, connecting rods, gudgeon pins and bearing caps for cracks. Lay the connecting rods on a flat surface, and look along the length to see if it appears bent or twisted. If you have doubts about their condition, get them measured at an engineering workshop. Inspect the small-end bush bearing in the connecting rod for signs of wear or cracking.

18 Using a micrometer, measure the diameter of all four pistons at a point 10 mm from the bottom of the skirt, at right angles to the gudgeon pin axis **(see illustration)**. Compare the measurements with those listed in the Specifications. If the piston diameter is out of the tolerance band listed for its particular size, then it must be renewed. **Note:** *If the cylinder block was rebored during a previous overhaul, oversize pistons may already have been fitted.* Record all of the measurements and use them to check the piston clearances when the cylinder bores are measured, later in this Chapter.

19 Locate a new piston ring in the appropriate groove and measure the ring-to-groove clearance using a feeler blade **(see illustration)**. Note that the rings are of different widths, so use the correct ring for the

7.13 The piston crown on a diesel engine

7.18 Using a micrometer, measure the diameter of all four pistons

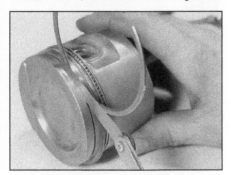

7.19 Measuring the piston ring-to-groove clearance using a feeler blade

7.21a The piston crown is marked with an arrow which must point towards the timing belt end of the engine

groove. Compare the measurements with those listed; if the clearances are outside of the tolerance band, then the piston must be renewed. Confirm this by checking the width of the piston ring with a micrometer.

20 Examine the small-end bearing and gudgeon pin for wear and damage. If excessive, the gudgeon pin will have to be renewed and a new bush fitted to the connecting rod. This work must be entrusted to an engine overhaul specialist or engineering works.

21 The orientation of the piston with respect to the connecting rod must be correct when the two are reassembled. The piston crown is marked with an arrow (which may be obscured by carbon deposits) **(see illustration)**; this must point towards the timing belt end of the engine when the piston is installed. The connecting rod and its bearing cap both have recesses machined into them, close to their mating surfaces - these recesses must both face the same way as the arrow on the piston crown (ie towards the timing belt end of the engine) when correctly installed **(see illustration)**. Reassemble the two components to satisfy this requirement.

22 Lubricate the gudgeon pin and small-end bush with clean engine oil. Slide the pin into the piston, engaging the connecting rod small-end. Fit two new circlips to the piston at either end of the gudgeon pin. Repeat this operation for the remaining pistons.

8 Crankshaft -
removal and inspection

Removal

Note: *If no work is to be done on the pistons and connecting rods, then removal of the cylinder head and pistons will not be necessary. Instead, the pistons need only be pushed far enough up the bores so that the connecting rods are positioned clear of the crankpins. The use of an engine stand is strongly recommended.*

1 With reference to Chapter 2A or 2B as applicable, carry out the following:

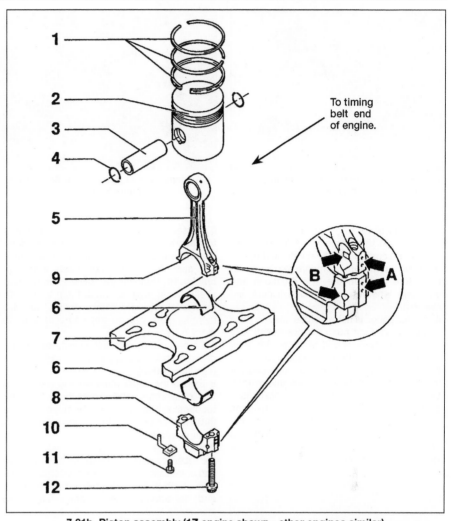

To timing belt end of engine.

7.21b Piston assembly (1Z engine shown - other engines similar)

1 Piston rings	6 Big-end bearing shell	10 Oil jet for piston cooling
2 Piston	7 Top of cylinder block	(where applicable)
3 Gudgeon pin	8 Big-end bearing cap	11 Oil jet retaining screw
4 Circlip	9 Locating dowel (where	12 Big-end bearing cap bolts
5 Connecting rod	applicable)	

A Connecting rod/bearing cap identification marks
B Connecting rod/bearing cap orientation marks

a) *Remove the timing belt and crankshaft sprocket.*
b) *Remove the clutch components and flywheel or driveplate (as applicable).*
c) *Remove the sump, baffle plate* **(see illustration)**, *oil pump and pick-up tube.*
d) *Remove the front and rear crankshaft oil seals and housings.*

2 Remove the pistons and connecting rods or disconnect them from the crankshaft as described in Section 7 (see Note above).

3 With the cylinder block upside down on the bench, carry out a check of the crankshaft endfloat as follows. **Note:** *This can only be accomplished when the crankshaft is still installed in the cylinder block/crankcase, but is free to move.* Set up a DTI gauge so that the probe is in line with the crankshaft axis and is

in contact with a fixed point on the end of the crankshaft. Push the crankshaft along its axis

8.1 Removing the baffle plate

8.3 Measuring crankshaft endfloat using a DTI gauge

8.4 Measuring crankshaft endfloat using feeler blades

8.5 Manufacturer's identification markings on the main bearing caps (arrowed)

to the end of its travel, and then zero the gauge. Push the crankshaft fully the other way, and record the endfloat indicated on the dial **(see illustration)**. Compare the result with the figure given in the Specifications and establish whether new thrustwashers are required.

4 If a dial gauge is not available, feeler blades can be used. First push the crankshaft fully towards the flywheel end of the engine, then use a feeler blade to measure the gap between cylinder No 3 crankpin web and the main bearing thrustwasher **(see illustration)**. Compare the results with the Specifications.

5 Observe the manufacturer's identification marks on the main bearing caps. The number indicates the cap position in the crankcase, as counted from the timing belt end of the engine **(see illustration)**.

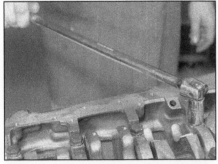

8.6a Loosening the main bearing cap bolts

6 Loosen the main bearing cap bolts half a turn at a time, until they can be removed **(see illustrations)**. Using a soft-faced mallet, strike the caps lightly to free them from the crankcase. Recover the lower main bearing shells, using tape to attach them to the cap for safekeeping. Mark them to aid identification, but do not score or scratch them in any way.

7 Carefully lift the crankshaft out, taking care not to dislodge the upper main bearing shells **(see illustration)**.

8 Extract the upper main bearing shells from the crankcase, and tape them to their respective bearing caps. Remove the two thrustwasher bearings from either side of No 3 bearing saddle.

9 With the shell bearings removed, observe the recesses machined into the bearing caps and crankcase - these provide location for the lugs which protrude from the shell bearings and so prevent them from being fitted incorrectly.

Inspection

10 Wash the crankshaft in a suitable solvent and allow it to dry. Flush the oil holes thoroughly, to ensure they are not blocked.

11 Inspect the main bearing and crankpin journals carefully. If uneven wear, cracking, scoring or pitting are evident then the crankshaft should be reground by an engineering workshop, and refitted to the engine with undersize bearings.

12 Use a micrometer to measure the diameter of each main bearing journal **(see illustration)**. Taking a number of measurements on the surface of each journal will reveal if it is worn unevenly. Differences in diameter measured at 90° intervals indicate that the journal is out of round. Differences in diameter measured along the length of the journal, indicate that the journal is tapered. Again, if wear is detected, the crankshaft must be reground by an engineering workshop, and undersize bearings will be needed.

13 Check the oil seal journals at either end of the crankshaft. If they appear excessively scored or damaged, they may cause the new seals to leak when the engine is reassembled. It may be possible to repair the journal; seek the advice of an engineering workshop or your Audi/VAG dealer.

14 Measure the crankshaft runout by setting up a DTI gauge on the centre main bearing and rotating the shaft in V-blocks. The maximum deflection of the gauge will indicate the runout. Take precautions to protect the bearing journals and oil seal mating surfaces from damage during this procedure. A maximum runout figure is not quoted by the manufacturer, but use the figure of 0.03 mm as a rough guide. If the runout exceeds this figure, crankshaft renewal should be considered - consult your Audi/VAG dealer or an engine rebuilding specialist for advice.

15 Refer to Section 11 for details of main and big-end bearing inspection.

8.6b Removing the main bearing cap bolts

8.7 Lifting the crankshaft from the crankcase

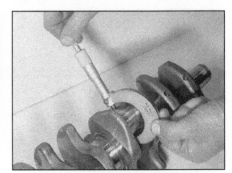

8.12 Use a micrometer to measure the diameter of each main bearing journal

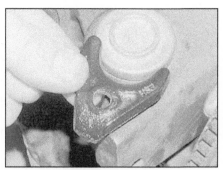

9.2a Remove the clamp . . .

9.2b . . . then lift out the bearing . . .

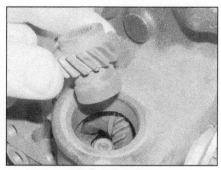

9.2c . . . and gear

9 Intermediate shaft - removal and refitting

Removal

1 Refer to Chapter 2A, 2B, 5B and 9 as applicable and carry out the following. Note that as the engine is out of the car, some of the preliminary procedures will not be necessary:
a) Remove the timing belt.
b) Remove the intermediate shaft sprocket.
c) Remove the distributor on engine code ADP.
d) Remove the brake vacuum pump on diesel engines.
2 On engine codes ADR, AFY, AEB, APU, AJL, unbolt the clamp and bearing and remove the oil pump drive gear from the rear of the cylinder block. Use a magnet to lift the gear out. Note which way the gear is fitted as

it is possible to fit it upside down, causing damage to the gears **(see illustrations)**.
3 Before the shaft is removed, the endfloat must be checked. Anchor a DTI gauge to the cylinder block with its probe in line with the intermediate shaft centre axis. Push the shaft into the cylinder block to the end of its travel, zero the DTI gauge and then draw the shaft out to the opposite end of its travel. Record the maximum deflection and compare the figure with that listed in Specifications - renew the shaft if the endfloat exceeds this limit **(see illustration)**.
4 Slacken the retaining bolts and withdraw the intermediate shaft flange. Recover the O-ring seal, then press out the oil seal **(see illustrations)**.
5 Withdraw the intermediate shaft from the cylinder block and inspect the drive gear at the end of the shaft; if the teeth show signs of excessive wear, or are damaged in any way, the shaft should be renewed.

6 If the oil seal has been leaking, check the shaft mating surface for signs of scoring or damage.

Refitting

7 Liberally oil the intermediate shaft bearing surfaces and drive gear, then guide the shaft into the cylinder block and engage the journal at the leading end with its support bearing.
8 Press a new shaft oil seal into its housing in the intermediate shaft flange and fit a new O-ring seal to the inner sealing surface of the flange.
9 Lubricate the inner lip of the seal with clean engine oil, and slide the flange and seal over the end of the intermediate shaft. Ensure that the O-ring is correctly seated, then fit the flange retaining bolts and tighten them to the specified torque. Check that the intermediate shaft can rotate freely.
10 On engine codes ADR, AFY, AEB, APU, AJL, insert the oil pump drive gear in the aperture at the rear of the cylinder block and engage it with the splined oil pump shaft. Make sure the gear is inserted the correct way around so that it is fully engaged with the gear on the end of the intermediate shaft. Refit the bearing together with oil seal and secure with the clamp and bolt tightened to the specified torque.
11 With reference to Chapter 2A, 2B, 5B and 9 as applicable, carry out the following:
a) Refit the brake vacuum pump on diesel engines.
b) Refit the sprocket to the intermediate shaft and tighten the centre bolt to the specified torque.
c) Refit the timing belt.
d) Refit the distributor on engine code ADP.

9.3 Check the intermediate shaft endfloat using a DTI gauge

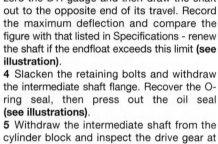

9.4a Slacken the retaining bolts (arrowed) . . .

9.4b . . . and withdraw the intermediate shaft flange

9.4c Press out the oil seal . . .

9.4d . . . then recover the O-ring seal

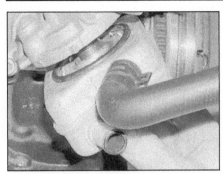

10.1a Removing the oil cooler . . .

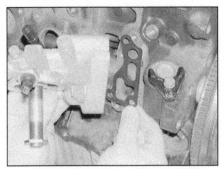

10.1b . . . and the oil filter mounting housing and gasket (ADR engine)

10.1c Removing the coolant pump housing (ADR engine)

10 Cylinder block/crankcase - cleaning and inspection

Cleaning

1 Remove all external components as applicable including lifting eyes, mounting brackets, the coolant pump and housing, viscous fan idler, oil cooler and filter mounting housing **(see illustrations)**, fuel injection pump mounting bracket and electrical switches/sensors from the block. For complete cleaning, the core plugs should ideally be removed. Drill a small hole in the plugs, then insert a self-tapping screw into the hole. Extract the plugs by pulling on the screw with a pair of grips, or by using a slide hammer.

2 Scrape all traces of gasket and sealant from the cylinder block/crankcase, taking care not to damage the sealing surfaces.

3 Remove all oil gallery plugs (where fitted). The plugs are usually very tight - they may have to be drilled out, and the holes re-tapped. Use new plugs when the engine is reassembled.

4 If the casting is extremely dirty, it should be steam-cleaned. After this, clean all oil holes and galleries one more time. Flush all internal passages with warm water until the water runs clear. Dry thoroughly, and apply a light film of oil to all mating surfaces and cylinder bores, to prevent rusting. If you have access to compressed air, use it to speed up the drying process, and to blow out all the oil holes and galleries.

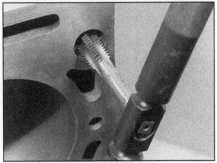

10.6 To clean the cylinder block threads, run a correct-size tap into the holes

⚠️ *Warning: Wear eye protection when using compressed air!*

5 If the castings are not very dirty, you can do an adequate cleaning job with hot, soapy water and a stiff brush. Take plenty of time, and do a thorough job. Regardless of the cleaning method used, be sure to clean all oil holes and galleries very thoroughly, and to dry all components well. Protect the cylinder bores as described above, to prevent rusting.

6 All threaded holes must be clean, to ensure accurate torque readings during reassembly. To clean the threads, run the correct-size tap into each of the holes to remove rust, corrosion, thread sealant or sludge, and to restore damaged threads **(see illustration)**. If possible, use compressed air to clear the holes of debris produced by this operation. **Note:** *Take extra care to exclude all cleaning liquid from blind tapped holes, as the casting may be cracked by hydraulic action if a bolt is threaded into a hole containing liquid.*

7 Apply suitable sealant to the new oil gallery plugs, and insert them into the holes in the block. Tighten them securely.

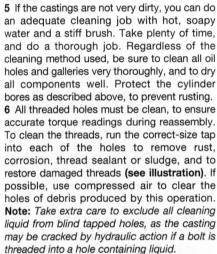

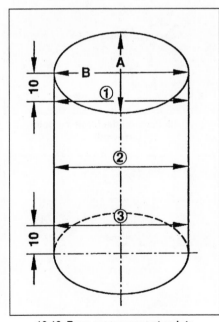

10.12 Bore measurement points

8 If the engine is not going to be reassembled immediately, cover it with a large plastic bag to keep it clean; protect all mating surfaces and the cylinder bores as described above, to prevent rusting.

Inspection

9 Visually check the casting for cracks and corrosion. Look for stripped threads in the threaded holes. If there has been any history of internal water leakage, it may be worthwhile having an engine overhaul specialist check the cylinder block/crankcase with professional equipment. If defects are found, have them renewed or if possible, repaired.

10 Check the cylinder bores for scuffing or scoring. Any evidence of this kind of damage should be cross-checked with an inspection of the pistons (see Section 7 of this Chapter). If the damage is in its early stages, it may be possible to repair the block by reboring it. Seek the advice of an engineering workshop.

11 To allow an accurate assessment of the wear in the cylinder bores to be made, their diameter must be measured at a number of points, as follows. Insert a bore gauge into bore No 1 and take three measurements in line with the crankshaft axis; one at the top of the bore, roughly 10 mm below the top of the bore, one halfway down the bore and one at a point roughly 10 mm above the bottom of the bore. **Note:** *Stand the cylinder block squarely on a workbench during this procedure, inaccurate results may be obtained if the measurements are taken when the engine mounted on a stand.*

12 Rotate the bore gauge through 90°, so that it is at right angles to the crankshaft axis and repeat the measurements detailed in paragraph 11 **(see illustration)**. Record all six measurements, and compare them with the data listed in the Specifications. If the difference in diameter between any two cylinders exceeds the wear limit, or if any one cylinder exceeds its maximum bore diameter, then *all four* cylinders will have to be rebored and oversize pistons will have to be fitted.

13 Use the piston diameter measurements recorded earlier (see Section 7) to calculate the piston-to-bore clearances. Figures are not available from the manufacturer, so seek the advice of your Audi/VAG dealer or engine reconditioning specialist.

14 Place the cylinder block on a level work surface, crankcase downwards. Use a straight edge and a set of feeler blades to measure the distortion of the cylinder head mating surface in both planes. A maximum figure is not quoted by the manufacturer, but use the figure of 0.05 mm as a rough guide. If the measurement exceeds this figure, repair may be possible by machining - consult your dealer for advice.

15 Before the engine can be reassembled, the cylinder bores must be honed. This process involves using an abrasive tool to produce a fine, cross-hatch pattern on the inner surface of the bore. This has the effect of seating the piston rings, resulting in a good seal between the piston and cylinder. There are two types of honing tool available to the home mechanic, both are driven by a rotary power tool, such as a drill. The bottle brush hone is a stiff, cylindrical brush with abrasive stones bonded to its bristles. The more conventional surfacing hone has abrasive stones mounted on spring-loaded legs. For the inexperienced home mechanic, satisfactory results will be achieved more easily using the Bottle Brush hone. **Note:** *If you are unwilling to tackle cylinder bore honing, an engineering workshop will be able to carry out the job for you at a reasonable cost.*

16 Carry out the honing as follows; you will need one of the honing tools described above, a power drill, a supply of clean rags, some honing oil and a pair of safety glasses.

17 Fit the honing tool in the drill chuck. Lubricate the cylinder bores with honing oil and insert the honing tool into the first bore, compressing the stones to allow it to fit. Turn on the drill and as the tool rotates, move it up and down in the bore at a rate that produces a fine cross-hatch pattern on the surface. The lines of the pattern should ideally cross at about 50 to 60° **(see illustration)**, although some piston ring manufacturer's may quote a different angle; check the literature supplied with the new rings.

⚠️ *Warning: Wear safety glasses to protect your eyes from debris flying off the honing tool.*

18 Use plenty of oil during the honing process. Do not remove any more material than is necessary to produce the required finish. When removing the hone tool from the bore, do not pull it out whilst it is still rotating; maintain the up/down movement until the chuck has stopped, then withdraw the tool whilst rotating the chuck by hand, in the normal direction of rotation.

19 Wipe out the oil and swarf with a rag and proceed to the next bore. When all four bores have been honed, thoroughly clean the whole cylinder block in hot soapy water to remove all traces of honing oil and debris. The block is clean when a clean rag, moistened with new engine oil does not pick up any grey residue when wiped along the bore.

20 Apply a light coating of engine oil to the mating surfaces and cylinder bores to prevent rust forming.

21 Refit all the components removed in paragraph 1.

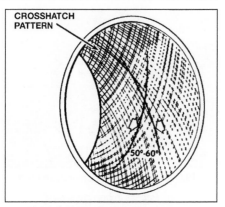

11 Main and big-end bearings - inspection and selection

Inspection

1 Even though the main and big-end bearings should be renewed during the engine overhaul, the old bearings should be retained for close examination, as they may reveal valuable information about the condition of the engine **(see illustration)**.

2 Bearing failure can occur due to lack of lubrication, the presence of dirt or other foreign particles, overloading the engine, or corrosion. Regardless of the cause of bearing failure, the cause must be corrected before the engine is reassembled, to prevent it from happening again.

3 When examining the bearing shells, remove them from the cylinder block/crankcase, the main bearing caps, the connecting rods and the connecting rod big-end bearing caps. Lay them out on a clean surface in the same general position as their location in the engine. This will enable you to match any bearing problems with the corresponding crankshaft journal. *Do not* touch any shell's internal bearing surface with your fingers while checking it, or the delicate surface may be scratched.

4 Dirt and other foreign matter gets into the engine in a variety of ways. It may be left in the engine during assembly, or it may pass through filters or the crankcase ventilation system. It may get into the oil, and from there into the bearings. Metal chips from machining operations and normal engine wear are often present. Abrasives are sometimes left in engine components after reconditioning, especially when parts are not thoroughly cleaned using the proper cleaning methods. Whatever the source, these foreign objects often end up embedded in the soft bearing material, and are easily recognised. Large particles will not embed in the bearing, but will score or gouge the bearing and journal. The best prevention for this cause of bearing failure is to clean all parts thoroughly, and keep everything spotlessly-clean during engine assembly. Frequent and regular engine oil and filter changes are also recommended.

5 Lack of lubrication (or lubrication breakdown) has a number of interrelated causes. Excessive heat (which thins the oil), overloading (which squeezes the oil from the bearing face) and oil leakage (from excessive bearing clearances, worn oil pump or high engine speeds) all contribute to lubrication breakdown. Blocked oil passages, which usually are the result of misaligned oil holes in a bearing shell, will also oil-starve a bearing, and destroy it. When lack of lubrication is the cause of bearing failure, the bearing material

10.17 Cylinder bore honing pattern

is wiped or extruded from the steel backing of the bearing. Temperatures may increase to the point where the steel backing turns blue from overheating.

6 Driving habits can have a definite effect on bearing life. Full-throttle, low-speed operation (labouring the engine) puts very high loads on bearings, tending to squeeze out the oil film. These loads cause the bearings to flex, which produces fine cracks in the bearing face (fatigue failure). Eventually, the bearing material will loosen in pieces, and tear away from the steel backing.

7 Short-distance driving leads to corrosion of bearings, because insufficient engine heat is produced to drive off the condensed water and corrosive gases. These products collect in the engine oil, forming acid and sludge. As the oil is carried to the engine bearings, the acid attacks and corrodes the bearing material.

8 Incorrect bearing installation during engine assembly will lead to bearing failure as well.

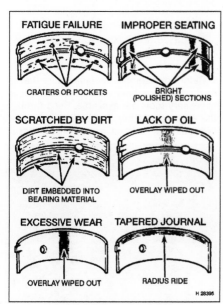

11.1 Typical bearing failures

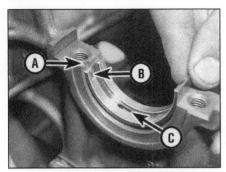

13.3 Bearing shells correctly refitted

A Recess in bearing saddle
B Lug on bearing shell
C Oil hole

Tight-fitting bearings leave insufficient bearing running clearance, and will result in oil starvation. Dirt or foreign particles trapped behind a bearing shell result in high spots on the bearing, which lead to failure.
9 *Do not* touch any shell's internal bearing surface with your fingers during reassembly as there is a risk of scratching the delicate surface, or of depositing particles of dirt on it.
10 As mentioned at the beginning of this Section, the bearing shells should be renewed as a matter of course during engine overhaul. To do otherwise is false economy.

Selection - main and big-end bearings

11 Main and big-end bearings for the engines described in this Chapter are available in standard sizes and a range of undersizes to suit reground crankshafts. Refer to the Specifications for details.
12 The running clearances will need to be checked when the crankshaft is refitted with its new bearings (see Section 13).

12 Engine overhaul - reassembly sequence

1 Before reassembly begins, ensure that all new parts have been obtained, and that all necessary tools are available. Read through the entire procedure to familiarise yourself with the work involved, and to ensure that all

13.8 Lay a piece of Plastigauge on each journal, in line with the crankshaft axis

items necessary for reassembly of the engine are at hand. In addition to all normal tools and materials, thread-locking compound will be needed. A suitable tube of liquid sealant will also be required for the joint faces that are without gaskets. It is recommended that the manufacturer's own products are used, which are specially formulated for this purpose; the relevant product names are quoted in the text of each Section where they are required.
2 In order to save time and avoid problems, engine reassembly should ideally be carried out in the following order:
  a) *Crankshaft (see Section 13).*
  b) *Piston/connecting rod assemblies (see Section 14 and 15).*
  c) *Oil pump (see Chapter 2A or 2B).*
  d) *Sump (see Chapter 2A or 2B).*
  e) *Flywheel/driveplate (see Chapter 2A or 2B).*
  f) *Cylinder head (see Chapter 2A or 2B).*
  g) *Timing belt tensioner, sprockets and timing belt (see Chapter 2A or 2B).*
  h) *Inlet and exhaust manifolds (see the relevant part of Chapter 4).*
  i) *Engine external components and ancillaries (see list in Section 5 of this Chapter).*
3 At this stage, all engine components should be absolutely clean and dry, with all faults repaired. The components should be laid out (or in individual containers) on a completely clean work surface.

13 Crankshaft - refitting and running clearance check

1 Crankshaft refitting is the first stage of engine reassembly following overhaul. At this point, it is assumed that the crankshaft, cylinder block/crankcase and bearings have been cleaned, inspected and reconditioned or renewed. Where removed, the oil jets must be refitted at this stage and their mounting bolts tightened to the specified torque.
2 Place the cylinder block on a clean, level worksurface, with the crankcase facing upwards. Wipe out the inner surfaces of the main bearing caps and crankcase with a clean cloth - they must be kept spotlessly clean.
3 Clean the rear surface of the new bearing shells with a cloth and lay them on the bearing saddles in the crankcase. Ensure that the orientation lugs on the shells engage with the recesses in the saddles, and that the oil holes are correctly aligned **(see illustration)**. Do not hammer or otherwise force the bearing shells into place. It is critically important that the surfaces of the bearings are kept free from damage and contamination.
4 Fit the thrust bearings either side of the No 3 bearing saddle. Use a small quantity of grease to hold them in place. Ensure that they are seated correctly in the machined recesses, with the oil grooves facing outwards **(see illustration)**.
5 Give the newly-fitted main bearing shells

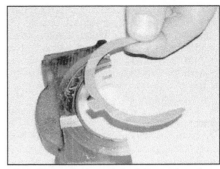

13.4 Fitting the crankshaft thrust bearings

and the crankshaft journals a final clean with a cloth. Check that the oil holes in the crankshaft are free from dirt, as any left here will become embedded in the new bearings when the engine is first started.
6 Carefully lay the crankshaft in the crankcase, taking care not to dislodge the bearing shells.

Running clearance check

7 When the crankshaft and bearings are refitted, a clearance must exist between them to allow lubricant to circulate. This clearance is impossible to check using feeler blades, so Plastigauge is used. This is a thin strip of soft plastic that is crushed between the bearing shells and journals when the bearing caps are tightened up. The change in its width then indicates the size of the clearance gap.
8 Cut off pieces of Plastigauge, just shorter than the length of the crankshaft journal. Lay a piece on each journal, in line with its axis **(see illustration)**.
9 Wipe off the rear surfaces of the new lower half main bearing shells and fit them to the main bearing caps, ensuring the locating lugs engage correctly **(see illustration)**.
10 Wipe the front surfaces of the bearing shells and, if available, give them a light coating of silicone release agent - this will prevent the Plastigauge from sticking to the shell. Fit the caps in their correct locations on the bearing saddles, using the manufacturer's markings as a guide. Ensure that they are correctly orientated - the caps should be fitted such that the recesses for the bearing shell locating lugs are on the same side as those in the bearing saddle.

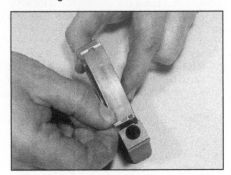

13.9 Fit the new lower half main bearing shells to the main bearing caps

11 Working from the centre bearing cap, tighten the bolts one half turn at a time until they are all correctly torqued to their first stage. Do not let the crankshaft turn at all whilst the Plastigauge is in place. Progressively unbolt the bearing caps and remove them, taking care not to dislodge the Plastigauge.

12 The width of the crushed Plastigauge can now be measured, using the scale provided **(see illustration)**. Use the correct scale, as both imperial and metric are printed. This measurement indicates the running clearance - compare it with that listed in Specifications. If the clearance is outside the tolerance, it may be due to dirt or debris trapped under the bearings; try cleaning them again and repeat the clearance check. If the results are still unacceptable, re-check the journal diameters and the bearing sizes. If the Plastigauge is thicker at one end, the journals may be tapered, and will require regrinding.

13 When you are satisfied that the clearances are correct, carefully remove the remains of the Plastigauge from the journals and bearings faces. Use a soft, plastic or wooden scraper as anything metallic is likely to damage the surfaces.

Crankshaft - final refitting

14 Lift the crankshaft out of the crankcase. Wipe off the surfaces of the bearings in the crankcase and the bearing caps.

15 Liberally coat the bearing shells in the crankcase with clean engine oil of the appropriate grade **(see illustration)**.

16 Lower the crankshaft into position so that

13.12 Measure the width of the crushed Plastigauge using the scale provided

No 1 cylinder crankpin is at BDC, ready for fitting No 1 piston.

17 Lubricate the lower bearing shells in the main bearing caps with clean engine oil, then fit the thrustwashers to each side of bearing cap No 3, noting that the lugs protruding from the washers engage the recesses in the side of the bearing cap **(see illustrations)**. Make sure that the locating lugs on the shells are still engaged with the corresponding recesses in the caps.

18 Fit the main bearing caps in the correct order and orientation - No 1 bearing cap must be at the timing belt end of the engine and the bearing shell locating recesses in the bearing saddles and caps must be adjacent to each other **(see illustrations)**. Insert the bearing cap bolts and hand tighten them only.

19 Working from the centre bearing cap outwards, tighten the retaining bolts to their specified torques and angles in the stages given **(see illustrations)**.

13.15 Lubricate the upper bearing shells . . .

20 Check that the crankshaft rotates freely by turning it manually. If resistance is felt, re-check the running clearances, as described above.

21 Carry out a check of the crankshaft endfloat as described at the beginning of Section 8. If the thrust surfaces of the crankshaft have been checked and new thrust bearings have been fitted, then the endfloat should be within specification.

22 Refit the pistons and connecting rods or reconnect them to the crankshaft as described in Section 15.

23 With reference to Chapter 2A or 2B as applicable, carry out the following:

a) *Refit the crankshaft front and rear oil seal housings, together with new oil seals.*
b) *Refit the oil pump and pick-up tube, baffle plate and sump.*
c) *Refit the flywheel and clutch or driveplate (as applicable).*
d) *Refit the crankshaft sprocket and timing belt.*

13.17a . . . and lower bearing shells with clean engine oil . . .

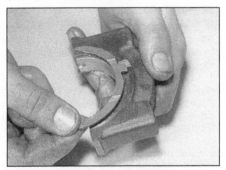

13.17b . . . then fit the thrustwashers each side of the bearing cap

13.18a Fitting No 3 main bearing cap

13.18b Fitting No 1 main bearing cap

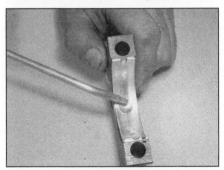

13.19a Tighten the main bearing cap bolts to the specified torque . . .

13.19b . . . and angle

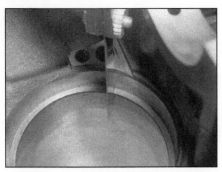

14.5 Checking a piston ring end gap using a feeler blade

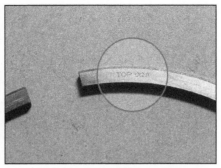

14.7 Piston ring TOP marking

14 Pistons and piston rings - assembly

1 At this point it is assumed that the pistons have been correctly assembled to their respective connecting rods and that the piston ring-to-groove clearances have been checked. If not, refer to the end of Section 7.
2 Before the rings can be fitted to the pistons, the end gaps must be checked with the rings fitted into the cylinder bores.
3 Lay out the piston assemblies and the new ring sets on a clean work surface so that the components are kept together in their groups during and after end gap checking. Place the crankcase on the work surface on its side, allowing access to the top and bottom of the bores.
4 Take the No 1 piston top ring and insert it into the top of the bore. Using the No 1 piston, push the ring close to the bottom of the bore, at the lowest point of the piston travel. Ensure that it is perfectly square in the bore.
5 Use a set of feeler blades to measure the gap between the ends of the piston ring. The correct blade will just pass through the gap with a minimal amount of resistance **(see illustration)**. Compare this measurement with that listed in Specifications. Check that you have the correct ring before deciding that a gap is incorrect. Repeat the operation for the remaining rings.
6 If new rings are being fitted, it is unlikely that the end gaps will be too small. If a measurement is found to be undersize, it must be corrected or there is the risk that the ends of the ring may contact each other during operation, possibly resulting in engine damage. This is achieved by gradually filing down the ends of the ring, using a file clamped in a vice. Fit the ring over the file such that both its ends contact opposite faces of the file. Move the ring along the file, removing small amounts of material at a time. Take great care as the rings are brittle and form sharp edges if they fracture. Remember to keep the rings and piston assemblies in the correct order.
7 When all the piston ring end gaps have been verified, they can be fitted to the pistons. Work from the lowest ring groove (oil control ring)

upwards. Note that the oil control ring comprises two side rails separated by a expander ring. Note also that the two compression rings are different in cross-section, and so must be fitted in the correct groove and the right way up, using a piston ring fitting tool. Both of the compression rings have marks stamped on one side to indicate the top facing surface. Ensure that these marks face up when the rings are fitted **(see illustration)**.
8 Distribute the end gaps around the piston, spaced at 120° intervals to the each other.
Note: *If the piston ring manufacturer supplies specific fitting instructions with the rings, follow these exclusively.*

15 Piston/connecting rod assemblies - refitting and big-end bearing clearance check

Big-end running clearance check

Note: *At this point, it is assumed that the crankshaft has been fitted to the engine, as described in Section 13.*
1 As with the main bearings, a running clearance must exist between the big-end crankpin and its bearing shells to allow oil to circulate. There are two methods of checking the size of the running clearance, as described in the following paragraphs.
2 Place the cylinder block on a clean, level worksurface, with the crankcase facing upwards. Position the crankshaft such that crankpin No 1 is at BDC.

15.12a Lubricate the pistons . . .

3 The first method is the least accurate and involves fitting the big-end bearing caps to the connecting rods away from the crankshaft, but with the bearing shells in place. **Note:** *Correct orientation of the bearing caps is critical; refer to the notes in Section 7.* The internal diameter formed by the assembled big-end is then measured using internal vernier calipers. The diameter of the respective crankpin is then subtracted from this measurement and the result is the running clearance.
4 The second method of carrying out this check involves the use of Plastigauge, in the same manner as the main bearing running clearance check (see Section 13) and is much more accurate than the previous method. Clean all crankpins with a cloth. With crankpin No 1 at BDC initially, place a strand of Plastigauge on the crankpin journal.
5 Fit the upper big-end bearing shell to the connecting rod, ensuring that the locating lug and recess engage correctly. Temporarily refit the piston/connecting rod assembly to the crankshaft, then refit the big-end bearing caps, using the manufacturer's markings to ensure that they are fitted the correct way around.
6 Tighten the bearing cap nuts/bolts to the Stage 1 torque. Take care not to disturb the Plastigauge or rotate the connecting rod during the tightening process.
7 Dismantle the assembly without rotating the connecting rod. Use the scale printed on the Plastigauge envelope to determine the big-end bearing running clearance and compare it with the figures listed in Specifications.
8 If the clearance is significantly different from that expected, the bearing shells may be the wrong size (or excessively worn, if the original shells are being re-used). Make sure that no dirt or oil was trapped between the bearing shells and the cap or connecting rod when the clearance was measured. Re-check the diameter of the crankpin. Note that if the Plastigauge was wider at one end than at the other, the crankpin may be tapered. When the problem is identified, fit new bearing shells or have the crankpins reground to a listed undersize, as appropriate.
9 Upon completion, carefully scrape away all traces of the Plastigauge material from the crankshaft and bearing shells. Use a plastic or wooden scraper, which will be soft enough to prevent scoring of the bearing surfaces.

Piston and connecting rod assemblies - final refitting

10 Note that the following procedure assumes that the crankshaft main bearing caps are in place (see Section 13).
11 Ensure that the bearing shells are correctly fitted, as described at the beginning of this Section. If new shells are being fitted, ensure that all traces of the protective grease are cleaned off using paraffin. Wipe dry the shells and connecting rods with a lint-free cloth.
12 Lubricate the cylinder bores, the pistons, piston rings and upper bearing shells with clean engine oil **(see illustrations)**. Lay out

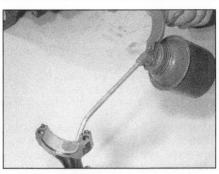

15.12b ... and big-end upper bearing shells with clean engine oil

15.16 Using a hammer handle to tap the piston into its bore

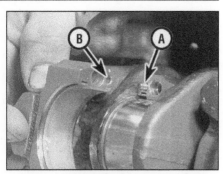

15.17 Fitting a big-end bearing cap

A Dowel (diesel engines only)
B Locating hole (diesel engines only)

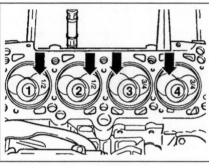

15.18 Piston orientation and coding on diesel engines

each piston/connecting rod assembly in order on a worksurface. Where the bearing caps are secured with nuts, pad the threaded ends of the bolts with insulating tape to prevent them scratching the crankpins and bores when the pistons are refitted.

13 Start with piston/connecting rod assembly No 1. Make sure that the piston rings are still spaced as described in Section 14, then clamp them in position with a piston ring compressor.

14 Insert the piston/connecting rod assembly into the top of cylinder No 1. Lower the big-end in first, guiding it to protect the cylinder bores. Where oil jets are located at the bottoms of the bores, take particular care not to break them off when guiding the connecting rods onto the crankpins.

15 Ensure that the orientation of the piston in its cylinder is correct - the piston crown, connecting rods and big-end bearing caps have markings, which must point towards the timing belt end of the engine when the piston is installed in the bore - refer to Section 7 for details.

16 Using a block of wood or hammer handle against the piston crown, tap the assembly into the cylinder until the piston crown is flush with the top of the cylinder **(see illustration)**.

17 Ensure that the bearing shell is still correctly installed. Liberally lubricate the crankpin and both bearing shells with clean engine oil. Taking care not to mark the cylinder bores, tap the piston/connecting rod assembly down the bore and onto the crankpin. Remove the insulating tape from the threaded ends of the bolts where applicable and oil the threads and undersides of the bolt

heads. Fit the big-end bearing cap, tightening its retaining nuts/bolts finger-tight at first **(see illustration)**. Note that the orientation of the bearing cap with respect to the connecting rod must be correct when the two components are reassembled. The connecting rod and its corresponding bearing cap both have recesses machined into them, close to their mating surfaces - these recesses must both face in the same direction as the arrow on the piston crown (ie towards the timing belt end of the engine) when correctly installed - refer to the illustrations in Section 7 for details.

18 On diesel engines, the piston crowns are specially shaped to improve the engine's combustion characteristics. Because of this, pistons 1 and 2 are different to pistons 3 and 4. When correctly fitted, the larger inlet valve chambers on pistons 1 and 2 must face the flywheel/driveplate end of the engine, and the larger inlet valve chambers on the remaining pistons must face the timing belt end of the engine. New pistons have number markings on their crowns to indicate their type - 1/2 denotes piston 1 or 2, 3/4 indicates piston 3 or 4 **(see illustration)**.

19 Tighten the retaining bolts/nuts to the specified Stage 1 torque **(see illustration)**.

20 Angle-tighten the retaining bolts/nuts to the specified Stage 2 angle **(see illustration)**.

21 Refit the remaining three piston/connecting rod assemblies in the same way.

22 Rotate the crankshaft by hand. Check that it turns freely; some stiffness is to be expected if new parts have been fitted, but there should be no binding or tight spots.

Diesel engines

23 If new pistons are fitted or if a new short engine is installed, the projection of the piston crowns above the cylinder head at TDC must be measured, to determine the type of head gasket that should be fitted.

24 Turn the cylinder block over (so that the crankcase is facing downwards) and rest it on a stand or wooden blocks. Anchor a DTI gauge to the cylinder block, and zero it on the head gasket mating surface. Rest the gauge probe on No 1 piston crown and turn the crankshaft slowly by hand so that the piston reaches TDC. Measure and record the maximum projection at TDC **(see illustration)**.

25 Repeat the measurement for the remaining pistons and record.

26 If the measurements differ from piston to piston, take the highest figure and use this to

15.19 Tighten the big-end bearing cap bolts/nuts to the Stage 1 setting ...

15.20 ... then angle-tighten them to the Stage 2 setting

15.24 Measuring the piston projection with a dial gauge

determine the head gasket type that must be used - refer to the Specifications for details.

27 Note that if the original pistons have been refitted, then a new head gasket of the same type as the original item must be fitted.

All engines

28 Refer to Part A or B of this Chapter (as applicable) and refit the oil pump and pickup, sump and baffle plate, flywheel and cylinder head.

16 Engine -
initial start-up after overhaul and reassembly

1 Refit the remainder of the engine components in the order listed in Section 12 of this Chapter. Refit the engine to the vehicle as described in Section 4 of this Chapter. Double-check the engine oil and coolant levels and make a final check that everything has been reconnected. Make sure that there are no tools or rags left in the engine compartment.

Petrol models

2 Remove the spark plugs, referring to Chapter 1A for details.

3 The engine must be immobilised such that it can be turned over using the starter motor, without starting - disable the fuel pump by unplugging the fuel pump power relay from the relay board with reference to the relevant Part of Chapter 4, and also disable the ignition system by disconnecting the wiring from the ignition module.

Caution: To prevent damage to the catalytic converter, it is important to disable the fuel system.

4 Turn the engine using the starter motor until the oil pressure warning lamp goes out. If the lamp fails to extinguish after several seconds of cranking, check the engine oil level and oil filter security. Assuming these are correct, check the security of the oil pressure switch cabling - do not progress any further until you are satisfied that oil is being pumped around the engine at sufficient pressure.

5 Refit the spark plugs, and reconnect the wiring to the fuel pump relay and ignition module.

Diesel models

6 Disconnect the electrical cable from the fuel cut-off valve at the fuel injection pump - refer to Chapter 4B for details.

7 Turn the engine using the starter motor until the oil pressure warning lamp goes out.

8 If the lamp fails to extinguish after several seconds of cranking, check the engine oil level and oil filter security. Assuming these are correct, check the security of the oil pressure switch cabling - do not progress any further until you are satisfied that oil is being pumped around the engine at sufficient pressure.

9 Reconnect the fuel cut-off valve cable.

All models

10 Start the engine, but be aware that as fuel system components have been disturbed, the cranking time may be a little longer than usual.

11 While the engine is idling, check for fuel, water and oil leaks. Don't be alarmed if there are some odd smells and the occasional plume of smoke as components heat up and burn off oil deposits.

12 Assuming all is well, keep the engine idling until hot water is felt circulating through the top hose.

13 On diesel models, check the fuel injection pump timing and engine idle speed, as described in Chapter 4B.

14 After a few minutes, recheck the oil and coolant levels, and top-up as necessary.

15 There is no need to re-tighten the cylinder head bolts once the engine has been run following reassembly.

16 If new pistons, rings or crankshaft bearings have been fitted, the engine must be treated as new, and run-in for the first 600 miles (1000 km). *Do not* operate the engine at full-throttle, or allow it to labour at low engine speeds in any gear. It is recommended that the engine oil and filter are changed at the end of this period.

Chapter 3
Cooling, heating and ventilation systems

Contents

Degrees of difficulty

| Easy, suitable for novice with little experience | | Fairly easy, suitable for beginner with some experience | | Fairly difficult, suitable for competent DIY mechanic | | Difficult, suitable for experienced DIY mechanic | | Very difficult, suitable for expert DIY or professional | 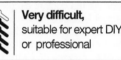 |

Specifications

General
Maximum system pressure . . . . 1.2 to 1.5 bar

Thermostat
Opening temperature . . . . 87°C (approx.)
Minimum valve lift . . . . at least 8 mm

Torque wrench settings

	Nm	lbf ft
Alternator/power steering pump bracket:		
Bracket to cylinder block	25	18
Strut to cylinder block	25	18
Strut to bracket	40	30
Coolant pump:		
Housing-to-block studs/bolts:		
Petrol engines	20	15
Diesel engines:		
Stage 1	20	15
Stage 2	Angle-tighten a further 90°	
Pump-to-housing bolts	10	7
Pulley bolts	25	18
Drain plug	30	22
Cooling fan switch	25	18
Thermostat housing bolts	10	7
Viscous cooling fan coupling/drive pulley shaft bolt	45	33
Viscous cooling fan coupling to drive pulley bolts	10	7

1 General information and precautions

General information

1 The cooling system is of the pressurised type, comprising a coolant pump, an aluminium radiator, cooling fan(s), a thermostat, heater matrix, and all associated hoses and switches. The coolant pump is driven either by the auxiliary drivebelt or the camshaft timing belt, depending on model. All models are fitted with a viscous-coupled primary cooling fan, which is driven by the auxiliary drivebelt, and an auxiliary cooling fan which is electrically-operated. The system functions as follows.

2 When the engine is cold, the coolant in the engine is pumped around the cylinder block and head passages, and through an engine oil cooler (where fitted). After cooling the cylinder bores, combustion surfaces and valve seats, the coolant passes through the heater, and is returned via the cylinder block to the coolant pump. The thermostat is initially closed, preventing the cold coolant from the radiator entering the engine.

3 When the coolant in the engine reaches a predetermined temperature, the thermostat opens. The cold coolant from the radiator is then allowed to enter the engine through the bottom hose and the hot coolant from the engine flows through the top hose to the radiator. As the coolant circulates through the radiator, it is cooled by the inrush of air when the car is in forward motion. The airflow is supplemented by the action of the cooling fan(s) when necessary. As the coolant reduces in temperature, it passes to the bottom of the radiator and the cycle is repeated.

4 The operation of the primary cooling fan is controlled by a viscous coupling. The coupling is driven by the auxiliary drivebelt and transmits drive to the fan through a temperature-sensitive fluid coupling arrangement. At lower temperatures the fan blade is allowed to spin freely on the coupling. At a predetermined temperature (around 75ºC), an internal valve in the coupling opens, which effectively locks-up the coupling, and transmits drive to the fan. Once the temperature drops again, the valve closes and the fan is allowed to spin freely again.

5 The operation of the electrically-operated auxiliary cooling fan is controlled by a thermostatic switch. At a predetermined coolant temperature, the switch/sensor actuates the fan. The switch then cuts the power supply to the fan when the coolant temperature has reduced sufficiently.

6 On models with an automatic transmission unit, a transmission fluid cooler is built into the radiator. The transmission unit is linked to the radiator by two pipes and the fluid is circulated around the cooler to keep its temperature stable under arduous operating conditions.

Precautions

⚠️ **Warning: Do not attempt to remove the expansion tank filler cap, or to disturb any part of the cooling system, while the engine is hot, as there is a high risk of scalding. If the expansion tank filler cap must be removed before the engine and radiator have fully cooled (even though this is not recommended), the pressure in the cooling system must first be relieved. Cover the cap with a thick layer of cloth to avoid scalding, and slowly unscrew the filler cap until a hissing sound is heard. When the hissing has stopped, indicating that the pressure has reduced, slowly unscrew the filler cap until it can be removed; if more hissing sounds are heard, wait until they have stopped before unscrewing the cap completely. At all times, keep well away from the filler cap opening, and protect your hands.**

⚠️ **Warning: Do not allow antifreeze to come into contact with your skin, or with the painted surfaces of the vehicle. Rinse off spills immediately, with plenty of water. Never leave antifreeze lying around in an open container, or in a puddle in the driveway or on the garage floor. Children and pets are attracted by its sweet smell, but antifreeze can be fatal if ingested.**

⚠️ **Warning: If the engine is hot, the electric cooling fan may start rotating even if the engine is not running. Be careful to keep your hands, hair, and any loose clothing well clear when working in the engine compartment.**

⚠️ **Warning: Refer to Section 10 for precautions to be observed when working on models equipped with air conditioning.**

2 Cooling system hoses - disconnection and renewal

Note: *Refer to the warnings given in Section 1 of this Chapter before proceeding. Hoses should only be disconnected once the engine has cooled sufficiently to avoid scalding.*

1 If the checks described in the relevant part of Chapter 1 reveal a faulty hose, it must be renewed as follows.

2 First drain the cooling system (see the relevant part of Chapter 1). If the coolant is not due for renewal, it may be re-used, providing it is collected in a clean container.

3 To disconnect a hose, use a screwdriver to slacken the clips, then move them along the hose, clear of the relevant inlet/outlet. Carefully work the hose free. The hoses can be removed with relative ease when new - on an older car, they may have stuck.

4 If a hose proves to be difficult to remove, try to release it by rotating its ends before attempting to free it. Gently prise the end of

the hose with a blunt instrument (such as a flat-bladed screwdriver), but do not apply too much force, and take care not to damage the pipe stubs or hoses. Note in particular that the radiator inlet stub is fragile; do not use excessive force when attempting to remove the hose. If all else fails, cut the hose with a sharp knife, then slit it so that it can be peeled off in two pieces. Although this may prove expensive if the hose is otherwise undamaged, it is preferable to buying a new radiator. Check first, however, that a new hose is readily available.

5 When fitting a hose, first slide the clips onto the hose, then work the hose into position. On some hose connections alignment marks are provided on the hose and union; if marks are present, ensure they are correctly aligned.

 TOOL TiP *If the hose is stiff, use a little soapy water as a lubricant, or soften the hose by soaking it in hot water. Do not use oil or grease, which may attack the rubber.*

6 Ensure the hose is correctly routed, then slide each clip back along the hose until it passes over the flared end of the relevant inlet/outlet, before tightening the clip securely.

7 Refill the cooling system with reference to the relevant part of Chapter 1.

8 Check thoroughly for leaks as soon as possible after disturbing any part of the cooling system.

3 Radiator - removal, inspection and refitting

Removal

1 Disconnect the battery negative lead then remove the front bumper as described in Chapter 11.

2 Drain the cooling system as described in the relevant part of Chapter 1.

3 Where applicable, unplug the wiring connector from the cooling fan switch which is screwed into the radiator.

4 Disconnect the radiator top and bottom coolant hoses, noting the correct fitted locations **(see illustrations)**.

5 On models with automatic transmission, wipe clean the area around the fluid pipe unions on the radiator. Slacken and remove the retaining bolts then carefully ease both pipes out from the radiator. Plug the pipe ends and cooler ports to minimise fluid loss and prevent the entry of dirt into the hydraulic system. Discard the sealing rings from the pipe end fittings, new ones must be used on refitting.

6 On models equipped with air conditioning, slacken and remove the nuts and bolts securing the condenser to the radiator and any nuts/bolts securing the refrigerant pipe clips in

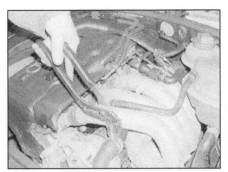

3.4a Release the clip . . .

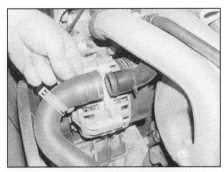

3.4b . . . and disconnect the radiator top coolant hose

4 Thermostat - removal, testing and refitting

1 The thermostat is located on the left-hand side of the front of the cylinder block. On later 1.6 litre models (engine code AHL) where the coolant pump is driven by the camshaft timing belt, the thermostat is fitted to a housing on the front of the cylinder block, to the left of the coolant pump. On all other models, it is fitted to the base of coolant pump housing and access is best from underneath the vehicle, once the undercover has been removed.

Removal

Engine code AHL

2 Disconnect the battery negative lead.
3 Place the lock carrier in the service position as described in Chapter 11.
4 Drain the cooling system as described in Chapter 1A.
5 Remove the auxiliary drivebelt as described in Chapter 1A.
6 Disconnect the radiator top hose as described in Section 3.
7 Pull the engine oil dipstick tube from the guide stub on the cylinder block.
8 Remove the alternator, with reference to Chapter 5A.
9 Release the radiator bottom hose from the thermostat housing stub.
10 Slacken and withdraw the securing bolts and remove the thermostat housing cover. Lift the thermostat from its housing and recover the sealing ring. A new sealing ring must be used on refitting **(see illustration)**.

All other models

11 Disconnect the battery negative lead.
12 Drain the cooling system as described in Chapter 1A or 1B as applicable.
13 If necessary, to improve access, release the retaining clip and disconnect the coolant hose from the thermostat cover.

position. Free the condenser from the radiator and support it to prevent excessive strain being placed on the pipes. **Do not** disconnect the refrigerant pipes (see Section 10).
7 On models equipped with air conditioning, unplug the wiring from the pressure switch at the right hand side of the radiator.
8 Undo the retaining screws and remove plastic covers from the left- and right-hand sides of the radiator. Where necessary also undo the retaining screws securing the intake duct to the top of the radiator **(see illustration)**.
9 Undo the bolts securing the power steering fluid cooler to the front of the radiator and position it clear **(see illustration)**. Tie the cooler to the body to prevent any strain being placed on the hoses.
10 Withdraw the upper radiator retaining pins, then pivot the radiator towards the front of the engine compartment and lift it away from its lower mountings. On models with air conditioning, take great care to avoid damaging the condenser as the radiator is removed.

Inspection

11 If the radiator has been removed due to suspected blockage, reverse-flush it as described in Section 32 of the relevant part of Chapter 1. Clean dirt and debris from the radiator fins, using an air line (in which case, wear eye protection) or a soft brush. Be careful, as the fins are sharp, and easily damaged.
12 If necessary, a radiator specialist can

perform a flow test on the radiator, to establish whether an internal blockage exists.
13 A leaking radiator must be referred to a specialist for permanent repair. Do not attempt to weld or solder a leaking radiator, as damage to the plastic components may result.
14 If the radiator is to be sent for repair or renewed, remove all hoses switches (where fitted).
15 Inspect the condition of the radiator mounting rubbers, and renew them if necessary.

Refitting

16 Refitting is a reversal of removal, bearing in mind the following points.
  a) *Ensure that the radiator is correctly engaged with its mounting rubbers and that the upper retaining pins are securely refitted.*
  b) *On models with automatic transmission, fit new sealing rings to the fluid pipe end fittings, lubricating them with fresh transmission fluid to ease installation. Ease both pipes fully into position before refitting the retaining bolts and tighten them securely.*
  c) *Make sure all coolant hoses are correctly reconnected and securely retained by their clips.*
  d) *Refill the cooling system as described in the relevant part of Chapter 1.*
  e) *On models with automatic transmission, on completion check the transmission fluid level and, if necessary, top-up as described in the relevant part of Chapter 1.*

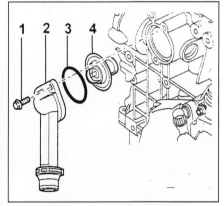

4.10 Thermostat and housing - 1.6 litre models (engine code AHL)

1 Bolt	*3 Sealing ring*
2 Housing	*4 Thermostat*

3.8 Undo the retaining screws and remove plastic covers from the left- and right-hand sides of the radiator

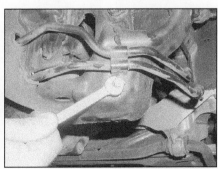

3.9 Undo the bolts securing the power steering fluid cooler to the front of the radiator and position it clear

4.14a Unscrew the retaining bolts and remove the thermostat housing cover . . .

4.14b . . . and sealing ring from the engine

4.15 Remove the thermostat from its housing

14 Unscrew the retaining bolts and remove the thermostat housing cover and sealing ring from the engine **(see illustrations)**. Discard the sealing ring; a new one must be used on refitting.
15 Remove the thermostat, noting which way around it is fitted **(see illustration)**.

Testing

16 A rough test of the thermostat may be made by suspending it with a piece of string in a container full of water. Heat the water to bring it to the boil - the thermostat must be fully open by the time the water boils. If not, renew it.
17 If a thermometer is available, the precise opening temperature of the thermostat may be determined; compare with the figures given in the Specifications. The opening temperature should also be marked on the thermostat.
18 A thermostat which fails to close as the water cools must also be renewed.

Refitting

All models

19 Refitting is a reversal of removal, noting the following points:
a) Use a new thermostat housing cover sealing ring.

b) On engine code AHL, ensure that the curved section of the thermostat body is positioned vertically.
c) Tighten the housing retaining bolts to the specified torque setting.
d) Refill the cooling system as described in Chapter 1A or 1B (as applicable)
e) On completion reconnect the battery.

5 Cooling fan(s) - testing, removal and refitting

Electric auxiliary cooling fan

Testing

1 Current supply to the cooling fans is via the ignition switch, a fuse and a pair of series resistors. The circuit is completed by the cooling fan thermostatic switch, which is mounted in the left-hand side of the radiator.
2 If a fan does not appear to work, run the engine until normal operating temperature is reached, then allow it to idle. The fan should cut in within a few minutes (before the temperature gauge needle enters the red section, or before the coolant temperature warning light comes on).
3 If not, switch off the ignition and disconnect

the wiring plug from the cooling fan switch. Bridge the relevant two contacts in the wiring plug (see *Wiring Diagrams* at the end of this Chapter 12 - most models have two-stage switches) using a length of spare wire, and switch on the ignition. If the fan now operates, the switch is probably faulty, and should be renewed.
4 If the fan still fails to operate, check that battery voltage is available at the feed wire to the switch; if not, then there is a fault in the feed wire (possibly due to a fault in the fan motor, or a blown fuse). If there is no problem with the feed, check that there is continuity between the switch earth terminal and a good earth point on the body; if not, then the earth connection is faulty, and must be re-made.
5 If the switch and the wiring are in good condition, the fault must lie in the motor itself. The motor can be checked by disconnecting it from the wiring loom and connecting a 12-volt supply directly to it.

Removal

6 Remove the radiator (see Section 3).
7 Slacken and remove the retaining bolts and remove the fan shroud assembly from the rear of the radiator **(see illustrations)**.
8 Unclip the motor wiring from the rear of the shroud then undo the retaining nuts and pull the motor assembly away from the shroud. On

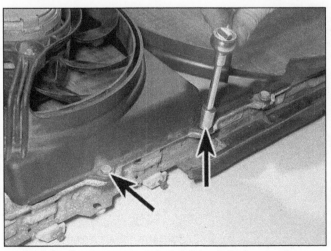

5.7a Slacken and remove the retaining bolts (arrowed) . . .

5.7b . . . and remove the fan shroud assembly from the rear of the radiator

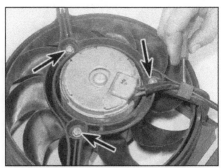

5.8a Unclip the motor wiring from the rear of the shroud then undo the retaining nuts (arrowed) and separate the motor and shroud

5.8b Where necessary, bend back the lockwasher tab and unscrew the retaining nut (note: may have left hand thread) . . .

some models it will be necessary to detach the fan blade from the motor to gain the necessary clearance required; bend back the lockwasher tab and unscrew the retaining nut (the nut may have a left-hand thread on some models) to free the fan **(see illustrations)**. If the motor is faulty, the complete unit must be renewed, as no spares are available.

Refitting

9 Fit the motor assembly to the shroud and securely tighten its retaining nuts. Ensure the motor wiring is correctly routed and clipped securely in position. Where necessary, seat the fan blade on the motor spindle then refit the lockwasher and retaining nut. Tighten the nut and secure it in position by bending up one of the lockwasher tabs.
10 Refit the shroud assembly to the radiator and securely tighten its retaining bolts.
11 Refit the radiator as described in Section 3.

Viscous-coupled cooling fan

Testing

12 The operation of the viscous coupling cannot be easily checked by the home mechanic. The only check which can be performed is a visual one to check the coupling assembly for signs of fluid leakage and the fan blade for signs of damage. When the coupling is cold, the fan should spin freely on the coupling and when it is hot (temperature above approximately 75°C), the coupling should lock up, causing the fan to

rotate. If there is any doubt about the operation of the coupling, it should be renewed.

Removal

Note: *It is likely that a peg spanner (Audi tool no. 3212 or suitable alternative) will be required to retain the drive pulley whilst the coupling is unscrewed.*
13 Place the lock carrier in the service position as described in Chapter 11.
14 Remove the auxiliary drivebelt as described in Chapter 2A or 2B as applicable.
15 Undo the retaining bolts and separate the fan blades from the coupling, noting which way around the fan blades are fitted **(see illustration)**.
16 Counterhold the drive pulley with a 5x60 mm bolt engaged with the small holes located around the pulley rim. Pass an 8mm Allen key through the drive pulley mounting bracket, and engage it with the rear of the pulley shaft bolt. Slacken and withdraw the bolt and remove the drive pulley and viscous coupling from the engine **(see illustration)**.
17 If required, the viscous coupling unit can be separated from the drive pulley by slackening and withdrawing the securing bolts.

Refitting

18 Refit the viscous coupling to the drive pulley (where removed) and tighten its retaining bolts to the specified torque.
19 Manoeuvre the drive pulley and coupling into position, then insert the shaft bolt and tighten it to the specified torque using a

suitable 8mm hex bit inserted through the rear of the drive pulley housing, whilst counter holding the drive pulley with the 5x60 mm bolt, as during removal.
20 Refit the fan blade unit ensuring that it is mounted the correct way around.
21 Refit the auxiliary drivebelt as described in Chapter 2A or 2B as applicable.
22 Refit the lock carrier as described in Chapter 11.

6 Cooling system electrical switches and sensors - testing, removal and refitting

Electrically-operated cooling fan thermostatic switch

Testing

1 Testing of the switch is described in Section 5, as part of the electric cooling fan test procedure.

Removal

Note: *The engine and radiator should be allowed to cool completely before the switch is removed.*
2 The switch is located in the left-hand side of the radiator, just above the bottom hose stub, and on most models can be reached from above. Where this is not the case, firmly apply the handbrake then jack up the front of the vehicle and support it on axle stands. Remove the retaining screws and fasteners and remove the undercover to be able to access the switch from below.
3 Disconnect the battery negative lead.
4 Drain the cooling system to just below the level of the switch (as described in the relevant part of Chapter 1). Alternatively, have ready a suitable bung to plug the switch aperture in the radiator when the switch is removed. If this method is used, take great care not to damage the radiator, and do not use anything which will allow foreign matter to enter the radiator.
5 Disconnect the wiring plug from the switch.

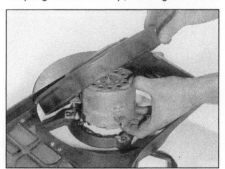

5.8c . . . and separate the motor and fan blade

5.15 Undo the retaining bolts and separate the fan blades from the coupling

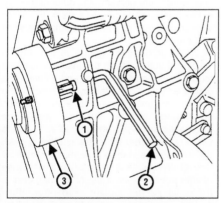

5.16 Viscous coupling drive pulley removal

1 5 x 60 mm bolt   3 Drive pulley
2 8 mm Allen key

6.10 Cooling system sensor location (1.8 litre model shown)

1 *Coolant temperature gauge/warning light sensor*
2 *Fuel injection system coolant temperature sensor*

6 Carefully unscrew the switch from the radiator, and recover the sealing washer (where fitted). If the system has not been drained, plug the switch aperture to prevent further coolant loss.

Refitting

7 If the switch was originally fitted using a sealing ring, use a new sealing ring on refitting. Where no sealing ring was fitted, clean the switch threads thoroughly and coat them with fresh sealing compound.

8 Refitting is a reversal of removal. Tighten the switch to the specified torque and refill (or top-up) the cooling system as described in the relevant part of Chapter 1.

9 On completion, start the engine and run it until it reaches normal operating temperature. Continue to run the engine, and check that the cooling fan cuts in and out correctly.

Coolant temperature gauge/warning light sensor

Testing

10 On all models, the coolant temperature gauge/warning light sensor is located in the coolant outlet union on the left-hand side/rear of the cylinder head (**see illustration**). Where two sensors are present, the outer of the two is the temperature gauge sensor (the inner sensor serves the engine management system).

11 The temperature gauge is fed with a stabilised voltage from the instrument panel feed (via the ignition switch and a fuse). The gauge earth is controlled by the sensor. The sensor contains a thermistor - an electronic component whose electrical resistance decreases at a predetermined rate as its temperature rises. When the coolant is cold, the sensor resistance is high, current flow through the gauge is reduced, and the gauge needle points towards the blue (cold) end of the scale. As the coolant temperature rises and the sensor resistance falls, current flow increases, and the gauge needle moves towards the upper end of the scale. If the sensor is faulty, it must be renewed.

12 The temperature warning light is fed with a voltage from the instrument panel. The light earth is controlled by the sensor. The sensor is effectively a switch, which operates at a predetermined temperature to earth the light and complete the circuit.

13 The sensors for both the gauge and warning light are incorporated in a single, four-pin unit.

14 If the gauge develops a fault, first check the other instruments; if they do not work at all, check the instrument panel electrical feed. If the readings are erratic, there may be a fault in the voltage stabiliser, which will necessitate renewal of the stabiliser (the stabiliser is integral with the instrument panel printed circuit board - see Chapter 12). If the fault lies in the temperature gauge alone, check it as follows.

15 If the gauge needle remains at the cold end of the scale when the engine is hot, disconnect the sensor wiring plug, and earth the relevant wire to the cylinder head. If the needle then deflects when the ignition is switched on, the sensor unit is proved faulty, and should be renewed. If the needle still does not move, remove the instrument panel (Chapter 12) and check the continuity of the wire between the sensor unit and the gauge, and the feed to the gauge unit. If continuity is shown, and the fault still exists, then the gauge is faulty, and the gauge unit should be renewed.

16 If the gauge needle remains at the hot end of the scale when the engine is cold, disconnect the sensor wire. If the needle then returns to the cold end of the scale when the ignition is switched on, the sensor unit is proved faulty, and should be renewed. If the needle still does not move, check the remainder of the circuit as described previously.

17 The same basic principles apply to testing the warning light. The light should illuminate when the relevant sensor wire is earthed.

Removal

18 Either partially drain the cooling system to just below the level of the sensor (as described in Chapter 1A or 1B), or have ready a suitable plug which can be used to plug the sensor aperture whilst it is removed. If a plug is used, take great care not to damage the sensor unit aperture, and do not use anything which will allow foreign matter to enter the cooling system.

19 On diesel engines, prise out the covers then unscrew the retaining nuts and remove the top cover from the engine to gain access to the sensor.

20 On all engines, disconnect the wiring connector from the sensor and identify whether the sensor is a push-fit or a screw-fit.

21 On screw-fit sensors, unscrew the sensor from the engine and recover its sealing washer.

22 On push-fit sensors, depress the sensor unit and slide out its retaining clip. Withdraw the sensor from the engine and recover its sealing ring.

Refitting

23 On screw-fit sensors, fit a new sealing washer then fit the sensor, tightening it securely.

24 On push-fit sensor units, fit a new sealing ring then push the sensor fully into its aperture and secure it in position with the retaining clip.

25 Reconnect the wiring connector then refill the cooling system as described in the relevant part of Chapter 1 or top-up as described in *Weekly checks*. On diesel engines, refit the top cover to the engine unit.

Engine management system coolant temperature sensor

26 On all models, the temperature gauge/warning light sensor is located in the coolant outlet union on the left-hand side/rear of the cylinder head. Where two sensors are present the temperature gauge one is the outer one (the inner sensor serves the fuel gauge/warning light).

27 The sensor is a thermistor (see paragraph 11) housed in a two-pin unit. The fuel injection/engine management electronic control unit (ECU) supplies the sensor with a set voltage and then, by measuring the current flowing in the sensor circuit, it determines the engine's temperature. This information is then used, in conjunction with other inputs, to control the injector timing, the idle speed, etc. It is also used to determine the glow plug pre-heating and post-heating times.

28 If the sensor circuit should fail to provide adequate information, the ECU's back-up facility will override the sensor signal. In this event, the ECU assumes a predetermined setting which will allow the fuel injection/engine management system to run, albeit at reduced efficiency. When this occurs, the warning light on the instrument panel will come on, and the advice of a Audi/VAG dealer should be sought. The sensor itself can only be tested using special Audi/VAG diagnostic equipment. *Do not* attempt to test the circuit using any other equipment, as there is a high risk of damaging the ECU.

Removal and refitting

29 Refer to the information given in paragraphs 18 to 25.

---

7 Coolant pump -
removal and refitting

Early 1.6 litre models (engine code AHL)

Removal

1 Disconnect the battery negative cable, then drain the cooling system as described in Chapter 1A.

2 Place the lock carrier in the service position, as described in Chapter 11.

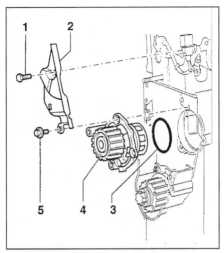

7.7 Coolant pump mounting details - 1.6 litre models (engine code ADP)

1 Bolt	3 Seal
2 Timing belt	4 Coolant pump
cover	5 Bolt

3 Remove the auxiliary drivebelt as described in Chapter 2A.

4 Remove the viscous-coupled cooling fan unit as described in Section 5.

5 With reference to *Timing belt - removal, inspection and refitting* in Chapter 2A, disengage the timing belt from the camshaft and coolant pump sprockets. There is no need to release the belt from the crankshaft sprocket - this means that the crankshaft auxiliary belt pulley and lower timing belt cover can remain in place.

6 Undo the screws and remove the upper section of the timing belt inner cover.

7 Slacken and withdraw the coolant pump securing bolts. Carefully withdraw the pump from the cylinder block and recover the sealing ring **(see illustration)**.

Refitting

8 Ensure that the pump and housing mating surfaces are clean and free from all traces of corrosion.

9 Obtain a new sealing ring and moisten it with undiluted coolant additive of the specified type (see *Recommended lubricants and fluids*). Position the sealing ring in its housing on the cylinder block.

10 Fit the coolant pump to the cylinder block, ensuring that the plug insert in the pump flange faces downwards.

11 Insert the retaining bolts and tighten them evenly and progressively to the specified torque.

12 Refit the inner timing belt cover, then refit the timing belt as described in Chapter 2A.

13 Refit the viscous-coupled cooling fan unit.

14 Refit the lock carrier and tighten the securing bolts to the specified torque (see Chapter 11).

15 On completion refill the cooling system as described in the relevant Part of Chapter 1, then reconnect the battery.

7.25a Unscrew the retaining studs/ bolts . . .

All other petrol engines (excluding engine code AHL)

Removal

16 Disconnect the battery negative cable, then drain the cooling system as described in Chapter 1A.

17 Place the lock carrier in the service position, as described in Chapter 11.

18 Remove the main auxiliary drivebelt as described in Chapter 2A. Note that on vehicles so equipped, the air conditioning compressor drivebelt does not need to be removed.

19 Remove the viscous-coupled cooling fan unit as described in Section 5.

20 Counterhold the power steering pump pulley by passing a screwdriver through the hole in the pulley and bracing it against the pump mounting bracket. Unbolt the outer section of the coolant pump pulley assembly and remove the V-belt.

21 Release the retaining clips and disconnect the coolant hoses from the back of the coolant pump housing and the thermostat housing.

22 Remove the alternator with reference to Chapter 5A.

23 Remove the power steering pump from its mounting bracket, as described in Chapter 10, noting that there is no need to disconnect the hydraulic pipe/hose(s) from the pump. Secure the pump clear of its mounting bracket using cable ties or wire.

24 Slacken and remove the nuts/bolts (as applicable) and remove the alternator and/or

7.25c Recover the sealing ring which is fitted between the housing and block and discard it

7.25b . . . and remove the coolant pump/ thermostat housing assembly from the engine

power steering pump bracket(s) from the engine to gain the necessary clearance required to enable the coolant pump housing assembly to be removed.

25 Unscrew the retaining studs/bolts (as applicable) securing the coolant pump/thermostat housing to the block and remove the housing assembly from the engine. **Note:** *On some engines it will be necessary to unscrew the bolt(s) that secure the timing belt cover to the housing assembly (see Chapter 2).* Recover the sealing ring which is fitted between the housing and block and discard it; a new one should be used on refitting **(see illustrations)**.

26 With the assembly on a bench, unscrew the retaining bolts and remove the pump from the housing **(see illustration)**. Discard the gasket, a new one must be used on refitting. Note it is not possible to overhaul the pump. If it is faulty, the unit must be renewed. Note the fitted position of the 'hammer head' bolt in the coolant pump housing.

Refitting

27 Ensure that the pump and housing mating surfaces are clean and dry and position a new gasket on the housing.

28 Fit the coolant pump to the housing and evenly tighten its retaining bolts to the specified torque setting. Ensure that the 'hammer head' pump-to-housing bolt (which also secures the belt cover in position) is fitted before the pump/housing assembly is bolted to the engine.

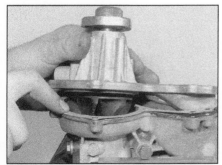

7.26 Unscrew the retaining bolts and remove the pump from the housing

29 Fit the new sealing ring to the housing assembly recess and refit the housing to the cylinder block. Refit the retaining studs/bolts (as applicable) and tighten them to the specified torque setting.
30 Connect the coolant hoses to the housing and securely tighten their retaining clips.
31 Refit the alternator/power steering pump bracket(s) and tighten the retaining nut/bolts to the specified torque setting.
32 Assemble the two halves of the coolant pump pulley and fit the V-belt over it. Refit the pulley and belt to the coolant pump and insert the pulley retaining bolts. Tighten the bolts to the specified torque setting, whilst rotating the pulley by hand to prevent the V-belt from being trapped.
33 Refit the power steering pump to the mounting bracket (see Chapter 10)
34 Refit the alternator (see Chapter 5A).
35 Refit the main auxiliary drivebelt as described in Chapter 2A.
36 Refit the viscous-coupled cooling fan unit as described in Section 5.
37 Refit the lock carrier as described in Chapter 11.
38 On completion refill the cooling system as described in the relevant Part of Chapter 1, then reconnect the battery.

Diesel engines

Note: *On diesel engines, new pump housing-to-cylinder block bolts/studs will be required on refitting.*

Removal

39 Disconnect the battery negative cable, then drain the cooling system as described in Chapter 1B.
40 Place the lock carrier in the service position, as described in Chapter 11.
41 Remove the main auxiliary drivebelt as described in the relevant part of Chapter 2B. Note that on vehicle so equipped, the air conditioning compressor drivebelt does not need to be removed.
42 Remove the viscous-coupled cooling fan unit as described in Section 5.
43 Counterhold the coolant pump pulley using a strap wrench, then unbolt the pulley from the pump hub and remove it.
44 Slacken and withdraw the coolant pump securing bolts. Carefully withdraw the pump from the cylinder block and recover the sealing ring **(see illustration)**.

Refitting

45 Ensure that the pump and housing mating surfaces are clean and dry, then position a new sealing ring on the pump.

46 Insert the pump retaining bolts and tighten them evenly and progressively to the specified torque.
47 Refit the main auxiliary drivebelt as described in Chapter 2B.
48 Refit the viscous-coupled cooling fan unit as described in Section 5.
49 Refit the lock carrier as described in Chapter 11.
50 On completion refill the cooling system as described in the relevant Part of Chapter 1, then reconnect the battery.

---

8 Heating and ventilation system - general information

1 The heating/ventilation system consists of a fully adjustable blower motor (housed behind the facia), face level vents in the centre and at each end of the facia, and air ducts to the front footwells.
2 The heater control unit is located in the facia, and the controls operate flap valves to deflect and mix the air flowing through the various parts of the heating/ventilation system. The flap valves are contained in the air distribution housing, which acts as a central distribution unit, passing air to the various ducts and vents.
3 Cold air enters the system through the grille at the rear of the engine compartment. If required, the airflow is boosted by the blower, and then flows through the various ducts, according to the settings of the controls. Stale air is expelled through ducts at the rear of the vehicle. If warm air is required, the cold air is passed over the heater matrix, which is heated by the engine coolant.
4 The outside air supply to the vehicle can be closed off which is useful to prevent unpleasant odours entering from outside the vehicle. This is achieved either by setting the blower motor switch to position 0 or by operating the recirculation switch (depending on model). This facility should only be used briefly, as the recirculated air inside the vehicle will soon become stale.

---

9 Heater/ventilation components - removal and refitting

General information

1 The information in this Section is only applicable to models equipped with a manually-operated conventional heating system, without air conditioning. On models with air conditioning, removal and refitting of the heater/ventilation/air conditioning system components is described in Section 11.

Heater/ventilation control unit

Removal

2 Disconnect the battery negative lead, then

7.44 Coolant pump mounting details - diesel models

1	Pulley hub	5	Seal
2	Bolt	6	Seal
3	Bolt	7	Housing
4	Coolant pump	8	Thermostat

9	Seal
10	Bolt
11	Thermostat housing cover

9.4 Carefully pull the knobs from the heater control rotary switch shafts

9.5a Remove the trim pieces . . .

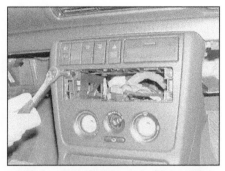

9.5b . . . then slacken and withdraw the screws from the corners of the audio unit aperture

remove the centre console as described in Chapter 11.

3 Remove the audio unit as described in Chapter 12.

4 Carefully pull the knobs from the heater control rotary switch shafts **(see illustration)**.

5 Remove the trim pieces, then slacken and withdraw the screws from the corners of the audio unit aperture **(see illustrations)**.

6 Using a small flat bladed screwdriver as a lever, carefully prise the trim panel from the front section of the centre console **(see illustration)**. Pad the screwdriver blade with tape to avoid damaging the trim panel and facia.

7 On later models, slacken and withdraw the screws from the corners of the heater control unit aperture. Note the fitted locations of the spring clips **(see illustration)**.

8 Remove the front section of the centre console, with reference to Chapter 11.

9 Undo the screws and lift off the centre console switch panel. The heater control unit can them be withdrawn from the rear of the switch panel after removing the securing screws. On later models, there is no need to remove the switch panel as the heater control unit releases from the front; note the fitted locations of the spring clips **(see illustrations)**.

10 Disconnect the wiring connector(s) from the rear of the panel **(see illustration)**.

11 Note the correct fitted location of each control cable (the cable end fittings are colour-coded) then detach them from the control panel **(see illustration)**. The outer cables are either clipped in position, and can

be released by carefully levering back the panel retaining tangs from below using a flat-bladed screwdriver, or are retained by a self-tapping screw.

12 Once the wiring and cable are detached, remove the control panel from the vehicle.

Refitting

13 Refitting is a reversal of removal, but ensure that the control cables (where fitted) are securely reconnected to their original locations. Check the operation of the controls prior to refitting the centre console. **Note:** *If the cable retaining tangs are damaged on removal, holes are provided in the control unit to secure the outer cable end fittings in position with self-tapping screws* **(see illustrations)**.

9.6 Carefully prise the trim panel from the front section of the centre console

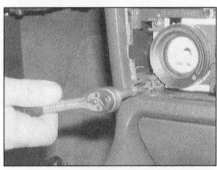

9.7 On later models, slacken and withdraw the screws from the corners of the heater control unit aperture

9.9a On later models, undo the screws and release the heater control unit from the switch panel

9.9b Note the fitted locations of the spring clips

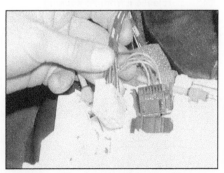

9.10 Unplug the wiring connector(s) from the rear of the panel

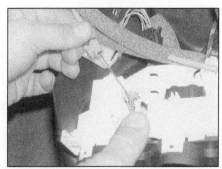

9.11 Note the correct fitted location of each control cable then detach them from the rear of the control panel

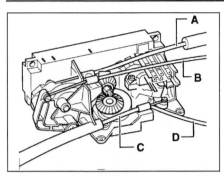

9.13a Heater control unit cable connection details

A *Footwell/defrost flap; RHD = green, LHD = White*
B *Central flap; RHD = yellow, LHD = Black*
C *Fresh air shut-off flap; RHD = Brown, LHD = Blue*
D *Temperature control flap; RHD = Orange, LHD = Red*

Blower motor

14 Disconnect the cable from the battery negative terminal.
15 Refer to Chapter 11 and remove the glovebox assembly from the facia.
16 On later models, remove the series resistor/thermal fuse unit, as described in the next sub-section.
17 Unplug the motor wiring connector from the series resistor/thermal fuse unit (early models) or the side of the motor housing (later models) **(see illustration)**.
18 On early models, release the retaining

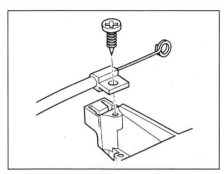

9.13b If the cable retaining tangs are damaged on removal, holes are provided in the control unit to secure the outer cable end fittings in position with self-tapping screws

catch, then rotate the motor unit clockwise and withdraw it from its housing.
19 On later models, grasp the motor mounting plate and slide it downwards to release it from its housing. Undo the securing screws and separate the motor from the mounting plate **(see illustrations)**.

Blower motor resistor/thermal fuse

Removal - early models

20 Remove the glovebox as described in Chapter 11. The resistor/fuse unit is mounted on the side of the blower motor housing.
21 Unplug the two wiring connectors from the side of the resistor/fuse unit baseplate.
22 Depress the retaining catches and

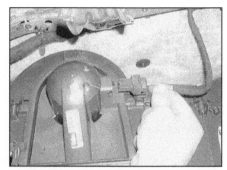

9.17 Unplug the motor wiring connector from the side of the motor housing (later models)

withdraw the unit from the blower motor housing.

Removal - later models

23 Remove the glovebox as described in Chapter 11. The resistor/fuse unit is mounted on the rear of the blower motor housing.
24 Unplug the wiring connector from the rear of the resistor/fuse unit baseplate **(see illustration)**.
25 Undo the securing screws and remove the baseplate from the blower motor housing **(see illustrations)**.
26 Drill out the two studs securing the resistor/fuse to the baseplate **(see illustration)**.
27 Release the securing catches, then unplug resistor/fuse unit from the baseplate and remove it from the vehicle.

Refitting

28 Refitting is the reverse of removal. On

9.19a On later models, grasp the motor mounting plate . . .

9.19b . . . and slide it downwards to release it from its housing

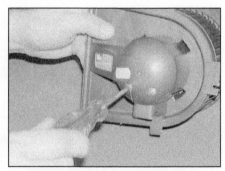

9.19c Undo the securing screws . . .

9.19d . . . and separate the motor from the mounting plate

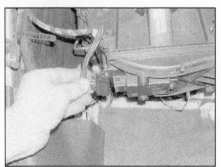

9.24 Unplug the wiring connector from the rear of the resistor/fuse unit baseplate

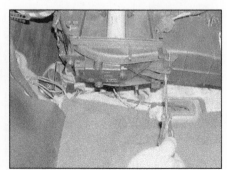

9.25a Undo the securing screws . . .

9.25b ... and remove the baseplate from the blower motor housing

9.26 Drill out the two studs securing the resistor/fuse to the baseplate

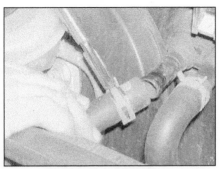

9.32a Release the clips ...

early models, it may be necessary to secure the resistor mounting plate in position with self tapping screws, using the lugs provided. On later models, secure the resistor/fuse unit to the baseplate using 3.2 x 10 mm screws.

Heater unit

Removal

29 Ensure that engine has cooled completely before starting work.
30 Open the bonnet and at the rear of the engine compartment, locate the heater matrix hoses and trace them back to the point where they connect to bulkhead stub pipes.
31 Place a draining container underneath the hoses, to catch the coolant that will escape when they are disconnected.
32 Apply proprietary hose clamps to both heater hoses, then release the clips and disconnect the hoses from the bulkhead stubs

(see illustrations). Allow the coolant from the heater circuit to collect in the draining container.
33 If you have access to a source of compressed air, apply it carefully at *low pressure* to the left hand bulkhead stub and blow the remainder of the coolant from the heater matrix.

 Warning: Always wear eye protection when working with compressed air.

34 If you do not have access to compressed air, bear in mind that a larger volume of coolant will remain in the heater circuit and that this may escape as the heater unit is removed from the inside of the car.
35 Prise the rubber grommet from the bulkhead aperture, then slide it off the pipe stubs and remove it from the engine compartment **(see illustration)**.
36 Remove the entire facia panel as

described in Chapter 11, noting that on early models, the heater unit is secured to the rear of the facia.

Models up to 1996

37 Unplug the wiring between the heater unit and the facia. Label each connection to avoid confusion on refitting.
38 Undo the securing screws and release the heater unit from the rear of the facia panel. Remove the unit from the vehicle, keeping it upright to avoid spilling the residual coolant.

Models from 1997

39 Undo the bolts and remove the left and right hand facia support brackets from the floorpan **(see illustrations)**.
40 Unclip the rear passenger air ducts from the front of the footwell vent unit. Remove the securing screws and detach the footwell vent unit from the base of the heater unit **(see illustrations)**.

9.32b ... and disconnect the heater hoses from the bulkhead stubs

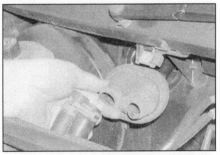

9.35 Prise the rubber grommet from the bulkhead aperture, then slide it off the pipe stubs

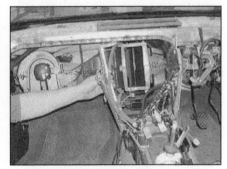

9.39a Undo the bolts and remove the left ...

9.39b ... and right hand facia support brackets from the floorpan

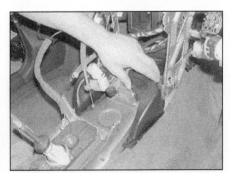

9.40a Unclip the rear passenger air ducts from the front of the footwell vent unit

9.40b Remove the securing screws and detach the footwell vent unit from the base of the heater unit

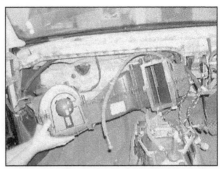

9.43 Slacken and withdraw the securing screws and lift the heater unit from the vehicle

41 Unplug the wiring heater unit wiring at the multiway connectors. Label each connection to avoid confusion on refitting. Release the wiring from the support clips on the side of the heater unit.

42 Slacken and withdraw the securing screws and lift the heater unit away from the bulkhead, towards the passenger's side of the vehicle. The heater unit gasket may be stuck to the bulkhead - carefully rock the housing from side-to-side until the gasket releases.

43 Remove the unit from the vehicle, keeping it upright to avoid spilling the residual coolant (see illustration).

Refitting

44 Refitting is the reverse of removal, noting the following points.
  a) Use a new housing gasket if the original is damaged.
  b) Ensure the ducts, elbows and gaiter are all securely joined to the housing and the wiring/cables are correctly routed before securing the housing in position.
  c) Ensure the coolant hoses are securely reconnected to the matrix; the feed hose from the cylinder head must be connected to the left hand union and the return hose to the coolant pump to the right hand union.
  d) Ensure that the rubber grommet is securely seated over the bulkhead stub pipes.
  e) On completion, top-up and bleed the cooling system as described in the relevant part of Chapter 1.

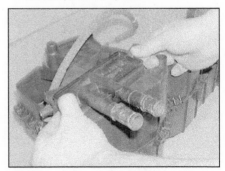

9.46b ... depress the locking catches ...

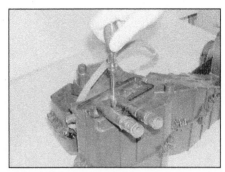

9.46a With the housing on a bench, undo the screw ...

Heater matrix

Removal

45 Remove the heater unit as described earlier in this Section. Note that on models up to 1996, the heater unit need not be detached from the facia panel.

46 With the housing on a bench, undo the screw, depress the locking catches and withdraw the heater matrix from the top of the heater unit (see illustration). Protect your hands as you do this - the matrix fins are sharp and can cause injury.

Refitting

47 Refitting is a reversal of removal. New heater matrices will be supplied with self-adhesive foam padding strips - these should be affixed to the edges of the core and the upper flange before the matrix is inserted into the heater unit.

Fresh air/recirculation flap valve motor (models from 1997)

Removal

48 Disconnect the negative cable from the battery terminal.

49 Remove the glove box assembly as described in Chapter 11.

50 The flap valve motor is located on the right hand side of the blower motor housing.

51 Unplug the wiring connector from the side of the motor.

52 Undo the securing screw and carefully withdraw the motor from the housing, manoeuvring the control lever through the housing aperture.

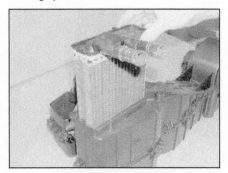

9.46c ... and withdraw the heater matrix from the top of the heater unit

Refitting

53 Refitting is a reversal of removal. If the position of the motor control lever makes refitting difficult, temporarily reconnect the battery and operate the recirculation switch, until the control lever is positioned horizontally with respect to the motor body.

---

10 Air conditioning system - general information and precautions

General information

1 An air conditioning system is available on certain models. It combines a conventional air heating system with an air cooling and dehumidifying system. This allows greater control over the temperature and humidity of the air inside the car, giving increased comfort and rapid window demisting.

2 The cooling side of the system works in the same way as a domestic refrigerator. Refrigerant gas, contained in a sealed network of alloy pipes, is drawn into a belt-driven compressor, and is forced through a condenser mounted on the front of the radiator. On entering the condenser, the refrigerant changes state from gas to liquid and releases heat, which is absorbed by the air flowing into the front of the engine compartment through the condenser. The liquid refrigerant passes through an expansion valve to an evaporator, where it changes from liquid under high pressure to gas under low pressure. This change in state is accompanied by a drop in temperature, which cools the evaporator. Air passing through the evaporator is cooled before flowing into the air distribution unit. The refrigerant then returns to the compressor, and the cycle begins again.

3 The cooled air passes to the air distribution unit, where it is blended with hot air blown through the heater matrix, to achieve the desired temperature in the passenger compartment. When the air conditioning system is operating in Automatic mode, a series of air valves controlled by servo motors automatically regulate the cabin temperature by blending hot and cold air.

4 The heating side of the system works in the same way as on models without air conditioning (see Section 9).

5 The operation of the system is managed by an electronic control unit, which controls the electric cooling fan, the compressor, and the facia-mounted warning light. Any problems with the system should be referred to a VAG dealer. The system has a built-in, self-diagnostic capability, but specialist equipment is needed to interpret the information it produces.

Precautions

6 When working on a vehicle equipped with air conditioning, it is necessary to observe

special precautions whenever dealing with any part of the air conditioning system, or its associated components. If for any reason the refrigerant lines must be disconnected, you must entrust this task to a VAG dealer or an air conditioning specialist. Similarly, the system can only be evacuated and recharged by a dealer or air conditioning specialist.

⚠️ **Warning: The air conditioning system contains a pressurised liquid refrigerant. If the system is discharged in an uncontrolled manner without the aid of specialist equipment, the refrigerant will boil as soon as it is exposed to the atmosphere, causing severe frostbite if it comes into contact unprotected skin. In addition, certain refrigerants, in the presence of a naked flame (including a lit cigarette), will oxidise to form a highly poisonous gas. It is therefore extremely dangerous to disconnect any part of the air conditioning system without specialised knowledge and equipment.**

7 Uncontrolled discharging of the refrigerant can also be damaging to the environment, as certain refrigerants contain CFCs.

8 Do not operate the air conditioning system if it is known to be short of refrigerant, as this will damage the compressor.

11 Air conditioning system components - removal and refitting

⚠️ **Warning: Do not attempt to discharge the refrigerant circuit yourself (refer to the precautions given in Section 10). Have the air conditioning system discharged by a qualified refrigeration engineer. On completion, have the engineer fit new O-rings to the line connections and evacuate and re-charge the system.**

Compressor

Removal

1 Disconnect the negative cable from the battery terminal.

2 Place the lock carrier in the service (see Chapter 11).

3 Have the air conditioning system discharged by a qualified engineer.

4 Remove the auxiliary drivebelt as described in the relevant part of Chapter 2.

5 Unscrew the retaining bolts and disconnect the refrigerant lines from the compressor. Remove the O-ring seals and discard them - new ones must be used on reconnection. Plug the open pipes and ports to prevent the ingress of moisture.

6 Unplug the wiring for the clutch unit, and where applicable, the shaft speed sensor at the connectors at the rear of the compressor.

7 Unscrew the three (Nippondenso compressor) or four (Zexel compressor) securing bolts from the front of the

compressor, then remove the compressor from its mounting bracket.

Refitting

8 Refitting is a reversal of the removal procedure; ensure that all fixings are tightened to the specified torque, where given. On completion, have the refrigerant engineer fit new O-rings to the line connections and then evacuate and re-charge the refrigerant circuit.

Evaporator/heater matrix housing

Caution: Before removing the evaporator/heater matrix housing, the air conditioning control system components must be set in a reference condition. This work should be entrusted to a VAG dealer as it requires access to dedicated test equipment.

Removal

9 Ensure that engine has cooled completely before starting work.

10 Have the air conditioning system discharged by a qualified engineer, then have the air conditioning control system components set in a reference condition by an Audi dealer.

11 Disconnect the negative cable from the battery terminal.

12 Open the bonnet and at the rear of the engine compartment, locate the heater matrix hoses and trace them back to the point where they connect to bulkhead stub pipes.

13 Place a draining container underneath the hoses, to catch the coolant that will escape when they are disconnected.

14 Apply proprietary hose clamps to both heater hoses, then slacken the clips and disconnect the hoses from the bulkhead stubs. Allow the coolant from the heater circuit to collect in the draining container.

15 If you have access to a source of compressed air, apply it carefully at *low pressure* to the left hand bulkhead stub and blow the remainder of the coolant from the heater matrix.

⚠️ **Warning: Always wear eye protection when working with compressed air.**

16 If you do not have access to compressed air, bear in mind that a larger volume of coolant will remain in the heater circuit and that this may escape as the housing is removed from the inside of the car.

17 Prise the rubber grommet from the bulkhead aperture, then slide it off the pipe stubs and remove it from the engine compartment.

18 Locate the aluminium air conditioning refrigerant pipes and trace them back to the engine compartment bulkhead. Unscrew the centre bolt and disconnect the pipes at the union. Remove the O-ring seals and discard them - new ones must be used on reconnection. Plug the open pipes to prevent the ingress of moisture.

19 Release the rubber grommet from the bulkhead aperture and slide it off the refrigerant pipe unions.

20 Unplug the wiring to the low pressure switch, then disconnect the control system vacuum supply hose. Tape both together so that they will pass easily through the bulkhead aperture when the housing is removed from the inside of the car.

21 Remove the entire facia panel as described in Chapter 11, noting that the evaporator/heater matrix housing is secured to the rear of the facia.

Models up to 1996

22 Unplug the wiring between the evaporator/heater matrix housing and the facia. Label each connection to avoid confusion on refitting.

23 Undo the securing screws and release the evaporator/heater matrix housing from the rear of the facia panel. Remove the housing from the vehicle, keeping it upright to avoid spilling the residual coolant.

Models from 1997

24 Unbolt the facia support brackets from the floorpan.

25 Unclip the rear passenger air ducts from the front of the footwell vent unit. Remove the securing screws and detach the footwell vent unit from the base of the evaporator/heater matrix housing.

26 Unplug the wiring for the evaporator/ heater matrix housing at the multiway connectors. Label each connection to avoid confusion on refitting. Release the wiring from the support clips on the side of the housing.

27 Slacken and withdraw the securing screws and lift the evaporator/heater matrix housing away from the bulkhead, towards the passenger's side of the vehicle. The housing gasket may be stuck to the bulkhead - carefully rock the housing from side-to-side until the gasket releases.

28 Remove the housing from the vehicle, keeping it upright to avoid spilling the residual coolant.

Refitting

29 Refitting is a reversal of removal. Refitting is the reverse of removal, noting the following points.

a) Use a new housing gasket if the original is damaged.

b) Ensure that the condensate drain pipe is correctly positioned on the rear of the evaporator/heater matrix housing.

c) Ensure the ducts, elbows and gaiter are all securely joined to the housing and the wiring/cables are correctly routed before securing the housing in position.

d) Ensure the coolant hoses are securely reconnected to the matrix; the feed hose from the cylinder head must be connected to the left hand union and the return hose to the coolant pump to the right hand union (with the vent hole incorporated).

e) *Ensure that the rubber grommets are securely seated in the bulkhead apertures.*
f) *Top-up and bleed the cooling system as described in the relevant part of Chapter 1.*
g) *On completion, have the refrigerant engineer fit new O-rings to the line connections and then evacuate and re-charge the refrigerant circuit.*

Blower motor

Removal

30 Disconnect the negative cable from the battery terminal.
31 Refer to Chapters 11 and 12, and carry out the following:
a) *Remove the glovebox from the facia*
b) *Remove the passenger airbag mounting bracket.*
32 Working under the facia in the passenger footwell, unplug the wiring connector from the rear of the blower motor unit.
33 Remove the four screws, then rotate the blower motor unit slightly and withdraw it from the heater matrix/evaporator housing. On models from 1997 onwards, the motor can now be detached from its baseplate by unplugging the wiring connectors and releasing the retaining catches.

Removal

34 Refitting is a reversal of removal.

Blower motor control unit

Removal

35 Disconnect the negative cable from the battery terminal.
36 Refer to Chapter 11 and carry out the following:
a) *Remove the glovebox from the facia*
b) *Remove the passenger airbag mounting bracket.*
37 The control unit is located to the right hand side of the blower motor unit.
38 Unplug the wiring connector from the unit, then undo the securing screw and withdraw the unit from the heater matrix/evaporator housing.

Refitting

39 Refitting is a reversal of removal.

Control system components

Caution: Before removing any of the air conditioning control system components, the system must be set in a reference condition. This work should be entrusted to an Audi dealer, as it requires access to dedicated test equipment.

Control panel

40 Have the air conditioning control system set in a reference condition by an Audi dealer.
41 Remove the audio unit as described in Chapter 12.
42 Undo the four securing screws, then using a small flat bladed screwdriver as a lever, detach the trim panel from the centre console.
43 Remove the two securing screws, recover the spring clips and withdraw the control panel from the centre console On later models, the control panel is secured in position with four spring clips and is removed by reaching through the audio unit aperture and pushing the control panel forwards.
44 Unplug the temperature sensor air ducting from the top of the control panel.
45 Depress the retaining catches and unplug the multiway connectors from the rear of the control panel. Remove the unit from the vehicle.
46 Refitting is a reversal of removal, noting the following points:
a) *Ensure that the air temperature sensor ducting is correctly reconnected.*
b) *Ensure that the trim securing clips are correctly positioned behind the control panel securing screws.*
c) *If the control panel has been renewed, it must be initialised by an Audi dealer using specialised test equipment before it can be operated.*

Flap valve positioning motors

47 Refer to Chapter 11 and remove the facia.
48 Remove the screws and detach the facia support bracket from the floorpan above the transmission tunnel.
49 Disconnect the footwell air distribution vent from the base of the evaporator/heater matrix housing.
50 The flap valve positioning motors are located on the side of the evaporator/heater matrix housing and is identified As follows:
a) *Footwell/defroster valve - yellow wiring connector.*
b) *Temperature flap valve - violet wiring connector.*
c) *Centre flap valve - green wiring connector.*
51 Unplug the wiring connector, then disconnect the operation lever from the motor shaft.
52 Remove the retaining screws and withdraw the motor from the housing. Note that the footwell/defroster valve is retained by a bracket.
53 Refitting is a reversal of removal. On

completion, the air conditioning control system must be initialised by a Audi dealer using specialised test equipment.

Temperature sensors

54 On early models, the interior temperature sensor is integrated into the centre console trim panel. Removal is as follows.
55 Undo the four securing screws, then using a small flat bladed screwdriver as a lever, detach the trim panel from the centre console.
56 Disconnect the air ducting from the rear of the sensor, and remove the panel/sensor from the vehicle.
57 The sensor blower motor (mounted behind the centre console front panel, to the left of the sensor can be removed by disconnecting the wiring and removing the securing screws.
58 Refitting is a reversal of removal.
59 On later models, additional sensors are mounted in the individual air ducts leading to the footwell and face level vents. These can be removed by disconnecting the wiring, then rotating the sensor unit and withdrawing it from the ducting.

Sunlight photo-sensor

60 Carefully prise the cover panel from the centre windscreen defroster vent.
61 Undo the screw and withdraw the sensor form the vent. Disconnect the wiring and tie the connector back to prevent it from disappearing down inside the facia.
62 Refitting is a reversal of removal.

Vacuum reservoir

63 Remove the evaporator/heater matrix housing as described earlier in this Section.
64 Disconnect the vacuum hoses from the ports on the side of the vacuum unit. Make a careful note of their order of connection to aid refitting.
65 Remove the screws and detach the vacuum reservoir from the housing.
66 Refitting is a reversal of removal.

Vacuum diaphragm unit

67 Remove the evaporator/heater matrix housing as described earlier in this Section.
68 Undo the vacuum diaphragm unit securing screws.
69 Disconnect the diaphragm unit shaft from the actuator lever.
70 Remove the unit from the evaporator/heater matrix housing.
71 Refitting is a reversal of removal. Adjust the length of the diaphragm unit shaft to 50 mm before reconnecting it to the actuator lever.

Chapter 4 Part A:
Fuel system - multipoint petrol injection

Contents

Degrees of difficulty

Easy, suitable for novice with little experience	Fairly easy, suitable for beginner with some experience	Fairly difficult, suitable for competent DIY mechanic	Difficult, suitable for experienced DIY mechanic	Very difficult, suitable for expert DIY or professional

Specifications

System type

Engine code AHL (1595 cc)	Simos
All other engines	Bosch Motronic 3.2 injection

Recommended fuel

Minimum octane rating:
Engine codes ADP, AHL, ADR, APT, APW, AEB, APU, AJL:	
For best performance	95 RON
Slight loss of power	91 RON
Engine code AFY (not fitted with catalytic converter)	88 RON (unleaded or leaded)

Fuel system data

Fuel pump type	Electric, immersed in fuel tank
Fuel pump delivery rate (battery voltage 12 V)	260 cm³/15 secs
Regulated fuel pressure at idling speed:	
Vacuum hose fitted	3.5 bar (approx)
Vacuum hose disconnected	4.0 bar (approx)
Minimum holding pressure (after 10 minutes)	2.5 bar
Engine idle speed (non-adjustable, electronically controlled):	
Engine codes ADP, ADR (to 06/96)	820 to 900 rpm
Engine codes ADR (from 07/96), AFY, AEB, AJL	780 to 900 rpm
Engine code AHL	760 to 960 rpm
Engine codes APT, APW	810 to 910 rpm
Engine code APU	740 to 860 rpm
Idle CO content (non-adjustable, electronically controlled)	0.1 to 1.1 %
Injector electrical resistance (at room temperature):	
Engine code ADP	14 to 16 ohms
Engine codes ADR, AEB, AFY, AEB, APU, AJL	11 to 13 ohms
Engine code AHL	14 to 17 ohms
Engine code APT, APW	12 to 13 ohms
Engine speed sender resistance:	
Engine code ADP, ADR, AFY, AEB, APU, AJL	480 to 1000 ohms
Engine code AHL	730 to 1000 ohms
Engine code APT, APW	450 to 1000 ohms

Torque wrench settings

	Nm	lbf ft
Catalytic converter to turbocharger	30	22
Coolant pipe to inlet manifold (ADP, AEB, APU, AJL)	10	7
Coolant return pipe to turbocharger	30	22
Coolant supply pipe to turbocharger	25	18
Fuel rail to inlet manifold	10	7
Fuel tank filler neck	25	18
Fuel tank mounting bolts	25	18
Inlet manifold:		
ADP, AHL	20	15
ADR, AFY, AEB, APU, AJL	10	7
Inlet manifold support brackets	20	15
Lambda sensor	50	37
Oil return pipe to turbocharger	10	7
Oil supply pipe to turbocharger	25	18
Turbocharger bracket:		
To turbocharger	40	30
To cylinder block	45	33
Turbocharger to exhaust manifold	35	26

1 General information and precautions

General information

The Bosch and Simos multipoint petrol injection systems described in this Chapter are self-contained engine management systems, which control both the fuel injection and ignition (see illustrations 1.1a to 1.1e). This Chapter deals with the fuel system components only, however refer to Chapter 5B for details of the ignition system.

The fuel injection system comprises a fuel tank, an electric fuel pump, a fuel filter, fuel supply and return lines, a throttle body, an air mass sensor, a fuel rail and four electronic injectors, a fuel pressure regulator, and an electronic control unit (ECU), together with its associated sensors, actuators and wiring. The component layout varies according to the system - refer to the relevant Section for details.

A turbocharger is fitted to engine codes AEB, APU and AJL.

The air mass sensor is located on the air cleaner outlet to the throttle body. Fuel is supplied under pressure to a fuel rail, and then passes to four electronic injectors. The duration of the injection period is determined by the ECU which switches the injectors on and off as required.

The fuel pump delivers a constant supply of fuel through a cartridge filter. The fuel is supplied to a fuel rail, and the fuel pressure regulator maintains a constant fuel pressure to the fuel injectors and returns excess fuel to the tank via the return line. The constant fuel flow system helps to reduce fuel temperature and prevents vaporisation.

The ECU controls starting and warm-up enrichment together with idle speed regulation and Lambda control. Idle speed control is achieved partly by an electronic throttle valve positioning module, on the side of the throttle body and partly by the ignition

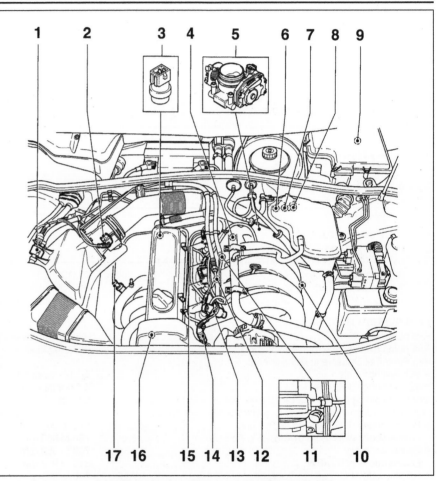

1.1a Simos components on the engine code AHL

1 Activated charcoal canister valve
2 Airflow meter
3 Coolant temperature sensor
4 Ignition coils and output
5 Throttle body
6 Lambda probe wiring connector
7 Engine speed sensor wiring connector
8 Knock sensor wiring connector
9 ECU
10 Inlet air temperature sender
11 Engine speed sender
12 Knock sensor
13 Fuel pressure regulator
14 Hall sender wiring
15 Injectors
16 Hall sender
17 Lambda probe

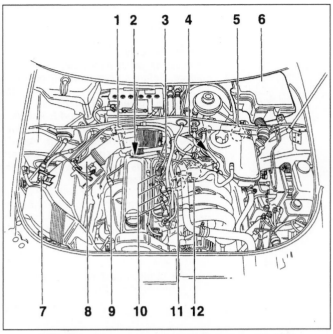

1.1b Motronic components on the engine code ADP

1 Ignition coil
2 Coolant temperature sender
3 Distributor with Hall sender
4 Throttle valve potentiometer
5 Wiring connectors for Lambda probe, engine speed sender and knock sensor
6 ECU
7 Activated charcoal filter solenoid
8 Airflow meter
9 Lambda probe
10 Injectors
11 Knock sensor
12 Engine speed sender

1.1c Motronic components on the engine code ADR

1 Ignition coils and HT leads
2 Coolant temperature sender
3 Throttle valve potentiometer
4 Wiring connectors for Lambda probe, engine speed sender and knock sensors 1 and 2
5 ECU
6 Activated charcoal filter solenoid
7 Airflow meter
8 Lambda probe
9 Injectors
10 Hall sender
11 Knock sensor 1
12 Knock sensor 2
13 Engine speed sender

system. Manual adjustment of the idle speed is not possible.

Inlet air is drawn into the engine through the air cleaner, which contains a renewable paper filter element.

The exhaust gas oxygen content is constantly monitored by the ECU via the Lambda sensor, which is mounted on the exhaust manifold. The ECU then uses this information to adjust the air/fuel ratio. Manual adjustment of the idle speed exhaust CO content is not possible. A catalytic converter is fitted to the exhaust system on all except very early models. A fuel evaporative control system is fitted, and the ECU controls the operation of the activated charcoal canister - refer to Chapter 4C for further details.

It should be noted that fault diagnosis of all the engine management systems described in this Chapter is only possible with dedicated electronic test equipment. Problems with the system operation should therefore be referred to an Audi/VAG dealer for assessment. Once the fault has been identified, the removal and refitting sequences detailed in the following Sections will then allow the appropriate component(s) to be renewed as required.

Note: *Throughout this Chapter, vehicles are frequently referred to by their engine code, rather than by engine capacity - refer to Chapter 2A for engine code listings.*

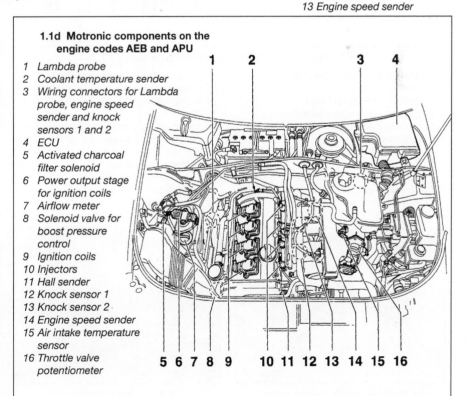

1.1d Motronic components on the engine codes AEB and APU

1 Lambda probe
2 Coolant temperature sender
3 Wiring connectors for Lambda probe, engine speed sender and knock sensors 1 and 2
4 ECU
5 Activated charcoal filter solenoid
6 Power output stage for ignition coils
7 Airflow meter
8 Solenoid valve for boost pressure control
9 Ignition coils
10 Injectors
11 Hall sender
12 Knock sensor 1
13 Knock sensor 2
14 Engine speed sender
15 Air intake temperature sensor
16 Throttle valve potentiometer

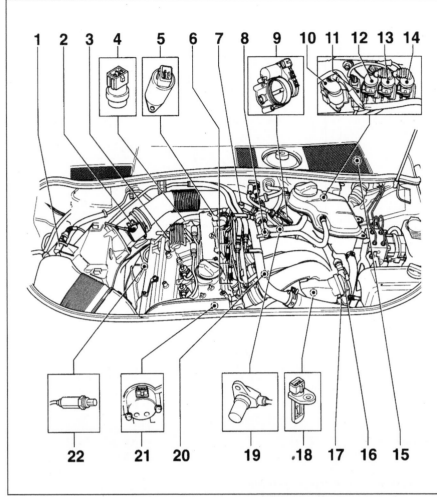

1.1e **Motronic components on the engine code APT**

1 *Activated charcoal filter solenoid*	12 *Wiring connector for speed sender*
2 *Airflow meter*	13 *Wiring connector for knock sensor 2*
3 *Ignition coils and HT leads*	14 *Wiring connector for knock sensor 1*
4 *Coolant temperature sensor*	15 *ECU*
5 *Camshaft adjustment valve*	16 *Inlet manifold change-over vacuum unit*
6 *Injectors*	17 *Inlet manifold change-over valve*
7 *Fuel pressure regulator*	18 *Inlet air temperature sensor*
8 *Knock sensor 2*	19 *Engine speed sender*
9 *Throttle valve potentiometer*	20 *Knock sensor 1*
10 *Wiring connector for Lambda probe*	21 *Hall sender*
11 *Wiring connector for oil sensors*	22 *Lambda probe*

2 Air cleaner and inlet ducts - removal and refitting

Removal

1 Remove the air cleaner cover and air ducts, then prise open the retaining clips and lift the upper cover from the air cleaner body (**see illustrations**). Note that the airflow meter is attached to the upper cover.

2 Remove the air cleaner filter element (see Chapter 1A for more details).

3 Loosen the clip and disconnect the air duct from the airflow meter on the air cleaner. Also disconnect the crankcase ventilation hoses (**see illustrations**).

4 Disconnect the wiring from the airflow meter and remove the upper cover from the engine compartment. If necessary, remove the airflow meter from the upper cover with reference to Section 4 or 5.

5 Unscrew the mounting bolt and remove the air cleaner body from the engine compartment (**see illustrations**). If necessary remove the rubber mountings from the body. Check the condition of the mountings and renew them if necessary.

6 On non-turbo models, remove the air duct from between the air cleaner and throttle body by releasing the clips (**see illustrations**).

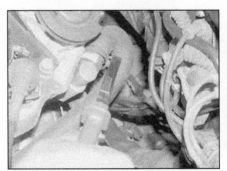

2.1a **Remove the air cleaner cover . . .**

2.1b **. . . side air duct . . .**

2.1c **. . . and front air duct**

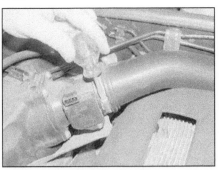

2.3a Loosen the clip . . .

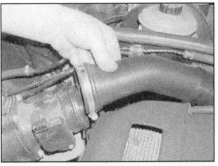

2.3b . . . and disconnect the air duct from the airflow meter

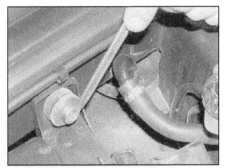

2.5a Unscrew the bolt . . .

2.5b . . . and remove the air cleaner body from the engine compartment

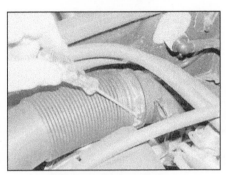

2.6a Loosen the clips . . .

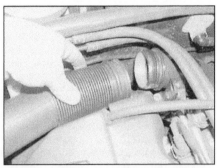

2.6b . . . and remove the air duct from between the air cleaner and throttle body

7 On turbo models, remove the air duct from between the air cleaner and intercooler

Refitting

8 Refitting is a reversal of removal.

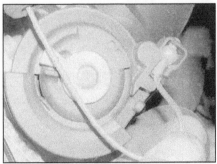

3.1 Disconnecting the accelerator cable from the segment

3.2 Removing the accelerator outer cable from the support

3 Accelerator cable -
removal, refitting and adjustment

Note: *Models fitted with engine codes APT, APU and APW do not have an accelerator cable, and there is no mechanical link between the throttle pedal and throttle body. An electric servomotor on the side of the throttle body operates the throttle valve and the accelerator pedal incorporates position senders.*

Removal

1 Disconnect the accelerator cable from the segment on the throttle body by turning the segment to open the throttle, then releasing the cable and end fitting **(see illustration)**.
2 Note the position of the adjustment clip in

the ferrule at the end of the outer cable, then slide the cable from the rubber grommet on the support **(see illustration)**. Remove the grommet from the support.
3 Release the accelerator cable from its supports in the engine compartment.
4 Inside the vehicle, remove the facia panel lower trim panel/storage compartment below the steering wheel.
5 Reach up under the facia, and disconnect the inner cable from the top of the accelerator pedal.
6 On automatic transmission models, disconnect the kick-down switch wiring from the outer cable on the engine compartment rear panel in the engine compartment.
7 At the engine compartment rear panel, slide out the cable retaining clip **(see illustrations)**. **Note:** *On manual transmission models, the clip is located behind the panel.*

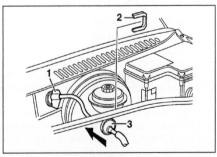

3.7a Accelerator cable retainer (1), clip (2) and grommet (3) on manual transmission models

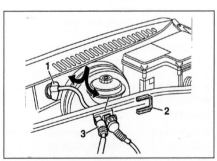

3.7b Accelerator cable retainer (1), clip (2) and grommet (3) on automatic transmission models

8 At the bulkhead below the windscreen, turn the cable retainer anticlockwise a quarter turn (90°) to align the triangular clip with its hole, then withdraw the accelerator cable into the engine compartment and remove it from the vehicle.

Refitting

9 Refitting is a reversal of removal, but adjust the cable as follows. Make sure that the outer cable is located securely in the bulkhead.

Adjustment

10 At the throttle body, adjust the position of the metal clip on the outer cable so that when the accelerator pedal is depressed fully, the throttle valve is held wide open to its end stop **(see illustration)**. With the pedal fully released, there must be a maximum of 1 mm slack in the inner cable.

11 On automatic transmission models, check that the kick-down switch is heard to click audibly as the cable reaches the end of its stroke. A further check can be made on automatic transmission models using an ohmmeter. Disconnect the wiring from the kick-down switch on the accelerator cable at the rear engine compartment panel and connect an ohmmeter across the two terminals. With the throttle pedal released, infinity resistance should be shown on the ohmmeter, indicating that the switch contacts are separated. Have an assistant slowly depress the throttle pedal. When the pedal is nearly at the end of its stroke, the reading must show zero resistance indicating that the switch internal contacts have closed at the kick-down point.

---

4 Bosch Motronic engine management system - component removal and refitting

Note: *Observe the precautions in Section 1 before working on any component in the fuel system. The ignition must be switched off at all times.*

Airflow meter

Removal

1 The airflow meter is located on the air cleaner upper cover. First prise open the retaining clips and lift the upper cover from the air cleaner body.
2 Loosen the clip and disconnect the air duct from the airflow meter.
3 Disconnect the wiring from the airflow meter.
4 Undo the mounting screws then remove the airflow meter. Recover the gasket.

Refitting

5 Refitting is a reversal of removal, but fit a new gasket or O-ring as applicable.

Throttle valve potentiometer

Note: *The potentiometer is matched to the throttle body during manufacture, and is not*

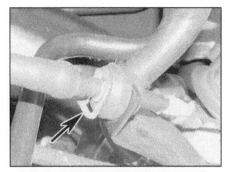

3.10 Accelerator cable adjustment clip

available separately - if defective, a complete throttle body assembly will be required.

Removal

6 Unplug the harness connector from the potentiometer/throttle switch.
7 Remove the retaining screws and lift the potentiometer/throttle switch away from the throttle body. Recover the O-ring seal.

Refitting

8 Refitting is a reversal of removal, noting the following:
  a) *Renew the O-ring seal if necessary.*
  b) *Ensure that the drive engages correctly with the throttle spindle extension.*
  c) *On vehicles with automatic transmission, the potentiometer must be matched to the automatic transmission Electronic Control Unit (ECU) - this operation requires access to dedicated electronic test equipment, refer to an Audi/VAG dealer for advice.*

Inlet manifold air temperature sensor

Removal

9 Where fitted, the sensor is threaded into the inlet manifold near the throttle body.
10 Unplug the harness connector from the sensor.
11 Unscrew the bolts and remove the sensor from the manifold.

Refitting

12 Refitting is a reversal of removal, however observe the correct tightening torque.

Throttle valve positioner

Removal and refitting

13 The throttle valve positioner is incorporated in a multiple housing incorporating the throttle valve potentiometer and idling switch. Besides controlling the idling speed of the engine, the positioner also functions as a damper when the throttle is closed.
14 The removal and refitting procedure is similar to that described earlier in this Section for the potentiometer. However, note that when the voltage supply to the unit is interrupted, the throttle valve moves into a mechanically set basic position. After refitting the unit, the basic setting procedure must be

carried out by an Audi/VAG dealer using the test instrument VAG 1551 or 1552.
15 Do not attempt to open the multiple housing.

Road speed sensor

Removal and refitting

16 Where fitted, the road speed sensor is incorporated in the speedometer and the signal is processed by the Motronic control unit. The signal is used to stabilise the idling and to minimise the jolting effect when the automatic transmission changes gear. Any fault with the sensor must be checked by an Audi/VAG dealer, and if necessary the speedometer unit in the instrument panel should be renewed with reference to Chapter 12.

Coolant temperature sensor

Removal

17 The coolant temperature sensor is located on the rear of the cylinder head on all engines.
18 Drain approximately one quarter of the coolant from the engine with reference to Chapter 1A.
19 Disconnect the wiring from the sensor.
20 Unscrew the sensor or extract the retaining clip and remove the sensor. Recover the sealing washer.

Refitting

21 Refitting is a reversal of removal, but fit a new washer. Where applicable, tighten the sensor securely. Refer to Chapter 1A and top-up the cooling system.

Engine speed sensor

Removal

22 The engine speed sensor is mounted on the rear, left-hand side of the cylinder block, adjacent to the mating surface of the block and transmission bellhousing, just behind the oil filter. If necessary, drain the engine oil and remove the oil filter and cooler to improve access with reference to Chapter 1A.
23 Unplug the harness connector from the sensor.
24 Unscrew the retaining bolt and withdraw the sensor from the cylinder block.

Refitting

25 Refitting is a reversal of removal.

Throttle body

26 On models with an accelerator cable, refer to Section 3 and detach the accelerator cable from the throttle valve lever.
27 Loosen the clips and detach the inlet air ducting from the throttle body.
28 Unplug the harness connector from the throttle potentiometer.
29 Disconnect the vacuum hose from the port on the throttle body, then where necessary release the wiring harness from the guide clip.
30 Unscrew and remove the through-bolts, then lift the throttle body away from the inlet manifold. Recover and discard the gasket.

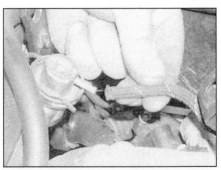

4.34 Disconnecting the vacuum hose from the fuel pressure regulator

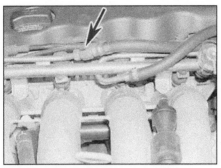

4.36 Fuel supply line union

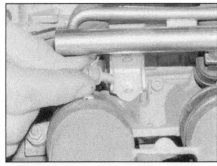

4.40a Unscrew the mounting bolts . . .

4.40b . . . and withdraw the fuel rail with injectors from the inlet manifold

4.41a Pull out the clip . . .

4.41b . . . and withdraw the injectors from the fuel rail

31 If required, refer to the relevant sub-Section and remove the throttle potentiometer.

Refitting

32 Refitting is a reversal of removal, noting the following:

a) *Use a new throttle body-to-inlet manifold gasket.*
b) *Ensure that all vacuum hoses and electrical connectors are refitted securely.*
c) *Where applicable, refer to Section 3 and adjust the accelerator cable.*

Fuel injectors and fuel rail

Removal

33 Disconnect the battery negative (earth) lead (see Chapter 5A).
34 Disconnect the vacuum hose from the fuel pressure regulator on the fuel rail **(see illustration)**.
35 Temporarily remove the fuel tank filler cap and refit it in order to release any pressure.
36 Wrap some rag around the fuel supply line union located over the fuel rail **(see illustration)**, and also place a suitable container beneath the union to catch any spilt fuel. Unscrew the union nut while holding the union bolt with another spanner, and allow the fuel to drain into the container. Remove the rag.
37 Unscrew the return union and disconnect the return fuel line.
38 Disconnect the wiring from each of the injectors. Label the wiring to aid correct refitting later.
39 On engine codes ADR, AEB and APU dis-

connect the wiring from the Hall sender.
40 Unscrew the mounting bolts, then carefully lift the fuel rail together with the injectors from the inlet manifold **(see illustrations)**.
41 With the assembly on the bench, pull out the clips and release each of the injectors from the fuel rail. Recover the O-ring seals **(see illustrations)**.

Refitting

42 Refit the injectors and fuel rail by following the removal procedure in reverse, noting the following points:

a) *Renew the injector O-ring seals, and smear them with a little clean engine oil before fitting them. When fitting the front O-ring, do not remove the plastic cap from the head of the injector but leave it in position and lift the O-ring over it.*

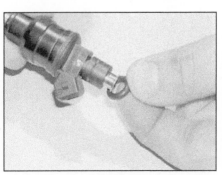

4.41c Remove the O-ring seals from the injectors

b) *Ensure that the injector retaining clips are securely seated.*
c) *Check that the fuel supply and return lines are reconnected correctly. Check the sealing washers and if necessary renew them.*
d) *Check that all vacuum and electrical connections are remade correctly and securely.*
e) *Reconnect the battery as described in Chapter 5A.*
f) *On completion, start the engine and check for fuel leaks.*

Fuel pressure regulator

Removal

43 Remove the engine top cover where necessary, then depressurise the fuel system as described in Section 9.
44 Disconnect the vacuum hose from the pressure regulator **(see illustration)**.

4.44 Disconnecting the vacuum hose from the pressure regulator

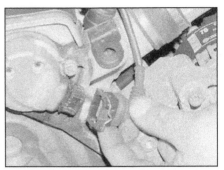

4.49 Disconnecting the wiring from the Hall sender

45 Place a cloth rag beneath the regulator to catch any spilt fuel.

46 Pull out the retaining spring clip, then lift the regulator from the fuel rail. Recover the O-ring seals.

Refitting

47 Refit the fuel pressure regulator by following the removal procedure in reverse, but renew the O-ring seals and ensure that the regulator retaining clip is secure.

Hall sender

Note: *This sub-Section does not cover the Hall sender removal on engine code ADP, which is located in the distributor.*

Removal

48 Remove the timing belt outer cover with reference to Chapter 2A, Section 4.

49 Release the clip and disconnect the wiring multiplug from the Hall sender **(see illustration)**.

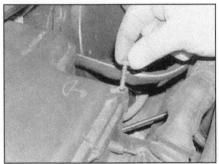

4.60a Undo the screws . . .

4.61a Release the spring retainer . . .

4.52 Lambda sensor on engine code ADR

50 Unscrew the mounting bolts and withdraw the Hall sender from the front of the cylinder head. Recover the gasket.

Refitting

51 Refitting is a reversal of removal, but renew the gasket and tighten the mounting bolts securely.

Lambda sensor

Removal

52 Except on engine codes AEB, APU and AJL (turbocharged), the Lambda sensor is located on the exhaust manifold on the right-hand side of the engine **(see illustration)**. On engine codes AEB, APU and AJL, the sensor is located on the top of the catalytic converter which is attached to the rear of the turbocharger on the right-hand side of the engine.

4.60b . . . and lift off the ECU cover

4.61b . . . to release the electronic control unit

53 The wiring connector for the Lambda sensor is located on the left-hand side of the bulkhead, beneath the coolant expansion tank. Undo the tank mounting screws and disconnect the low coolant wiring, then position the tank to one side. **Do not** disconnect any of the coolant hoses from the tank. Disconnect the Lambda wiring and release the cables from the plastic ties.

54 Unscrew and remove the sensor, taking care to avoid damaging the sensor probe as it is removed. **Note:** *As the wiring flying lead remains connected to the sensor, a special slotted socket may be used to remove the sensor.*

Refitting

55 Apply a little anti-seize grease to the sensor threads, but avoid contaminating the probe tip. **Note:** *New Lambda sensors may be supplied with fitting paste on the threads.*

56 Refit the sensor and tighten it to the correct torque.

57 Reconnect the wiring and secure with the plastic ties.

Electronic control unit (ECU)

Caution: Always wait at least 30 seconds after switching off the ignition before disconnecting the wiring from the ECU. When the wiring is disconnected, all the learned values are erased, however any contents of the fault memory are retained. After reconnecting the wiring, the basic settings must be reinstated by an Audi/VAG dealer using a special test instrument. Note also that if the ECU is renewed, the identification of the new ECU must be transferred to the immobiliser control unit by an Audi/VAG dealer.

Removal

58 The electronic control unit is located on the bulkhead at the rear of the engine compartment. On RHD models it is on the right-hand side, and on LHD models it is on the left-hand side.

59 Disconnect the battery negative (earth) lead (see Chapter 5A).

60 Undo the screws and lift off the cover **(see illustrations)**. **Note:** *On early LHD models, a hole is provided in the cowl panel for access to the rear mounting bolt, however on later models it is necessary to unclip the cowl panel for access to the bolt.*

61 Release the spring retainer with a screwdriver and lift up the electronic control unit **(see illustrations)**.

62 Prise open the clip and release the wiring connector from the ECU.

 Warning: Wait a minimum of 30 seconds after switching off the ignition, before disconnecting the ECU wiring connector.

63 Withdraw the ECU from the bulkhead.

Refitting

64 Refitting is a reversal of removal, but press the clip down until it snaps into position

4.64 Firmly press down the ECU retaining clip

(see illustration). Reconnect the battery as described in Chapter 5A.

5 Simos engine management system - component removal and refitting

Note: *Observe the precautions in Section 1 before working on any component in the fuel system. The ignition must be switched off at all times.*

Airflow meter

Removal

1 Disconnect the battery negative (earth) lead (see Chapter 5A). Also remove the engine top cover where necessary.
2 With reference to Section 2, slacken the clips and disconnect the air ducting from the airflow meter, at the rear of the air cleaner housing.
3 Unplug the harness connector from the airflow meter.
4 Remove the retaining screws and extract the meter from the air cleaner housing. Recover the O-ring seal.
Caution: Handle the airflow meter carefully - its internal components are easily damaged.

Refitting

5 Refitting is a reversal of removal. Renew the O-ring seal if it appears damaged.

Throttle valve potentiometer

6 The throttle valve potentiometer is an integral part of the throttle body - refer to the information in the relevant sub-Section.

Inlet air temperature sensor

Removal

7 The sensor is mounted on the left-hand rear of the inlet manifold.
8 Disconnect the wiring from the sensor.
9 Unscrew the sensor from the inlet manifold, and recover the O-ring seal.

Refitting

10 Refitting is a reversal of removal but fit a new O-ring seal and tighten the sensor securely.

Road speed sensor

11 The road speed sensor is mounted on the transmission - refer to Chapter 7A.

Coolant temperature sensor

Removal

12 The coolant temperature sensor is mounted in the coolant outlet elbow on the rear of the cylinder head. Remove the engine top cover where necessary.
13 Disconnect the wiring from the sensor.
14 Refer to Chapter 1A, and drain approximately one quarter of the coolant from the engine.
15 Extract the retaining clip and lift the sensor from the coolant elbow - be prepared for an amount of coolant loss. Recover the O-ring.

Refitting

16 Refit the sensor by reversing the removal procedure, using a new O-ring. Refer to Chapter 1A and top-up the cooling system.

Engine speed sensor

Removal

17 The engine speed sensor is mounted on the rear, left-hand side of the cylinder block, adjacent to the mating surface of the block and transmission bellhousing, just behind the oil filter. If necessary, drain the engine oil and remove the oil filter and cooler to improve access with reference to Chapter 1A.
18 Unplug the harness connector from the sensor.
19 Unscrew the retaining bolt and withdraw the sensor from the cylinder block.

Refitting

20 Refitting is a reversal of removal.

Throttle body

Removal

21 Refer to Section 4 and detach the accelerator cable from the throttle valve lever.
22 Slacken the clips and detach the inlet air ducting from the throttle body.
23 Unplug the harness connector from the throttle positioning valve module.
24 Disconnect the vacuum hose from the port on the throttle body, then release the wiring harness from the guide clip.
25 Refer to Chapter 3, and drain approximately one quarter of the coolant from the engine. Slacken the clips and disconnect the coolant hoses from the ports on the throttle body, making a careful note of their fitted positions.
26 Disconnect the charcoal filter emission control system vacuum hose from the port on the throttle body.
27 Unscrew and remove the bolts, then lift the throttle body away from the inlet manifold. Recover and discard the gasket.

Refitting

28 Refitting is a reversal of removal, noting the following:
a) Use a new throttle body-to-inlet manifold gasket.
b) Observe the correct tightening torque when refitting the throttle body bolts.
c) Ensure that all the vacuum hoses and electrical connectors are refitted securely.
d) Refer to Chapter 1A and top-up the cooling system.
e) Check and if necessary adjust the accelerator cable.

Fuel injectors and fuel rail

Removal

29 Disconnect the battery negative (earth) lead (see Chapter 5A). Also remove the engine top cover where necessary.
30 Disconnect the vacuum hose from the fuel pressure regulator on the fuel rail.
31 Temporarily remove the fuel tank filler cap and refit it in order to release any pressure.
32 Wrap some rag around the fuel supply line union located over the fuel rail, and also place a suitable container beneath the union to catch any spilt fuel. Unscrew the union nut while holding the union bolt with another spanner, and allow the fuel to drain into the container. Remove the rag.
33 Unscrew the return union and disconnect the return fuel line.
34 Disconnect the wiring from each of the injectors. Label the wiring to aid correct refitting later.
35 Unscrew the mounting bolts, then carefully lift the fuel rail together with the injectors from the inlet manifold.
36 With the assembly on the bench, pull out the clips and release each of the injectors from the fuel rail. Recover the O-ring seals.

Refitting

37 Refit the injectors and fuel rail by following the removal procedure in reverse, noting the following points:
a) Renew the injector O-ring seals if they appear worn or damaged.
b) Ensure that the injector retaining clips are securely seated.
c) Check that the fuel supply and return hoses are reconnected correctly. Check the sealing washers and if necessary renew them.
d) Check that all vacuum and electrical connections are remade correctly and securely.
e) Reconnect the battery as described in Chapter 5A.
f) On completion, start the engine and check for fuel leaks.

Fuel pressure regulator

Removal

38 Remove the engine top cover where necessary, then depressurise the fuel system as described in Section 9.

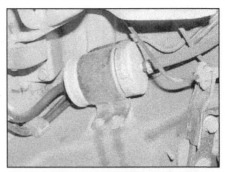

6.1 Fuel filter situated underneath the rear of the vehicle

39 Disconnect the vacuum hose from the pressure regulator.

40 Place a cloth rag beneath the regulator to catch any spilt fuel.

41 Pull out the retaining spring clip, then lift the regulator from the fuel rail. Recover the O-ring seals.

Refitting

42 Refit the fuel pressure regulator by following the removal procedure in reverse, but renew the O-ring seals and ensure that the regulator retaining clip is secure.

Hall sender

Removal

43 Remove the camshaft sprocket with reference to Chapter 2A

44 Note the location of the Hall sender and if necessary mark it in relation to the cylinder head. Disconnect the wiring from the sender.

45 Unbolt the rear timing cover from the cylinder head.

46 Unscrew the remaining bolts and remove the Hall sender from the cylinder head.

Refitting

47 Refitting is a reversal of removal, but make sure that the sender base plate is central before tightening the retaining bolts.

Lambda sensor

Removal

48 The Lambda sensor is located on the exhaust manifold on the right-hand side of the engine.

49 The wiring connector for the Lambda sensor is located on the left-hand side of the bulkhead, beneath the coolant expansion tank.

50 Undo the tank mounting screws and disconnect the low coolant wiring, then position the tank to one side. **Do not** disconnect any of the coolant hoses from the tank. Disconnect the Lambda wiring and release the cables from the plastic ties.

51 Unscrew and remove the sensor, taking care to avoid damaging the sensor probe as it is removed. **Note:** *As the wiring flying lead remains connected to the sensor, a special slotted socket may be used to remove the sensor.*

Refitting

52 Apply a little anti-seize grease to the sensor threads, but avoid contaminating the probe tip. **Note:** *New Lambda sensors may be supplied with fitting paste on the threads.*

53 Refit the sensor and tighten it to the correct torque.

54 Reconnect the wiring and secure with the plastic ties.

Electronic control unit (ECU)

Caution: Always wait at least 30 seconds after switching off the ignition before disconnecting the wiring from the ECU. When the wiring is disconnected, all the learned values are erased, however any contents of the fault memory are retained. After reconnecting the wiring, the basic settings must be reinstated by an Audi/VAG dealer using a special test instrument. Note also that if the ECU is renewed, the identification of the new ECU must be transferred to the immobiliser control unit by an Audi/VAG dealer.

Removal

55 The electronic control unit is located on the bulkhead at the rear of the engine compartment. On RHD models it is on the right-hand side, and on LHD models it is on the left-hand side.

56 Disconnect the battery negative (earth) lead (see Chapter 5A).

57 Undo the screws and lift off the cover. **Note:** *On early LHD models, a hole is provided in the cowl panel for access to the rear mounting bolt, however on later models it is necessary to unclip the cowl panel for access to the bolt.*

58 Release the spring retainer and lift up the electronic control unit.

59 Prise open the clip and release the wiring connector from the ECU.

 Warning: Wait a minimum of 30 seconds after switching off the ignition, before disconnecting the ECU wiring connector.

60 Withdraw the ECU from the bulkhead.

Refitting

61 Refitting is a reversal of removal. Reconnect the battery as described in Chapter 5A.

6 Fuel filter - renewal

Note: *Observe the precautions in Section 1 before working on fuel system components.*

1 The fuel filter is situated underneath the rear of the vehicle, in front of the fuel tank **(see illustration)**. To gain access to the filter, chock the front wheels, then jack up the rear of the vehicle and support it securely on axle stands.

2 Depressurise the fuel system with reference to Section 9.

3 If available, fit hose clamps to the filter inlet and outlet hoses. These are not essential, but even with the system depressurised, there will still be an amount of petrol in the pipes (and the old filter), and this will siphon out when the pipes are disconnected. Even with hose clamps fitted, the old filter will contain some fuel, so have some rags ready to soak up any spillage.

4 Loosen the hose clips and detach the hoses from the filter. If crimp-type clips are used, discard them and fit worm-type clips when reassembling. Similarly, if the fuel hoses show any sign of perishing or cracking, particularly at the hose ends or where the hose enters the metal end fitting, renew the hoses.

5 Before removing the filter, note any direction-of-flow markings on the filter body, and check against the new filter - the arrow should point in the direction of fuel flow (towards the front of the car).

6 It may be possible to slide the filter from the mounting at this stage, but if it is tight unbolt the mounting from the underbody and remove the filter on the bench.

7 Fit the new filter into position, with the flow marking arrow correctly orientated. With the filter located in the mounting, insert and tighten the mounting bolts.

8 Reconnect the fuel hoses using new clips if necessary. Ensure that no dirt is allowed to enter the hoses or filter connections. Remove the hose clamps.

9 Start the engine noting that there may be a delay as the system re-pressurises and the new filter fills with fuel. Let the engine run for several minutes while you check the filter hose connections for leaks, then switch it off.

 Warning: Dispose safely of the old filter; it will be highly flammable, and may explode if thrown on a fire.

7 Fuel pump and gauge sender unit - removal and refitting

Note: *Observe the precautions in Section 1 before working on fuel system components. A special Audi/VAG tool is required to unscrew the inner section of the baffle housing.*

Removal

1 The fuel pump and gauge sender unit are combined in one assembly, mounted in the fuel tank. Access is via a hatch provided in the load space floor. Removal of the unit exposes the contents of the tank to the atmosphere, so extreme care must be exercised to prevent fire. The area inside and around the car must be well ventilated to prevent a build-up of fuel fumes. If possible, remove the unit when the fuel tank is nearly empty, or alternatively syphon the fuel from the tank into a suitable container.

2 Depressurise the fuel system as described in Section 9.

7.5 View of the fuel pump and gauge sender unit with the hatch removed

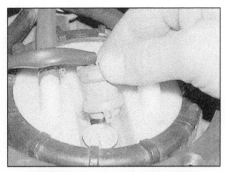

7.6 Disconnecting the wiring plug

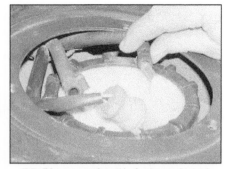

7.7 Disconnecting the fuel supply and return hoses

3 Ensure that the vehicle is parked on a level surface, then disconnect the battery negative (earth) lead (see Chapter 5A).

4 Refer to Chapter 11 and remove the trim from the load space floor.

5 Slacken and remove the access hatch screws and lift the hatch away from the floorpan **(see illustration)**.

6 Unplug the wiring connector from the pump/sender unit **(see illustration)**.

7 Place rags beneath the fuel and vent hoses to catch spilt fuel. Slacken the clips and disconnect the fuel supply and return hoses **(see illustration)**. Identify each hose for position.

8 Note the location of the arrows, then unscrew the plastic ring securing the pump/

sender unit in the tank. Audi/VAG technicians use a special tool to unscrew the ring, however two screwdrivers engaged with the slots in the ring and crossed over each other may be used with success. Alternatively use a pair of large water pump pliers **(see illustrations)**.

9 Remove the flange and seal from the fuel tank aperture.

10 Disconnect the fuel gauge sender wiring and release it from the inside of the flange **(see illustration)**.

11 Squeeze the ferrule and pull the fuel return pipe from the bottom of the flange **(see illustration)**.

12 Turn the inner section of the baffle housing anticlockwise approximately 15°, then lift out the fuel pump together with the inner section

of the baffle housing **(see illustration)**. Audi technicians use a special tool which engages the cut-outs in the top of the fuel pump, and it is recommended that this tool is obtained if at all possible. It may be possible to use an alternative tool, however the plastic is quite flexible and may be broken easily. If the fuel pump is to be renewed, drain all fuel from the old unit. The flange may be removed from the fuel pump if necessary by loosening the clip and disconnecting the intermediate supply pipe, however, note the fitted position of the pipe to ensure correct refitting.

13 To remove the fuel gauge sender, reach inside the fuel tank and depress the retaining tab on the side of the baffle housing. Carefully lift out the sender **(see illustrations)**.

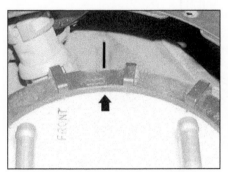

7.8a Note the alignment arrows

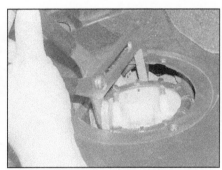

7.8b Using a pair of large water pump pliers to loosen the plastic ring

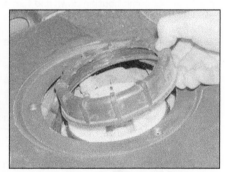

7.8c Removing the plastic ring

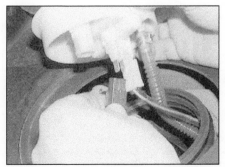

7.10 Disconnecting the fuel gauge sender wiring from the bottom of the flange

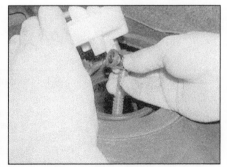

7.11 Disconnecting the fuel return pipe from the bottom of the flange

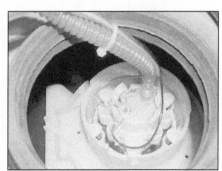

7.12 View of the baffle housing inner section through the top of the fuel tank

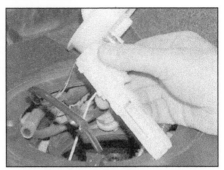

7.13a Removing the fuel gauge sender from the fuel tank

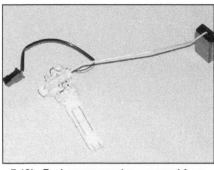

7.13b Fuel gauge sender removed from the fuel tank

14 Inspect the float on the sender unit swinging arm for punctures and fuel ingress, and renew it if it appears damaged. Inspect the rubber seal from the fuel tank aperture and renew it if necessary. Inspect the sender unit wiper and track; clean off any dirt and debris that may have accumulated and look for breaks in the track.

Refitting

15 Insert the fuel gauge sender in the baffle housing and press it down until it engages the retaining clip.
16 If the flange was removed from the fuel pump, reconnect the intermediate supply pipe and tighten the clip. Position the pipe **(see illustration)**.
17 Insert the fuel pump and inner baffle housing in the outer baffle housing so that the notch in the upper edge is aligned with the first mark on the housing. Using the spanner, push the fuel pump/housing down and turn it clockwise until it is aligned with the second mark on the housing.
18 Reconnect the fuel return pipe to the bottom of the flange.
19 Attach the fuel gauge sender wiring to the inside of the flange, and reconnect it to the bottom of the flange. The wiring must be wrapped once around the fuel return pipe.
20 Smear the new rubber seal with clean fuel, then locate it on the flange and refit the flange in the tank aperture.

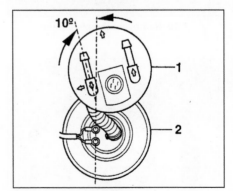

7.16 Position the pipe on the flange as shown

1 Flange
2 Inner section of baffle housing

21 Screw on and tighten the plastic ring. To ensure the align-ment arrows are opposite each other when the ring is fully tight, turn the flange slightly anti-clockwise while the ring is being tightened.
22 Reconnect the fuel supply and return hoses and tighten the clips.

23 Reconnect the wiring connector to the pump/sender unit.
24 Refit the access hatch and tighten the screws.
25 Refit the trim to the load space floor.
26 Reconnect the battery negative (earth) lead (see Chapter 5A).

8 Fuel tank -
removal and refitting

Note: *Observe the precautions in Section 1 before working on fuel system components.*

Removal

1 Before the tank can be removed, it must be drained of as much fuel as possible. As no drain plug is provided, it is preferable to remove the tank when it is nearly empty. Alternatively, syphon or hand-pump the fuel from the tank into a suitable safe container **(see illustration)**.

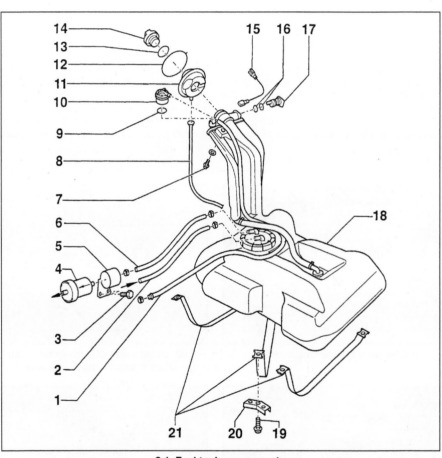

8.1 Fuel tank components

1 Breather pipe to activated charcoal filter	7 Bolt	15 Earth lead
2 Fuel return from fuel rail	8 Overflow hose	16 O-ring seals
3 Bolt	9 O-ring seal	17 Vent valve
4 Fuel filter	10 Gravity valve	18 Fuel tank
5 Mounting bracket	11 Rubber cup	19 Fuel tank mounting bolts
6 Fuel feed to fuel rail	12 Retaining ring	20 Bracket
	13 Gasket	21 Fuel tank mounting straps
	14 Filler cap	

2 Disconnect the battery negative (earth) lead (see Chapter 5A).
3 Refer to Chapter 11 and remove the trim from the load space floor.
4 Slacken and remove the access hatch screws and lift the hatch away from the floorpan.
5 Unplug the wiring connector from the pump/sender unit. **Do not** disconnect the fuel supply and return hoses.
6 Open the fuel tank filler flap and wipe clean the area around the filler neck. Using a screwdriver, carefully lever out the clamping ring from the rubber cup on the filler neck.
7 Press the rubber cup through the body aperture.
8 Chock the front wheels, then jack up the rear of the vehicle and support on axle stands (see *Jacking and vehicle support*). Remove the right-hand rear roadwheel.
9 Remove the right-hand rear wheelarch liner.
10 Unscrew the bolt securing the filler neck and protection plate to the body. Note that the bolt also secures the earth wire.
11 Where fitted, remove the rear underbody splash guard from in front of the rear axle.
12 At the front of the tank, identify the positions of the supply and return hoses, and the fuel evaporative carbon canister hose on the underbody. Loosen the clips and disconnect the hoses. Be prepared for some loss of fuel by placing a suitable container beneath the tank.
13 Support the fuel tank with a trolley jack and piece of wood.
14 Mark the positions of the support straps to ensure correct refitting, then unbolt and remove them **(see illustrations)**. Note the position of the earth cable on the rearmost mounting.
15 With the help of an assistant, lower the fuel tank to the ground and remove from under the vehicle.
16 If the tank is contaminated with sediment or water, remove the fuel pump/sender unit (see Section 7) and swill the tank out with clean fuel. The tank is injection moulded from a synthetic material and if damaged, it should be renewed. However, in certain cases it may be possible to have small leaks or minor damage repaired by a suitable specialist.

Refitting

17 Refitting is the reverse of the removal procedure noting the following points:
a) When lifting the tank back into position take care to ensure none of the hoses get trapped between the tank and vehicle underbody.
b) Ensure that all pipes and hoses are correctly routed and secured.
c) It is important that the earth cable is correctly refitted to the strap and filler neck. Connect an ohmmeter between the metal ring on the filler neck and a bare metal part of the body, and check that the reading is zero resistance.
d) Tighten the tank retaining strap bolts.

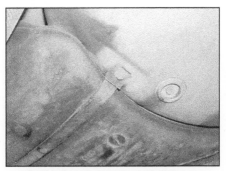

8.14a Fuel tank rear mounting . . .

e) On completion, refill the tank with fuel and thoroughly check for signs of leakage prior to taking the vehicle out on the road.
f) Reconnect the battery as described in Chapter 5A.

9 Fuel injection system - depressurisation

Note: *Observe the precautions in Section 1 before working on fuel system components.*

> ⚠️ **Warning: The following procedure will merely relieve the pressure in the fuel system - remember that fuel will still be present in the system components and take precautions accordingly before disconnecting any of them.**

1 The fuel system referred to in this Section comprises the tank-mounted fuel pump and sender, the fuel filter, the fuel rail and injectors, the fuel pressure regulator and the metal pipes and flexible hoses of the fuel lines between these components. All these contain fuel which will be under pressure while the engine is running and/or while the ignition is switched on. The pressure will remain for some time after the ignition has been switched off and must be relieved before any of these components are disturbed for servicing work.
2 Disconnect the battery negative (earth) lead (see Chapter 5A).
3 Open the fuel filler flap and briefly remove the filler cap to relieve any pressure in the fuel tank. Refit the cap.

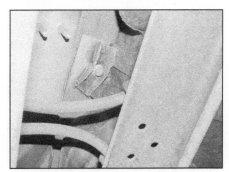

8.14b . . . and front mounting

4 Where applicable, remove the engine top cover.
5 Place some cloth rags beneath the fuel supply pipe union located over the fuel rail on the inlet manifold. Also wrap a cloth around the union.
6 Using two spanners, loosen the union nut and release the fuel pressure. Leave the union nut loose and the rags in position while working on the fuel system.
7 On completion of the work, tighten the union nut using the two spanners.

10 Inlet manifold - removal and refitting

Note: *Observe the precautions in Section 1 before working on fuel system components.*

Removal

1 Disconnect the battery negative (earth) lead (see Chapter 5A).
2 Where applicable, remove the engine top cover(s).
3 Drain the cooling system as described in Chapter 1A. Alternatively on non-turbo models, fit hose clamps to the two hoses leading to the throttle body.
4 If the coolant has been drained, loosen the clips and disconnect the two coolant hoses from the coolant expansion tank located on the left-hand side of the engine.
5 Undo the screws and lift the expansion tank, then disconnect the wiring from the low lever warning switch. Remove the tank from the engine compartment. Where the coolant has not been drained, position the tank to the rear of the engine compartment away from the inlet manifold.
6 Disconnect the accelerator cable from the throttle body and support bracket (refer to Section 3).
7 On models with cruise control, disconnect the actuator rod at the throttle body.
8 Disconnect the vacuum hose from the ACF (activated charcoal filter) valve at the inlet manifold.
9 Disconnect the brake servo vacuum hose from the inlet manifold.
10 On non-turbo models, remove the air inlet duct from between the air cleaner and throttle body, and where necessary also disconnect the crankcase breather hose. Withdraw the duct from the engine compartment.
11 On turbo models, loosen the clip and disconnect the inlet duct from the throttle body on the left-hand side of the engine.
12 Disconnect the wiring and fuel pressure regulator hose from the throttle body. Loosen the clips and disconnect the coolant hoses from the throttle body. Remove the throttle body from the inlet manifold with reference to Sections 4 or 5.
13 On engine codes ADR and AFY manufactured up to 07/1997, disconnect the wiring from the air temperature sensor.

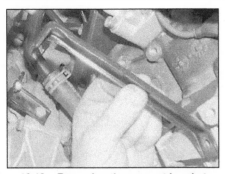

10.18a Removing the support bracket from the inlet manifold

14 On engine codes ADR and AFY manufactured from 08/1997-on, disconnect the wiring from the air temperature sensor and inlet manifold change-over valve.
15 Unscrew the fuel rail mounting bolts, then carefully remove the fuel rail and injectors from the inlet manifold and position to the rear of the engine compartment on a clean cloth. On engine codes ADR, AFY, AHL, AEB, APU and AJL, also disconnect the wiring from the Hall sender on the front of the engine.
16 On engine code ADP, unbolt the upper coolant pipe from the top of the inlet manifold, then loosen the clips and disconnect the hoses from each end of the pipe. Remove the pipe from the engine.
17 On engine codes AEB, APU and AJL, disconnect the hoses from the upper coolant pipe, then unbolt the pipe from the inlet manifold and flange at the rear of the cylinder head.

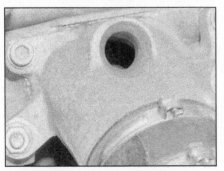

10.19a Engine oil dipstick location on engine code ADR

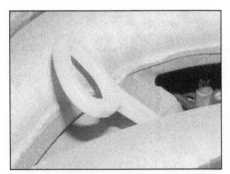

10.20a Unscrew the nuts and bolts . . .

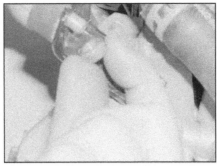

10.18b Unscrewing the inlet manifold support mounting nuts

18 Unscrew and remove the bolts/nuts securing the support brackets to the inlet manifold. Also unscrew the nuts from the mounting rubbers (see illustrations).
19 Pull out the engine oil level dipstick from its tube. On engine code ADR, note the location of the coolant hose between the central tubes of the inlet manifold (see illustrations).
20 Unscrew the nuts and bolts securing the inlet manifold to the cylinder head. Withdraw the inlet manifold and recover the gasket (see illustrations).

Refitting

21 Refitting is the reverse of the removal procedure noting the following points:
a) Clean the contact faces of the inlet manifold and cylinder head, and fit a new gasket.
b) Tighten nut and bolts to the specified torque where given.

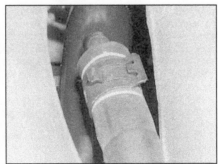

10.19b Coolant hose location on engine code ADR

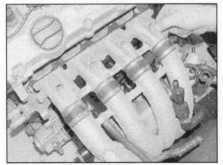

10.20b . . . then withdraw the inlet manifold from the cylinder head . . .

c) Check and if necessary adjust the accelerator cable as described in Section 3.
d) Refill/top-up the cooling system with reference to Chapter 1A.
e) Reconnect the battery as described in Chapter 5A.

11 Fuel injection system - testing and adjustment

1 If a fault appears in the fuel injection system first ensure that all the system wiring connectors are securely connected and free of corrosion. Then ensure that the fault is not due to poor maintenance; ie, check that the air cleaner filter element is clean, the spark plugs are in good condition and correctly gapped, the cylinder compression pressures are correct, the ignition timing is correct and the engine breather hoses are clear and undamaged, referring to Chapters 1A, 2A and 5B for further information.
2 If these checks fail to reveal the cause of the problem the vehicle should be taken to an Audi/VAG dealer for testing. A diagnostic connector is incorporated in the engine management system wiring harness, into which dedicated electronic test equipment can be plugged. The test equipment is capable of 'interrogating' the engine management system ECU electronically and accessing its internal fault log. In this manner, faults can be pinpointed quickly and simply, even if their occurrence is intermittent. Testing all the system components individually in an attempt to locate the fault by elimination is a time consuming operation that is unlikely to be fruitful (particularly if the fault occurs dynamically) and carries high risk of damage to the ECU's internal components.
3 Experienced home mechanics equipped with an accurate tachometer and a carefully-calibrated exhaust gas analyser may be able to check the exhaust gas CO content and the engine idle speed. If these are found to be out of specification, then the vehicle must be taken to a Audi/VAG dealer for assessment. Neither the air/fuel mixture (exhaust gas CO content) nor the engine idle speed are manually adjustable, therefore incorrect test results indicate a fault within the fuel injection system.

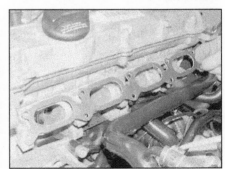

10.20c . . . and recover the gasket

12 Turbocharger -
general information, removal and refitting

Note: *This Section applies to engine codes AEB, APU and AJL only.*

General information

1 The turbocharger is mounted directly on the exhaust manifold. Lubrication is provided by an oil supply pipe that runs from the engine oil filter mounting. Oil is returned to the sump via a return pipe that connects to the side of the sump. The turbocharger unit has an integral wastegate valve and vacuum actuator diaphragm, which is used to control the boost pressure applied to the inlet manifold.

2 The turbocharger's internal components rotate at a very high speed, and as such are very sensitive to contamination; a great deal of damage can be caused by small particles of dirt, particularly if they strike the delicate turbine blades.

Caution: Thoroughly clean the area around all oil pipe unions before disconnecting them, to prevent the ingress of dirt. Store dismantled components in a sealed container to prevent contamination. Cover the turbocharger air inlet ducts to prevent debris entering, and clean using lint-free cloths only.

Removal

3 Apply the handbrake, then jack up the front of the vehicle and support it on axle stands (see *Jacking and vehicle support*). Remove the engine compartment undershield.

4 Remove the engine top cover where applicable.

5 On models with air conditioning, loosen the pivot and tension bolts and move the tensioner roller upwards to release the tension on the drivebelt. Slip the drivebelt from the crankshaft, compressor and tensioner pulleys. Unbolt the compressor and tie it to one side with reference to Chapter 3. **Do not** disconnect the refrigerant lines from the compressor.

6 Unbolt and remove the turbocharger support bracket.

7 Unbolt the oil return pipe either from the turbocharger or sump and recover the gasket.

8 Loosen the clips and disconnect the air supply and feed hoses from the turbocharger.

9 Fit hose clamps to the coolant supply and return hoses on the turbocharger. Alternatively, drain the cooling system with reference to Chapter 1A.

10 Unscrew the union bolt and disconnect the coolant supply pipe. Recover the gaskets.

11 Disconnect the vacuum hose from the pressure regulating valve capsule.

12 Unscrew the bolt securing the coolant supply pipe to the pressure regulating valve bracket.

13 Remove the air cleaner as described in Section 2.

14 Remove the engine top cover.

15 Unbolt the crankcase breather pipe at the cylinder head cover and heat shield.

16 Unscrew the two bolts securing the oil supply pipe to the heat shield, then remove the heat shield.

17 Loosen the clip and disconnect the coolant return pipe from the rigid pipe on the turbocharger. Leave the rigid pipe in position on the turbocharger.

18 Unscrew the union nut and disconnect the oil supply pipe. Use two spanners to do this, one to hold the adapter stationary in the turbocharger.

19 Unscrew the nuts and disconnect the exhaust front pipe/catalytic converter from the turbocharger. Push the front pipe to the rear and recover the gasket.

20 Unscrew the bolts securing the turbocharger to the exhaust manifold. Swivel the turbocharger to one side, then unscrew the union bolt and remove the coolant supply pipe and gasket. Withdraw the turbocharger from the engine compartment.

Refitting

All engines

21 Refit the turbocharger by following the removal procedure in reverse, noting the following points:

a) *Renew all gaskets.*
b) *Renew all self-locking nuts.*
c) *Before reconnecting the oil supply pipe, fill the turbocharger with fresh oil using an oil can.*
d) *Tighten all nuts and bolts to the specified torque where given.*
e) *When the engine is started after refitting, allow it to idle for approximately one minute to give the oil time to circulate around the turbine shaft bearings.*
f) *Top up and bleed the cooling system with reference to Chapter 1A.*

13 Intercooler -
removal and refitting

Note: *This Section applies to engine codes AEB, APU and AJL only.*

Removal

1 Apply the handbrake, then jack up the front of the vehicle and support it on axle stands (see *Jacking and vehicle support*). Remove the engine compartment undertray.

2 The intercooler is located on the left-hand side of the engine compartment, and access to it is achieved by moving the complete front panel (the lock carrier assembly) away from the front of the car as far as possible, but without disconnecting the radiator hoses or electrical wiring. To do this, first remove the front bumper as described in Chapter 11, then unscrew the three quick-release clips from the noise insulation panel and unbolt the air duct from between the lock carrier and the air cleaner. On the left-hand side of the radiator, release the wiring from the clips. Unscrew the bolts securing the lock carrier assembly to the underbody channels, then unscrew the upper side bolts located behind the headlight units. With the help of an assistant, pull the complete assembly away from the front of the car as far as possible. Audi technicians use special tools to hold the assembly, however support bars may be made out of threaded metal rod screwed into the underbody channels.

3 Loosen the clip and disconnect the top hose from the intercooler.

4 Remove the air duct from the front of the intercooler. Recover the rubber grommets.

5 Loosen the clip and disconnect the bottom hose from the intercooler.

6 Pull the bottom of the intercooler out from the mounting grommet, then unhook it from the upper mounting grommets. Withdraw it downwards from under the car. If necessary, remove the grommets from the mounting bracket.

Refitting

7 Refitting is a reversal of removal.

Chapter 4 Part B:
Fuel system - diesel

Contents

Degrees of difficulty

| Easy, suitable for novice with little experience | | Fairly easy, suitable for beginner with some experience | | Fairly difficult, suitable for competent DIY mechanic | | Difficult, suitable for experienced DIY mechanic | | Very difficult, suitable for expert DIY or professional | |

Specifications

General

Maximum engine speed	N/A (ECU controlled)
Engine idle speed	N/A (ECU controlled)
Engine fast idle speed	N/A (ECU controlled)

Fuel injection pump

Injection pump timing (DTI reading)	0.7 ± 0.02 mm

Turbocharger

Type	Garrett
Maximum boost pressure (without charge pressure control)	1.550 to 1.750 bar

Torque wrench settings

	Nm	lbf ft
EGR pipe to exhaust manifold (engine codes AFN and AHH)	25	18
EGR valve to inlet manifold	25	18
Fuel cut-off solenoid	40	30
Fuel filler neck	25	18
Fuel pipe unions to injection pump and injectors	25	18
Fuel tank retaining strap bolts	25	18
Heat shield to exhaust manifold (engine codes 1Z, AFF and AHU)	25	18
Injection pump cover	10	7
Injection pump mounting	25	18
Injection pump sprocket:		
Except AHH engine	45	33
Engine code AHH:		
Stage 1	20	15
Stage 2	Angle-tighten 90°	
Injection pump timing plug	20	15
Injector clamp nut	20	15
Injector pipe unions	25	18
Inlet manifold to cylinder head	25	18
Oil supply pipe bracket to exhaust manifold (engine		
codes AFN and AHH)	25	18
Oil supply pipe to turbocharger	25	18
Turbocharger oil return pipe to cylinder block	30	22
Turbocharger to catalytic converter	25	18
Turbocharger to exhaust manifold	30	22

1 General information and precautions

General information

The fuel system comprises a fuel tank, a fuel injection pump, an engine-bay mounted fuel filter with an integral water separator, fuel supply and return lines and four fuel injectors. All engines are fitted with a turbocharger.

The injection pump is driven at half crankshaft speed by the camshaft timing belt. Fuel is drawn from the fuel tank, through the filter by the injection pump, which then distributes the fuel under very high pressure to the injectors via separate delivery pipes.

The direct-injection fuelling system is controlled electronically by a diesel engine management system, comprising an Electronic Control Unit (ECU) and its associated sensors, actuators and wiring.

Basic injection timing is set mechanically by the position of the pump on its mounting bracket. Dynamic timing and injection duration are controlled by the ECU and are dependant on engine speed, throttle position and rate of opening, inlet air flow , inlet air temperature, coolant temperature, fuel temperature, ambient pressure (altitude) and manifold depression information, received from sensors mounted on and around the engine. Closed loop control of the injection timing is achieved by means of an injector needle lift sensor. Note that injector No 3 is fitted with the needle lift sensor.

Two-stage injectors are used, which improve the engine's combustion charac-teristics, leading to quieter running and better exhaust emissions.

In addition, the ECU manages the operation of the Exhaust Gas Recirculation (EGR) emission control system, the turbocharger boost pressure control system and the glow plug control system.

It should be noted that fault diagnosis of the diesel engine management system is only possible with dedicated electronic test equipment. Problems with the system's operation should therefore be referred to an Audi/VAG dealer for assessment. Once the fault has been identified, the removal/refitting sequences detailed in the following Sections will then allow the appropriate component(s) to be renewed as required.

Note: *Throughout this Chapter, vehicles are frequently referred to by their engine code, rather than by engine capacity - refer to Chapter 2B for engine code listings.*

Precautions

Many of the operations described in this Chapter involve the disconnection of fuel lines, which may cause an amount of fuel spillage. Before commencing work, refer to the warnings below and the information in *Safety first!* at the beginning of this manual.

2.5a Unscrew the mounting bolt . . .

⚠ *Warning: When working on any part of the fuel system, avoid direct contact skin contact with diesel fuel - wear protective clothing and gloves when handling fuel system components. Ensure that the work area is well ventilated to prevent the build up of diesel fuel vapour.*

Fuel injectors operate at extremely high pressures and the jet of fuel produced at the nozzle is capable of piercing skin, with potentially fatal results. When working with pressurised injectors, take care to avoid exposing any part of the body to the fuel spray. It is recommended that a diesel fuel systems specialist should carry out any pressure testing of the fuel system components.

Under no circumstances should diesel fuel be allowed to come into contact with coolant hoses - wipe off accidental spillage immediately. Hoses that have been contaminated with fuel for an extended period should be renewed. diesel fuel systems are particularly sensitive to contamination from dirt, air and water. Pay particular attention to cleanliness when working on any part of the fuel system, to prevent the ingress of dirt. Thoroughly clean the area around fuel unions before disconnecting them. Store dismantled components in sealed containers to prevent contamination and the formation of condensation. Only use lint-free cloths and clean fuel for component cleansing.

2.5b . . . and remove the air cleaner body from the engine compartment

2 Air cleaner and inlet ducts - removal and refitting

Removal

1 Disconnect the wiring from the airflow meter on the air cleaner cover. Also disconnect the small hose.
2 Release the wiring and hose from the clip on the air cleaner cover.
3 Loosen the clip and disconnect the air inlet duct from the air cleaner cover.
4 Release the spring clips and withdraw the air cleaner cover, then remove the filter element (see Chapter 1B for more details). Handle the airflow meter carefully, as it is a delicate component.
5 Unscrew the mounting bolt and remove the air cleaner from the right-hand side of the engine compartment **(see illustrations)**.
6 To remove the remaining ducting, apply the handbrake, then jack up the front of the vehicle and support it on axle stands (see *Jacking and vehicle support*). Remove the splash guard from under the radiator.
7 Loosen the clips and disconnect the U-shaped hose from the intercooler and air pipe on the left-hand side of the engine compartment.
8 Loosen the clip and disconnect the air cleaner hose from the right-hand side of the air pipe, then unbolt and remove the air pipe.
9 Loosen the clips and disconnect the rear air ducts from the intercooler and inlet manifold. Disconnect the wiring and hoses as applicable, then unscrew the mounting bolts and remove the ducts.

Refitting

10 Refitting is a reversal of removal.

3 Accelerator position sender - removal, refitting and adjustment

Removal

1 Refer to Chapter 11 and remove the trim panels from under the steering column area of the facia, to gain access to the pedal cluster.
2 Disconnect the wiring from the accelerator position sender on the top of the accelerator pedal bracket.
3 Unscrew the bolts and remove the accelerator position sender and bracket from the floor.
4 Detach the operating rod from the pedal, then unclip the pedal from the mounting bracket.
5 Note the position of the operating rod cam on the position sender spindle, then undo the nut and remove the washer, and disconnect the cam.
6 Undo the screws and remove the position sender from the bracket.

Refitting and adjustment

7 Locate the position sender on the bracket, then insert and tighten the screws.

8 Locate the operating rod and cam on the spindle and secure with the nut and washer. Make sure that the cam is the correct way round. The extended edge of the cam must be aligned with the centre of the mounting bolt hole **(see illustration)**.

9 Clip the pedal on the mounting bracket, then adjust the sender as follows.

10 Position the pedal stop so that the letters HS (Hand Shift) are visible on the outer surface of the stop. This applies to both manual and automatic transmission models for the adjustment procedure.

11 Depress the pedal until it touches the stop, then adjust the length of the operating rod so that the point of kick-down is just reached. Some trial and error will be necessary by connecting the rod eyelet to the pedal, then disconnecting it again to make any necessary adjustment. The point of kick-down can be felt as the sender cam reaches the end of its stroke.

12 On manual transmission models, leave the pedal stop in its present position with the letters HS visible. However, on automatic transmission models, turn the stop through 180° so that the letters AG (Automatic Gearbox) are visible.

13 With the operating rod attached to the pedal, refit the pedal bracket to the floor and tighten the mounting bolts.

14 Reconnect the wiring for the position sender.

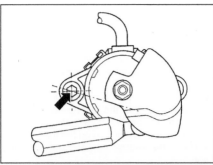

3.8 The extended edge of the cam must be aligned with the centre of the mounting bolt hole

15 Refit the trim panels beneath the steering column.

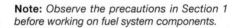

4 Fuel gauge sender unit - removal and refitting

Note: *Observe the precautions in Section 1 before working on fuel system components.*

Removal

1 The fuel gauge sender unit is mounted in the fuel tank. Access is via a hatch provided in the load space floor. Removal of the unit exposes the contents of the tank to the atmosphere, so extreme care must be exercised to prevent fire. The area inside and around the car must be well ventilated to prevent a build-up of fuel fumes. If possible,

remove the unit when the fuel tank is nearly empty, or alternatively syphon the fuel from the tank into a suitable container.

2 Ensure that the vehicle is parked on a level surface, then disconnect the battery negative (earth) lead (see Chapter 5A).

3 Refer to Chapter 11 and remove the trim from the load space floor.

4 Unscrew and remove the access hatch screws and lift the hatch away from the floorpan.

5 Unplug the wiring connector from the sender unit **(see illustration)**.

6 Place rags beneath the fuel supply and return hoses to catch spilt fuel. Loosen the clips and disconnect the fuel supply and return hoses. Identify each hose for position **(see illustrations)**.

7 Note the location of the arrows, then unscrew the plastic ring securing the sender unit in the tank. Audi/VAG technicians use a special tool to unscrew the ring, however two screwdrivers engaged with the slots in the ring and crossed over each other may be used with success. Alternatively use a pair of large water pump pliers **(see illustrations)**.

8 Carefully lift the fuel gauge sender unit and seal from the fuel tank.

9 Inspect the float on the sender unit swinging arm for punctures and fuel ingress, and renew the sender unit if it appears damaged. Inspect the rubber seal from the fuel tank aperture and renew it if necessary. Inspect the sender unit wiper and track; clean off any dirt and debris that may have accumulated and look for breaks in the track.

4.5 Disconnecting the wiring from the sender unit

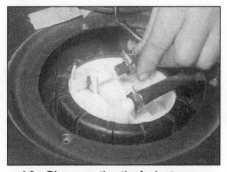

4.6a Disconnecting the fuel return . . .

4.6b . . . and supply hoses from the sender unit

4.7a Using a pair of grips, unscrew the plastic securing ring . . .

4.7b . . . and remove it

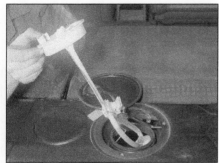

4.7c Removing the sender unit

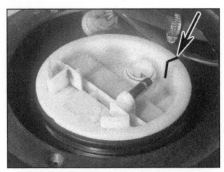

4.11 Align the sender unit marks before fitting the securing ring

Refitting

10 Insert the fuel gauge sender unit into the fuel tank together with a new seal. Note that the seal must be fitted dry.

11 Align the notch/line on the sender with the arrow on the fuel tank, then screw on and tighten the plastic plug **(see illustration)**. To ensure the alignment arrows are opposite each other when the ring is fully tight, turn the flange slightly anticlockwise while the ring is being tightened.

12 Reconnect the fuel supply and return hoses and tighten the clips.

13 Reconnect the wiring connector to the sender unit.

14 Refit the hatch and tighten the screws.

15 Refit the trim to the load space floor.

16 Reconnect the battery negative (earth) lead (see Chapter 5A).

5 Fuel tank -
removed and refitting

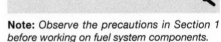

Note: *Observe the precautions in Section 1 before working on fuel system components.*

Removal

1 Before the tank can be removed, it must be drained of as much fuel as possible. As no drain plug is provided, it is preferable to remove the tank when it is nearly empty. Alternatively, syphon or hand-pump the fuel from the tank into a suitable safe container.

2 Disconnect the battery negative (earth) lead (see Chapter 5A).

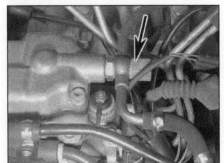

6.6 The fuel return union bolt is fitted with a non-return valve

3 Refer to Chapter 11 and remove the trim from the load space floor.

4 Unscrew and remove the access hatch screws and lift the hatch away from the floorpan.

5 Unplug the wiring connector for the sender unit. **Do not** disconnect the fuel supply and return hoses.

6 Open the fuel tank filler flap and wipe clean the area around the filler neck. Using a screwdriver, carefully lever out the clamping ring from the rubber cup on the filler neck.

7 Press the rubber cup through the body aperture.

8 Chock the front wheels, then jack up the rear of the vehicle and support on axle stands (see *Jacking and vehicle support*). Remove the right-hand rear roadwheel.

9 Remove the right-hand rear wheelarch liner.

10 Unscrew the bolt securing the filler neck and protection plate to the body. Note that the bolt also secures the earth wire.

11 Where fitted, remove the rear underbody splash guard from in front of the rear axle.

12 At the front of the tank, identify the positions of the supply and return hoses. Loosen the clips and disconnect the hoses. Be prepared for some loss of fuel by placing a suitable container beneath the tank.

13 Support the fuel tank with a trolley jack and piece of wood.

14 Mark the positions of the support straps to ensure correct refitting, then unbolt and remove them. Note the position of the earth cable on the rearmost mounting.

15 With the help of an assistant, lower the fuel tank to the ground and remove from under the vehicle.

16 If the tank is contaminated with sediment or water, remove the sender unit (see Section 4) and swill the tank out with clean fuel. The tank is injection moulded from a synthetic material and if damaged, it should be renewed. However, in certain cases it may be possible to have small leaks or minor damage repaired by a suitable specialist.

Refitting

17 Refitting is the reverse of the removal procedure noting the following points:

a) *When lifting the tank back into position take care to ensure none of the hoses get trapped between the tank and vehicle underbody.*

6.8 Loosening the fuel pipe union nuts

b) *Ensure that all pipes and hoses are correctly routed and secured.*

c) *Before fully tightening the fuel tank mounting strap bolts, push the fuel tank fully to the right-hand side.*

d) *It is important that the earth cable is correctly refitted to the strap and filler neck. Connect an ohmmeter between the metal ring on the filler neck and a bare metal part of the body, and check that the reading is zero resistance.*

e) *On completion, refill the tank with fuel and thoroughly check for signs of leakage prior to taking the vehicle out on the road.*

f) *Reconnect the battery as described in Chapter 5A.*

6 Fuel injection pump -
removal, refitting and adjustment

Note: *Observe the precautions in Section 1 before working on fuel system components. A suitable dial gauge and adapter will be required for the initial setting of the injection pump.*

Removal

1 Disconnect the battery negative (earth) lead (see Chapter 5A) and position it away from the terminal.

2 Unscrew the nuts and remove the plastic cover from the top of the engine.

3 Unclip and remove the upper outer timing cover.

4 Remove the camshaft cover as described in Chapter 2B

5 Set the engine to the No 1 TDC position as described in Chapter 2B The use of the camshaft locking bar is necessary for this procedure.

6 Unscrew the union bolts and disconnect the fuel inlet and return hoses from the injection pump. Note that the union bolt with the non-return valve is fitted to the return line **(see illustration)**. Recover the sealing washers.

7 Note and identify the wiring connections on the fuel injection pump, then disconnect them.

8 Unscrew the union nuts securing the fuel pipes to the injectors and fuel injection pump, and remove them as a complete set **(see illustration)**. Hold the adapters stationary with a further spanner. Take care not to bend the pipes.

9 Cover the open pipes and ports to prevent the ingress of dust and dirt **(see Haynes Hint)**.

10 Refer to Chapter 2B and remove the timing belt.

Except engine code AHH

11 Hold the injection pump sprocket stationary using a suitable tool engaged with the holes in the sprocket **(see illustration)**.

12 Unscrew the injection pump sprocket nut approximately 1 turn.

13 Using a suitable puller, release the sprocket from the injection pump shaft **(see illustration)**. **Do not** strike the puller hard in

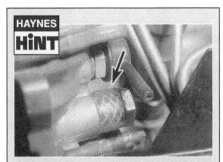

Fit a short length of hose over the banjo bolt (arrowed) so that the drillings are covered, then thread the bolt back into its injection pump port

an attempt to release the sprocket, otherwise the injection pump may be damaged.

14 Unscrew the nut and remove the sprocket. Recover the Woodruff key from the slot in the shaft **(see illustrations)**.

Engine code AHH

15 Mark the two-piece injection pump sprocket and hub in relation to each other, then hold the sprocket stationary using a home-made tool as described in paragraph 11. Unscrew and remove the three bolts and remove the sprocket from the hub. Note that the bolts must be renewed each time they are loosened, so obtain new bolts before commencing the refitting procedure.

Caution: On no account should the injection pump sprocket hub centre bolt be loosened, as this will alter the basic

6.11 Using a home-made tool to hold the injection pump sprocket stationary

injection timing which can only be reset by a VAG dealer or fuel injection specialist.

All engine codes

16 If necessary, mark the position of the injection pump in relation to the mounting bracket as a guide to refitting. Unscrew the front bolts securing the injection pump to the mounting bracket. The two inner bolts are accessed from the front of the inner timing cover, and the remaining bolt is accessed from the injection pump side of the mounting bracket.

17 Unscrew the rear mounting bolt and withdraw the injection pump from the mounting bracket **(see illustration)**.

Refitting and adjustment

18 Locate the injection pump in the mounting bracket and refit the rear mounting bolt. Tighten the bolt and conical nut to the specified torque to centralise the pump.

6.13 Attach a two-legged puller to the injection pump sprocket

19 Rotate the injection pump as necessary to centralise it within the slotted holes at the front of the mounting bracket, then refit the front mounting bolts and hand-tighten them at this stage. If the original pump is being refitted, align the previously made marks and fully tighten the mounting bolts.

Except engine code AHH

20 Insert the Woodruff key in the slot in the shaft, then refit the sprocket and nut. Hold the sprocket stationary with the tool used for removal, and tighten the nut to the specified torque.

21 Align the TDC pin holes and insert the pin to lock the sprocket in the TDC position.

Engine code AHH

22 Locate the injection pump sprocket on its hub and align the previously-made marks. Insert three new bolts and hand-tighten them at this stage.

All engine codes

23 Refit the timing belt and tensioner as described in Chapter 2B.

24 Before refitting the wiring and fuel pipes, carry out the following adjustment.

25 Check that the TDC timing marks are correctly aligned with each other with reference to Chapter 2B, then remove the locking bar from the rear of the camshaft, and the pin from the pump sprocket.

Except engine code AHH

26 Unscrew the timing plug from the rear of the injection pump and fit a dial gauge. A suitable adapter will be required **(see illustrations)**. Recover the seal from the hole.

6.14a Lift off the pump sprocket . . .

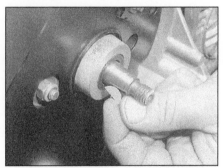

6.14b . . . and recover the Woodruff key

6.17 Removing the injection pump rear mounting bolt

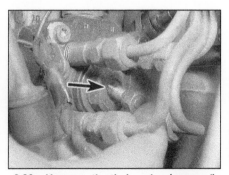

6.26a Unscrew the timing plug (arrowed) from the pump head and recover the seal

6.26b Screw the dial gauge into the pump head

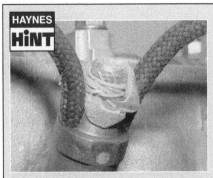

Cut the fingertips from an old pair of rubber gloves and secure them over the fuel ports with elastic bands

27 Preload the dial gauge by 2 mm then slowly turn the engine anticlockwise until the needle on the gauge stops moving. Now set the dial gauge with 1 mm preload and zero the gauge.

28 Slowly turn the engine clockwise until the TDC mark on the flywheel/driveplate is aligned with the edge of the timing aperture in the transmission housing. Do not turn the engine further than the TDC mark - if the engine is turned too far, repeat the preload procedure again.

29 Check the reading on the dial gauge which will indicate the commencement of injection. This should be 0.7 ± 0.02 mm.

30 If adjustment is required, loosen the pump mounting bolts by about 1 turn, then rotate the pump as necessary until the required setting is achieved.

31 Tighten the pump mounting bolts to the specified torque, then repeat the procedure and check that the injection timing is correct.

32 Remove the dial gauge then refit and tighten the timing plug.

All engine codes

33 Refit the fuel pipes to the injectors and fuel injection pump and tighten the union nuts to the specified torque.

34 Reconnect the wiring to the injection pump.

35 Refit the fuel inlet and return hoses together with new sealing washers and tighten the union bolts to the specified torque.

Make sure that the union bolt with the non-return valve is fitted to the return line.

36 Refit the camshaft cover with reference to Chapter 2B, then refit the upper outer timing cover.

37 Reconnect the battery negative (earth) lead (see Chapter 5A).

38 The injection pump must now be bled using a hand-operated vacuum pump. The Audi vacuum pump includes a container in the hose to receive the fuel as it is drawn from the pump. Connect the pump to the return union on the injection pump and operate the vacuum pump until fuel free of bubbles flows into the container. Do not allow the fuel to enter the vacuum pump.

39 Refit the return hose, then start the engine and check for fuel leaks.

40 The injection timing must now be checked and adjusted dynamically by an Audi dealer who will have the equipment necessary to carry out the check.

41 After making an adjustment to the injection pump timing, always loosen the fuel pipe union nuts and re-tighten them to relieve any tension which may cause them to fracture after constant vibration.

42 Refit the plastic cover to the top of the engine.

---

7 Injectors - general information, removal and refitting

Note: *Observe the precautions in Section 1 before working on fuel system components.*

⚠️ **Warning: Exercise extreme caution when working on the fuel injectors. Never expose the hands or any part of the body to injector spray, as the high working pressure can cause the fuel to penetrate the skin, with possibly fatal results. You are strongly advised to have any work which involves testing the injectors under pressure carried out by a dealer or fuel injection specialist.**

General information

1 Injectors do deteriorate with prolonged use and it is reasonable to expect them to need reconditioning or renewal after 60 000 miles

(100 000 km) or so. Accurate testing, overhaul and calibration of the injectors must be left to a specialist. A defective injector which is causing knocking or smoking can be located without dismantling as follows.

2 Run the engine at a fast idle. Slacken each injector union in turn, placing rag around the union to catch spilt fuel and being careful not to expose the skin to any spray. When the union on the defective injector is slackened, the knocking or smoking will stop.

Removal

Note: *Take care not to allow dirt into the injectors or fuel pipes during this procedure. Do not drop the injectors or allow the needles at their tips to become damaged. The injectors are precision-made to fine limits and must not be handled roughly.*

3 Cover the alternator with a clean cloth or plastic bag to prevent the possibility of fuel being spilt onto it.

4 Carefully clean around the injectors and pipe union nuts and disconnect the return pipes from the injectors.

5 Wipe clean the pipe unions then slacken the union nuts securing the injector pipes to the injectors and the relevant union nuts securing the pipes to the rear of the injection pump (the pipes are removed as one assembly); as each pump union nut is slackened, retain the adapter with a suitable open-ended spanner to prevent it being unscrewed from the pump. With the union nuts undone remove the injector pipes from the engine. Cover the injector and pipe unions to prevent the entry of dirt into the system **(see Haynes Hint)**.

6 Disconnect the wiring for the needle stroke transmitter from injector No 3.

7 Unscrew the injector clamp retaining nuts or bolts (as applicable). Remove the washers, then remove the clamps and collars **(see illustrations)**.

8 Withdraw the injectors from the cylinder head **(see illustration)**. If they are tight, ease them out by turning them with a spanner on their flats. If they are seized in position, Audi technicians use a slide hammer tool which is screwed onto the pipe union thread. Note that the injector second from rear is higher than the rest (No 3 cylinder on 4-cylinder engines),

7.7a Unscrew the bolt . . .

7.7b . . . and remove the clamp . . .

7.7c . . . and spacer

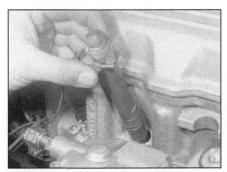

7.8 Removing an injector from the cylinder head

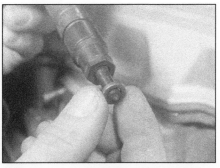

7.10a Locate a new heat shield washer on the injector before refitting it

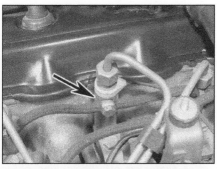

7.10b The needle lift sensing injector is fitted second from the rear on all engines

and incorporates a needle lift sensing device which sends a signal to the engine management ECU.

9 Using a screwdriver, hook out the copper heat shield washers from the injector recesses in the cylinder head. New ones must be obtained for refitting.

Refitting

10 Insert the injectors into position, using new copper heat shield washers. Make sure that the injector with the needle stroke transmitter is located in No 3 position **(see illustrations)**.

11 Fit the mounting collars and retaining clamps, and secure in position with the washers and nuts or bolts (as applicable), tightened to the specified torque.

12 Reconnect the wiring for the needle stroke transmitter on injector No 3.

13 Refit the injector pipes and tighten the union nuts to the specified torque setting.

14 Reconnect the leak-off pipes to the injectors.

15 Start the engine and check that it runs correctly.

---

8 Diesel engine management system - component removal and refitting

Note: *Observe the precautions in Section 1 before working on the fuel system.*

Coolant temperature sensor

Removal

1 The coolant temperature sensor is located on the rear of the cylinder head.

2 Refer to Chapter 1B and drain approximately one quarter of the coolant from the engine.

3 Disconnect the wiring, then unscrew and remove the sensor.

Refitting

4 Refitting is a reversal of removal, but tighten the sensor to the specified torque. Top-up the cooling system with reference to Chapter 1B.

Engine speed sensor

Removal

5 The engine speed sensor is mounted on the

rear left-hand side of the cylinder block, adjacent to the mating surface of the block and transmission bellhousing.

6 Trace the wiring back from the sensor to the connector and disconnect it.

7 Undo the retaining screw and withdraw the sensor from the cylinder block.

Refitting

8 Refitting is a reversal of removal.

Fuel cut-off valve

Removal

9 The fuel cut-off valve is located on top of the distributor head on the fuel injection pump. First clean the area around the valve to prevent dust and dirt entering the fuel system.

10 To remove the valve, unscrew the nut and disconnect the wiring.

11 Unscrew the valve and remove the O-ring, spring and plunger.

Refitting

12 Refitting is a reversal of removal, but clean all components before fitting and tighten the valve to the specified torque.

Start of injection valve

Removal

13 The start of injection valve is located just below the distributor head on the fuel injection pump. First clean the area around the valve to prevent dust and dirt entering the fuel system.

14 Undo the screw and withdraw the valve from the injection pump. Be prepared for some loss of fuel.

15 Recover the outer O-ring, strainer and inner O-ring.

16 Disconnect the wiring at the connector.

Refitting

17 Refitting is a reversal of removal, but clean all components before fitting and tighten the screw securely.

Charge pressure control valve

Removal

18 The charge pressure control valve is located behind the right-hand headlight. First disconnect the plastic air duct from the inlet duct and intermediate duct leading to the air cleaner.

19 Disconnect the wiring.

20 Remove the vacuum hoses, noting their order of connection carefully to aid correct refitting.

21 Unscrew the mounting nuts and withdraw the valve.

Refitting

22 Refitting is a reversal of removal.

Air intake charge pressure/temperature sensor

Removal

23 The air intake charge pressure/temperature sensor is located on the air duct leading from the intercooler to the inlet manifold, at the left-hand rear of the engine compartment **(see illustration)**. First disconnect the wiring.

24 Undo the screws and remove the sensor from the air duct.

Refitting

25 Refitting is a reversal of removal.

Air mass meter

Removal

26 The air mass meter is located in the air cleaner upper cover **(see illustration)**.

27 Disconnect the plastic air duct from the inlet duct and intermediate duct leading to the air cleaner.

28 Loosen the clip and disconnect the air inlet hose from the airflow meter.

29 Prise open the retaining clips and lift the upper cover from the air cleaner body together with the airflow meter. Disconnect

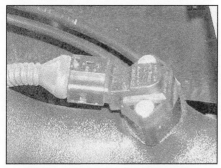

8.23 Air intake charge pressure/temperature sensor

the wiring from the meter and remove the assembly.

30 The airflow meter and shield may be unbolted from the upper cover and also the intermediate air duct removed. Handle the airflow meter carefully, as it is a delicate component. Recover the sealing collar.

Refitting

31 Refitting is a reversal of removal.

Electronic control unit (ECU)

Caution: Always wait at least 30 seconds after switching off the ignition before disconnecting the wiring from the ECU. When the wiring is disconnected, all the learned values are erased, however any contents of the fault memory are retained. After reconnecting the wiring, the basic settings must be reinstated by an Audi/VAG dealer using a special test instrument. Note also that if the ECU is renewed, the identification of the new ECU must be transferred to the immobiliser control unit by an Audi/VAG dealer.

Removal

32 The electronic control unit is located on the bulkhead at the rear of the engine compartment. On RHD models it is on the right-hand side, and on LHD models it is on the left-hand side.

33 Disconnect the battery negative (earth) lead (see Chapter 5A).

34 Undo the screws and lift off the cover. **Note:** *On early LHD models, a hole is provided in the cowl panel for access to the rear mounting bolt, however on later models it is necessary to unclip the cowl panel for access to the bolt.*

35 Using a screwdriver, release the spring retainer from the top of the ECU. Lift the electronic control unit from the mounting box for access to the wiring connector. **Note:** *On some models it may be necessary to remove the auxiliary relay carrier toegether with the auxiliary fuse box.*

36 Prise open the clip and release the wiring connector from the ECU.

 Warning: Wait a minimum of 30 seconds after switching off the ignition, before disconnecting the ECU wiring connector.

37 Withdraw the ECU from the bulkhead. If necessary, the mounting box can be removed by unscrewing the retaining nuts and releasing the peg from the location hole.

Refitting

38 Refitting is a reversal of removal. When refitting the cover, press it down firmly by hand, then progressively tighten the retaining screws. Reconnect the battery as described in Chapter 5A.

System relay and glow plug fusebox

Removal

39 The system relay is located beneath the

8.26 Air mass meter (AFN engine)

ECU cover. First disconnect the battery negative (earth) lead (see Chapter 5A).

40 Undo the screws and lift off the cover.

41 To remove the relay, pull it directly from the fusebox. To remove the fusebox, disconnect the wiring then unbolt the fusebox.

Refitting

42 Refitting is a reversal of removal.

Clutch and brake pedal switches

Removal and refitting

43 The clutch and brake pedal switches send signals to the ECU which automatically adjusts the injection pump timing. Refer to Chapters 6 and 9 for information on their removal and refitting.

Fuel temperature sensor

Removal

44 The fuel temperature sender is located on top of the injection pump, below the cover.

45 Undo the screws and lift the top cover from the injection pump. Recover the gasket.

46 Undo the screws and remove the fuel temperature sensor.

Refitting

47 Refitting is a reversal of removal. Tighten the pump top cover screws securely.

---

9 Turbocharger - general information, removal and refitting

General information

1 A turbocharger is fitted to all diesel engines, and is mounted directly on the exhaust manifold. Lubrication is provided by an oil supply pipe that runs from the engine oil filter mounting. Oil is returned to the sump via a return pipe that connects to the side of the cylinder block. The turbocharger unit has an integral wastegate valve and vacuum actuator diaphragm, which is used to control the boost pressure applied to the inlet manifold.

2 The turbocharger's internal components rotate at a very high speed, and as such are very sensitive to contamination; a great deal of damage can be caused by small particles

of dirt, particularly if they strike the delicate turbine blades.

Caution: Thoroughly clean the area around all oil pipe unions before disconnecting them, to prevent the ingress of dirt. Store dismantled components in a sealed container to prevent contamination. Cover the turbocharger air inlet ducts to prevent debris entering, and clean using lint-free cloths only.

Removal

3 Apply the handbrake, then jack up the front of the vehicle and support it on axle stands (see *Jacking and vehicle support*). Remove the engine compartment undershield.

4 Remove the engine top cover where applicable.

5 On models with air conditioning, loosen the pivot and tension bolts and move the tensioner roller upwards to release the tension on the drivebelt. Slip the drivebelt from the crankshaft, compressor and tensioner pulleys. Unbolt the compressor and tie it to one side with reference to Chapter 3. **Do not** disconnect the refrigerant lines from the compressor.

6 Loosen the clips and disconnect the right-hand air inlet hose.

7 Unscrew the union bolt and disconnect the oil return pipe from the right-hand side of the cylinder block. Plug or cover the pipe and aperture to prevent entry of dust and dirt.

8 Unscrew the turbocharger-to-exhaust manifold mounting bolts but leave the two front bolts loose to support the unit.

9 Remove the air cleaner assembly as described in Section 2.

10 Loosen the clips and disconnect the front air inlet hose from the turbocharger.

11 Unscrew the union nut and disconnect the oil supply pipe from the turbocharger **(see illustration)**.

12 Note the location of the two vacuum hoses then disconnect them from the wastegate control unit **(see illustration)**.

13 Unscrew and remove the nuts securing the turbocharger to the catalytic converter **(see illustration)**.

14 Remove the last two mounting bolts, and withdraw the turbocharger from the exhaust manifold and catalytic converter. Recover the gasket.

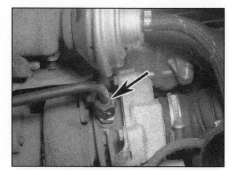

9.11 Turbocharger oil supply pipe and union nut

Refitting

15 Refit the turbocharger by following the removal procedure in reverse, noting the following points:

a) *Renew the gasket.*

b) *Renew all self-locking nuts.*

c) *Before reconnecting the oil supply pipe, fill the turbocharger with fresh oil using an oil can.*

d) *Tighten all nuts and bolts to the specified torque where given.*

e) *When the engine is started after refitting, allow it to idle for approximately one minute to give the oil time to circulate around the turbine shaft bearings.*

9.12 Vacuum pipe on the turbocharger boost pressure control valve

9.13 Turbocharger to catalytic converter mounting nuts

10 Intercooler - removal and refitting

Removal

1 Apply the handbrake, then jack up the front of the vehicle and support it on axle stands (see *Jacking and vehicle support*). Remove the engine compartment undertray.

2 The intercooler is located on the left-hand side of the engine compartment, and access to it is achieved by moving the complete front panel (the lock carrier assembly) away from the front of the car as far as possible, but without disconnecting the radiator hoses or electrical wiring. To do this, first remove the front bumper as described in Chapter 11, then unscrew the three quick-release clips from the noise insulation panel and unbolt the air duct from between the lock carrier and the air cleaner. On the left-hand side of the radiator, release the wiring from the clips. Unscrew the bolts securing the lock carrier assembly to the underbody channels, then unscrew the upper side bolts located behind the headlight units. With the help of an assistant, pull the complete assembly away from the front of the car as far as possible. Audi technicians use special tools to hold the assembly, however support bars may be made out of threaded

metal rod screwed into the underbody channels.

3 Loosen the clip and disconnect the top hose from the intercooler.

4 Remove the air duct from the front of the intercooler. Recover the rubber grommets.

5 Loosen the clip and disconnect the bottom hose from the intercooler **(see illustration)**.

6 Pull the bottom of the intercooler out from the mounting grommet, then unhook it from the upper mounting grommets. Withdraw it downwards from under the car **(see illustration)**. If necessary, remove the grommets from the mounting bracket.

Refitting

7 Refitting is a reversal of removal.

11 Inlet manifold - removal and refitting

Engine codes 1Z, AFF and AHU

Removal

1 Remove the turbocharger as described in Section 10.

2 Loosen the clip and disconnect the air duct from the inlet manifold.

3 Disconnect the vacuum hose from the EGR control valve.

4 Unscrew the two bolts securing the EGR

control valve to the inlet manifold.

5 Unscrew the nuts and remove the small heatshield from the front of the exhaust manifold.

6 Unscrew the mounting nuts and remove the inlet manifold from the cylinder head. Recover the gaskets from the inlet manifold and EGR control valve.

Refitting

7 Refitting is a reversal of removal, using new manifold and EGR valve gaskets.

Engine codes AFN and AHH

Removal

8 Unbolt the EGR valve and pipe from the inlet and exhaust manifolds and move the assembly to one side. It is not necessary to disconnect the vacuum hose from the EGR valve.

9 Loosen the clip and disconnect the air duct from the inlet manifold.

10 Unbolt the oil supply pipe bracket from the exhaust manifold.

11 Unscrew the mounting nuts and remove the inlet manifold from the cylinder head. Recover the gaskets from the inlet manifold and EGR control valve.

Refitting

12 Refitting is a reversal of removal, using new manifold and EGR valve gaskets.

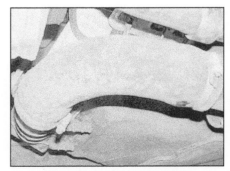

10.5 Intercooler bottom hose

10.6 Intercooler bottom mounting

Chapter 4 Part C:
Emission control and exhaust systems

Contents

Degrees of difficulty

Easy, suitable for novice with little experience	**Fairly easy,** suitable for beginner with some experience	**Fairly difficult,** suitable for competent DIY mechanic 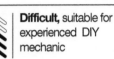	**Difficult,** suitable for experienced DIY mechanic	**Very difficult,** suitable for expert DIY or professional

Specifications

Torque wrench settings	Nm	lbf ft
Catalytic converter to front pipe	25	18
Catalytic converter to turbocharger (engine codes AEB, APU, AJL) . . .	30	22
EGR valve to inlet manifold	25	18
Exhaust clamp bolts	40	30
Exhaust manifold	25	18
Exhaust mounting brackets to underbody	25	18
Front exhaust pipe to manifold (engine codes ADP, ADR, AFY, AHL)	30	22
Front pipe to bracket on gearbox (engine codes AEB, APU, AJL)	25	18
Semi-flexible pipe to EGR valve and exhaust manifold	25	18

1 General information

Emission control systems

All petrol engine models are designed to use unleaded petrol and are controlled by engine management systems that are programmed to give the best compromise between driveability, fuel consumption and exhaust emission production. In addition, a number of systems are fitted that help to minimise other harmful emissions. A crankcase emission control system is fitted, which reduces the release of pollutants from the engines lubrication system, and a catalytic converter is fitted which reduces exhaust gas pollutant. An evaporative loss emission control system is fitted which reduces the release of gaseous hydrocarbons from the fuel tank.

All diesel-engined models have a crankcase emission control system, and in addition are fitted with a catalytic converter, and an Exhaust Gas Recirculation (EGR) system to reduce exhaust emissions.

Crankcase emission control

To reduce the emission of unburned hydrocarbons from the crankcase into the atmosphere, the engine is sealed and the blow-by gases and oil vapour are drawn from inside the crankcase, through a wire mesh oil separator, into the inlet tract to be burned by the engine during normal combustion.

Under conditions of high manifold depression the gases will be sucked positively out of the crankcase. Under conditions of low manifold depression the gases are forced out of the crankcase by the (relatively) higher crankcase pressure. If the engine is worn, the raised crankcase pressure (due to increased blow-by) will cause some of the flow to return under all manifold conditions. All diesel engines have a pressure regulating valve on the camshaft cover, to control the flow of gases from the crankcase.

Exhaust emission control - petrol models

To minimise the amount of pollutants which escape into the atmosphere, all petrol models are fitted with a three-way catalytic converter in the exhaust system. The fuelling system is of the closed-loop type, in which a Lambda sensor in the exhaust system provides the engine management system ECU with constant feedback, enabling the ECU to adjust the air/fuel mixture to optimise combustion.

The Lambda sensor has a heating element built-in that is controlled by the ECU through the Lambda sensor relay to quickly bring the sensor's tip to its optimum operating temperature. The sensor's tip is sensitive to oxygen and relays a voltage signal to the ECU that varies according on the amount of oxygen in the exhaust gas. If the inlet air/fuel mixture is too rich, the exhaust gases are low in oxygen so the sensor sends a low-voltage signal, the voltage rising as the mixture weakens and the amount of oxygen rises in the exhaust gases. Peak conversion efficiency of all major pollutants occurs if the inlet air/fuel mixture is maintained at the chemically-correct ratio for the complete combustion of petrol of 14.7 parts (by weight) of air to 1 part of fuel (the stoichiometric ratio). The sensor output voltage alters in a large step at this point, the ECU using the signal change as a reference point and correcting the inlet air/fuel mixture accordingly by altering the fuel injector pulse width. Details of the Lambda sensor removal and refitting are given in Chapter 4A.

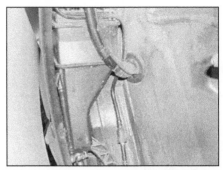

2.9 Charcoal canister location behind the front right-hand wheel arch liner

Exhaust emission control - diesel models

An oxidation catalyst is fitted in the exhaust system of all diesel engined models. This has the effect of removing a large proportion of the gaseous hydrocarbons, carbon monoxide and particulates present in the exhaust gas.

An Exhaust Gas Recirculation (EGR) system is also fitted to all diesel engined models. This reduces the level of nitrogen oxides produced during combustion by introducing a proportion of the exhaust gas back into the inlet manifold, under certain engine operating conditions, via a plunger valve. The system is controlled electronically by the diesel engine management ECU.

Evaporative emission control - petrol models

To minimise the escape of unburned hydrocarbons into the atmosphere, an evaporative loss emission control system is fitted to all petrol models. The fuel tank filler cap is sealed and a charcoal canister is mounted underneath the right-hand wing to collect the petrol vapours released from the fuel contained in the fuel tank. It stores them until they can be drawn from the canister (under the control of the fuel-injection/ignition system ECU) via the purge valve(s) into the inlet tract, where they are then burned by the engine during normal combustion.

To ensure that the engine runs correctly when it is cold and/or idling and to protect the catalytic converter from the effects of an over-rich mixture, the purge control valve(s) are not opened by the ECU until the engine has warmed up, and the engine is under load; the valve solenoid is then modulated on and off to allow the stored vapour to pass into the inlet tract.

Exhaust systems

On petrol models with engine codes ADP, ADR and AFY, the exhaust system comprises the exhaust manifold (with Lambda sensor), front pipe, catalytic converter, intermediate pipe and silencer, and tailpipe and silencer. On petrol models with engine code AHL, the exhaust system comprises the exhaust manifold (with Lambda sensor), front pipe and integral catalytic converter, intermediate pipe and silencer, and tailpipe and silencer. On petrol models with engine codes AEB, APU and AJL, the exhaust system comprises the exhaust manifold, turbocharger, catalytic converter with Lambda sensor, front pipe, intermediate pipe and silencer, and tailpipe and silencer.

On all diesel models, the exhaust system comprises the exhaust manifold, turbocharger, front pipe and integral catalytic converter, a short connecting pipe, intermediate pipe and silencer, and tailpipe and silencer. The system is supported by rubber bushes and/or rubber mounting rings.

Initially, the exhaust intermediate and rear sections are manufactured as one unit, however they are available separately as service items.

2 Evaporative loss emission control system - information and component renewal

Information

1 The evaporative loss emission control system consists of the purge valve, the activated charcoal filter canister and a series of connecting vacuum hoses.

2 The purge valve is located in the front right-hand corner of the engine compartment, in the vacuum line between the charcoal canister and the inlet manifold. The charcoal canister is mounted inside the right-hand front wheel housing behind the wheel arch liner, in front of the A-pillar.

Component renewal

Purge valve

3 Ensure that the ignition is switched off, then unplug the wiring harness from the purge valve at the connector.

4 Loosen the clips and disconnect the vacuum hoses. Note which way round the valve is fitted.

5 Refitting is a reversal of removal.

Charcoal canister

6 Apply the handbrake, then jack up the front of the vehicle and support it on axle stands (see *Jacking and vehicle support*). Remove the right-hand front roadwheel.

7 Refer to Chapter 11, and partially remove the rear of the right-hand front wheel arch liner to give access to the charcoal canister.

8 Disconnect the vacuum and breather hoses, noting which ports they connect to.

9 Undo the mounting screws and remove the charcoal canister (see illustration).

10 Refitting is a reversal of removal.

3 Crankcase emission system - general information

1 The crankcase emission control system consists of hoses connecting the crankcase to the air cleaner or inlet manifold. A pressure regulating valve is fitted to all diesel engines. Oil separator units are fitted to some petrol engines.

2 The system requires no attention other than to check at regular intervals that the hoses, valve and oil separator are free of blockages and in good condition.

4 Exhaust Gas Recirculation (EGR) system - information and component removal

Note: *The EGR system is only fitted to diesel engines.*

Information

1 The EGR system consists of the EGR valve, the modulator valve and a series of connecting vacuum hoses.

2 The EGR valve is mounted on a flange joint at the inlet manifold and is connected to a second flange joint at the exhaust manifold by a semi-flexible pipe.

Component renewal

EGR valve

3 Disconnect the vacuum hose from the port on the EGR valve (see illustration).

4 Unscrew the nuts and bolts and disconnect the semi-flexible connecting pipe from the EGR valve flange and from the exhaust manifold. The pipe is attached to the exhaust manifold by two nuts, and to the EGR valve by bolts (see illustrations). Recover the gaskets.

4.3 Vacuum hose on the EGR valve (AFN engine)

4.4a EGR valve (AFN engine)

4.4b EGR valve pipe-to-exhaust manifold mounting nuts (AFN engine)

4.4c EGR valve pipe-to-exhaust manifold mounting nuts (1Z engine)

4.5 EGR valve and mounting bolts (1Z engine)

5 Unscrew and remove the bolts securing the EGR valve to the inlet manifold flange and lift off the EGR valve **(see illustration)**. Recover the gasket.

6 Refitting is a reversal of removal, but use new flange joint gaskets and self-locking nuts.

5 Exhaust manifold - removal and refitting

Petrol engine models

Removal

1 Apply the handbrake, then jack up the front of the vehicle and support it on axle stands (see *Jacking and vehicle support*). Remove the splash guard from the bottom of the engine compartment.

2 Remove the air cleaner and trunking as described in Chapters 4A or 4B (as applicable). Also remove the engine top cover where necessary.

3 Except on engine codes AEB, APU and AJL, remove the Lambda sensor from the exhaust manifold as described in Chapter 4A.

4 On engine codes AEB, APU and AJL, unscrew the turbocharger support bracket bolts several turns only. Also unbolt the oil supply pipe from the heat shield.

5 Unbolt the heat shield from over the exhaust manifold where necessary.

6 Except on engine codes AEB, APU and AJL, unscrew the nuts and disconnect the exhaust front pipe from the exhaust manifold.

Recover the gasket and push the front pipe to the rear away from the manifold.

7 On engine codes AEB, APU and AJL, unscrew the three bolts securing the turbocharger to the exhaust manifold, and lower the turbocharger, then recover the gasket. Plug the opening in the turbocharger with rag to prevent entry of any foreign objects.

8 Progressively unscrew and remove the nuts and washers, and withdraw the exhaust manifold from the studs on the cylinder head. Recover the gasket.

Refitting

9 Clean thoroughly the mating surfaces of the manifold and cylinder head.

10 Refitting is a reversal of removal, but fit new gaskets, renew self-locking nuts, and tighten the nuts to the specified torque. On engine codes AEB, APU and AJL, fit the exhaust manifold, then the turbocharger to the manifold, and finally the turbocharger to the cylinder block. Refer to Chapter 4A for add-itional tightening torques.

Diesel engine models

Removal

11 Remove the turbocharger as described in Chapter 4B.

12 Unbolt and remove the heat shield.

13 Remove the inlet manifold as described in Chapter 4B.

14 Unscrew the bolt securing the oil supply pipe to the exhaust manifold.

15 On engine codes 1Z, AFF and AHU only, unbolt and remove the EGR recirculation pipe.

16 Progressively unscrew and remove the nuts and washers, and withdraw the exhaust manifold from the studs on the cylinder head. Recover the gaskets.

Refitting

17 Clean thoroughly the mating surfaces of the manifold and cylinder head.

18 Refitting is a reversal of removal, but fit new gaskets, renew self-locking nuts, and tighten the nuts to the specified torque.

6 Exhaust system - component renewal

 Warning: Allow ample time for the exhaust system to cool before starting work. In particular, note that the catalytic converter runs at very high temperatures. If there is any chance that the system may still be hot, wear suitable gloves.

Removal

1 Each exhaust section can be removed individually, however because the system is located above the rear axle, the complete system cannot be removed complete.

2 To remove part of the system, first jack up the front or rear of the car and support it on axle stands (see *Jacking and vehicle support*). Alternatively position the car over an inspection pit or on car ramps.

Front pipe (and catalytic converter on petrol engine code AHL and all diesel engines)

Note: *Handle the flexible, braided section of the front pipe carefully, and do not bend it excessively.*

3 Working under the car, unbolt the floor crossmember from the underbody.

4 Remove the air cleaner assembly as described in Chapter 4A or 4B.

5 Unscrew the nuts and disconnect the front pipe from the exhaust manifold (or catalytic converter on engine codes AEB, APU, AJL). Recover the gasket **(see illustrations)**.

6 Support the intermediate (or catalytic converter/short pipe) exhaust section on a trolley jack, then unscrew the flange bolts and separate the front pipe. Recover the gasket.

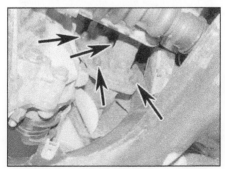

6.5a Unscrew the exhaust front pipe-to-manifold bolts . . .

6.5b . . . and remove the gasket

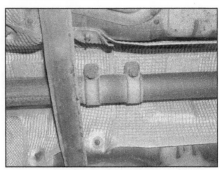

6.9 Clamp securing catalytic converter to intermediate section (ADR engine)

6.23a Mounting at the front of the tailpipe and silencer

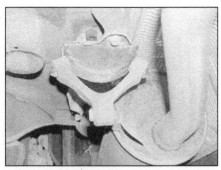

6.23b Mounting at the rear of the tailpipe and silencer

Catalytic converter (engine codes ADP, ADR, AFY)

7 Working under the car, support the front pipe and intermediate section on axle stands or trolley jacks.

8 Unscrew the flange bolts and separate the catalytic converter from the front pipe. Recover the gasket.

9 Note the fitted position of the clamp (the bolts should be on the left-hand side of the clamp, and the lower ends of the bolts should not be below the bottom of the intermediate pipe), then unscrew the clamp bolts and separate the catalytic converter from the intermediate section **(see illustration)**.

Catalytic converter (engine codes AEB, APU, AJL)

10 Remove the Lambda sensor as described in Chapter 4A, Section 4.

11 Unscrew and remove the bolts securing the catalytic converter to the front pipe. Recover the gasket.

12 Unbolt the exhaust system bracket from the gearbox and lower the front pipe.

13 Unscrew the flange nuts and remove the catalytic converter from the turbocharger. Recover the gasket. Withdraw the catalytic converter from under the car.

Short pipe (engine codes 1Z, AHU, AHH, AFN, AFF)

14 Unscrew the flange bolts and separate the short pipe from the catalytic converter.

15 Unscrew the clamp bolts and separate the short pipe from the intermediate section. Withdraw the short pipe from under the car.

Intermediate pipe and silencer

16 Working under the car, support the front pipe on an axle stand or trolley jack.

17 If the original intermediate/tail pipe is fitted, it will be necessary to cut through the middle pipe in order to separate it from the tailpipe and silencer. The pipe has an indentation to indicate where the cut must be made. Using a hacksaw, cut through the pipe at right-angles.

18 If the service pipe has been fitted, unscrew the clamp bolts and separate the intermediate pipe from the tailpipe.

19 Note the fitted position of the clamp attaching the intermediate pipe to the catalytic converter or short pipe (the bolts should be on the left-hand side of the clamp, and the lower ends of the bolts should not be below the bottom of the pipe), then unscrew the clamp bolts and separate the catalytic converter.

20 Disconnect the rubber mounting and withdraw the intermediate pipe and silencer from under the car.

Tailpipe and silencer

21 If the original intermediate/tail pipe is fitted, it will be necessary to cut through the middle pipe in order to separate it from the tailpipe and silencer. The pipe has an indentation to indicate where the cut must be made. Using a hacksaw, cut through the pipe at right-angles.

22 If the service pipe has been fitted, unscrew the clamp bolts and separate the tailpipe from the intermediate pipe. Note that the fitted position of the clamp should be with the bolts facing the rear of the car, and the bolt ends should not be below the bottom of the pipe.

23 Disconnect the rubber mountings and withdraw the tailpipe and silencer from under the car **(see illustrations)**.

Refitting

24 Each section is refitted by a reversal of the removal sequence, noting the following points.

a) *Ensure that all traces of corrosion have been removed from the flanges or pipe ends and renew all necessary gaskets.*

b) *Inspect the rubber mountings for signs of damage or deterioration and renew as necessary.*

c) *Prior to tightening the exhaust system mounting, ensure that all rubber mountings are correctly located and that there is adequate clearance between the exhaust system and vehicle underbody.*

7 Catalytic converter - general information and precautions

1 The catalytic converter is a reliable and simple device which needs no maintenance in itself, but there are some facts which an owner should be aware of if the converter is to function properly for its full service life.

Petrol models

a) *DO NOT use leaded petrol - the lead will coat the internal precious metals, reducing their converting efficiency and will eventually destroy the converter.*

b) *Always keep the ignition and fuel systems well-maintained in accordance with the manufacturer's schedule.*

c) *If the engine develops a misfire, do not drive the car at all (or at least as little as possible) until the fault is cured.*

d) *DO NOT push- or tow-start the car - this will soak the catalytic converter in unburned fuel, causing it to overheat when the engine does start.*

e) *DO NOT switch off the ignition at high engine speeds.*

f) *The catalytic converter, used on a well-maintained and well-driven car, should last between 50 000 and 100 000 miles - if the converter is no longer effective it must be renewed.*

Petrol and diesel models

g) *DO NOT use fuel or engine oil additives - these may contain substances harmful to the catalytic converter.*

h) *Remember that the catalytic converter operates at very high temperatures. DO NOT, therefore, park the car in dry undergrowth, over long grass or piles of dead leaves after a long run.*

i) *Remember that the catalytic converter is FRAGILE - do not strike it with tools during servicing work.*

Chapter 5 Part A:
Starting and charging systems

Contents

Degrees of difficulty

Easy, suitable for novice with little experience	Fairly easy, suitable for beginner with some experience	Fairly difficult, suitable for competent DIY mechanic 	Difficult, suitable for experienced DIY mechanic	Very difficult, suitable for expert DIY or professional

Specifications

General
System type . . . .   12-volt, negative earth

Starter motor
Type . . . .   Pre-engaged

Battery
Ratings . . . .   44 to 80 Ah (depending on model and market)

Alternator
Type . . . .   Bosch or Valeo
Rating . . . .   70, 90 or 120 amp
Minimum brush length . . . .   5.0 mm

Torque wrench settings

	Nm	lbf ft
Alternator mounting bolts:		
Diesel engine	25	18
Petrol engine lower	45	33
Petrol engine upper	25	18
Battery clamp bolt	15	11
Starter motor:		
Bracket to cylinder block (petrol engines)	22	16
To transmission	65	48

1 General information and precautions

General information

The engine electrical system consists mainly of the charging and starting systems. Because of their engine-related functions, these are covered separately from the body electrical devices such as the lights, instruments, etc which are covered in Chapter 12. On petrol engine models refer to Part B of this Chapter for information on the ignition system, and on Diesel models refer to Part C for the pre-heating system.

The electrical system is of the 12-volt negative earth type.

The battery may of the low maintenance or maintenance-free (sealed for life) type and is charged by the alternator, which is belt-driven from the crankshaft pulley.

The starter motor is of the pre-engaged type, with an integral solenoid. On starting, the solenoid moves the drive pinion into engagement with the flywheel/driveplate ring gear before the starter motor is energised. Once the engine has started, a one-way clutch prevents the motor armature being driven by the engine until the pinion disengages from the flywheel.

Further details of the various systems are given in the relevant Sections of this Chapter. While some repair procedures are given, the usual course of action is to renew the component concerned. The owner whose interest extends beyond mere component renewal should obtain a copy of the *Automobile Electrical & Electronic Systems Manual*, available from the publishers of this manual.

Precautions

⚠️ *Warning: It is necessary to take extra care when working on the electrical system to avoid damage to semi-conductor devices (diodes and transistors), and to avoid the risk of personal injury. In addition to the precautions given in Safety first!, observe the following when working on the system:*

Always remove rings, watches, etc before working on the electrical system. Even with the battery disconnected, capacitive discharge could occur if a component's live terminal is earthed through a metal object. This could cause a shock or nasty burn.

Do not reverse the battery connections. Components such as the alternator, electronic control units, or any other components having semi-conductor circuitry could be irreparably damaged.

Never disconnect the battery terminals, the alternator, any electrical wiring or any test instruments when the engine is running.

Do not allow the engine to turn the alternator when the alternator is not connected.

Never test for alternator output by 'flashing' the output lead to earth.

Always ensure that the battery negative lead is disconnected when working on the electrical system.

If the engine is being started using jump leads and a slave battery, connect the batteries *positive-to-positive* and *negative-to-negative* (see *Jump starting* at the beginning of the manual). This also applies when connecting a battery charger.

Before using electric-arc welding equipment on the car, *disconnect the battery, alternator and components such as electronic control units* to protect them from the risk of damage.

Caution: The radio/cassette fitted as standard equipment has a built-in security code to deter thieves. If the power source to the unit is cut, the anti-theft system will activate. Even if the power source is immediately reconnected, the radio/cassette unit will not function until the correct security code has been entered. Therefore, if you do not know the correct security code for the radio/cassette unit, do not disconnect the battery negative terminal or remove the radio/cassette unit from the vehicle.

2 Battery - testing and charging

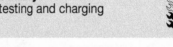

Standard and low-maintenance battery - testing

1 If the vehicle covers a small annual mileage, it is worthwhile checking the specific gravity of the electrolyte every three months to determine the state of charge of the battery. Use a hydrometer to make the check, and compare the results with the following table. Note that the specific gravity readings assume an electrolyte temperature of 15°C (60°F); for every 10°C (18°F) below 15°C (60°F) subtract 0.007. For every 10°C (18°F) above 15°C (60°F) add 0.007.

	Above 25°C	Below 25°C
Fully charged	1.210 to 1.230	1.270 to 1.290
70% charged	1.170 to 1.190	1.230 to 1.250
Discharged	1.050 to 1.070	1.110 to 1.130

2 If the battery condition is suspect, first check the specific gravity of electrolyte in each cell. A variation of 0.040 or more between any cells indicates loss of electrolyte or deterioration of the internal plates.

3 If the specific gravity variation is 0.040 or more, the battery should be renewed. If the cell variation is satisfactory but the battery is discharged, it should be charged as described later in this Section.

Maintenance-free battery - testing

4 In cases where a sealed for life maintenance-free battery is fitted, topping-up and testing of the electrolyte in each cell is not possible. The condition of the battery can therefore only be tested using a battery condition indicator or a voltmeter.

5 Certain models may be fitted with a maintenance-free battery, with a built-in charge condition indicator. The indicator is located in the top of the battery casing, and indicates the condition of the battery from its colour. If the indicator shows green, then the battery is in a good state of charge. If the indicator turns darker, eventually to black, then the battery requires charging, as described later in this Section. If the indicator shows clear/yellow, then the electrolyte level in the battery is too low to allow further use, and the battery should be renewed. **Do not attempt to charge, load or jump start a battery when the indicator shows clear/yellow.**

6 If testing the battery using a voltmeter, connect the voltmeter across the battery and note the voltage. The test is only accurate if the battery has not been subjected to any kind of charge for the previous six hours. If this is not the case, switch on the headlights for 30 seconds, then wait four to five minutes before testing the battery after switching off the headlights. All other electrical circuits must be switched off, so check that the doors and tailgate are fully shut when making the test.

7 If the voltage reading is less than 12.2 volts, then the battery is discharged, whilst a reading of 12.2 to 12.4 volts indicates a partially discharged condition.

8 If the battery is to be charged, remove it from the vehicle and charge it as described later in this Section.

Standard and low maintenance battery - charging

Note: *The following is intended as a guide only. Always refer to the manufacturer's recommendations (often printed on a label attached to the battery) before charging a battery.*

9 Charge the battery at a rate equivalent to 10% of the battery capacity (eg for a 45 Ah battery charge at 4.5 A) and continue to charge the battery at this rate until no further rise in specific gravity is noted over a four-hour period.

10 Alternatively, a trickle charger charging at the rate of 1.5 amps can safely be used overnight.

11 Specially rapid boost charges which are claimed to restore the power of the battery in 1 to 2 hours are not recommended, as they can cause serious damage to the battery plates through overheating.

12 While charging the battery, note that the temperature of the electrolyte should never exceed 37.8°C (100°F).

Maintenance-free battery - charging

Note: *The following is intended as a guide only. Always refer to the manufacturer's recommendations (often printed on a label attached to the battery) before charging a battery.*

13 This battery type takes considerably longer to fully recharge than the standard type, the time taken being dependent on the extent of discharge, but it can take anything up to three days.

14 A constant voltage type charger is required, to be set, when connected, to 13.9 to 14.9 volts with a charger current below 25 amps. Using this method, the battery should be useable within three hours, giving a voltage reading of 12.5 volts, but this is for a partially-discharged battery and, as mentioned, full charging can take far longer.

15 If the battery is to be charged from a fully-discharged state (condition reading less than 12.2 volts), have it recharged by your local automotive electrician, as the charge rate is higher and constant supervision during charging is necessary.

3 Battery - disconnection, removal and refitting

Note: *If the vehicle has a security-coded radio, check that you have a copy of the code number before disconnecting the battery cable; refer to the caution in Section 1.*

Disconnection and removal

1 The battery is located at the rear of the engine compartment, on the bulkhead **(see illustration)**.

2 Loosen the clamp nut and disconnect the battery negative (–) lead from the terminal **(see illustrations)**.

3 Lift the plastic flap where fitted, then loosen the clamp nut and disconnect the battery positive (+) lead from the terminal.

4 At the base of the battery, unscrew the retaining clamp bolt and remove the clamp.

5 Where fitted, disconnect the vent pipe from the battery. Note on some models the vent incorporates a flashback arrester.

6 Carefully lift out the battery and withdraw it from the engine compartment

Refitting

7 Clean the battery mounting and apply a little grease to the threads of the clamp bolt.

8 Place the battery in position and refit the clamp. Tighten the bolt to the specified torque.

9 Where fitted, refit the vent pipe.

10 Reconnect the battery positive (+) lead to the terminal and tighten the clamp nut.

11 Reconnect the battery negative (–) lead to the terminal and tighten the clamp nut.

12 Re-activate the radio by inserting the security code.

4 Alternator/charging system - testing in vehicle

Note: *Refer to Section 1 of this Chapter before starting work.*

1 If the charge warning light fails to illuminate when the ignition is switched on, first check the alternator wiring connections for security. If satisfactory, check that the warning light bulb has not blown, and that the bulbholder is secure in its location in the instrument panel. If the light still fails to illuminate, check the continuity of the warning light feed wire from the alternator to the bulbholder. If all is satisfactory, the alternator is at fault and should be renewed or taken to an auto-electrician for testing and repair.

2 Similarly, if the charge warning light comes on with the ignition, but is then slow to go out when the engine is started, this may indicate an impending alternator problem. Check all the items listed in the preceding paragraph, and refer to an auto-electrical specialist if no obvious faults are found.

3 If the charge warning light illuminates when the engine is running, stop the engine and check that the drivebelt is correctly tensioned (see Chapter 1A or 1B) and that the alternator connections are secure. If all is so far satisfactory, check the alternator brushes and slip rings as described in Section 6. If the fault persists, the alternator should be renewed, or taken to an auto-electrician for testing and repair.

4 If the alternator output is suspect even though the warning light functions correctly, the regulated voltage may be checked as follows.

5 Connect a voltmeter across the battery terminals, and start the engine.

6 Increase the engine speed until the voltmeter reading remains steady; the reading should be approximately 12 to 13 volts, and no more than 14 volts.

7 Switch on as many electrical accessories (eg, the headlights, heated rear window and heater blower) as possible, and check that the alternator maintains the regulated voltage at around 13 to 14 volts.

8 If the regulated voltage is not as stated, this

3.1 Battery location at the rear of the engine compartment

may be due to worn brushes, weak brush springs, a faulty voltage regulator, a faulty diode, a severed phase winding or worn or damaged slip rings. The brushes and slip rings may be checked (see Section 6), but if the fault persists, the alternator should be renewed or taken to an auto-electrician.

5 Alternator - removal and refitting

Removal

1 Disconnect the battery negative lead and position it away from the terminal - refer to the precautions in Section 1.

2 On petrol engine code AHL, press the engine oil dipstick guide tube up from its guide.

3 On petrol engine codes AEB, APU and AJL, loosen the clip and disconnect the intercooler air duct from the throttle housing.

4 Remove the main drivebelt as described in Chapter 2A or 2B as applicable.

5 Remove the viscous fan unit with reference to Chapter 3. Briefly, it is removed by inserting an Allen key from behind, while holding the unit stationary with a temporary bolt inserted from behind, resting on the engine cylinder block.

Petrol engines

6 Unscrew and remove the alternator upper mounting bolt **(see illustration)**.

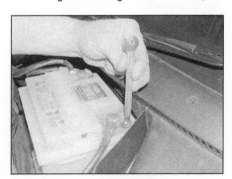

3.2a Loosen the clamp nut . . .

3.2b . . . and disconnect the battery negative (–) lead from the terminal

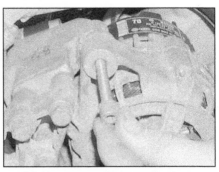

5.6 Unscrew and remove the upper mounting bolt (ADR)

5.7a Alternator lower mounting bolt (ADR)

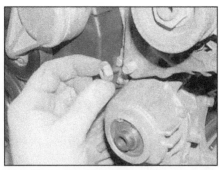

5.7b Removing the nut from the alternator lower mounting bolt

7 Unscrew the nut from the alternator lower mounting bolt, then swivel the alternator to one side and withdraw the lower mounting bolt from the front **(see illustrations)**.

8 Carefully release the support plastic tie from the alternator wiring **(see illustration)**.

9 Undo the nuts and disconnect the main cable and charging warning light wire from the rear of the alternator.

10 On engine code AHL, remove the wiring connector from the rear of the left-hand side headlight and remove the cap from the hydraulic fluid reservoir.

11 Push the coolant pipe to one side, and withdraw the alternator from the engine.

Diesel engines

12 Undo the nuts and disconnect the main cable and charging warning light wire from the rear of the alternator, then disconnect the wire from the DF terminal.

13 Carefully release the support plastic tie from the alternator wiring.

14 Support the alternator, then unscrew and remove the mounting bolts.

15 Push the coolant pipe to one side, and withdraw the alternator from the engine.

Refitting

16 Refitting is a reversal of removal. Refer to Chapter 2A or 2B as applicable for details of refitting the main drivebelt. Tighten the alternator mounting bolts to the specified torque.

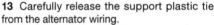

6 Alternator -
brush holder/regulator
module renewal

1 Remove the alternator, as described in Section 5.

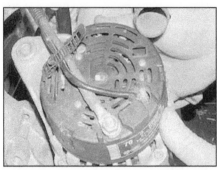

5.8 Wiring on the rear of the alternator

2 Place the alternator on a clean work surface, with the pulley facing down.

Bosch alternator

3 Undo the screws, then prise open the clips and lift the plastic cover from the rear of the alternator **(see illustrations)**.

4 Undo the two screws and carefully remove the voltage regulator/brush holder from the alternator **(see illustrations)**.

Valeo alternator

5 Undo the three nuts and remove the plastic cover from the rear of the alternator **(see illustration)**.

6 Undo the two nuts and single screw, and carefully remove the voltage regulator/brush holder from the alternator.

7 Press the plastic cap from the voltage regulator/brush holder.

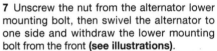

6.3a On the Bosch alternator, undo the retaining screws (arrowed) . . .

6.3b . . . then prise open the clips . . .

6.3c . . . and lift the plastic cover from the rear of the alternator (Bosch)

6.4a Undo the screws . . .

6.4b . . . and remove the voltage regulator/brush holder (Bosch)

All types

8 Measure the free length of the brush contacts - where applicable, take the measurement from the manufacturer's emblem (A) etched on the side of the brush contact, to the shallowest part of the curved end face of the brush (B) **(see illustration)**. Check the measurement with the Specifications; renew the module if the brushes are worn below the minimum limit.

9 Clean and inspect the surfaces of the slip rings, at the end of the alternator shaft **(see illustration)**. If they are excessively worn, or damaged, the alternator must be renewed.

10 Reassemble the alternator by following the dismantling procedure in reverse. On completion, refer to Section 5 and refit the alternator.

7 Starting system - testing

Note: *Refer to Section 1 of this Chapter before starting work.*

1 If the starter motor fails to operate when the ignition key is turned to the appropriate position, the following possible causes may be to blame:

a) *The battery is faulty.*
b) *The electrical connections between the switch, solenoid, battery and starter motor are somewhere failing to pass the necessary current from the battery through the starter to earth.*
c) *The solenoid is faulty.*
d) *The starter motor is mechanically or electrically defective.*

2 To check the battery, switch on the headlights. If they dim after a few seconds, this indicates that the battery is discharged - recharge (see Section 2) or renew the battery. If the headlights glow brightly, operate the ignition switch and observe the lights. If they

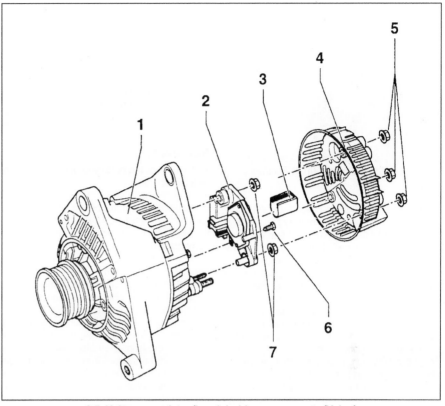

6.5 Voltage regulator/brush holder components (Valeo)

1 Alternator	4 Plastic cover
2 Voltage regulator/brush holder	5 Nuts
3 Plastic cap	

dim, then this indicates that current is reaching the starter motor, therefore the fault must lie in the starter motor. If the lights continue to glow brightly (and no clicking sound can be heard from the starter motor solenoid), this indicates that there is a fault in the circuit or solenoid - see following paragraphs. If the starter motor turns slowly when operated, but the battery is in good condition, then this indicates that either the starter motor is faulty, or there is considerable resistance somewhere in the circuit.

3 If a fault in the circuit is suspected, disconnect the battery leads (including the earth connection to the body), the starter/solenoid wiring and the engine/transmission earth strap. Thoroughly clean the connections, and reconnect the leads and wiring, then use a

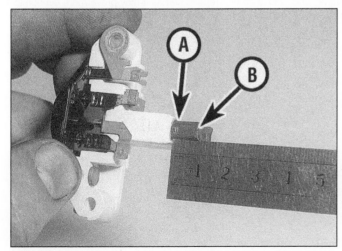

6.8 Measuring the alternator brush length - for A and B see text

6.9 Inspect the surfaces of the slip rings (arrowed) at the end of the alternator shaft

8.6 Starter motor (ADR engine)

voltmeter or test light to check that full battery voltage is available at the battery positive lead connection to the solenoid, and that the earth is sound. Smear petroleum jelly around the battery terminals to prevent corrosion - corroded connections are amongst the most frequent causes of electrical system faults.

4 If the battery and all connections are in good condition, check the circuit by disconnecting the wire from the solenoid blade terminal. Connect a voltmeter or test light between the wire end and a good earth (such as the battery negative terminal), and check that the wire is live when the ignition switch is turned to the start position. If it is, then the circuit is sound - if not the circuit wiring can be checked as described in Chapter 12.

5 The solenoid contacts can be checked by connecting a voltmeter or test light between the battery positive feed connection on the starter side of the solenoid, and earth. When the ignition switch is turned to the start position, there should be a reading or lighted bulb, as applicable. If there is no reading or lighted bulb, the solenoid is faulty and should be renewed.

6 If the circuit and solenoid are proved sound, the fault must lie in the starter motor. Begin checking the starter motor by removing it (see Section 8), and checking the brushes. If the fault does not lie in the brushes, the motor windings must be faulty. In this event, it may

be possible to have the starter motor overhauled by a specialist, but check on the availability and cost of spares before proceeding, as it may prove more economical to obtain a new or exchange motor.

8 Starter motor -
    removal and refitting

Removal

1 Disconnect the battery negative (earth) lead (see Section 3).

2 Apply the handbrake, then jack up the front of the vehicle and support it on axle stands (see *Jacking and vehicle support*). Remove the splash guard from under the engine compartment.

3 On models with air conditioning, move the complete front panel (the lock carrier assembly) away from the front of the car as far as possible, but without disconnecting the radiator hoses or electrical wiring. To do this, first remove the front bumper as described in Chapter 11, then unscrew the three quick-release clips from the noise insulation panel and unbolt the air duct from between the lock carrier and the air cleaner. On the left-hand side of the radiator, release the wiring from the clips. Unscrew the bolts securing the lock carrier assembly to the underbody channels, then unscrew the upper side bolts located behind the headlight units. With the help of an assistant, pull the complete assembly away from the front of the car as far as possible. Audi technicians use special tools to hold the assembly, however support bars may be made out of threaded metal rod and screwed into the underbody channels. **Note:** *Even on models without air conditioning, it may be helpful to move the lock carrier assembly away from the front of the car to gain improved access to the starter motor.*

4 On models with air conditioning, loosen the pivot and tension bolts and move the tensioner roller upwards to release the tension

on the drivebelt. Slip the drivebelt from the crankshaft, compressor and tensioner pulleys, then refer to Chapter 3 and unbolt the air conditioning compressor from the engine. Tie the compressor to one side away from the engine compartment.

 Warning: Do not disconnect the air conditioning refrigerant circuit.

5 On diesel engine code AFN only, unbolt and remove the turbocharger support bracket from the right-hand side of the engine. Also undo the nuts and remove the cable holder from the starter motor.

6 Unscrew the nut and disconnect the main cable from the terminal at the top of the starter motor **(see illustration)**.

7 Disconnect the trigger wire from the solenoid terminal.

8 On petrol engines, unscrew and remove the bolt securing the starter bracket to the cylinder block.

9 Unscrew the nut and remove the cable support from the starter motor bracket.

10 Unscrew and remove the two remaining bolts securing the starter motor to the transmission.

11 Lift the starter motor and withdraw it forwards from the bellhousing aperture.

Refitting

12 Refit the starter motor by following the removal procedure in reverse. Tighten the mounting bolts to the specified torque.

9 Starter motor -
    testing and overhaul

If the starter motor is thought to be defective, it should be removed from the vehicle and taken to an auto-electrician for assessment. In the majority of cases, new starter motor brushes can be fitted at a reasonable cost. However, check the cost of repairs first as it may prove more economical to purchase a new or exchange motor.

Chapter 5 Part B:
Ignition system - petrol engines

Contents

Degrees of difficulty

| Easy, suitable for novice with little experience | | Fairly easy, suitable for beginner with some experience | | Fairly difficult, suitable for competent DIY mechanic | | Difficult, suitable for experienced DIY mechanic | | Very difficult, suitable for expert DIY or professional | |

Specifications

General

Type:

Engine code ADP (1595 cc)	Bosch Motronic 3.2 injection
Engine code AHL (1595 cc)	Simos
Engine code ADR (1781 cc)	Bosch Motronic 3.2 injection
Engine code AFY (1781 cc)	Bosch Motronic 3.2 injection
Engine code APT (1781 cc)	Bosch Motronic 3.2 injection
Engine code APW (1781 cc)	Bosch Motronic 3.2 injection
Engine codes AEB and APU (1781 cc)	Bosch Motronic 3.2 injection
Engine code AJL (1781 cc)	Bosch Motronic 3.2 injection

Ignition coil

Primary winding resistance:

Engine codes ADP and AHL	0.5 to 1.5 ohms
Engine codes AEB, APU and AJL	0.4 to 0.6 ohms

Secondary resistance:

Engine codes ADP and AHL	5000 to 9000 ohms
Engine codes AEB, APU and AJL	N/A

Note: *The twin-spark ignition coils on other engines cannot be tested using conventional equipment, but require the use of a diode tester.*

Rotor arm

Resistance (engine code ADP) . . . . 1000 ohms

Ignition timing

Engine codes ADR, AHL, AFY, APT, APW, AEB, APU, AJL	Controlled by engine management system
Engine code ADP	0° ± 3°

Spark plugs

See Chapter 1A Specifications

Torque wrench setting	Nm	lbf ft
Knock sensor mounting bolt	20	15

1 General information

The Bosch and Simos systems described in this Chapter are self-contained engine management systems, which control both the fuel injection and ignition. This Chapter deals with the ignition system components only - refer to Chapter 4A for details of the fuel system components.

The ignition system comprises the spark plugs, HT leads, distributor (engine code ADP), electronic ignition coil(s), and Electronic Control Unit (ECU) together with its associated sensors, actuators and wiring. The component layout varies from system to system but the basic operation is the same for all models.

The basic operation is as follows: the ECU supplies a voltage to the input stage of the ignition coil which causes the primary windings in the coil to be energised. The supply voltage is periodically interrupted by the ECU and this results in the collapse of primary magnetic field, which then induces a much larger voltage in the secondary coil, called the HT voltage. This voltage is directed, via the HT leads, to the spark plug in the cylinder currently on its ignition stroke. The spark plug electrodes form a gap small enough for the HT voltage to arc across, and the resulting spark ignites the fuel/air mixture in the cylinder. The timing of this sequence of events is critical and is regulated solely by the ECU.

The ECU calculates and controls the ignition timing primarily according to engine speed, crankshaft position, throttle position and inlet air temperature, received from sensors mounted on and around the engine. Other parameters that affect ignition timing are coolant temperature and engine knock. Again, these are monitored via sensors mounted on the engine. On all engines, the coil dwell angle is controlled by a Hall transmitter in the distributor (engine code ADP) or on the front of the inlet camshaft.

A knock sensor is mounted on the cylinder block in order to detect engine pre-ignition (or 'pinking') before it actually becomes audible. If pre-ignition occurs, the ECU retards the ignition timing of the cylinder that is pre-igniting in steps until the pre-ignition ceases. The ECU then advances the ignition timing of that cylinder in steps until it is restored to normal, or until pre-ignition occurs again.

Except on engines fitted with the Simos engine management systems, idle speed control is achieved partly by an electronic throttle valve positioning module, mounted on the side of the throttle body and partly by the ignition system, which gives fine control of the idle speed by altering the ignition timing. On the Simos system, the ECU controls the idle speed through ignition timing and injection period. Manual adjustment of the engine idle speed is not necessary or possible.

It should be noted that comprehensive fault diagnosis of all the engine management systems described in this Chapter is only possible with dedicated electronic test equipment. Problems with the systems operation that cannot be pinpointed by following the basic guidelines in Section 2 should therefore be referred to an Audi/VAG dealer for assessment. Once the fault has been identified, the removal/refitting sequences detailed in the following Sections will then allow the appropriate component(s) to be renewed as required.

Note: *Throughout this Chapter, vehicles are frequently referred to by their engine code, rather than by engine capacity - refer to Chapter 2A for engine code listings.*

2 Ignition system - testing

⚠️ *Warning: Extreme care must be taken when working on the system with the ignition switched on; it is possible to get a substantial electric shock from a vehicle's ignition system. Persons with cardiac pacemaker devices should keep well clear of the ignition circuits, components and test equipment. Always switch off the ignition before disconnecting or connecting any component and when using a multi-meter to check resistances.*

General

1 Most ignition system faults are likely to be due to loose or dirty connections or to 'tracking' (unintentional earthing) of HT voltage due to dirt, dampness or damaged insulation, rather than by the failure of any of the system's components. Always check all wiring thoroughly before condemning an electrical component and work methodically to eliminate all other possibilities before deciding that a particular component is faulty.

2 The practice of checking for a spark by holding the live end of an HT lead a short distance away from the engine is not recommended.

Engine will not start

3 If the engine either will not turn over at all, or only turns very slowly, check the battery and starter motor. Connect a voltmeter across the battery terminals (meter positive probe to battery positive terminal), then disable the ignition by disconnecting the wiring from the coil. Note the voltage reading obtained while turning over the engine on the starter for a maximum of ten seconds. If the reading obtained is less than approximately 9.5 volts, first check the battery, starter motor and charging systems (see Chapter 5A).

4 If the engine turns over at normal speed but will not start on models with a distributor cap, check the HT circuit by connecting a timing light (following the manufacturer's instruct-

ions) and turning the engine over on the starter motor. If the light flashes, voltage is reaching the spark plugs, so these should be checked first. If the light does not flash, check the HT leads themselves followed by the distributor cap, carbon brush and rotor arm using the information given in Chapter 1A. If there is a spark, check the fuel system for faults referring to the relevant part of Chapter 4 for further information.

5 On models without a distributor cap, check the HT leads and ignition coil with reference to Section 3 of this Chapter.

6 If there is still no spark, then the problem must lie within the engine management system. The vehicle should be referred to an Audi/VAG dealer for assessment.

Engine misfires

7 An irregular misfire suggests either a loose connection or intermittent fault on the primary circuit.

8 With the ignition switched off, check carefully through the system ensuring that all connections are clean and securely fastened. Check the LT circuit as described above.

9 Check that the HT coil, the distributor cap (where applicable) and the HT leads are clean and dry. Check the leads themselves and the spark plugs (by substitution, if necessary), then where applicable check the distributor cap, carbon brush and rotor arm.

10 Regular misfiring is almost certainly due to a fault in the HT leads, spark plugs or, where applicable, the distributor cap.

11 If HT voltage is not present on one particular lead, the fault will be in that lead or in the distributor cap where fitted. If HT is present on all leads, the fault will be in the spark plugs.

Other problems

12 Problems with the system's operation that cannot be pinpointed by following the guidelines in the preceding paragraphs should be referred to a Audi/VAG dealer for assessment.

3 HT coil - removal, testing and refitting

Removal

1 On engine code ADP, the ignition coil is located on the right-hand side of the bulkhead, at the rear of the engine compartment. On engine code ADR, AFY, APT and APW, the ignition coil is located on the camshaft cover, over spark plugs 3 and 4; HT leads 3 and 4 are integral with the ignition coil and HT leads 1 and 2 are conventional. On engine code AHL, the ignition coil is located on the middle of the bulkhead at the rear of the engine compartment. On engine codes AEB, APU and AJL, the four ignition coils are located directly above the spark plugs.

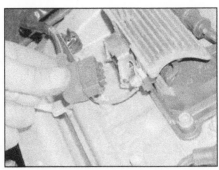

3.3a Disconnect the wiring . . .

3.3b . . . then disconnect the earth cable . . .

3.3c . . . and unbolt the ignition coil from the camshaft cover

2 On engine codes ADP and AHL, disconnect the low tension wiring from the coil on the bulkhead, then disconnect the HT lead. Unbolt the coil from the bulkhead.

3 On engine codes ADR, AFY, APT and APW, remove the engine top cover, then disconnect the wiring from the ignition coil by first lifting the locking clamp. Unscrew the nut and disconnect the earth cable. Carefully pull the HT leads from Nos 1 and 2 spark plugs, by pulling on the end fittings and not the leads themselves. Unscrew the mounting nuts, then pull up the coil assembly at the same time disconnecting the HT leads from Nos 3 and 4 spark plugs **(see illustrations)**. Recover the gasket.

4 On engine codes AEB, APU and AJL, remove the engine top cover, then disconnect the wiring from each of the ignition coils. Unscrew the bolt and disconnect the earth wire from the front of the camshaft cover and move the wiring to one side. Unscrew the mounting bolts and carefully lift the ignition coils from the camshaft cover, at the same time disconnecting the HT extensions from the spark plugs. Recover the gaskets from the coils. If necessary, the HT extensions can be removed from the bottom of the coils.

Testing

5 On engine codes ADP and AHL, disconnect the low tension and HT wiring, then connect an ohmmeter between the two low tension wiring terminals (terminals 1 and 15). Check that the primary resistance is as given in the Specifications. Now check that the secondary resistance between terminals 4 (HT) and 15 is as given in the Specifications **(see illustration)**.

6 On engine codes ADR, AFY, APT and APW, no tests are possible on the coil assembly, however the current supply can be checked by disconnecting the wiring plug and connecting an ammeter between the central terminal and earth. With the ignition switched on, battery voltage should be recorded on the ammeter.

7 On engine codes AEB, APU and AJL, the best method of testing a coil is to replace it with another known good coil. Alternatively, unplug the wiring from each **injector** one at a time to determine which cylinder is not firing. Once the misfiring cylinder is located, the spark plug can be removed for inspection. If

the spark plug proves in order and provided the engine is generally in good condition, the coil is proved faulty and should be renewed. Note that coils may be interchanged between cylinders.

Refitting

8 Refitting is a reversal of removal. On engine codes ADR, AFY, APT and APW, depress the locking clamp to secure the wiring.

4 Distributor -
removal, inspection and refitting

Note: *This Section applies to engine code ADP only.*

Removal

1 The distributor is located on the left-hand rear of the engine and is driven from the top of the oil pump shaft, which is driven from the intermediate shaft.

2 Set the engine to TDC on No 1 cylinder as described in Chapter 2A, Section 2.

3 Disconnect the HT lead from the ignition coil on the bulkhead, then identify the spark plug HT leads for position and disconnect them.

4 Unplug the Hall sensor cable from the distributor body at the connector.

5 Prise off the retaining clips, then lift off the distributor cap. Check at this point that the

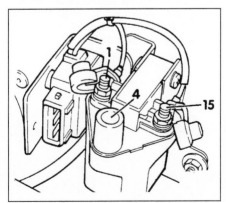

3.5 Ignition coil terminal positions

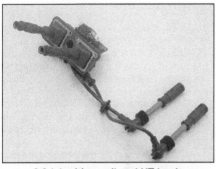

3.3d Ignition coil and HT leads

centre of the rotor arm electrode is aligned with the cylinder No 1 marking on the distributor body **(see illustration)**.

6 Mark the relationship between the distributor body and the cylinder block by scribing lines on each.

7 Unscrew the bolt and remove the clamp, then withdraw the distributor from the cylinder block. Recover the O-ring seal **(see illustration)**. **Note:** *As the distributor is removed, the rotor arm will turn anticlockwise.*

Inspection

8 Recover the O-ring seal from the bottom of the distributor and inspect it. Renew it if necessary.

9 Inspect the teeth of the distributor drive gear for signs of wear or damage. Any slackness will affect ignition timing. Renew the distributor if the teeth of the drive gear appear worn or chipped.

4.5 Centre of rotor arm electrode aligned with the cylinder No 1 mark

4.7 Unscrew the bolt then remove the clamp and withdraw the distributor

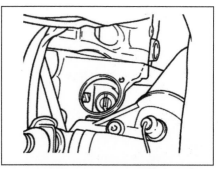

4.11 The oil pump drive tongue must be aligned with the axis of the crankshaft

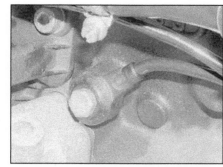

6.5 Knock sensor on engine code ADR

Refitting

10 Check that the engine is still set to TDC on cylinder No 1 cylinder.

11 Check that the oil pump shaft drive tongue is aligned with the axis of the crankshaft **(see illustration)**. If not, turn it with a screwdriver.

12 Fit the new O-ring, then insert the distributor and loosely fit the clamp and securing bolt; it will be necessary to make allowance for the shaft to turn slightly clockwise as it engages the intermediate shaft drive gear. Rotate the distributor body such that the alignment marks made during removal line up.

13 The shaft is engaged correctly when the centre of the rotor arm electrode is pointing directly at the No 1 cylinder mark on the distributor body - It may take a few attempts to get this right, as the helical drive gears make the alignment difficult to judge. Tighten the distributor clamp bolt.

14 Refit the distributor cap and secure with the clips.

15 Reconnect the Hall sensor cable.

16 Reconnect the spark plug HT leads and the main HT lead to the ignition coil.

17 It will now be necessary to have the ignition timing checked and if necessary adjusted - refer to Section 5.

5 Ignition timing - checking and adjusting

A distributor is fitted to engine code ADP,

and it is possible to make a basic setting of the ignition timing on this engine, however it is recommended that this work is carried out by an Audi/VAG dealer using dedicated equipment, as the system can be checked for fault codes at the same time. On all other engine codes, the ignition timing is under the control of the engine management system ECU and is not manually adjustable. The vehicle must be taken to an Audi/VAG dealer if the timing requires checking.

6 Ignition system sensors - removal and refitting

1 Many of the engine management system sensors provide signals for both the fuel injection and ignition systems. Those specific to the ignition system are detailed in this Section.

2 Those sensors that are common to both systems are detailed in Chapter 4A. These include the airflow meter, throttle valve potentiometer, inlet manifold air temperature sensor, throttle valve positioner, road speed sensor, coolant temperature sensor, engine speed sensor, and Hall sender.

Knock sensor

Removal

3 A knock sensor is located on the left-hand rear of the cylinder block. On engine codes ADR, AEB, APU, AFY, and AJL, two sensors are fitted next to each other.

4 Unplug the wiring from the sensor at the connector.

5 Unscrew the mounting bolt and remove the sensor **(see illustration)**.

Refitting

6 Refitting is a reversal of removal, but note that the sensor's operation will be affected if its mounting bolt is not tightened to exactly the right torque.

Hall-effect sensor (engine code ADP)

7 This sensor is an integral part of the distributor assembly. It can be removed and renewed separately, however special tooling may be required to dismantle the distributor. It is therefore recommended that this operation is entrusted to an automotive electrical specialist.

7 Rotor arm - removal and refitting

1 Prise off the retaining clips, then lift off the distributor cap.

2 Pull the rotor arm from the end of the distributor shaft. If necessary, remove the dust cover.

3 Inspect the distributor cap contacts and clean them if necessary.

4 Fit the new rotor arm using a reversal of the removal procedure - ensure that the rotor arm alignment lug engages with the recess in the distributor shaft, before refitting the distributor cap.

Chapter 5 Part C:
Pre-heating systems - diesel models

Contents

Degrees of difficulty

| Easy, suitable for novice with little experience | | Fairly easy, suitable for beginner with some experience | | Fairly difficult, suitable for competent DIY mechanic | | Difficult, suitable for experienced DIY mechanic | | Very difficult, suitable for expert DIY or professional | |

Specifications

Glow plugs

Current consumption .... 8 amps per glow plug

Torque wrench setting	Nm	lbf ft
Glow plug to cylinder head	15	11

1 General information

To assist cold starting, diesel engined models are fitted with a pre-heating system, which comprises four glow plugs, a glow plug control unit (incorporated in the ECU), a facia mounted warning lamp and the associated electrical wiring.

The glow plugs are miniature electric heating elements, encapsulated in a metal case with a probe at one end and electrical connection at the other. Each inlet tract has a glow plug threaded into it, which is positioned directly in line with the incoming spray of fuel. When the glow plug is energised, the fuel passing over it is heated, allowing its optimum combustion temperature to be achieved more readily in the combustion chamber.

The duration of the pre-heating period is governed by the glow plug control unit, which monitors the temperature of the engine via the coolant temperature sensor and alters the pre-heating time to suit the conditions.

A facia mounted warning lamp informs the driver that pre-heating is taking place. The lamp extinguishes when sufficient pre-heating has taken place to allow the engine to be started, but power will still be supplied to the glow plugs for a further period until the engine is started. If no attempt is made to start the engine, the power supply to the glow plugs is switched off to prevent battery drain and glow plug burn-out. Note that if a fault occurs in the engine management system while the car is moving, the glow plug warning lamp will start flashing and the system will then switch to fail-safe mode. Should this occur, the car must be taken to an Audi/VAG dealer for fault diagnosis.

2.10 Removing a glow plug from the cylinder head

2.12 Tightening a glow plug with a torque wrench

2 Glow plugs -
testing, removal and refitting

Testing

1 If the system malfunctions, testing is ultimately by substitution of known good units, but some preliminary checks may be made as described in the following paragraphs.

2 Connect a voltmeter or 12 volt test lamp between the glow plug supply cable and a good earth point on the engine.

Caution: Make sure that the live connection is kept well clear of the engine and bodywork.

3 Have an assistant activate the pre-heating system by turning on the ignition, and check that the battery voltage is applied to the glow plug electrical connection. Note that the voltage will drop to zero when the pre-heating period ends.

4 If no supply voltage can be detected at the glow plug, then the supply cabling must be faulty.

5 To locate a faulty glow plug, first disconnect the battery negative cable and position it away from the terminal.

6 Remove the supply cabling from the glow plug terminal, and connect an ammeter between the cable and terminal. Measure the steady state current consumption (ignore the initial current surge which will be about 50% higher). Compare the result with the Specifications - high current consumption (or no current draw at all) indicates a faulty glow plug.

7 As a final check, remove the glow plugs and inspect them visually, as described in the next sub-Section.

Removal

8 Disconnect the battery negative (earth) lead (see Chapter 5A).

9 Remove the nuts and washers from the glow plug terminals. Lift off the bus bar.

10 Unscrew and remove the glow plug(s) **(see illustration)**.

11 Inspect the glow plug stems for signs of damage. A badly burned or charred stem may be an indication of a faulty fuel injector; refer to Chapter 4B for greater detail.

Refitting

12 Refitting is a reversal of removal, but tighten the glow plug to the specified torque **(see illustration)**.

Chapter 6
Clutch

Contents

Degrees of difficulty

Easy, suitable for novice with little experience	**Fairly easy,** suitable for beginner with some experience	**Fairly difficult,** suitable for competent DIY mechanic 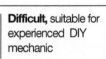	**Difficult,** suitable for experienced DIY mechanic	**Very difficult,** suitable for expert DIY or professional

Specifications

General

Type	Single dry plate, diaphragm spring with spring-loaded hub
Operation	Hydraulic with slave and master cylinders
Friction plate diameter	210 mm, 228 mm, or 240 mm (according to model)

Torque wrench settings

	Nm	lbf ft
Clutch master cylinder mounting bolts	20	15
Clutch pedal bracket mounting bolt:		
Long Torx bolt (from inside engine compartment - also secures		
brake master cylinder and servo)	25	18
Short hex socket-head bolt (from inside passenger compartment) . .	25	18
Clutch pedal shaft securing bolt	5	4
Clutch slave cylinder mounting bolt	25	18
Hydraulic pipe union to master/slave cylinder	15	11
Pressure plate-to-flywheel bolt	22	16

1 General information

The clutch is of single dry plate type, incorporating a diaphragm spring pressure plate, and is hydraulically operated.

The clutch cover (pressure plate) is bolted to the rear face of the flywheel, and the friction disc is located between the pressure plate and the flywheel friction surface. The disc hub is splined to the transmission input shaft and is free to slide along the splines. Friction lining material is riveted to each side of the disc and the disc hub incorporates cushioning springs to absorb transmission shocks and ensure a smooth take-up of drive. On all engines except engine code AHL, the flywheel is manufactured in two parts instead of the conventional single unit; the friction surface has a limited buffered movement in relation to the main flywheel mass bolted to the rear of the crankshaft. This has the effect of absorbing the initial clutch engagement shock and makes for a smoother gearchange.

When the clutch pedal is depressed, the slave cylinder pushrod moves the release lever forwards, and the release bearing is forced onto the diaphragm spring fingers. As the centre of the spring is pushed in, the outer part of the spring moves out and releases the pressure plate from the friction disc. Drive then ceases to be transmitted to the transmission.

When the clutch pedal is released, the diaphragm spring forces the pressure plate into contact with the linings on the friction disc, and at the same time pushes the disc slightly forward along the input shaft splines into engagement with the flywheel. The friction disc is now firmly sandwiched between the pressure plate and flywheel. This causes drive to be taken up.

An over-centre spring is fitted to the clutch pedal to equalise the operating effort over the full pedal stroke.

As the linings wear on the friction disc, the pressure plate rest position moves closer to the flywheel resulting in the 'rest' position of the diaphragm spring fingers being raised. The hydraulic system requires no adjustment since the quantity of hydraulic fluid in the circuit automatically compensates for wear every time the clutch pedal is operated.

2 Hydraulic system - bleeding

⚠️ **Warning: Hydraulic fluid is poisonous; thoroughly wash off spills from bare skin without delay. Seek immediate medical advice if any fluid is swallowed or gets into the eyes. Certain types of hydraulic fluid are inflammable and may ignite when brought into contact with hot components. Hydraulic fluid is also an effective paint stripper. If spillage occurs onto painted bodywork or fittings, it should be washed off immediately, using copious quantities of cold water. It is also hygroscopic (i.e. it can absorb moisture from the air) which then renders it useless. Old fluid may have suffered contamination, and should never be re-used.**

1 If any part of the hydraulic system is dismantled, or if air has accidentally entered the system, the system will need to be bled. The presence of air is characterised by the pedal having a spongy feel and it results in difficulty in changing gear.

2 The design of the clutch hydraulic system does not allow bleeding to be carried out using the conventional method of pumping the clutch pedal. In order to remove all air present in the system, it is necessary to use pressure bleeding equipment. This is available from auto accessory shops at relatively low cost.

3 The pressure bleeding equipment should be connected to the brake/clutch hydraulic fluid reservoir in accordance with the manufacturer's instructions. The system is bled through the bleed screw of the clutch slave cylinder, which is located at the top of the transmission housing. Access is best achieved by jacking up the front of the vehicle and supporting it on axle stands (see *Jacking and vehicle support*). Where necessary, remove the splash guard from under the transmission.

4 The system is bled until the fluid being ejected is free from air bubbles. The bleed screw is then closed and the bleeding equipment disconnected and removed.

5 Check the operation of the clutch to see that it is satisfactory. If air still remains in the system, repeat the bleeding operation.

6 Discard any fluid which is bled from the system, even if it looks clean. Hydraulic fluid absorbs water and its re-use can cause internal corrosion of the master and slave cylinders, leading to excessive wear and failure of the seals.

3 Clutch pedal - removal and refitting

Right-hand drive models

Removal

1 Remove the storage compartment/panel from below the steering column (refer to Chapter 11 if necessary). Unclip the cover then undo the retaining screws and pull the storage compartment from the clips in the facia. This will allow access to the pedal bracket.

2 Where fitted, disconnect the wiring and pull out the switch above the clutch pedal.

3 Using a screwdriver, extract the clip and release the clutch master cylinder pushrod from the pedal.

4 Unscrew the pivot bolt from the left-hand end of the pedal pivot, then withdraw the lever and lower the clutch pedal from the bracket, at the same time releasing it from the over-centre spring. Note the position of the bush, bearings, spacers and caps to ensure correct reassembly.

5 If necessary, the bearings can be renewed separate to the pedal **(see illustration)**.

Refitting

6 Refitting is a reversal of removal but grease the bearings and bush first. Refer to Chapter 9 and make sure that the brake pedal is refitted correctly.

Left-hand drive models

Removal

7 Remove the storage compartment/panel from below the steering column (refer to Chapter 11 if necessary). Unclip the cover then undo the retaining screws and pull the storage compartment from the clips in the facia. This will allow access to the pedal bracket.

8 Where fitted, disconnect the wiring and pull out the switch above the clutch pedal.

9 Using a screwdriver, release the clutch master cylinder pushrod pin securing clip

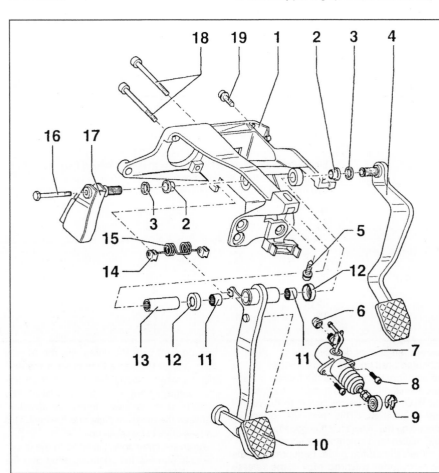

3.5 Pedal components on right-hand drive models

1 Mounting bracket	8 Socket head bolt	15 Over-centre spring
2 End bush	9 Clip	16 Bolt
3 Washer	10 Clutch pedal	17 Brake lever
4 Brake pedal	11 Needle roller bearing	18 Brake master cylinder and servo mounting bolts
5 Bracket mounting bolt	12 Cap	
6 Seal	13 Main bush	19 Bracket mounting bolt
7 Clutch master cylinder	14 Bearing	

from the pedal by twisting it upwards then pulling it from the pedal. Pull up the pedal to disconnect it from the pushrod **(see illustration)**.

10 Prise the pedal retaining clip from the groove in the left-hand end of the pivot shaft.

11 Unscrew the shaft retaining bolt, then press the shaft to the right until the clutch pedal can be removed from the bracket.

12 Prise the over-centre spring from the slots in the pedal bracket.

Refitting

13 Refitting is a reversal of removal, but do not refit the shaft retaining bolt until the pedal pivot shaft clip has been fitted.

---

4 Master cylinder -
removal, overhaul and refitting

Note: *Refer to the warning at the beginning of Section 2 regarding the hazards of working with hydraulic fluid.*

Removal

1 The clutch master cylinder is located inside the car on the clutch and brake pedal mounting bracket. Hydraulic fluid for the unit is supplied from the brake master cylinder reservoir.

Right-hand drive models

2 Before proceeding, place cloth rags on the carpet inside the car to prevent damage from spilt brake fluid.

3 In the engine compartment, clamp the hydraulic fluid hose leading from the brake fluid reservoir to the clutch master cylinder using a brake hose clamp.

4 Pull the hydraulic supply hose from the clutch master cylinder on the bulkhead.

5 Unscrew the union nut and disconnect the hydraulic line from the master cylinder. Tape over or plug the line to prevent loss of fluid or entry of dust.

6 Inside the car, remove the storage compartment/panel from below the steering column (refer to Chapter 11 if necessary). Unclip the cover then undo the retaining screws and pull the storage compartment from the clips in the facia. This will allow access to the pedal bracket.

7 Where fitted, disconnect the wiring and pull out the switch above the clutch pedal.

8 Disconnect the master cylinder pushrod from the peg on the clutch pedal by prising off the retaining clip.

9 Unscrew the mounting bolts using an Allen key, and withdraw the master cylinder from the pedal bracket. Make sure that the rubber seal remains fitted to the flange on the master cylinder.

Left-hand drive models

10 Remove the engine management ECU from the left-hand side of the bulkhead (see Chapter 4A, Section 4 or 5). To do this on early

models, unbolt the cover from the electronics box, using a socket through the hole in the cowl panel to reach the rear bolt. Later models are not provided with a hole in the cowl, and the cowl must be unclipped for access to the rear bolt.

11 Where applicable, remove the auxiliary relay carrier and auxiliary fusebox.

12 Disconnect the wiring at the connector, then pull the engine wiring harness together with the rubber grommet through the opening in the electronics box. Unscrew the retaining nuts at the rear of the electronics box, then release the box from the location peg at the front and withdraw the box from the bulkhead.

13 Before proceeding, place cloth rags on the carpet inside the car to prevent damage from spilt brake fluid.

14 Using a brake hose clamp, clamp the hydraulic fluid hose leading from the brake

fluid reservoir to the clutch master cylinder.

15 Pull the hose from the clutch master cylinder on the bulkhead.

16 On early models, unscrew the union nut and disconnect the hydraulic line from the master cylinder. The union nut is partially concealed by the brake vacuum servo unit. On later models, prise out the clip with a screwdriver, then pull the hydraulic line from the master cylinder. Tape over or plug the line to prevent loss of fluid or entry of dust.

17 Using a Torx key, unscrew and remove the brake master cylinder mounting bolts.

18 Inside the car, remove the storage compartment/panel from below the steering column (refer to Chapter 11 if necessary). Unclip the cover then undo the retaining screws and pull the storage compartment from the clips in the facia. This will allow access to the pedal bracket.

3.9 Clutch pedal components on left-hand drive models

1 *Mounting bracket*	6 *Clutch pedal*	12 *Over-centre spring*
2 *Pivot pin*	7 *Pushrod pin*	13 *Pivot pin locking bolt*
3 *Clip*	8 *Clip*	14 *Seal*
4 *Bracket mounting bolt*	9 *Clutch master cylinder*	15 *Brake master cylinder and*
5 *Brake pedal*	10 *Socket head bolt*	*servo mounting bolts*
	11 *Over-centre spring holders*	

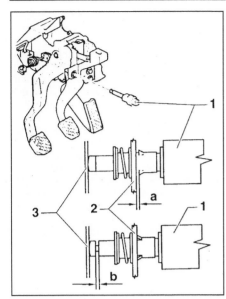

4.31 Clutch pedal switch adjustment

1 Switch   3 Clutch pedal
2 Mounting bracket

a and b = 0.5 mm maximum

19 Using a screwdriver, release the clutch master cylinder pushrod pin securing clip from the pedal by twisting it upwards then pulling it from the pedal. Pull up the pedal to disconnect it from the pushrod.
20 Using an Allen key, unscrew the clutch master cylinder mounting bolts and also the upper pedal bracket bolt, then pull the bracket and master cylinder slightly out and withdraw the master cylinder. Make sure that the rubber seal remains fitted to the flange on the master cylinder.

Overhaul

21 Repair kits are not available from Audi, but they may be available from a motor factor.
22 To overhaul the master cylinder, first clean the exterior surfaces.
23 Prise off the rubber boot and remove the pushrod. If necessary, loosen the locknut, unscrew the clevis and locknut, and remove the pushrod from the rubber boot. Note the distance between the pushrod eye centre and the mounting flange to ensure correct refitting.

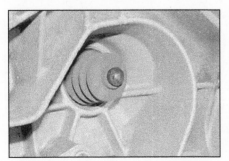

5.15 View of the clutch slave cylinder in the transmission casing, with the engine removed

24 Extract the circlip from the mouth of the cylinder , and withdraw the washer, piston and spring noting that the smaller end of the spring contacts the piston.
25 Clean the components, and examine them for wear and deterioration. If the piston and bore are worn excessively, or if corrosion is evident, renew the complete cylinder. If they are in good condition, remove the seals from the piston and renew them.
26 Dip the new seals in hydraulic fluid, and fit them on the piston, using the fingers only to manipulate them into position. Make sure that the seal lips face the spring end of the piston.
27 Insert the spring in the cylinder, then dip the piston in hydraulic fluid and carefully insert it.
28 Fit the washer, then locate the circlip in the groove.
29 Apply a little grease to the end of the pushrod, then locate it on the piston and fit the rubber boot.
30 Screw on the locknut and clevis then adjust the distance between the centre of the eye and the bulkhead face of the mounting flange to 139.0 ± 0.5 mm on RHD models, or 165.0 ± 0.5 mm on LHD models.

Refitting

31 Refitting is a reversal of removal, but tighten the master cylinder mounting bolts and the hydraulic hose union to the specified torques. Apply a little grease to the clevis pin eye before refitting it. Bleed the clutch hydraulic system as described in Section 2. On LHD models, before refitting the electronics box check the bulkhead gasket and if necessary renew it. On completion, check the setting of the clutch pedal switch as follows. With the pedal released, the gap between the switch plunger and the main body of the switch must be not more than 0.5 mm. Also the gap between the pedal bracket and the retaining tabs of the switch must not be more than 0.5 mm. To adjust the switch, turn it as required **(see illustration)**.

---

5 Slave cylinder -
   removal, overhaul and refitting

Note: *Refer to the warning at the beginning of Section 2 regarding the hazards of working with hydraulic fluid.*

Removal

1 The slave cylinder is located on top of the transmission. Although access is possible from the engine compartment, it may be considered better to raise the front of the car for access from below.
2 Apply the handbrake, then jack up the front of the vehicle and support it on axle stands (see *Jacking and vehicle support*).
3 Clamp the rubber section of the hydraulic hose leading from the master cylinder to the slave cylinder using a brake hose clamp, to prevent loss of hydraulic fluid.

4 Unscrew the union nut and disconnect the hydraulic line from the slave cylinder. Tape over or plug the end of the line and the slave cylinder aperture.
5 Unscrew the mounting bolt and withdraw the slave cylinder. As the cylinder is being removed, recover the hose support bracket.

Overhaul

6 Repair kits are not available from Audi, but they may be available from a motor factor.
7 To overhaul the slave cylinder, first clean the exterior surfaces.
8 Prise off the rubber boot and remove the pushrod.
9 Extract the special spring clip from the mouth of the cylinder , and withdraw the piston and spring.
10 Clean the components, and examine them for wear and deterioration. If the piston and bore are worn excessively, or if corrosion is evident, renew the complete cylinder. If they are in good condition, remove the seal from the piston and renew it.
11 Dip the new seal in hydraulic fluid, and fit it on the piston, using the fingers only to manipulate it into position. Make sure that the seal lip faces the spring end of the piston.
12 Insert the spring in the cylinder, then dip the piston in hydraulic fluid and carefully insert it.
13 Hold the piston depressed with a screwdriver then press a new spring clip into the mouth of the cylinder, making sure that the legs of the clip grip the cylinder.
14 Fit the pushrod, followed by the rubber boot.

Refitting

15 Refitting is a reversal of removal, but smear a little lithium grease to the outer surface of the rubber boot before locating the slave cylinder in the transmission aperture **(see illustration)**. Tighten the mounting bolt and union to the specified torque and finally bleed the system as described in Section 2. The end of the pushrod which contacts the release lever should be lightly lubricated with a molybdenum disulphide grease and care must be taken to ensure that the pushrod actually engages with the depression in the lever. The slave cylinder must be pressed into the transmission casing before the mounting bolt can be inserted. For easier refitting, a special mounting bolt with a locating extension can be obtained from Audi. Due to the limited access and the fact that the slave cylinder must be pushed against the considerable force of the internal return spring, refitting should be made in stages. First fully insert the cylinder (without the hose support bracket), ensuring that the bolt hole is correctly aligned, then refit the hose support bracket so that the front tags are engaged with the cut-out in the cylinder. With the cylinder held in this position, insert the mounting bolt and tighten to the specified torque. Finally locate the hydraulic line on the support bracket.

6.3a Use an Allen key to unscrew the clutch pressure plate bolts

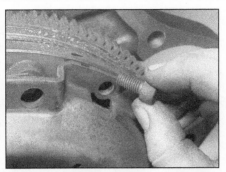

6.3b Removing the clutch pressure plate bolts

6.4 Removing the pressure plate and friction disc from the flywheel

6 Clutch disc and pressure plate - removal, inspection and refitting

⚠️ *Warning: Dust created by clutch wear and deposited on the clutch components may contain asbestos, which is a health hazard. DO NOT blow it out with compressed air or inhale any of it. DO NOT use petrol or petroleum-based solvents to clean off the dust. Brake system cleaner or methylated spirit should be used to flush the dust into a suitable receptacle. After the clutch components are wiped clean with clean rags, dispose of the contaminated rags and cleaner in a sealed container.*

Removal

1 Access to the clutch is obtained by removing the transmission as described in Chapter 7A.
2 Mark the clutch pressure plate and flywheel in relation to each other.
3 Hold the flywheel stationary, then unscrew the clutch pressure plate bolts progressively in diagonal sequence using an Allen key **(see illustrations)**. With the bolts unscrewed two or three turns, check that the pressure plate is not binding on the dowel pins. If necessary, use a screwdriver to release the pressure plate.
4 Remove all the bolts, then lift the clutch pressure plate and friction disc from the flywheel **(see illustration)**.

Inspection

5 Clean the pressure plate, disc and flywheel. Do not inhale the dust, as it may contain asbestos which is dangerous to health.
6 Examine the fingers of the diaphragm spring for wear or scoring **(see illustration)**. If the depth of wear exceeds half the thickness of the fingers, a new pressure plate assembly must be fitted.
7 Examine the pressure plate for scoring, cracking and discoloration. Light scoring is acceptable, but if excessive, a new pressure plate assembly must be fitted.
8 Examine the friction disc linings for wear and cracking, and for contamination with oil or grease **(see illustration)**. The linings are worn excessively if they are worn down to, or near, the rivets. Check the disc hub and splines for wear, by temporarily fitting it on the transmission input shaft. Renew the friction disc as necessary.
9 Examine the flywheel friction surface for scoring, cracking and discoloration (caused by overheating). If excessive, it may be possible to have the flywheel machined by an engineering works, otherwise it should be renewed.
10 Ensure that all parts are clean, and free of oil or grease, before reassembling. Apply just a small amount of high-melting-point grease to the splines of the friction disc hub. Note that new pressure plates and clutch covers may be coated with protective grease. It is only permissible to clean the grease away from the friction disc lining contact area. Removal of the grease from other areas will shorten the service life of the clutch.

Refitting

11 Commence reassembly by locating the friction disc on the flywheel, with the raised,

6.6 Examine the fingers of the diaphragm spring for wear or scoring

6.8 Examine the friction disc linings for wear and cracking

6.11 Locating the friction disc on the flywheel

6.12 Locating the clutch pressure plate over the friction disc

torsion spring side of the hub facing outwards. If necessary, the centralising tool (see paragraph 14) may be used to hold the disc on the flywheel at this stage **(see illustration)**.

12 Locate the clutch pressure plate on the disc, and fit it onto the location dowels **(see illustration)**. If refitting the original pressure

6.15 Tightening the clutch pressure plate bolts

plate, make sure that the previously-made marks are aligned.

13 Insert the bolts finger-tight to hold the pressure plate in position.

14 The friction disc must now be centralised, to ensure correct alignment of the transmission input shaft with the spigot bearing in the crankshaft. To do this, a proprietary tool may be used, or alternatively, use a wooden mandrel made to fit inside the friction disc and flywheel spigot bearing. Insert the tool through the friction disc into the spigot bearing, and make sure that it is central.

15 Tighten the pressure plate bolts progressively and in diagonal sequence, until the specified torque setting is achieved, then remove the centralising tool **(see illustration)**.

16 Check the release bearing in the transmission bellhousing for smooth operation, and if necessary renew it with reference to Section 7.

17 Refit the transmission with reference to Chapter 7A.

7 Release bearing and lever - removal, inspection and refitting

Removal

1 Remove the transmission as described in Chapter 7A **(see illustration)**.

2 Use a screwdriver to prise the release lever from the ball stud inside the transmission bellhousing. If this proves difficult, push the spring clip from the pivot end of the release lever by pushing it through the hole. This will release the pivot end of the lever from the ball stud. Now withdraw the lever together with the release bearing from the guide sleeve **(see illustrations)**.

7.1 Transmission bellhousing and clutch release lever and bearing with the engine removed

7.2a Push the spring clip to release the arm from the pivot stud

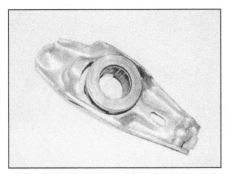

7.2b Release lever and bearing removed from the transmission

7.3a Using a screwdriver to release the bearing from the arm

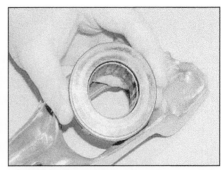

7.3b Removing the bearing from the arm

3 Use a screwdriver to depress the plastic tabs and separate the bearing from the lever **(see illustrations)**.
4 Remove the plastic pivot from the ball stud. The release lever locates on the plastic pivot.

Inspection

5 Spin the release bearing by hand, and check it for smooth running. Any tendency to seize or run rough will necessitate renewal of the bearing. If it is to be re-used, wipe it clean with a dry cloth; on no account should the bearing be washed in a liquid solvent, otherwise the internal grease will be removed.

Refitting

6 Commence refitting by lubricating the ball stud and plastic pivot with a little copper grease **(see illustration)**. Smear a little grease on the release bearing surface which contacts the diaphragm spring fingers and the release lever, and also on the guide sleeve.
7 Fit the spring onto the release lever, and make sure the plastic pivot is in place on the ball stud. Refit the lever together with the bearing and press the release lever onto the ball stud until the spring holds it in position **(see illustrations)**.

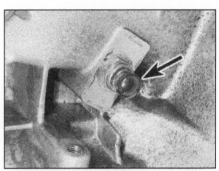

7.6 Lubricate the ball stud with a little copper grease

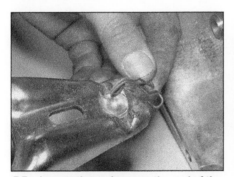

7.7a Locate the spring over the end of the release lever . . .

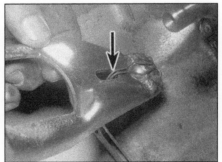

7.7b . . . and press the spring into the hole . . .

7.7c . . . then press the release lever onto the ball stud until the spring clip holds it in position

Chapter 7 Part A:
Manual transmission

Contents

Degrees of difficulty

Easy, suitable for novice with little experience	Fairly easy, suitable for beginner with some experience	Fairly difficult, suitable for competent DIY mechanic	Difficult, suitable for experienced DIY mechanic	Very difficult, suitable for expert DIY or professional

Specifications

General

Type	Transmission mounted on rear of engine, with drive flanges to front wheels. Five forward speeds and reverse, synchromesh on all gears, integral final drive
Lubricant capacities	See Chapter 1A or 1B

Torque wrench settings	Nm	lbf ft
Engine-to-transmission bolts:		
M10	45	33
M12	65	48
Gearchange adjustment bolt	23	17
Guide sleeve bolt:		
Aluminium casing*	35	26
Magnesium casing*	25	18
Multi-function switch:		
Aluminium casing*	25	18
Magnesium casing*	15	11
Oil filler plug	25	18

On magnesium casings the code MgAl9Zn1 appears just in front of the left-hand driveshaft, and on the bottom of the casing behind the left-hand driveshaft.

1 General information

The five-speed manual transmission is bolted to the rear of the in-line engine. The front-wheel-drive configuration transmits the power to a differential unit located at the front of the transmission, through driveshafts, to the front wheels. All gears including reverse incorporate a synchromesh engagement.

Gearshift is by a floor-mounted lever. A single shift rod connects the bottom of the lever to the transmission, and the shift rod is connected to a single shift rod which protrudes from the rear of the transmission **(see illustrations)**.

2 Gearchange linkage - adjustment

Standard gearchange models

1 Apply the handbrake, then jack up the front of the vehicle and support it on axle stands (see *Jacking and vehicle support*). Select neutral.
2 Working under the car, remove the heatshield from the underbody for access to the bottom of the gearchange. For improved access, remove the exhaust front downpipe and catalytic converter (see Chapter 4C).
3 Loosen the clamp bolt attaching the gearchange rod to the adjustment fork on the bottom of the gearchange lever **(see illustration)**. Do not remove the bolt.
4 Working inside the car, unscrew and remove the knob from the top of the gearstick, then unclip and remove the gaiter.
5 Remove the noise insulation around the bottom of the gearstick housing.
6 Check that the ball housing is horizontal. If not, loosen the two nuts, adjust the position of the housing, and re-tighten the nuts.

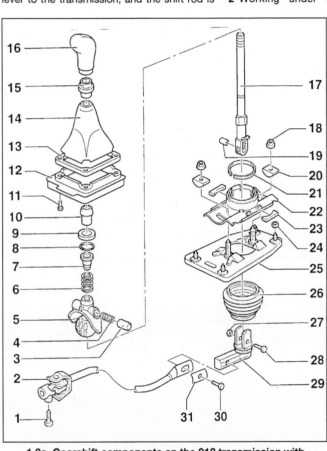

1.2a Gearshift components on the 012 transmission with standard gearchange

1 Bolt	11 Screw	22 Housing
2 Gearchange selector rod	12 Lower frame	23 Buffer
	13 Upper frame	24 Nut
3 Bush	14 Gaiter	25 Plate
4 Spring	15 Bush	26 Bellows
5 Ball stop	16 Knob	27 Nut
6 Spring	17 Gear lever	28 Bolt
7 Spacer	18 Nut	29 Selector fork
8 Circlip	19 Spacer	30 Bolt
9 Collar	20 Spacer	31 Clamp
10 Bush	21 Clip	

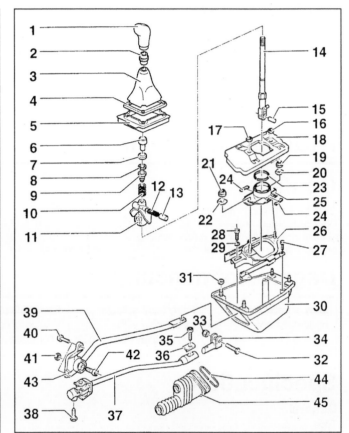

1.2b Gearshift components on the 012 transmission with short-travel gearchange

1 Knob	16 Nut	31 Nut
2 Bush	17 Nut	32 Bolt
3 Gaiter	18 Noise insulation	33 Nut
4 Upper frame	19 Nut	34 Selector fork
5 Lower frame	20 Spacer	35 Bolt
6 Bush	21 Nut	36 Clamp
7 Collar	22 Spacer	37 Front selector rod
8 Circlip	23 Circlip	38 Bolt
9 Spacer	24 Buffer	39 Front pushrod
10 Spring	25 Housing	40 Bolt
11 Ball stop	26 Rear pushrod	41 Nut
12 Spring	27 Bolt	42 Bolt
13 Bush	28 Bolt	43 Retainer
14 Gear lever	29 Washer	44 Ring
15 Spacer	30 Housing	45 Bellows

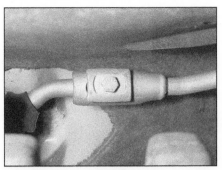

2.3 Gearshift adjustment bolt and clamp (standard gearchange)

7 Have an assistant hold the gear lever in a vertical position to that the distance between the ends of the curved ball stop are the same on both sides with the lever positioned slightly to the rear. The gear lever is now in the 3rd/4th neutral position **(see illustrations)**.
8 Make sure the transmission gear selector rod is positioned in neutral, then tighten the adjustment bolt beneath the car.
9 Check that all gear positions can be selected without difficulty.
10 Refit the underbody heatshield together with the exhaust downpipe and catalytic converter (where removed).
11 Refit the noise insulation, gaiter and gear knob, and lower the car to the ground.

Short-travel gearchange models

12 Working inside the car, unscrew and remove the knob from the top of the gearstick, then unclip and remove the gaiter.
13 Remove the noise insulation around the bottom of the gearstick housing.
14 Measure the distance between the rear pushrod and body as shown **(see illustration)**. If it is not 37 mm, loosen the pushrod bolt, re-position the pushrod, and tighten the bolt.
15 Working through the gearstick aperture, loosen the clamp bolt attaching the gearchange rod to the adjustment fork on the gearchange lever. Do not remove the bolt.
16 Check that the ball housing is horizontal. If not, loosen the two nuts, adjust the position of the housing, and re-tighten the nuts.

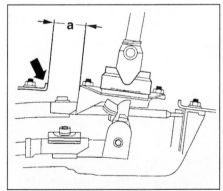

2.14 On the short-travel gearchange, the distance shown must be 37.0 mm

17 Have an assistant hold the gear lever in a vertical position to that the distance between the ends of the curved ball stop are the same on both sides with the lever positioned slightly to the rear. The gear lever is now in the 3rd/4th neutral position.
18 Make sure the transmission gear selector rod is positioned in neutral, then tighten the adjustment bolt.
19 Refit the noise insulation, gaiter and gear knob, and lower the car to the ground.

3 Manual transmission - removal and refitting

Removal

1 Select a solid, level surface to park the vehicle upon. Give yourself enough space to move around it easily. Apply the handbrake and chock the rear wheels.
2 Apply the handbrake, then jack up the front of the vehicle and support it on axle stands (see *Jacking and vehicle support*). Remove the splash guard from under the engine compartment.
3 Disconnect the battery negative (earth) lead (see Chapter 5A).
4 Remove the air cleaner assembly as described in Chapter 4A or 4B.
5 On turbocharged models, undo the screws and lift the coolant expansion tank from its location and move it to one side without disconnecting the coolant hoses. Disconnect the Lambda sensor wiring on the bulkhead.
6 Refer to Chapter 4C, and remove the exhaust front pipe and catalytic converter. Take care not to bend excessively the flexible section of the front pipe.
7 Unscrew and remove the transmission-to-engine bolts accesible from above (ie the engine compartment).
8 Unbolt the splash guard support bracket from under the front of the engine compartment.
9 Using an Allen key, unbolt the heat shields from over the inner end of the right-hand driveshaft.
10 Support the transmission on a trolley jack, then unbolt the right-hand transmission mounting complete with rubber bush.

3.11 Driveshaft connection to drive flange on side of transmission

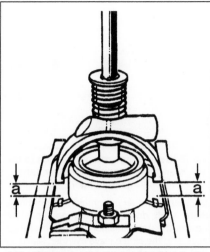

2.7a Distance 'a' must be equal on both sides of the curved ball stop

2.7b Using a steel rule to centralise the gear lever

11 Refer to Chapter 8 and detach the driveshafts from the transmission flanges **(see illustration)**. Rest the driveshafts on the suspension links.
12 Disconnect the wiring from the speedometer sender on the transmission.
13 Disconnect the wiring from the reversing light switch on the transmission.
14 Check that all wiring has been disconnected from the transmission and transmission-to-engine bolts.
15 Remove the starter motor with reference to Chapter 5A. If preferred, the wiring may be left connected, and the starter supported to one side.
16 Unscrew the bolt and disconnect the gearchange rod from the rear of the transmission **(see illustration)**.
17 On models with a short-travel gearchange, unscrew the bolt and detach the steady bar.
18 Make sure that the transmission is adequately supported, then unscrew the remaining bolts securing the transmission to the engine.
19 Unscrew the bolt securing the left-hand transmission mounting to the rubber mounting.
20 With the help of an assistant, withdraw the transmission from the locating dowels on

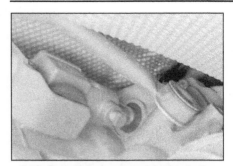

3.16 Gearchange rod connection to the rear of the transmission (standard gearchange)

the rear of the engine, making sure that the input shaft does not hang on the clutch. Lower the transmission sufficient to gain access to the clutch slave cylinder. Make sure that the driveshafts are supported clear of the transmission.

> ⚠ **Warning: Make sure that the transmission remains steady on the jack head. Keep the transmission level until the input shaft is fully withdrawn from the clutch friction plate.**

21 Unbolt the slave cylinder from the transmission, and tie it to one side. **Note:** *Do not depress the clutch pedal with the slave cylinder removed.*

22 Lower the transmission to the ground.

Refitting

23 Before refitting the transmission, make sure that the location dowels are correctly positioned in the engine cylinder block rear face. Also make sure that the starter motor lower mounting bolt is positioned in the transmission, as it cannot be inserted with the transmission in its normal position.

24 Refitting the transmission is a reversal of the removal procedure, but note the following points:

a) Check the rear rubber mountings and renew them if necessary.

b) Apply a little high-melting-point grease to the splines of the transmission input shaft.
c) Tighten all nuts and bolts to the specified torque where given.
d) On completion, refer to Section 2 and check the gearchange linkage adjustment.

4 Manual transmission overhaul - general information
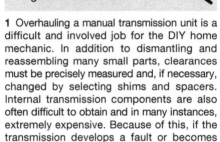

1 Overhauling a manual transmission unit is a difficult and involved job for the DIY home mechanic. In addition to dismantling and reassembling many small parts, clearances must be precisely measured and, if necessary, changed by selecting shims and spacers. Internal transmission components are also often difficult to obtain and in many instances, extremely expensive. Because of this, if the transmission develops a fault or becomes noisy, the best course of action is to have the unit overhauled by a specialist repairer or to obtain an exchange reconditioned unit.

2 Nevertheless, it is not impossible for the more experienced mechanic to overhaul the transmission if the special tools are available and the job is carried out in a deliberate step-by-step manner, to ensure that nothing is overlooked.

3 The tools necessary for an overhaul include internal and external circlip pliers, bearing pullers, a slide hammer, a set of pin punches, a dial test indicator and possibly a hydraulic press. In addition, a large, sturdy workbench and a vice will be required.

4 During dismantling of the transmission, make careful notes of how each component is fitted to make reassembly easier and accurate.

5 Before dismantling the transmission, it will help if you have some idea of where the problem lies. Certain problems can be closely related to specific areas in the transmission which can make component examination and

renewal easier. Refer to the *Fault finding* Section in this manual for more information.

5 Multi-function switch - removal and refitting

Removal

1 The multi-function switch is located on top of the transmission **(see illustration)**.

2 Apply the handbrake, then jack up the front of the vehicle and support it on axle stands (see *Jacking and vehicle support*).

3 Disconnect the wiring connector, then unscrew the bolts securing the switch lead to the top of the transmission

4 Note the fitted position of the switch, then unscrew the bolt and remove the switch retainer plate.

5 Withdraw the multi-function switch from the transmission. Recover the O-ring seal.

Refitting

6 To refit the switch first clean the switch location in the transmission. Fit a new O-ring seal, then insert the switch in the previously noted position.

7 Refit the retainer plate and tighten the bolt.

8 Secure the lead to the top of the transmission and tighten the bolts.

9 Reconnect the wiring, then lower the vehicle to the ground.

6 Speedometer transducer - removal and refitting

Removal

1 All transmissions are fitted with an electronic speedometer transducer on the left-hand side of the transmission, just above the driveshaft drive flange **(see illustration)**.

5.1 Multi-function switch

6.1 Speedometer transducer (1) and multi-function switch connector (2)

This device measures the rotational speed of the transmission final drive and converts the information into an electronic signal, which is then sent to the speedometer module in the instrument panel. On certain models, the signal is also used as an input by the engine management system ECU.

2 Apply the handbrake, then jack up the front of the vehicle and support it on axle stands (see *Jacking and vehicle support*).

3 Disconnect the wiring from the transducer.

4 Depress the retainer, then turn the speedometer drive and withdraw it from the transmission. Take care not to damage the drive as the electronic components are delicate. Recover the gasket **(see illustration)**.

Refitting

5 Refitting is a reversal of removal, but renew the gasket.

7 Oil seals - renewal

Driveshaft flange oil seals

1 Apply the handbrake, then jack up the front of the vehicle and support it on axle stands (see *Jacking and vehicle support*). Remove the relevant roadwheel.

2 Refer to Chapter 8 and unbolt the heatshield, then unscrew the bolts and remove the relevant driveshaft from the transmission drive flange. Tie the driveshaft away from the transmission, and wrap the inner joint in a plastic bag, in order to prevent entry of dust and dirt. Turn the steering as necessary to move the driveshaft away from the flange.

3 Position a suitable container beneath the transmission to catch spilled oil.

4 The drive flange is held in position by a circlip, and in order to remove the flange, it is necessary to release the circlip. To do this, locate a suitable distance piece (such as a chisel) between the flange and the final drive cover or transmission casing (as applicable), then screw a bolt through the flange onto the distance piece. As the bolt is tightened, the flange will be forced outwards and the circlip released from its groove. If the flange is tight, turn it 180° and repeat the removal procedure.

5 With the flange out, note the fitted depth of the oil seal in the housing, then prise it out using a large flat-bladed screwdriver.

6 Clean all traces of dirt from the area around the oil seal aperture, then apply a smear of grease to the lips of the new oil seal.

7 Ensure the seal is correctly positioned, with its sealing lip facing inwards, and tap it squarely into position, using a suitable tubular drift (such as a socket) which bears only on the hard outer edge of the seal. If the surface of the flange is good, make sure the seal is fitted at the same depth in its housing as originally noted; it should be 5.5 mm below

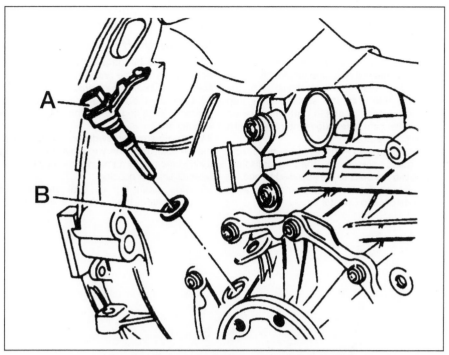

6.4 Speedometer transducer (A) and gasket (B)

the outer edge of the transmission. If the surface of the flange is worn, fit the oil seal at a depth of 6.5 mm.

8 Clean the oil seal and apply a smear of multi-purpose grease to its lips.

9 It is recommended that the circlip on the inner end of the drive flange is renewed whenever the flange is removed. To do this, mount the flange in a soft-jawed vice, then prise off the old circlip and fit the new one **(see illustration)**. Lightly grease the circlip.

10 Insert the drive flange through the oil seal and engage it with the differential gear. Using a suitable drift, drive the flange fully into the gear until the circlip is felt to engage.

11 Refit the driveshaft (see Chapter 8).

12 Refit the roadwheel, then lower the vehicle to the ground. Check and if necessary top up the transmission oil level.

Input shaft oil seal

13 The transmission must be removed for access to the input shaft oil seal. Refer to Section 3 of this Chapter.

14 Remove the clutch release bearing and lever with reference to Chapter 6.

15 Unscrew the bolts and remove the guide sleeve from inside the bellhousing. Recover the gasket. Do not disturb any shims located on the input shaft.

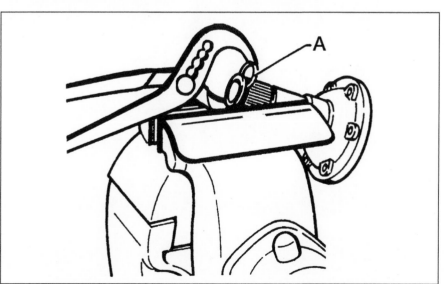

7.9 Fitting a new circlip to the groove in the transmission drive flange

16 Using a punch or drift, carefully drive the oil seal from its fitted position in the guide sleeve .

17 Wipe clean the oil seal seating.

18 Smear a little multi-purpose grease on the lips of the new oil seal, and locate the seal in the guide sleeve with the sealing lip facing the gearbox side. Tap the seal squarely into position, using a suitable drift which bears only on the hard outer edge of the seal, until it is against the stop.

19 Using a new O-ring and new bolts, refit the guide sleeve to the transmission, tightening the bolts to the specified torque.

20 Refit the clutch release bearing and lever with reference to Chapter 6.

21 Refit the transmission with reference to Section 3 of this Chapter.

Selector shaft oil seal

22 Apply the handbrake, then jack up the front of the vehicle and support it on axle stands (see *Jacking and vehicle support*).

23 Unscrew the locking bolt and slide the gearshift coupling from the transmission selector shaft.

24 Using a small screwdriver, carefully prise the oil seal from the transmission housing taking care not to damage the surface of the selector shaft or housing.

25 Wipe clean the oil seal seating and selector shaft, then smear a little multi-purpose grease on the new oil seal lips and locate the seal over the end of the shaft. Make sure the closed side of the seal faces outwards. To prevent damage to the oil seal, temporarily wrap some adhesive tape around the end of the shaft.

26 Tap the oil seal squarely into position, using a suitable tubular drift which bears only on the hard outer edge of the seal. The seal should be inserted until it is 1.0 mm below the surface of the transmission.

27 Refit the gearshift coupling and tighten the locking bolt.

28 Lower the vehicle to the ground.

Chapter 7 Part B:
Automatic transmission

Contents

Degrees of difficulty

Easy, suitable for novice with little experience		Fairly easy, suitable for beginner with some experience		Fairly difficult, suitable for competent DIY mechanic		Difficult, suitable for experienced DIY mechanic		Very difficult, suitable for expert DIY or professional	

Specifications

General

Type	Electro-hydraulically controlled planetary gearbox providing four forward speeds and one reverse speed. Drive transmitted through hydrodynamic torque converter

Designation:

All models except petrol turbo	01N 4-speed
Petrol turbo models	01V 5-speed
Automatic transmission fluid capacity	See Chapter 1A or 1B

Torque wrench settings

	Nm	lbf ft
Automatic transmission selector cable support bolt	23	17
Bracket for fluid pipe	10	7
Torque converter to driveplate	85	63
Fluid pipes to transmission	20	15
Fluid pipe union	25	18
Transmission bellhousing-to-engine bolts:		
M10	45	33
M12	65	48
Transmission mounting:		
Centre bolt	40	30
To body	23	17
To transmission	40	30

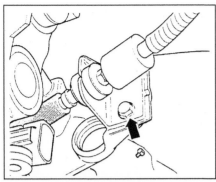

2.9 Selector cable support bracket bolt on the transmission

1 General information

The automatic transmission is a four or five speed unit, incorporating a hydrodynamic torque converter with and a planetary gearbox.

Gear selection is achieved by means of a floor mounted, seven position selector lever. The positions are P (Park), R (Reverse), N (Neutral), D (Drive), 3 (3rd gear lock), 2 (2nd gear lock), 1 (1st gear lock). The transmission has a kick-down feature which provides greater acceleration when the accelerator pedal is depressed to the floor.

The overall operation of the transmission is managed by the engine management electronic control unit (ECU) and as a result there are no manual adjustments. Comprehensive fault diagnosis can therefore only be carried out using dedicated electronic test equipment.

Due to the complexity of the transmission and its control system, major repairs and overhaul operations should be left to an Audi/VAG dealer, who will be equipped to carry out fault diagnosis and repair. The information in this Chapter is therefore limited to a description of the removal and refitting of the transmission as a complete unit. The removal, refitting and adjustment of the selector cable is also described.

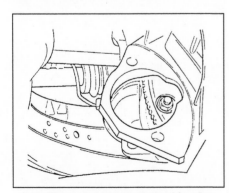

2.16 The torque converter-to-driveplate nuts are accessed through the starter motor aperture

2 Automatic transmission - removal and refitting

Removal

1 Select a solid, level surface to park the vehicle upon. Give yourself enough space to move around it easily. Apply the handbrake and chock the rear wheels.

2 Apply the handbrake, then jack up the front of the vehicle and support it on axle stands (see *Jacking and vehicle support*). Remove both front roadwheels.

3 Remove the engine undershield panel and remove the noise insulation .

4 Disconnect the battery negative (earth) lead (see Chapter 5A) and position it away from the terminal.

5 Where necessary, unscrew the nuts and remove the top cover from the engine.

6 Remove the exhaust front downpipe with reference to Chapter 4C, taking care not to bend the flexible coupling. Also, where necessary, unbolt the downpipe mounting bracket from the transmission.

7 Disconnect the wiring from the speedometer sender.

8 Identify the wiring connections on the rear of the transmission, then unplug them. Loosen and detach the wiring support, and position the wiring to one side.

9 With the selector lever in position P, carefully disconnect the inner cable from the transmission lever, then unbolt the support bracket **(see illustration)**. Position the cable to one side.

10 Using an Allen key, unbolt the heat shields from over the inner end of the right-hand driveshaft.

11 Refer to Chapter 8 and detach the driveshafts from the transmission flanges. Tie the driveshafts away from the transmission.

12 Unbolt the right-hand transmission mounting complete with rubber bush and shield.

13 Position a suitable container beneath the transmission to collect spilt hydraulic fluid.

14 Detach the hydraulic pipes from the transmission, and recover the sealing rings. On petrol models without air conditioning, unscrew the bolts and withdraw the pipes. On all other models, unscrew the union nuts located beneath the left-hand side of the radiator and also the nuts located beneath the front of the transmission, and remove the pipes completely. Plug the apertures in the transmission housing to prevent entry of dust and dirt.

15 Remove the starter motor as described in Chapter 5A.

16 Turn the engine to locate one of the torque converter-to-driveplate nuts in the starter motor aperture **(see illustration)**. Unscrew and remove the nut while preventing the engine from turning using a wide-bladed screwdriver engaged with the ring gear teeth

on the driveplate. Unscrew the remaining two nuts, turning the engine a third of a turn at a time to locate them.

17 Unscrew the transmission-to-engine mounting bolts accessible from under the car.

18 Support the engine with a hoist or support bar located on the front wing inner channels. If necessary, remove the bonnet as described in Chapter 11 in order to position the hoist over the engine. Due to the weight of the automatic transmission, the engine should be supported using both the front and rear lifting eyes. Depending on the engine, temporarily remove components as necessary to attach the hoist.

19 Support the transmission with a trolley jack or stand.

20 On petrol turbo models, mark the location of the subframe beneath the engine compartment, then loosen only the front subframe bolts. Remove the remaining subframe bolts and lower the rear of the subframe. **Note:** *It is important that the subframe is refitted in its correct position otherwise the handling of the car will be affected and excessive wear will occur.*

21 Unscrew and remove the transmission-to-engine mounting bolts accessible from over the engine.

22 With the help of an assistant, withdraw the transmission from the locating dowels on the rear of the engine, making sure that the torque converter remains fully engaged with the transmission input shaft. If necessary, use a lever to release the torque converter from the driveplate.

23 When the locating dowels are clear of their mounting holes, lower the transmission to the ground using the jack. Strap a restraining bar across the front of the bellhousing to keep the torque converter in position.

> ⚠ *Warning: Make sure that the transmission remains steady on the jack head. Take care to prevent the torque converter from falling out as the transmission is removed.*

24 Where necessary, remove the intermediate plate from the locating dowels.

Refitting

25 Refitting the transmission is a reversal of the removal procedure, but note the following points:

a) *As the torque converter is refitted, ensure that the drive pins at the centre of the torque converter hub engage with the recesses in the automatic transmission fluid pump inner wheel.*

b) *Tighten the bellhousing bolts and torque converter-to-driveplate nuts to the specified torque. Always renew self-locking nuts and bolts.*

c) *Renew the O-ring seals on the fluid pipes and filler tube attached to the transmission casing.*

d) *Tighten the transmission mounting bolts to the correct torque.*

e) *Check the final drive oil level and transmission fluid level as described in Chapter 1A or 1B.*

f) *On completion, refer to Section 4 and check the gear selector cable adjustment.*

3 Automatic transmission overhaul - general information

In the event of a fault occurring, it will be necessary to establish whether the fault is electrical, mechanical or hydraulic in nature, before repair work can be contemplated. Diagnosis requires detailed knowledge of the transmissions operation and construction, as well as access to specialised test equipment, and so is deemed to be beyond the scope of this manual. It is therefore essential that problems with the automatic transmission are referred to an Audi/VAG dealer for assessment.

Note that a faulty transmission should not be removed before the vehicle has been assessed by a dealer, as fault diagnosis is carried out with the transmission in situ.

4 Selector/lock cable - removal, refitting and adjustment

Removal

1 Move the selector lever to the P position
2 Apply the handbrake, then jack up the front of the vehicle and support it on axle stands (see *Jacking and vehicle support*).
3 Working under the vehicle, undo the screws and lower the heatshield from the gearshift mounting bracket onto the exhaust. Slide the heatshield forwards.
4 Release the cover from the bottom of the selector lever bracket by pressing the fastener to the rear **(see illustration)**.

5 Disconnect the inner cable by squeezing the clip to release the cable from the selector lever. Pull the outer cable from the support, then pull out the locking element and remove the cover and cable from the bottom of the selector lever assembly. Take care not to bend the cable excessively.
6 At the transmission end of the cable, use a screwdriver to prise the end of the inner cable up from the transmission lever.
7 Unscrew the bolt and detach the support bracket with cable from the side of the transmission.
8 Loosen the locknuts and detach the cable from the bracket. Withdraw the cable from under the car.

Refitting

9 Refitting is a reversal of removal, but lightly grease the cable end fittings. Before lowering the car to the ground and before reconnecting the cable to the transmission lever, adjust the cable as follows.

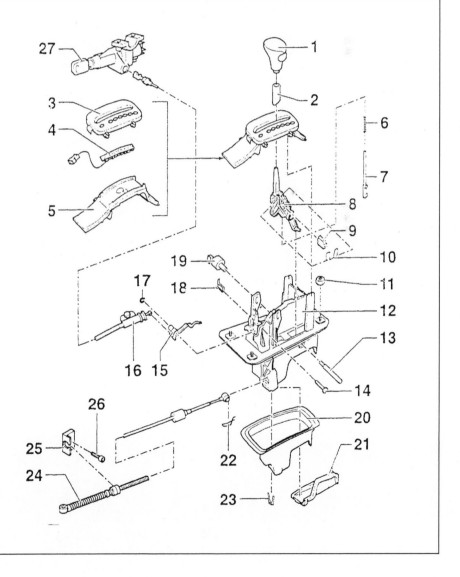

4.4 Selector components

1 Knob
2 Sleeve
3 Display
4 Light guide
5 Guide
6 Spring
7 Connecting rod
8 Selector lever
9 Engagement element
10 Spring clip
11 Nut
12 Bracket
13 Pivot
14 Pin
15 Lever
16 Locking cable
17 Washer
18 Spring
19 Lock solenoid
20 Rubber housing
21 Cover
22 Clip
23 Locking element
24 Selector lever cable
25 Support bracket
26 Bolt
27 Ignition/starter switch

Adjustment

10 Move the selector lever inside the car to the P position.

11 Move the selector lever on the transmission to the P position, which is the rear stop. Make sure that both front wheels are locked by attempting to turn them in the same direction at the same time. **Note:** *Even though the transmission is locked, it will still be possible to turn the front wheels in* **opposite** *directions, since the differential gears are able move in relation to each other.*

12 Loosen the bolt(s) securing the selector cable to the transmission.

13 Press the cable end onto the selector lever, then check that the cable is free of any stress by moving it side to side several times. Now tighten the cable securing bolt.

14 Check the adjustment by selecting P. With the brake pedal released, check that the selector lever cannot be moved out of the P position with the lever button pressed. Now depress the brake pedal and check that the lock solenoid releases enabling the selector lever to be moved to any position with the lever button pressed. Check that the display agrees with the actual position of the lever.

15 Select position N. With the brake pedal released, check that the selector lever is locked. Depress the pedal and check that the selector lever can be moved to any position. Note that it is only possible to select R with the button pressed.

16 On RHD models, check that it is only possible to operate the starter motor in positions P and N with the button released.

17 Lower the car to the ground.

Chapter 8
Driveshafts

Contents

Degrees of difficulty

Easy, suitable for novice with little experience	**Fairly easy,** suitable for beginner with some experience	**Fairly difficult,** suitable for competent DIY mechanic	**Difficult,** suitable for experienced DIY mechanic	**Very difficult,** suitable for expert DIY or professional

Specifications

Lubrication

Type:
Ball-and-cage joints	G 000 603 grease*

Tripod-type joint:
88 mm diameter joint	G 000 603 grease*
98 mm diameter joint	G 000 633 grease*

Amount per joint:
Petrol engine models with manual transmission:
  Outer joint:
88 mm diameter joint	100 g
98 mm diameter joint	120 g

  Inner joint:
100 mm diameter joint	110 g
108 mm diameter joint	120 g

Models with automatic transmissions and diesel models:
  Outer joint:
88 mm diameter joint	100 g
98 mm diameter joint	120 g
Inner joint	As supplied in repair kit*

*See your VAG dealer for details

Torque wrench settings

	Nm	lbf ft
Driveshaft-to-transmission flange bolts:		
M8 bolts	40	30
M10 bolts	77	57
Hub bolt:		
M14 bolt:		
Stage 1	115	85
Stage 2	Angle-tighten a further 180°	
M16 bolt:		
Stage 1	190	140
Stage 2	Angle-tighten a further 180°	
Upper suspension arm, pinch bolt nut	40	30

1 General information

1 Drive is transmitted from the differential to the front wheels by means of two steel driveshafts or either solid or hollow construction (depending on model). Both driveshafts are splined at their outer ends, to accept the wheel hubs, and are secured to the hub by a large bolt. The inner end of each driveshaft is bolted to the transmission drive flanges.

2 Constant velocity (CV) joints are fitted to each end of the driveshafts, to ensure the smooth and efficient transmission of drive at all the angles possible as the roadwheels move up and down with the suspension, and as they turn from side to side under steering. On petrol engine models with a manual transmission unit, both inner and outer constant velocity joints are of the ball-and-cage type. On all diesel engine models and petrol engine models with automatic transmission, the outer joint is of the ball-and-cage type, but the inner joint is of the tripod type.

3 Rubber or plastic gaiters are secured over both CV joints with steel clips. These contain the grease that is packed into the joint, and also protect the joint from the ingress of dirt and debris.

2.8 Withdrawing the driveshaft from the wheel arch

2.12a Manoeuvre the driveshaft into position, engaging the splines with those of the hub . . .

2.12b . . . and fit the new hub bolt

2 Driveshafts - removal and refitting

Removal

1 Remove the wheel trim/hub cap (as applicable) then partially slacken the hub bolt with the vehicle resting on its wheels. Also slacken the wheel bolts.

2 Chock the rear wheels of the car, firmly apply the handbrake, then jack up the front of the car and support it on axle stands. Remove the appropriate front roadwheel. Whilst the wheel is removed, refit at least one of the wheel bolts to ensure the brake disc remains correctly positioned on the hub.

3 Remove the retaining screws and fasteners and remove the undercover from beneath the engine/transmission unit to gain access to the driveshafts. Where necessary, also unbolt the heatshield from the transmission housing to improve access to the inner joint.

4 On models equipped with ABS, remove the wheel sensor from the hub as described in Chapter 9. Release the sensor wiring from the locating bracket on the brake caliper.

5 Unscrew the pinch bolt and separate the front and rear upper suspension arm balljoints from the top of the hub carrier (see Chapter 10, Section 5 for details). Discard the nut, a new one should be used on refitting.

Caution: Do not unbolt the steering track rod from the hub carrier.

6 Slacken and remove the hub bolt. If the bolt was not slackened with the wheels on the ground, refit at least two roadwheel bolts to the front hub, tightening them securely, then have an assistant firmly depress the brake pedal to prevent the front hub from rotating, whilst you slacken and remove the hub bolt. Alternatively, a tool can be fabricated from two lengths of steel strip (one long, one short) and a nut and bolt; the nut and bolt forming the pivot of a forked tool.

7 Slacken and remove the bolts securing the inner driveshaft joint to the transmission flange and recover the reinforcing plates (where fitted) from underneath the bolts. Support the driveshaft by suspending it with wire or string - do not allow it to hang under its weight, or the joint may be damaged.

8 Swivel the hub carrier towards the rear of the wheel arch to free the driveshaft inner joint from transmission flange. Move the joint to one side then free the outer joint splines from the hub and manoeuvre the driveshaft out from underneath the vehicle **(see illustration)**. On driveshafts where the inner joint is exposed, remove the gasket from the driveshaft inner joint face and discard it; a new one should be used on refitting. **Note:** *Do not allow the vehicle to rest on its wheels with one or both driveshafts removed, as damage to the wheel bearing(s) may result. If moving the vehicle is unavoidable, temporarily insert the outer end of the driveshaft(s) in the hub(s) and tighten the driveshaft bolt(s). Support the inner end(s) of the driveshaft(s) to avoid damage.*

Refitting

9 Before installing the driveshaft, examine the driveshaft oil seal in the transmission for signs of damage or deterioration. If necessary, on manual transmissions, renew it as described in Chapter 7A.

10 Thoroughly clean the driveshaft outer joint and hub splines and the mating surfaces of the inner joint and transmission flange. Check that all gaiter clips are securely fastened.

11 On a driveshaft where the inner joint is exposed (ball-and-cage type), fit a new gasket to the inner joint face by peeling off its backing foil and sticking it securely to the joint.

12 Manoeuvre the driveshaft into position, engaging the splines with those of the hub, and slide the outer joint into position. Fit the new hub bolt, tightening it by hand only at this stage **(see illustrations)**.

13 Align the driveshaft inner joint with the transmission flange then refit the retaining bolts and where fitted (on ball-and-cage type joints) the reinforcing plates. Tighten all bolts by hand then, working in a diagonal sequence, tighten them to the specified torque **(see illustrations)**. Where necessary, refit the heatshield to the transmission housing and securely tighten its retaining bolts.

14 Refit the front and rear upper suspension arms to top of the hub, insert the pinch bolt, then fit the new retaining nut and tighten it to the specified torque (see Chapter 10).

2.13a Align the driveshaft inner joint with the transmission flange . . .

2.13b . . . then refit the retaining bolts and the reinforcing plates

2.13c Tighten all bolts to the specified torque

15 On models with ABS refit the wheel sensor to the hub as described in Chapter 9. Refit the ABS wiring to the brake caliper bracket.

16 Refit the undercover and roadwheel then lower the vehicle to the ground and tighten the wheel bolts to the specified torque (see Chapter 1A or 1B).

17 With the vehicle resting on its wheels, tighten the hub bolt to the specified stage 1 torque then angle-tighten it through the specified stage 2 angle, using an angle-measuring gauge to ensure accuracy **(see illustrations)**. If an angle gauge is not available, use white paint to make alignment marks between the bolt head and hub/wheel prior to tightening; the marks can then be used to check that the bolt has been rotated through the correct angle.

18 Refit the wheel trim/hub cap (as applicable).

3 Driveshafts - overhaul

1 Remove the driveshaft from the vehicle as described in Section 2 and proceed as described under the relevant sub-heading.

Outer joint (all models)

Note: *A long M16 bolt/threaded rod will be useful during this procedure (see paragraph 4).*
2 Secure the driveshaft in a vice equipped with soft jaws, and release the gaiter retaining

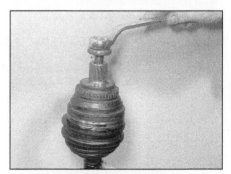

3.4 Using the hub bolt to draw the outer CV joint off of the driveshaft

2.17a With the vehicle resting on its wheels, tighten the hub bolt to the specified stage 1 torque . . .

clips. If necessary, the retaining clips can be cut to release them.

3 Fold back the rubber gaiter to expose the outer constant velocity joint. Scoop out the excess grease and dispose of it.

4 It is now necessary to remove the outer constant velocity joint from the driveshaft. This is most easily achieved using a long M16 bolt/threaded bar; screw the bolt/bar in through the hub bolt threads until it contacts the end of the driveshaft then turn the bolt/bar to force the joint off **(see illustration)**. **Note:** *If the original hub bolt is threaded along the entire length of its shank, the bolt can be used.* If a bolt/bar is not available, use a hammer and suitable soft metal drift to sharply strike the inner member of the outer joint to drive it off the end of the shaft, taking great care not to damage the joint. On models with hollow driveshafts, it will first be necessary to displace the inner circlip (using circlip pliers) from its groove at the inner surface of the joint, to allow the dished washer and the plastic spacer ring to be slid along the driveshaft, away from the joint.

5 Once the joint assembly has been removed, remove the circlip from the groove in the driveshaft splines, and discard it. A new circlip must be fitted on reassembly.

6 Slide the spacer and dished washer off from the driveshaft, noting their correct fitted locations, and remove the rubber gaiter.

7 With the constant velocity joint removed

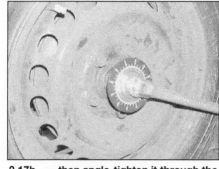

2.17b . . . then angle-tighten it through the specified stage 2 angle

from the driveshaft, thoroughly clean the joint using paraffin, or a suitable solvent, and dry it thoroughly. Carry out a visual inspection of the joint.

8 Move the inner splined driving member from side-to-side, to expose each ball in turn at the top of its track. Examine the balls for cracks, flat spots, or signs of surface pitting.

9 Inspect the ball tracks on the inner and outer members. If the tracks have widened, the balls will no longer be a tight fit. At the same time, check the ball cage windows for wear or cracking between the windows.

10 If the constant velocity joint is found to be worn or damaged, it will be necessary to renew the joint, or the complete driveshaft (where the joint is not available separately). Refer to your Audi/VAG dealer for further information on parts availability. If the joint is in satisfactory condition, obtain a repair kit; the genuine Audi/VAG kit consists of a new gaiter, circlip, spring washer and spacer, retaining clips, and the correct type and quantity of grease.

11 Tape over the splines on the end of the driveshaft, then slide the new gaiter onto the shaft **(see illustration)**. Remove the tape.

12 Fit the dished washer, ensuring its convex surface is facing inwards, then slide on the spacer with its flatter surface facing the dished washer **(see illustrations)**.

13 Fit the new circlip making sure it is correctly located in the driveshaft groove **(see illustration)**.

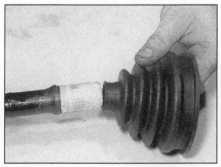

3.11 Tape over the driveshaft splines then slide the new gaiter along the shaft

3.12a Fit the dished washer with its convex surface facing inwards . . .

3.12b . . . then slide on the spacer with its flatter surface facing the dished washer

3.13 Fit the new circlip to the driveshaft groove

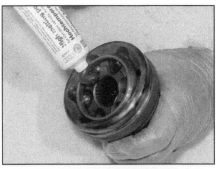

3.14 Work the grease well into the ball tracks of the outer joint

3.15a Locate the outer joint on the driveshaft splines . . .

3.15b . . . and tap it over the circlip

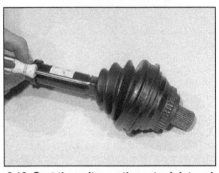

3.16 Seat the gaiter on the outer joint and driveshaft then lift its inner lip to equalise air pressure inside the gaiter

3.17a Fit the inner and outer retaining clips . . .

14 Work the grease well into the ball tracks of the outer joint then fill the gaiter with any excess (see illustration).

15 Locate the outer joint on the driveshaft splines and slide it on until the inner member abuts the circlip. Tap the joint outer member sharply with hammer and soft-metal drift to force the inner member over the circlip and fully onto the driveshaft (see illustrations). Pull on the joint assembly to make sure the joint is securely retained by the circlip.

16 Locate the outer lip of the gaiter in the groove on the joint outer member then lift the inner lip of the gaiter to equalise the air pressure inside (see illustration).

17 Fit both the inner and outer retaining clips to the gaiter and secure each one in position by compressing its raised section. In the absence of the special tool, carefully compress each clip using a pair of side cutters taking great care not to cut through the clip (see illustrations).

18 Check that the constant velocity joint moves freely in all directions, then refit the driveshaft to the vehicle as described in Section 2.

Inner joint

Petrol engine models with manual transmission

Note: *The inner joint is a very tight fit on the driveshaft and removal/refitting will therefore require the use of a hydraulic press and suitable adapters. If this equipment is not available, gaiter renewal must be entrusted to an Audi/VAG dealer or other suitably-equipped garage.*

19 Secure the driveshaft in a vice equipped with soft jaws then, using a hammer and

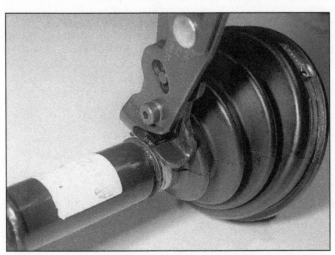

3.17b . . . and secure them in position by carefully compressing their raised sections . . .

3.17c . . . taking great care not to cut through the clip

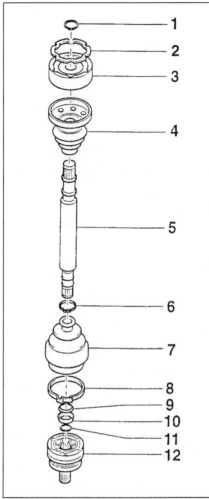

3.19 Exploded view of driveshaft - petrol engine models with manual transmission

1 Circlip	6 Retaining clip
2 Gasket	7 Outer gaiter
3 Inner constant	8 Retaining clip
velocity joint	9 Dished washer
4 Inner gaiter and	10 Spacer
locating plate	11 Circlip
5 Driveshaft	12 Outer joint

punch, carefully tap the gaiter locating plate off from the inner constant velocity joint outer member **(see illustration)**.

20 Remove the circlip from the inner end of the driveshaft.

21 Remove the inner constant velocity joint from the driveshaft by securely supporting the joint outer member and pressing the driveshaft out from the inner member.

22 Release the gaiter inner retaining clip and remove the gaiter from the driveshaft.

23 Clean and inspect the inner joint as described in paragraphs 7 to 9.

24 If the constant velocity joint is found to be worn or damaged, it will be necessary to renew the joint, or the complete driveshaft (where no joint components are available separately). Refer to your Audi/VAG dealer for

3.34 Check the inner joint rollers and bearings for wear

further information on parts availability. If the joint is in satisfactory condition, obtain a repair kit; the genuine Audi/VAG kit consists of a new gaiter, locating plate, circlip, retaining clips, and the correct type and quantity of grease.

25 Tape over the splines on the end of the driveshaft, then slide the new gaiter onto the shaft. Remove the tape and fit the locating plate to the driveshaft gaiter.

26 Securely clamp the driveshaft then press the inner joint onto the shaft, ensuring it is fitted the right way around. Secure the joint in position with the new circlip making sure it is correctly located in the driveshaft groove.

27 Work the grease well into the ball tracks of the joint then fill the gaiter with any excess.

28 Wipe clean the mating surfaces of the gaiter locating plate and joint. Apply a smear of sealant (Audi/VAG recommend the use of D-3 sealant - available from your Audi/VAG dealer) to the locating plate then align the locating plate holes with those on the joint outer member and tap the plate firmly onto the joint.

29 Ensure the outer lip is correctly engaged with the locating plate then lift the inner lip of the gaiter to equalise the air pressure inside.

30 Fit both the inner and outer retaining clips to the gaiter and secure each one in position by compressing its raised section. In the absence of the special tool, carefully compress each clip using a pair of side cutters taking great care not to cut through the clip

31 Check that the constant velocity joint moves freely in all directions, then refit the driveshaft to the vehicle as described in Section 2.

Diesel engine models and petrol engine models with automatic transmission

Note: *Check parts availability with your VAG dealer before proceeding; at the time of writing inner gaiters were only available for 32mm diameter driveshafts.*

32 Remove the outer constant velocity joint as described above in paragraphs 2 to 6. It is recommended that the outer joint gaiter is also renewed, regardless of its apparent condition.

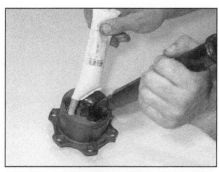

3.36 Work the grease well into the bearing tracks and rollers

33 Release the retaining clips then slide the inner gaiter off from the driveshaft. If necessary, cut the gaiter to release it from the shaft.

34 Thoroughly clean the joint using paraffin, or a suitable solvent, and dry it thoroughly. Check the tripod joint bearings and joint outer member for signs of wear, pitting or scuffing on their bearing surfaces. Check that the bearing rollers rotate smoothly and easily around the tripod joint, with no traces of roughness **(see illustration)**.

35 If on inspection, the tripod joint or outer member reveal signs of wear or damage, it will be necessary to renew the complete driveshaft assembly, since the joint is not available separately. If the joint is in satisfactory condition, obtain a repair kit consisting of a new gaiter, retaining clips, and the correct type and quantity of grease. Although not strictly necessary, it is also recommended that the outer constant velocity joint gaiter is renewed, regardless of its apparent condition.

36 On reassembly, pack the inner joint with the grease supplied. Work the grease well into the bearing tracks and rollers, while twisting the joint **(see illustration)**.

37 Clean the shaft, using emery cloth to remove any rust or sharp edges which may damage the gaiter. Tape over the splines on the end of the driveshaft and grease the driveshaft ridges to prevent possible damage to the inner gaiter on installation.

38 Ease the inner gaiter onto and along the driveshaft and carefully lever it over driveshaft ridge, taking great care not to damage it **(see illustrations)**. Locate the outer lip in the

3.38a Tape over the driveshaft splines then slide the inner gaiter into position ...

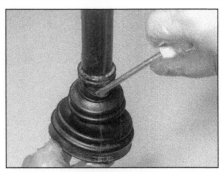

3.38b ... levering it carefully over the driveshaft ridge

groove on the joint outer member and seat the inner lip correctly on the driveshaft.

39 Lift the inner lip of the gaiter to equalise the air pressure inside then fit both the inner and outer retaining clips. Secure each clip in

3.39a Seat the gaiter in position then lift the inner lip to equalise the air pressure inside

3.39b Fit the retaining clips to the gaiter . . .

3.39c ... and secure them in position by carefully compressing their raised sections

position by compressing its raised section **(see illustrations)**. In the absence of the special tool, carefully compress each clip using a pair of side cutters taking great care not to cut through the clip.

40 Refit the outer constant velocity joint as described in paragraphs 11 to 17 **(see illustration)**.

41 Check that both constant velocity joints move freely in all directions, then refit the driveshaft to the vehicle as described in Section 2.

4 Driveshaft overhaul -
general information

1 If any of the checks described in Chapter 1A or 1B reveal wear in any driveshaft joint, first remove the roadwheel trim or centre cap (as

appropriate) and check that the hub bolt is tight. If the bolt is loose, obtain a new bolt and tighten it to the specified torque (see Section 2). If the bolt is tight, refit the centre cap/trim and repeat the check on the other hub bolt.

2 Road test the vehicle, and listen for a metallic clicking from the front as the vehicle is driven slowly in a circle on full-lock. If a clicking noise is heard, this indicates wear in the outer constant velocity joint; this means that the joint must be renewed.

3 If vibration, consistent with road speed, is felt through the car when accelerating, there is a possibility of wear in the inner constant velocity joints.

4 To check the joints for wear, remove the driveshafts, then dismantle them as described in Section 3; if any wear or free play is found, the affected joint must be renewed. Refer to your Audi/VAG dealer for information on the availability of driveshaft components.

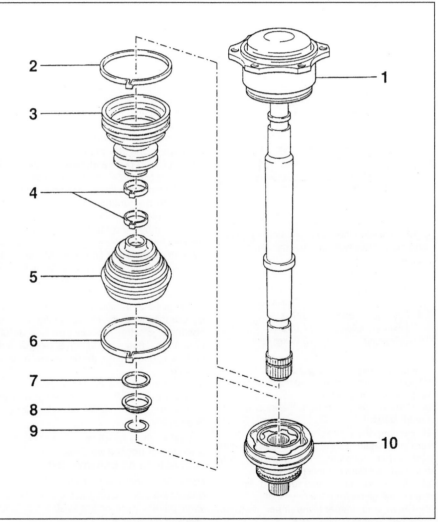

3.40 Exploded view of driveshaft - diesel engine and automatic transmission models

1 Inner joint	4 Retaining clip	8 Spacer
2 Retaining clip	5 Outer gaiter	9 Circlip
3 Inner gaiter	6 Retaining clip	10 Outer joint
	7 Dished washer	

Chapter 9
Braking system

Contents

Degrees of difficulty

| **Easy,** suitable for novice with little experience | **Fairly easy,** suitable for beginner with some experience | **Fairly difficult,** suitable for competent DIY mechanic | **Difficult,** suitable for experienced DIY mechanic | **Very difficult,** suitable for expert DIY or professional |

Specifications

Front brakes

	ATE/Teves calipers	Lucas calipers
Type	Disc, with single-piston sliding caliper	
Disc diameter	280 mm	288 mm
Disc thickness:		
Solid discs:		
New	13 mm	15 mm
Minimum	11 mm	13 mm
Ventilated discs:		
New	22 mm	25 mm
Minimum	20 mm	23 mm
Maximum disc run-out (all types)	0.05 mm	
Brake pad friction material thickness (all types):		
New	14 mm	
Minimum	2 mm	

Rear brakes

Disc diameter	245 mm
Disc thickness:	
New	10 mm
Minimum thickness	8 mm
Maximum disc run-out	0.05 mm
Brake pad friction material thickness:	
New	12mm
Minimum	2 mm

Servo

Pushrod balljoint to servo unit mating surface dimension:	
LHD models	159.0 ± 0.5 mm
RHD models	173.2 ± 0.5 mm

Torque wrench settings

	Nm	lbf ft
ABS hydraulic unit nuts	10	7
Brake pedal shaft to operating lever bolt	25	18
Front brake caliper (ATE/Teves):		
Guide pins	25	18
Mounting bracket bolts	125	92
Wiring/brake hose bracket bolt	10	7
Front brake caliper (Lucas):		
Guide pin bolts*	30	22
Mounting bracket bolts	125	92
Wiring/brake hose bracket bolt	10	7
Handbrake lever mounting nuts	25	18
Hydraulic pipe union nuts	15	11
Master cylinder retaining nuts	50	37
Rear brake caliper:		
Guide pin bolt*	30	22
Mounting bracket bolt	95	70
Vacuum servo to bulkhead/pedal bracket bolts (T45)	25	18

* Use new fasteners

1 General information

1 The braking system is of the servo-assisted, dual-circuit hydraulic type. The arrangement of the hydraulic system is such that each circuit operates one front and one rear brake from a tandem master cylinder. Under normal circumstances, both circuits operate in unison. However, in the event of hydraulic failure in one circuit, full braking force will still be available at two diagonally opposite road wheels.

2 All models have disc brakes fitted at the front and rear wheels as standard. ABS is also fitted as standard on all models (refer to Section 18 for further information on ABS operation).

3 The front and rear disc brakes are actuated by single-piston sliding type calipers, which ensure that equal pressure is applied to each disc pad. The handbrake mechanism is built into the rear calipers.

4 On all models, the handbrake provides an independent mechanical (rather than hydraulic) means of rear brake application.

5 Because diesel engines have no throttle valve, there is insufficient vacuum in the inlet manifold to operate the braking system servo effectively at all times. To overcome this problem, a vacuum pump is fitted to models with diesel engines, to provide sufficient vacuum to operate the servo unit. The pump is mounted to the side of the cylinder block and is driven by the auxiliary shaft.

Note: *When servicing any part of the system, work carefully and methodically; also observe scrupulous cleanliness when overhauling any part of the hydraulic system. Always renew components (in axle sets, where applicable) if in doubt about their condition, and use only genuine Audi/VAG replacement parts, or at least those of known good quality. Note the warnings given in Safety first and at relevant points in this Chapter concerning the dangers of asbestos dust and hydraulic fluid.*

2 Hydraulic system - bleeding

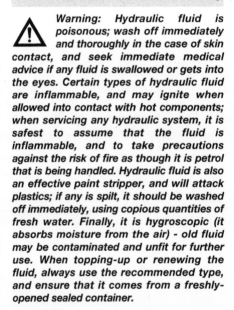

⚠️ *Warning: Hydraulic fluid is poisonous; wash off immediately and thoroughly in the case of skin contact, and seek immediate medical advice if any fluid is swallowed or gets into the eyes. Certain types of hydraulic fluid are inflammable, and may ignite when allowed into contact with hot components; when servicing any hydraulic system, it is safest to assume that the fluid is inflammable, and to take precautions against the risk of fire as though it is petrol that is being handled. Hydraulic fluid is also an effective paint stripper, and will attack plastics; if any is spilt, it should be washed off immediately, using copious quantities of fresh water. Finally, it is hygroscopic (it absorbs moisture from the air) - old fluid may be contaminated and unfit for further use. When topping-up or renewing the fluid, always use the recommended type, and ensure that it comes from a freshly-opened sealed container.*

General

1 The correct operation of any hydraulic system is only possible after removing all air from the components and circuit; this is achieved by bleeding the system.

2 During the bleeding procedure, add only clean, unused hydraulic fluid of the recommended type; *never* re-use fluid that has already been bled from the system. Ensure that a sufficient quantity of new fluid is available before starting work.

3 If there is any possibility of incorrect fluid being already in the system, the brake components and circuit must be flushed completely with uncontaminated, correct fluid, and new seals should be fitted to the various components.

4 If hydraulic fluid has been lost from the system, or air has entered because of a leak, ensure that the fault is cured before proceeding further.

5 Park the vehicle on level ground, securely chock the wheel then release the handbrake.

6 Check that all pipes and hoses are secure, unions tight and bleed screws closed. Clean any dirt from around the bleed screws.

7 Unscrew the master cylinder reservoir cap, and top the master cylinder reservoir up to the MAX level line; refit the cap loosely, and remember to maintain the fluid level at least above the MIN level line throughout the procedure, or there is a risk of further air entering the system.

8 There are a number of one-man, do-it-yourself brake bleeding kits currently available from motor accessory shops. It is recommended that one of these kits is used whenever possible, as they greatly simplify the bleeding operation, and also reduce the risk of expelled air and fluid being drawn back into the system. If such a kit is not available, the basic (two-man) method must be used, which is described in detail below.

9 If a kit is to be used, prepare the vehicle as described previously, and follow the kit manufacturer's instructions, as the procedure may vary slightly according to the type being used; generally, they are as outlined below in the relevant sub-section.

10 Whichever method is used, the same sequence must be followed (see paragraphs 11 to 13) to ensure the removal of all air from the system.

Bleeding sequence

11 If the system has been only partially disconnected, and suitable precautions were taken to minimise fluid loss, it should be necessary only to bleed that part of the system (ie the primary or secondary circuit).

12 If the complete system is to be bled, then it should be done working in the following sequence:

   a) Right-hand rear brake.
   b) Left-hand rear brake.
   c) Right-hand front brake.
   d) Left-hand front brake.

Bleeding - basic (two-man) method

13 Collect a clean glass jar, a suitable length of plastic or rubber tubing which is a tight fit over the bleed screw, and a ring spanner to fit the screw. The help of an assistant will also be required.

14 Remove the dust cap from the first screw in the sequence. Fit the spanner and tube to the screw, place the other end of the tube in the jar, and pour in sufficient fluid to cover the end of the tube.

15 Ensure that the master cylinder reservoir fluid level is maintained at least above the MIN level line throughout the procedure.

16 Have the assistant fully depress the brake pedal several times to build up pressure, then maintain it on the final downstroke.

17 While pedal pressure is maintained, unscrew the bleed screw (approximately one turn) and allow the compressed fluid and air to flow into the jar.

18 The assistant should maintain pedal pressure, following it down to the floor if necessary, and should not release it until instructed to do so. When the flow stops, tighten the bleed screw again, have the assistant release the pedal slowly, and recheck the reservoir fluid level.

19 Repeat the steps given in paragraphs 16 to 18 inclusive until the fluid emerging from the bleed screw is free from air bubbles. If the master cylinder has been drained and refilled, and air is being bled from the first screw in the sequence, allow approximately five seconds between cycles for the master cylinder passages to refill.

20 When no more air bubbles appear, tighten the bleed screw securely, remove the tube and spanner, and refit the dust cap. Do not overtighten the bleed screw.

21 Repeat the procedure on the remaining screws in the sequence, until all air is removed from the system and the brake pedal feels firm again. On completion, lower the vehicle to the ground (where necessary).

Bleeding - using a one-way valve kit

22 As their name implies, these kits consist of a length of tubing with a one-way valve fitted, to prevent expelled air and fluid being drawn back into the system; some kits include a translucent container, which can be positioned so that the air bubbles can be more easily seen flowing from the end of the tube.

23 The kit is connected to the bleed screw, which is then opened **(see illustration)**. The user returns to the driver's seat, depresses the brake pedal with a smooth, steady stroke, and slowly releases it; this is repeated until the expelled fluid is clear of air bubbles.

24 Note that these kits simplify work so much that it is easy to forget to watch the master cylinder reservoir fluid level; ensure that this is maintained at least above the MIN level line at all times, otherwise air will be reintroduced into the system.

Bleeding - using a pressure-bleeding kit

25 These kits are usually operated by the reservoir of pressurised air contained in the spare tyre. However, note that it will probably be necessary to reduce the pressure to a lower level than normal; refer to the instructions supplied with the kit.

26 By connecting a pressurised, fluid-filled container to the master cylinder reservoir, bleeding can be carried out simply by opening each screw in turn (in the specified sequence), and allowing the fluid to flow out until no more air bubbles can be seen in the expelled fluid.

27 This method has the advantage that the large reservoir of fluid provides an additional safeguard against air being drawn into the system during bleeding.

28 Pressure-bleeding is particularly effective when bleeding difficult systems, or when bleeding the complete system at the time of routine fluid renewal.

All methods

29 When bleeding is complete, and firm pedal feel is restored, wash off any spilt fluid, tighten the bleed screws securely, and refit their dust caps.

30 Check the hydraulic fluid level in the master cylinder reservoir, and top-up if necessary (see *Weekly checks*).

31 Discard any hydraulic fluid that has been bled from the system; it will not be fit for re-use.

32 Check the feel of the brake pedal. If it feels at all spongy, air must still be present in the system, and further bleeding is required. Failure to bleed satisfactorily after a reasonable repetition of the bleeding procedure may be due to worn master cylinder seals. **Note:** *If difficulty is experienced in bleeding the braking circuit on models with antilock brakes (ABS), this maybe due to air being trapped in the ABS hydraulic unit. If this is the case then the vehicle should be taken to a Audi/VAG dealer so that the system can be bled using special electronic test equipment.*

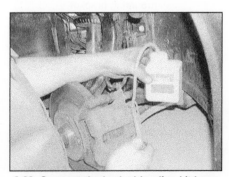

2.23 Connect the brake bleeding kit hose to the caliper bleed nipple, then open the nipple using a spanner

3 Hydraulic pipes and hoses - renewal

Caution: On models equipped with ABS, disconnect the battery before disconnecting any braking system hydraulic union and do not reconnect the battery until after the hydraulic system has been reconnected and the fluid reservoir is topped up. Failure to do this could lead to air entering the hydraulic unit requiring the unit to be bled using special Audi/VAG test equipment (see Section 2).

Note: *Before starting work, refer to the note at the beginning of Section 2 concerning the dangers of hydraulic fluid.*

1 If any pipe or hose is to be renewed, minimise fluid loss by first removing the master cylinder reservoir cap, then tightening it down onto a piece of polythene to obtain an airtight seal. Alternatively, flexible hoses can be sealed, if required, using a proprietary brake hose clamp; metal brake pipe unions can be plugged (if care is taken not to allow dirt into the system) or capped immediately they are disconnected. Place a wad of rag under any union that is to be disconnected, to catch any spilt fluid.

2 If a flexible hose is to be disconnected, unscrew the brake pipe union nut before removing the spring clip which secures the hose to its mounting bracket.

3 To unscrew the union nuts, it is preferable to obtain a brake pipe spanner of the correct size; these are available from most large motor accessory shops. Failing this, a close-fitting open-ended spanner will be required, though if the nuts are tight or corroded, their flats may be rounded-off if the spanner slips. In such a case, a self-locking wrench is often the only way to unscrew a stubborn union, but it follows that the pipe and the damaged nuts must be renewed on reassembly. Always clean a union and surrounding area before disconnecting it. If disconnecting a component with more than one union, make a careful note of the connections before disturbing any of them.

4 If a brake pipe is to be renewed, it can be obtained, cut to length and with the union nuts and end flares in place, from Audi/VAG dealers. All that is then necessary is to bend it to shape, following the line of the original, before fitting it to the car. Alternatively, most motor accessory shops can make up brake pipes from kits, but this requires very careful measurement of the original, to ensure that the replacement is of the correct length. The safest answer is usually to take the original to the shop as a pattern.

5 On refitting, do not overtighten the union nuts. It is not necessary to exercise brute force to obtain a sound joint.

6 Ensure that the pipes and hoses are correctly routed, with no kinks, and that they are secured in the clips or brackets provided. After fitting, remove the polythene from the

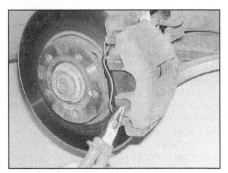

4.2 Unclip the pad retaining spring and remove it from the brake caliper

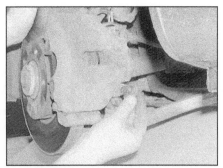

4.3 Remove the end caps from the guide bushes to gain access to the caliper guide pin bolts

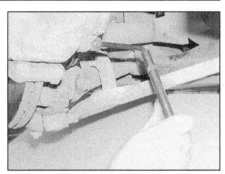

4.4a Slacken . . .

reservoir, and bleed the hydraulic system as described in Section 2. Wash off any spilt fluid, and check carefully for fluid leaks.

4 Front brake pads - renewal

Warning: Renew both sets of front brake pads at the same time - never renew the pads on only one wheel, as uneven braking may result. Note that the dust created by wear of the pads may contain asbestos, which is a health hazard. Never blow it out with compressed air, and don't inhale any of it. An approved filtering mask should be worn when working on the brakes. DO NOT use petrol

or petroleum-based solvents to clean brake parts; use brake cleaner or methylated spirit only.

1 Apply the handbrake, then jack up the front of the vehicle and support it on axle stands. Remove the front roadwheels. Whilst the wheels are removed, refit at least one wheel bolt to each hub to ensure the brake discs remain correctly positioned on the hubs.

Models with ATE/Teves calipers

2 Carefully unclip the pad retaining spring and remove it from the brake caliper **(see illustration)**.

3 Remove the end caps from the guide bushes to gain access to the caliper guide pin bolts **(see illustration)**.

4 Slacken and remove the caliper guide bolts, then lift the caliper away from the mounting

bracket **(see illustrations)**. Tie the caliper to the suspension strut using a suitable piece of wire; do not allow it to hang unsupported from the flexible brake hose.

5 Unclip the inner pad from the caliper piston and remove the outer pad from the mounting bracket **(see illustrations)**.

Models with Lucas calipers

6 Slacken and remove the caliper upper and lower guide pin bolts whilst counterholding the guide pins with an open ended spanner **(see illustration)**. Note that new bolts must be used on refitting.

7 Lift the caliper away from the mounting bracket. Tie the caliper to the suspension strut using a suitable piece of wire; do not allow it to hang unsupported from the flexible brake hose **(see illustrations)**.

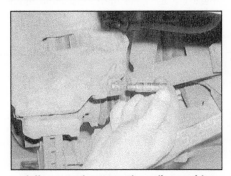

4.4b . . . and remove the caliper guide bolts . . .

4.4c . . . then lift the caliper away from the mounting bracket

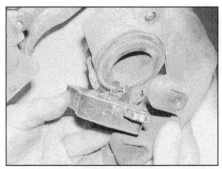

4.5a Unclip the inner pad from the caliper piston . . .

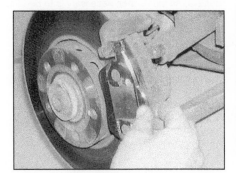

4.5b . . . and remove the outer pad from the mounting bracket

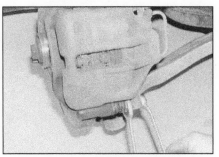

4.6 Slacken and remove the caliper guide pin bolts whilst counterholding the guide pins with an open ended spanner

4.7a Lift the caliper away from the mounting bracket

4.7b Tie the caliper to the suspension strut using a suitable piece of wire; do not allow it to hang unsupported from the flexible brake hose

4.8a Remove the inner . . .

4.8b . . . and outer pads from the caliper mounting bracket

8 Remove the inner and outer pads from the caliper mounting bracket. Ensure that the circular heatshield plate remains clipped into the end face of the piston **(see illustrations)**.

All models

9 First measure the thickness of each brake pad's friction material **(see illustration)**. If either pad is worn at any point to the specified minimum thickness or less, all four pads must be renewed. Also, the pads should be renewed if any are fouled with oil or grease; there is no satisfactory way of degreasing friction material, once contaminated. If any of the brake pads are worn unevenly, or are fouled with oil or grease, trace and rectify the cause before reassembly.

10 If the brake pads are still serviceable, carefully clean them using a clean, fine wire brush or similar, paying particular attention to the sides and back of the metal backing. Clean out the grooves in the friction material, and pick out any large embedded particles of dirt or debris. Carefully clean the pad locations in the caliper mounting bracket.

Models with ATE/Teves calipers

11 Prior to fitting the pads, check that the

guide pin bolts are free to slide easily in the caliper body bushes, and are a reasonably tight fit. Brush the dust and dirt from the caliper and piston, but **do not** inhale it, as it is injurious to health. Inspect the dust seal around the piston for damage, and the piston for evidence of fluid leaks, corrosion or damage. If any of these components requires attention, refer to Section 8.

12 If new brake pads are to be fitted, the caliper piston must be pushed back into the cylinder to make room for them. Either use a piston retraction tool, a G-clamp or use suitable pieces of wood as levers. Clamp off the flexible brake hose leading to the caliper then connect a brake bleeding kit to the caliper bleed nipple. Open the bleed nipple as the piston is retracted; the surplus brake fluid will then be collected in the bleed kit vessel **(see illustration)**.

Note: The ABS unit contains hydraulic components that are very sensitive to impurities in the brake fluid. Even the smallest particles can cause the system to fail through blockage. The pad retraction method described here prevents any debris in the brake fluid expelled from the caliper from

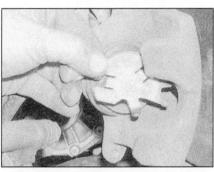

4.8c Ensure that the circular heatshield plate remains clipped into the end face of the piston

being passed back to the ABS hydraulic unit.
13 Clip the inner pad into the caliper piston and fit the outer pad to the mounting bracket, ensuring its friction material is against the brake disc. Note that the outer pad has an arrow stamped onto its outer lower edge; this should point in the normal direction of rotation of the brake disc. If new pads are being fitted, remove the adhesive foil backing (where fitted) from the outer pad and clean off any sticky residue.

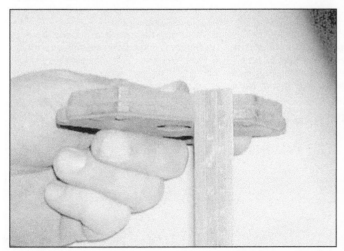

4.9 Measure the thickness of each brake pad's friction material

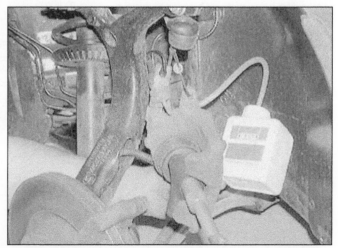

4.12 Using a retraction tool to push the piston back into the caliper. Note the clamp connected to the brake hose and the brake bleeding kit connected to the caliper bleed nipple

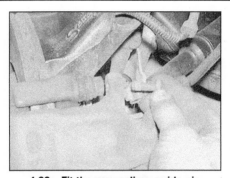

4.14 Refit the caliper guide bolts and tighten them to the specified torque setting

4.22a Fit the new caliper guide pin bolts . . .

4.22b . . . and tighten them to the specified torque setting

14 Manoeuvre the caliper into position then refit the caliper guide bolts and tighten them to the specified torque setting (see illustration).
15 Refit the end caps to the caliper guide bushes and clip the wear sensor wiring onto the lower cap.
16 Fit the pad retaining spring, ensuring its ends are correctly located in the caliper body holes. Press the inner edge of the spring into position so that its ends are firmly in contact with the surface of the brake pad.

Models with Lucas calipers

17 Prior to fitting the pads, check that the guide pins are free to slide easily in the caliper body bushes.
18 Brush the dust and dirt from the caliper and piston, but do not inhale it, as it is injurious to health. Inspect the dust seal around the piston for damage, and the piston for evidence of fluid leaks, corrosion or damage. If any of these components requires attention, refer to Section 8.
19 If new brake pads are to be fitted, the caliper piston must be pushed back into the cylinder to make room for them; refer to the information given in paragraph 12.
20 Clip the inner pad into the caliper piston and fit the outer pad to the mounting bracket, ensuring its friction material is against the brake disc. If new pads are being fitted, remove the adhesive foil backing (where fitted) from the outer pad and clean off any sticky residue.
21 Fit the caliper over the brake pads, ensuring that the butterfly clips on the outer edge of the brake pads bear against the inner surface of the caliper body without jamming in

the caliper inspection aperture. Note: New caliper guide pin bolts must be used.
22 Fit the new caliper guide pin bolts and tighten them to the specified torque setting, counterholding the guide pin with an open ended spanner (see illustrations).

All models

23 Depress the brake pedal repeatedly, until the pads are pressed into firm contact with the brake disc, and normal (non-assisted) pedal pressure is restored.
24 Repeat the above procedure on the remaining front brake caliper.
25 Refit the roadwheels, then lower the vehicle to the ground and tighten the roadwheel bolts to the specified torque setting (see Chapter 1A or 1B).
26 Check (and if necessary top-up) the hydraulic brake fluid level as described in Weekly checks.

⚠ Warning: New pads will not give full braking efficiency until they have bedded in. Be prepared for this, and avoid hard braking as much as possible for the first hundred miles or so after pad renewal.

5 Rear brake pads - renewal

⚠ Warning: Renew both sets of rear brake pads at the same time - never renew the pads on only one wheel, as uneven braking may result. Note

that the dust created by wear of the pads may contain asbestos, which is a health hazard. Never blow it out with compressed air, and don't inhale any of it. An approved filtering mask should be worn when working on the brakes. DO NOT use petrol or petroleum-based solvents to clean brake parts; use brake cleaner or methylated spirit only.

Note: The caliper guide pin bolts must be renewed whenever they are unscrewed.
1 Chock the front wheels, then jack up the rear of the vehicle and support it on axle stands. Remove the rear wheels. Whilst the wheels are removed, refit at least one wheel bolt to each hub to ensure the brake discs remain correctly positioned on the hubs.
2 Referring to Section 16, release the handbrake lever then back off the handbrake cable adjuster to obtain maximum freeplay in the cables and ensure both caliper handbrake levers are against their stops.
3 Slacken and remove the caliper guide pin bolts, counterholding the guide pins with an open ended spanner to prevent them from rotating (see illustration). Discard the guide pin bolts - new bolts must be used on refitting.
4 Lift the caliper away from the brake pads, and tie it to the suspension strut using a suitable piece of wire. Do not allow the caliper to hang unsupported on the flexible brake hose(see illustrations).
5 Withdraw the two brake pads from the caliper mounting bracket (see illustrations).
6 First measure the thickness of each brake pad (including the backing plate). If either pad is worn at any point to the specified minimum

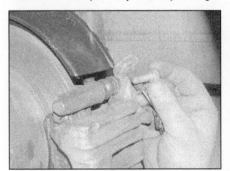

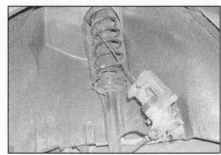

5.3 Slacken and remove the caliper guide pin bolts

5.4a Lift the caliper away from the brake pads . . .

5.4b . . . and tie it to the suspension strut using a piece of wire; do not allow the caliper to hang unsupported on the hose

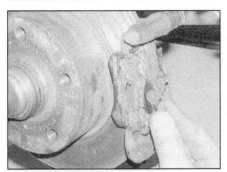

5.5a Withdraw the outer . . .

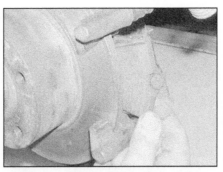

5.5b . . . and inner pad from the caliper mounting bracket

5.9 Using a retraction tool to push the piston back into the caliper

thickness or less, **all four** pads must be renewed. Also, the pads should be renewed if any are fouled with oil or grease; there is no satisfactory way of degreasing friction material, once contaminated. If any of the brake pads are worn unevenly, or fouled with oil or grease, trace and rectify the cause before reassembly. New brake pads are available from Audi/VAG dealers.

7 If the brake pads are still serviceable, carefully clean them using a clean, fine wire brush or similar, paying particular attention to the sides and back of the metal backing. Clean out the grooves in the friction material (where app-licable), and pick out any large embedded particles of dirt or debris. Carefully clean the pad locations in the caliper body/mounting bracket.

8 Prior to fitting the pads, check that the guide pins are free to slide easily in the caliper bracket, and check that the rubber guide pin gaiters are undamaged. Brush the dust and dirt from the caliper and piston, but **do not** inhale it, as it is injurious to health. Inspect the dust seal around the piston for damage, and the piston for evidence of fluid leaks, corrosion or damage. If attention to any of these components is necessary, refer to Section 9.

9 If new brake pads are to be fitted, it will be necessary to retract the piston fully into the caliper bore, by rotating it in a clockwise direction using a retraction tool, or a pair of circlip pliers **(see illustration)**. The excess brake fluid must be ejected via the caliper bleed nipple; refer to the information given in Section 4, paragraph 12.

10 Where applicable, peel the protective sheet from the pad backing plates, then fit the pads in the mounting bracket, ensuring that each pad's friction material is facing the brake disc.

11 Slide the caliper back into position over the pads ensuring the pad anti-rattle springs are correctly positioned against the inner surface of the caliper body and are not jammed in the inspection aperture. **Note:** New guide pin bolts must be used when the caliper is refitted.

12 Press the caliper into position, then install the new guide pin bolts, tightening them to the specified torque setting whilst retaining the guide pins with an open-ended spanner.

13 Repeat the above procedure on the remaining rear brake caliper.

14 Depress the brake pedal repeatedly to force the pads into firm contact with the discs. Once normal pedal feel has returned, check that the discs rotate freely.

15 Refit the roadwheels then lower the vehicle to the ground and tighten the roadwheel bolts to the specified torque setting (see Chapter 1A or 1B).

16 Check (and if necessary top-up) the hydraulic fluid level as described in *Weekly checks.*

⚠️ **Warning: New pads will not give full braking efficiency until they have bedded in. Be prepared for this, and avoid hard braking as much as possible for the first hundred miles or so after pad renewal.**

6 Front brake disc - inspection, removal and refitting

Note: *Before starting work, refer to the note at the beginning of Section 4 concerning the dangers of asbestos dust.*

Inspection

Note: *If either disc requires renewal, BOTH should be renewed at the same time, to ensure even and consistent braking. New brake pads should also be fitted.*

1 Apply the handbrake, then jack up the front of the car and support it on axle stands. Remove the appropriate front roadwheel. Whilst the wheel is removed, refit at least one of the wheel bolts to ensure the brake disc remains correctly positioned on the hub; if necessary fit spacers to the wheel bolts to clamp the disc firmly in position.

2 Slowly rotate the brake disc so that the full area of both sides can be checked; remove the brake pads if better access is required to the inboard surface. Light scoring is normal in the area swept by the brake pads, but if heavy scoring or cracks are found, the disc must be renewed.

3 It is normal to find a lip of rust and brake dust around the disc's perimeter; this can be scraped off if required. If, however, a lip has formed due to excessive wear of the brake pad swept area, then the disc's thickness must be measured using a micrometer. Take

measurements at several places around the disc, at the inside and outside of the pad swept area; if the disc has worn at any point to the specified minimum thickness or less, the disc must be renewed.

4 If the disc is thought to be warped, it can be checked for run-out. First secure the disc firmly to the hub by refitting at least two roadwheel bolts - fit plain washers to the roadwheel bolts to ensure that the disc is properly seated on the hub.

5 Either use a dial gauge mounted on any convenient fixed point, while the disc is slowly rotated, or use feeler blades to measure (at several points all around the disc) the clearance between the disc and a fixed point, such as the caliper mounting bracket **(see illustration)**. If the measurements obtained are at the specified maximum or beyond, the disc is excessively warped, and must be renewed; however, it is worth checking first that the hub bearing is in good condition (Chapter 10).

6 Check the disc for cracks, especially around the wheel bolt holes, and any other wear or damage, and renew if necessary.

Removal

7 Slacken and remove the two bolts securing the brake caliper mounting bracket to the strut. Slide the whole caliper assembly off the hub and away from the disc and tie the assembly to the front coil spring, using a piece of wire or string, to avoid placing any strain on the hydraulic brake hose. The caliper mounting bracket can be unbolted and removed separately if required (see Section 8).

6.5 Using a DTI gauge to measure disc runout

6.8 Removing a front brake disc

7.4a Using a hammer and a large flat-bladed screwdriver or similar, carefully tap and prise the cap . . .

7.4b . . . out of the centre of the brake disc

8 Use chalk or paint to mark the relationship of the disc to the hub, then remove all the wheel bolts and washers used to secure the disc in position and remove the disc **(see illustration)**. If it is tight, lightly tap its rear face with a hide or plastic mallet to free it from the hub.

Refitting

9 Refitting is the reverse of the removal procedure, noting the following points:

a) *Ensure that the mating surfaces of the disc and hub are clean and flat.*

b) *On refitting, align (if applicable) the marks made on removal.*

c) *If a new disc has been fitted, use a suitable solvent to wipe any preservative coating from the disc, before refitting the caliper. Note that new brake pads should always be fitted when the disc is renewed.*

d) *Prior to installation, clean the caliper bracket mounting bolts. Slide the caliper into position, making sure the pads pass either side of the disc, and tighten the caliper bracket bolts to the specified torque setting.*

e) *Refit the roadwheel then lower the vehicle to the ground and tighten the wheel bolts to the specified torque (see Chapter 1A or 1B). Apply the footbrake several times to force the pads back into contact with the disc before driving the vehicle.*

7 Rear brake disc - inspection, removal and refitting

Note: *Before starting work, refer to the note at the beginning of Section 5 concerning the dangers of asbestos dust.*

Inspection

Note: *If either disc requires renewal, BOTH should be renewed at the same time, to ensure even and consistent braking. New brake pads should be fitted also.*

1 Firmly chock the front wheels, engage 1st gear (or P), then jack up the rear of the car and support it on axle stands (see *Jacking and vehicle support*). Remove the appropriate rear roadwheel.

2 Inspect the disc as described in Section 6.

Removal

3 Unscrew the two bolts securing the brake caliper mounting bracket in position, then slide the whole caliper assembly off the disc. Using a piece of wire or string, tie the caliper to the rear suspension coil spring, to avoid placing any strain on the hydraulic brake hose. The caliper mounting bracket can be unbolted and removed separately if required (see Section 9).

4 Using a hammer and a large flat-bladed screwdriver or similar, carefully tap and prise the cap out of the centre of the brake disc **(see illustrations)**. Renew the cap if it is distorted during removal.

5 Extract the split pin from the hub nut, and remove the locking ring. Discard the split pin; a new one must be used on refitting **(see illustrations)**.

6 Slacken and remove the rear hub nut, then slide off the toothed washer and remove the outer bearing from the centre of the disc **(see illustrations)**.

7 The disc can now be slid off the stub axle **(see illustration)**.

7.5a Extract the split pin from the hub nut . . .

7.5b . . . and remove the locking ring

7.6a Slacken and remove the rear hub nut . . .

7.6b . . . then slide off the toothed washer . . .

7.6c . . . and remove the outer bearing from the centre of the disc

7.7 The disc can now be slid off the stub axle

7.11a Gradually slacken the hub nut . . .

7.11b . . . until the position is found where it is just possible to move the toothed washer from side-to-side using a screwdriver

Refitting

8 If a new disc is been fitted, use a suitable solvent to wipe any preservative coating from the disc. If necessary, install the bearing races, inner bearing and oil seal as described in Chapter 10, and thoroughly grease the outer bearing. **Note:** *On models fitted with ABS, the reluctor ring will have to be heated so that it can be removed from the old disc and fitted to the new one.*

9 Apply a smear of grease to the disc oil seal, and slide the disc assembly onto the stub axle.

10 Fit the outer bearing and toothed thrust-washer, ensuring its tooth is correctly engaged in the axle slot.

11 Refit the hub nut, tightening it to the point where it just contacts the washer whilst rotating the brake disc to settle the hub bearings in position. Gradually slacken the hub nut until the position is found where it is just possible to move the toothed washer from side-to-side using a screwdriver **(see illustrations)**. **Note:** *Only a small amount of force should be needed to move the washer.*

12 When the hub nut is correctly positioned, refit the locking ring and secure it in position with a new split pin. Trim the legs and bend them over to lock the pin in position **(see illustrations)**.

13 Fit the cap to the centre of the brake disc, driving it fully into position.

14 Before refitting the brake caliper, make sure that both sides of the disc are completely clean. Slide the caliper into position over the disc, making sure the pads pass either side of the disc. Tighten the caliper mounting bolts to the specified torque setting.

15 Refit the roadwheel, then lower the vehicle to the ground and tighten the wheel bolts to the specified torque setting (see Chapter 1A or 1B).

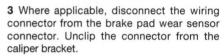

8 Front brake caliper - removal, overhaul and refitting

Caution: On models equipped with ABS, disconnect the battery before disconnecting any braking system hydraulic union and do not reconnect the battery until after the hydraulic system has been reconnected and fluid reservoir topped up. Failure to do this could lead to air entering the hydraulic unit requiring the unit to be bled using special Audi/VAG test equipment.

Note: *Before starting work, refer to the note at the beginning of Section 2 concerning the dangers of hydraulic fluid, and to the warning at the beginning of Section 4 concerning the dangers of asbestos dust.*

Removal

1 Apply the handbrake, then jack up the front of the vehicle and support it on axle stands. Remove the front roadwheels. Whilst the wheels are removed, refit at least one wheel bolt to the hub to ensure the brake disc remains correctly positioned on the hub.

2 Minimise fluid loss by first removing the master cylinder reservoir cap, and then tightening it down onto a piece of polythene, to obtain an airtight seal. Alternatively, use a brake hose clamp, a G-clamp or a similar tool to clamp the flexible hose.

3 Where applicable, disconnect the wiring connector from the brake pad wear sensor connector. Unclip the connector from the caliper bracket.

4 Clean the area around the caliper brake pipe union then unscrew the union nut. Unbolt the mounting bracket from the caliper and position the pipe clear. Plug/cover the pipe end and caliper union to minimise fluid loss and prevent the entry of dirt into the hydraulic system. Wash off any spilt fluid immediately with cold water.

5 On models with ATE/Teves calipers, carefully lever the pad retaining spring out position and remove it from the brake caliper using a flat-bladed screwdriver. Remove the end caps from the guide bushes then slacken and remove the caliper guide bolts.

6 On models with Lucas calipers, counter-hold the guide pins with an open ended spanner, then unscrew and remove both guide pin bolts.

7 Lift the caliper out of position, freeing it from the pad wear sensor wiring (where applicable). Remove the inner brake pad from the piston and the outer brake pad from the caliper mounting bracket. Unbolt and remove the caliper mounting bracket.

Overhaul

8 With the caliper on the bench, wipe away all traces of dust and dirt, but *avoid inhaling the dust, as it is injurious to health.*

9 Withdraw the partially ejected piston from the caliper body, and remove the dust seal.

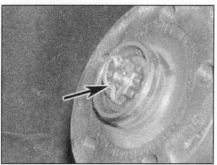

7.12a Secure the locking ring in position with a new split pin

7.12b Trim the legs and bend them over to lock the pin in position

> **HAYNES HiNT** *If the piston cannot be withdrawn by hand, it can be forced out by applying compressed air to the brake hose union hole. Only low pressure should be required, such as that generated by a foot pump. Even using low pressure, the piston will be ejected with considerable force; place a block of soft wood in the caliper to prevent damage to the end of the piston, and avoid getting your fingers trapped between the piston and caliper.*

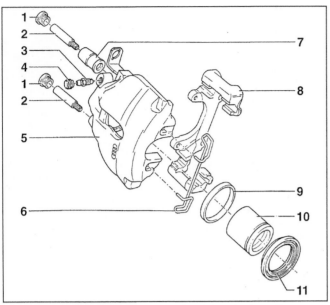

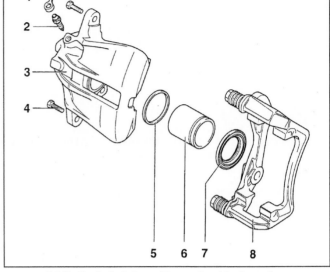

8.14a Exploded view of Teves/ATE front brake caliper

1 Dust cap	6 Pad retaining	9 Piston seal
2 Guide bolts	spring	10 Piston
3 Bleed screw	7 Guide sleeves	11 Dust seal
4 Dust cap	8 Caliper mounting	
5 Caliper	bracket	

8.14b Exploded view of Lucas front brake caliper

1 Dust cap	4 Guide pin bolts	7 Dust seal
2 Bleed screw	5 Piston seal	8 Caliper mounting
3 Caliper	6 Piston	bracket

10 Using a soft flat bladed instrument, such as a plastic spatula, extract the piston hydraulic seal, taking great care not to damage the caliper bore.

11 Thoroughly clean all components, using only methylated spirit, isopropyl alcohol or clean brake fluid as a cleaning medium. Never use mineral-based solvents such as petrol or paraffin, as they will attack the hydraulic system's rubber components. Dry the components immediately, using compressed air or a clean, lint-free cloth. Use compressed air to blow clear the fluid passages.

12 Check all components, and renew any that are worn or damaged. Check particularly the cylinder bore and piston; these should be renewed (note that this means the renewal of the complete body assembly) if they are scratched, worn or corroded in any way. Similarly check the condition of the guide bolts and the bushes in the caliper body; both bolts should be undamaged and (when

cleaned) a reasonably tight sliding fit in the bushes. If there is any doubt about the condition of any component, renew it.

13 If the assembly is fit for further use, obtain the appropriate repair kit; the components are available from Audi/VAG dealers in various combinations. All rubber seals should be renewed as a matter of course; these should never be re-used.

14 On reassembly, ensure that all components are clean and dry **(see illustrations)**.

15 Soak the piston and the new piston (fluid) seal in clean hydraulic fluid. Smear clean fluid on the cylinder bore surface.

16 Fit the new piston (fluid) seal, using only your fingers (no tools) to manipulate it into the cylinder bore groove.

17 Fit the new dust seal to the rear of the piston and seat the outer lip of the seal in the caliper body groove. Carefully ease the piston squarely into the cylinder bore using a twisting

motion. Press the piston fully into position and seat the inner lip of the dust seal in the piston groove.

18 If the guide bushes are being renewed, push the old bushes out from the body and press the new ones into position, making sure they are correctly seated.

19 Prior to refitting, fill the caliper with fresh hydraulic fluid by slackening the bleed screw and pumping the fluid through the caliper until bubble-free fluid is expelled from the union hole.

Refitting

20 Bolt the caliper mounting bracket to the hub carrier; use clean bolts and tighten them to the specified torque **(see illustrations)**. Refit the brake pads to the piston and caliper mounting bracket, with reference to Section 4. Manoeuvre the caliper into position over the brake pads.

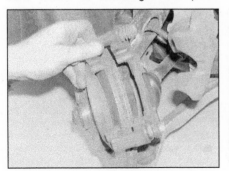

8.20a Fit the caliper mounting bracket to the hub carrier . . .

8.20b . . . use new bolts . . .

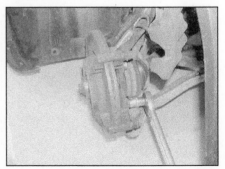

8.20c . . . and tighten them to the specified torque

21 Fit the caliper guide pins/guide pin bolts (as applicable), tightening them to the specified torque setting, and refit the end caps to the guide bushes. **Note:** *On models with Lucas calipers, new guide pin bolts must be fitted.*

22 Reconnect the brake pipe to the caliper and refit the mounting bracket to the caliper. Tighten the bracket retaining bolt and the brake pipe union nut to their specified torque settings.

23 Fit the pad retaining spring, ensuring its ends are correctly located in the caliper body holes.

24 Ensure the wiring is correctly routed through the loop on the lower cap then clip the pad wear sensor wiring connector onto its bracket on the caliper. Securely reconnect the wiring connector.

25 Remove the brake hose clamp or polythene (where fitted) and bleed the hydraulic system as described in Section 2. Note that, providing the precautions described were taken to minimise brake fluid loss, it should only be necessary to bleed the relevant front brake.

26 Refit the roadwheel, then lower the vehicle to the ground and tighten the roadwheel bolts to the specified torque (see Chapter 1A or 1B).

9 Rear brake caliper - removal, overhaul and refitting

Caution: *On models equipped with ABS, disconnect the battery before disconnecting any braking system hydraulic union and do not reconnect the battery until after the hydraulic system has reconnected and fluid reservoir topped up. Failure to do this could lead to air entering the hydraulic unit requiring the unit to be bled using special Audi/VAG test equipment.*
Note: *Before starting work, refer to the note at the beginning of Section 2 concerning the dangers of hydraulic fluid, and to the warning at the beginning of Section 5 concerning the dangers of asbestos dust.*

Removal

Note: *New guide pin bolts must be used on refitting.*

1 Chock the front wheels, then jack up the rear of the vehicle and support it on axle stands. Remove the relevant rear wheel. Whilst the wheel is removed, refit at least one wheel bolt to the hub to ensure the brake disc remains in position.

2 Referring to Section 16, release the handbrake lever then back off the handbrake cable adjuster to obtain maximum freeplay in the cables.

3 Free the handbrake cable from the caliper lever then remove the retaining clip and free the outer cable from the caliper body.

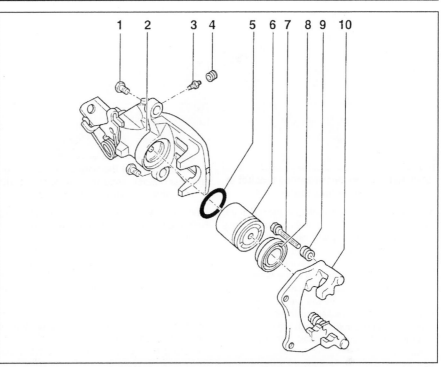

9.13 Exploded view of the rear brake caliper

1 Self locking bolt	4 Dust cap	7 Guide pin	10 Caliper mounting
2 Caliper	5 Piston seal	8 Dust seal	bracket
3 Bleed screw	6 Piston	9 Dust sleeve	

4 Minimise fluid loss by first removing the master cylinder reservoir cap, and then tightening it down onto a piece of polythene, to obtain an airtight seal. Alternatively, use a brake hose clamp, a G-clamp or a similar tool to clamp the flexible hose.

5 Clean the area around the caliper brake hose then slacken the union.

6 Slacken and remove the caliper guide pin bolts, using a slim open-ended spanner to prevent the guide pins from rotating. Discard the guide pin bolts - new bolts must be used on refitting.

7 Lift the brake caliper away from the its mounting bracket and unscrew it from the end of the brake hose. Plug/cover the hose end and caliper union to minimise fluid loss and prevent the entry of dirt into the hydraulic system. Wash off any spilt fluid immediately with cold water. Remove the inner and outer brake pads from the caliper mounting bracket. Unbolt and remove the caliper mounting bracket.

Overhaul

Note: *It is not possible to overhaul the brake caliper handbrake mechanism. If the mechanism is faulty, or fluid is leaking from the handbrake lever seal the caliper assembly must be renewed.*

8 With the caliper on the bench, wipe away all traces of dust and dirt, but avoid inhaling the dust, as it is injurious to health.

9 Remove the piston from the caliper bore by rotating it in an anti-clockwise direction. This

can be achieved using a suitable pair of circlip pliers engaged in the caliper piston slots. Once the piston turns freely but does not come out any further, the piston is held in only by its seal and can be withdrawn by hand.

10 Remove the dust seal from the piston then, using a blunt flat bladed instrument, carefully extract the piston hydraulic seal from the caliper bore. Take great care not to mark the caliper surface.

11 Withdraw the guide pins from the caliper mounting bracket, and remove the guide sleeve gaiters.

12 Inspect all the caliper components (as described for the front brake caliper in Section 8), and renew as necessary, noting that the handbrake mechanism must **not** be dismantled.

13 On reassembly, ensure all components are clean and dry **(see illustration)**.

14 Soak the piston and the new piston (fluid) seal in clean hydraulic fluid. Smear clean fluid on the cylinder bore surface. Fit the new piston (fluid) seal, using only your fingers (not tools) to manipulate into the cylinder bore groove.

15 Fit the new dust seal to the rear of the piston and seat the outer lip of the seal in the caliper body groove. Carefully ease the piston squarely into the cylinder bore using a twisting motion. Turn the piston in a clockwise direction, using the method employed on dismantling, until it is fully retracted into the caliper bore then seat the inner lip of the dust seal in the piston groove.

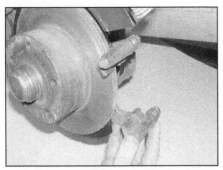

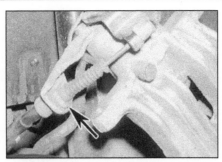

9.18 Refit the caliper mounting bracket to the rear hub carrier

9.22 Reconnect the handbrake cable to the rear caliper, securing it in position with the retaining clip (arrowed)

16 Apply the grease supplied in the repair kit, or a copper-based brake grease or anti-seize compound, to the guide pins. Fit the new gaiters to the guide pins and fit the pins to the caliper mounting bracket, ensuring that the gaiters are correctly located in the grooves on both the pins and caliper bracket.

17 Prior to refitting, fill the caliper with fresh hydraulic fluid by slackening the bleed screw and pumping the fluid through the caliper until bubble-free fluid is expelled from the union hole.

Refitting

18 Bolt the caliper mounting bracket to the rear hub carrier; use clean bolts and tighten

them to the specified torque **(see illustration)**. Refit the brake pads to the caliper mounting bracket with reference to Section 5.

19 Screw the caliper fully onto the brake hose, then manoeuvre the caliper into position over the pads then fit the new guide pin bolts, tightening them to the specified torque setting.

20 Remove the brake hose clamp or polythene (where used) and securely tighten the brake hose union.

21 Bleed the hydraulic system as described in Section 2. Note that, providing the precautions described were taken to minimise brake fluid loss, it should only be necessary to bleed the relevant rear brake.

22 Reconnect the handbrake cable to the caliper **(see illustration)**, securing it in position with the retaining clip, and adjust the cable as described in Section 14.

23 Refit the roadwheel, then lower the vehicle to the ground and tighten the roadwheel bolts to the specified torque (see Chapter 1A or 1B).

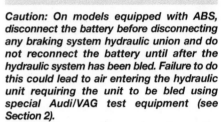

10 Master cylinder -
removal, overhaul and refitting

Caution: On models equipped with ABS, disconnect the battery before disconnecting any braking system hydraulic union and do not reconnect the battery until after the hydraulic system has been bled. Failure to do this could lead to air entering the hydraulic unit requiring the unit to be bled using special Audi/VAG test equipment (see Section 2).

Note: *Before starting work, refer to the warning at the beginning of Section 2 concerning the dangers of hydraulic fluid.*

Removal

1 Raise the front of the vehicle and rest it securely on axle stands. Remove the left hand front road wheel.

2 Connect a length of hose to the left hand front brake caliper bleed screw, then direct the other end of the hose into a suitable receptacle, as described in Section 2. Open the bleed screw and then depress the brake pedal repeatedly to expel as much brake fluid as possible from the master cylinder. When the fluid flow ceases, close the bleed screw.

3 Pad the area underneath the master cylinder with absorbent rags, to catch any fluid spills. Disconnect the clutch master cylinder feed hose from the side of the brake master cylinder and plug the outlet to minimise fluid loss.

4 Disconnect the wiring plug from the brake fluid level sender unit.

5 Wipe clean the area around the brake pipe unions on the side of the master cylinder, and place absorbent rags beneath the pipe unions to catch any surplus fluid. Make a note of the correct fitted positions of the unions, then unscrew the union nuts and carefully withdraw the pipes. Plug or tape over the pipe ends and master cylinder orifices, to minimise the loss of brake fluid, and to prevent the entry of dirt into the system. Wash off any spilt fluid immediately with cold water.

6 Pull the sealing strip from the upper edge of the bulkhead, in front of the brake master cylinder. Release the wiring loom from its retaining clips and lift it up to allow the master cylinder to be removed.

7 Slacken and remove the two nuts securing the master cylinder to the vacuum servo unit, then withdraw the unit from the engine compartment. Recover the sealing ring fitted to the rear of the master cylinder and discard it; a new one must be used on refitting **(see illustration)**. **Note:** *The Torx head bolts which*

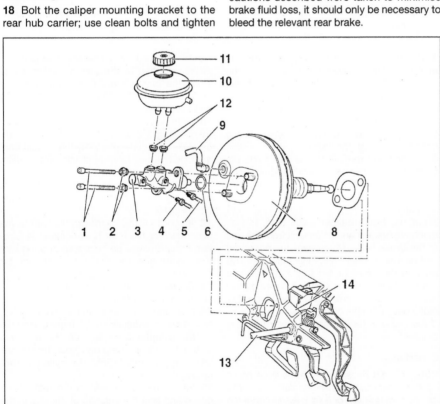

10.7 Exploded view of the master cylinder/brake vacuum servo

1 T45 Torx bolt	6 Seal	11 Cap
2 Self locking nut	7 Servo	12 Sealing plugs
3 Master cylinder	8 Gasket	13 Fluid supply hose
4 Brake pipe	9 Vacuum hose	14 Engine compartment
5 Brake pipe	10 Fluid reservoir	bulkhead

secure the servo unit is position are threaded into the same studs as the master cylinder mounting nuts and should not be disturbed if only the master cylinder is to be removed.

Overhaul

8 If the master cylinder is faulty, it must be renewed. Repair kits are not available from Audi/VAG dealers, so the cylinder must be treated as a sealed unit.

9 The only items which can be renewed are the mounting seals for the fluid reservoir; if these show signs of deterioration, pull off the reservoir and remove the old seals. Lubricate the new seals with clean brake fluid, and ease them into the master cylinder ports. When fitting the rear seal, take care to ensure that the seal engages correctly with the pushrod circuit filling tube and ensure that the seal projects from the rear of its housing by approximately 1 mm. Once both seals are correctly fitted, ease the fluid reservoir into position and push it fully home.

Refitting

10 Remove all traces of dirt from the master cylinder and servo unit mating surfaces, and fit a new sealing ring to the rear of the master cylinder body.

11 Fit the master cylinder to the servo unit, ensuring that the servo unit pushrod enters the master cylinder bore centrally. Have an assistant depress the brake pedal slightly, so that pushrod is moved towards the master cylinder.

12 Refit the master cylinder mounting nuts and tighten them to the specified torque.

13 Wipe clean the brake pipe unions, then refit them to the master cylinder ports and tighten them to the specified torque.

14 Reconnect the clutch master cylinder hose to the fluid reservoir and securely tighten the retaining clip.

15 Reconnect the fluid level sender unit wiring connector.

16 Clip the wiring loom into position and refit the sealing strip to the upper edge of the bulkhead.

17 Refill the master cylinder reservoir with new fluid, and bleed the brake and clutch hydraulic systems, as described in Section 2 and Chapter 6 respectively.

11 Brake pedal - removal and refitting

Removal

1 Disconnect the battery negative terminal.

2 Remove the brake master cylinder as described in Section 10.

3 Remove the brake servo vacuum unit.

4 Disconnect the hydraulic pipe from the rear of the clutch master cylinder, as described in Chapter 6. Pad the surrounding area with absorbent rags, to catch any fluid spillage.

5 On right hand drive models, unscrew and withdraw the pedal bracket securing screw, located on the bulkhead at the rear of the engine compartment, behind the servo unit mountings.

6 Remove the trim panels underneath the drivers side of the facia, as necessary to gain access to the base of the steering column.

7 Turn the steering wheel until the front road wheels are set the in the straight-ahead position. Ensure that the wheel remains in this position throughout the remainder of the procedure.

8 Unscrew the nut from the pinch bolt securing the universal joint at the base of the steering column to the steering gear. Rotate the bolt through half turn and withdraw it from the joint.

9 Secure the lower section of the steering column to the upper section using a length of wire. This is to ensure that when the steering column is detached from the steering gear, the two sections of the column do not become separated.

Caution: Do not allow the upper and lower sections of the steering column to become separated whilst the steering column is detached from the steering gear. Ensure that the steering wheel and roadwheels do not move until the steering column is reconnected or the airbag contact unit may become misaligned, leading to the failure of the airbag system.

10 Pull the steering column universal joint off the steering gear pinion and move it to one side.

11 Release the brake light switch from its mounting bracket and position it to one side. Where applicable, detach the vacuum control valves from the brackets above the brake and clutch pedals and position them to one side.

12 On petrol engine models, detach the accelerator cable from the accelerator pedal as described in Chapter 4A.

13 Slacken and remove the nut securing the pedal bracket assembly to the bulkhead, then manoeuvre the assembly out from underneath the facia. Take care to avoid damaging the immobiliser control unit as the assembly is withdrawn.

14 On right hand drive models, unscrew the securing bolt and remove the servo pushrod operating lever from the left hand side of the clutch pedal. Withdraw the brake pedal from the assembly.

15 On left hand drive models, remove the securing clips and withdraw the pivot shaft from the brake and clutch pedals. Remove the brake pedal from the assembly.

16 Examine all components for signs of wear or damage, renewing them as necessary.

Refitting

17 Apply a smear of multi-purpose grease to the pedal pivot bore and the pushrod clevis pin.

18 The remainder of the refitting procedure is a reversal of the removal procedure, noting the following points:

a) *Do not remove the wire securing the upper and lower sections of the steering column together until the universal joint has been refitted to the steering gear pinion.*

b) *Delay the final tightening of the pedal bracket securing nut until the brake vacuum servo unit has been refitted.*

c) *Tighten all fixings to the correct torque, where specified.*

d) *Refit the accelerator cable as described in Chapter 4A.*

e) *Refit the brake servo vacuum unit as described in Section 12.*

f) *Refit the brake master cylinder as described in Section 10.*

g) *Refit and adjust the stop-light switch as described in Section 17.*

h) *Refit the cruise control system vacuum valves.*

i) *Bleed the brake and clutch hydraulic systems as described in Section 2 and Chapter 6 respectively.*

12 Vacuum servo unit - testing, removal and refitting

Testing

1 To test the operation of the servo unit, depress the footbrake several times to exhaust the vacuum, then start the engine whilst keeping the pedal firmly depressed. As the engine starts, there should be a noticeable give in the brake pedal as the vacuum builds up. Allow the engine to run for at least two minutes, then switch it off. If the brake pedal is now depressed it should feel normal, but further applications should result in the pedal feeling firmer, with the pedal stroke decreasing with each application.

2 If the servo does not operate as described, first inspect the servo unit check valve as described in Section 13. On diesel engine models, also check the vacuum pump as described in Section 20.

3 If the servo unit still fails to operate satisfactorily, the fault may lie within the unit itself. Repairs to the unit are not possible - if faulty, the servo unit must be renewed.

Removal

4 Remove the master cylinder as described in Section 10.

5 Carefully ease the vacuum hose connection out from the servo unit, taking care not to damage the grommet.

6 Undo the retaining screws and remove the storage compartment panel from the driver's side of the facia.

7 Working underneath the facia, locate the servo unit pushrod and note how it is connected to the brake pedal. On right hand drive models, the pushrod connects to a remote operating lever, which is located to the left of the clutch pedal. On left hand drive

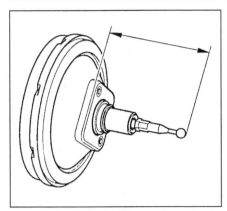

12.10 Check that the distance from the tip of the pushrod ball joint to the servo unit mating surface is as specified

models it is connected directly to the rear of the brake pedal. In both installations, the pushrod is equipped with a ball joint. To disconnect the pushrod from the remote operating lever/pedal, depress the locking tabs of the ball joint retaining clip and raise the brake pedal, until the push rod ball joint can be felt to disengage.

8 Slacken and remove the Torx bolts securing the servo unit to the pedal mounting bracket and bulkhead.

9 Manoeuvre the servo unit out of position. Recover the gasket which is fitted between the servo and bulkhead. Examine the gasket for signs of wear or damage and renew if necessary.

Refitting

10 Prior to refitting, check that the distance from the tip of the pushrod ball joint to the servo unit mating surface (without the gasket in place) is as specified **(see illustration)**. If adjustment is necessary, slacken the locknut and rotate the pushrod. Once the distance is correctly set, hold the pushrod and securely tighten the locknut.

11 Ensure the servo unit and bulkhead mating surfaces are clean, fit the gasket to the rear of the servo unit and manoeuvre the unit into position.

12 From inside the vehicle, make sure the pushrod is correctly engaged with the rear of the pedal, or the remote operating lever (as

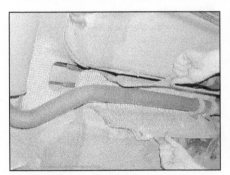

14.5a Remove the exhaust system heat shields . . .

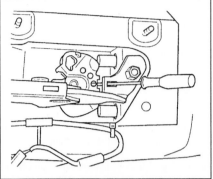

14.4 Pass a screwdriver through the hole in the handbrake lever mounting bracket and lock the handbrake cable compensator pulley in position, to prevent it from turning

applicable) then press the pushrod firmly into position until the ball joint can be felt to engage. Lift the brake pedal by hand to check that the pushrod is securely reconnected.

13 Refit the servo unit securing bolts and tighten them to the specified torque.

14 Adjust the operation of the brake light switch as described in section 17.

15 Refit the storage compartment panel to the underside of the facia.

16 Ease the vacuum hose end fitting into position in the servo unit, taking care not to displace the rubber grommet.

17 Refit the master cylinder as described in Section 10.

18 Bleed the brake hydraulic system as described in Section 2.

19 Bleed the clutch hydraulic system as described in Chapter 6.

13 Vacuum servo unit check valve - removal, testing and refitting

Removal

Note: *The valve is an integral part of the servo unit vacuum hose and is not available separately.*

1 Carefully ease the vacuum hose connection out from the servo unit, taking care not to damage the grommet.

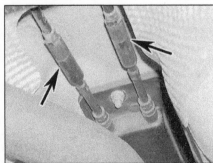

14.5b . . . to gain access to the handbrake cable adjuster collars (arrowed)

2 Work back along the hose, freeing it from all the relevant retaining clips whilst noting its correct routing.

3 Slacken the retaining clip(s) then disconnect the vacuum hose from the manifold and/or vacuum pump (as applicable) and remove it from the vehicle.

Testing

4 Examine the vacuum hose for signs of damage, and renew if necessary. The valve may be tested by blowing through it in both directions. Air should flow through the valve in one direction only - when blown through from the servo unit end of the valve. Renew the valve if this is not the case.

5 Examine the servo unit rubber sealing grommet and hose(s) linking the main hose to the manifold/pump (as applicable) for signs of damage or deterioration, and renew as necessary.

Refitting

6 Ensure the sealing grommet is in position in the servo unit then carefully ease the vacuum hose end fitting into position, taking great care not to displace or damage the grommet.

7 Ensure the hose is correctly routed then connect it to the pump/manifold and securely tighten the retaining clip(s).

8 On completion, start the engine and check the check valve-to-servo unit connection for signs of air leaks.

14 Handbrake - adjustment

1 Depress the brake pedal firmly, to settle the rear brake self adjustment mechanism.

2 Chock the front wheels, then jack up the rear of the vehicle and support it on axle stands. Fully release the handbrake lever.

3 Remove the ashtray unit from the rear section of the centre console, as described in Chapter 11.

4 Pass a screwdriver through the hole in the handbrake lever mounting bracket and lock the handbrake cable compensator pulley in position, to prevent it from turning **(see illustration)**.

5 Working underneath the vehicle, locate the handbrake adjuster collars, which are located above the exhaust pipe. Access can be gained by removing the exhaust system heat shields **(see illustrations)**.

6 Working on the first adjustment collar, remove the locking ring, then rotate the collar anticlockwise until it reaches its end stop. Counterhold the rear section of the handbrake cable using an open ended spanner on the hex nut provided as you do this **(see illustrations)**.

7 Grasp the handbrake cable either side of the adjustment collar and push them together firmly, so that the collar takes up all the slack between the two sections of the handbrake cable.

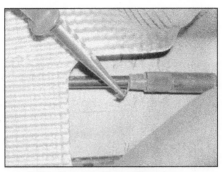

14.6a Remove the locking ring . . .

8 Rotate the adjustment collar clockwise, until the slot for the locking ring is just visible, then insert the locking ring into its slot.

9 Repeat the steps in paragraphs 6 to 8 on the remaining adjustment collar.

10 Pull the two sections of the adjustment collar apart on either cable until the slack in both handbrake cables has been taken up. Ensure that the brake caliper handbrake levers remain seated on their stops as you do this.

11 Working inside the vehicle, remove the screwdriver to free the handbrake cable compensator pulley, then apply and release the handbrake lever firmly at least three times.

12 Return to the underside of the vehicle and turn the adjustment collars on both handbrake cables until a gap of approximately 1 mm (but not greater than 1.5 mm) can seen between the caliper handbrake levers and their end stops **(see illustration)**.

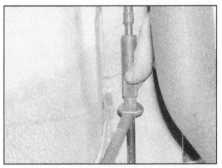

14.6b . . . then rotate the collar anticlockwise until it reaches its end stop, whilst counterholding the rear section of the handbrake cable using a spanner

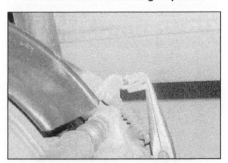

16.4a Remove the metal clip and disconnect the handbrake cable outer from its mounting lug

13 Check on both handbrake cables that the adjustment collars have not been turned to the extent that the coloured rubber O-rings inside the collars have been exposed. If this is the case, the handbrake cables may be stretched beyond the limit of adjustment, or the rear brake pads may be excessively worn.

14 Check the operation of the handbrake and repeat the adjustment procedure as necessary.

15 Once the handbrake is correctly adjusted (both brakes securely lock the wheels with the lever applied and spin freely when the lever is released), lower the vehicle to the ground.

15 Handbrake lever - removal and refitting

Removal

1 Remove the rear section of the centre console as described in Chapter 11.

2 Unscrew the two nuts that secure the handbrake lever to the floorpan.

3 Disengage the handbrake cable from the base of the lever, then free the handbrake lever from its mountings and remove it from the vehicle.

Refitting

4 Refitting is a reversal of removal, but adjust the handbrake, as described in Section 14, before the rear section of the centre console is refitted.

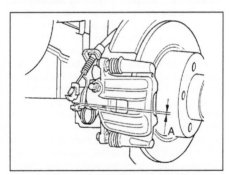

14.12 Turn the adjustment collar until a gap of between 1.0 and 1.5mm (A) can seen between the caliper handbrake lever and the end stop

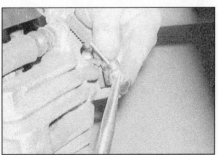

16.4b Release the cable inner from its lever and withdraw the cable from the caliper

16 Handbrake cables - removal and refitting

Removal

1 The handbrake cable consists of two sections, a right- and a left-hand section, which are linked to the lever by a compensator plate. Each section can be removed individually as follows.

2 Undo the nuts and remove the exhaust system heatshields to gain access to the front end of the handbrake cable.

3 Remove the locking ring from the first handbrake cable adjustment collar and rotate the collar anticlockwise as far as possible. Grasp the front and rear sections of the handbrake cable either side of the adjustment collar and push them firmly together to obtain maximum free play. Repeat this operation on the second handbrake cable.

4 Working at the first rear brake caliper, remove the metal clip and disconnect the handbrake cable outer from its mounting lug. Release the cable inner from its lever and withdraw the cable from the caliper **(see illustrations)**. Repeat this operation at the remaining caliper.

5 Work back along the length of each handbrake cable, noting its correct routing, and free it from all the relevant retaining clips and fixings, including those on the rear suspension beam.

6 Undo the nuts and remove the exhaust system rear silencer heatshield to gain access to the handbrake cable clamp plate. Release the spring clips and free the cables from the floorpan.

7 Carefully prise the handbrake cable grommets from the underside of the handbrake lever housing.

8 Working inside the vehicle, unhook the handbrake cables from the compensator pulley at the rear of the handbrake lever, by inserting a screwdriver through the hole provided in the handbrake lever mounting bracket **(see illustration)**.

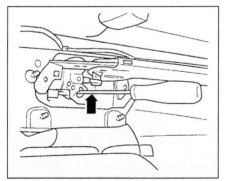

16.8 Unhook the handbrake cables from the rear of the handbrake lever, by inserting a screwdriver through the hole in the handbrake lever mounting bracket

17.3 Unplug the wiring connector from the rear of the switch body

9 Withdraw the handbrake cables via the underside of the car.

Refitting

10 Refitting is a reversal of the removal procedure, ensuring that the cable is correctly routed and retained by all the necessary clips and ties. In particular, make sure that the cable grommets seat correctly in the underside of the handbrake lever housing. On completion, adjust the operation of the handbrake as described in Section 14.

17 Stop-light switch - removal, refitting and adjustment

Removal

1 The stop-light switch is located on the pedal bracket behind the facia. On models with cruise control there are two switches on the brake pedal, the stop-light switch is the upper of the two. The lower cruise control switch can be identified by the vacuum hoses leading to it.
2 Undo the retaining screws and remove the storage compartment panel/trim panel from the underside of the facia on the driver's side.
3 Disconnect the battery negative cable, then unplug the wiring connector from the rear of the switch body **(see illustration)**.
4 Depress the brake pedal, then unscrew and remove the lower locknut from the front of the switch.
5 Withdraw the switch and remove it from the bracket. If the switch retaining clip and washer are a loose fit, remove them and store with the switch.

Refitting and adjustment

6 Ensure the clip is securely fitted to the pedal bracket.
7 On some models, where adjustment of the stop light switch has not previously been carried out, an upper locknut may not be fitted. To permit adjustment, an M12x1.5 nut must be threaded on to the switch shaft before the switch is refitted to its mounting bracket.
8 Fit the spring washer to the switch, then depress the brake pedal and engage the

switch with its retaining clip, pushing it fully into position.
9 Fit the lower locknut to the switch, then allow the brake pedal to slowly pivot back to its rest position, so that the pedal just bears against the switch plunger.
10 Adjust the position of the switch in its bracket by turning the upper and lower locknuts such that the protrusion of the plunger from the front of the switch is between 0.1 and 0.5 mm. Tighten the lower locknut when this dimension is correct.
11 Reconnect the wiring connector, and check the operation of the stop-lights. If the stop-light switch does not function correctly it must be renewed.
12 Refit the storage compartment/trim panel to the facia. On completion, reconnect the battery negative cable.

18 Anti-lock braking system (ABS) - general information

Note: *On models equipped with traction control, the ABS unit is a dual function unit, controlling both the Anti-Lock Braking system (ABS), the Electronic Differential Locking (EDL) and/or Anti-Slip Regulation (ASR) system functions.*

1 ABS is fitted as standard to all models in the range. The system comprises a hydraulic unit, an electronic control unit (ECU) and four roadwheel sensors. The hydraulic unit contains the eight hydraulic solenoid valves (two for each brake - one inlet and one outlet) and the electrically driven return pump. The purpose of the system is to prevent the road wheels locking during heavy braking. This is achieved by automatic release of the brake on the relevant wheel, followed by re-application of the brake. In the case of the rear wheels, both rear brakes are released and applied at the same time.
2 The solenoid valves are controlled by the ECU, which itself receives signals from the four wheel sensors (front sensors are fitted to the hubs and the rear sensors are fitted to the rear axle), which monitor the speed of rotation of each wheel. By comparing these signals, the ECU can determine the speed at which the vehicle is travelling. It can then use this speed to determine when a wheel is decelerating at an abnormal rate, compared to the speed of the vehicle, and therefore predicts when a wheel is about to lock. During normal operation, the system functions in the same way as a non-ABS braking system.
3 If the ECU senses that a wheel is about to lock, it closes the relevant outlet solenoid valves in the hydraulic unit, which then isolates the relevant brake on the wheel which is about to lock from the master cylinder, effectively sealing-in the hydraulic pressure.
4 If the speed of rotation of the wheel continues to decrease at an abnormal rate, the ECU opens the inlet solenoid valves on the

relevant brake and operates the electrically driven return pump which pumps the hydraulic fluid back into the master cylinder, releasing the brake. Once the speed of rotation of the wheel returns to an acceptable rate, the pump stops; the solenoid valves switch again, allowing the hydraulic master cylinder pressure to return to the caliper, which then re-applies the brake. This cycle can be carried out many times a second.
5 The action of the solenoid valves and return pump creates pulses in the hydraulic circuit. When the ABS system is functioning, these pulses can be felt through the brake pedal.
6 On models with a traction control system, the ABS system also performs the Electronic Differential Lock (EDL) and traction control/Anti-Slip Regulation (ASR) functions. If under acceleration the ECU senses that a wheel is spinning, it uses the hydraulic unit to gradually apply the brake on that wheel until traction is regained. Once the wheel regains traction, the brake is released.
7 The operation of the ABS system is entirely dependent on electrical signals. To prevent the system responding to any inaccurate signals, a built-in safety circuit monitors all signals received by the ECU. If an inaccurate signal or low battery voltage is detected, the ABS system is automatically shut down, and the warning light on the instrument panel is illuminated, to inform the driver that the ABS system is not operational. Normal braking should still be available, however.
8 Earlier models were fitted with Bosch ABS 5.0, where the electronic control unit (ECU) is mounted remotely from the hydraulic unit. Later models were fitted with Bosch ABS 5.3, where the ECU and hydraulic unit are combined.
9 If a fault does develop in the ABS system, the vehicle must be taken to a Audi/VAG dealer for fault diagnosis and repair.

19 Anti-lock braking system (ABS) components - removal and refitting

Hydraulic unit

Caution: Disconnect the battery before disconnecting any braking system hydraulic union and do not reconnect the battery until after the hydraulic system has reconnected and fluid reservoir topped up. Failure to do this could lead to air entering the hydraulic unit requiring the unit to be bled using special Audi/VAG test equipment (see Section 2).
Note: *Audi state that the operation of the hydraulic unit should be checked using special test equipment after refitting. Bearing this in mind, it is recommended that removal and refitting of the unit is entrusted to a Audi/VAG dealer. If you decide to remove/refit the unit yourself, ensure that the operation of the braking system is checked at the earliest opportunity by a Audi/VAG dealer.*

Removal

1 Disconnect the battery negative terminal.
2 Where necessary, undo the retaining screw and remove the plastic relay cover from the hydraulic unit.
3 Release the locking bar and disconnect the main wiring connector from the hydraulic unit.
4 Where necessary, unscrew the retaining nut and disconnect the earth lead from the regulator.
5 Raise the front of the vehicle and rest it securely on axle stands, then remove the left hand front road wheel.
6 Connect a length of hose to the left hand front brake caliper bleed screw, then direct the other end of the hose into a suitable receptacle, as described in Section 2. Open the bleed screw and then depress the brake pedal through one full stroke and hold it in this position, using a suitable weight, or a wedge such as a block of wood. When the expelled brake fluid has collected into the receptacle, close the bleed screw. **Note:** *The brake pedal must be held in the depressed position until the brake pipes have been reconnected to the hydraulic unit, at the end of this procedure.*
7 Wipe clean the area around all the pipes unions and mark the locations of the hydraulic fluid pipes to ensure correct refitting. Unscrew the union nuts and disconnect the pipes from the regulator assembly. Be prepared for fluid spillage, and plug the open ends of the pipes and the hydraulic unit unions, to prevent dirt ingress and further fluid loss.
8 Slacken the hydraulic unit mounting nuts and remove the assembly from the engine compartment. If necessary, the mounting bracket can then be unbolts and remove from the vehicle. Renew the regulator mountings if they show signs of wear or damage. **Note:** *Keep the hydraulic unit upright to minimise the risk of fluid loss, and to prevent air locks inside the unit.*

Refitting

Note: *New hydraulic units are supplied pre-filled with brake fluid and fully bled; it is vitally important that the union plugs are not removed until the brake pipes are reconnected as loss of fluid will introduce air into the unit.*

9 Manoeuvre the hydraulic unit into position in the mounting bracket and tighten the mounting nuts to the specified torque setting.
10 Remove the plugs and reconnect the hydraulic pipes to the correct unions on the hydraulic unit and tighten the union nuts to the specified torque.
11 Securely reconnect the wiring connector to the hydraulic unit and (where necessary) refit the cover.
12 Fill the brake fluid reservoir with fresh fluid (see *Weekly checks*) and reconnect the battery.
13 Remove the weight/wedge from the brake pedal and then bleed the entire braking hydraulic system as described in Section 2. Thoroughly check the operation of the braking

19.21 Removing an ABS front wheel speed sensor

system before using the vehicle on the road. Have the operation of the ABS system checked by a Audi/VAG dealer at the earliest possible opportunity.

Electronic control unit (ECU) - models with Bosch ABS 5.0

Removal

14 Remove the rear seat cushion as described in Chapter 11 to gain access to the ECU.
15 Slacken and remove the retaining screws and lift the ECU away from the floorpan.
16 Ensure that the ignition is switched off, then release the retaining clip and disconnect the wiring connector from the ECU. Remove the ECU from the vehicle.

Refitting

17 Refitting is the reverse of removal ensuring the wiring connector is securely reconnected.

Front wheel sensor

Removal

18 Disconnect the battery negative lead.
19 Apply the handbrake, then jack up the front of the vehicle and support securely on axle stands. To improve access, remove the roadwheel.
20 Trace the wiring back from the sensor, releasing it from all the relevant clips and ties whilst noting its correct routing, and disconnect the wiring connector.
21 Carefully pull the sensor out from the hub

carrier assembly and remove it from the vehicle. With the sensor removed, slide the rubber seal and clamping sleeve out from the hub carrier **(see illustration)**.

Refitting

22 Ensure that the mating faces of the sensor, clamping ring and hub carrier are clean and dry then lubricate clamping sleeve and wheel sensor surfaces with a small quantity of copper based grease.
23 Press the clamping sleeve fully into the hub carrier then insert the wheel sensor together with the rubber seal. Ensure the sensor wiring is correctly positioned then push the sensor firmly into position until it is fully home in the hub carrier.
24 Ensure the sensor is securely retained then work along the sensor wiring, making sure it is correctly routed, securing it in position with all the relevant clips and ties. Reconnect the wiring connector.
25 Refit the wheel (where removed) then lower the vehicle and (where necessary) tighten the wheel bolts to the specified torque (see Chapter 1A or 1B). Reconnect the battery negative terminal.

Rear wheel sensor

Removal

26 Disconnect the battery negative lead.
27 Remove the rear seat cushion (see Chapter 11) and locate the rear wheel sensor ABS wiring connectors. Unplug the relevant connector and free the wiring from its retaining clips.
28 Chock the front wheels, then jack up the rear of the vehicle and support it on axle stands. To improve access, remove the appropriate roadwheel.
29 Working underneath the vehicle, trace the wiring back from the sensor, releasing it from all the relevant clips. Undo the retaining bolts and remove the wiring protective cover from the rear axle then release the wiring grommet from body and pull the wiring through so that it is free to be removed with the sensor.
30 Carefully pull the sensor out from axle assembly and remove it from the vehicle. With the sensor removed, slide the clamping sleeve out of position **(see illustrations)**.

19.30a Remove the sensor from axle assembly (stub axle and brake caliper removed for clarity)

19.30b Slide the clamping sleeve out of position

Refitting

31 Ensure that the mating faces of the sensor, clamping ring and axle are clean and dry then lubricate the clamping sleeve and wheel sensor surfaces with a little copper based grease.

32 Press the clamping sleeve fully into the axle then insert the wheel sensor. Ensure the sensor wiring is correctly positioned then push the sensor firmly into position until it is fully home in the axle.

33 Ensure the sensor is securely retained then work along the sensor wiring, making sure it is correctly routed, securing it in position with all the relevant clips and ties. Refit the wiring protective cover to the axle, tighten its retaining screws securely, then feed the wiring connector up through the body and seat the wiring grommet correctly in position.

34 Refit the roadwheel then lower the vehicle to the ground and tighten the wheel bolts to the specified torque (see Chapter 1A or 1B).

35 Reconnect the sensor wiring connect then refit the seat cushion and reconnect the battery negative terminal.

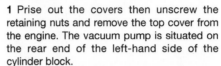

20 Vacuum pump (diesel engine models) - removal and refitting

Removal

1 Prise out the covers then unscrew the retaining nuts and remove the top cover from the engine. The vacuum pump is situated on the rear end of the left-hand side of the cylinder block.

2 Release the retaining clip, and disconnect the vacuum hose from the top of pump.

3 Slacken and remove the retaining bolt and remove the pump retaining clamp from the cylinder block.

4 Withdraw the vacuum pump from the cylinder block, and recover the sealing ring. Discard the sealing ring, a new one should be used on refitting.

Refitting

5 Fit the new sealing to the vacuum pump and apply a smear of oil to it to aid installation.

20.6 On refitting, ensure that the slot in the vacuum pump drive gear (arrowed) aligns with the dog on the drive shaft

6 Manoeuvre the vacuum pump into position, making sure that the slot in the drive gear aligns with the dog on the drive shaft **(see illustration)**.

7 Refit the retaining clamp and securely tighten its retaining bolt.

8 Reconnect the vacuum hose to the pump, and secure it in position with the retaining clip.

9 Refit the top cover to the engine and securely tighten its retaining nuts.

Chapter 10
Suspension and steering

Contents

Degrees of difficulty

Easy, suitable for novice with little experience	**Fairly easy,** suitable for beginner with some experience	**Fairly difficult,** suitable for competent DIY mechanic	**Difficult,** suitable for experienced DIY mechanic	**Very difficult,** suitable for expert DIY or professional

Specifications

Wheel alignment and steering angles

Note: Models built from 1998 onwards were fitted with an aluminium upper transverse arm mounting bracket; this replaced the steel version fitted to earlier models. Note the difference in front suspension settings.

Front wheel alignment (models with steel upper transverse arm mounting bracket):
   Toe setting:
      Standard . . . . +10' ± 2'
      At 20° steering angle . . . . -1° 20' ± 30'
   Camber:
      Standard setting:*
         Standard suspension (code 1BA) . . . . -25' ± 25'
         Sports suspension (code 1BE) . . . . -40' ± 25'
         Heavy duty running gear (code 1BP) . . . . -25' ± 25'
         Heavy duty suspension (code 1BB) . . . . -15' ± 25'
         Heavy duty suspension (code 1BT) . . . . -30' ± 25'
      Maximum difference between sides . . . . ± 30'
Front wheel alignment (models with aluminium upper transverse arm mounting bracket):
   Toe setting:
      Standard . . . . +10' ± 2'
      At 20° steering angle . . . . -1° 20' ± 30'
   Camber:
      Standard setting:*
         Standard suspension (code 1BA) . . . . -35' ± 25'
         Sports suspension (code 1BE) . . . . -50' ± 25'
         Heavy duty running gear (code 1BP) . . . . -35' ± 25'
         Heavy duty suspension (code 1BB) . . . . -20' ± 25'
         Heavy duty suspension (code 1BT) . . . . -30' ± 25'
      Maximum difference between sides . . . . ± 30'

Wheel alignment and steering angles (continued)

Rear wheel alignment:

Toe setting:*

Standard suspension (code 1BA)	+20' + 15' -10'
Sports suspension (code 1BE)	+28' +15' -10'
Heavy duty running gear (code 1BP)	+20' + 15' -10'
Heavy duty suspension (code 1BB)	+14' + 15' - 10'
Heavy duty suspension (code 1BT)	+17' + 15' - 10'
Maximum deviation of direction of travel from longitudinal axis of vehicle	± 15'

Camber:

Standard setting	-1° 30' ± 20'
Maximum difference between sides	30'

The suspension type code is stamped on the vehicle identification (VIN) plate

Roadwheels

Type	Pressed-steel or aluminium alloy (depending on model)

Size:

Normal roadwheels	6J x 15, 7J x 15, 7J x 16 (depending on model)
Spare wheel ('space saver' type)	4B x 15
Tyre pressures	Refer to *Weekly checks*

Torque wrench settings

	Nm	lbf ft
Front suspension		
Anti-roll bar drop link**:		
Link to anti-roll bar nut*:		
Early models with ball joints	Not available	
Later models with rubber bushes:		
Stage 1	40	30
Stage 2	Angle-tighten a further 90°	
Link to suspension lower arm nut*:		
Stage 1	40	30
Stage 2	Angle-tighten a further 90°	
Anti-roll bar mounting clamp nuts*	25	18
Hub bolt:		
M14 bolt:		
Stage 1	115	85
Stage 2	Angle-tighten a further 180°	
M16 bolt:		
Stage 1	190	140
Stage 2	Angle-tighten a further 180°	
Lower suspension arms:		
Front lower arm to hub carrier balljoint nut*	100	74
Front lower arm to subframe nut *:		
Stage 1	80	59
Stage 2	Angle-tighten a further 90°	
Rear lower arm to hub carrier balljoint nut*	100	74
Rear lower arm to subframe nut *:		
Stage 1	90	66
Stage 2	Angle-tighten a further 90°	
Subframe:		
Front mounting bracket bolts *	75	55
Main mounting bolts *:		
Stage 1	110	81
Stage 2	Angle-tighten a further 90°	
Rear mounting bracket bolts *:		
Underside of bolt head plain	25	18
Underside of bolt head ribbed	75	55
Suspension strut:		
Lower mounting nut to suspension arm *	90	66
Piston rod nut *	60	44
Upper mounting nuts *	20	15

Fit new nut/bolt

Note: *On models with electrical discharge headlamps, do not confuse the vehicle level sensor connecting rod with the anti-roll bar drop link – the tightening torque for the level sensor connecting rod nut is minimal.*

Torque wrench settings (continued)

	Nm	lbf ft
Front suspension (continued)		
Upper suspension arms:		
Bracket to bodywork bolts	75	55
Front upper arm to hub carrier clamp bolt nut*	40	30
Rear upper arm to hub carrier clamp bolt nut*	50	37
Upper arm to bracket nut*:		
Stage 1	50	37
Stage 2	Angle-tighten a further 90°	
Rear suspension		
Axle pivot bolt and nut *:		
Stage 1	80	59
Stage 2	Angle-tighten a further 90°	
Axle pivot bracket securing bolts *	75	55
Hub nut	adjust as described in text (Section 8)	
Suspension strut:		
Lower mounting bolt nut *:		
Stage 1	50	37
Stage 2	Angle-tighten a further 90°	
Shock absorber piston nut *	25	18
Upper mounting bolts	25	18
Stub axle bolts	30	22
Steering		
Power steering pump mounting bolts	20	15
Steering column:		
Mounting bolts	23	17
Universal joint clamp bolt nut	30	22
Steering gear:		
Hydraulic pipe union bolts:		
Supply pipe	40	30
Return pipe	50	37
Hydraulic pipe retaining bracket bolt	20	15
Centring hole plug	13	10
Mounting bolts	65	48
Steering damper to track rod nut	10	7
Steering damper to steering gear housing bolt	35	26
Steering wheel retaining bolt *	60	44
Track rod:		
Adjustment locknut	40	30
Balljoint to hub carrier nut *	50	37
Toe curve adjustment bolt	7	5
Track rod to steering gear	100	74
Roadwheels		
Wheel bolts	120	89

*Fit new nut/bolt

1 General information

1 The front suspension is fully independent, utilising four transverse arms (two upper and two lower) and a solid upright (or hub carrier) in an unequal-length, double-wishbone configuration. Coil spring-over-telescopic shock absorber struts are connected between the front lower transverse arm and upper transverse arm mounting bracket. The hub carriers house the wheel bearings, brake calipers and the hub/disc assemblies, and are connected to the upper and lower transverse arms by means of balljoints. A front anti-roll bar is fitted to all models; the anti-roll bar is rubber-mounted onto the subframe, and is connected to the front lower transverse arms via a drop link. The subframe provides mountings for all the lower suspension components as well as the engine and transmission mountings.

2 The rear suspension comprises a torsion beam axle with trailing arms, which are connected to the body via rubber bushes. The axle is attached to the lower ends of the rear suspension struts which incorporate coil springs and telescopic shock absorbers. A rear anti-roll bar is fitted to reduce body roll.

3 The suspension type code is stamped on the vehicle identification (VIN) plate and on the identification label in the spare wheel well **(see illustration)**.

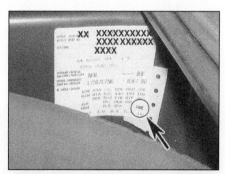

1.3 The suspension type code is stamped on the vehicle identification (VIN) plate and on the identification label in the spare wheel well (arrowed)

4 The steering column has a flexible coupling at its lower end and is secured to the steering gear pinion by means of a clamp bolt.

5 The steering gear is mounted onto the vehicle body and is connected by two track rods, with balljoints at their outer ends, to bosses projecting rearwards from the suspension hub carriers. The track rod ends are threaded, to facilitate adjustment. The hydraulic steering system is powered by a belt-driven pump, which is driven off the crankshaft pulley.

2 Front hub bearings - renewal

Note: *The bearing is a sealed, pre-adjusted and pre-lubricated, double-row roller type, and is intended to last the car's entire service life without maintenance or attention. Never overtighten the hub bolt in an attempt to adjust the bearing.*

Note: *A hydraulic press will be required to dismantle and rebuild the assembly; if such a tool is not available, a large bench vice and spacers (such as large sockets) may serve as an adequate substitute. The bearing's inner races are an interference fit on the hub; if the inner race remains on the hub when it is pressed out of the hub carrier, a knife-edged bearing puller will be required to remove it.*

1 Park the vehicle on a level surface, switch off the ignition, apply the handbrake firmly and select first gear.

2 Remove the wheel trim/hub centre cap and then slacken the driveshaft bolt by a few turns, with reference to Chapter 8, Section 2.

3 Raise the front of the vehicle and rest it securely on axle stands. Remove the appropriate front road wheel.

4 On vehicles equipped with electrical discharge headlamps, release the clip and disconnect the vehicle level sensor connecting rod from the front lower transverse arm; see Chapter 12 for details.

5 Refer to Chapter 9 and carry out the following:

  a) *Unbolt the brake caliper, together with its mounting bracket, from the hub carrier and suspend it from coil spring.*

  b) *Remove the brake disc.*

  c) *Remove the ABS wheel speed sensor from the base of the hub carrier. Release the ABS wheel sensor wiring from its retaining clips in the wheel arch and secure it away from the work area.*

6 Undo the screws and detach the brake disc shield from the hub carrier.

7 Undo the securing nuts, then separate the front and rear lower transverse arms from the base of the hub carrier, with the aid of a ball joint splitter (see Section 5). Avoid damaging the rubber gaiters.

8 Unbolt the track rod balljoint from the hub carrier, as described in Section 21.

9 Undo the securing nut and extract the clamp bolt from the top of the hub carrier (see Section 5). Separate the front and rear upper transverse arm ball joints from the top of the hub carrier, but do not force the slots apart with a screwdriver or similar, in an attempt to free the balljoint pins. Take care to avoid damaging the balljoint rubber gaiters.

10 Grasp the hub carrier and gradually draw it off the driveshaft. Use a hub puller if the driveshaft is a tight fit in the hub.

11 Support the base of the hub carrier securely on blocks or in a vice. Using a tubular spacer which bears only on the inner end of the hub flange, press the hub flange out of the bearing. If the bearing's inner race remains on the hub, remove it using a bearing puller (see note above).

12 Securely support the outer face of the hub carrier then, using a tubular spacer which bears only on the inner race, press the complete bearing assembly out from the strut.

13 Thoroughly clean the hub and hub carrier, removing all traces of dirt and grease, and polish away any burrs or raised edges which might hinder reassembly. Check both for cracks or any other signs of wear or damage, and renew them if necessary.

14 Securely support the inner face of the base of the hub carrier and locate the bearing in the strut bore. Make sure the larger diameter inner race of the bearing is facing outwards (towards the hub flange) then press the bearing into position using a tubular spacer which bears only on the outer race. Ensure the bearing enters the hub carrier squarely and is pressed fully into position.

15 Securely support the outer face of the hub flange, and locate the hub bearing inner race over the end of the hub flange. Using a tubular spacer which bears only on the inner race, press the bearing onto the hub until it seats against the shoulder.

16 Check that the hub flange rotates freely, without any sign of roughness or sticking.

17 Offer the hub carrier up to the wheel arch and pass the driveshaft through the centre of the hub. Fit the new driveshaft bolt, but hand tighten it only at this stage.

18 Reconnect the lower transverse arms to the base of the hub carrier as described in

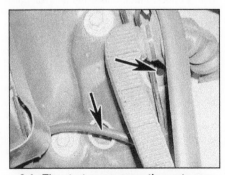

3.4a The strut upper mounting nuts are accessed via two holes (arrowed), located in the scuttle to the rear of the engine compartment

Section 5. Fit new self locking nuts and tighten them to the specified torque.

19 Reconnect the upper transverse arms to the top of the hub carrier as described in Section 5. Refit the clamp bolt, together with a new self locking nut and tighten it to the specified torque. Press down on both transverse arms as you tighten the nut, to ensure that the balljoints are properly seated in the hub carrier.

20 Reconnect the steering track rod balljoint to the hub as described in Section 21. Fit a new securing nut and tighten it, and the adjustment bolt, to their respective specified torque.

21 Refit the brake disc shield and tighten the retaining screws securely.

22 Carry out the following with reference to the appropriate sections of Chapter 9:

  a) *Refit the ABS wheel speed sensor to the hub carrier and secure the wiring with the clips in the wheel arch.*

  b) *Refit the brake disc.*

  c) *Refit the brake caliper.*

23 On vehicles equipped with electrical discharge headlamps, fasten the clip to reconnect the vehicle level sensor connecting rod to the front lower transverse arm; see Chapter 12 for details.

24 Refit the road wheel, tighten the bolts to the specified torque and lower the vehicle to the ground.

25 Tighten the driveshaft bolt to the specified torque, as described in Chapter 8 Section 2, then refit the hub cap/wheel trim.

26 On completion, it is essential that the front wheel alignment is checked and if necessary adjusted either by an Audi dealer or a suitably equipped tyre specialist.

3 Front suspension strut - removal and refitting

Removal

1 Remove the wheel trim/hub cap (as applicable) and slacken the wheel bolts by half a turn with the vehicle resting on its wheels.

2 Chock the rear wheels of the car, firmly apply the handbrake, then jack up the front of the car and support it securely on axle stands. Remove the appropriate front road wheel.

3 On vehicles equipped with electrical discharge headlamps, release the clip and disconnect the vehicle level sensor connecting rod from the front lower transverse arm; see Chapter 12 for details.

4 The strut upper mounting nuts are accessed via two holes, located in the scuttle to the rear of the engine compartment and plugged with rubber grommets. Support the underside of the hub carrier on a trolley jack or an axle stand, then prise out the grommets and unscrew the strut upper mounting nuts using a socket wrench and long extension bar **(see illustrations)**.

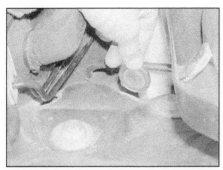

3.4b Prise out the rubber grommets . . .

3.4c . . . then unscrew the strut upper mounting nuts using a socket wrench and long extension bar

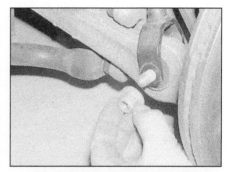

3.8 Undo the nut and remove the suspension strut lower mounting bolt from the transverse arm

3.9 Disengage the strut upper mounting studs from the mounting bracket and withdraw the strut from the wheel arch

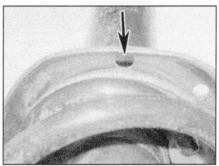

3.10 Ensure that the alignment hole (arrowed) in the strut coil spring lower seat faces inwards towards the vehicle

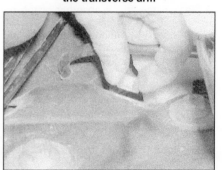

3.14 Fit new nuts to the strut upper mounting studs

5 Release the ABS wheel speed sensor from its mounting clips and position it away from the suspension strut (see Chapter 9, Section 19).
6 Working in the wheel arch, undo the securing nut and extract the clamp bolt from the top of the hub carrier (see Section 5). Separate the front and rear upper transverse arm ball joints from the top of the hub carrier, but do not force the slots apart with a screwdriver or similar, in an attempt to free the balljoint pins. Take care to avoid damaging the balljoint rubber gaiters.
7 Undo the securing nuts, then separate the rear lower transverse arm from the base of the hub carrier, with the aid of a ball joint splitter - avoid damaging the rubber gaiters (see Section 5). This allows the strut lower mounting bolt to be withdrawn from the front lower transverse arm.
8 Undo the nut and remove the suspension strut lower mounting bolt from the transverse arm **(see illustration)**.
9 Disengage the strut upper mounting studs from the mounting bracket and withdraw the strut from the wheel arch **(see illustration)**.

Refitting

10 Offer up the suspension strut to the wheel arch and engage the upper mounting studs with the mounting bracket. Ensure that the alignment hole in the strut coil spring lower seat faces inwards towards the vehicle **(see illustration)**.
11 Bolt the strut lower mounting to the lower transverse arm, fit a new securing nut but

hand tighten it only at this stage.
12 Reconnect the lower transverse arm to the base of the hub carrier as described in Section 5. Fit a new self locking nut and tighten it to the specified torque.
13 Reconnect the upper transverse arms to the top of the hub carrier as described in Section 5. Refit the clamp bolt, together with a new self locking nut and tighten it to the specified torque. Press down on both transverse arms as you tighten the nut, to ensure that the balljoints are properly seated in the hub carrier.
14 Fit new nuts to the strut upper mounting studs and tighten them to the specified torque **(see illustration)**. Refit the rubber grommets to the scuttle access holes.
15 Refit the ABS wheel speed sensor to its retaining clips.

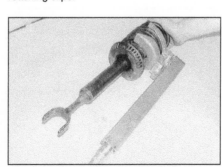

4.2 Compress the coil spring evenly and progressively until tension is relieved from the spring seats

16 On vehicles equipped with electrical discharge headlamps, fasten the clip to reconnect the vehicle level sensor connecting rod to the front lower transverse arm; see Chapter 12 for details.
17 Refit the road wheel and tighten the bolts to the specified torque, then lower the vehicle to the ground.
18 With the vehicle resting on its wheels, tighten the suspension strut lower mounting bolt nut to the specified torque.

4 Front suspension strut - overhaul

⚠️ *Warning: Before attempting to dismantle the front suspension strut, a suitable tool to hold the coil spring in compression must be obtained. Adjustable coil spring compressors are readily-available, and are recommended for this operation. Any attempt to dismantle the strut without such a tool is likely to result in damage or personal injury.*
1 With the strut removed from the car, clean away all external dirt. If required, mount the strut upright in a vice to provide stability. Pad the vice jaws with wood or aluminium, to prevent damage to the strut lower mountings.
2 Fit the spring compressor and compress the coil spring evenly and progressively until tension is relieved from the spring seats **(see illustration)**.

4.3 Slacken the shock absorber piston nut whilst retaining the piston with a suitable Allen key

4.4a Remove the nut . . .

4.4b . . . then lift off the mounting plate . . .

3 Slacken the shock absorber piston nut whilst retaining the piston with a suitable Allen key **(see illustration)**. This can achieved using either a spanner with an angled head, or by turning the socket with a 'crows foot' adapter, or by using a socket with a centre hole large enough to allow the Allen key to pass through and a hex fitting at the top; the socket can then be turned with an open ended spanner.
4 Remove the nut, then lift off the mounting plate followed by the washer, the upper spring seat and upper spring support **(see illustrations)**.
5 Remove the dust gaiter, rubber bump stop and protective cap from the shock absorber piston, then lift off the coil spring (together with the compressors) **(see illustrations)**.
6 Remove the lower spring support **(see**

illustration), then if required, loosen the lower spring seat from the shock absorber body by tapping it lightly with a soft faced mallet.
7 Examine the shock absorber for signs of fluid leakage. Check the piston rod for signs of pitting along its entire length, and check the shock absorber body for signs of damage or serious corrosion. While holding it in an upright position, test the operation of the shock absorber by moving the piston through a full stroke, and then through short strokes of 50 to 100 mm. In both cases, the resistance felt should be smooth and continuous. If the resistance is jerky, or uneven, or if there is any visible sign of wear or damage to the shock absorber, renewal will be necessary. **Note:** *Shock absorbers must be renewed in pairs, to preserve the handling characteristics of the vehicle..*

8 Inspect all other components for signs of damage or deterioration, and renew as required.
9 Refit the lower spring seat to the shock absorber body, such that the alignment hole is positioned at 90° to the axis of the strut lower mounting bolt.
10 Refit the lower spring support, ensuring that it engages correctly with the recess in the lower spring seat.
11 Slide the protective cap, bump stop rubber and dust gaiter onto the end of the piston rod and press them firmly into position. Ensure the lower end of the dust gaiter is correctly engaged with the strut base.
12 Refit the compressed coil spring to the strut base, ensuring that the end of the coil bears against the corresponding stop on the spring support **(see illustration)**.

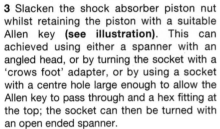

4.4c . . . followed by the washer . . .

4.4d . . . the upper spring seat and upper spring support

4.5a Remove the dust gaiter, rubber bump stop and protective cap from the shock absorber piston . . .

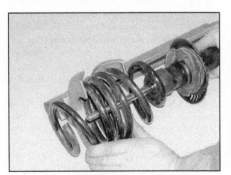

4.5b . . . then lift off the coil spring (together with the compressors)

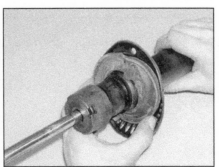

4.6 Remove the lower spring support

4.12 Ensure that the end of the coil spring bears against the stop (arrowed) on the spring support

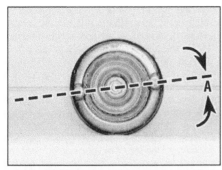

4.13a Fit the upper spring seat such that the alignment hole is positioned at an angle (A) of 11° to the longitudinal axis of the strut lower mounting bolt (shown by a length of welding rod)

13 Fit the upper spring support and spring seat, washer and upper mounting to the top of the strut, such that the spring seat alignment hole is positioned at 11° to the longitudinal axis of the strut lower mounting bolt. If the assembly has been carried out correctly, the upper end of the coil spring should be positioned against the stop on the underside of the upper spring seat **(see illustrations)**.

14 Fit a new piston rod nut, then retain the shock absorber piston rod using the method employed during removal and tighten the nut to the specified torque.

15 Ensure all components are correctly seated and both spring ends are in contact with their stops then progressively release the spring compressor and remove it from the strut.

16 Refit the strut to the vehicle as described in Section 3.

5 Front suspension transverse arms - removal, overhaul and refitting

Front and rear upper arms

Note: *Later models equipped with sports or heavy duty suspension have a buffer plate fitted above the upper rear transverse suspension arm. In addition, the upper rear transverse suspension arm on **all** models from*

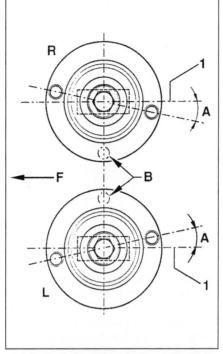

4.13b Note the difference in angle offset between the right and left-hand struts

A	Angle = 11± 2°	L Left-hand strut
B	Lower spring seat	R Right-hand strut
	alignment holes	1 Axis of strut lower
F	Direction of travel	mounting bolt

1997 onwards have an integral buffer stop. If the rear upper suspension arm is renewed, the later revised version should be used regardless of whether the vehicle is fitted with a buffer plate.

Removal

1 Chock the rear wheels, firmly apply the handbrake, then jack up the front of the vehicle and support on axle stands. Remove the appropriate front roadwheel.

2 Whilst the wheel is removed, refit at least one wheel bolt to ensure the brake disc remains correctly positioned on the hub.

3 On vehicles equipped with electrical discharge headlamps, release the clip and disconnect the vehicle level sensor connecting

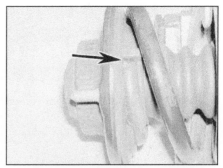

4.13c The upper end of the coil spring should be positioned against the stop (arrowed) on the underside of the upper spring seat

rod from the front lower transverse arm; see Chapter 12 for details.

4 Carefully prise the ABS wheel speed sensor wiring from its retaining clips.

5 Undo the securing nut and extract the clamp bolt from the top of the hub carrier. Separate the front and rear upper transverse arm ball joints from the top of the hub carrier, but do not force the slots apart with a screwdriver or similar, in an attempt to free the balljoint pins **(see illustrations)**. Take care to avoid damaging the balljoint rubber gaiters.

6 Undo the securing nut, then separate the rear lower transverse arm from the base of the hub carrier, with the aid of a ball joint splitter (avoid damaging the rubber gaiter). This allows the strut lower mounting bolt to be withdrawn from the front lower transverse arm.

7 Undo the nut and remove the suspension strut lower mounting bolt from the front transverse arm (see Section 4).

8 The upper transverse arm mounting bracket bolts are located in the scuttle, to the rear of the engine compartment **(see illustration)**. Unscrew the three bolts and remove the mounting bracket, the suspension strut and both upper transverse arms as an assembly. There may be plastic washers fitted to the underside of the bolts; these are factory assembly components which do not need to be refitted, once removed. **Note:** *Make a careful note of the fitted positions of any*

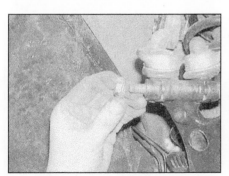

5.5a Undo the securing nut . . .

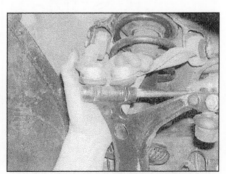

5.5b . . . and extract the clamp bolt from the top of the hub carrier

5.5c Separate the ball joints from the top of the hub carrier

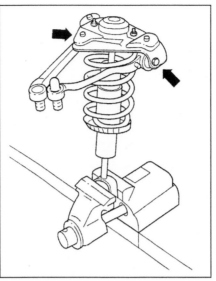

5.8 The upper transverse arm mounting bracket bolts (arrowed) are located in the scuttle, to the rear of the engine compartment

shims fitted underneath the heads of the transverse arm mounting bracket bolts; they must be refitted in the same positions to preserve the front suspension alignment settings.

9 Mount the lower end of the strut in a bench vice, then slacken and remove the nut and bolt securing the appropriate upper transverse arm to the mounting bracket **(see illustration)**.

Overhaul

10 Thoroughly clean the arm and the area around the arm mountings, removing all traces of dirt, thread locking compound and underseal if necessary, then check carefully for cracks, distortion or any other signs of wear or damage, paying particular attention to the inner pivot bush and balljoint. The balljoint is an integral part of the lower arm and cannot be renewed separately. If the arm or balljoint are damaged then the complete assembly must be renewed.

11 Renewal of the inner pivot bush will require the use of a hydraulic press and several spacers and is therefore best entrusted to a Audi/VAG dealer or garage with access to the necessary equipment. If such equipment is available, press out the old bush

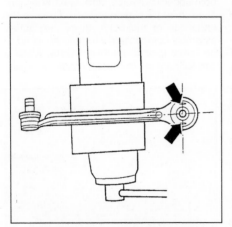

5.11 Ensure the bush is correctly positioned so that the cavities are aligned with the centre axis of the arm

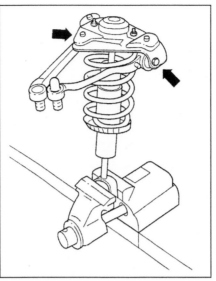

5.9 Slacken and remove the nuts and bolts (arrowed) securing the appropriate upper transverse arm to the mounting bracket

and install the new one using a spacer which bears only on the bush outer edge. Ensure the bush is correctly positioned so that the cavities are aligned with the centre axis of the arm, as shown **(see illustration)**.

Refitting

12 Offer up the transverse arm to the mounting bracket, insert a new securing bolt and screw on a new securing nut.

13 Position the transverse arm such that the vertical distance between the front edge of the mounting bracket and the arm is 47 mm **(see illustration)**. Hold the arm in this position and tighten the securing nut to the specified stage 1 and 2 torque settings. This ensures that the rubber bush is not stressed when the vehicle is lowered onto its wheels.

14 Refit the suspension strut, transverse arms and mounting bracket to the wheel arch as an assembly. Insert the mounting bracket

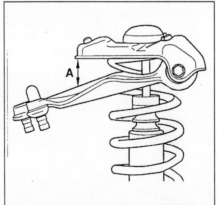

5.13 Position the transverse arm such that the vertical distance (A) between the front edge of the mounting bracket and the arm is 47 mm

securing bolts, together with the shims (where fitted), using the notes made during removal to ensure that the shims are correctly positioned. Tighten the bolts to the specified torque.

15 Bolt the strut lower mounting to the lower transverse arm, fit a new securing nut but hand tighten it only at this stage.

16 Bolt the rear lower transverse arm to the base of the hub carrier, then fit a new securing nut and tighten it to the specified torque.

17 Reconnect the upper transverse arm balljoints to the top of the hub carrier. Refit the clamp bolt, together with a new self locking nut and tighten it to the specified torque **(see illustration)**. Press down on both transverse arms as you tighten the nut, to ensure that the balljoints are properly seated in the hub carrier.

18 Refit the ABS wheel speed sensor wiring to its retaining clips.

19 On vehicles equipped with electrical discharge headlamps, fasten the clip to reconnect the vehicle level sensor connecting rod to the front lower transverse arm; see Chapter 12 for details.

20 Refit the road wheel and tighten the bolts to the specified torque, then lower the vehicle to the ground.

21 With the vehicle resting on its wheels, tighten the suspension strut lower mounting bolt nut to the specified torque.

22 On completion, have the front wheel alignment checked and if necessary adjusted by an Audi dealer or a suitably equipped tyre specialist.

Rear lower arm

Removal

23 Chock the rear wheels, firmly apply the handbrake, then jack up the front of the vehicle and support on axle stands. Remove the appropriate front roadwheel.

24 Whilst the wheel is removed, refit at least one wheel bolt to ensure the brake disc remains correctly positioned on the hub.

25 Undo the securing nut, then separate the transverse arm from the base of the hub carrier, with the aid of a ball joint splitter - avoid damaging the rubber gaiter **(see illustrations)**.

5.17 Tighten the new clamp bolt nut to the specified torque

5.25a With the aid of a ball joint splitter . . .

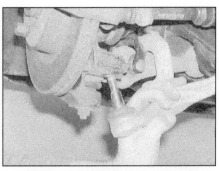

5.25b . . . .separate the rear lower transverse arm from the base of the hub carrier

26 Slacken and remove the nut from the bolt at the inboard end of the transverse arm. To allow the bolt to be withdrawn, the corner of the subframe must be lowered slightly. To do this, unscrew and remove the two support plate bolts, then slacken and withdraw the subframe securing bolt. Note that the bolt is threaded through the inner of the two sets of subframe bolt holes.

27 Lower the subframe slightly, withdraw the transverse arm inboard securing bolt then remove the arm from the vehicle.

Overhaul

28 Thoroughly clean the arm and the area around the arm mountings, removing all traces of dirt, thread locking compound and underseal if necessary, then check carefully for cracks, distortion or any other signs of wear or damage, paying particular attention to the inner pivot bush and balljoint. Note that the inner bush has a hydraulic action; fluid leakage indicates that the bush has been damaged and must be renewed. The balljoint is an integral part of the lower arm and cannot be renewed separately. If the arm or balljoint are damaged then the complete assembly must be renewed.

29 Renewal of the inner pivot bush will require the use of a hydraulic press and several spacers and is therefore best entrusted to a Audi/VAG dealer or garage with access to the necessary equipment. If such equipment is available, press out the old bush and install the new one using a spacer which bears only on the bush outer edge. Ensure the bush is correctly positioned so that the cavities are aligned with the centre axis of the arm.

Refitting

30 Refitting is a reversal of removal noting the following points:
 a) *Use new transverse arm and subframe securing nuts and bolts.*
 b) *Delay tightening the transverse arm inboard securing bolt until the vehicle is resting on its roadwheels.*
 c) *Ensure that the transverse arm inboard securing bolt passes through the inner of the two sets of subframe bolt holes.*

 d) *Tighten all fixings to the correct torque, where specified*

Front lower arm

Removal

31 Chock the rear wheels, firmly apply the handbrake, then jack up the front of the vehicle and support on axle stands. Remove the appropriate front roadwheel.

32 Whilst the wheel is removed, refit at least one wheel bolt to ensure the brake disc remains correctly positioned on the hub.

33 On vehicles equipped with electrical discharge headlamps, release the clip and disconnect the vehicle level sensor connecting rod from the front lower transverse arm; see Chapter 12 for details.

34 Undo the securing nut, then separate the front lower transverse arm from the base of the hub carrier, with the aid of a ball joint splitter (avoid damaging the rubber gaiter).

35 Undo the nut and remove the suspension strut lower mounting bolt from the front transverse arm.

36 Remove the securing nut and detach the anti-roll bar drop link, from the transverse arm as described in Section 6.

37 Unscrew the nut and withdraw the transverse arm inboard securing bolt, then remove the transverse arm from the vehicle. Note that the bolt is threaded through the inner of the two sets of subframe bolt holes.

Overhaul

38 Thoroughly clean the arm and the area around the arm mountings, removing all traces of dirt, thread locking compound and underseal if necessary, then check carefully for cracks, distortion or any other signs of wear or damage, paying particular attention to the inner and strut pivot bushes and balljoint. The balljoint is an integral part of the lower arm and cannot be renewed separately. If the arm or balljoint are damaged then the complete assembly must be renewed.

39 Renewal of the inner and strut pivot bushes will require the use of a hydraulic press and several spacers and is therefore best entrusted to a Audi/VAG dealer or garage with access to the necessary equipment. If such equipment is available, press out the old

bush and install the new one using a spacer which bears only on the bush outer edge. Ensure the bush is correctly positioned so that the cavities are aligned with the centre axis of the arm.

Refitting

40 Refitting is a reversal of removal noting the following points:
 a) *Use new transverse arm and strut securing nuts and bolts.*
 b) *To avoid damaging the bushes, delay tightening the transverse arm inboard securing nut the strut securing nut and the anti-roll bar drop link securing nut to their final torque settings until the vehicle is resting on its roadwheels.*
 c) *Ensure that the transverse arm inboard securing bolt passes through the inner of the two sets of subframe bolt holes.*
 d) *Tighten all fixings to the correct torque, where specified.*

---

6 Front suspension anti-roll bar - removal and refitting

Removal

1 The anti-roll bar must be removed/refitted with the vehicle resting on its wheels. For this reason the following operation will be much easier if the vehicle can be positioned over an inspection pit. Alternatively drive the vehicle onto ramps to increase the clearance between the front of the vehicle and the ground.

2 Remove the fasteners and retaining clips and remove the undercover from beneath the engine/transmission to gain access to the anti-roll bar mounting clamps.

3 Slacken and remove the nuts and bolts securing both the anti-roll bar mounting clamps to the subframe. Remove the clamps and discard the nuts; new ones should be used on refitting.

4 Unscrew the securing nuts and detach the drop links from the lower transverse arms each side. Note that on later models with rubber bushed joints, rather than the balljoints fitted to earlier models, the drop link is secured with separate nuts and bolts. On both versions, discard the nuts as new ones should be used on refitting

5 Unscrew the nuts securing the anti-roll bar ends to the drop links and discard them; new nuts should be used on refitting. On later models the drop links are secured by separate nuts and bolts (refer to the note in the previous paragraph). Where applicable, remove the washer and rear bush from each end of the bar, noting their correct fitted positions.

6 As they are removed, note that the drop link-to-lower arm mounting bushes are fitted with their concave side facing the wishbone.

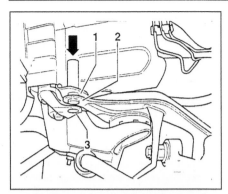

7.21 Pass a wooden dowel (arrowed) through each of the alignment holes in the front corners of the subframe

1 *Bracket (upper)*   3 *Bracket (lower)*
2 *Subframe*

On later models, the drop links have rubber bushes instead of balljoints; the arrow marked on the side of this version of the link must point towards the front of the vehicle when correctly fitted.

7 Lower the anti-roll bar, and remove it from under the vehicle.

8 Renew the anti-roll bar if it is damaged or distorted. Renew the mounting bushes if they are perished or worn.

Refitting

9 Mount the drop links onto the anti-roll bar, then fit the bolts (where applicable) and fit new securing nuts - hand tighten them only at this stage. Ensure that the concave side of the drop link faces the front of the vehicle. On later models, the arrow on the side of the drop link points towards the front of the vehicle.

10 Manoeuvre the anti-roll bar into position and engage the ends of the drop links with the lower arms. Insert the securing bolts, or the ball joints studs (as applicable) through the lugs in the lower arms.

11 Screw on the new drop link retaining nuts, tightening them lightly only at this stage.

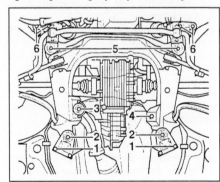

7.24 Subframe mounting bolt details

1 *Rear mounting bracket bolts*
2 *Main mounting bolts*
3 *Transmission mounting bolts*
4 *Transmission mounting bolts*
5 *Main mounting bolts*
6 *Front mounting bracket bolts*

12 Refit the mounting clamps to the anti-roll bar mounting bushes. Ensure both clamps are correctly located on the bushes then fit the retaining bolts and new nuts. Tighten the retaining nuts lightly only at this stage.

13 Rock the vehicle from side to side, to settle the anti-roll bar in position. Tighten all four anti-roll bar drop link nuts to the specified torque settings. Also tighten the anti-roll bar mounting clamp bolt nuts to the specified torque.

14 Refit the undercover and tighten the fixings securely.

<table>
<tr><td>7</td><td>Front suspension subframe - removal and refitting</td></tr>
</table>

Removal

1 Chock the rear wheels, firmly apply the handbrake, then jack up the front of the vehicle and support on axle stands.

2 Remove both front roadwheels. Whilst the wheel is removed, refit at least one wheel bolt to ensure the brake discs remain correctly positioned on the hub.

3 Remove the fasteners and retaining clips and remove the undercover from beneath the engine/transmission unit.

4 Referring to Chapter 2A or 2B, attach a lifting bracket to the rear of the engine and support the weight of the engine/transmission unit, using either a lifting beam or an engine hoist.

5 On vehicles equipped with electrical discharge headlamps, release the clip and disconnect the ride height sensor connecting rod from the front lower transverse arm; see Chapter 12 for details.

6 Carefully prise the ABS wheel speed sensor wiring from its retaining clips.

7 Unbolt the anti-roll bar drop links from both lower suspension arms, with reference to Section 6.

8 Unbolt the inboard ends of both rear lower transverse arms from the subframe with reference to Section 5. Note that this will entail unbolting the rear corners of the subframe from the underside of the vehicle and lowering it slightly to allow the transverse arm bolts to be withdrawn.

9 Unbolt the lower ends of both suspension struts from the front lower transverse arms with reference to Section 3.

10 Unbolt the inboard ends of both front lower transverse arms from the subframe with reference to Section 5.

11 Suspend the hub carrier, suspension strut and transverse arms from the inside of the wheel arch using lengths of wire to avoid straining the suspension bushes and ball joints.

12 Ensure that the engine and transmission are securely suspended by the lifting equipment, then unbolt the right and left hand transmission mountings from the subframe.

13 Slacken and withdraw the two subframe securing bolts, located to the rear of the anti-roll bar clamp brackets.

14 Slacken the four subframe securing bolts located forward of the anti-roll bar clamps brackets, until the subframe can be released from its mountings. Do not remove the bolts completely.

15 Carefully lower the subframe and withdraw it from the underside of the vehicle.

Overhaul

16 Renewal of the bonded subframe bushes requires access to a hydraulic press and a number of specially shaped extraction/fitment tools. Fabrication of alternative tools is not recommended due to the risk of damage to the subframe bush mountings. For this reason, it's best to entrust bush renewal work to an Audi dealer.

Refitting

Note: All subframe mounting nuts and bolts must be renewed.

17 Offer the subframe up the underside of the engine compartment and engage the front mountings with their respective brackets. Fit the new subframe front mounting bolts, but do not fully tighten them at this stage.

18 Reconnect the transmission mountings to the subframe.

19 Reconnect the lower end of the suspension strut to the front lower transverse arm with reference to Section 3, then reconnect the front and rear lower transverse arms to the subframe with reference to Section 5. Do not fully tighten the securing nuts and bolts at this stage.

20 Refit the electrical discharge headlamp ride height sensor pushrod to the front lower transverse arm with reference to Chapter 12 (where applicable).

21 Obtain two lengths of wooden dowel, each roughly 15 mm in diameter and 150 mm in length. Working through the wheel arches, pass a dowel through each of the alignment holes in the front corners of the subframe. Adjust the position of the subframe until both dowels pass through all three alignment holes on each side **(see illustration)**.

22 Refit the mounting brackets at the rear corners of the subframe, insert the new brackets securing bolts and tighten them lightly. With the brackets in place, fit new subframe rear mounting bolts and tighten them lightly.

23 Remove the engine hoist/support bar (as applicable) then tighten the subframe and suspension mounting bolts in the order given in the following paragraphs.

24 Tighten the four main subframe securing bolts to their specified first and second stage torques **(see illustration)**.

25 Tighten the four subframe front mounting bracket bolts to their specified torques.

26 Tighten the four subframe rear mounting bracket bolts to their specified torques.

27 Tighten the transmission mounting bolts to their specified torques, with reference to Chapter 7A or 7B as applicable.
28 Tighten the front and rear lower transverse arm inboard securing bolts to their specified torques, with reference to Section 5.
29 Refit the anti-roll bar drop link with reference to Section 6. Use new securing nuts and tighten them to the specified torques.
30 Tighten the strut-to-front lower transverse arm securing nut to the specified torque (see Section 4).
31 Refit the ABS wheel speed sensor wiring to its retaining clips (see Chapter 9, Section 19).
32 Securely refit the undercover then refit the roadwheels and lower the vehicle to the ground. Tighten the wheel bolts to the specified torque.
33 On completion, have the front wheel alignment and steering angles checked and if necessary adjusted at the earliest possible opportunity.

8 Rear wheel bearings - adjustment

1 Chock the front wheels and select first gear, or Park, as applicable. Jack up the rear of the vehicle and support it securely on axle stands.
2 Carefully prise the dust cap from the brake disc to expose the hub nut.
3 Extract the split pin, remove the locking ring and loosen the hub nut slightly.

9.3 The races can be driven out using a suitable soft metal drift

9.5b ... and insert it into position

4 Re-tighten the hub nut slowly, up to the point where it only just touches the thrustwasher. Rotate the hub as the nut is tightened, to ensure that the bearings are correctly seated. Back the nut off a fraction so that the washer can just be seen to slide to one side, when pushed with a screwdriver **(see illustration)**. Fit the locking ring and insert a new split pin to secure.
5 Beware of overtightening the hub nut, as this will cause premature bearing wear. If you are adjusting a bearing which has been in service for some time, when play has been noted, do not overtighten to compensate for wear - this is potentially dangerous as it could cause the wheel bearing to seize in use.
6 Smear a liberal amount of grease into the dust cap, then carefully drive the cap into position.
7 If a new bearing has been fitted, it is advisable to check for play after a few hundred miles. Re-adjust the bearing if necessary.

9 Rear wheel bearings - renewal

1 The rear wheel bearings are housed in the rear brake disc/hub. Refer to Chapter 9 Section 7 for removal details.
2 Wipe clean the inner bearing and seal. Note the direction of fitting, then lever the seal from the hub. Take care not to damage the ABS wheel speed sensor rotor. Extract the inner bearing from the hub.

9.5a Lubricate the inner bearing with grease ...

9.6a Fit the new oil seal ...

8.4 Adjust the rear wheel bearing as described in the text

3 The races can be driven out using a suitable soft metal drift, but take care not to damage the hub or ABS speed sensor rotor **(see illustration)**.
4 Clean the bearing race locations in the hub. Use a tube drift of suitable diameter to drive or press the new races into position in the hub each side. Ensure that they are squarely and fully inserted. If using the old bearings, be sure to keep the original bearings and races together. Never interchange new bearings with old races, or vice-versa.
5 Lubricate the inner bearing with grease, and insert it into position **(see illustrations)**.
6 Support the hub with its outboard face down, and carefully drive the new oil seal into position, taking care not to damage the ABS speed sensor rotor, where applicable. Lubricate the oil seal lip ready for refitting to the stub axle **(see illustrations)**.
7 With reference to Chapter 9, Section 7, pack the hub with grease, then refit it to the stub axle, followed by the outer bearing, thrustwasher and hub retaining nut. Adjust the bearing as described in Section 8, then refit the locking ring, split pin and dust cap.

10 Rear stub axle - removal and refitting

Removal

1 Remove the disc/hub assembly as described in Section 9.

9.6b ... and carefully drive it into position using a suitable tubular drift

10.2a Slacken and remove the bolts securing the disc backplate in position . . .

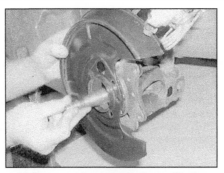

10.2b . . . and remove it along with the stub axle

10.5 Tighten the stub axle/heat shield retaining bolts to the specified torque setting

2 Slacken and remove the bolts securing the disc backplate in position and remove it along with the stub axle **(see illustrations)**.
3 Inspect the stub axle for signs of damage such as scoring and renew if necessary. Do not attempt to straighten it.

Refitting

4 Ensure the mating surfaces of the axle, stub axle and backplate are clean and dry. Check the backplate for signs of damage, and remove any burrs with a fine file or emery cloth.
5 Manoeuvre the stub axle and backplate assembly into position and refit the retaining bolts. Tighten the retaining bolts to the specified torque setting in a diagonal sequence **(see illustration)**.
6 Refit the disc/hub as described in Section 9.

11 Rear suspension strut - removal and refitting

Removal

1 Chock the front wheels, then jack up the rear of the car and support it on axle stands. Remove the relevant rear roadwheel.
2 Position a trolley jack underneath the rear axle and raise it until it is supporting the axle weight.
3 Slacken and remove the nut then withdraw the lower mounting bolt which secures the strut to the axle **(see illustrations)**. Discard the nut and bolt; new items should be used on refitting.
4 Working inside the vehicle, remove the trim panel from the side of the load space to

expose the strut upper mounting bolts. Alternatively, remove the rear seat back as described in Chapter 11; a cut-out in the rear bulkhead then allows access to the strut upper mounting bolts.
5 Slacken and remove the strut upper mounting bolts then rotate the strut to disengage the upper mounting lugs. Lower the axle slightly until the strut assembly can be manoeuvred out from underneath the vehicle **(see illustrations)**. Discard the mounting nuts; new ones should be used on refitting.
6 Recover the gasket from the upper mountings; it may still be stuck inside the wheel arch. Discard the gasket - a new item must be used on refitting.

Refitting

7 Fit a new gasket in position on the strut upper mounting.
8 Manoeuvre the strut into position in the rear wheel arch, then rotate it until the upper mounting lugs can be felt to engage **(see illustration)**. Fit the new upper mounting bolts and tighten them to the specified torque setting.
9 Refit the load space trim panel/rear seat back rest, as applicable.
10 Raise the axle and locate the strut lower mounting on the axle brackets. Fit the new lower mounting bolt and screw on the new nut. Do not tighten the nut yet.
11 Refit the roadwheel then lower the vehicle to the ground and tighten the wheel bolts to the specified torque.

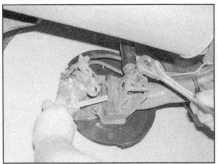

11.3a Slacken and remove the nut . . .

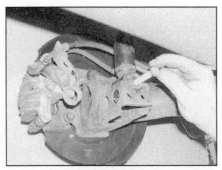

11.3b . . . then withdraw the strut lower mounting bolt

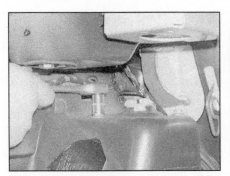

11.5a Slacken and remove the strut upper mounting bolts . . .

11.5b Manoeuvre the strut assembly from the wheel arch

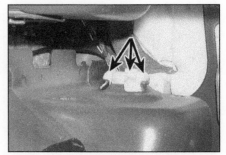

11.8 Rotate the strut until the upper mounting lugs (arrowed) can be felt to engage

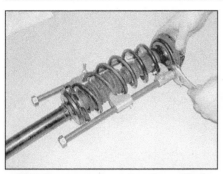

12.2 Compress the coil spring until all tension is relieved from the spring seats

12 With the vehicle resting on its wheels, rock the car to settle the strut in position, then tighten the lower mounting nut to the specified torque setting.

12.5a Remove the nut . . .

12.5b . . . then lift off the dished washer . . .

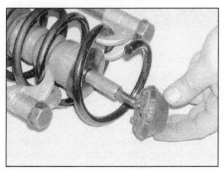

12.6a Slide off the bearing ring . . .

12.3 Prise the plastic cap from the top of the strut, together with its O-ring seal

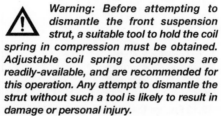

12 Rear suspension strut - overhaul

> ⚠️ **Warning: Before attempting to dismantle the front suspension strut, a suitable tool to hold the coil spring in compression must be obtained. Adjustable coil spring compressors are readily-available, and are recommended for this operation. Any attempt to dismantle the strut without such a tool is likely to result in damage or personal injury.**

1 With the strut removed from the car, clean away all external dirt, then mount it upright in a vice. Make alignment marks between the mounting plate, coil spring, lower seat and shock absorber body as these will be helpful on reassembly.

12.5c . . . bearing . . .

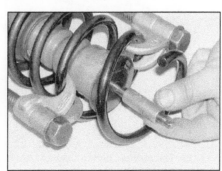

12.6b . . . spacer . . .

12.4 Slacken the damper rod nut whilst retaining the damper rod with a suitable tool

2 Fit the spring compressor and compress the coil spring until tension is relieved from the spring seats **(see illustration)**.
3 Prise the plastic cap from the top of the strut, together with its O-ring, to expose the strut damper rod nut **(see illustration)**.
4 Slacken the damper rod nut whilst retaining the damper rod with a suitable Allen key or spanner **(see illustration)**.
5 Remove the nut then lift off the dished washer, bearing, upper spring plate together with its gasket, upper spring seat **(see illustrations)**.
6 Slide off the spacer (where fitted), bearing ring, lower washer and O-ring. Withdraw the bump stop and its lower support ring and plastic bellows followed by the protective cap. Remove the coil spring and compressors, then extract the packing ring and the lower spring seat from the shock absorber body **(see illustrations)**.

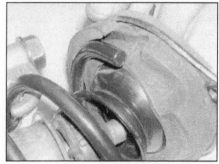

12.5d . . . and upper spring plate and seat

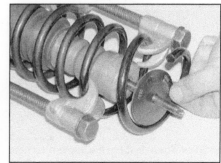

12.6c . . . lower washer . . .

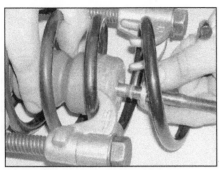

12.6d ... and O-ring

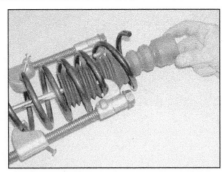

12.6e Withdraw the bump stop and its lower support ring and plastic bellows ...

12.6f ... followed by the protective cap

12.11 Ensure that the lower end of the coil spring abuts the lower spring seat stop (arrowed)

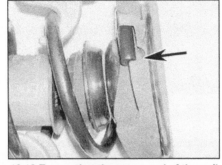

12.12 Ensure that the upper end of the coil spring abuts the upper spring seat stop (arrowed)

7 Examine the shock absorber for signs of fluid leakage. Check the piston for signs of pitting along its entire length, and check the shock body for signs of damage. While holding it in an upright position, test the operation of the shock absorber by moving the piston through a full stroke, and then through short strokes of 50 to 100 mm. In both cases, the resistance felt should be smooth and continuous. If the resistance is jerky, or uneven, or if there is any visible sign of wear or damage to the shock absorber, renewal will be necessary.

Caution: Shock absorbers must be renewed in pairs. Different versions of shock absorbers are fitted to different models - ensure that you have the correct version for your vehicle.

8 Inspect all other components for signs of damage or deterioration, and renew any that are suspect.
9 Fit the spring lower seat and packing ring to the shock absorber ensuring that their end stops are positioned at 90° to the lower mounting bolt axis.
10 Slide the protective cap over the damper rod then refit the plastic bellows, followed by the lower support ring, bump stop, O-ring, lower washer, bearing ring and spacer.
11 Refit the coil spring to the shock absorber. Make sure that the spring end abuts the spring seat stop **(see illustration)**.
12 Lubricate the upper spring seat with talcum powder then fit it to the upper end of the coil spring ensuring its stop (indicated by the marking 'Federanfang') is correctly

located against the spring end **(see illustration)**.
13 Fit the upper spring seat to the spring plate, using the alignment marks made on dismantling to ensure it is correctly positioned. The upper mounting bolt holes must be positioned at 45° to the axis of the strut lower mounting bolt lug. Note also that the nuts welded to the underside of the spring plate flange must engage with the corresponding recesses in the top of the spring seat **(see illustrations)**.
14 Fit the spring seat/plate assembly to the damper rod, then fit the bearing followed by the dished washer. Fit a new gasket to the supper spring plate.
15 Fully extend the piston rod and screw on the new nut. Counterhold the damper rod to prevent it from rotating and tighten the nut to the specified torque.
16 With the main components now assembled, check that lower end of the coil spring abuts the stop on the lower spring seat.
17 Press the cap, together with its O-ring, into position on the upper spring plate. Ensure that the x- shaped lugs on the cap are aligned perpendicularly to the axis of the strut lower mounting bolt **(refer to illustration 12.13a)**.
18 Ensure all components are correctly positioned then carefully release the spring compressor and remove it from the strut.
19 Refit the strut to the vehicle as described in Section 11.

13 Rear axle assembly - removal and refitting

Removal

1 Chock the front wheels, engage 1st gear (or P), then slacken the rear roadwheel bolts. Raise and support the vehicle at the rear on axle stands (see *Jacking and vehicle support*). Remove the rear roadwheels.
2 Remove the screws securing the heatshield above the exhaust system intermediate pipe. Slide the heatshield to one side to allow access to the handbrake cable adjustment collars, as described in Chapter 9 Section 14.

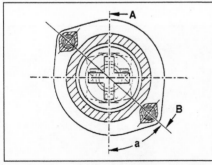

12.13a The axis (B) of the upper mounting bolt holes must be positioned at an angle (a) of 45° to the axis (A) of the strut lower mounting bolt lug

12.13b The nuts welded to the underside of the spring plate flange must engage with the corresponding recesses (arrowed) in the top of the spring seat

14.4 Unplug the airbag contact unit wiring connector

With reference to Chapter 9 Section 16, disconnect the handbrake cables from each rear brake, then detach the cables from the clips securing it to the axle.

3 Clamp the rubber section of the rear brake pipes to minimise fluid loss, then unscrew the unions and disconnect the brake hydraulic lines from each rear brake. Plug the open unions to prevent the ingress of dirt.

4 On models fitted with electric discharge headlamps, disconnect the ride height sensor pushrod from the axle beam; refer to Chapter 12 for details.

5 Position jacks or stands under the axle each side to support its weight.

6 Unbolt and remove the strut lower mounting bolt each side, and detach the struts from the axle, as described in Section 11 of this Chapter.

7 Disconnect the ABS wheel speed sensor from the rear of the stub axle carrier as described in Chapter 9, Section 19. Release the wiring from its clips to free it from the axle assembly then position it away from the work area.

8 Check that all associated fittings are clear of the axle. Cover the stub axles and brake assemblies to ensure that they do not get damaged or dirty as the axle assembly is removed. Ensure that the axle is securely supported. If possible, engage the services of an assistant to help in steadying the axle assembly as it is detached and lowered from the vehicle.

9 Unscrew and remove the pivot bolt nut each side, then withdraw the bolts and lower the axle from the pivot/mountings. Lower and remove the axle assembly from under the vehicle.

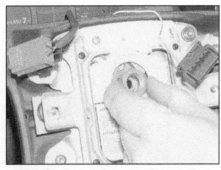

14.5 Slacken and remove the steering wheel securing nut/bolt

10 If the mounting/pivot bushes are worn, they must be renewed. Remove the outer bush, then the inner bush, using a suitable puller or the proprietary Audi extraction tool. It is important that the mounting is not driven out, or else the seating would be enlarged.

11 Dip the new bushes in soapy water, to lubricate them for ease of fitting. Press each bush in from the outside with a puller, ensuring that the arrow markings on the outer face point to the front.

Refitting

12 Refitting is a reversal of the removal procedure. When the axle is raised into position, loosely assemble the retaining bolts and nuts until the axle is fully located before tightening them fully to the specified torque settings. The pivot bolt nuts must only be tightened when the vehicle is standing on its roadwheels.

13 When reconnecting the brake hydraulic lines, handbrake cables and ABS wiring, ensure that everything is correctly routed and secured. Bleed the hydraulic system, adjust the handbrake and refit the ABS wheel speed sensor as described in Chapter 9, Section 19.

14 On models fitted with electric discharge headlamps, reconnect the ride height sensor pushrod to the axle beam with reference to Chapter 12.

15 On completion, the rear wheel alignment must be checked. The rear axle overall toe-out cannot be adjusted as the axle is a rigid assembly, but the toe out at the individual wheels can be altered by slackening the securing bolts and repositioning the axle pivot

mounting brackets. However, this should only be attempted if the appropriate wheel alignment checking equipment is available. For this reason it is recommended that the operation is carried out by an Audi dealer, or a suitably equipped tyre specialist.

14 Steering wheel - removal and refitting

⚠ *Warning: Refer to the precautions given in Chapter 12 before handling airbag system components.*

Removal

1 Remove the airbag unit as described in Chapter 12.

2 Position the front wheels in the straight-ahead position and engage the steering lock.

3 Slacken and remove the retaining screws then unclip the upper shroud and remove it from the steering column.

4 Locate the airbag contact unit wiring connector and disconnect it **(see illustration)**. On models equipped with a multi-function steering wheel, unplug the switch and heating element wiring at the connector.

5 Slacken and remove the steering wheel securing nut/bolt (as applicable) then mark the steering wheel and steering column shaft in relation to each other **(see illustration)**. Discard the nut/bolt; a new one must be used on refitting.

6 Lift the steering wheel off the column splines, taking care not to damage the contact unit wiring. **Do not** rotate the contact unit whilst the wheel is removed; tape it in position to prevent movement **(see illustrations)**.

Refitting

7 Refitting is a reversal of removal, noting the following points **(see illustration)**:
a) *Use the markings made during removal to ensure that the alignment between the steering wheel and column is correct.*
b) *Fit a new steering wheel securing bolt/nut and tighten it to the correct torque.*
c) *On completion, refit the airbag unit as described in Chapter 12.*

14.6a Lift the steering wheel off the column splines

14.6b Tape the airbag contact unit in position, to prevent movement

14.7 Fit a new steering wheel securing nut and tighten it to the correct torque

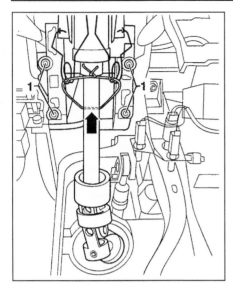

15.12 Secure the lower section of the steering column to the upper section using a length of wire

 15 Steering column - removal, inspection and refitting

⚠ *Warning: Refer to the precautions given in Chapter 12, regarding the safe handling of airbag system components, before proceeding.*

Removal

1 Turn the steering wheel until the front road wheels are set the in the straight-ahead position.

Caution: Ensure that the steering column and road wheels remains in the straight-ahead position throughout the remainder of this procedure, or the airbag contact unit may become misaligned, leading to the failure of the airbag system.

2 Disconnect the battery negative lead. **Note:** *If the vehicle has a security-coded radio, check that you have a copy of the code number before disconnecting the battery. Refer to your Audi dealer if in doubt.*

3 Remove the drivers airbag from the steering wheel, as described in Chapter 12.

4 Remove the steering wheel from the steering column, as described in Section 14.

⚠ *Warning: Pay close attention to the precautions listed in Chapter 12 before working on any component in the airbag system.*

5 If not already done, remove the screws and withdraw the steering column shrouds.

6 Remove the screws and detach the combination switches from the steering column, as described in Chapter 12.

7 Undo the cable ties and release the wiring harness from the steering column.

8 Detach and remove the lower facia trim/storage tray and insulation panels on the

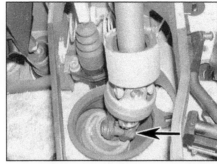

15.13 Unscrew the nut from the pinch bolt (arrowed) securing the universal joint at the base of the steering column to the steering gear

driver's side. Detach and remove the lower column/bulkhead cover.

9 Disconnect the ignition switch/steering column lock wiring connector (see Section 16).

10 On models with automatic transmission, disconnect the transmission selector lock cable from the ignition switch as follows. Move the transmission selector lever to the Park position. Insert the ignition key and turn it clockwise to the first (On) position. Lift the locking lever at the rear of the ignition switch housing up slightly, then withdraw the locking cable from the rear of the housing.

11 Remove the remaining trim panels underneath the drivers side of the facia, as necessary to gain access to the base of the steering column.

12 Secure the lower section of the steering column to the upper section using a length of wire. This is to ensure that when the steering column is detached from the steering gear, the two sections of the column do not become separated **(see illustration)**.

Caution: Do not allow the upper and lower sections of the steering column to become separated whilst the steering column is detached from the steering gear, as this can cause the internal components to become detached and misaligned.

13 Unscrew the nut from the pinch bolt securing the universal joint at the base of the steering column to the steering gear. Rotate the bolt through half turn and withdraw it from the joint **(see illustration)**.

15.15 Remove the four steering column mounting bolts (arrowed)

14 Pull the steering column universal joint off the steering gear pinion and move it to one side.

15 Remove the four steering column mounting bolts and withdraw the column assembly from the vehicle **(see illustration)**.

16 Check the various components for excessive wear. If the column has been damaged in any way, it must be renewed as a unit.

17 If required, remove the ignition switch/steering column lock, as described in Section 16.

Refitting

18 Refitting is a reversal of the removal procedure, noting the following points:

19 Ensure that the protective plastic cap is still in place on the pivot bolt that protrudes from the left hand side of the steering column. If the cap has been lost, cover the end of the bolt with thick adhesive tape to prevent the wiring harness from chaffing.

20 Where applicable, refit the ignition switch/column lock as described in Section 16.

21 Fit the four steering column upper securing bolts, but do not tighten them yet.

22 Insert the pinch bolt that secures the universal joint at the base of the steering column to the steering gear, and secure by rotating it through half a turn anticlockwise. Refit the nut and tighten it to the specified torque.

23 Now tighten the four upper steering column securing bolts to the specified torque.

24 Remove the wire that was used to secure the upper and lower sections of the steering column together.

25 On models with automatic transmission, to refit the selector lever locking cable, move the gear selector lever to the Park position, and turn the ignition key to the ON position. Inserting the end of the locking cable into the rear of the ignition switch housing and push it firmly home, until the locking bar can be heard to engage. Test the operation of the cable as follows: (1) it should be only possible to move the selector lever from the Park position to other gear positions with the ignition key in the On position (2) it should only be possible to remove the ignition key from the switch with the selector lever in the Park position and the ignition key in the Off position.

26 Refit the lower facia trim/storage tray and insulation panels on the driver's side. Refit the lower column/bulkhead cover.

27 Refit the combination switches as described in Chapter 12.

28 Refit the steering wheel as described in Section 14.

29 Refit the drivers airbag as described in Chapter 12.

30 As a safety precaution against accidental airbag detonation, ensure that no-one is inside the car then reconnect the battery negative cable.

31 On completion, ensure that the steering action, and the operation of the column switches, is satisfactory.

16.3 Unplug the wiring connector from the side of the key sensor ring

16.5 Insert a length of 2mm diameter welding rod with a chamfered point (arrowed) into the access hole until it is felt to contact the retaining tang

16.6 Withdraw the lock cylinder from its housing

16 Ignition switch/ steering column lock - removal and refitting

Lock cylinder

Removal

Note: Removal of the lock cylinder requires the use of the vehicle's spare ignition key, which is fitted with a narrow-profile, moulded plastic grip. The grip fitted to the standard key, fitted with a built-in immobiliser transmitter and/or lock illumination torch is too bulky to be used in the removal procedure.

1 Remove the steering wheel, as described in Section 14.
2 Remove the steering column combination switches as described in Chapter 12.
3 Carefully unplug the wiring connector from the side of the key sensor ring (**see illustration**).
4 Insert the spare key (see note at the beginning of this sub-Section) into the ignition switch and turn it to the On position. In this position, a small hole which allows access to the lock cylinder retaining tang hole is exposed.
5 Insert a thin screwdriver or a length of 2mm diameter welding rod (chamfered at the end) into the access hole until it is felt to contact the retaining tang (**see illustration**).
6 Hold the screwdriver/rod in position, then grasp the key and withdraw the lock cylinder from its housing (**see illustration**).

Refitting

7 Fit the key to the new lock cylinder and turn it to the On position.
8 Slide the new lock cylinder into position, until the retaining tang can be heard to engage with a click.
9 Pull lightly on the key to check that the cylinder is securely held in position.
10 Reconnect the wiring to the sensor ring, checking that the connector is pushed fully home.
11 Refit the steering column combination switches as described in Chapter 12.
12 Refit the steering wheel as described in Section 14.

Ignition switch

Removal

Note: The lock cylinder does not have to be removed to complete this procedure.
13 Remove the steering wheel, as described in Section 14.
14 Remove the steering column combination switches as described in Chapter 12.
15 Unplug the multi-way wiring connector from the rear of the ignition switch (**see illustration**).
16 Carefully scoop the locking compound from the two bolt holes on the left hand side of the lock cylinder housing, to expose the heads of the ignition switch securing screws.
17 Undo the ignition switch securing screws

and withdraw the switch from the lock cylinder housing (**see illustrations**).

Refitting

18 Ensure the switch is correctly positioned (rotated as far anti-clock wise as possible) then refit it to the rear of the lock cylinder housing. Ensure the switch is correctly engaged with the lock and slide it fully into position.
19 Clean the threads of the retaining screws then apply a drop of locking compound to each screw. Refit the screws to the lock assembly and tighten them securely. Apply a drop of locking compound to the heads of both screws after they have been tightened.
20 Refit the wiring connector to the rear of the ignition switch.
21 Refit the steering column combination switches as described in Chapter 12.
22 Refit the steering wheel as described in Section 14.

17 Steering gear assembly - removal, overhaul and refitting

Right-hand drive models

Removal

1 Disconnect the battery negative terminal. Access to the steering rack is very poor with the engine in position and cannot be easily improved.

16.15 Unplug the multi-way wiring connector from the rear of the ignition switch

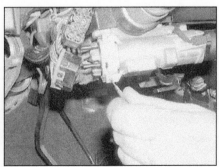

16.17a Undo the ignition switch securing screws . . .

16.17b . . . and withdraw the switch from the lock cylinder housing

2 Release the clips and remove the cover from the top of the plenum chamber.
3 Remove the battery as described in Chapter 5A.
4 Unscrew the securing bolts and remove the battery tray.
5 Remove the air cleaner and its associated ducting, as described in the relevant part of Chapter 4.
6 Remove the remaining trim panels underneath the drivers side of the facia, as necessary to gain access to the base of the steering column.
7 Secure the lower section of the steering column to the upper section using a length of wire. This is to ensure that when the steering column is detached from the steering gear, the two sections of the column do not become separated.
Caution: Do not turn the steering wheel or allow the upper and lower sections of the steering column to become separated whilst the steering column is detached from the steering gear, as this can cause the column's internal components to become detached and misaligned.

8 Unscrew the nut from the pinch bolt securing the universal joint at the base of the steering column to the steering gear. Rotate the bolt through half a turn and withdraw it from the joint.
9 Pull the steering column universal joint off the steering gear pinion and move it to one side. Detach the pinion plastic cowling from the bulkhead and withdraw it into the vehicle.
10 Firmly apply the handbrake then jack up the from of the vehicle and support it on axle stands. Remove both front roadwheels. Whilst the wheels are removed secure the discs to the hubs with a least one roadwheel bolt each.
11 Remove the right-hand hub carrier assembly as described in Section 2, paragraphs 1 to 10. Remove the left-hand track rod balljoint pinch-bolt and retaining bolt, and separate the balljoint from the hub carrier. Take care to avoid damaging the track rod bellows as you do this.
12 Unbolt the bottom of the right hand suspension strut from the suspension lower arm as described in Section 3, but do not slacken or remove the strut upper mounting nuts.
13 Unscrew the three bolts and remove the

upper transverse arm mounting bracket, the suspension strut and both upper transverse arms as an assembly from the right hand wheel arch. Note that the bolts are accessible from the plenum chamber, to the rear of the engine compartment. There may be plastic washers fitted to the underside of the bolts; these are factory assembly components which do not need to be refitted, once removed. **Note**: *Make a careful note of the fitted positions of any shims fitted underneath the heads of the transverse arm mounting bracket bolts; they must be refitted in the same positions to preserve the front suspension alignment settings.*
14 Undo the plastic nut, prise out the clips and remove the section of the inner wheel arch liner that shrouds the point where the track rod end enters the engine compartment.
15 Using brake hose clamps, clamp both the supply and return hoses near the power steering fluid reservoir. This will minimise fluid loss during subsequent operations.
16 Mark the unions to ensure that they are correctly positioned on reassembly, then unscrew the feed and return pipe union bolts from the steering gear assembly; be prepared for fluid spillage, and position a suitable container beneath the pipes whilst unscrewing the union bolts. Disconnect both pipes and recover the sealing rings; discard the rings new ones must be used on refitting. Plug the pipe ends and steering gear orifices, to prevent fluid leakage and to keep dirt out of the hydraulic system.
17 Free the power steering pipes from the retaining clips on the underside of the steering gear housing and position them clear of the underside of the steering gear.
18 Unbolt and remove the heat shield from the front of the steering gear.
19 On models with air conditioning, disconnect the wiring connector from the pressure switch on the steering gear housing.
20 Slacken and remove the bolts securing the steering gear in position. There are three bolts in total; two either side of the pinion housing at the right hand side of the steering gear (one accessible from above the housing and one accessible from below), the third is located at the left hand end of the steering gear, and is accessible from above via the plenum chamber.
21 Make a note of the correct routing of all wiring and hoses around the steering gear to ensure they are correctly positioned on refitting.
22 With the aid of an assistant, free the steering gear pinion from the bulkhead then manoeuvre the steering gear out of position via the right hand wheelarch aperture. Take great care not to damage any wiring/hoses or the rubber gaiter as the steering gear is removed.
23 With the steering gear removed, check the pinion housing gaiter for signs of damage or deterioration and renew if necessary **(see illustration)**.

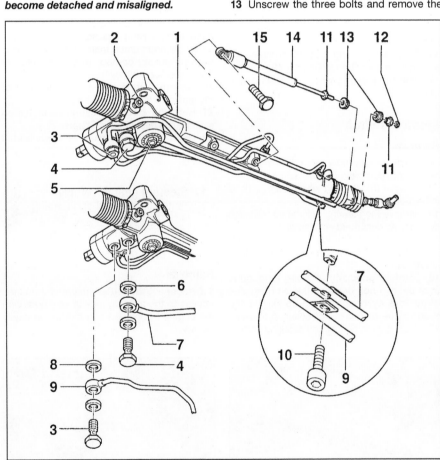

17.23 Steering gear and associated components - RHD models

1 Steering gear	*6 Sealing washer*	*11 Bush*
2 Inspection hole and bolt	*7 Return pipe*	*12 Nut*
3 Banjo bolt	*8 Sealing ring*	*13 Bush*
4 Banjo bolt	*9 Supply pipe*	*14 Damper*
5 Adjustment screw	*10 Bolt*	*15 Bolt*

Overhaul

24 Examine the steering gear assembly for signs of wear or damage, and check that the rack moves freely throughout the full length of its travel, with no signs of roughness or excessive free play between the steering gear pinion and rack. Inspect all the steering gear fluid unions for signs of leakage, and check that all union bolts are securely tightened.

25 It is possible to overhaul the steering gear assembly housing components, but this task should be entrusted to a Audi/VAG dealer. The only components which can be renewed easily by the home mechanic are the steering gear gaiters (rubber bellows), the track rod balljoints. Track rod balljoint and steering gear rubber bellows renewal procedures are covered elsewhere in this Chapter.

Refitting

26 Before the steering gear can be refitted, it must be centred as follows. Remove the socket head bolt from the tapped inspection hole at the side of the pinion gear housing. Move the right hand track rod by hand until the alignment hole - drilled into the surface of the steering rack - is visible through the inspection hole. Obtain a bolt of the same thread as that removed from the inspection hole and file the end of it to a conical point. Thread the bolt into the inspection hole and turn it until the pointed end engages with the drilled alignment hole in the steering rack; check that the rack is immobilised by trying to move the right hand track rod end. The steering gear is now locked in the centre position **(see illustration)**.

27 With the aid of an assistant, carefully manoeuvre the steering gear into position, ensuring that the wiring/hoses are all correctly routed around the steering gear.

28 Fit the two steering gear securing bolts that are accessed from above, but only hand tighten them, at this stage.

29 Fit the remaining steering gear securing bolt from below and tighten it to its specified torque. On completion, tighten the two upper securing bolts to their specified torque settings **(see illustration)**.

30 Position the rigid hydraulic pipes in their retaining clips on the underside of the steering gear, then reconnect the feed and return pipes to the steering gear, positioning a new sealing ring on each side of each end fitting, then screw in the union bolts. Ensure the pipes are correctly routed, then tighten both union bolts to their respective specified torque settings. Tighten the hydraulic pipe retaining clip bolt(s) securely. Remove the clamps from the fluid reservoir hoses.

31 Working inside the vehicle, from the drivers footwell, press the flexible gaiter over the steering gear pinion and into position on the bulkhead.

32 Reconnect the universal joint at the base of the steering column to the steering gear pinion. Insert the pinch bolt and secure by rotating it through half a turn anticlockwise.

Refit the nut and hand tighten it.

33 Remove the wire that was used to secure the upper and lower sections of the steering column together.

34 Remove the home-made locking bolt from the inspection hole on the side of the steering gear, then refit the original socket head bolt to seal the inspection hole and tighten to the specified torque.

35 Now tighten the universal joint pinch bolt at the base of the steering column to the specified torque.

36 Refit the trim panels to the underside of the drivers side of the facia.

37 Refit the plastic cover to the inside of the wheelarch, over the track rod end, and secure it with the press stud clips and the plastic nut(s). Reconnect the left-hand track rod balljoint and tighten the bolts to the specified torque.

38 Refit the upper suspension arm mounting bracket to the inside of the wheel arch, ensuring that the shims (if fitted) are replaced in their original positions, as noted during removal. Insert the three securing bolts and tighten them to the specified torque.

39 Refit the bottom of the right hand suspension strut to the suspension lower arm as described in Section 3. Tighten the securing nut and bolt to the specified torque.

40 Refit the right hand hub carrier assembly as described in Section 2, paragraphs 17 to 23 of this Chapter. Take care to avoid damaging the track rod bellows as you do this.

41 Refit the heat shield panel to the front of the steering gear.

42 On models with air conditioning, reconnect the wiring to the pressure switch on the steering gear hydraulic pipe.

43 Refit the roadwheels then lower the vehicle to the ground and tighten the wheel bolts to the specified torque.

44 Tighten the driveshaft bolt to the specified torque, as described in Chapter 8 Section 2, then refit the hub cap/wheel trim.

45 Refit the battery tray and tighten the retaining bolts securely, then refit the battery with reference to Chapter 5A. Refit the cover panel over the plenum chamber.

46 Refit the air cleaner and its associated ducting with reference to the relevant section of Chapter 4.

47 Top up the power steering fluid with reference to Weekly Checks, then bleed the hydraulic system with reference to Section 19.

48 On completion, have the front wheel alignment checked by a VAG dealer.

Left-hand drive models

Removal

49 Apply the handbrake and chock the rear wheels, then loosen the front roadwheel bolts. Raise and support the front of the vehicle on axle stands (see *Jacking and vehicle support*). Remove both front roadwheels.

50 Remove the battery from the engine compartment as described in Chapter 5A, then unbolt and remove the battery tray.

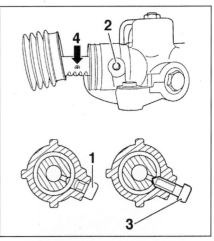

17.26 Steering rack centring details

1 *Socket head bolt*   3 *Centring bolt*
2 *Inspection hole*   4 *Alignment hole*

51 Turn the steering wheel to the centre position then remove the ignition key to engage the steering lock.

Caution: Ensure that the steering column and road wheels remains in the straight-ahead position throughout the remainder of this procedure, or the airbag contact unit may become misaligned, leading to the failure of the airbag system.

52 Working inside the vehicle, detach and remove the lower facia trim/storage tray and insulation panels on the driver's side. Detach and remove the lower column/bulkhead cover

53 Remove the remaining trim panels underneath the drivers side of the facia, as necessary to gain access to the base of the steering column.

54 Secure the lower section of the steering column to the upper section using a length of wire. This is to ensure that when the steering column is detached from the steering gear, the two sections of the column do not become separated.

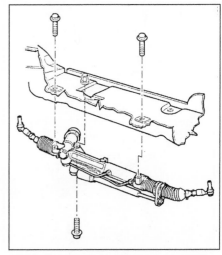

17.29 Steering gear securing bolt details - RHD models

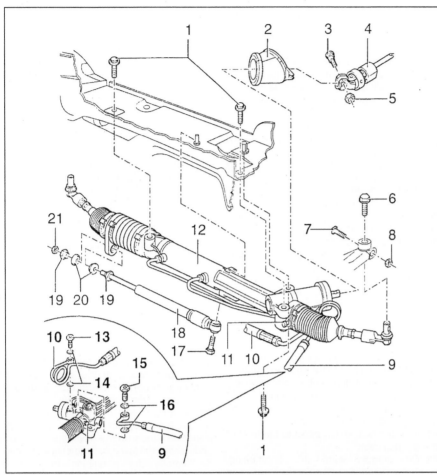

17.64 Steering gear and associated components - LHD models

1 Bolt	6 Bolt	11 Inspection hole	16 Sealing ring
2 Boot	7 Bolt	and bolt	17 Bolt
3 Eccentric pinch	8 Nut	12 Steering gear	18 Damper
bolt	9 Return pipe	13 Banjo bolt	19 Bush
4 Steering column	10 Supply pipe	14 Sealing ring	20 Bush
5 Nut		15 Banjo bolt	21 Nut

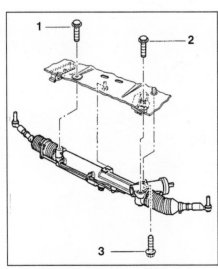

**17.66 Steering gear securing bolt
tightening sequence - LHD models**

the steering gear. Take care to avoid causing damage to the hoses by pinching.

59 Undo the plastic nut, prise out the clips and remove the section of the inner wheel arch liner that shrouds the point where the track rod end enters the engine compartment.

60 Unscrew the unions and disconnect the fluid supply and return lines from the steering gear. Clean the connections before they are detached. Drain any fluid remaining in the system into a container for disposal. Tie the lines back away from the work area, and seal off their ends to prevent further leakage and the possible ingress of dirt.

61 Refer to Section 21, and unbolt the track-rod end balljoints from the hub carrier.

62 Unscrew and remove the steering gear mounting bolts from the bodywork.

63 Check that all connections are free and clear of the steering gear, then unclip the plastic collar from the pinion housing and withdraw the steering gear from the vehicle via the left hand wheel arch.

64 If the steering gear is known to be damaged or worn beyond an acceptable level, it may have to be renewed. However, it is possible to have the steering gear overhauled - consult a VAG dealer or specialist repairer for further advice **(see illustration)**.

Refitting

65 Before the steering gear can be refitted, it must be centred as follows. Remove the socket head bolt from the tapped inspection hole at the side of the pinion gear housing. Move the right hand track rod by hand until the alignment hole - drilled into the surface of the steering rack - is visible through the inspection hole. Obtain a bolt of the same thread as that removed from the inspection hole and file the end of it to a conical point. Thread the bolt into the inspection hole and turn it until the pointed end engages with the drilled alignment hole in the steering rack; check that the rack is immobilised by trying to move the right hand track rod end. The steering gear is now locked in the centre position **(refer to illustration 17.26)**.

66 Manoeuvre the steering gear into position in the engine compartment. Insert the three securing bolts, then tighten them to their specified torques in the sequence shown **(see illustration)**. On completion, remove the locking bolt from the alignment hole, then refit the original plug to seal the steering gear.

67 The remainder of the refitting procedure is a reversal of removal, noting the following points:

a) *The fluid lines will need to be connected as the steering gear is raised into position. Take care to keep the connections clean and tighten the unions to their specified torques, using new sealing washers where applicable.*

b) *Tighten all fixings to the specified torque wrench settings.*

c) *Refer to Section 21 to reconnect the track-rod ends.*

Caution: Do not allow the upper and lower sections of the steering column to become separated whilst the steering column is detached from the steering gear, as this can cause the internal components to become detached and misaligned.

55 Unscrew the nut from the pinch bolt securing the universal joint at the base of the steering column to the steering gear. Rotate the bolt through half turn and withdraw it from the joint.

56 Pull the steering column universal joint off the steering gear pinion and move it to one side. Unclip the pinion cover from the bulkhead and withdraw it into the vehicle.

57 Siphon the fluid from the power steering fluid reservoir. If a suitable implement is not readily available to siphon the fluid from the system, it can be drained into a container when the hydraulic lines are detached from the steering gear.

58 To minimise fluid leakage, apply hose clamps to the fluid pipes leading to and from

d) Top up the fluid level as described in Weekly checks and bleed the system as described in Section 19.

e) Finally, have the wheel alignment checked and if necessary adjusted by a VAG dealer.

18 Steering gear rubber bellows - renewal

1 The steering gear bellows can be removed and refitted with the steering gear unit in situ or removed from the vehicle.

2 Measure the exposed amount of adjustment thread showing on the inboard side of the track-rod end balljoint locknut. This will act as a guide to the adjustment position when refitting the balljoint to the rod. Loosen off the locknut, and detach the balljoint from the track-rod as described in Section 21.

3 Unscrew and remove the locking nut from the track-rod.

4 Release the retaining clips and withdraw the bellows from the steering gear and track-rod.

5 Refit in the reverse order of removal. Smear the inner bore of the bellows with lubricant prior to fitting to ease its assembly. Renew the balljoint locknuts. Use new clips to retain the bellows and ensure that the end of the bellows locates correctly in the groove machined into the trackrod, without twisting.

6 On completion, have the front wheel alignment checked and if necessary adjusted (see Section 24).

19 Power steering system - bleeding

1 This procedure will only be necessary when any part of the hydraulic system has been disconnected.

2 Referring to Weekly checks, remove the fluid reservoir filler cap, and top-up with the specified fluid to the MAX level mark on the dipstick.

3 Jack up the front of the vehicle and support it on axle stands to remove the weight from the front wheels

4 With the engine stopped, quickly move the steering from lock-to-lock ten times to purge out the trapped air, then top-up the level in the fluid reservoir. Repeat this procedure until the fluid level in the reservoir does not drop any further.

5 Lower the vehicle to the ground again and if necessary, top-up the fluid level to the MAX level mark.

6 Start the engine and allow it to idle for approximately two minutes; during this time turn the steering from lock to lock ten times. Whilst the engine is running, keep an eye on the fluid level in the reservoir. Once air bubbles stop appearing in the fluid reservoir, switch off the engine.

7 Check that fluid level is up to the upper mark on the power steering fluid reservoir, topping-up if necessary then securely refit the reservoir cap.

8 If an abnormal noise is heard from the fluid lines when the steering wheel is turned, it indicates that there is still air in the system. This should escape through the course of normal driving after covering approximately 10 to 20 km. If the noise persists, it may be necessary to repeat the bleeding process.

20 Power steering pump - removal and refitting

Removal

1 Firmly apply the handbrake then jack up the front of the vehicle and support it on axle stands.

2 Remove the retaining screws and fasteners and remove the undercover from beneath the engine/transmission unit.

3 Move the lock carrier crossmember at the front of the engine compartment to the service position; refer to Chapter 11 for details.

4 Refer to the relevant part of Chapter 2 and remove the ribbed auxiliary drivebelt.

5 Remove the pulley from the coolant pump with reference to Chapter 3.

6 Using brake hose clamps, clamp both the supply and return hoses near the power steering fluid reservoir. This will minimise fluid loss during subsequent operations.

7 Wipe clean the area around the power steering pump fluid pipe unions and hose connections.

8 Unscrew the union bolt and disconnect fluid delivery pipe from the pump; be prepared for fluid spillage, and position a suitable container beneath the pipe whilst unscrewing the union bolt. Disconnect the pipe and recover the sealing rings; discard the rings new ones must be used on refitting. Plug the pipe end and steering pump orifice, to minimise fluid leakage and to keep dirt out of the hydraulic system.

9 Slacken the clip and disconnect the fluid supply hose from the rear of the power steering pump. Plug the end of the hose and cover the pump fluid port to prevent contamination.

10 Slacken and remove the pump mounting bolts and withdraw the pump from its bracket.

11 If the power steering pump is faulty it must be renewed. The pump is a sealed unit and cannot be overhauled.

Refitting

12 If a new pump is to be fitted, it must be primed with fluid prior to fitting, to ensure adequate lubrication during its initial stages of operation. Failure to do this could cause noisy operation and may lead to early pump failure. To prime the pump, pour the specified grade of hydraulic fluid into the fluid supply port on the pump, and simultaneously rotate the pump pulley. When the fluid exits from the fluid delivery union, it is primed and ready for use.

13 Manoeuvre the pump into position, then refit its mounting bolts and tighten them to the specified torque.

14 Fit a new sealing ring to each side of the hydraulic delivery pipe end fitting then reconnect the pipe to the pump and screw in the union bolt. Ensure the pipe is correctly routed then tighten the union bolt to the specified torque.

15 Reconnect the supply hose to the pump and secure it in position with the retaining clip. Remove the hose clamps used to minimise fluid loss.

16 Refit the pulley to the coolant pump with reference to Chapter 3.

17 Refit and tension the auxiliary drivebelt(s) as described in the relevant part of Chapter 1.

18 Refit the lock carrier crossmember to the front of the engine compartment, as described in Chapter 11.

19 Refit the engine compartment undercover, ensuring it is securely held by all its retaining screws and fasteners.

20 On completion, top up the hydraulic system as described in Weekly Checks, then bleed the system as described in Section 19.

21 Track rod balljoint - removal and refitting

Removal

1 Apply the handbrake, then jack up the front of the vehicle and support it on axle stands. Remove the appropriate front roadwheel. Whilst the wheel is removed, secure the brake disc to the hub with a roadwheel bolt.

2 Slacken and withdraw the adjustment bolt, followed by the securing nut and bolt then push down on the track rod to detach it from the rear of the hub carrier (see illustration).

3 To give greater clearance, unscrew the plastic nuts and extract the press-fit clips then detach the plastic track rod cover from the wheel arch.

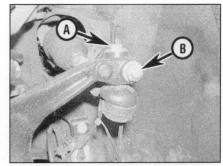

21.2 Track rod ball joint adjustment bolt (A) and securing nut and bolt (B)

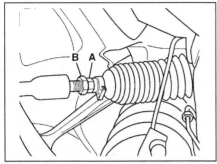

21.8 Trackrod adjustment flats (A) and lock nut (B)

4 If the balljoint is to be re-used, use a straight-edge and a scriber, or similar, to mark its relationship to the track rod adjustment nut.

5 Hold the track rod adjustment flats, and unscrew the balljoint locknut by a quarter of a turn. Do not move the locknut from this position, as it will serve as a handy reference mark on refitting.

6 Counting the **exact** number of turns necessary to do so, unscrew the balljoint assembly from the track rod.

7 Carefully clean the balljoint and the threads. Renew the balljoint if its movement is sloppy or too stiff, if excessively worn, or if damaged in any way; carefully check the stud taper and threads. If the balljoint gaiter is damaged, the complete balljoint assembly must be renewed; it is not possible to obtain the gaiter separately.

Refitting

8 Screw the balljoint onto the track rod by the number of turns noted on removal. This should bring the balljoint locknut to within a quarter of a turn from the track rod, with the alignment marks that were made on removal (if applicable) lined up. Counterhold the trackrod adjustment flats and tighten the lock nut to the specified torque **(see illustration)**.

9 Locate the balljoint spigot in the rear of the hub carrier then fit the retaining bolt together with a new nut, followed by the adjustment bolt and tighten them to the specified torque settings.

10 Refit the roadwheel, then lower the vehicle to the ground and tighten the roadwheel bolts to the specified torque.

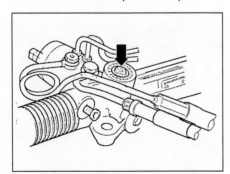

23.3 Steering gear adjustment screw (arrowed) - LHD models shown

11 Check and, if necessary, adjust the front wheel alignment as described in Section 24.

22 Track rod - removal and refitting

Removal

1 Apply the handbrake, then jack up the front of the vehicle and support it on axle stands. Remove the appropriate front roadwheel. Whilst the wheel is removed, secure the brake disc to the hub with a roadwheel bolt.

2 Slacken and withdraw the adjustment bolt, followed by the securing nut and bolt then push down on the track rod balljoint to detach it from the rear of the hub carrier.

3 Unscrew the plastic nuts and extract the press-fit clips, then detach the plastic track rod cover from the wheel arch.

4 Release the retaining clips and slide the rubber bellows towards the outboard end of the trackrod; this will expose the large integral hex nut at the inner end of the track rod.

5 Hold the track rod hex nut securing using a large open ended spanner, and unscrew the track rod from the end of the steering gear.

6 If the balljoint is to be re-used, use a straight-edge and a scriber, or similar, to mark its relationship to the track rod adjustment nut. Remove the balljoint from the track rod with reference to Section 21. **Note:** *If both track rods are to be removed, and the L and R markings on the track rod balljoints are no longer visible, mark the rods to avoid confusion on refitting.*

Refitting

7 Refitting is a reversal of removal noting the following points:
a) *Tighten the track rod to the specified torque, using a suitable 'crows foot' adapter.*
b) *Ensure that the rubber bellows is securely refitted, using new clips where necessary.*
c) *On completion have the front wheel alignment checked and if necessary adjusted.*

23 Steering gear - adjustment

1 With the vehicle stationary and the engine switched off, turn the steering wheel from side to side. If there is any undue slackness in the steering gear, resulting in noise or rattles the steering gear can be adjusted as follows.

2 Apply the handbrake and chock the rear wheels. Raise and support the front of the vehicle on axle stands (see *Jacking and vehicle support*).

3 Have an assistant turn the steering wheel back and forth by half a turn in each direction.

Tighten the self-locking adjustment screw by approximately one eighth of a turn at a time until the rattling or looseness is eradicated **(see illustration)**.

4 Lower the vehicle to the ground, then road test the car. If the steering fails to self-centre after cornering, loosen the adjustment screw a fraction at a time until it does.

5 If, when the correct self-centring point is reached, there is still excessive play in the steering, retighten the adjuster nut a fraction to take up the play.

6 If the adjustment procedures listed above do not provide satisfactory steering adjustment, it is probable that the steering gear is worn beyond an acceptable level, and it must be removed and overhauled.

24 Wheel alignment and steering angles - general information

Definitions

1 A car's steering and suspension geometry is defined in four basic settings - all angles are expressed in degrees; the steering axis is defined as an imaginary line drawn through the axis of the suspension strut, extended where necessary to contact the ground.

2 **Camber** is the angle between each roadwheel and a vertical line drawn through its centre and tyre contact patch, when viewed from the front or rear of the car. Positive camber is when the roadwheels are tilted outwards from the vertical at the top; negative camber is when they are tilted inwards. The individual front wheel camber angles cannot be adjusted, but the overall camber angle between both front wheels can be balanced out by repositioning the suspension subframe. The rear wheel camber angle is also specified but no adjustment is possible.

3 **Castor** is the angle between the steering axis and a vertical line drawn through each roadwheels centre and tyre contact patch, when viewed from the side of the car. Positive castor is when the steering axis is tilted so that it contacts the ground ahead of the vertical; negative castor is when it contacts the ground behind the vertical. The castor angle is not adjustable.

4 **Toe** is the difference, viewed from above, between lines drawn through the roadwheel centres and the car's centre-line. Toe-in is when the roadwheels point inwards, towards each other at the front, while toe-out is when they splay outwards from each other at the front.

5 The front wheel toe setting is adjusted by screwing the track rod adjusters in or out of its balljoints, to alter the effective length of the track rod assembly. The overall rear wheel toe setting cannot be altered, but the individual toe angles can be balanced out by repositioning the rear axle assembly.

Checking and adjustment

6 Due to the special measuring equipment necessary to check the wheel alignment and steering angles, and the skill required to use it properly, the checking and adjustment of these settings is best left to a Audi/VAG dealer or similar expert. Note that most tyre-fitting shops now possess sophisticated checking equipment. The following is provided as a guide, should the owner decide to carry out a DIY check.

Front wheel toe setting

7 To check the toe setting, a tracking gauge must first be obtained. Two types of gauge are available, and can be obtained from motor accessory shops. The first type measures the distance between the front and rear inside edges of the roadwheels with the vehicle stationary. The second type, known as a scuff plate, measures the actual position of the contact surface of the tyre, in relation to the road surface, with the vehicle in motion. This is achieved by pushing or driving the front tyre over a plate, which then moves slightly according to the scuff of the tyre, and shows this movement on a scale. Both types have their advantages and disadvantages, but either can give satisfactory results if used correctly and carefully.

8 For the measurements to be accurate it is important that the vehicle is unladen except, for a full tank of fuel and the spare wheel and vehicle tool kit, and that the tyres are correctly inflated (see *Weekly checks*). Rock the vehicle several times to settle all suspension components in position and ensure the front wheels are positioned in the straight-ahead position before taking any measurements.

9 If adjustment is necessary, apply the parking brake then jack up the front of the vehicle and support it securely on axle stands.

10 First clean the track rod adjuster threads; if they are corroded, apply penetrating fluid before starting adjustment.

11 Hold the adjuster stationary and slacken the balljoint and track rod locknuts. Alter the length of the track rod by rotating the adjuster as necessary; shortening the track rod length will reduce toe-in/increase toe-out.

12 When the setting is correct, hold the track rod adjuster and tighten both locknuts to the specified torque setting.

13 If after adjustment, the steering wheel spokes are no longer horizontal when the wheels are in the straight-ahead position, remove the steering wheel and reposition it (see Section 14).

14 Check that the toe setting has been correctly adjusted by lowering the vehicle to the ground and re-checking the toe setting; re-adjust if necessary.

Chapter 11
Bodywork and fittings

Contents

Degrees of difficulty

Easy, suitable for novice with little experience	**Fairly easy,** suitable for beginner with some experience	**Fairly difficult,** suitable for competent DIY mechanic	**Difficult,** suitable for experienced DIY mechanic	**Very difficult,** suitable for expert DIY or professional

Specifications

Torque wrench settings	Nm	lbf ft
Bonnet hinge bolts	21	15
Bonnet lock bolts	10	7
Boot lid (Saloon) mounting nuts	21	15
Door hinge bolts	30	22
Door lock screws	10	7
Door mirror bolt	12	9
Front bumper mounting tube-to-bodywork bolts	45	33
Front bumper-to-mounting tube bolts	23	17
Lock carrier/front cross-panel retaining bolts	10	7
Rear bumper-to-bodywork	23	17
Rear centre seat belt inertia reel (Avant)	55	41
Seat belt anchor bolts	50	37
Seat belt front stalk mounting bolt	60	44
Seat belt inertia reel bolt	50	37
Seat belt-to-height adjuster bolt	23	17
Tailgate (Avant) mounting nuts	21	15
Window component carrier-to-door bolts	30	22
Window motor to regulator	7	5

1 General description

Two body types are produced - the four-door Saloon and the five-door Avant estate. The body is of all-steel construction, and incorporates calculated impact crumple zones at the front and rear, with a central safety cell passenger compartment.

During manufacture, the underbody is treated with underseal, and as a further anti-rust aid, some of the more exposed body panels are galvanised. The bumpers and wheel arch liners are plastic mouldings, for durability and strength.

2 Maintenance - bodywork and underframe

The general condition of a vehicle's bodywork is the one thing that significantly affects its value. Maintenance is easy, but needs to be regular. Neglect, particularly after minor damage, can lead quickly to further deterioration and costly repair bills. It is important also to keep watch on those parts of the vehicle not immediately visible, for instance the underside, inside all the wheel arches, and the lower part of the engine compartment.

The basic maintenance routine for the bodywork is washing - preferably with a lot of water, from a hose. This will remove all the loose solids which may have stuck to the vehicle. It is important to flush these off in such a way as to prevent grit from scratching the finish. The wheel arches and underframe need washing in the same way, to remove any accumulated mud which will retain moisture and tend to encourage rust. Paradoxically enough, the best time to clean the underframe and wheel arches is in wet weather, when the mud is thoroughly wet and soft. In very wet weather, the underframe is usually cleaned of large accumulations automatically, and this is a good time for inspection.

Periodically, except on vehicles with a wax-based underbody protective coating, it is a good idea to have the whole of the underframe of the vehicle steam-cleaned, engine compartment included, so that a thorough inspection can be carried out to see what minor repairs and renovations are necessary. Steam cleaning is available at many garages, and is necessary for the removal of the accumulation of oily grime, which sometimes is allowed to become thick in certain areas. If steam-cleaning facilities are not available, there are some excellent grease solvents available which can be brush-applied; the dirt can then be simply hosed off. Note that these methods should not be used on vehicles with wax-based underbody protective coating, or the coating will be removed. Such vehicles should be inspected annually, preferably just before Winter, when the underbody should be washed down, and any damage to the wax coating repaired. Ideally, a completely fresh coat should be applied. It would also be worth considering the use of wax-based protection for injection into door panels, sills, box sections, etc, as an additional safeguard against rust damage, where such protection is not provided by the vehicle manufacturer.

After washing paintwork, wipe off with a chamois leather to give an unspotted clear finish. A coat of clear protective wax polish will give added protection against chemical pollutants in the air. If the paintwork sheen has dulled or oxidised, use a cleaner/polisher combination to restore the brilliance of the shine. This requires a little effort, but such dulling is usually caused because regular washing has been neglected. Care needs to be taken with metallic paintwork, as special non-abrasive cleaner/polisher is required to avoid damage to the finish. Always check that the door and ventilator opening drain holes and pipes are completely clear, so that water can be drained out. Brightwork should be

treated in the same way as paintwork. Windscreens and windows can be kept clear of the smeary film which often appears, by proprietary glass cleaner. Never use any form of wax or other body or chromium polish on glass.

3 Maintenance - upholstery and carpets

Mats and carpets should be brushed or vacuum-cleaned regularly, to keep them free of grit. If they are badly stained, remove them from the vehicle for scrubbing or sponging, and make quite sure they are dry before refitting. Seats and interior trim panels can be kept clean by wiping with a damp cloth. If they do become stained (which can be more apparent on light-coloured upholstery), use a little liquid detergent and a soft nail brush to scour the grime out of the grain of the material. Do not forget to keep the headlining clean in the same way as the upholstery. When using liquid cleaners inside the vehicle, do not over-wet the surfaces being cleaned. Excessive damp could get into the seams and padded interior, causing stains, offensive odours or even rot. If the inside of the vehicle gets wet accidentally, it is worthwhile taking some trouble to dry it out properly, particularly where carpets are involved. *Do not leave oil or electric heaters inside the vehicle for this purpose.*

4 Minor body damage - repair

Repairs of minor scratches in bodywork

If the scratch is very superficial, and does not penetrate to the metal of the bodywork, repair is very simple. Lightly rub the area of the scratch with a paintwork renovator or a very fine cutting paste to remove loose paint from the scratch, and to clear the surrounding bodywork of wax polish. Rinse the area with clean water.

Apply touch-up paint to the scratch using a fine paint brush; continue to apply fine layers of paint until the surface of the paint in the scratch is level with the surrounding paintwork. Allow the new paint at least two weeks to harden, then blend it into the surrounding paintwork by rubbing the scratch area with a paintwork renovator or a very fine cutting paste. Finally, apply wax polish.

Where the scratch has penetrated right through to the metal of the bodywork, causing the metal to rust, a different repair technique is required. Remove any loose rust from the bottom of the scratch with a penknife, then apply rust-inhibiting paint to prevent the formation of rust in the future. Using a rubber

or nylon applicator, fill the scratch with bodystopper paste. If required, this paste can be mixed with cellulose thinners to provide a very thin paste which is ideal for filling narrow scratches. Before the stopper-paste in the scratch hardens, wrap a piece of smooth cotton rag around the top of a finger. Dip the finger in cellulose thinners, and quickly sweep it across the surface of the stopper-paste in the scratch; this will ensure that the surface of the stopper-paste is slightly hollowed. The scratch can now be painted over as described earlier in this Section.

Repairs of dents in bodywork

When deep denting of the vehicle's bodywork has taken place, the first task is to pull the dent out, until the affected bodywork almost attains its original shape. There is little point in trying to restore the original shape completely, as the metal in the damaged area will have stretched on impact, and cannot be reshaped fully to its original contour. It is better to bring the level of the dent up to a point which is about 3 mm below the level of the surrounding bodywork. In cases where the dent is very shallow anyway, it is not worth trying to pull it out at all. If the underside of the dent is accessible, it can be hammered out gently from behind, using a mallet with a wooden or plastic head. Whilst doing this, hold a suitable block of wood firmly against the outside of the panel, to absorb the impact from the hammer blows and thus prevent a large area of the bodywork from being 'belled-out'.

Should the dent be in a section of the bodywork which has a double skin, or some other factor making it inaccessible from behind, a different technique is called for. Drill several small holes through the metal inside the area - particularly in the deeper section. Then screw long self-tapping screws into the holes, just sufficiently for them to gain a good purchase in the metal. Now the dent can be pulled out by pulling on the protruding heads of the screws with a pair of pliers.

The next stage of the repair is the removal of the paint from the damaged area, and from an inch or so of the surrounding 'sound' bodywork. This is accomplished most easily by using a wire brush or abrasive pad on a power drill, although it can be done just as effectively by hand, using sheets of abrasive paper. To complete the preparation for filling, score the surface of the bare metal with a screwdriver or the tang of a file, or alternatively, drill small holes in the affected area. This will provide a good 'key' for the filler paste.

To complete the repair, see the Section on filling and respraying.

Repairs of rust holes or gashes in bodywork

Remove all paint from the affected area, and from an inch or so of the surrounding 'sound' bodywork, using an abrasive pad or a wire brush on a power drill. If these are not available, a few sheets of abrasive paper will do the job most effectively. With the paint removed, you will be able to judge the severity of the corrosion, and therefore decide whether to renew the whole panel (if this is possible) or to repair the affected area. New body panels are not as expensive as most people think, and it is often quicker and more satisfactory to fit a new panel than to attempt to repair large areas of corrosion.

Remove all fittings from the affected area, except those which will act as a guide to the original shape of the damaged bodywork (eg headlight shells etc). Then, using tin snips or a hacksaw blade, remove all loose metal and any other metal badly affected by corrosion. Hammer the edges of the hole inwards, to create a slight depression for the filler paste.

Wire-brush the affected area to remove the powdery rust from the surface of the remaining metal. Paint the affected area with rust-inhibiting paint; if the back of the rusted area is accessible, treat this also.

Before filling can take place, it will be necessary to block the hole in some way. This can be achieved with aluminium or plastic mesh, or aluminium tape.

Aluminium or plastic mesh, or glass-fibre matting, is probably the best material to use for a large hole. Cut a piece to the approximate size and shape of the hole to be filled, then position it in the hole so that its edges are below the level of the surrounding bodywork. It can be retained in position by several blobs of filler paste around its periphery.

Aluminium tape should be used for small or very narrow holes. Pull a piece off the roll, trim it to the approximate size and shape required, then pull off the backing paper (if used) and stick the tape over the hole; it can be overlapped if the thickness of one piece is insufficient. Burnish down the edges of the tape with the handle of a screwdriver or similar, to ensure that the tape is securely attached to the metal underneath.

Bodywork repairs - filling and respraying

Before using this Section, see the Sections on dent, deep scratch, rust holes and gash repairs.

Many types of bodyfiller are available, but generally speaking, those proprietary kits which contain a tin of filler paste and a tube of resin hardener are best for this type of repair which can be used directly from the tube. A wide, flexible plastic or nylon applicator will be found invaluable for imparting a smooth and well-contoured finish to the surface of the filler.

Mix up a little filler on a clean piece of card or board - measure the hardener carefully (follow the maker's instructions on the pack), otherwise the filler will set too rapidly or too slowly. Using the applicator, apply the filler paste to the prepared area; draw the applicator across the surface of the filler to achieve the correct contour and to level the surface. When a contour that approximates to the correct one is achieved, stop working the paste - if you carry on too long, the paste will become sticky and begin to 'pick-up' on the applicator. Continue to add thin layers of filler paste at 20-minute intervals, until the level of the filler is just proud of the surrounding bodywork.

Once the filler has hardened, the excess can be removed using a metal plane or file. From then on, progressively-finer grades of abrasive paper should be used, starting with a 40-grade production paper, and finishing with a 400-grade wet-and-dry paper. Always wrap the abrasive paper around a flat rubber, cork, or wooden block - otherwise the surface of the filler will not be completely flat. During the smoothing of the filler surface, the wet-and-dry paper should be periodically rinsed in water. This will ensure that a very smooth finish is imparted to the filler at the final stage.

At this stage, the 'dent' should be surrounded by a ring of bare metal, which in turn should be encircled by the finely 'feathered' edge of the good paintwork. Rinse the repair area with clean water, until all the dust produced by the rubbing-down operation has gone.

Spray the whole area with a light coat of primer - this will show up any imperfections in the surface of the filler. Repair these imperfections with fresh filler paste or bodystopper, and again smooth the surface with abrasive paper. If bodystopper is used, it can be mixed with cellulose thinners, to form a thin paste which is ideal for filling small holes. Repeat this spray-and-repair procedure until you are satisfied that the surface of the filler, and the feathered edge of the paintwork, are perfect. Clean the repair area with clean water, and allow to dry fully.

The repair area is now ready for final spraying. Paint spraying must be carried out in a warm, dry, windless and dust-free atmosphere. This condition can be created artificially if you have access to a large indoor working area, but if you are forced to work in the open, you will have to pick your day very carefully. If you are working indoors, dousing the floor in the work area with water will help to settle the dust which would otherwise be in the atmosphere. If the repair area is confined to one body panel, mask off the surrounding panels; this will help to minimise the effects of a slight mis-match in paint colours. Bodywork fittings (eg chrome strips, door handles etc) will also need to be masked off. Use genuine masking tape, and several thickness of newspaper, for the masking operations.

Before starting to spray, agitate the aerosol can thoroughly, then spray a test area (an old tin, or similar) until the technique is mastered. Cover the repair area with a thick coat of primer; the thickness should be built up using several thin layers of paint, rather than one thick one. Using 400 grade wet-and-dry paper, rub down the surface of the primer until it is smooth. While doing this, the work area should be thoroughly doused with water, and the wet-and-dry paper periodically rinsed in water. Allow to dry before spraying on more paint.

Spray on the top coat, again building up the thickness by using several thin layers of paint. Start spraying at one edge of the repair area, and then, using a side-to-side motion, work until the whole repair area and about 2 inches of the surrounding original paintwork is covered. Remove all masking material 10 to 15 minutes after spraying on the final coat of paint.

Allow the new paint at least two weeks to harden, then, using a paintwork renovator or a very fine cutting paste, blend the edges of the paint into the existing paintwork. Finally, apply wax polish.

Plastic components

With the use of more and more plastic body components by the vehicle manufacturers (eg bumpers, spoilers, and in some cases major body panels), rectification of more serious damage to such items has become a matter of either entrusting repair work to a specialist in this field, or renewing complete components. Repair of such damage by the DIY owner is not feasible, owing to the cost of the equipment and materials required for effecting such repairs. The basic technique involves making a groove along the line of the crack in the plastic, using a rotary burr in a power drill. The damaged part is then welded back together, using a hot air gun to heat up and fuse a plastic filler rod into the groove. Any excess plastic is then removed, and the area rubbed down to a smooth finish. It is important that a filler rod of the correct plastic is used, as body components can be made of a variety of different types (eg polycarbonate, ABS, polypropylene).

Damage of a less serious nature (abrasions, minor cracks etc) can be repaired by the DIY owner using a two-part epoxy filler repair material which can be used directly from the tube. Once mixed in equal proportions, this is used in similar fashion to the bodywork filler used on metal panels. The filler is usually cured in twenty to thirty minutes, ready for sanding and painting.

If the owner is renewing a complete component himself, or if he has repaired it with epoxy filler, he will be left with the problem of finding a suitable paint for finishing which is compatible with the type of plastic used. At one time, the use of a universal paint was not possible, owing to the complex range of plastics met with in body component applications. Standard paints, generally speaking, will not bond to plastic or rubber satisfactorily, but professional matched paints, to match any plastic or rubber finish, can be obtained from some dealers. However, it is now possible to obtain a plastic body parts finishing kit which consists of a pre-primer treatment, a primer and coloured top coat. Full instructions are normally supplied with a kit, but basically the method of use is to first apply the pre-primer to the component concerned, and allow it to dry for up to 30 minutes. Then the primer is applied, and left to dry for about an hour before finally applying the special-coloured top coat. The result is a correctly coloured component, where the paint will flex with the plastic or rubber, a property that standard paint does not normally possess.

5 Major body damage - repair

Where serious damage has occurred, or large areas need renewal due to neglect, it means that complete new panels will need welding-in, and this is best left to professionals. If the damage is due to impact, it will also be necessary to check completely the alignment of the bodyshell, and this can only be carried out accurately by an Audi dealer using special jigs. If the body is left misaligned, it is primarily dangerous, as the car will not handle properly, and secondly, uneven stresses will be imposed on the steering, suspension and possibly transmission, causing abnormal wear, or complete failure, particularly to such items as the tyres.

6 Door rattles - tracing and rectification

1 Check first that the door is not loose at the hinges, and that the latch is holding the door firmly in position. Check also that the door lines up with the aperture in the body. If the door is out of alignment, adjust it as described in Section 23.
2 If the latch is holding the door in the correct position, but the latch still rattles, the lock mechanism is worn and should be renewed.
3 Other rattles from the door could be caused by wear in the window operating mechanism, interior lock mechanism, loose glass channels or loose wiring.

7 Bonnet and strut - removal, refitting and adjustment

Bonnet

Removal

1 Fully open the bonnet, then place some cardboard or rags beneath the corners by the hinges to protect the bodywork.
2 Disconnect the windscreen washer tubes from the nozzles on the bonnet, and release the hose from retaining clips.
3 Prop the bonnet open using two stout lengths of wood, one positioned at each corner. Alternatively, enlist the help of an assistant to support the bonnet.
4 Disconnect the gas strut from the bonnet, with reference to the information given later in this section.
5 Mark the location of the hinges with a pencil, then loosen the four hinge-to-bonnet retaining bolts (two each side).
6 Support the bonnet as the securing bolts are unscrewed, then withdraw the bonnet from the car.

Refitting and adjustment

7 Refitting is a reversal of removal. Ensure that the hinges are adjusted to their original positions. Close the bonnet very carefully initially; misalignment may cause the edges of the bonnet to damage the bodywork. If necessary, adjust the hinges to their original positions and check that the bonnet is level with the surrounding bodywork. If necessary, adjust the height of the bonnet front edge by screwing the rubber buffers in or out.
8 Check that the bonnet lock operates in a satisfactory manner. In particular, check that the safety catch holds the bonnet after the bonnet release cable has been pulled.

Strut

Removal

9 Prop the bonnet open using two stout lengths of wood, one positioned at each corner. Alternatively, enlist the help of an assistant to support the bonnet.
10 Release the circlips from the strut upper and lower mountings, using a suitable pair of thin-nosed pliers.
11 Withdraw the pivot pin from the upper mounting and slide the base of the strut off its lower mounting bracket spigot.

Refitting

12 Refitting is a reversal of removal, noting that the thicker end of the strut must face towards the bonnet

8 Bonnet lock and release cable - removal and refitting

Removal

1 Open the bonnet and locate the bonnet lock mechanism, mounted underneath the crossmember at the front of the engine compartment (see illustration). Slacken and withdraw the four securing bolts and withdraw the lock mechanism from the crossmember.
2 Disengage the nipple at the end of the release cable inner from the arm at the rear of the lock mechanism, using a pair of thin-nosed pliers. Withdraw the cable from the lock mechanism.

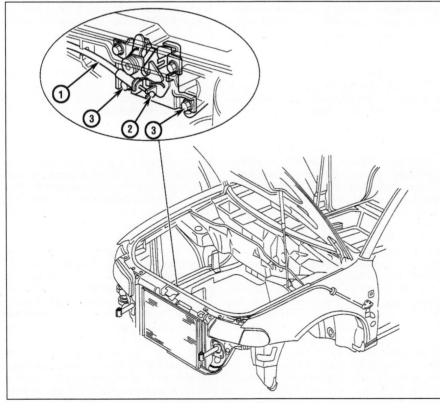

8.1 Bonnet lock mechanism

1 Release cable   *2 Nipple*   *3 Securing bolts*

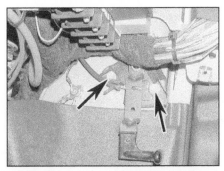

8.6 Unscrew securing bolts (arrowed) and detach the handle mechanism and its bracket from the bodywork

3 Free the release cable from all its retaining clips in the engine compartment.

4 Working in the drivers footwell, unclip the cover panel from the right hand end of facia, then undo the screws, and release the trim panel/storage tray beneath the steering column from its retaining clips.

5 Undo the screws and release the trim panel from the base of the right hand A-pillar.

6 Unscrew securing bolts and detach the handle mechanism and its bracket from the bodywork **(see illustration)**.

7 Attach a suitable length of strong cord to the end of the release cable at the lock mechanism end, then carefully draw the cable through into the footwell.

8 Undo the cord from the cable, and leave the cord ends exposed in the engine compartment and footwell.

9.2 Undo the screws to release the trailing edges of the bumper from the wheel arch liner

9.5 Unscrew and remove the bumper retaining bolts from below

Refitting

9 Refit in the reverse order of removal. Tie the inner end of the cable to the exposed cord in the footwell, carefully pull the cable through to the lock mechanism, then untie the cord.

10 When positioning the cable in the engine compartment, ensure that it is re-routed correctly to avoid kinks, sharp bends and chaffing. Check for satisfactory operation of the cable and the lock before closing the bonnet. Ensure that the bonnet locks properly when closed, and also that the safety catch operates correctly when the bonnet release cable is actuated.

9 Bumpers - removal and refitting

Front bumper

Removal

Note: *Under no circumstances should the vehicle be driven with the front bumper and bumper brackets not securely fitted, as in this condition the front crossmember which supports the engine is no longer properly secured.*

1 Open the bonnet.

2 Working at each front wheel arch in turn, undo the screws to release the trailing edges of the bumper from the wheel arch liner **(see illustration)**.

9.3 Release the retaining lugs and prise the grilles from both sides of the bumper

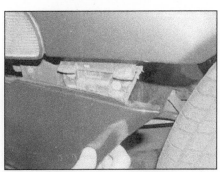

9.6a Free the trailing edges of the bumper from their securing brackets

3 Release the retaining lug and prise the grilles from both sides of the bumper **(see illustration)**.

4 Where bumper-mounted foglights are fitted, remove the foglight unit from the bumper, referring to Chapter 12, Section 7, as necessary. On certain models, the ambient temperature sensor is mounted on the rear surface of the bumper; unplug the wiring from it at the connector.

5 Unscrew and remove the two bumper retaining bolts from below **(see illustration)**.

6 Carefully withdraw the bumper assembly by sliding it squarely away from the front of the vehicle. Where headlight washers are fitted, pull the bumper out to the point where the washer hose can be detached from its bumper-to-crosspanel connection before fully withdrawing the bumper. If the bumper sticks in position, free the trailing edges one at a time by grasping the lower edge of the bumper just forward of the wheel arch and pivoting it upwards and away from the wing, to release it from its securing bracket **(see illustrations)**. **Note:** *The height of the bumper can be altered by adjusting the position of the threaded sleeves, inside the bumper mounting tubes.*

7 If required, the front air dam (where fitted) can be removed from the lower edge of the bumper by extracting the expander rivets and releasing the retaining tabs. To remove an expander rivet, first press in the central pin, then extract the rivet body using a pair of pliers. Refit with the central pin pulled out; when the rivet body is fully inserted, press in the central pin until it is flush with the rivet body.

8 The impact-absorbing bumper mounting tubes can be removed from the bodywork by slackening and withdrawing the mounting bolts. On refitting, ensure that the correct tightening torque for the mounting bolts is observed.

Refitting

9 Refitting is a reversal of removal. Tighten the bumper retaining bolts to the specified torque. On completion, check for satisfactory operation of the headlight washers, foglights and ambient temperature sensor, as applicable.

9.6b Carefully withdraw the bumper assembly by sliding it squarely away from the front of the vehicle

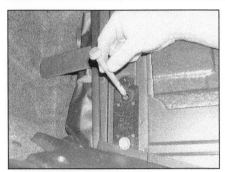

9.11 Unscrew and remove the four rear bumper retaining bolts (two at each side)

9.12a Carefully withdraw the bumper assembly by sliding it squarely away from the rear of the vehicle

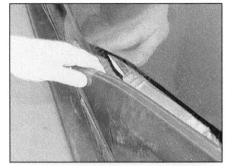

9.12b If the bumper sticks in position, unclip the leading edges from their securing brackets one at a time

Rear bumper

Removal

10 Working at each rear wheel arch in turn, undo the screws to release the leading edges of the bumper from the wheel arches.

11 Working in the luggage area, fold back the floor covering for access, then unscrew and remove the two retaining bolts at each side **(see illustration)**. On Avant models, it will be necessary to remove the trim panel from the top of the load space sill, followed by the left hand side load space trim panel and floor carpet, to gain access to one of the bolts on the left hand side.

12 Carefully withdraw the bumper assembly by sliding it squarely away from the rear of the vehicle. If the bumper sticks in position, free the leading edges one at a time by grasping the lower edge of the bumper just to the rear of the wheel arch and pivoting it upwards and away from the wing, to release it from its securing bracket **(see illustrations)**.

13 The impact-absorbing bumper mounting tubes can be removed from the bumper by slackening and withdrawing the mounting screws. On refitting, ensure that the correct tightening torque for the mounting screws is observed.

14 If required, the trim strip at the upper edge of the bumper can be removed by releasing the securing tabs.

Refitting

15 Refit in the reverse order of removal. Loosely fit all retaining bolts and screws

before fully tightening them. Tighten the retaining bolts to the specified torque **(see illustration)**.

10 Lock carrier/ front crossmember - removal and refitting

General information

1 The lock carrier/front crossmember is the name given to the section of bodywork that is mounted across the front of the engine compartment. A number of major components, including the bonnet lock mechanism, front bumper, radiator, automatic transmission fluid cooler and front light clusters are mounted on the lock carrier. The construction of the Audi A4 bodywork is such that the lock carrier and its associated components can be removed without being extensively dismantled. In addition, the lock carrier can be moved forward several centimetres to a 'service position' without having to disconnect the various hoses, pipes and wiring harnesses that serve the components mounted on it. In this position, access to components at the front of the engine compartment is greatly improved.

Removal

2 Disconnect the battery negative lead. **Note**: *If the vehicle has a security-coded radio, check that you have a copy of the code number before disconnecting the battery. Refer to your Audi dealer if in doubt.*

9.15 Tighten the bumper retaining bolts to the specified torque

3 Refer to Section 9 and remove the front bumper.

4 Undo the screws and remove the noise insulation tray from the underside of the engine compartment **(see illustration)**.

5 Disconnect the release cable from the bonnet lock mechanism with reference to Section 8.

6 Remove the securing screw(s) and detach the air inlet grille and ducting from the lock carrier **(see illustration)**.

7 Locate the wiring harness connectors for the headlight units, headlight beam aim control motors, direction indicators and at the left hand corner of the engine compartment and disconnect them **(see illustration)**. Also disconnect the wiring from the temperature sender located at the rear lower edge of the radiator, adjacent to the bottom hose stub pipe.

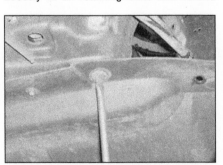

10.4 Undo the screws and remove the noise insulation tray from the underside of the engine compartment

10.6 Detach the air inlet ducting from the lock carrier

10.7 Unplug the wiring harness connectors from the headlight units

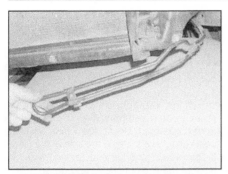

10.10 Unbolt the power steering fluid cooler from the lock carrier

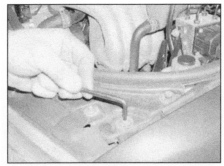

10.13 Unscrew and remove the bolts securing the lock carrier to the top of the front wing

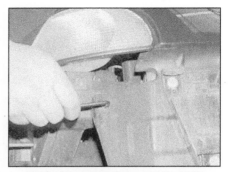

10.14 Unscrew and remove the bolts securing the lock carrier to the side of each front wing

8 Drain the coolant as described in the relevant Part of Chapter 1, then disconnect the coolant hoses from the radiator as described in Chapter 3, Section 3.

9 On models with air conditioning, unbolt the condenser from the lock carrier and secure it to a suitable point at the front of the engine compartment using cable ties or wire.

Caution: Do not allow the condenser to hang by its refrigerant pipes, as the strain may cause them to fracture.

⚠ *Warning: Do not disconnect the refrigerant pipes from the condenser (refer to the precautions in Chapter 3 regarding the dangers of air conditioning system refrigerant).*

10 Unbolt the power steering fluid cooler from the lock carrier and secure it to a suitable point at the underside of the engine compartment using cable ties or wire **(see illustration)**. On models with automatic transmission, repeat this process at the automatic transmission fluid cooler.

11 On turbo charged models, remove the securing screws and detach the intercooler air duct from the lock carrier.

12 Release the ends of the lock carrier rubber sealing strip from each front wing; there is no need to remove the strip from the lock carrier completely.

13 Unscrew and remove the two bolts securing the lock carrier to the top of the front wing on each side of the vehicle **(see illustration)**.

14 Unscrew and remove the bolts (one each side, located underneath the front direction indicator unit) securing the lock carrier to the side of each front wing **(see illustrations)**.

15 Enlist the help of an assistant to support the lock carrier during this final stage. Unscrew and remove the front bumper mounting tube bolts (four in the right hand side, three on the left hand side) then withdraw the lock carrier/cross-panel from the front of the vehicle **(see illustrations)**.

Refitting

16 Refit in the reverse order of removal. Check the operation of the front lights, and the bonnet lock and safety catch, on completion. Refill and bleed the cooling system as described in Chapter 1A or 1B, and have the headlights checked for correct beam alignment.

Setting the lock carrier in the service position

Note: *To carry out this procedure, it will necessary to fabricate two service tools, using two 300 mm lengths of threaded rod and a selection of hex nuts.*

17 Disconnect the battery negative lead.

Note: *If the vehicle has a security-coded radio, check that you have a copy of the code number before disconnecting the battery. Refer to your Audi dealer if in doubt.*

18 Refer to Section 9 and remove the front bumper.

19 Undo the quick release bolts and release

the front edge of the engine compartment noise insulation panel from the underside of the lock carrier; there is no need to remove the panel completely.

20 Remove the securing screw(s) and detach the air inlet grille/ducting from the lock carrier.

21 Slacken and withdraw the right hand uppermost bolt from the right hand bumper mounting tube. Thread one of the home made service tools into the hole vacated by the bolt and thread one of the hex nuts to the end of the tool. Thread the second tool into the hole located to the left of the bumper left hand mounting tube **(see illustration)**.

22 Remove the remainder of the bolts securing the lock carrier in position, with reference to paragraphs 13 to 15 in the previous sub-Section.

23 Carefully draw the lock carrier away from the front of the engine compartment until the rearmost of the two bolts on either side of the upper surface of the lock carrier line up with the first of the two corresponding holes at the front of each wing. Re-insert the securing bolts to retain the lock carrier in position. Adjust the hex nuts on the two home made service tools so that the lock carrier is held securely and cannot swing on the upper mounting bolts.

24 The lock carrier can be refitted by following the removal procedure in reverse. Ensure that all fixings are tightened to the correct torque wrench setting, where specified. On completion, have the headlights checked for correct beam alignment.

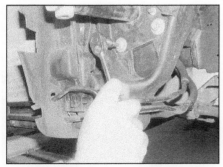

10.15a Unscrew and remove the front bumper mounting tube bolts . . .

10.15b . . . then withdraw the lock carrier/cross-panel from the front of the vehicle

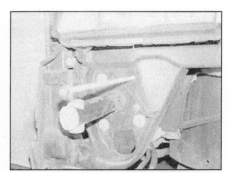

10.21 Use lengths of threaded rod for supporting the lock carrier

12.2a Remove the securing screws and detach the grab handle . . .

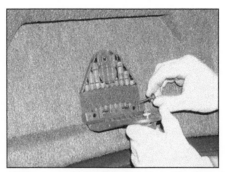

12.2b . . . and warning triangle holder from the bootlid

2 Remove the securing screws and detach the warning triangle holder and grab handle from the bootlid **(see illustrations)**.
3 Slacken and withdraw the flock-covered screws, then unclip the trim panel from the bootlid **(see illustrations)**.
4 Unplug the wiring connectors from the lock switch and rear light units, then release the grommet and withdraw the wiring harness from the bootlid. Unclip the wiring from the guide channel clipped to the side of the hinge.
5 Disconnect the central locking vacuum hose at the line connector and unclip it from the hinge guide channel.
6 Prise the spring clips from the upper and lower balljoints using a small screwdriver, then release the gas strut from the bootlid hinge **(see illustrations)**.
7 Mark the relationship between the bootlid and the hinges by drawing around the outside of each hinge with a marker pen.
8 Place cloths or pieces of cardboard over the surfaces of the rear wings, to prevent damage during removal.
9 Enlist the aid of an assistant to support the bootlid, then unscrew and remove the hinge-to-boot lid retaining nuts **(see illustration)**, and lift the lid clear.

11 Front wheel arch liners - removal and refitting

Removal

1 Chock the rear wheels, apply the handbrake, then loosen the relevant front wheel bolts. Jack up and support the front of the car on axle stands (see *Jacking and vehicle support*). Remove the relevant roadwheel.
2 The liner is secured by expanding plastic rivets and screws. The rivets may be of the type that have to be prised out, or they may have a central pin that has to be pressed through the rivet body first, before the rivet is prised free.
3 When applicable, remove the liner securing screws.

4 Lower the liner out of position, and manoeuvre it out from under the front wing. Recover the rivet expander pins, as necessary.

Refitting

5 Refitting is a reversal of removal. Renew any fasteners which were broken on removal. When fitting the expanding-type rivets, place the rivet body into position with the central pin retracted, then press pin into the rivet body until it is flush with the top of the rivet.

Refitting

10 Refit in the reverse order of removal. Check the lid for correct alignment, and if necessary loosen off the hinge bolts to adjust, then retighten them; there should be an even gap of approximately 3 mm between the outside edge of the bootlid and the surrounding bodywork. The height of the bootlid can be adjusted by slackening the bolts and altering the position of the rubber buffers located on the rear lower corners of the bootlid.

12 Boot lid - removal and refitting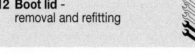

Removal

1 Raise the boot lid, then remove warning triangle from its holder.

13 Boot lid lock and lock cylinder - removal and refitting

1 Where applicable, detach and remove the trim from inside the boot lid, as described in Section 12.

12.3a Slacken and withdraw the flock-covered screws . . .

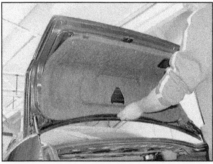

12.3b . . . then unclip the trim panel from the bootlid

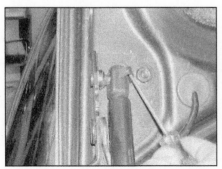

12.6a Prise the spring clips from the upper balljoints . . .

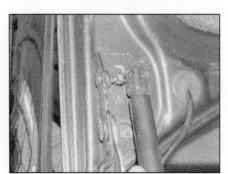

12.6b . . . then release the gas strut from the bootlid hinge

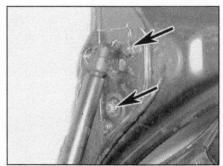

12.9 Unscrew and remove the hinge-to-boot lid retaining nuts (arrowed)

13.2 Disconnect the operating rod from the lock

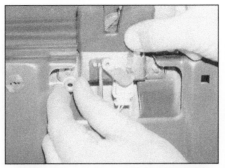

13.3a Unscrew the retaining nuts and withdraw the lock unit from the boot lid . . .

13.3b As it is withdrawn, unplug the wiring connector from the lock

Lock unit

Removal

2 Disconnect the lock operating rod from the lock **(see illustration)**.

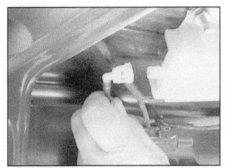

13.5 Unplug the central locking vacuum hose from the lock cylinder unit

3 Mark the fitted position of the lock with a marker pen, then unscrew the retaining nuts and withdraw the lock unit from the boot lid. As it is withdrawn, unplug the wiring connector from the lock **(see illustrations)**.

Refitting

4 Refit in the reverse order of removal.

Lock cylinder unit

Removal

5 Unplug the central locking vacuum hose from the lock cylinder unit **(see illustration)**.
6 Unscrew the retaining nuts and withdraw the lock cylinder unit from the boot lid **(see illustrations)**.
7 On models with central locking, detach the operating rod from the joint by unclipping the plastic tag and rotating the joint whilst pulling the rod from the lever.
8 Disconnect the wiring from the lock cylinder

unit as it becomes accessible **(see illustration)**.
9 If required, the vacuum unit can be removed by depressing the locking tab with a screwdriver. The central locking switch unit can be removed in a similar manner **(see illustrations)**.

Refitting

10 Refit in the reverse order of removal.

---

14 Tailgate (Avant models) - removal and refitting

Removal

1 Open the tailgate, then unscrew the trim panel/grab handle securing bolt at the centre of the lower edge of the tailgate **(see illustration)**.

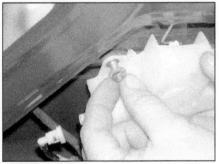

13.6a Unscrew the retaining nuts . . .

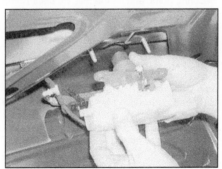

13.6b . . . and withdraw the lock cylinder unit from the boot lid

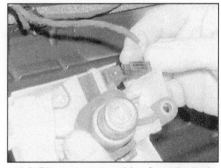

13.8 Disconnect the wiring from the lock cylinder unit as it becomes accessible

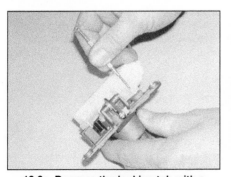

13.9a Depress the locking tab with a screwdriver . . .

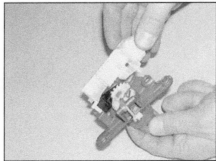

13.9b . . . and remove the vacuum unit

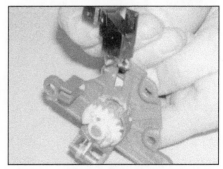

13.9c . . . the central locking switch unit can be removed in a similar manner

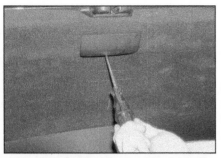

14.1 Unscrew the trim panel/grab handle securing bolt at the centre of the lower edge of the tailgate

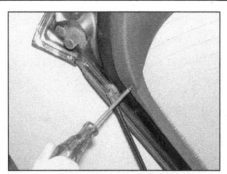

14.2a Undo the screws . . .

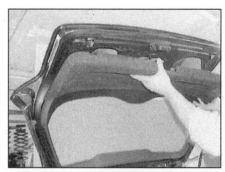

14.2b . . . then carefully prise the lower section of the trim panel from the tailgate

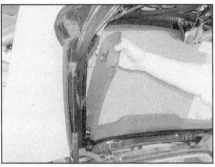

14.2c Similarly, unclip the upper section of the trim panel from the tailgate rear window aperture

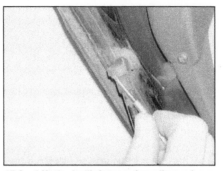

15.2a Lift the balljoints spring clips using a screwdriver . . .

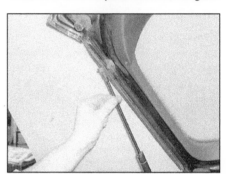

15.2b . . . and prise the strut balljoint free from its stud

2 Undo the screws at the left and right hand sides, then carefully prise the lower section of the trim panel from the tailgate using just enough force to overcome the spring clips. Similarly, unclip the upper section of the trim panel from the tailgate rear window aperture **(see illustrations)**.
3 Disconnect the wiring from the tailgate components (lock switch, wiper motor, rear light units and demister element) at the connectors. Note the routing and attachment locations of the wires.
4 Unplug the central locking vacuum hose from the tailgate at the line connector.
5 Mark the relationship between the tailgate and its hinges using a felt tip pen.

6 Enlist the aid of an assistant to help support the tailgate, then detach the tailgate strut with reference to Section 15.
7 Unscrew and remove the tailgate-to-hinge securing bolts, and lift the tailgate clear of the vehicle.

Refitting

8 Refit in the reverse order of removal. Check that the tailgate is correctly aligned before fully tightening the tailgate hinge bolts.
9 The fit and closing tension of the tailgate can be adjusted by altering the positions of the rubber buffers at the upper and lower edges of the tailgate.

15 Tailgate support strut(s) -
removal and refitting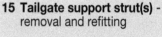

Removal

1 Open the tailgate and support it with a prop (or with the aid of an assistant).
2 Disconnect the strut at the upper and lower balljoints by lifting the spring clips, and prising the joint free **(see illustrations)**.
3 If a strut is defective in operation, it must be renewed. Do not attempt to dismantle and repair the strut. Note that the struts are filled with pressurised gas, and so should not be punctured or disposed of by incineration.

Refitting

4 Refit in the reverse order of removal. The thinner, piston rod end of the strut must be attached to the bodywork. Ensure that the strut is securely engaged with the balljoints.

16 Tailgate lock and lock cylinder (Avant models) -
removal and refitting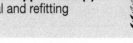

1 Refer to Section 13 and proceed as described for the boot lid lock unit and/or the boot lid lock cylinder, as required **(see illustrations)**.

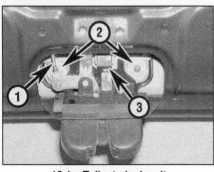

16.1a Tailgate lock unit (Avant models)

1 Operating rod
2 Securing nuts
3 Courtesy light switch

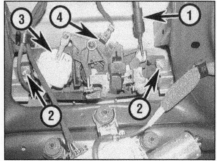

16.1b Tailgate lock cylinder unit (Avant models)

1 Operating rod
2 Securing nuts
3 Vacuum actuator unit
4 Central locking switch

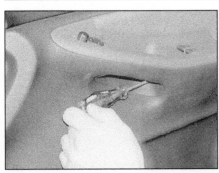

17.1a Remove the screw . . .

17.1b . . . and withdraw the grab handle from the door trim panel

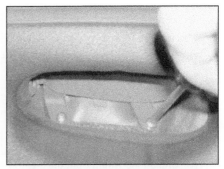

17.2 Slacken and withdraw the two screws exposed by the removal of the grab handle moulding

17 Door trim panel -
removal and refitting

Front/rear door panel

Removal

1 Open the door and remove the screw from the grab handle internal moulding. Withdraw the moulding from the door **(see illustrations)**.
2 Slacken and withdraw the two screws exposed by the removal of the grab handle moulding **(see illustration)**.

3 On models with manual front windows, insert a flat bladed screwdriver underneath the winder handle knob and lever against the trim to detach it from the winder handle. Undo the securing screw and remove the winder handle from its shaft, together with its spacer **(see illustrations)**.
4 Undo the screw at the front and rear of the upper edge of the door trim panel **(see illustrations)**.
5 Lift the trim panel up squarely, to disengage the mounting hooks on the rear of the panel from the door.
6 Unhook the operating cable from the rear of the interior handle, as it becomes accessible **(see illustration)**.

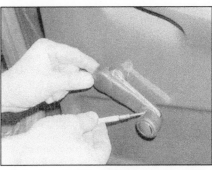

17.3a Lever against the trim to detach it from the winder handle

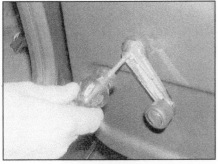

17.3b Undo the securing screw . . .

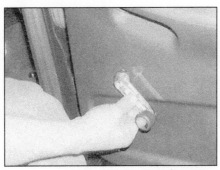

17.3c . . . and remove the winder handle from its shaft . . .

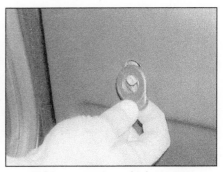

17.3d . . . together with its spacer

17.4a Undo the screw at the rear . . .

17.4b . . . and front of the upper edge of the door trim panel

17.6 Unhook the operating cable from the rear of the interior handle

17.7 Unplug the wiring from the electric window/mirror/central locking switches, and the door mounted speakers

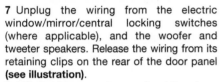

17.8 Lift the trim panel away from the door

17.9 Removing the waterproof membrane from the trim panel

7 Unplug the wiring from the electric window/mirror/central locking switches (where applicable), and the woofer and tweeter speakers. Release the wiring from its retaining clips on the rear of the door panel **(see illustration)**.

8 Lift the trim panel away from the door, noting the fitted positions of the moulded packing pieces mounted along the upper edge of the door **(see illustration)**.

9 If required, the waterproof membrane can be removed by carefully passing the wiring harness connectors through the membrane and releasing it from the mounting hooks on the rear of the trim panel **(see illustration)**.

Refitting

10 Refit in the reverse order of removal. Guide the door locking knob through the hole at the upper edge of the trim panel, and ensure that the wiring and connections are

secure and correctly routed, clear of the window regulator and latch/lock components.

18 Central locking system - general

Refer to the information given in Chapter 12.

19 Door lock - removal and refitting

Removal

1 Fully close the window. Refer to Section 17 and remove the door trim panel and the waterproof membrane.

2 Refer to Section 21 and remove the window

component carrier from the door. **Note:** *On early models where a anti-theft panel is not fitted above the lock mechanism, it is not necessary to remove the window component carrier to gain access to the lock.*

3 Unclip and remove the anti-theft panel from the lock mechanism (where fitted).

4 Carefully release the locking button, exterior handle and lock cylinder operating rods from the lock mechanism **(see illustration)**. Make a note of the fitted locations of each rod.

5 Disconnect the vacuum hose from the central locking actuator **(see illustration)**.

6 Undo the two retaining screws, and withdraw the lock unit, together with its base plate from the door **(see illustrations)**.

7 Unhook the interior handle operation cable from the lock unit, then unplug the switch wiring **(see illustrations)**.

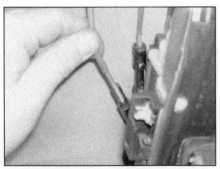

19.4 Release the lock operating rods from the lock mechanism

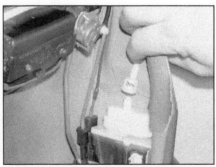

19.5 Disconnect the vacuum hose from the central locking actuator

19.6a Undo the two retaining screws . . .

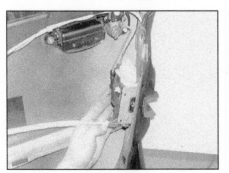

19.6b . . . and withdraw the lock unit from the door

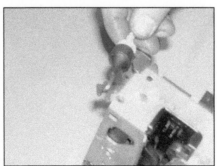

19.7a Unhook the interior handle operation cable from the lock unit . . .

19.7b . . . then unplug the switch wiring

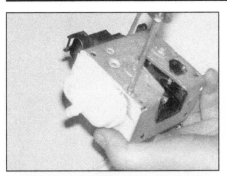

19.8a To remove the vacuum actuator unit, undo the screw . . .

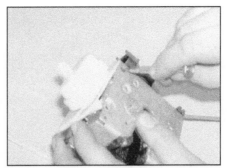

19.8b . . . depressing its locking tab with a small screwdriver . . .

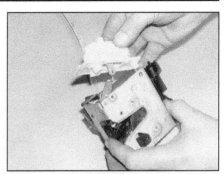

19.8c . . . and withdraw the unit from the lock

8 If required the vacuum actuator unit can be removed by removing the securing screw, depressing its locking tab with a small screwdriver and withdrawing the unit (**see illustrations**).

Refitting

9 Refitting is a reversal of the removal procedure (**see illustration**).

20 Door handles and lock cylinder - removal and refitting

Exterior door handle

Removal

1 Fully close the window. Refer to Section 17 and remove the door trim panel and the waterproof membrane.
2 Refer to Section 21 and remove the window component carrier from the door.
3 Rotate the locking element to release it from the rear of the handle and lock cylinder (**see illustrations**).

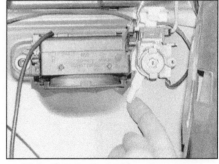

20.3a Rotate the locking element . . .

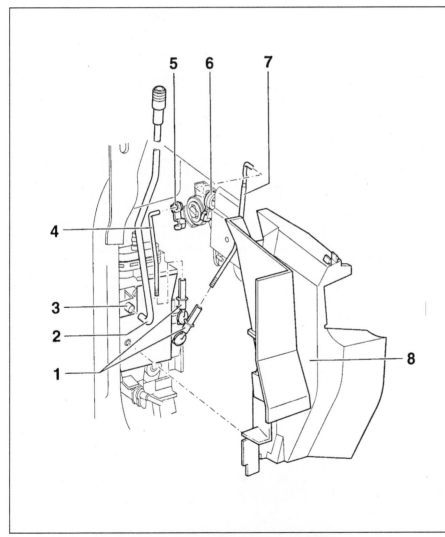

19.9 Door lock and operating rod details

1 Clip
2 Locking knob rod
3 Clip
4 Lock cylinder rod
5 Bush
6 Bush
7 Door lock rod
8 Anti-theft panel

20.3b . . . and release it from the rear of the handle and lock cylinder

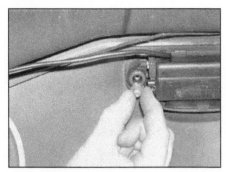

20.4a Slacken and withdraw the securing screw . . .

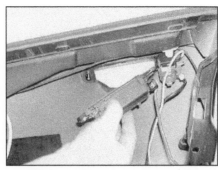

20.4b . . . then remove the handle assembly from the door

20.5 Remove the escutcheon from the outer surface of the door

20.6a Using a small flat bladed screwdriver . . .

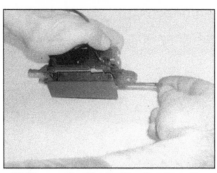

20.6b . . . prise the locking bar from the rear of the handle . . .

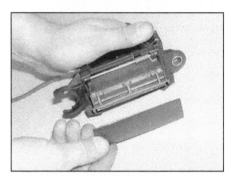

20.6c . . . and detach the trim panel

4 Slacken and withdraw the securing screw, then remove the handle assembly from the door **(see illustrations)**, leaving the lock cylinder housing in place.
5 Remove the escutcheon from the outer surface of the door **(see illustration)**.
6 If required, prise the locking bar from the rear of the handle using a small flat bladed screwdriver and detach the trim panel **(see illustrations)**.

Refitting

7 Refitting is a reversal of removal.

Lock cylinder

Removal

8 Remove the exterior door handle as described in the previous sub-section.
9 Where applicable, trace the wiring for the central locking switch and/or lock de-icing element, from the rear of the lock cylinder housing to the door wiring harness and unplug at the wiring connectors **(see illustration)**.
10 Withdraw the lock cylinder housing from the door **(see illustration)**.

11 To remove the lock cylinder from its housing, insert the key, then remove the circlip from the rear of the lock cylinder. Slide off the driver plate followed by the spring, turn the lock cylinder through 180°, then withdraw it from the handle assembly.
12 To fit the new lock cylinder, insert the lock cylinder into the housing and turn it to the left using the key. Refit the spring, driver plate and circlip. To align the driver plate correctly, ensure that the half-tooth on the driver plate engages with the corresponding half-tooth on the microswitch drive pinion **(see illustrations)**.

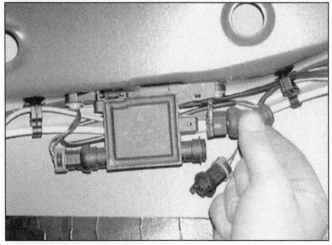

20.9 Disconnecting the wiring for the lock cylinder de-icer heating element

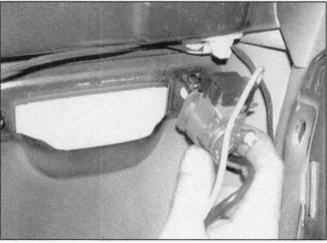

20.10 Withdraw the lock cylinder housing from the door

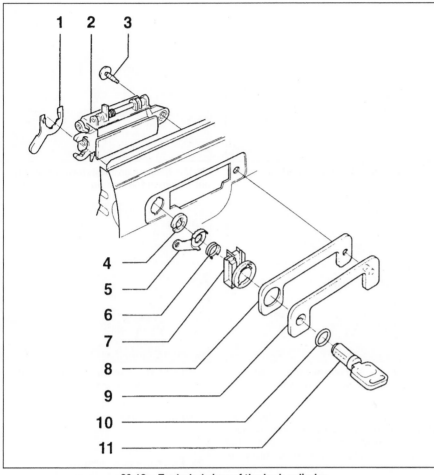

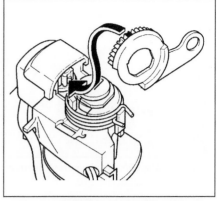

20.12b To align the driver plate correctly, ensure that the half-tooth on the driver plate engages with the corresponding half-tooth on the microswitch drive pinion

20.12a Exploded view of the lock cylinder

1 Locking element	5 Driver plate	9 Escutcheon
2 Handle	6 Spring	10 Seal
3 Screw	7 Housing	11 Lock cylinder
4 Circlip	8 Plate	and key

20.14a Release the spring-loaded retaining tab at the rear of the handle . . .

Interior door handle

13 With reference to Section 17, remove the door trim panel and the waterproof membrane.

14 Release the spring-loaded retaining tab at the rear of the handle and withdraw the handle assembly from the door trim panel **(see illustrations)**.

15 Refitting is a reversal of removal.

3 Draw around the two window glass clamps with a permanent marker to record the relationship between the clamp jaws and the glass. This will aid alignment during refitting.

4 Slacken the bolts and release the window glass from the clamps **(see illustrations)**.

5 Lift the window glass from the door **(see illustration)**.

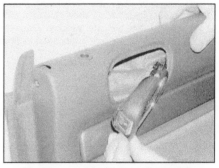

20.14b . . . and withdraw the handle assembly from the door trim panel

21 Door window and regulator - removal and refitting

Front door window glass

Removal

1 Lower the window glass to the half-way position, then disconnect the battery negative cable.

2 Remove the door trim and waterproof membrane as described in Section 17.

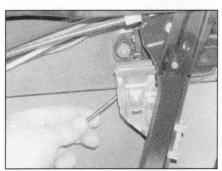

21.4a Slacken the bolts . . .

21.4b . . . and release the window glass from the clamps

21.5 Lift the window glass from the door

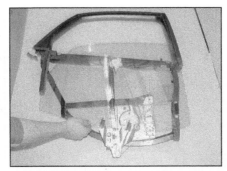

21.7 Removing the rear window glass

21.12a Slacken and withdraw the securing bolts - two at the leading edge (arrowed) . . .

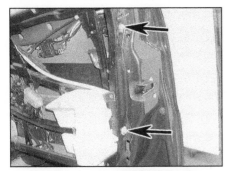

21.12b . . . two at the trailing edge (arrowed) . . .

21.12c . . . and remove the window component carrier from the door

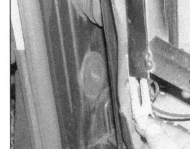

21.12d Recover the wedge-shaped adjustment block

Refitting

6 Refitting is a reversal of removal.

Rear door window glass

7 Remove the window component carrier from the rear door as described in the following sub-section, then slacken the clamps and remove the window glass as described in the previous sub-section (**see illustration**).

Component carrier/regulator

Removal

8 Lower the window glass to the half-way position, then disconnect the battery negative cable.
9 Remove the door trim and waterproof membrane as described in Section 17.

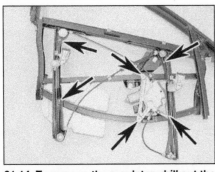

21.14 To remove the regulator, drill out the pop-rivets (arrowed) that secure the regulator to the window component carrier (front door shown)

10 Unplug the wiring from the window motor (where applicable), then release the wiring harness from the window component carrier.
11 Using a marker pen, mark the position of the wedge-shaped adjustment block in relation to the door and carrier. The block is fitted between the lower leading edge of the door and window component carrier.
12 Slacken and withdraw the four securing bolts (two at the leading edge of the door, two at the trailing edge) and remove the window component carrier from the door. Recover the wedge-shaped adjustment block (**see illustrations**).
13 Place the window component carrier face up on a clean work surface.
14 To remove the regulator, drill out the pop-rivets (six on the front door, four on the rear door) and detach the regulator from the window component carrier (**see illustration**).

Refitting

15 Refit the window regulator and window component carrier to the door by following the removal procedure in reverse, but note the following points:
a) *Fit new regulator securing pop-rivets.*
b) *When refitting the window component carrier, fit the wedge-shaped adjustment block according to the marks made during removal, to preserve the alignment of the window in relation to the B-pillar and roofline.*
c) *Ensure that the interior handle operating cable passes between the window guide channel and the upright member of the window component carrier.*

d) *Tighten all fixings to the correct torque where specified.*

22 Electrically-operated windows - general information and motor renewal

Window switches

1 Refer to Chapter 12, Section 6.

Window winder motors

Removal

2 Fully close the window then remove the door inner trim panel as described in Section 17. To further improve access to the motor, remove window component carrier from the door as described in Section 21.
3 Tape the window glass to the frame to prevent it falling down when the motor is removed.
4 If the motor is being removed with the window frame in position, disconnect the wiring connector from the motor.
5 Undo the screws securing the motor to the regulator mechanism then carefully prise off the motor and remove it.

Refitting

6 Fit the motor, aligning it with the regulator mechanism, and refit the retaining screws. Evenly and progressively tighten the retaining screws in a diagonal sequence to draw the motor squarely down onto the regulator then tighten them to the specified torque.

25.4a The rear sunroof drain tubes terminate behind the leading edges of the rear bumper . . .

25.4b . . . but can also be accessed by removing the load space side trim panels . . .

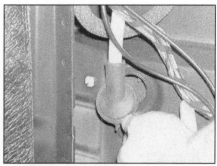

25.4c . . . and prising out the tube grommet

7 Reconnect the wiring connector to the motor and remove the tape from the glass.

8 Refit the window component carrier (where removed) to the door as described in Section 21.

9 Prior to refitting the trim panel, reconnect the battery and window switch and check the operation of the window. **Note:** *On models where the windows are equipped with a safety system which automatically opens the window should anything become trapped, it will be necessary to initiate the motor as follows. Switch the ignition on and then off again then raise the window fully hold the switch in the closed position for four seconds, then lower the window and check that it opens fully.*

10 Once the window operation is known to be correct, refit the inner trim panel as described in Section 17.

23 Doors - removal and refitting

Removal

1 Remove the door trim and insulation panel as described in Section 17.

2 Unclip the trim panel from the lower A-pillar. Disconnect the door wiring harness at the multiway connector, and unplug the central locking vacuum pipe at the union.

3 Remove the window component carrier as described in Section 21.

4 Get an assistant to support the weight of the door, or support it with blocks. If blocks are used, make sure the door will be securely supported (it is a heavy and awkward component), and pad the blocks with some rag to prevent damage to the underside of the door.

5 Mark the relationship between the lower hinge and the door, using a marker pen.

6 Unscrew and remove the bolts that secure the lower hinge to the door.

7 At the upper hinge, remove the plug and extract the hinge pin clamp bolt.

8 Remove the door by lifting it upwards, to separate the upper hinge and remove it from the vehicle.

9 Clean the bolt threads with a wire brush, and the nut threads with a tap, and treat them with thread-locking fluid when refitting the door.

Refitting

10 Refitting is a reversal of the removal procedure. Use the markings made during removal to ensue that the lower hinge is positioned correctly on the door. Note that the hinges have elongated mounting holes to allow the position of the door to be adjusted.

11 On completion, shut the door and check it for closure and alignment. Check the depth at which the striker enters the lock. If adjustment is required, slacken the securing bolts and reposition the striker plate.

24 Windscreen, rear window glass and rear side window glass - general information

The windscreen, rear window glass, and rear side window glass are directly bonded to the metalwork. Their removal and refitting requires the use of special tools not readily available to the home mechanic. This work should therefore be left to a Audi dealer, or a specialist glass replacement company.

25 Sunroof - general

1 A sliding/tilting sunroof is fitted to some models. When fitted correctly, the sunroof in the fully closed position should be level with, or no more than 1.0 mm lower than, the roof panel, at the leading edge. The rear edge must be level with, or no more than 1.0 mm higher than, the roof panel at the rear.

2 Removal and refitting, and adjustments to the sunroof, are best entrusted to an Audi garage, as specialised tools are required.

3 The sunroof panel motor can be removed and refitted as described in Chapter 12. If the motor malfunctions when the sunroof is in the open position, it can be wound shut manually.

To do this, unclip the plastic panel from the driver's end of the facia, then release the manual cranking tool which is clipped to the inner surface of the panel. Open the small hatch towards the rear of the overhead console, to provide access to the underside of the sunroof motor and insert the cranking tool into the hole at the end of the motor shaft. The tool can then be turned to close the sunroof as required.

4 If the sunroof water drain hoses become blocked, they may be cleared by probing them with a length of suitable cable (an old speedometer drive cable is ideal). The front drain tubes terminates just below the A-pillars, between the upper and lower front door hinges. The rear drain tubes terminate behind the leading edges of the rear bumper, but can also be accessed by removing the load space side trim panels and prising out the tube grommet **(see illustrations)**.

26 Door mirror components - removal and refitting

Mirror glass

Renewal

⚠ **Warning: Wear gloves and eye protection when carrying out this operation, particularly if the mirror glass is broken.**

1 Adjust the position of the mirror glass so that the lower edge of the glass protrudes from the mirror housing.

2 Line the edges of the mirror housing with masking tape, to prevent damage during mirror glass removal.

3 Using a wide-bladed wooden or plastic wedge, inserted between the lower edge of the glass and housing, carefully prise the mirror free from its retaining clips. When the lower edge of the mirror is felt to unclip, move the implement to the top of the housing and carefully lever at the upper edge of the mirror glass until it releases fully. Do not use excessive force as this may crack the mirror glass or housing **(see illustration)**.

26.3 Using a wide-bladed instrument, carefully prise the mirror free from its retaining clips

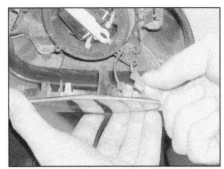

26.4 Unplug the wiring from the heating element connectors at the rear of the mirror glass

26.5 Ensure that the friction finger at the outer edge of the mirror glass enters the guide channel (arrowed) in the side of the mirror housing

4 Where applicable, unplug the wiring from the heating element connectors at the rear of the mirror glass **(see illustration)**.
5 Reconnect the heater element wiring to the

rear of the new mirror glass (where applicable) then fit the new mirror glass to the housing, ensuring that the friction finger at the outer edge of the glass enters the guide channel in the side of the mirror housing **(see illustration)**. Press firmly at the centre of the mirror glass to engage the retaining clip. On completion, check the operation of the mirror adjustment mechanism using the adjustment knob/buttons.

release the securing tabs using a small screwdriver and remove the cover panel **(see illustrations)**.
9 Remove the three mirror housing securing screws **(see illustration)**.
10 Lift the housing from the mirror body **(see illustration)**.
11 Fit the new mirror housing using a reversal of the removal procedure.

26.8a Slacken and withdraw the two screws . . .

Mirror housing

Renewal

6 The body-coloured mirror housing can be renewed without removing the mirror assembly from the door.
7 Remove the mirror glass as described in the previous sub-section.
8 Slacken and withdraw the two screws located underneath the mirror housing, then

Complete mirror assembly

Removal

12 Refer to Section 17 and remove the door trim panel.
13 Prise free and remove the triangular trim piece from the inside of the door. Remove the foam rubber padding **(see illustrations)**.
14 Unplug the mirror wiring harness at the connector **(see illustration)**.

26.8b . . . release the securing tabs . . .

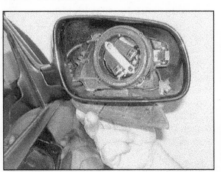

26.8c . . . and remove the cover panel

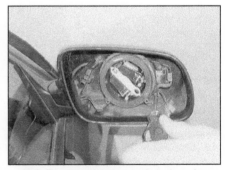

26.9 Remove the three mirror housing securing screws

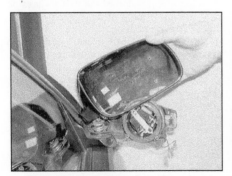

26.10 Lift the housing from the mirror body

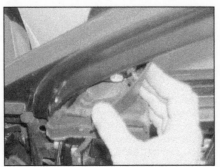

26.13 Remove the triangular trim piece from the inside of the door

26.14 Unplug the mirror wiring harness at the connector

26.15a Undo the retaining bolt . . .

26.15b . . . and withdraw the mirror from the door

15 Undo the retaining bolt and withdraw the mirror from the door **(see illustrations)**. Pass the wiring harness connector through the door aperture and recover the rubber seal.
16 To remove the mirror adjustment

mechanism, first remove the mirror glass as described earlier in this section. Undo the securing screws and remove the mechanism from the mirror body.

Refitting

17 Refitting the mirror is a reversal of the removal procedure. Check the operation of the mirror adjustment on completion.

27 Centre console - removal and refitting

Rear section

Removal

1 With the handbrake lever pulled on, prise out the securing pin at the base of the handbrake grip, and pull the handbrake lever grip free. Withdraw the trim from the handbrake lever **(see illustrations)**.
2 Prise the plastic plugs from the front lower edges of the console and remove the securing screws beneath **(see illustrations)**.
3 Remove the ashtray from the rear end of the console, then undo the retaining nut in the base of the ashtray recess **(see illustration)**.
4 Where applicable, release the diagnostic connector from its position adjacent to the ashtray **(see illustration)**.
5 Partially withdraw the console, disconnect the ashtray/cigar lighter wiring, then remove the console, by lifting it from the rear up and over the handbrake lever **(see illustration)**.

Refitting

6 Refitting is a reversal of the removal procedure. Ensure that the ashtray/cigar lighter wiring is reconnected and that the

27.1a Prise out the securing pin at the base of the handbrake grip . . .

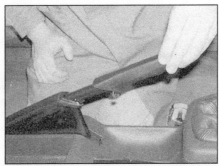

27.1b . . . and pull the handbrake lever grip free

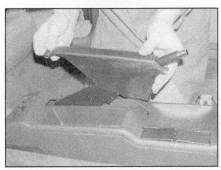

27.1c Withdraw the trim from the handbrake lever

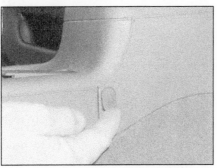

27.2a Prise the plastic plugs from the front lower edges of the console . . .

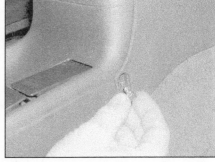

27.2b . . . and remove the securing screws beneath

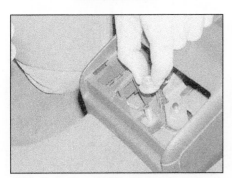

27.3 Undo the retaining nut in the base of the ashtray recess

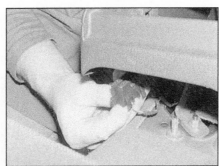

27.4 Release the diagnostic connector from its position adjacent to the ashtray

27.5 Remove the console from the vehicle

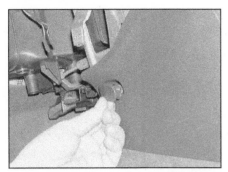

27.10a Prise the plastic plugs from the front lower edges of the console . . .

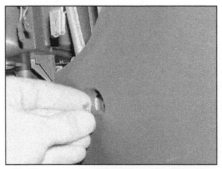

27.10b . . . and remove the securing nuts beneath

27.11 Unclip and remove the gear lever gaiter . . .

diagnostic connector is refitted in the correct position.

Front Section

Removal

7 Remove the rear section of the centre console as described in the previous sub-section.

8 Remove the radio/cassette unit as described in Chapter 12.

9 On vehicles with a manual heating system, pull the knobs from the heater controls (see Chapter 3). Remove the four securing screws at the corners of the radio aperture and release the console trim panel from its retaining clips.

10 Prise the plastic plugs from the front lower edges of the console and remove the securing nuts beneath **(see illustrations)**.

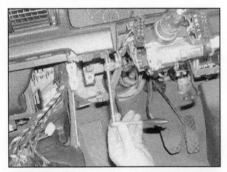

28.9a The facia securing bolts are located as follows: one to left of the steering column . . .

11 On models with manual transmission, unscrew the gear lever knob, then unclip and remove the gear lever gaiter **(see illustration)**. On models with automatic transmission, carefully unclip the trim/gear indicator panel, lift it over the gear shift lever and remove it from the console.

12 Partially withdraw the console, disconnect the ashtray/cigar lighter wiring, then remove the console from the facia **(see illustration)**.

Refitting

13 Refitting is a reversal of removal. Ensure that the clips at the front lower edges of the console engage with the facia support framework, and that all wiring is correctly routed.

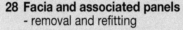

28 Facia and associated panels
- removal and refitting

Removal

1 Disconnect the battery negative lead. **Note:** *If the vehicle has a security-coded radio, check that you have a copy of the code number before disconnecting the battery. Refer to your Audi dealer if in doubt.*

2 Remove the front and rear sections of the centre console, as described in Section 27.

3 Remove the switch panel and heater control panel as described in Chapter 3 Section 9.

4 On models equipped with a passenger

27.12 . . . then remove the console from the facia

airbag, refer to Chapter 12 and remove the airbag unit from the facia.

5 Remove the steering wheel as described in Chapter 10.

6 Remove the steering column stalk switches, as described in Chapter 12.

7 Unscrew the screws from the front and side of the driver's storage shelf, then unclip the shelf from underneath the steering column.

8 Remove the securing screws and detach the upper and lower trim panels from the steering column.

9 Unscrew the securing bolts as shown; the bolts at the right and left hand ends of the facia are exposed by unclipping the plastic cover panels **(see illustrations)**.

10 The upper edge of the facia is secured by two retaining clips; carefully withdraw the facia assembly from the bulkhead to disengage the clips.

28.9b . . . one to the right of the steering column . . .

28.9c . . . two either side of the centre console support frame . . .

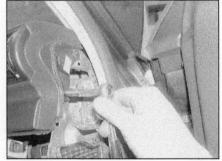

28.9d . . . two at the right hand end of the facia . . .

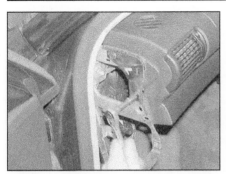

28.9e . . . one at the left hand end of the facia . . .

28.9f . . . and two securing the underside of the facia . . .

28.9g . . . to the bulkhead crossmember

11 Unplug the wiring from the rear of the instrument pack as the connectors become accessible, then remove the facia assembly from the vehicle **(see illustration)**.

Refitting

12 Refitting is a reversal of the removal process. Ensure that the heater control cables and all wiring harnesses are correctly routed and clipped in position.

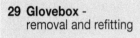

29 Glovebox - removal and refitting

Note: *Later models equipped with a passenger side airbag do not have a glovebox.*

Removal

1 Unclip the cover panel from the passengers end of the facia and undo the three retaining screws from the side and underside of the glovebox.
2 Open the glovebox lid and undo the two side retaining screws **(see illustration)**.
3 Partially withdraw the glovebox so that the illumination light wire can be disconnected, then remove the glovebox from the facia **(see illustrations)**.
4 If required the glovebox lid damping mechanism can be removed by extracting the hinge pin and then rotating the mechanism through quarter of a turn to disengage it from its mountings.

Refitting

5 Refit in the reverse order of removal.

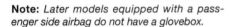

30 Interior mirror - removal and refitting

Manual mirror

1 Press the mirror support arm downwards at a slight angle and withdraw the mirror from the mounting.
2 To refit, position the support arm at 60° to 90° to the vertical, then turn it clockwise to the point where the lock spring is felt to engage.
3 If the mirror mounting plate becomes detached, clean away the old glue, then apply a suitable glass-to-metal glue in accordance with the glue manufacturer's instructions, and refit the mounting plate into position. Ensure that the plate is correctly orientated, so that when the mirror is fully fitted to it, the mirror support arm is vertical.

Automatic anti-glare mirror

4 Unclip the cover from the mirror support arm/cable guide.
5 Release the wiring from its clip and unplug the wiring connector.
6 Press the mirror support arm downwards at a slight angle to disengage the mirror from its mounting.

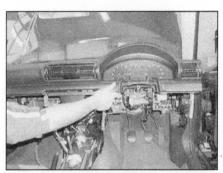

28.11 Removing the facia assembly from the vehicle

7 To refit, position the support arm at 60° to 90° to the vertical, then grasp the mirror body and turn it clockwise to the point where the lock spring is felt to engage. Do not hold the mirror by the support arm/cable guide as you do this as damage may result.
8 Reconnect the wiring, press it into its clip and refit the cable guide cover.
9 To test the operation of the mirror, cover the photo-sensor at the lower edge of the until the mirror glass lightens, then uncover the sensor and aim a light source at it; the mirror should quickly darken in response to the change in light level.

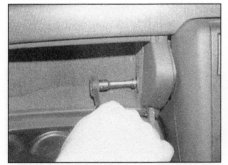

29.2 Open the glovebox lid and undo the two side retaining screws

29.3a Disconnect the illumination light wiring . . .

29.3b . . . then remove the glovebox from the facia

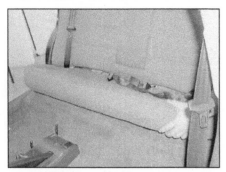

31.9a Grasp the front lower edge of the seat and pull it upwards . . .

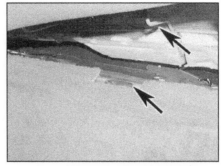

31.9b . . . to release the retaining pins from their sockets (arrowed)

31.13 Depress the locking buttons and remove the rear seat headrests from their guide tubes

31 Seats -
removal and refitting

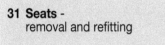

Note: *This information does not apply to models fitted with side impact airbags.*

Front seat

Removal

1 Move the seat rearwards to the extent of its travel and fold the backrest fully forward.
2 Disconnect the battery negative cable.
3 At the rear of the seat, prise out the trim cap and unscrew the securing bolt from the end of the outermost seat runner.
4 Unscrew the securing bolt and remove the rear inner seat mounting bracket.

5 At the front of the seat, Unscrew the securing nut and withdraw the bolt from the mounting bracket.
6 Extract the locking pin and slide the seat to the rear to release it from its mountings.
7 Unplug the wiring from the underside of the seat (where applicable) and remove the seat from the vehicle.

Refitting

8 Refit the seat in the reverse order of removal.

Rear seat bench

Removal

9 Grasp the front lower edge of the seat and pull it upwards, to release the retaining pins from their sockets **(see illustrations)**.

10 Slide the seat bench forward and remove it from the vehicle.

Refitting

11 Refit the seat bench in the reverse order of removal.

Rear seat backrest (fixed)

Removal

12 Remove the rear seat bench as described in the previous sub-section.
13 Depress the locking buttons and remove the rear seat headrests from their guide tubes **(see illustration)**.
14 Carefully prise the headrest guide tubes from the seat backrest **(see illustration)**.
15 Slacken and withdraw the securing screws from the lower edge of the seat backrest **(see illustration)**.
16 Lift the backrest upwards to disengage the upper mounting lugs, then remove the backrest from the vehicle **(see illustration)**.

Refitting

17 Refit the seat backrest in the reverse order of removal **(see illustrations)**.

Rear seat backrest (split)

18 Remove the rear seat bench as described previously in this section.
19 Where applicable, unbolt the rear centre seat belt lower anchor bracket from the bodywork.

31.14 Carefully prise the headrest guide tubes from the seat backrest

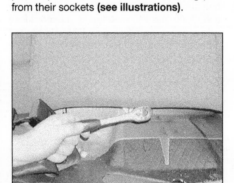

31.15 Slacken and withdraw the securing screws from the lower edge of the seat backrest

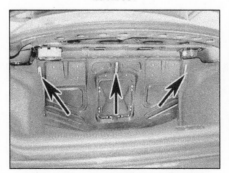

31.16 Remove the backrest from the vehicle

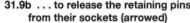

31.17a Ensure that the mounting lugs (arrowed) . . .

31.17b . . . engage with the slots in the rear bulkhead (viewed from the load space)

20 At the centre hinge between the two halves of the seat, remove the securing bolt and detach the locking clip. Lift the seat pivot pin out of the hinge, then slide the seat to one side to disengage the pivot pin at the opposite end from its socket **(see illustrations)**.

Refitting

21 Refit the seat backrest in the reverse order of removal. Ensure that the seat belt anchor bracket is tightened to the correct torque.

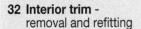

32 Interior trim -
removal and refitting

Interior trim panels

Removal

1 The interior trim panels are secured using either screws or various types of trim fasteners, usually studs or clips.
2 Check that there are no other panels overlapping the one to be removed; usually there is a sequence that has to be followed, and this will only become obvious on close inspection.
3 Remove all obvious fasteners, such as screws. If the panel will not come free, it is held by hidden clips or fasteners. These are usually situated around the edge of the panel and can be prised up to release them; note, however that they can break quite easily so replacements should be available. The best way of releasing such clips without the correct type of tool, is to use a large flat-bladed screwdriver. Note in many cases that the adjacent sealing strip must be prised back to release a panel.
4 When removing a panel, **never** use excessive force or the panel may be damaged; always check carefully that all fasteners or other relevant components have been removed or released before attempting to withdraw a panel.

Refitting

5 Refitting is the reverse of the removal procedure; secure the fasteners by pressing them firmly into place and ensure that all disturbed components are correctly secured to prevent rattles.

Carpets

6 The passenger compartment floor carpet is in one piece and is secured at its edges by screws or clips, usually the same fasteners used to secure the various adjoining trim panels.
7 Carpet removal and refitting is reasonably straightforward but very time-consuming because all adjoining trim panels must be removed first, as must components such as the seats, the centre console and seat belt lower anchorages.

31.20a At the centre hinge between the two halves of the seat, remove the securing bolt . . .

Headlining

8 The headlining is clipped to the roof and can be withdrawn only once all fittings such as the grab handles, sun visors, sunroof (if fitted), windscreen and rear quarter windows and related trim panels have been removed and the door, tailgate and sunroof aperture sealing strips (as applicable) have been prised clear.
9 Note that headlining removal requires considerable skill and experience if it is to be carried out without damage and is therefore best entrusted to an expert.

33 Seat belt tensioning mechanism -
general information

Later models are fitted with a seat belt tensioners that are integrated into the airbag control system. The system is designed to instantaneously take up any slack in the seat belt in the case of a direct or oblique frontal impact, therefore reducing the possibility of injury to the occupants. Each front seat is fitted with its own tensioner, which is situated behind the lower B-pillar trim panel.

The seat belt tensioner is triggered by a frontal impact above a pre-determined force. Lesser impacts and impacts to the rear of the vehicle will not trigger the system.

When the system is triggered, the explosive gas in the tensioner mechanism retracts and

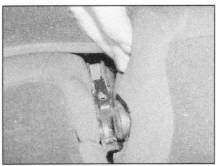

31.20c Lift the seat pivot pin out of the hinge . . .

31.20b . . . and detach the locking clip

locks the seat belt through a cable which acts on the inertia reel. This prevents the seat belt moving and keeps the occupant firmly in position in the seat. Once the tensioner has been triggered, the seat belt will be permanently locked and the assembly must be renewed, together with the impact sensors.

There is a risk of injury if the system is triggered inadvertently when working on the vehicle, and it is therefore strongly recommended that any work involving the seat belt tensioner system is entrusted to an Audi dealer. Note the following warnings before contemplating any work on the front seat belts.

⚠️ *Warning:*
Do not expose the tensioner mechanism to temperatures in excess of 100°C (212°F).
Always disconnect the battery negative lead before working on the seat belts (refer to the Warnings given in Chapter 12 relating to the airbag system).
If the tensioner mechanism is dropped, it must be renewed, even it has suffered no apparent damage.
Do not allow any solvents to come into contact with the tensioner mechanism.
Do not attempt to open the tensioner mechanism as it contains explosive gas.
Tensioners must be discharged before they are disposed of, but this task should be entrusted to a Audi dealer.

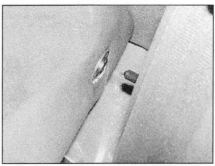

31.20d . . . and disengage the seat pivot pin at the opposite end from its socket

34 Seat belts - general

Note: *On later models equipped with front seat belt tensioners, refer to the warnings in Section 33 before working on the front seat belts.*

1 Periodically check the belts for fraying or other damage. If evident, renew the belt.

2 If the belts become dirty, wipe them with a damp cloth, using a little liquid detergent only.

3 Check the tightness of the anchor bolts, and if they are ever disconnected, make quite sure that the original sequence of fitting of washers, bushes, and anchor plate is retained.

4 Access to the front belt height adjuster and inertia reel units can be made by removing the trim from the B-pillar on the side concerned.

5 The rear seat belt anchorages can be checked by removing the rear seat bench. Access to the rear seat inertia reel units is made by removing the rear seat backrest, parcel shelf and luggage area side trim.

6 The torque wrench settings for the seat belt anchor bolts and other attachments are given in the Specifications at the start of this Chapter.

7 Never modify the seat belts, or alter the attachments to the body, in any way.

Chapter 12
Body electrical system

Contents

Degrees of difficulty

| Easy, suitable for novice with little experience | Fairly easy, suitable for beginner with some experience | Fairly difficult, suitable for competent DIY mechanic 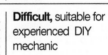 | Difficult, suitable for experienced DIY mechanic | Very difficult, suitable for expert DIY or professional |

Specifications

System type . . . . 12 volt, negative earth

Bulbs — Power rating (Watts)

Brake light (separate)	21
Brake and tail lights	21/5
Foglight (rear)	21
Headlights (halogen):	
Single bulb	60/55 (H4 type)
Twin bulbs:	
Main beam	55 (H7 type)
Dipped beam	55 (H7 type)
Fog lamp (front)	55 (H1 type)
Indicators	21
Number plate light	5
Reversing light	21
Sidelights	4
Tail light (separate)	5

Torque wrench settings

	Nm	lbf ft
Drivers airbag unit to steering wheel screws	8	6
Passenger airbag unit to facia screws	12	9
Rear window wiper arm nut	8	6
Rear window wiper mounting bracket nuts	8	6
Windscreen wiper arm nuts	16	12
Windscreen wiper linkage bolts	8	6

1 General information and precautions

⚠️ **Warning: Before carrying out any work on the electrical system, read through the pre-cautions given in 'Safety first!' at the beginning of this manual, and in Chapter 5A and 5B.**

1 The electrical system is of 12-volt negative earth type. Power for the lights and all electrical accessories is supplied by a lead/acid type battery which is charged by the alternator.

2 This Chapter covers repair and service procedures for the various electrical components not associated with the engine. Information on the battery, alternator and starter motor can be found in Chapter 5A.

3 It should be noted that prior to working on any component in the electrical system, the battery negative terminal should first be disconnected to prevent the possibility of electrical short-circuits and/or fires. **Note:** *If the vehicle has a security-coded radio, check that you have a copy of the code number before disconnecting the battery. Refer to your Audi dealer if in doubt.*

2 Electrical fault-finding - general information

Note: *Refer to the precautions given in 'Safety first!' and in Chapter 5 before starting work. The following tests relate to testing of the main electrical circuits, and should not be used to test delicate electronic circuits (such as anti-lock braking systems), particularly where an electronic control unit is used.*

General

1 Typically, electrical circuit consists of an electrical component, any switches, relays, motors, fuses, fusible links or circuit breakers related to that component, and the wiring and connectors which link the component to both the battery and the chassis. To help to pinpoint a problem in an electrical circuit, wiring diagrams are included at the end of this Chapter.

2 Have a good look at the appropriate wiring diagram, before attempting to diagnose an electrical fault, to obtain a complete understanding of the components included in the particular circuit concerned. The possible sources of a fault can be narrowed down by noting if other components related to the circuit are operating properly. If several components or circuits fail at one time, the problem is likely to be related to a shared fuse or earth connection.

3 An electrical problem will usually stem from simple cause, such as loose or corroded connections, a faulty earth connection, a blown fuse, a melted fusible link, or a faulty relay (refer to Section 3 for details of testing relays). Visually inspect the condition of all fuses, wires and connections in a problem circuit before testing the components. Use the wiring diagrams to determine which terminal connections will need to be checked in order to pinpoint the trouble-spot.

4 The basic tools required for electrical fault-finding include a circuit tester or voltmeter (a 12-volt bulb with a set of test leads can also be used for certain tests); a self-powered test light (sometimes known as a continuity tester); an ohmmeter (to measure resistance); a battery and set of test leads; and a jumper wire, preferably with a circuit breaker or fuse incorporated, which can be used to bypass suspect wires or electrical components. Before attempting to locate a problem with test instruments, use the wiring diagram to determine where to make the connections.

5 Sometimes, an intermittent wiring fault (usually caused to a poor or dirty connection, or damaged wiring insulation) can be pinpointed by performing a wiggle test on the wiring. This involves wiggling the wiring by hand to see if the fault occurs as the wiring is moved. It should be possible to narrow down the source of the fault to a particular section of wiring. This method of testing can be used in conjunction with any of the tests described in the following sub-Sections.

6 Apart from problems due to poor connections, two basic types of fault can occur in an electrical circuit: open-circuit, or short-circuit.

7 Largely, open-circuit faults are caused by a break somewhere in the circuit, which prevents current from flowing. An open-circuit fault will prevent a component from working, but will not cause the relevant circuit fuse to blow.

8 Low resistance or short-circuit faults are caused by a 'short'; a failure point which allows the current flowing in the circuit to 'escape' along an alternative route, somewhere in the circuit. This typically occurs when a positive supply wire touches either an earth wire, or an earthed component such as the bodyshell. Such faults are normally caused by a breakdown in wiring insulation, A short circuit fault will normally cause the relevant circuit fuse to blow.

9 Fuses are designed to protect a circuit from being overloaded. A blown fuse indicates that there may be problem in that particular circuit and it is important to identify and rectify the problem before renewing the fuse. Always renew a blown fuse with one of the correct current rating; fitting a fuse of a different rating may cause an overloaded circuit to overheat and even catch fire.

Finding an open-circuit

10 One of the most straightforward ways of finding an open circuit fault is by using a circuit test meter or voltmeter. Connect one lead of the meter to either the negative battery terminal or a known good earth. Connect the other lead to a connector in the circuit being tested, preferably nearest to the battery or fuse. Switch on the circuit, bearing in mind that some circuits are live only when the ignition switch is moved to a particular position. If voltage is present (indicated either by the tester bulb lighting or a voltmeter reading, as applicable), this means that the section of the circuit between the relevant connector and the battery is problem-free. Continue to check the remainder of the circuit in the same fashion. When a point is reached at which no voltage is present, the problem must lie between that point and the previous test point with voltage. Most problems can be traced to a broken, corroded or loose connection.

Finding a short-circuit

11 Loading the circuit during testing will produce false results and may damage your test equipment, so all electrical loads must be disconnected from the circuit before it can be checked for short circuits. Loads are the components which draw current from a circuit, such as bulbs, motors, heating elements, etc.

12 Keep both the ignition and the circuit under test switched off, then remove the relevant fuse from the circuit, and connect a circuit test meter or voltmeter to the fuse connections.

13 Switch on the circuit, bearing in mind that some circuits are live only when the ignition switch is moved to a particular position. If voltage is present (indicated either by the tester bulb lighting or a voltmeter reading, as applicable), this means that there is a short-circuit. If no voltage is present, but the fuse still blows with the load(s) connected, this indicates an internal fault in the load(s).

Finding an earth fault

14 The battery negative terminal is connected to 'earth':- the metal of the engine/transmission and the car body - and most systems are wired so that they only receive a positive feed, the current returning through the metal of the car body. This means that the component mounting and the body form part of that circuit. Loose or corroded mountings can therefore cause a range of electrical faults, ranging from total failure of a circuit, to a puzzling partial fault. In particular, lights may shine dimly (especially when another circuit sharing the same earth point is in operation), motors (eg. wiper motors or the radiator cooling fan motor) may run slowly, and the operation of one circuit may have an apparently unrelated effect on another. Note that on many vehicles, earth straps are used between certain components, such as the engine/transmission and the body, usually where there is no metal-to-metal contact between components due to flexible rubber mountings, etc.

15 To check whether a component is properly earthed, disconnect the battery and

connect one lead of an ohmmeter to a known good earth point. Connect the other lead to the wire or earth connection being tested. The resistance reading should be zero; if not, check the connection as follows.

16 If an earth connection is thought to be faulty, dismantle the connection and clean back to bare metal both the bodyshell and the wire terminal or the component earth connection mating surface. Be careful to remove all traces of dirt and corrosion, then use a knife to trim away any paint, so that a clean metal-to-metal joint is made. On reassembly, tighten the joint fasteners securely; if a wire terminal is being refitted, use serrated washers between the terminal and the bodyshell to ensure a clean and secure connection. When the connection is remade, prevent the onset of corrosion in the future by applying a coat of petroleum jelly or silicone-based grease or by spraying on (at regular intervals) a proprietary ignition sealer or a water dispersant lubricant.

3 Fuses and relays - general information

Main fuses

1 The fuses are located on a single panel at the right hand end of the facia.
2 Access to the fuses is gained by pulling open the cover panel **(see illustration)**.
3 Each fuse is numbered; the fuses' ratings and circuits they protect are listed on the rear face of the cover panel. A list of fuses is given at the end of this Chapter.
4 On some models (depending on specification), some additional fuses are located in separate holders next to the relays.
5 To remove a fuse, first switch off the circuit concerned (or the ignition), then pull the fuse out of its terminals. The wire within the fuse should be visible; if the fuse is blown the wire

will have a break in it, which will be visible through the plastic casing.
6 Always renew a fuse with one of an identical rating; never use a fuse with a different rating from the original or substitute anything else. Never renew a fuse more than once without tracing the source of the trouble. The fuse rating is stamped on top of the fuse; note that the fuses are also colour-coded for easy recognition.
7 If a new fuse blows immediately, find the cause before renewing it again; a short to earth as a result of faulty insulation is most likely. Where a fuse protects more than one circuit, try to isolate the defect by switching on each circuit in turn (if possible) until the fuse blows again. Always carry a supply of spare fuses of each relevant rating on the vehicle, a spare of each rating should be clipped into the base of the fusebox.

Fusible links

8 On diesel models, the glow plug electrical supply circuit is protected by a fusible link. The link is located inside a protective plastic box at the rear of the engine compartment, next to the heater intake vent. A melted link indicates a serious wiring fault or a glow plug failure - renewing the link should **not** be attempted without first diagnosing the cause of the problem.
9 Prior to renewing the link, first disconnect the battery negative cable. Unclip the cover to gain access to the metal link. Slacken the retaining screws, then slide the link out of position.
10 Fit the new link (noting the information given in paragraphs 6 and 7) then tighten its retaining screws securely and clip the cover into position.

Relays

11 The relays are mounted on common base, which is accessed by removing the trim panel from the underside of the steering column **(see illustration)**.

12 The relays are of sealed construction, and cannot be repaired if faulty. The relays are of the plug-in type, and may be removed by pulling directly from their terminals. In some cases, it will be necessary to prise the two plastic clips outwards before removing the relay.
13 If a circuit or system controlled by a relay develops a fault and the relay is suspect, operate the system; if the relay is functioning, it should be possible to hear it click as it is energised. If this is the case, the fault lies with the components or wiring of the system. If the relay is not being energised, then either the relay is not receiving a main supply or a switching voltage, or the relay itself is faulty. Testing is by the substitution of a known good unit, but be careful; while some relays are identical in appearance and in operation, others look similar but perform different functions.
14 To renew a relay, first ensure that the ignition switch is off. The relay can then simply be pulled out from the socket and the new relay pressed in.
Note: *The direction indicator/hazard warning relay is incorporated into the hazard warning light switch; see Section 6 for removal details.*

4 Ignition switch/ steering column lock - removal and refitting

Refer to the information given in Chapter 10.

5 Steering column combination switch - removal and refitting

Removal

1 Disconnect the battery negative lead (refer to Section 1).
2 Refer to Chapter 10 and remove the steering wheel.

3.2 The fuses are located on a single panel at the right hand end of the facia; access is gained by pulling open the cover panel

3.11 The relays (arrowed) are accessed by removing the trim panel from the underside of the steering column (steering wheel removed for clarity)

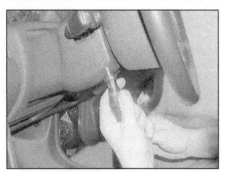

5.3a Undo the retaining screws . . .

5.3b . . . and remove the upper column shroud

5.3c Remove the screws and detach the grip from the steering column height adjustment lever

5.3d Undo the securing screws . . .

5.3e . . . and remove the lower column shroud

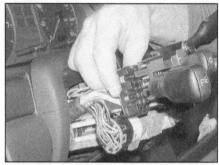

5.4 Unplug the wiring connectors from the rear of the switch assembly

3 Undo the retaining screws and remove the upper and lower column shrouds. Note that it will be necessary to remove the screws and

5.5a Slacken the clamp sleeve screw . . .

detach the grip from the steering column height adjustment lever **(see illustrations)**.
4 Unplug the wiring connectors from the rear of the switch assembly **(see illustration)**.
5 Slacken the clamp sleeve screw and remove the combination switch assembly from the steering column **(see illustrations)**.
6 Undo the securing screw and detach the relevant section of the switch assembly **(see illustrations)**.

Refitting

7 Refitting is a reversal of the removal procedure. Ensure that the wiring connections are securely made. Check for satisfactory operation on completion.

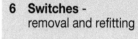

6 Switches - removal and refitting

Facia switch

1 Using a small screwdriver or similar tool, carefully prise the switch button out of the facia. Pad the blade of the screwdriver to prevent damage to the console and switch.
2 Extract the switch body from the console using a pair of long-nosed pliers, then unplug the connector from the rear of the switch.
3 Refitting is a reversal of removal.

5.5b . . . and remove the combination switch assembly from the steering column

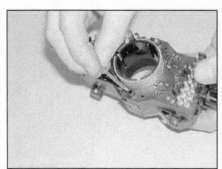

5.6a Undo the securing screw . . .

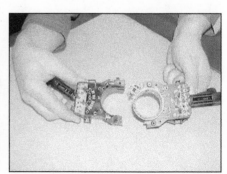

5.6b . . . and detach the relevant section of the switch assembly

6.4 Prise off the rubber cover . . .

6.6 Carefully withdraw the courtesy light switch from the body aperture

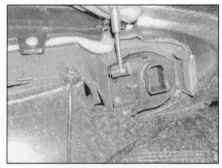

6.9a Compress the retaining lugs on the underside of the switch . . .

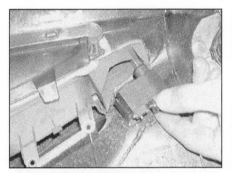

6.9b . . . and push it from the trim panel

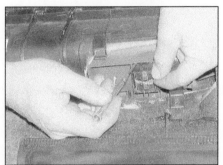

6.20a Depress the retaining tabs . . .

6.20b . . . and withdraw the switch from the door trim panel

Courtesy light switches

4 Prise off the rubber cover **(see illustration)**.
5 Unscrew the cross-head screw.
6 Carefully withdraw the switch from the body aperture **(see illustration)**. Disconnect the wiring and remove the switch. Make sure that the wiring does not drop back into the aperture by using tape or string to secure it.
7 Refitting is a reversal of removal.

Electric door mirror adjuster switch

8 Remove the door inner trim panel and detach the waterproof membrane from it, as described in Chapter 11.
9 Detach the wiring connector. Compress the retaining lugs on the underside of the switch and push it from the door trim panel **(see illustrations)**.
10 Refit in the reverse order of removal.

Sunroof control switch

11 Using a small screwdriver, prise out the interior light/switch console from the roof panel.
12 Unplug the wiring connector from the switch.
13 Pull the knob from the switch shaft, then unscrew the securing nut and remove the switch body from the roof panel.
14 Refit in the reverse order of removal.

Handbrake warning switch

15 Remove the rear section of the centre console as described in Chapter 11.
16 Undo the screw and remove the switch from the lever. On some models the switch may be simply clipped in place on the handbrake lever mounting bracket.

17 Detach the wiring connector from the switch.
18 Refit in the reverse order of removal.

Door-mounted electric window switches

19 Remove the door inner trim panel and detach the waterproof membrane from it, as described in Chapter 11.
20 Depress the retaining tabs and withdraw the switch from the door trim panel **(see illustrations)**.
21 Refitting is a reversal of removal.

Stop-light switch

22 Refer to Chapter 9.

Steering column combination switch

23 Refer to Section 5.

---

7 Exterior light units and bulbs - removal and refitting

1 Whenever a bulb is renewed, note the following points:
a) Disconnect the battery negative lead before starting work (see Section 1).
b) Remember that if the light has just been in use, the bulb may be extremely hot.
c) Always check the bulb contacts and holder, ensuring that there is clean metal-to-metal contact between the bulb and its live(s) and earth. Clean off any corrosion or dirt before fitting a new bulb.

d) Wherever bayonet-type bulbs are fitted, ensure that the live contact(s) bear firmly against the bulb contact.
e) Always ensure that the new bulb is of the correct rating and that it is completely clean before fitting it; this applies particularly to headlight/foglight bulbs (see below).

Headlight - main/dipped beam

Note: *This section does not cover dipped beam bulb renewal models fitted with electrical discharge headlamps; refer to Section 11 for renewal details.*
2 When working on the right-hand headlight, undo the two air intake duct securing screws from the lock carrier, then lift the duct and position it out of the way.
3 Depress the locking tabs and detach the cover panel from the rear of the headlamp unit **(see illustration)**.

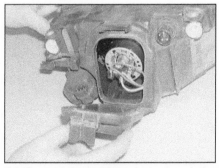

7.3 Depress the locking tabs to detach the panel (shown with unit removed for clarity)

7.4 Unplug the wiring connector from the rear of the bulb

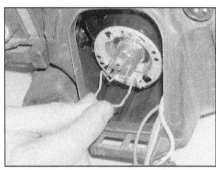

7.5a Release the metal retaining clip . . .

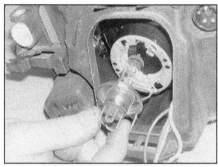

7.5b . . . and withdraw the bulb

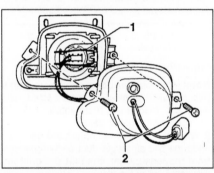

7.8 Withdraw the sidelight bulbholder and bulb from the rear of the light unit

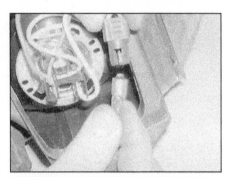

7.9 Depress and twist the sidelight bulb to remove it

Front foglamps

11 On models where the foglamps are incorporated into the headlamp unit, the bulb renewal procedure is the same as that described for the main and dipped beam headlight bulbs. Note that the fog light bulb occupies the lowermost position on models with composite headlamp units. On models where the foglamps are mounted in the front bumper/valence, reach behind the front bumper, undo the two screws and remove the cover from the rear of the foglamp unit. The bulb can then be removed after releasing the metal spring clip and unplugging the wiring connector. In both cases, ensure on refitting that the cut-out(s) on the edge of the bulb flange bear against the corresponding locating tab(s) on the bulbholder. If the beam requires vertical adjustment, prise free the adjacent grille/trim panel and rotate the foglamp adjustment screw, located at the lower inner edge of the lamp mounting flange **(see illustrations)**.

4 Unplug the wiring connector from the rear of the relevant bulb **(see illustration)**. Note that on models with composite headlamp

units, the dipped beam bulb occupies the outer position, the main beam bulb occupies the inner position. On other models, the main and dipped beam bulb are combined in a single unit.

5 Release the metal retaining clip and withdraw the bulb **(see illustrations)**.

6 Refitting is a reversal of removal. Do not touch the glass of the new bulb with bare fingers. If the glass is accidentally touched, clean it with methylated spirit.

Front direction indicator

12 Locate the locking bar at the rear of the direction indicator unit. Pivot the locking bar rearwards using a small screwdriver, then depress the locking tab and withdraw the direction indicator unit from the front of the vehicle **(see illustrations)**.

13 Rotate the bulbholder anticlockwise and withdraw it from the light unit **(see illustration)**.

14 Depress and rotate the bulb to remove it from the bulbholder **(see illustration)**.

15 Refitting is a reversal of removal. Engage

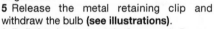

7.11a Foglamp bulb location (models with valence-mounted foglamps)

1 Spring clip   2 Rear cover screws

Sidelight

7 Remove the plastic cover from the rear of the headlight **(see illustration 7.3)**.

8 With draw the bulb and bulbholder from the rear of the light unit **(see illustration)**.

9 Depress and twist the bulb to remove it **(see illustration)**.

10 Refitting is a reversal of removal.

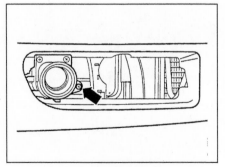

7.11b Foglamp adjustment screw (arrowed)

7.12a Pivot the locking bar rearwards using a small screwdriver (light unit removed from vehicle for clarity) . . .

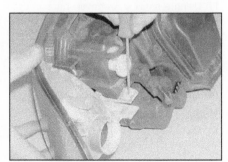

7.12b . . . then depress the locking tab and withdraw the direction indicator light unit from the front of the vehicle

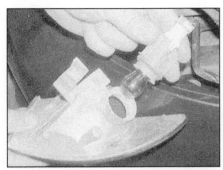

7.13 Rotate the bulbholder anticlockwise and withdraw it from the light unit

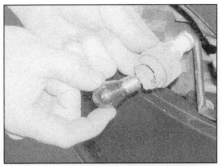

7.14 Depress and rotate the bulb to remove it from the bulbholder

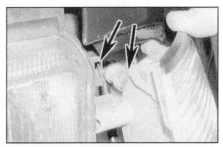

7.15 Engage the guide pegs (arrowed) at the inner edge of the direction indicator unit with those on the outer edge of the headlamp unit

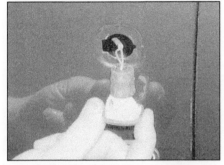

7.16a Release the lens from the bodywork . . .

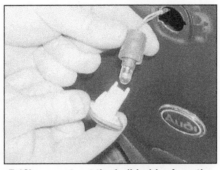

7.16b . . . extract the bulbholder from the lens . . .

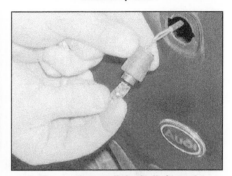

7.16c . . . then pull the bulb from the bulbholder

the guide pegs at the inner edge of the direction indicator unit with those on the outer edge of the headlamp unit **(see illustration)**. Ensure that the locking bar is securely pressed into place at the rear of the indicator unit.

Direction indicator side repeater light

16 Push the lens towards the front of the vehicle, then tilt it out at the rear to release the lens from the bodywork. Extract the bulbholder from the lens, then pull the bulb from the bulbholder **(see illustrations)**.
17 Refitting is a reversal of removal.

Rear combination lights - Saloon models

18 Remove the clips and fold the inner trim panel away from the side of the load space, to expose the rear of the light unit **(see illustration)**.

19 Depress the retaining clips and withdraw the bulbholder **(see illustration)**.
20 Press and twist the relevant bulb and withdraw it from the bulb holder **(see illustration)**.

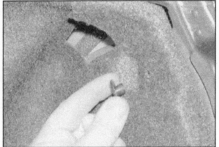

7.18 Remove the clips and fold the inner trim panel away from the side of the load space, to expose the rear of the light unit

21 To remove the light unit, remove the bulb-holder unit as described above, then unscrew and remove the retaining nuts. Remove the light unit and if required, unclip the trim panel from the lower edge **(see illustrations)**.

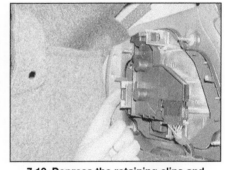

7.19 Depress the retaining clips and withdraw the bulbholder

7.20 Press and twist the relevant bulb and withdraw it from the from the bulb holder

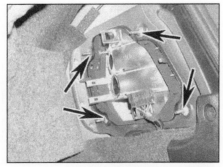

7.21a Unscrew and remove the retaining nuts (arrowed) . . .

7.21b . . . and remove the rear combination light unit from the bodywork (saloon model shown)

7.21c If required, unclip the trim panel from the lower edge of the light unit

7.22 On refitting, ensure that the seal is correctly positioned

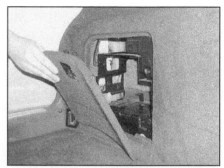

7.23a Open the access flap in the rear luggage area trim, to gain access to the rear of the light unit

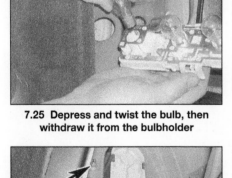

7.23b Undo the securing screws and remove the accessory rack

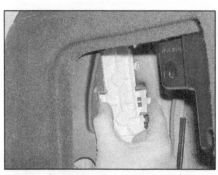

7.24a Compress the retaining clips . . .

7.24b . . . and withdraw the bulbholder

22 Refit in the reverse order of removal, ensuring that the seal is correctly positioned **(see illustration)**. On completion check for the satisfactory operation of all rear lights.

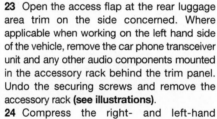

7.25 Depress and twist the bulb, then withdraw it from the bulbholder

Rear combination lights - Avant models

23 Open the access flap at the rear luggage area trim on the side concerned. Where applicable when working on the left hand side of the vehicle, remove the car phone transceiver unit and any other audio components mounted in the accessory rack behind the trim panel. Undo the securing screws and remove the accessory rack **(see illustrations)**.
24 Compress the right- and left-hand retaining clips towards the centre of the light unit, and withdraw the bulbholder **(see illustrations)**.
25 Depress and twist the bulb, then withdraw it from the bulbholder **(see illustration)**.
26 To remove the light unit, undo the retaining nuts and withdraw the unit from the bodywork **(see illustrations)**.

27 Refit in the reverse order of removal. Check the rear lights for satisfactory operation on completion.

Number plate light

28 The number plate lights are located in the boot lid or tailgate, just above the number plate. For better access to the retaining screws, open the boot lid or tailgate. Undo the two retaining screws and remove the relevant lens and bulbholder from the light unit **(see illustrations)**
29 Remove the bulb from its holder **(see illustration)**.
30 Refit in the reverse order of removal, and check the light for satisfactory operation.

High level brake light - saloon models

31 Unclip the cover from the parcel shelf **(see illustration)**.

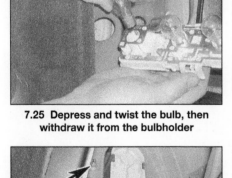

7.26a Rear combination light unit securing nuts (arrowed)

7.26b Undo the retaining nuts . . .

7.26c . . . and withdraw the unit from the bodywork

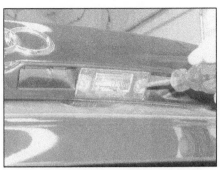

7.28a Undo the two retaining screws . . .

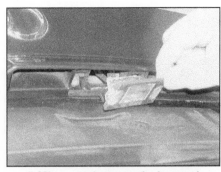

7.28b . . . and remove the lens and bulbholder from the light unit

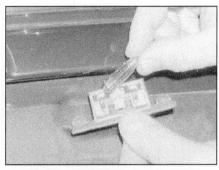

7.29 Remove the bulb from its holder

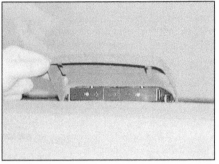

7.31 Unclip the cover from the parcel shelf

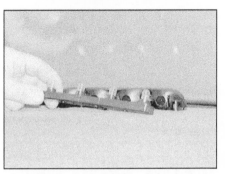

7.32 Unclip the bulbholder from the lens unit

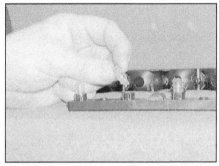

7.33 Pull the relevant bulb from the holder

32 Unclip the bulbholder from the lens unit **(see illustration)**.

33 Pull the relevant bulb from the holder **(see illustration)**.

34 Refitting is a reversal of removal.

High level brake light - Avant models

35 Remove the tailgate trim panel as described in Chapter 11, Section 14.

36 Undo the screws and detach the light unit from the tailgate **(see illustration)**.

37 Unclip the lens from the bulbholder **(see illustration)**.

38 Pull the relevant bulb from the holder **(see illustration)**.

39 Refitting is a reversal of removal.

8 Interior light bulbs - renewal

1 Whenever a bulb is renewed, note the following points:

a) *Disconnect the battery negative lead before starting work (see Section 1).*

b) *Remember that if the light has just been in use, the bulb may be extremely hot.*

c) *Always check the bulb contacts and holder, ensuring that there is clean metal-to-metal contact between the bulb and its live(s) and earth. Clean off any corrosion or dirt before fitting a new bulb.*

d) *Wherever bayonet-type bulbs are fitted,*

ensure that the live contact(s) bear firmly against the bulb contact.

e) *Always ensure that the new bulb is of the correct rating and that it is completely clean before fitting it.*

Interior/reading lights

Front passenger light unit

2 Unclip the lens from the light unit **(see illustration)**.

3 Remove the bulb from its holder. The courtesy light is fitted with a festoon bulb which can be prised from its spring contacts. The map reading lights are equipped with bayonet fit bulbs (depress, twist and withdraw to remove) **(see illustrations)**.

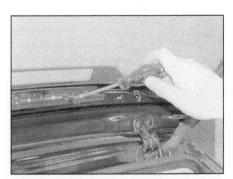

7.36 Undo the screws and detach the light unit from the tailgate

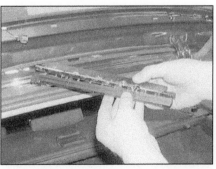

7.37 Unclip the lens from the bulbholder

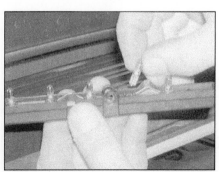

7.38 Pull the relevant bulb from the holder

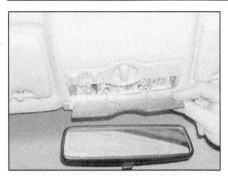

8.2 Unclip the lens from the front passenger light unit

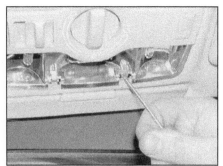

8.3a The courtesy light is fitted with a festoon style bulb

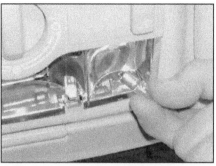

8.3b The map reading lights are equipped with bayonet fit bulbs

4 Refit in the reverse order of removal.

Rear passenger light unit

5 Prise free the light lens/unit, then twist and withdraw the combined bulb and bulbholder **(see illustrations)**.
6 Refit in the reverse order of removal.

Luggage area and glovebox lights

7 Prise free the light lens/unit and extract the festoon bulb from its holder.
8 Refit in the reverse order of removal, and check for satisfactory operation.

Sunvisor/vanity mirror light

9 Prise free the lens from the sunvisor. The festoon bulbs can be extracted from their holders in the visor **(see illustrations)**.

10 Refit in the reverse order of removal.

Instrument panel bulbs

11 Remove the instrument panel as described in Section 10.
12 To remove a bulb, twist the bayonet-fit bulbholder through quarter of a turn and withdraw it carefully **(see illustrations)**. Depending on type, the bulb may be integral with its holder, or it may withdrawn and renewed separately.
13 Refit in the reverse order of removal.

Cigar lighter illumination bulb

14 Open the ashtray, depress the locking tabs and withdraw the ashtray from its housing. Disconnect the wiring plug.
15 Leaving the cigar lighter in the panel, pull

free the bulbholder from the rear of the lighter, and extract the bulb from the holder.
16 Refit in the reverse order of removal.

Switch illumination bulbs

17 Switch illumination bulbs are usually built into the switch itself, and cannot be renewed separately. Refer to Section 6 and remove the switch - bulb renewal should then be self-evident, if it is possible; otherwise, renew the switch.

Heater control panel illumination bulb

18 Remove the heater control panel as described in Chapter 3.
19 Unclip the bezel and light guides from the front of the control panel **(see illustrations)**.

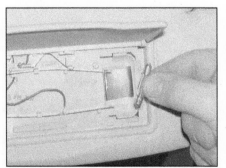

8.5a Prise free the rear passenger lens/light unit . . .

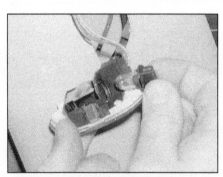

8.5b . . . then twist and withdraw the combined bulb and bulbholder

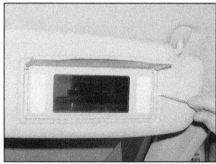

8.9a Prise free the lens from the sunvisor

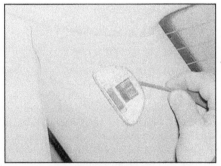

8.9b The festoon bulbs can be extracted from their holders in the visor

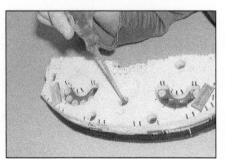

8.12a To remove an instrument panel bulb, twist the bayonet-fit bulbholder through quarter of a turn . . .

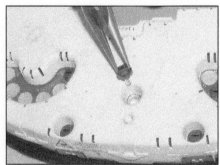

8.12b . . . and withdraw it carefully

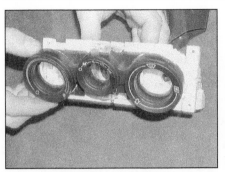

8.19a Unclip the bezel . . .

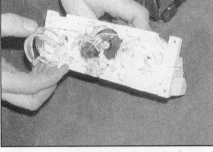

8.19b . . . and light guides from the front of
the heater control panel

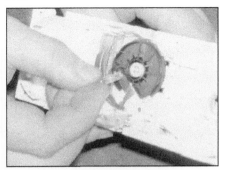

8.20 Pull the bulb from its holder

20 Pull the bulb from its holder **(see illustration)**.
21 Refit in the reverse order of removal.

9 Headlights -
removal, refitting
and beam adjustment

Headlight unit

Removal

1 Unplug the wiring from the rear of the headlamp unit **(see illustration)**.
2 Remove the adjacent direction indicator unit, with reference to Section 7.
3 Slacken and withdraw the headlamp securing bolts - one at the outer lower edge and two along the upper edge at the lock carrier.
4 Slide the headlight unit to the side, to

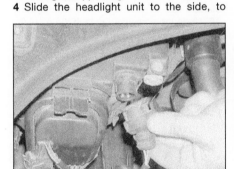

9.1 Unplug the wiring from the rear of the
headlamp unit

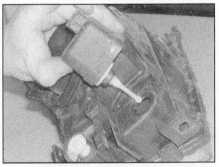

9.9 Withdraw the range control motor
from the headlight unit

disengage the locating peg at the lower inside edge.
5 Lift the headlight slightly, then pivot it forwards and withdraw it from the front of the vehicle **(see illustration)**.

Refitting

6 Refitting is a reversal of the removal procedure. On completion check for satisfactory operation, and have the headlight beam adjustment checked as soon as possible (see below).

Range control motor

Removal

7 Remove the headlight unit as described in the previous sub-Section.
8 Rotate the motor unit (clockwise for the left-hand headlight, anticlockwise for right-hand headlight) until it is felt to disengage from the rear of the headlight unit.

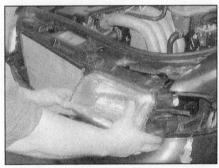

9.5 Withdraw the headlight unit from the
front of the vehicle

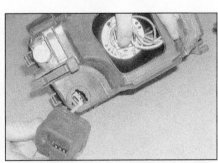

9.10 On refitting, lift the reflector to allow
the adjustment shaft ball joint to engage
with its socket

9 Tilt the unit to one side so that the ball joint at the end of the adjustment shaft disengages from the socket at the of the lens, then withdraw the motor from the headlight unit **(see illustration)**.

Refitting

10 Refitting is a reversal of removal. It may be necessary to lift the reflector to allow the adjustment shaft ball joint to engage with its socket **(see illustration)**. On completion, check for satisfactory operation, and have the headlight beam adjustment checked as soon as possible.

Beam adjustment

Halogen headlamps

11 Accurate adjustment of the headlight beam is only possible using optical beam setting equipment, and this work should therefore be carried out by a VAG dealer or suitably equipped workshop.
12 For reference, the headlights can be adjusted using the adjuster screws, accessible via the top of each light unit **(see illustration)**.
13 Some models are equipped with an electrically operated headlight beam adjustment system which is controlled through the switch in the facia. On these models, ensure that the switch is set to the basic 0 position before adjusting the headlight aim.

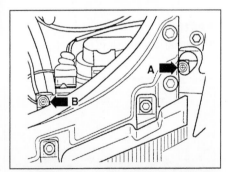

9.12 The headlight basic beam adjustment
can be altered using the adjuster screws,
accessible via the top of each light unit

*A Lateral (Bosch)/vertical (Valeo) adjustment
    screw*
*B Vertical (Bosch)/lateral (Valeo) adjustment
    screw*

10.4 Remove the trim panel from the lower edge of the instrument pack

10.5 Undo the two securing screws at the lower edge of the instrument pack

Electrical discharge headlights

14 The headlamp range is controlled dynamically by an electronic control unit which monitors the ride height of the vehicle via sensors fitted to the front and rear suspension. Beam adjustment can only be carried out using VAG test equipment.

10 Instrument panel - removal and refitting

Removal

1 Disconnect the battery negative lead (refer to Section 1).
2 Remove the steering wheel as described in Chapter 10.
3 Detach the upper section of the steering column trim panel as described at the beginning of Section 5.
4 Remove the trim panel from the lower edge of the instrument pack **(see illustration)**.
5 Undo the two securing screws at the lower edge of the instrument pack **(see illustration)**.
6 Withdraw the instrument pack and unplug the wiring connectors from the rear **(see illustrations)**.
7 Remove the instrument pack from the facia.

Refitting

8 Refitting is a reversal of removal.

10.6a Withdraw the instrument pack from the facia . . .

11 Electrical discharge headlamp system - component removal and refitting

General information

1 Electrical discharge headlamps were available as an optional extra on all A4 models covered in this manual. The headlamps are fitted with discharge bulbs, that produce light by means of an electric arc, rather than by heating a metal filament as in conventional halogen bulbs. The arc is generated by a starter circuit which operates at HT voltages. The intensity of the emitted light means that the headlamp beam has to be controlled dynamically to avoid dazzling other road users. An electronic control unit monitors the vehicle's pitch and overall ride height via sensors mounted on the front and rear suspension and adjusts the beam range accordingly, using the range control motors built into the headlamp units.

 Warning: The discharge bulb starter circuitry operate at extremely high voltages. To avoid the risk of electric shock, ensure that the battery negative cable is disconnected before working on the headlamp units.

Bulb renewal

Headlight main beam and sidelight

2 Main beam headlight and sidelight bulb renewal is the same as that described for

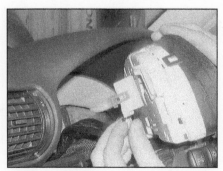

10.6b . . . and unplug the wiring connectors from the rear of the instrument pack

models with conventional headlights (see Section 7).

Headlight dipped beam

3 Ensure that the battery negative cable is disconnected.
4 Unclip the cover panel from the rear of the headlamp unit.
5 Unplug the connector from the rear of the headlight unit by turning the connector 90° anti-clockwise.
6 Turn the retaining ring anti-clockwise, and withdraw the bulb from the headlight unit.
7 Taking care to avoid touching the glass bulb, fit the new bulb, ensuring that the recesses engage with the corresponding tabs on the rear of the light unit.
8 Fit the retaining ring, ensuring that the recesses engage with the corresponding lugs on the rear of the bulb flange, then turn the ring clockwise to lock it in position.
9 Refit the connector and the cover panel, then reconnect the battery.

Starter unit
Removal

10 Ensure that the battery negative cable is disconnected.
11 Unclip the cover panel from the rear of the headlamp unit.
12 Unplug the connector from the rear of the headlight unit.
13 Depress the locking tabs to release the bush, then feed the cable through the starter unit rear cover.
14 Unplug the wiring connector from the starter unit.
15 Undo the screw and detach the mounting bar from the rear of the headlamp unit.
16 Release the starter unit from the head-lamp unit.

Refitting

17 Refitting is a reversal of removal.

Front ride height sensor
Removal

18 The sensor is mounted between the subframe and the front left hand transverse suspension arm.
19 Unplug the wiring connector from the sensor.
20 Compress the tabs with pliers and release the link rod securing clip from the suspension arm.
21 Unscrew the bolts and detach the sensor from its mounting bracket.

Refitting

22 Refitting is a reversal of removal.

Rear ride height sensor
Removal

23 The sensor is mounted between at the centre of the rear axle.
24 Unplug the wiring connector from the sensor.
25 Undo the bolt and release the link rod securing clip from the axle beam.

26 Unscrew the bolts and detach the sensor from its mounting bracket.

Refitting

27 Refitting is a reversal of removal.

Electronic control unit

Removal

28 The electronic control unit is mounted underneath the rear seat bench on the right hand side.

29 Remove the rear seat bench as described in Chapter 11.

30 Open the foam rubber casing and withdraw the control unit. Unplug the wiring connector and remove the unit from the vehicle.

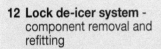

12 Lock de-icer system - component removal and refitting

General information

1 Certain models are fitted with an automatic lock de-icing system. An electronic control unit monitors a switch in the driver's door handle. When the handle is lifted, the unit supplies current to a heating element mounted in the door lock cylinder.

2 The only component that can be renewed separately is the electronic control unit. The heating element is an integral part of the lock cylinder and the switch is integral with the door handle.

3 To remove the control unit, first remove the door trim panel as described in Chapter 11.

4 Unplug the wiring connectors from the control unit then unscrew the securing bolts and remove the unit from the door **(see illustration)**.

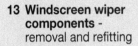

13 Windscreen wiper components - removal and refitting

Wiper blades

1 Refer to *Weekly checks*.

Wiper arms

2 If the wipers are not in their parked position, switch on the ignition, and allow the motor to automatically park.

3 Before removing an arm, mark its parked position on the glass with a strip of adhesive tape. Prise off the cover and unscrew the spindle nut. Remove the washer and ease the arm from the spindle by rocking it slowly from side to side.

4 Refitting is a reversal of removal, but before tightening the spindle nuts, position the wiper blades as marked before removal.

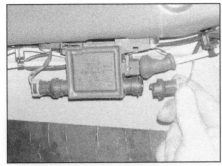

12.4 Unplug the wiring connectors from the door lock de-icer system control unit

Wiper motor

Removal

5 Disconnect the battery negative terminal.

6 Remove the wiper arms as described in the previous sub Section.

7 Unclip the left and right hand sections of the water deflector panel and remove it from behind the engine compartment bulkhead.

8 Slacken and remove the mounting bolts and manoeuvre the wiper motor assembly out of position, disconnecting the wiring connector as it becomes accessible. Recover the spacer which is fitted to the centre mounting.

9 To separate the motor from the linkage, carefully prise the linkage arm off from the motor balljoint then undo the three retaining bolts and remove the motor.

Refitting

10 Refitting is the reverse of removal ensuring the mounting bolts are tightened to the specified torque. Also ensure that the water deflector panel is correctly clipped in position.

14 Washer system - general

1 All models are fitted with a windscreen washer system. Estate models also have a tailgate washer, and some models are fitted with headlight washers.

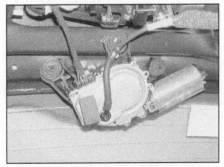

15.5 Tailgate wiper motor mounting plate bolts (arrowed)

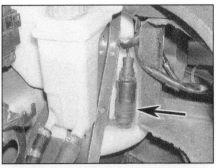

14.2 The windscreen washer fluid pump is attached to the side of the reservoir body

2 The fluid reservoir(s) for the windscreen washer (and where applicable, for the headlight washers) is/are located in the engine compartment on the left-hand side. On some models there is a separate reservoir for the headlamp washers, which is located adjacent to the main windscreen washer reservoir; a connecting pipe allows both reservoirs to be topped-up by a common filler neck. The fluid pump is attached to the side of the reservoir body **(see illustration)**.

3 The tailgate washer fluid reservoir is located behind the trim in the right hand side of the load space. The fluid pump is attached to the side of the reservoir body.

4 The reservoir fluid level must be regularly topped up with windscreen washer fluid containing an antifreeze agent, but not cooling system antifreeze - see *Weekly checks*.

5 The supply hoses are attached by rubber couplings to their various connections, and if required, can be detached by simply pulling them free from the appropriate connector.

6 The washer jets can be cleaned and adjusted using a needle. When adjusted correctly, the jets should be aimed at a point just above the centre of the wiper swept area.

7 The headlight washer jets are best adjusted using the VAG tool, and should therefore be entrusted to a VAG garage to set.

15 Tailgate wiper motor - removal and refitting

1 Disconnect the battery negative lead.

2 Remove the tailgate trim panel as described in Chapter 11, Section 14.

3 Remove the wiper arm and blade as described in Section 13, then unscrew the spindle nut. Remove the nut and washers.

4 Detach the wiring connector from the wiper motor, then disconnect the washer jet hose.

5 Undo the wiper motor mounting plate bolts and remove the wiper motor, complete with the mounting plate, from the tailgate **(see illustration)**.

6 Refit in the reverse order of removal. Refit the wiper arm and blade so that the arm is parked correctly.

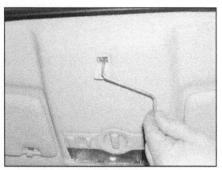

17.2 Insert the emergency cranking tool into the slot in the motor drive, push it upwards, and wind the roof shut by hand

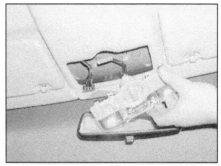

17.4 Remove the screws and lower the interior courtesy/map light unit away from the headlining

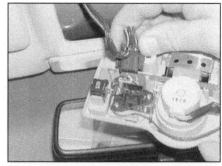

17.5 Unplug the wiring connector from the light unit

16 Horns - removal and refitting

Removal

1 The horns are located at the front end of the vehicle, on the left-hand side between the front bumper and the inner wing. Access to the horns is improved by unclipping and removing the wheel arch liner (see Chapter 11).

2 Disconnect the battery negative lead (see Section 1), then undo the horn unit retaining bolt and disconnect the wiring connector.

Refitting

3 Refit in the reverse order of removal. Check for satisfactory operation on completion.

17 Sunroof motor - removal and refitting

Closing sunroof manually

1 If the motor malfunctions when the roof panel is in the open position, it can be wound shut manually. To do this, prise the cover from the fusebox at the right hand end of the facia and unclip the emergency cranking tool from inside of the cover.

2 Open access hatch in the overhead switch console and insert the cranking tool into the slot in the motor drive, push it upwards, and wind the roof shut by hand **(see illustration)**.

Motor

Removal

3 Ensure that the sunroof is fully closed - refer to paragraphs 1 and 2 if the motor has failed. Disconnect the battery negative lead (refer to Section 1).

4 Remove the lens from the interior courtesy/map light unit (see Section 8). Remove the screws and lower the light unit away from the headlining **(see illustration)**.

5 Unplug the wiring connector from the light unit **(see illustration)**.

6 Remove the securing screws and detach the right and left hand sun visors from the roof. Similarly, remove both roof-mounted front grab handles.

7 Remove the securing screws and unclip the right and left hand trim panels from the B-pillars.

8 Fold down the headlining from the front to expose the sunroof motor.

9 Unplug the wiring connector from the sunroof motor.

10 Unscrew the securing bolt and detach the sunroof motor from its mounting bracket.

Refitting

11 Refit in the reverse order of removal, noting the following points:

a) Smear the drive pinion with a little grease before engaging the motor with the cables.

b) As with removal, it is important that the roof panel be in the closed position to ensure correct engagement. If the motor was activated whilst it was removed, or if a new motor is being fitted, it must be set for correct engagement before fitting. To do this, connect up the switch wiring to it and turn the switch to the closed position. This will activate the motor so that it is set at the closed position, ready for fitting.

c) Use new motor securing bolts and clean the threads of the corresponding mounting holes before refitting.

d) Check for satisfactory operation of the sunroof on completion.

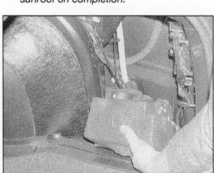

18.5 Withdraw the pump unit from the right-hand side of the luggage compartment

18 Central locking system - general information and component renewal

1 Most models are equipped with a central door locking system, which automatically locks all doors and the rear tailgate/boot lid in unison with the manual locking of either front door. The system is operated by a bi-pressure pump, which supplies vacuum to lock the doors, and pressure to unlock them. Apart from the central locking vacuum units and the bi-pressure pump, the door locks are identical to those on models without central locking - see Chapter 11.

2 Should the system develop a fault, the condition and security of the hoses should first be checked. A leak will cause the bi-pressure pump to run longer than five seconds, and if it runs for thirty-five seconds, an internal control unit will automatically switch it off.

Lock vacuum units

3 Refer to the information given in the relevant door/bootlid/tailgate lock removal sections in Chapter 11.

4 The fuel tank filler flap control is located behind the right-hand side trim panel in the luggage area, and can be removed by detaching the hose to the positioner unit, the flap-to-positioner control rod and the single retaining screw. Refit in the reverse order of removal.

Bi-pressure pump

5 Detach and remove the right-hand side trim in the luggage area. Withdraw the pump unit **(see illustration)**.

6 Remove the pump from its insulation jacket, then detach the wiring connector and the vacuum hoses, and remove the pump **(see illustrations opposite)**.

7 Refit in the reverse order of removal. Check for satisfactory operation of the pump before refitting the insulation and trim panel/floor cover.

18.6a Remove the pump from its insulation jacket . . .

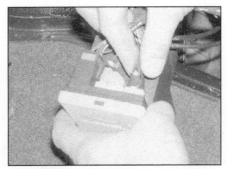

18.6b . . . then detach the wiring connector . . .

18.6c . . . and the vacuum hoses

19 Radio - removal and refitting

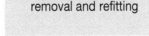

Note: *This Section applies only to standard-fit audio equipment.*

Removal

1 The radio is fitted with special mounting clips, requiring the use of special removal tools, which should be supplied with the vehicle, or may be obtained from an in-car entertainment specialist. Alternatively, it may be possible to make up some removal tools **(see illustration)**.

2 Disconnect the battery negative lead - refer to Section 1.

3 Insert the removal rods in the holes provided on the lower, or upper and lower edges of the radio unit (depending on model).

4 Slide the removal tools fully into the slots until they locate **(see illustration)**.

5 Withdraw the radio from the mounting case, then disconnect the loudspeaker, supply and aerial plugs. Note that some radio units also have a fuse fitted on the rear face.

Refitting

6 Refitting is a reversal of removal, but push the radio fully into its case until the spring clips are engaged. If the radio is of the security code type, it will be necessary to enter the code number before switching on the radio.

20 Radio aerial - removal and refitting

Roof-mounted aerial - Avant models

1 Disconnect the battery negative cable.

2 Prise the load space courtesy light unit from the headlining.

3 Unscrew the aerial mast from its base and prise off the conical cover beneath.

4 Unscrew the securing nut from the aerial base and lift off the seat.

5 Withdraw the aerial base through the headlining into the inside of the vehicle.

6 Slide back the insulation sleeving and unplug the radio coaxial cable from the aerial base. Where applicable, unplug the car phone coaxial and power supply cables from the aerial base.

7 Refitting is a reversal of removal.

Rear- and side-window mounted aerial

8 On all saloon models and some Avant models, the aerial is a ribbon element type, incorporated into the rear window demister element; the top three elements are not heated and form the HF (AM) aerial, the remaining elements are heated and form the VHF (FM) aerial. On higher specification Avant models, a roof mounted aerial is fitted in conjunction with a rear screen aerial and a rear side window ribbon element aerial; a control unit incorporated in the audio system then automatically selects the most suitable aerial for the frequency being received. To improve reception, an amplifier is fitted; this may be fitted under the rear parcel shelf trim, behind the load space side trim, behind the tailgate trim, or behind the D-pillar trim, depending on model and audio system specification. In the event of the element being damaged, repairs or renewal should be referred to a VAG garage or audio specialist.

21 Speakers - removal and refitting

1 The audio system speakers are fitted in the front and rear door trim panels, and in the rear parcel shelf trim panel. On Avant models, an additional sub-woofer is mounted behind the left hand load space trim panel. On all models, separate mid-range and high frequency tweeters are fitted in the front door trim panels.

Door-mounted mid-range speaker

2 To remove a door-mounted mid-range speaker, remove the appropriate door trim as described in Chapter 11. Detach the waterproof membrane from the rear of the trim panel. Undo the retaining screws, detach the wiring connectors and remove the speaker **(see illustration)**.

19.1 Radio removal tools

19.4 Slide the removal tools fully into the slots until they locate

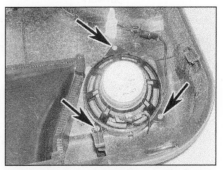

21.2 Undo the retaining screws (arrowed) and remove the door mounted mid-range speaker

21.3a Release the clip . . .

21.3b . . . and remove the speaker from the moulded trim

Door-mounted high frequency (tweeter) speaker

3 Remove the appropriate door trim as described in Chapter 11. Detach the waterproof membrane from the rear of the trim panel, then remove the door inner handle surround. The tweeter speaker is clipped into place - release the clips, unplug the wiring and remove the speaker from the moulded trim **(see illustrations)**.

4 Refit in the reverse order of removal. Note any direction-of-fitting markings on the rear of the speaker.

Rear parcel shelf speakers

5 Remove the rear seat bench and back rest as described in Chapter 11.

6 Detach the cover from the high level brake light as described in Section 7, then unplug the wring and remove the bulbholder.

7 Unbolt the rear seat belt lower anchor points from the bodywork, with reference to Chapter 11. Prise the seat belt height adjuster mechanisms from the rear parcel shelf.

8 Release the press-stud clips and release the parcel shelf from the bodywork. Note the location of the clips at the front lower edge and the securing hook on the underside (visible from the load space) **(see illustrations)**.

9 Undo the securing screws and lift the speakers from their housings. Unplug the wiring as it becomes accessible **(see illustrations)**.

10 Refit in the reverse order of removal. Note any direction-of-fitting markings on the rear of the speaker. Ensure that the new seat belt lower anchor bolts are used and tightened to the correct torque.

Sub-woofer (Avant models)

11 Remove the rear seat back rest and bench as described in Chapter 11.

12 Bend back the locking tabs at the base of the left and right hand rear seat back rest side padded panels, then unhook the upper end of the panels and remove them.

13 Prise off the seal strip from the left hand side of the tailgate aperture.

14 Undo the securing screws and remove the trim panel from the tailgate aperture lower sill.

15 Unclip the left hand rear seat belt trim and remove it from the load space trim panel.

16 Prise out the trim for the seat backrest catch and remove it from the trim panel.

17 Remove the load space tonneau (where fitted).

18 Remove the screws and detach the lashing eyelets from the left hand side of the load space.

19 Remove the securing screws and lift off the left hand load space side trim panel.

20 Undo the securing screws and remove the sub-woofer and its mounting plate from the resonator cavity. Unplug the wiring as It becomes accessible.

21 Refitting is a reversal of removal.

22 Airbag system - general information and precautions

⚠ *Warning: Before carrying out any operations on the airbag system, disconnect the battery negative terminal. When operations are complete, make sure no one is inside the vehicle when the battery is reconnected.*

Note that the airbag(s) must not be subjected to temperatures in excess of 90°C (194°F). When the airbag is removed, ensure that it is stored the correct way up to prevent possible inflation.

Do not allow any solvents or cleaning agents to contact the airbag assemblies. They must be cleaned using only a damp cloth.

The airbags and control unit are both sensitive to impact. If either is dropped or damaged they should be renewed.

Disconnect the airbag control unit wiring plug prior to using arc-welding equipment on the vehicle.

21.8a Release the parcel shelf from the bodywork

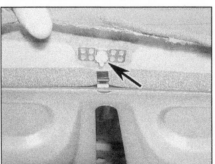

21.8b Note the location of the clips at the front lower edge . . .

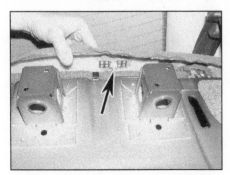

21.8c . . . and the securing hook on the underside (visible from the load space)

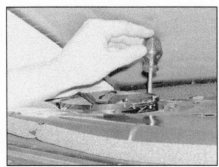

21.9a Undo the securing screws . . .

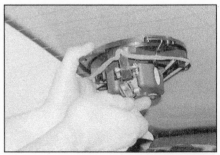

21.9b . . . and lift the speakers from their housings - unplug the wiring as it becomes accessible

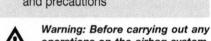

Both a driver's and passenger's airbag were fitted as standard to later models; on other models they were available as an optional extra. The driver's airbag is fitted to the centre of the steering wheel. The passenger's airbag is fitted to the upper surface of the facia, above the glovebox. The airbag system comprises of the airbag unit(s) (complete with gas generators), an impact sensor, the control unit and a warning light in the instrument panel. Seat mounted side air bags are also fitted on certain models, as are seat belt tensioners. These components are incorporated into the same airbag control system, the complexity of the removal and refitting procedures precludes their coverage in this manual.

The airbag system is triggered in the event of a direct or offset frontal impact above a predetermined force. The airbag is inflated within milliseconds, and forms a safety cushion between the driver and the steering wheel or (where applicable) the passenger and the facia. This prevents contact between the upper body and the steering wheel, column and facia, and therefore greatly reduces the risk of injury. The airbag then deflates almost immediately through vents in the side of the airbag.

Every time the ignition is switched on, the airbag control unit performs a self-test. The self-test takes approximately 3 seconds, and during this time the airbag warning light on the facia is illuminated. After the self-test has been completed, the warning light should go out. If the warning light fails to come on, remains illuminated after the initial 3-second period, or comes on at any time when the vehicle is being driven, there is a fault in the airbag system. The vehicle should then be taken to a VAG dealer for examination at the earliest possible opportunity.

23 Airbag system components - removal and refitting

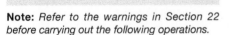

Note: *Refer to the warnings in Section 22 before carrying out the following operations.*

1 Disconnect the battery negative terminal (see Section 1).

Driver's airbag

Note: *New airbag retaining screws will be required on refitting.*
2 If require for improved access, slacken and remove the retaining screws, and remove the steering column upper and lower shrouds.
3 Slacken and remove the two Allen screws from the rear of the steering wheel, rotating the wheel as necessary to gain access to the screws.
4 Return the steering wheel to the straight-ahead position, then carefully lift the airbag assembly away from the steering wheel and disconnect the wiring connector(s) from the rear of the unit. Note that the airbag must not be knocked or dropped, and should be stored the correct way up with its padded surface uppermost.
5 On refitting, reconnect the wiring connector(s) and seat the airbag unit in the steering wheel, making sure the wire does not become trapped. Fit the new retaining screws and tighten them securely. Switch on the ignition, **then** reconnect the battery negative lead.

Passenger airbag

6 Remove the glovebox as described in Chapter 11.
7 Locate the airbag wiring connector, to the left of the airbag unit. Lift the connector out of its mounting bracket, then unplug the two halves of the connector.
8 Slacken and withdraw the securing screws and detach first the lower pair, then the side pair of air bag mounting brackets.
9 Undo the securing screws and remove the airbag unit from the facia. Note that the airbag must not be knocked or dropped, and should be stored the correct way up with its hinged surface uppermost
10 Refitting is a reversal of removal. Fit two new air bag-to-facia screws, and ensure that the wiring connector is securely reconnected and pressed into its mounting bracket to lock it in position.

11 Ensure that no-one is inside the vehicle. Switch on the ignition, **then** reconnect the battery negative lead.

Airbag wiring contact unit

12 Set the front wheels in the straight-ahead position, then remove the steering wheel as described in Chapter 10.
13 Taking care not to rotate the contact unit, undo the retaining screws and remove it from the steering wheel. Note that on some models, the slip ring contact unit is fitted to the front face of the steering column combination switch unit; depress the locking tabs to release the contact unit from switch unit.
14 On refitting, fit the unit to the steering wheel and securely tighten its retaining screws. On models where the contact unit is fitted to the combination switch unit, press the contact unit squarely into place until the locking tabs are felt to engage. If a new contact unit is being fitted, cut the cable-tie which is fitted to prevent the unit accidentally rotating.
15 Refit the steering wheel as described in Chapter 10.

24 Anti-theft alarm system - general information

Later models are fitted with an anti-theft alarm and immobiliser system as standard equipment.

Should the system become faulty, the vehicle should be taken to a VAG dealer for examination. They will have access to a special diagnostic tester which will quickly trace any fault present in the system.

AUDI A4 wiring diagrams 1995 to 1998

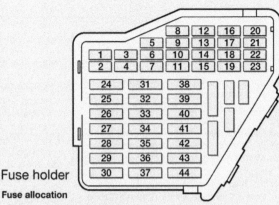

Fuse holder

Index to diagrams

1   Starting and charging
2   M3.2 Motronic fuel injection system (1.6 and 1.8 models)
3   Simos fuel injection system (1.6 models)
4   1.9 diesel direct injection system
5   Automatic gearbox (4-speed)
6   Brake and reversing lights, Headlight range control, Headlights, rear lights, glove box light
7   Foglights, turn signal lights, hazard warning lights
8   Interior lighting, dual tone horn, fresh air blower and heated rear window, cigarette lighter
9   Windscreen wash/wipe, headlight wash, exterior mirrors - heated and adjustable with retractable function
10 Electric windows, anti-lock braking system (front wheel drive)
11 Central locking
12 Instrument panel

*NB diagrams will differ slightly with model year. Diagrams shown are based on model year '96.

Earth locations

E1   In battery box
E2   In rear wiring loom
E3   In front wiring loom
E4   In front right wiring harness
E5   In diesel direct injection wiring loom
E6   In dash panel wiring loom
E7   In auto gearbox wiring harness
E8   In dash panel wiring loom
E9   In rear wiring loom
E10 In rear wiring loom
E11 In RH headlight wiring loom
E12 In LH headlight wiring loom
E13 At RH rear pillar
E14 Behind dash panel, LH side
E15 In Driver's side door wiring loom
E16 In window lifter wiring loom
E17 In alarm system wiring loom
E18 Bottom left 'A' pillar
E19 On hydraulic unit

H31652

Fuse allocation

1	5A	Heated washer jets
2	10A	Turn signals
3	5A	Relay for headlight washers. Lighting for: glove box, engine compartment, air conditioner, automatic gearbox, instrument cluster
4	5A	Number plate light
5	10A	Instrument cluster, seat heating, gearshift display, mirror switch, airbag warning lamp, outside temperature indicator, navigation system, parking aid
6	5A	Central locking
7	10A	Anti-lock brake system
8	5A	Telephone
9	10A	Heated mirrors and door locks
10	5A	Automatic headlight range control
11	5A	Cruise control (automatic gearbox)
12	10A	Power supply, on-board diagnosis
13	10A	Brake lights
14	10A	Interior lights, reading lights, anti-theft alarm, make-up mirror
15	10A	Instrument cluster, automatic gearbox (4-speed), air conditioner, navigation system
16	5A	Anti-lock brake system
17	10A	Heated door locks
18	10A	Main beam headlight, right
19	10A	Main beam headlight, left
20	15A	RH dipped beam headlight, headlight range control
21	15A	LH dipped beam headlight, headlight range control
22	5A	Rear and side lights, right
23	5A	Rear and side lights, left
24	25A	Windscreen wipers, washer pump, intermittent relay
25	30A	Heater blower, air conditioner
26	30A	Heated rear window, heated mirrors, air recirculation
27	-	-
28	15A	Fuel pump
29	20A	Engine management
30	20A	Sunroof
31	15A	Reversing lights, cruise control, automatic gearbox, diagnostic connector
32	20A	Engine management
33	15A	Cigarette lighter
34	15A	Engine management
35	30A	Electrical socket for trailer
36	15A	Front fog lights, rear fog light
37	20A	Telephone, radio
38	15A	Luggage compartment light, central locking
39	15A	Hazard warning lights
40	25A	Horn
41	25A	Anti-lock brake system (hydraulic modulator/pump)
42	40A	Blower
43	5A	S-contact (central locking, radio, navigation system)
44	30A	Seat heating

Wire colours

W White
R Red
Y Yellow
Br Brown
Bl Blue
Gr Grey
G Green
B Black
L Lilac

H31653

Key to items

1 Battery
2 Starter motor
3 Alternator
4 Ignition switch
5 Central electrics
   R4 bridge (manual gearbox) or starter inhibitor (automatic gearbox)
   R6 fuel pump relay or glow plugs relay (diesel)

6 3-point relay carrier (Diesel only)
   D9 fuse for glow plugs
7 13-point relay carrier
   R13 Starter inhibitor and reversing light relay
8 Glow plugs

Diagram 1

Key to symbols

20	Item number
—⊗—	Bulb
—•⁄ •—	Switch
	Multiple contact switch (ganged)
—◦⋈◦—	Fuse/ fusible link
▭	Solenoid actuator
▭	Resistor
▱	Variable resistor
	Internal connection in a component
—◦—	Wire conection, detachable
	Wire connection, fixed
G/Y	Wire colour (green wire with yellow tracer)
	Interconnecting line (thin line)
	Denotes alternative wiring variation
Diagram 5, Arrow B **B** **RH indicator signal**	Connections to other circuits
G102	Earth point with location code
Ⓜ	Pump/motor
	Dashed outline denotes part of a larger item, containing in this case an electronic or solid state device
	Gauge/meter

*   *Only Diesel models*
**   *Only models with automatic gearbox up to January '96*
***   *Only models with automatic gearbox from January '96*
**** *Only models with manual gearbox*

Starting and charging

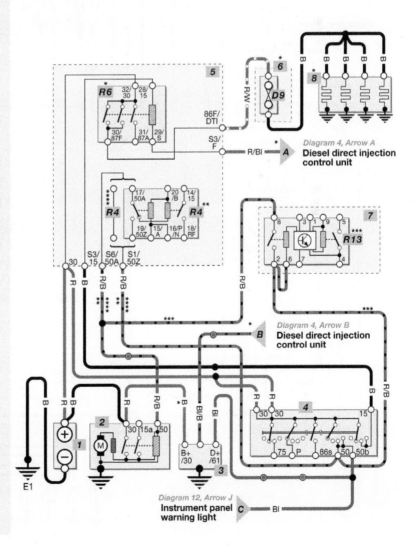

Wire colours

W White
R Red
Y Yellow
Br Brown
Bl Blue
Gr Grey
G Green
B Black
L Lilac

H31654

Key to items

1 Battery
4 Ignition switch
5 Central electrics
  R6 fuel pump relay or glow plugs relay (diesel)
10 Throttle valve control unit
11 Intake air temperature sender
12 Coolant temperature sender
13 Knock sensor 2
14 Knock sensor 1

15 Hall sender
16 Motronic control unit
17 Fuel pump
18 Air mass meter
19 Charcoal filter system solenoid
20 Lambda probe and heater
21 Injector, cylinder 1
22 Injector, cylinder 2
23 Injector, cylinder 3
24 Injector, cylinder 4

25 Engine speed sender
26 Fuse holder
27 Spark plugs
28 Ignition coil unit

*   Only on models with automatic gearbox
**   Only on models with air conditioning
*** Only on models with auto check system
**** Only on models without air conditioning

Diagram 2

**Typical M3.2 Motronic fuel injection system
(1.6 and 1.8 models)**

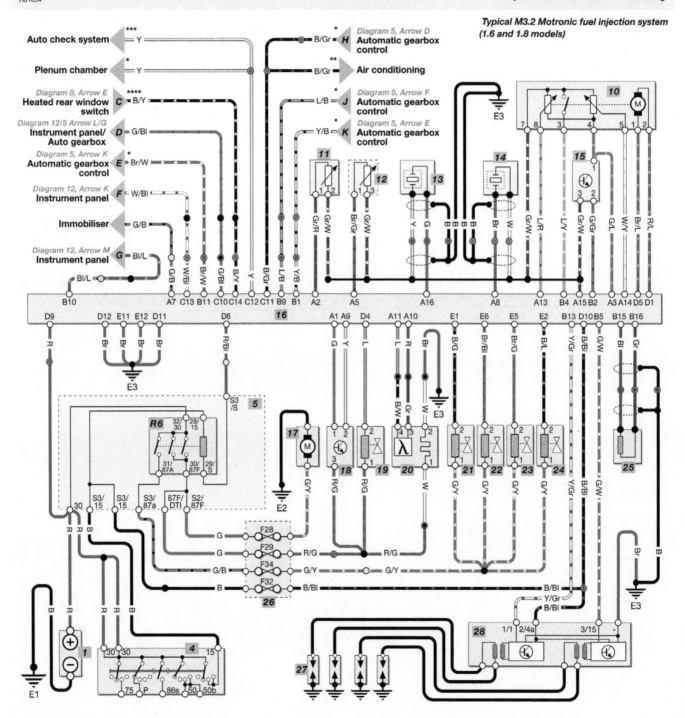

Wire colours

W White
R Red
Y Yellow
Br Brown
Bl Blue
Gr Grey
G Green
B Black
L Lilac

H31655

Key to items

1 Battery
4 Ignition switch
5 Central electrics
   R6 fuel pump relay or glow plugs relay (diesel)
10 Throttle valve control unit
11 Temperature sender
12 Coolant temperature sender
14 Knock sensor 1
15 Hall sender
16 Simos control unit
17 Fuel pump
18 Air mass meter
19 Charcoal filter system solenoid
20 Lambda probe and heater
21 Injector, cylinder 1
22 Injector, cylinder 2
23 Injector, cylinder 3
24 Injector, cylinder 4
25 Engine speed sender
26 Fuse holder
27 Spark plugs
28 Ignition coil unit

*   Only on models with automatic gearbox
**   Only on models with air conditioning
*** Only on models with auto check system
**** Only on models without air conditioning

Diagram 3

Typical Simos fuel injection system (1.6 models)

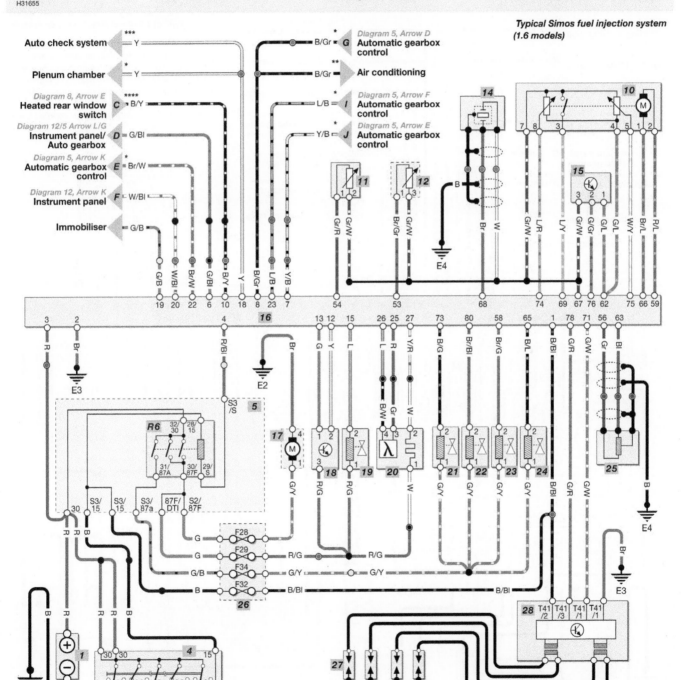

Wire colours

- **W** White
- **R** Red
- **Y** Yellow
- **Br** Brown
- **Bl** Blue
- **Gr** Grey
- **G** Green
- **B** Black
- **L** Lilac

H31656

Key to items

- **1** Battery
- **4** Ignition switch
- **5** Central electrics
- **6** 3-point relay carrier (diesel only)
  - **D1** high heater output relay
  - **D2** low heater output relay
  - **D3** direct injection system relay
  - **D6** engine electronics fuse
  - **D7** heater fuse 1
  - **D8** heater fuse 2
- **10** Throttle valve control unit
- **11** Temperature sender
- **12** Coolant temperature sender
- **16** Diesel injection control unit
- **18** Air mass meter
- **25** Engine speed sender
- **30** Throttle position sender & idle switch
- **31** EGR valve
- **32** Boost pressure control valve
- **33** Brake pedal switch
- **34** Clutch pedal switch
- **35** Heating elements (coolant)
- **36** Quantity adjuster
- **37** Needle lift sender

Diagram 4

Typical 1.9 diesel direct injection system

- ***** Only on models with automatic gearbox
- ****** Only on models with air conditioning
- ******* Only on models with auto check system
- ******** Only on models with 81kW TDI engine
- **#** Only on models with manual gearbox
- **##** Only on models with 66kW TDI engine
- **###** Only on models without air conditioning

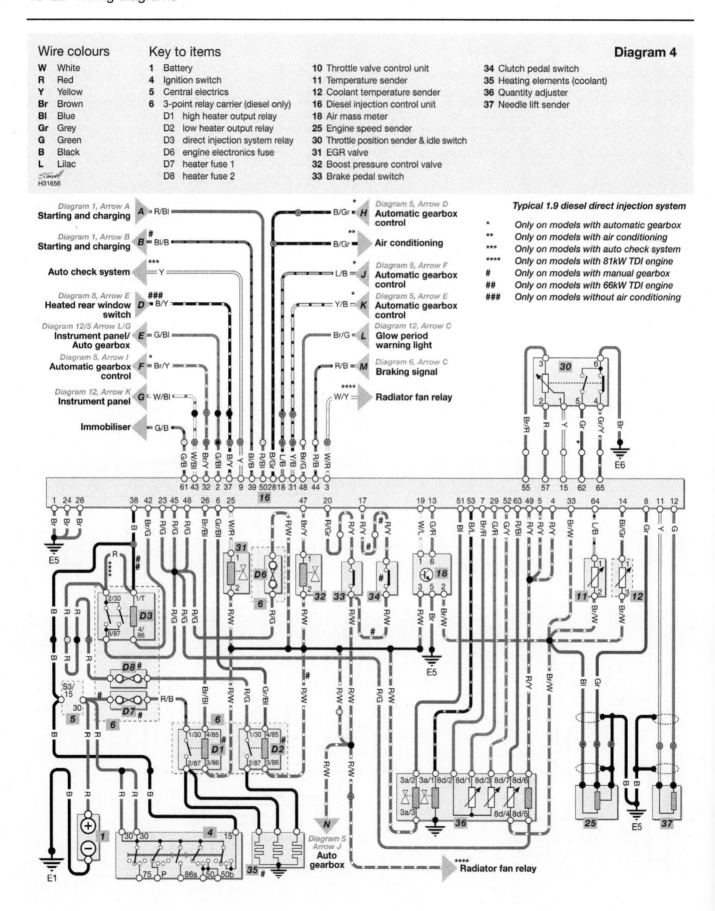

Wire colours

W White
R Red
Y Yellow
Br Brown
Bl Blue
Gr Grey
G Green
B Black
L Lilac

H31657

Key to items

1 Battery
4 Ignition switch
5 Central electrics
　R4　starter inhibitor and
　　　reversing light relay
7 13-point relay carrier
　R13 starter inhibitor and
　　　reversing light relay
10 Throttle valve control unit
26 Fuse holder

40 Kick down switch
41 Gearbox oil temp. sender and
　　solenoid valves 1 to 7
42 Multi function switch
43 Automatic gearbox control unit
44 Selector lever lock solenoid
45 Gear selector light bulb
46 Diagnostic connection
47 Gearbox speed sender
48 Road speed sender

* Only on models up to January '96
** Only on models from January '96
*** Only on 1.9TDI models
**** Only on 1.6/1.8 petrol engine models
\# Only on 1.6/1.8 models with cruise control
\#\# Only on 1.9 TDI models with cruise control

Diagram 5

Typical 4 speed automatic gearbox (type 01N)

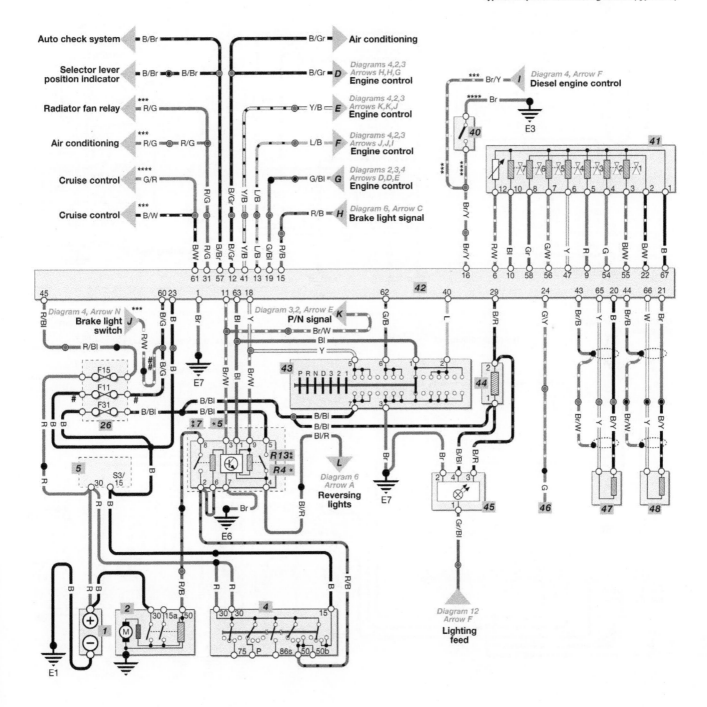

Wire colours

W	White
R	Red
Y	Yellow
Br	Brown
Bl	Blue
Gr	Grey
G	Green
B	Black
L	Lilac

H31658

Key to items

1	Battery
4	Ignition switch
5	Central electrics
26	Fuse holder
50	Lighting switch
51	Glove box light
52	Number plate light
53	LH headlight unit
54	RH headlight unit
55	LH rear light cluster
56	RH rear light cluster
57	Left beam control motor
58	Right beam control motor
59	Headlight range adjuster
60	Brake light switch
61	Reversing light switch
62	High level brake light

Diagram 6

*	Only on models with manual gearbox
**	Only on models from March '96
***	Only on models with atomatic gearbox

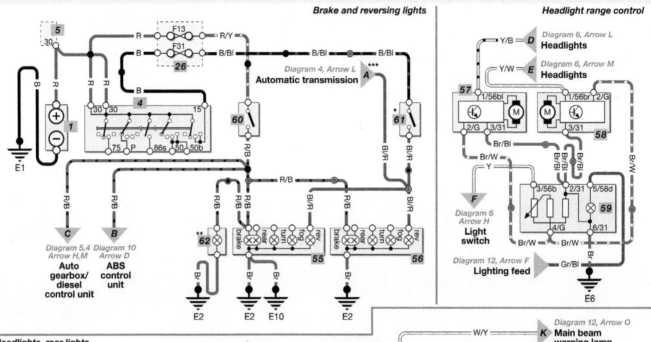

Brake and reversing lights

Headlight range control

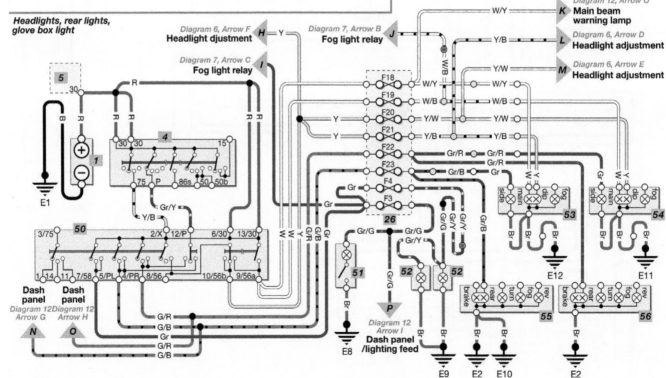

Headlights, rear lights, glove box light

Wire colours

W White
R Red
Y Yellow
Br Brown
Bl Blue
Gr Grey
G Green
B Black
L Lilac

H31659

Key to items

1 Battery
4 Ignition switch
5 Central electrics
   R1 'X' contact relay
7 13-point relay carrier
   R10 fog lights relay
26 Fuse holder
50 Lighting switch
53 LH headlight unit
54 RH headlight unit

55 LH rear light cluster
56 RH rear light cluster
65 Fog light switch
66 Rear fog light switch
67 Turn signal switch
68 Hazard lights switch and relay
69 LH side turn signal
70 RH side turn signal

Diagram 7

Foglights

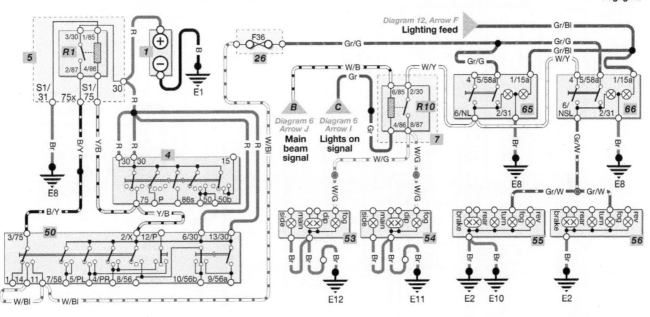

Turn signal lights, hazard warning lights

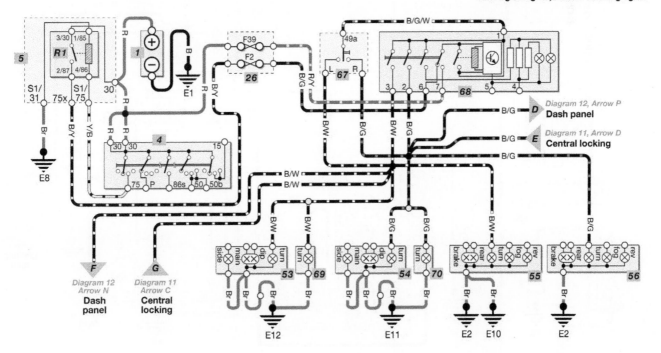

Wire colours

W   White
R   Red
Y   Yellow
Br Brown
Bl Blue
Gr Grey
G   Green
B   Black
L   Lilac

H31660

Key to items

1   Battery
4   Ignition switch
5   Central electrics
    R1 'X' contact relay
    R2 dual tone horn relay
26 Fuse holder
71 Boot light
72 Interior light, front
73 Boot light switch
74 Rear LH reading light

75 Rear RH reading light
76 Driver side illuminated mirror
77 Passenger side illuminated mirror
78 High tone horn
79 Low tone horn
80 Horn control
81 Cigarette lighter
82 Heated rear window switch
83 Series resistance for fresh air
    blower with fuse

84 Fresh air blower
85 Heated rear window
86 Fresh air blower switch

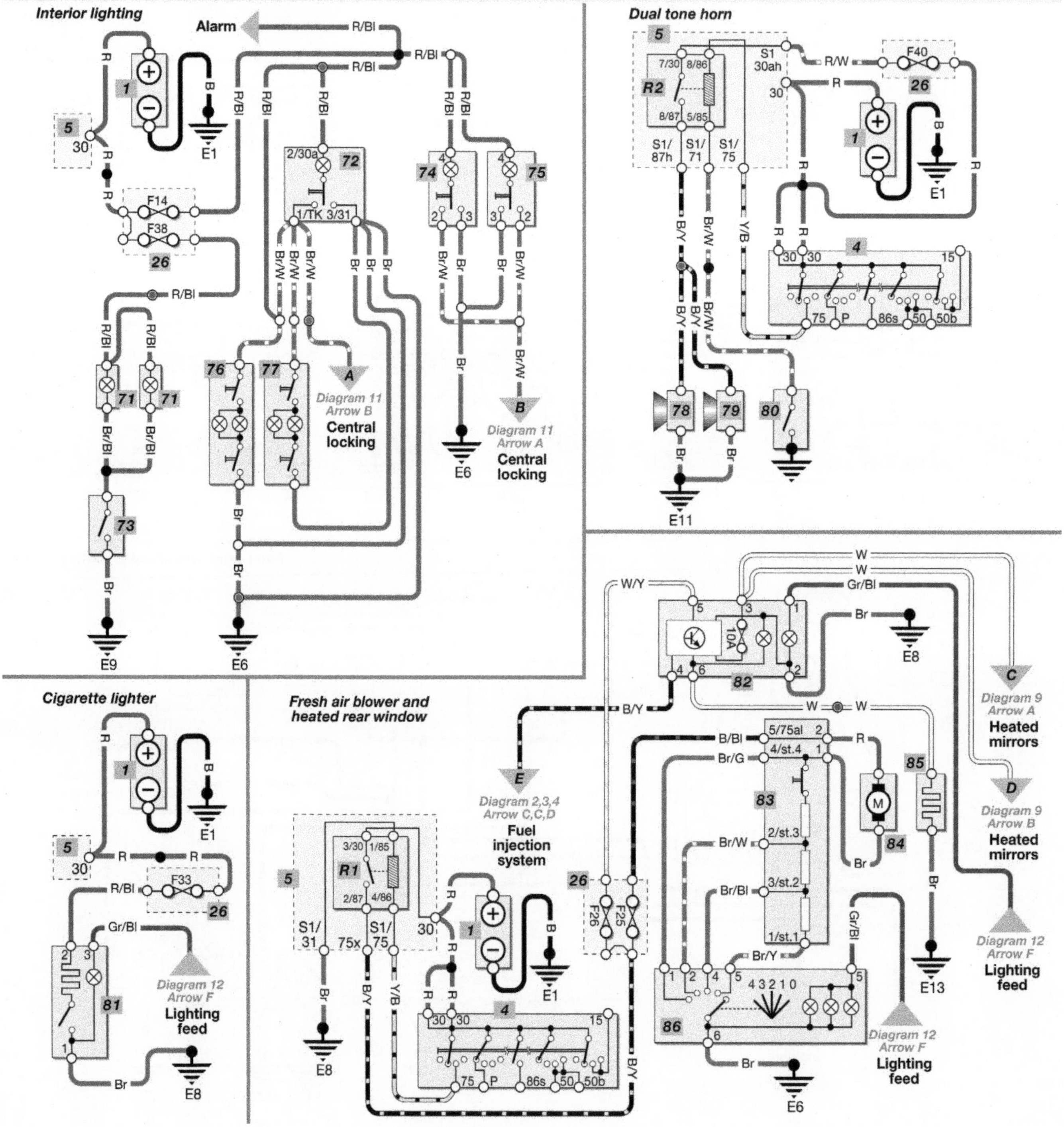

Diagram 8

Interior lighting

Dual tone horn

Cigarette lighter

Fresh air blower and heated rear window

Fuel injection system

Heated mirrors

Lighting feed

Diagram 9

Wire colours

W	White
R	Red
Y	Yellow
Br	Brown
Bl	Blue
Gr	Grey
G	Green
B	Black
L	Lilac

H31661

Key to items

1 Battery
4 Ignition switch
5 Central electrics
   R1 'X' contact relay
   R3 headlight washer relay
   R5 intermittent wipe relay
26 Fuse holder
90 Folding mirror control unit
91 Mirror adjustment switch
92 Driver side mirror heating and adjustment motors
93 Passenger side mirror heating and adjustment motors
94 Headlight washer pump
95 Wiper switch
96 Windscreen washer pump
97 Heater, RH washer jet
98 Heater, LH washer jet
99 Windscreen wiper motor

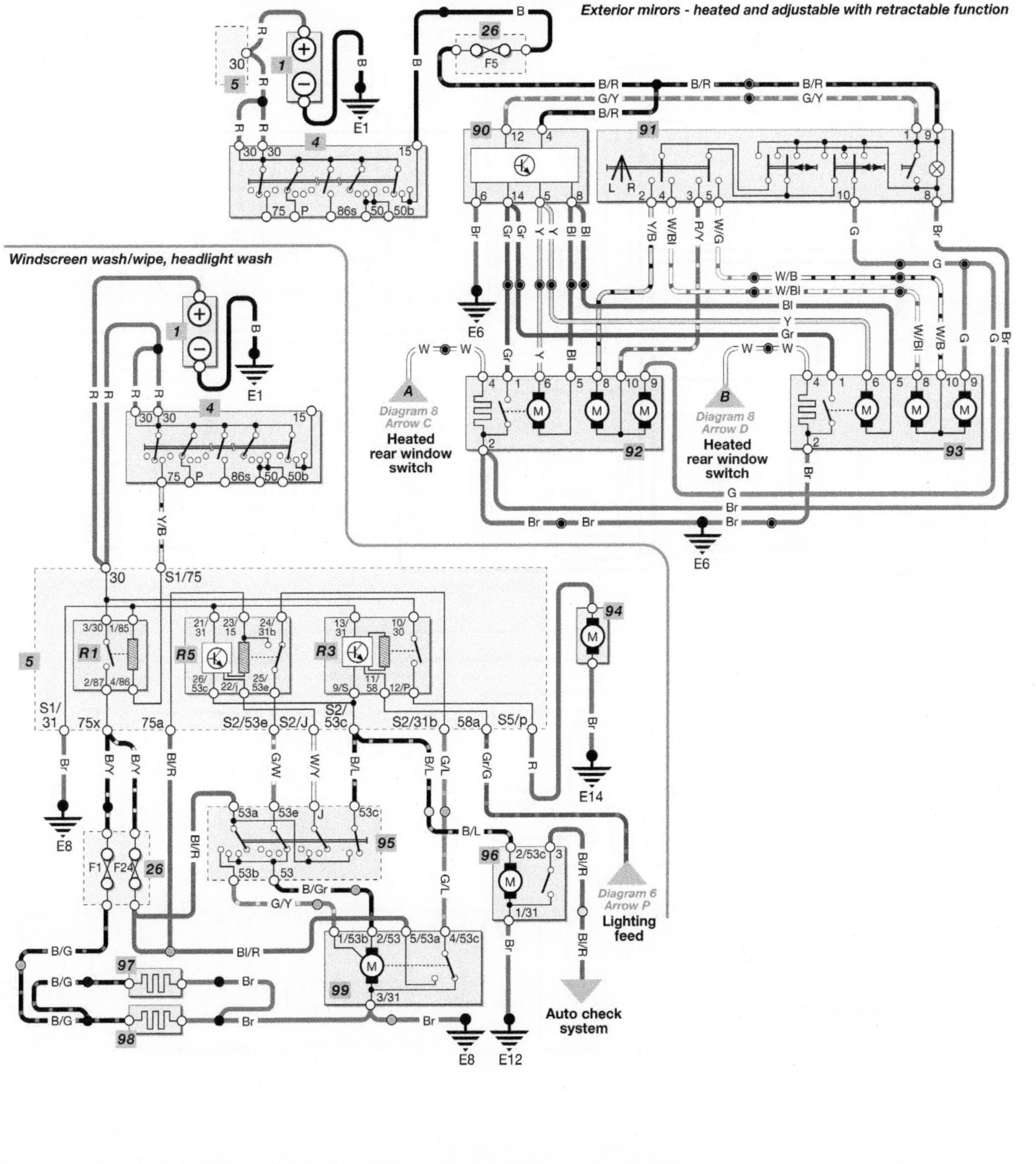
Exterior mirors - heated and adjustable with retractable function
Windscreen wash/wipe, headlight wash
Diagram 8
Arrow C
Heated rear window switch
Diagram 8
Arrow D
Heated rear window switch
Diagram 6
Arrow P
Lighting feed
Auto check system
E1
E6
E8
E12
E14
F5
F1
F24

Wire colours

W	White
R	Red
Y	Yellow
Br	Brown
Bl	Blue
Gr	Grey
G	Green
B	Black
L	Lilac

H31662

Key to items

1	Battery
4	Ignition switch
5	Central electrics
26	Fuse holder
100	Electric window control unit (* in driver's door)
101	Front RH window switch *
102	Rear LH window switch *
103	Rear RH window switch *
104	Rear window isolation switch
105	Front LH window switch *
106	Front RH window switch
107	Rear LH window switch
108	Rear RH window switch
109	Front LH window motor
110	Front RH window motor
111	Rear LH window motor
112	Rear RH window motor
113	Fuse for rear windows (30A)
114	Fuse for front windows (30A)
150	ABS hydraulic pump fuse (50A)
151	ABS hydraulic unit
152	Traction control switch
153	Traction control warning lamp
154	Control unit for ABS with EDL
155	Rear RH wheel speed sensor
156	Front RH wheel speed sensor
157	Rear LH wheel speed sensor
158	Front LH wheel speed sensor

Diagram 10

Electric windows

Anti-lock braking system

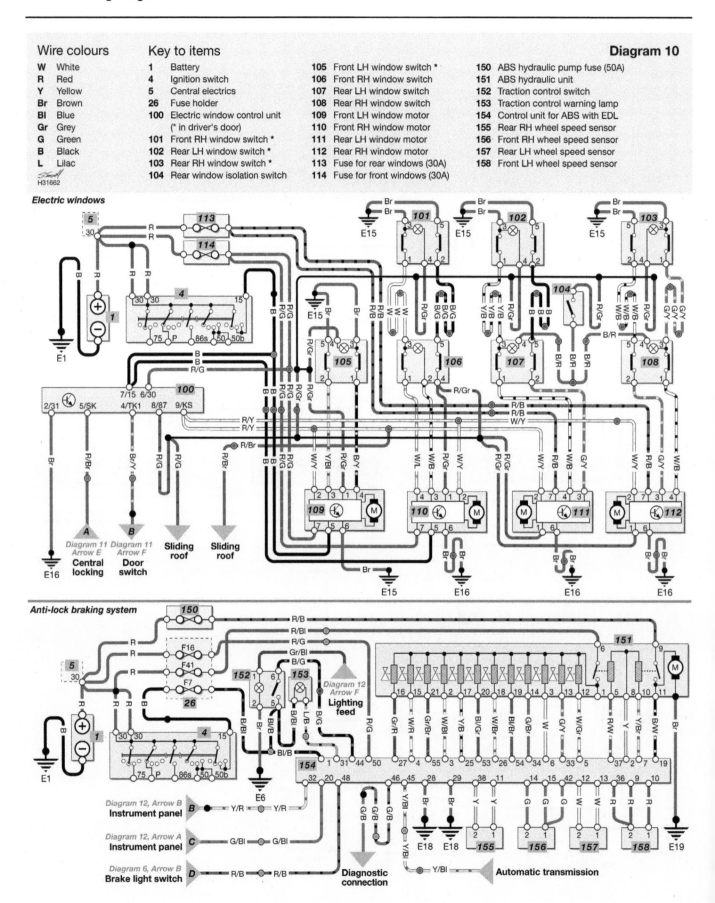

Wire colours

W White
R Red
Y Yellow
Br Brown
Bl Blue
Gr Grey
G Green
B Black
L Lilac

H31663

Key to items

1 Battery
4 Ignition switch
5 Central electrics
26 Fuse holder
120 Alarm and immobiliser fuse (15A)
121 Alarm system warning lamp
122 Ultra-sonic sensor control unit
123 Interior monitor switch
124 LH ultra-sonic sensor
125 RH ultra-sonic sensor

126 Motor for central locking, with control unit for interior lights switch off delay and anti theft system
127 Central locking and door contact switch (driver side)
128 Central locking and door contact switch (passenger side)
129 Rear LH door contact switch
130 Rear RH door contact switch
131 Lock cylinder contact switch

132 Door handle switch for alarm (driver side)
133 Door handle switch for alarm (passenger side)
134 Contact switch in tailgate
135 LH infrared sensor (central locking)
136 RH infrared sensor (central locking)
137 Horn for alarm system
138 Contact switch for alarm system

Diagram 11

Central locking system and interior lights switch-off delay

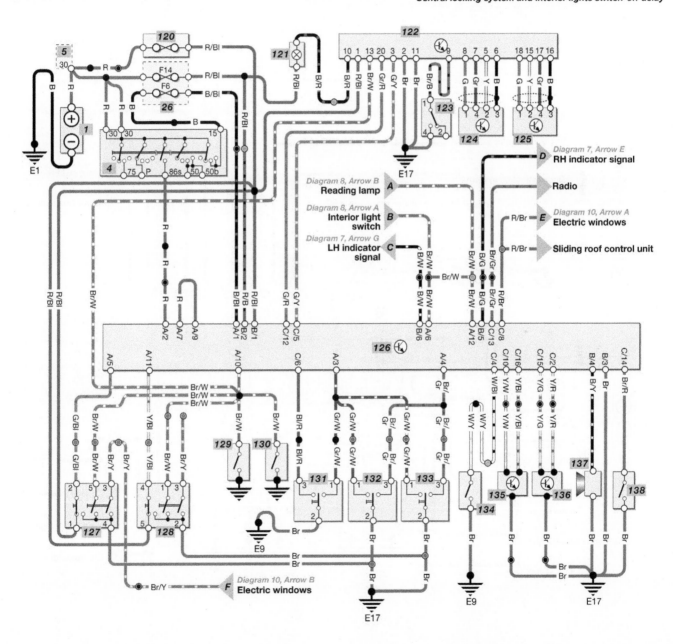

Wire colours

W	White
R	Red
Y	Yellow
Br	Brown
Bl	Blue
Gr	Grey
G	Green
B	Black
L	Lilac

S....ll
H31664

Key to items

1	Battery
4	Ignition switch
5	Central electrics
26	Fuse holder
140	Instrument Cluster
a	Analogue clock
b	Buzzer
d	Fuel gauge
e	Coolant temp. gauge
f	Tachometer

g	Oil temp. gauge
h	Speedometer
i	Charge warning lamp
j	Handbrake warning lamp
k	ABS warning lamp
l	Airbag warning lamp
n	Glow period lamp
o	Immobiliser warning lamp
p	RH turn signal
q	Main beam warning lamp

r	LH turn signal
141	Oil pressure switch
142	Oil temp. sender
143	Coolant level switch
144	Fuel level sender
145	Road speed sender
146	Coolant temp. sender
147	Handbrake switch

Diagram 12

Instrument panel

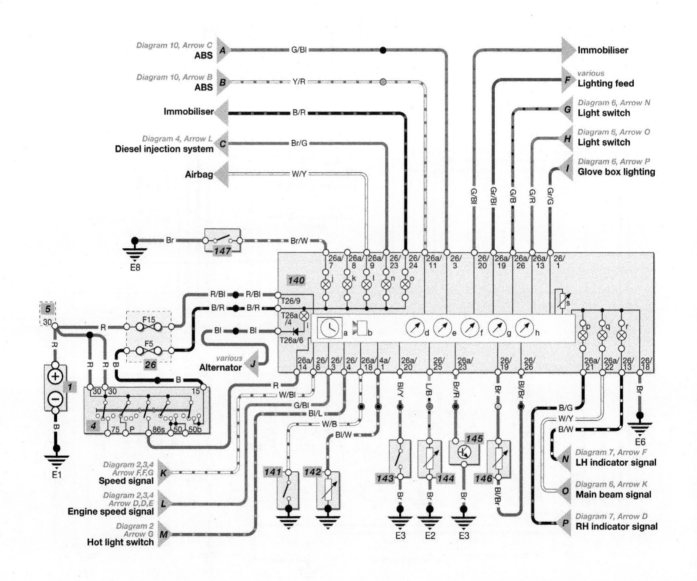

Dimensions and weights

Note: *All figures are approximate, and may vary according to model. Refer to manufacturer's data for exact figures.*

Dimensions
Overall length . . . . 4479 mm
Overall width . . . . 1733 mm
Overall height (unladen) . . . . 1415 mm
Turning circle . . . . 11.1 m

Weights
Kerb weight:
  Petrol engine models:
    1.6 litre . . . . 1185 kg (manual) or 1205 kg (automatic)
    1.8 litre . . . . 1220 kg (manual) or 1240 kg (automatic)
  Diesel engine models . . . . 1240 kg (manual) or 1260 kg (automatic)
Maximum towing weight:
  Trailer without brakes . . . . 630 to 690 kg
  Trailer with brakes . . . . 1350 to 1600 kg
Maximum roof rack load . . . . 75 kg

Conversion factors

Length (distance)

Inches (in)	x 25.4	= Millimetres (mm)	x 0.0394	= Inches (in)
Feet (ft)	x 0.305	= Metres (m)	x 3.281	= Feet (ft)
Miles	x 1.609	= Kilometres (km)	x 0.621	= Miles

Volume (capacity)

Cubic inches (cu in; in³)	x 16.387	= Cubic centimetres (cc; cm³)	x 0.061	= Cubic inches (cu in; in³)
Imperial pints (Imp pt)	x 0.568	= Litres (l)	x 1.76	= Imperial pints (Imp pt)
Imperial quarts (Imp qt)	x 1.137	= Litres (l)	x 0.88	= Imperial quarts (Imp qt)
Imperial quarts (Imp qt)	x 1.201	= US quarts (US qt)	x 0.833	= Imperial quarts (Imp qt)
US quarts (US qt)	x 0.946	= Litres (l)	x 1.057	= US quarts (US qt)
Imperial gallons (Imp gal)	x 4.546	= Litres (l)	x 0.22	= Imperial gallons (Imp gal)
Imperial gallons (Imp gal)	x 1.201	= US gallons (US gal)	x 0.833	= Imperial gallons (Imp gal)
US gallons (US gal)	x 3.785	= Litres (l)	x 0.264	= US gallons (US gal)

Mass (weight)

Ounces (oz)	x 28.35	= Grams (g)	x 0.035	= Ounces (oz)
Pounds (lb)	x 0.454	= Kilograms (kg)	x 2.205	= Pounds (lb)

Force

Ounces-force (ozf; oz)	x 0.278	= Newtons (N)	x 3.6	= Ounces-force (ozf; oz)
Pounds-force (lbf; lb)	x 4.448	= Newtons (N)	x 0.225	= Pounds-force (lbf; lb)
Newtons (N)	x 0.1	= Kilograms-force (kgf; kg)	x 9.81	= Newtons (N)

Pressure

Pounds-force per square inch (psi; lbf/in²; lb/in²)	x 0.070	= Kilograms-force per square centimetre (kgf/cm²; kg/cm²)	x 14.223	= Pounds-force per square inch (psi; lbf/in²; lb/in²)
Pounds-force per square inch (psi; lbf/in²; lb/in²)	x 0.068	= Atmospheres (atm)	x 14.696	= Pounds-force per square inch (psi; lbf/in²; lb/in²)
Pounds-force per square inch (psi; lbf/in²; lb/in²)	x 0.069	= Bars	x 14.5	= Pounds-force per square inch (psi; lbf/in²; lb/in²)
Pounds-force per square inch (psi; lbf/in²; lb/in²)	x 6.895	= Kilopascals (kPa)	x 0.145	= Pounds-force per square inch (psi; lbf/in²; lb/in²)
Kilopascals (kPa)	x 0.01	= Kilograms-force per square centimetre (kgf/cm²; kg/cm²)	x 98.1	= Kilopascals (kPa)
Millibar (mbar)	x 100	= Pascals (Pa)	x 0.01	= Millibar (mbar)
Millibar (mbar)	x 0.0145	= Pounds-force per square inch (psi; lbf/in²; lb/in²)	x 68.947	= Millibar (mbar)
Millibar (mbar)	x 0.75	= Millimetres of mercury (mmHg)	x 1.333	= Millibar (mbar)
Millibar (mbar)	x 0.401	= Inches of water (inH$_2$O)	x 2.491	= Millibar (mbar)
Millimetres of mercury (mmHg)	x 0.535	= Inches of water (inH$_2$O)	x 1.868	= Millimetres of mercury (mmHg)
Inches of water (inH$_2$O)	x 0.036	= Pounds-force per square inch (psi; lbf/in²; lb/in²)	x 27.68	= Inches of water (inH$_2$O)

Torque (moment of force)

Pounds-force inches (lbf in; lb in)	x 1.152	= Kilograms-force centimetre (kgf cm; kg cm)	x 0.868	= Pounds-force inches (lbf in; lb in)
Pounds-force inches (lbf in; lb in)	x 0.113	= Newton metres (Nm)	x 8.85	= Pounds-force inches (lbf in; lb in)
Pounds-force inches (lbf in; lb in)	x 0.083	= Pounds-force feet (lbf ft; lb ft)	x 12	= Pounds-force inches (lbf in; lb in)
Pounds-force feet (lbf ft; lb ft)	x 0.138	= Kilograms-force metres (kgf m; kg m)	x 7.233	= Pounds-force feet (lbf ft; lb ft)
Pounds-force feet (lbf ft; lb ft)	x 1.356	= Newton metres (Nm)	x 0.738	= Pounds-force feet (lbf ft; lb ft)
Newton metres (Nm)	x 0.102	= Kilograms-force metres (kgf m; kg m)	x 9.804	= Newton metres (Nm)

Power

Horsepower (hp)	x 745.7	= Watts (W)	x 0.0013	= Horsepower (hp)

Velocity (speed)

Miles per hour (miles/hr; mph)	x 1.609	= Kilometres per hour (km/hr; kph)	x 0.621	= Miles per hour (miles/hr; mph)

Fuel consumption*

Miles per gallon, Imperial (mpg)	x 0.354	= Kilometres per litre (km/l)	x 2.825	= Miles per gallon, Imperial (mpg)
Miles per gallon, US (mpg)	x 0.425	= Kilometres per litre (km/l)	x 2.352	= Miles per gallon, US (mpg)

Temperature

Degrees Fahrenheit = (°C x 1.8) + 32   Degrees Celsius (Degrees Centigrade; °C) = (°F - 32) x 0.56

It is common practice to convert from miles per gallon (mpg) to litres/100 kilometres (l/100km), where mpg x l/100 km = 282

Spare parts are available from many sources, including maker's appointed garages, accessory shops, and motor factors. To be sure of obtaining the correct parts, it will sometimes be necessary to quote the vehicle identification number. If possible, it can also be useful to take the old parts along for positive identification. Items such as starter motors and alternators may be available under a service exchange scheme - any parts returned should be clean.

Our advice regarding spare parts is as follows.

Officially appointed garages

This is the best source of parts which are peculiar to your car, and which are not otherwise generally available (eg, badges, interior trim, certain body panels, etc). It is also the only place at which you should buy parts if the vehicle is still under warranty.

Accessory shops

These are very good places to buy materials and components needed for the maintenance of your car (oil, air and fuel filters, light bulbs, drivebelts, greases, brake pads, touch-up paint, etc). Components of this nature sold by a reputable shop are of the same standard as those used by the car manufacturer.

Besides components, these shops also sell tools and general accessories, usually have convenient opening hours, charge lower prices, and can often be found close to home. Some accessory shops have parts counters where components needed for almost any repair job can be purchased or ordered.

Motor factors

Good factors will stock all the more important components which wear out comparatively quickly, and can sometimes supply individual components needed for the overhaul of a larger assembly (eg, brake seals and hydraulic parts, bearing shells, pistons, valves). They may also handle work such as cylinder block reboring, crankshaft regrinding, etc.

Tyre and exhaust specialists

These outlets may be independent, or members of a local or national chain. They frequently offer competitive prices when compared with a main dealer or local garage, but it will pay to obtain several quotes before making a decision. When researching prices, also ask what extras may be added - for instance fitting a new valve and balancing the wheel are both commonly charged on top of the price of a new tyre.

Other sources

Beware of parts or materials obtained from market stalls, car boot sales or similar outlets. Such items are not invariably sub-standard, but there is little chance of compensation if they do prove unsatisfactory. In the case of safety-critical components such as brake pads, there is the risk not only of financial loss, but also of an accident causing injury or death.

Second-hand components or assemblies obtained from a car breaker can be a good buy in some circumstances, but this sort of purchase is best made by the experienced DIY mechanic.

Vehicle identification numbers

Modifications are a continuing and unpublicised process in vehicle manufacture, quite apart from major model changes. Spare parts manuals and lists are compiled upon a numerical basis, the individual vehicle identification numbers being essential to correct identification of the component concerned.

When ordering spare parts, always give as much information as possible. Quote the car model, year of manufacture, body and engine numbers as appropriate.

The *vehicle identification plate* is situated at the rear of the engine compartment (see illustration). A further *vehicle identification sticker* is located under the rear luggage compartment floor covering (see illustration). The *vehicle identification number* is also repeated in the form of stamped numbers on the engine compartment rear panel (see illustration).

The *engine number* is stamped on the left-hand side of the cylinder block.

Other identification numbers or codes are stamped on major items such as the gearbox, etc. These numbers are unlikely to be needed by the home mechanic.

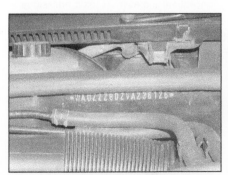

The *Vehicle Identification Number (VIN)* is situated at the rear of the engine compartment

A *vehicle identification sticker*, which includes the *engine code*, is located under the boot floor

The *vehicle identification number* is also repeated in the form of stamped numbers on the engine compartment rear panel

Whenever servicing, repair or overhaul work is carried out on the car or its components, observe the following procedures and instructions. This will assist in carrying out the operation efficiently and to a professional standard of workmanship.

Joint mating faces and gaskets

When separating components at their mating faces, never insert screwdrivers or similar implements into the joint between the faces in order to prise them apart. This can cause severe damage which results in oil leaks, coolant leaks, etc upon reassembly. Separation is usually achieved by tapping along the joint with a soft-faced hammer in order to break the seal. However, note that this method may not be suitable where dowels are used for component location.

Where a gasket is used between the mating faces of two components, a new one must be fitted on reassembly; fit it dry unless otherwise stated in the repair procedure. Make sure that the mating faces are clean and dry, with all traces of old gasket removed. When cleaning a joint face, use a tool which is unlikely to score or damage the face, and remove any burrs or nicks with an oilstone or fine file.

Make sure that tapped holes are cleaned with a pipe cleaner, and keep them free of jointing compound, if this is being used, unless specifically instructed otherwise.

Ensure that all orifices, channels or pipes are clear, and blow through them, preferably using compressed air.

Oil seals

Oil seals can be removed by levering them out with a wide flat-bladed screwdriver or similar implement. Alternatively, a number of self-tapping screws may be screwed into the seal, and these used as a purchase for pliers or some similar device in order to pull the seal free.

Whenever an oil seal is removed from its working location, either individually or as part of an assembly, it should be renewed.

The very fine sealing lip of the seal is easily damaged, and will not seal if the surface it contacts is not completely clean and free from scratches, nicks or grooves. If the original sealing surface of the component cannot be restored, and the manufacturer has not made provision for slight relocation of the seal relative to the sealing surface, the component should be renewed.

Protect the lips of the seal from any surface which may damage them in the course of fitting. Use tape or a conical sleeve where possible. Lubricate the seal lips with oil before fitting and, on dual-lipped seals, fill the space between the lips with grease.

Unless otherwise stated, oil seals must be fitted with their sealing lips toward the lubricant to be sealed.

Use a tubular drift or block of wood of the appropriate size to install the seal and, if the seal housing is shouldered, drive the seal down to the shoulder. If the seal housing is unshouldered, the seal should be fitted with its face flush with the housing top face (unless otherwise instructed).

Screw threads and fastenings

Seized nuts, bolts and screws are quite a common occurrence where corrosion has set in, and the use of penetrating oil or releasing fluid will often overcome this problem if the offending item is soaked for a while before attempting to release it. The use of an impact driver may also provide a means of releasing such stubborn fastening devices, when used in conjunction with the appropriate screwdriver bit or socket. If none of these methods works, it may be necessary to resort to the careful application of heat, or the use of a hacksaw or nut splitter device.

Studs are usually removed by locking two nuts together on the threaded part, and then using a spanner on the lower nut to unscrew the stud. Studs or bolts which have broken off below the surface of the component in which they are mounted can sometimes be removed using a stud extractor. Always ensure that a blind tapped hole is completely free from oil, grease, water or other fluid before installing the bolt or stud. Failure to do this could cause the housing to crack due to the hydraulic action of the bolt or stud as it is screwed in.

When tightening a castellated nut to accept a split pin, tighten the nut to the specified torque, where applicable, and then tighten further to the next split pin hole. Never slacken the nut to align the split pin hole, unless stated in the repair procedure.

When checking or retightening a nut or bolt to a specified torque setting, slacken the nut or bolt by a quarter of a turn, and then retighten to the specified setting. However, this should not be attempted where angular tightening has been used.

For some screw fastenings, notably cylinder head bolts or nuts, torque wrench settings are no longer specified for the latter stages of tightening, "angle-tightening" being called up instead. Typically, a fairly low torque wrench setting will be applied to the bolts/nuts in the correct sequence, followed by one or more stages of tightening through specified angles.

Locknuts, locktabs and washers

Any fastening which will rotate against a component or housing during tightening should always have a washer between it and the relevant component or housing.

Spring or split washers should always be renewed when they are used to lock a critical component such as a big-end bearing retaining bolt or nut. Locktabs which are folded over to retain a nut or bolt should always be renewed.

Self-locking nuts can be re-used in non-critical areas, providing resistance can be felt when the locking portion passes over the bolt or stud thread. However, it should be noted that self-locking stiffnuts tend to lose their effectiveness after long periods of use, and should then be renewed as a matter of course.

Split pins must always be replaced with new ones of the correct size for the hole.

When thread-locking compound is found on the threads of a fastener which is to be re-used, it should be cleaned off with a wire brush and solvent, and fresh compound applied on reassembly.

Special tools

Some repair procedures in this manual entail the use of special tools such as a press, two or three-legged pullers, spring compressors, etc. Wherever possible, suitable readily-available alternatives to the manufacturer's special tools are described, and are shown in use. In some instances, where no alternative is possible, it has been necessary to resort to the use of a manufacturer's tool, and this has been done for reasons of safety as well as the efficient completion of the repair operation. Unless you are highly-skilled and have a thorough understanding of the procedures described, never attempt to bypass the use of any special tool when the procedure described specifies its use. Not only is there a very great risk of personal injury, but expensive damage could be caused to the components involved.

Environmental considerations

When disposing of used engine oil, brake fluid, antifreeze, etc, give due consideration to any detrimental environmental effects. Do not, for instance, pour any of the above liquids down drains into the general sewage system, or onto the ground to soak away. Many local council refuse tips provide a facility for waste oil disposal, as do some garages. If none of these facilities are available, consult your local Environmental Health Department, or the National Rivers Authority, for further advice.

With the universal tightening-up of legislation regarding the emission of environmentally-harmful substances from motor vehicles, most vehicles have tamperproof devices fitted to the main adjustment points of the fuel system. These devices are primarily designed to prevent unqualified persons from adjusting the fuel/air mixture, with the chance of a consequent increase in toxic emissions. If such devices are found during servicing or overhaul, they should, wherever possible, be renewed or refitted in accordance with the manufacturer's requirements or current legislation.

OIL CARE
FOLLOW THE CODE
OIL BANK LINE
0800 66 33 66
www.oilbankline.org.uk

Note: It is antisocial and illegal to dump oil down the drain. To find the location of your local oil recycling bank, call this number free.

The jack supplied with the vehicle tool kit should only be used for changing the roadwheels - see *Wheel changing* at the front of this manual. When carrying out any other kind of work, raise the vehicle using a hydraulic trolley jack, and always supplement the jack with axle stands positioned under the vehicle jacking points.

When using a trolley jack or axle stands, always position the jack head or axle stand head under, or adjacent to one of the relevant wheel changing jacking points under the sills **(see illustration)**. Use a block of wood between the jack or axle stand and the sill.

Do not attempt to jack the vehicle under the front crossmember, the sump, or any of the suspension components.

The jack supplied with the vehicle locates in the jacking points on the underside of the sills - see *Wheel changing* at the front of this manual. Ensure that the jack head is correctly engaged before attempting to raise the vehicle.

Never work under, around, or near a raised vehicle, unless it is adequately supported in at least two places.

Wheel changing jacking points (arrowed)

Radio/cassette unit anti-theft system - precaution

The radio/cassette unit fitted as standard equipment by Audi is equipped with a built-in security code to deter thieves. If the power source to the unit is cut, the anti-theft system will activate. Even if the power source is immediately reconnected, the radio/cassette unit will not function until the correct security code has been entered. Therefore, if you do not know the correct security code for the unit, do not disconnect the battery negative lead, or remove the radio/cassette unit from the vehicle.

Introduction

A selection of good tools is a fundamental requirement for anyone contemplating the maintenance and repair of a motor vehicle. For the owner who does not possess any, their purchase will prove a considerable expense, offsetting some of the savings made by doing-it-yourself. However, provided that the tools purchased meet the relevant national safety standards and are of good quality, they will last for many years and prove an extremely worthwhile investment.

To help the average owner to decide which tools are needed to carry out the various tasks detailed in this manual, we have compiled three lists of tools under the following headings: *Maintenance and minor repair*, *Repair and overhaul*, and *Special*. Newcomers to practical mechanics should start off with the *Maintenance and minor repair* tool kit, and confine themselves to the simpler jobs around the vehicle. Then, as confidence and experience grow, more difficult tasks can be undertaken, with extra tools being purchased as, and when, they are needed. In this way, a *Maintenance and minor repair* tool kit can be built up into a *Repair and overhaul* tool kit over a considerable period of time, without any major cash outlays. The experienced do-it-yourselfer will have a tool kit good enough for most repair and overhaul procedures, and will add tools from the *Special* category when it is felt that the expense is justified by the amount of use to which these tools will be put.

Maintenance and minor repair tool kit

The tools given in this list should be considered as a minimum requirement if routine maintenance, servicing and minor repair operations are to be undertaken. We recommend the purchase of combination spanners (ring one end, open-ended the other); although more expensive than open-ended ones, they do give the advantages of both types of spanner.

☐ *Combination spanners:*
  Metric - 8 to 19 mm inclusive
☐ *Adjustable spanner - 35 mm jaw (approx.)*
☐ *Spark plug spanner (with rubber insert) -*
  petrol models
☐ *Spark plug gap adjustment tool -*
  petrol models
☐ *Set of feeler gauges*
☐ *Brake bleed nipple spanner*
☐ *Screwdrivers:*
  Flat blade - 100 mm long x 6 mm dia
  Cross blade - 100 mm long x 6 mm dia
  Torx - various sizes (not all vehicles)
☐ *Combination pliers*
☐ *Hacksaw (junior)*
☐ *Tyre pump*
☐ *Tyre pressure gauge*
☐ *Oil can*
☐ *Oil filter removal tool*
☐ *Fine emery cloth*
☐ *Wire brush (small)*
☐ *Funnel (medium size)*
☐ *Sump drain plug key (not all vehicles)*

Repair and overhaul tool kit

These tools are virtually essential for anyone undertaking any major repairs to a motor vehicle, and are additional to those given in the *Maintenance and minor repair* list. Included in this list is a comprehensive set of sockets. Although these are expensive, they will be found invaluable as they are so versatile - particularly if various drives are included in the set. We recommend the half-inch square-drive type, as this can be used with most proprietary torque wrenches.

The tools in this list will sometimes need to be supplemented by tools from the *Special* list:

☐ *Sockets (or box spanners) to cover range*
  in previous list (including Torx sockets)
☐ *Reversible ratchet drive (for use with*
  sockets)
☐ *Extension piece, 250 mm (for use with*
  sockets)
☐ *Universal joint (for use with sockets)*
☐ *Flexible handle or sliding T "breaker bar"*
  (for use with sockets)
☐ *Torque wrench (for use with sockets)*
☐ *Self-locking grips*
☐ *Ball pein hammer*
☐ *Soft-faced mallet (plastic or rubber)*
☐ *Screwdrivers:*
  Flat blade - long & sturdy, short (chubby),
  and narrow (electrician's) types
  Cross blade – long & sturdy, and short
  (chubby) types
☐ *Pliers:*
  Long-nosed
  Side cutters (electrician's)
  Circlip (internal and external)
☐ *Cold chisel - 25 mm*
☐ *Scriber*
☐ *Scraper*
☐ *Centre-punch*
☐ *Pin punch*
☐ *Hacksaw*
☐ *Brake hose clamp*
☐ *Brake/clutch bleeding kit*
☐ *Selection of twist drills*
☐ *Steel rule/straight-edge*
☐ *Allen keys (inc. splined/Torx type)*
☐ *Selection of files*
☐ *Wire brush*
☐ *Axle stands*
☐ *Jack (strong trolley or hydraulic type)*
☐ *Light with extension lead*
☐ *Universal electrical multi-meter*

Sockets and reversible ratchet drive

Brake bleeding kit

Torx key, socket and bit

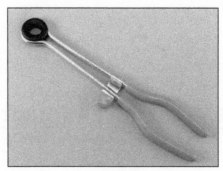
Hose clamp

Angular-tightening gauge

Special tools

The tools in this list are those which are not used regularly, are expensive to buy, or which need to be used in accordance with their manufacturers' instructions. Unless relatively difficult mechanical jobs are undertaken frequently, it will not be economic to buy many of these tools. Where this is the case, you could consider clubbing together with friends (or joining a motorists' club) to make a joint purchase, or borrowing the tools against a deposit from a local garage or tool hire specialist. It is worth noting that many of the larger DIY superstores now carry a large range of special tools for hire at modest rates.

The following list contains only those tools and instruments freely available to the public, and not those special tools produced by the vehicle manufacturer specifically for its dealer network. You will find occasional references to these manufacturers' special tools in the text of this manual. Generally, an alternative method of doing the job without the vehicle manufacturers' special tool is given. However, sometimes there is no alternative to using them. Where this is the case and the relevant tool cannot be bought or borrowed, you will have to entrust the work to a dealer.

- ☐ Angular-tightening gauge
- ☐ Valve spring compressor
- ☐ Valve grinding tool
- ☐ Piston ring compressor
- ☐ Piston ring removal/installation tool
- ☐ Cylinder bore hone
- ☐ Balljoint separator
- ☐ Coil spring compressors (where applicable)
- ☐ Two/three-legged hub and bearing puller
- ☐ Impact screwdriver
- ☐ Micrometer and/or vernier calipers
- ☐ Dial gauge
- ☐ Stroboscopic timing light
- ☐ Dwell angle meter/tachometer
- ☐ Fault code reader
- ☐ Cylinder compression gauge
- ☐ Hand-operated vacuum pump and gauge
- ☐ Clutch plate alignment set
- ☐ Brake shoe steady spring cup removal tool
- ☐ Bush and bearing removal/installation set
- ☐ Stud extractors
- ☐ Tap and die set
- ☐ Lifting tackle
- ☐ Trolley jack

Buying tools

Reputable motor accessory shops and superstores often offer excellent quality tools at discount prices, so it pays to shop around.

Remember, you don't have to buy the most expensive items on the shelf, but it is always advisable to steer clear of the very cheap tools. Beware of 'bargains' offered on market stalls or at car boot sales. There are plenty of good tools around at reasonable prices, but always aim to purchase items which meet the relevant national safety standards. If in doubt, ask the proprietor or manager of the shop for advice before making a purchase.

Care and maintenance of tools

Having purchased a reasonable tool kit, it is necessary to keep the tools in a clean and serviceable condition. After use, always wipe off any dirt, grease and metal particles using a clean, dry cloth, before putting the tools away. Never leave them lying around after they have been used. A simple tool rack on the garage or workshop wall for items such as screwdrivers and pliers is a good idea. Store all normal spanners and sockets in a metal box. Any measuring instruments, gauges, meters, etc, must be carefully stored where they cannot be damaged or become rusty.

Take a little care when tools are used. Hammer heads inevitably become marked, and screwdrivers lose the keen edge on their blades from time to time. A little timely attention with emery cloth or a file will soon restore items like this to a good finish.

Working facilities

Not to be forgotten when discussing tools is the workshop itself. If anything more than routine maintenance is to be carried out, a suitable working area becomes essential.

It is appreciated that many an owner-mechanic is forced by circumstances to remove an engine or similar item without the benefit of a garage or workshop. Having done this, any repairs should always be done under the cover of a roof.

Wherever possible, any dismantling should be done on a clean, flat workbench or table at a suitable working height.

Any workbench needs a vice; one with a jaw opening of 100 mm is suitable for most jobs. As mentioned previously, some clean dry storage space is also required for tools, as well as for any lubricants, cleaning fluids, touch-up paints etc, which become necessary.

Another item which may be required, and which has a much more general usage, is an electric drill with a chuck capacity of at least 8 mm. This, together with a good range of twist drills, is virtually essential for fitting accessories.

Last, but not least, always keep a supply of old newspapers and clean, lint-free rags available, and try to keep any working area as clean as possible.

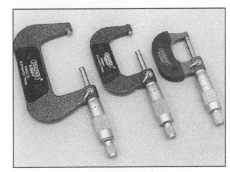

Micrometers

Dial test indicator ("dial gauge")

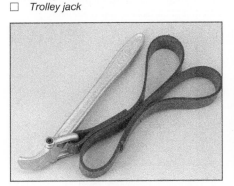

Strap wrench

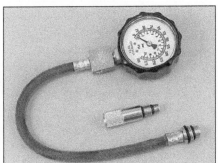

Compression tester

Fault code reader

This is a guide to getting your vehicle through the MOT test. Obviously it will not be possible to examine the vehicle to the same standard as the professional MOT tester. However, working through the following checks will enable you to identify any problem areas before submitting the vehicle for the test.

It has only been possible to summarise the test requirements here, based on the regulations in force at the time of printing. Test standards are becoming increasingly stringent, although there are some exemptions for older vehicles.

An assistant will be needed to help carry out some of these checks.

The checks have been sub-divided into four categories, as follows:

1 Checks carried out **FROM THE DRIVER'S SEAT**

2 Checks carried out **WITH THE VEHICLE ON THE GROUND**

3 Checks carried out **WITH THE VEHICLE RAISED AND THE WHEELS FREE TO TURN**

4 Checks carried out on **YOUR VEHICLE'S EXHAUST EMISSION SYSTEM**

---

1 Checks carried out **FROM THE DRIVER'S SEAT**

Handbrake

☐ Test the operation of the handbrake. Excessive travel (too many clicks) indicates incorrect brake or cable adjustment.
☐ Check that the handbrake cannot be released by tapping the lever sideways. Check the security of the lever mountings.

Footbrake

☐ Depress the brake pedal and check that it does not creep down to the floor, indicating a master cylinder fault. Release the pedal, wait a few seconds, then depress it again. If the pedal travels nearly to the floor before firm resistance is felt, brake adjustment or repair is necessary. If the pedal feels spongy, there is air in the hydraulic system which must be removed by bleeding.

☐ Check that the brake pedal is secure and in good condition. Check also for signs of fluid leaks on the pedal, floor or carpets, which would indicate failed seals in the brake master cylinder.
☐ Check the servo unit (when applicable) by operating the brake pedal several times, then keeping the pedal depressed and starting the engine. As the engine starts, the pedal will move down slightly. If not, the vacuum hose or the servo itself may be faulty.

Steering wheel and column

☐ Examine the steering wheel for fractures or looseness of the hub, spokes or rim.
☐ Move the steering wheel from side to side and then up and down. Check that the steering wheel is not loose on the column, indicating wear or a loose retaining nut. Continue moving the steering wheel as before, but also turn it slightly from left to right.
☐ Check that the steering wheel is not loose on the column, and that there is no abnormal

movement of the steering wheel, indicating wear in the column support bearings or couplings.

Windscreen, mirrors and sunvisor

☐ The windscreen must be free of cracks or other significant damage within the driver's field of view. (Small stone chips are acceptable.) Rear view mirrors must be secure, intact, and capable of being adjusted.

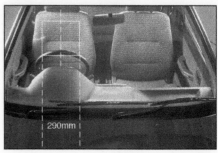

☐ The driver's sunvisor must be capable of being stored in the "up" position.

Seat belts and seats

Note: *The following checks are applicable to all seat belts, front and rear.*

☐ Examine the webbing of all the belts (including rear belts if fitted) for cuts, serious fraying or deterioration. Fasten and unfasten each belt to check the buckles. If applicable, check the retracting mechanism. Check the security of all seat belt mountings accessible from inside the vehicle.

☐ Seat belts with pre-tensioners, once activated, have a "flag" or similar showing on the seat belt stalk. This, in itself, is not a reason for test failure.

☐ The front seats themselves must be securely attached and the backrests must lock in the upright position.

Doors

☐ Both front doors must be able to be opened and closed from outside and inside, and must latch securely when closed.

2 Checks carried out WITH THE VEHICLE ON THE GROUND

Vehicle identification

☐ Number plates must be in good condition, secure and legible, with letters and numbers correctly spaced – spacing at (A) should be at least twice that at (B).

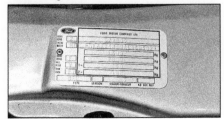

☐ The VIN plate and/or homologation plate must be legible.

Electrical equipment

☐ Switch on the ignition and check the operation of the horn.

☐ Check the windscreen washers and wipers, examining the wiper blades; renew damaged or perished blades. Also check the operation of the stop-lights.

☐ Check the operation of the sidelights and number plate lights. The lenses and reflectors must be secure, clean and undamaged.

☐ Check the operation and alignment of the headlights. The headlight reflectors must not be tarnished and the lenses must be undamaged.

☐ Switch on the ignition and check the operation of the direction indicators (including the instrument panel tell-tale) and the hazard warning lights. Operation of the sidelights and stop-lights must not affect the indicators - if it does, the cause is usually a bad earth at the rear light cluster.

☐ Check the operation of the rear foglight(s), including the warning light on the instrument panel or in the switch.

☐ The ABS warning light must illuminate in accordance with the manufacturers' design. For most vehicles, the ABS warning light should illuminate when the ignition is switched on, and (if the system is operating properly) extinguish after a few seconds. Refer to the owner's handbook.

Footbrake

☐ Examine the master cylinder, brake pipes and servo unit for leaks, loose mountings, corrosion or other damage.

☐ The fluid reservoir must be secure and the fluid level must be between the upper (**A**) and lower (**B**) markings.

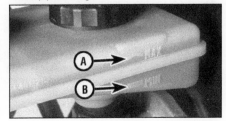

☐ Inspect both front brake flexible hoses for cracks or deterioration of the rubber. Turn the steering from lock to lock, and ensure that the hoses do not contact the wheel, tyre, or any part of the steering or suspension mechanism. With the brake pedal firmly depressed, check the hoses for bulges or leaks under pressure.

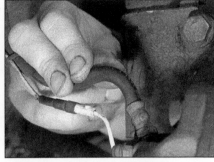

Steering and suspension

☐ Have your assistant turn the steering wheel from side to side slightly, up to the point where the steering gear just begins to transmit this movement to the roadwheels. Check for excessive free play between the steering wheel and the steering gear, indicating wear or insecurity of the steering column joints, the column-to-steering gear coupling, or the steering gear itself.

☐ Have your assistant turn the steering wheel more vigorously in each direction, so that the roadwheels just begin to turn. As this is done, examine all the steering joints, linkages, fittings and attachments. Renew any component that shows signs of wear or damage. On vehicles with power steering, check the security and condition of the steering pump, drivebelt and hoses.

☐ Check that the vehicle is standing level, and at approximately the correct ride height.

Shock absorbers

☐ Depress each corner of the vehicle in turn, then release it. The vehicle should rise and then settle in its normal position. If the vehicle continues to rise and fall, the shock absorber is defective. A shock absorber which has seized will also cause the vehicle to fail.

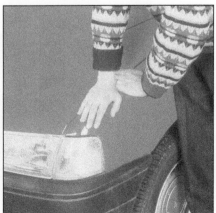

Exhaust system

☐ Start the engine. With your assistant holding a rag over the tailpipe, check the entire system for leaks. Repair or renew leaking sections.

3 Checks carried out **WITH THE VEHICLE RAISED AND THE WHEELS FREE TO TURN**

Jack up the front and rear of the vehicle, and securely support it on axle stands. Position the stands clear of the suspension assemblies. Ensure that the wheels are clear of the ground and that the steering can be turned from lock to lock.

Steering mechanism

☐ Have your assistant turn the steering from lock to lock. Check that the steering turns smoothly, and that no part of the steering mechanism, including a wheel or tyre, fouls any brake hose or pipe or any part of the body structure.

☐ Examine the steering rack rubber gaiters for damage or insecurity of the retaining clips. If power steering is fitted, check for signs of damage or leakage of the fluid hoses, pipes or connections. Also check for excessive stiffness or binding of the steering, a missing split pin or locking device, or severe corrosion of the body structure within 30 cm of any steering component attachment point.

Front and rear suspension and wheel bearings

☐ Starting at the front right-hand side, grasp the roadwheel at the 3 o'clock and 9 o'clock positions and rock gently but firmly. Check for free play or insecurity at the wheel bearings, suspension balljoints, or suspension mountings, pivots and attachments.

☐ Now grasp the wheel at the 12 o'clock and 6 o'clock positions and repeat the previous inspection. Spin the wheel, and check for roughness or tightness of the front wheel bearing.

☐ If excess free play is suspected at a component pivot point, this can be confirmed by using a large screwdriver or similar tool and levering between the mounting and the component attachment. This will confirm whether the wear is in the pivot bush, its retaining bolt, or in the mounting itself (the bolt holes can often become elongated).

☐ Carry out all the above checks at the other front wheel, and then at both rear wheels.

Springs and shock absorbers

☐ Examine the suspension struts (when applicable) for serious fluid leakage, corrosion, or damage to the casing. Also check the security of the mounting points.

☐ If coil springs are fitted, check that the spring ends locate in their seats, and that the spring is not corroded, cracked or broken.

☐ If leaf springs are fitted, check that all leaves are intact, that the axle is securely attached to each spring, and that there is no deterioration of the spring eye mountings, bushes, and shackles.

☐ The same general checks apply to vehicles fitted with other suspension types, such as torsion bars, hydraulic displacer units, etc. Ensure that all mountings and attachments are secure, that there are no signs of excessive wear, corrosion or damage, and (on hydraulic types) that there are no fluid leaks or damaged pipes.

☐ Inspect the shock absorbers for signs of serious fluid leakage. Check for wear of the mounting bushes or attachments, or damage to the body of the unit.

Driveshafts (fwd vehicles only)

☐ Rotate each front wheel in turn and inspect the constant velocity joint gaiters for splits or damage. Also check that each driveshaft is straight and undamaged.

Braking system

☐ If possible without dismantling, check brake pad wear and disc condition. Ensure that the friction lining material has not worn excessively, (A) and that the discs are not fractured, pitted, scored or badly worn (B).

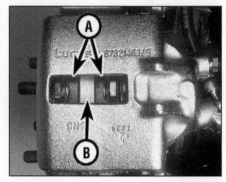

☐ Examine all the rigid brake pipes underneath the vehicle, and the flexible hose(s) at the rear. Look for corrosion, chafing or insecurity of the pipes, and for signs of bulging under pressure, chafing, splits or deterioration of the flexible hoses.

☐ Look for signs of fluid leaks at the brake calipers or on the brake backplates. Repair or renew leaking components.

☐ Slowly spin each wheel, while your assistant depresses and releases the footbrake. Ensure that each brake is operating and does not bind when the pedal is released.

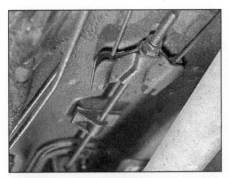

☐ Examine the handbrake mechanism, checking for frayed or broken cables, excessive corrosion, or wear or insecurity of the linkage. Check that the mechanism works on each relevant wheel, and releases fully, without binding.

☐ It is not possible to test brake efficiency without special equipment, but a road test can be carried out later to check that the vehicle pulls up in a straight line.

Fuel and exhaust systems

☐ Inspect the fuel tank (including the filler cap), fuel pipes, hoses and unions. All components must be secure and free from leaks.

☐ Examine the exhaust system over its entire length, checking for any damaged, broken or missing mountings, security of the retaining clamps and rust or corrosion.

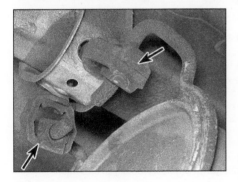

Wheels and tyres

☐ Examine the sidewalls and tread area of each tyre in turn. Check for cuts, tears, lumps, bulges, separation of the tread, and exposure of the ply or cord due to wear or damage. Check that the tyre bead is correctly seated on the wheel rim, that the valve is sound and properly seated, and that the wheel is not distorted or damaged.

☐ Check that the tyres are of the correct size for the vehicle, that they are of the same size

and type on each axle, and that the pressures are correct.

☐ Check the tyre tread depth. The legal minimum at the time of writing is 1.6 mm over at least three-quarters of the tread width. Abnormal tread wear may indicate incorrect front wheel alignment.

Body corrosion

☐ Check the condition of the entire vehicle structure for signs of corrosion in load-bearing areas. (These include chassis box sections, side sills, cross-members, pillars, and all suspension, steering, braking system and seat belt mountings and anchorages.) Any corrosion which has seriously reduced the thickness of a load-bearing area is likely to cause the vehicle to fail. In this case professional repairs are likely to be needed.

☐ Damage or corrosion which causes sharp or otherwise dangerous edges to be exposed will also cause the vehicle to fail.

4 Checks carried out on YOUR VEHICLE'S EXHAUST EMISSION SYSTEM

Petrol models

☐ The engine should be warmed up, and running well (ignition system in good order, air filter element clean, etc).

☐ Before testing, run the engine at around 2500 rpm for 20 seconds. Let the engine drop to idle, and watch for smoke from the exhaust. If the idle speed is too high, or if dense blue or black smoke emerges for more than 5 seconds, the vehicle will fail. Typically, blue smoke signifies oil burning (engine wear); black smoke means unburnt fuel (dirty air cleaner element, or other fuel system fault).

☐ An exhaust gas analyser for measuring carbon monoxide (CO) and hydrocarbons (HC) is now needed. If one cannot be hired or borrowed, have a local garage perform the check.

CO emissions (mixture)

☐ The MOT tester has access to the CO limits for all vehicles. The CO level is measured at idle speed, and at 'fast idle' (2500 to 3000 rpm). The following limits are given as a general guide:

At idle speed – Less than 0.5% CO
At 'fast idle' – Less than 0.3% CO
Lambda reading – 0.97 to 1.03

☐ If the CO level is too high, this may point to poor maintenance, a fuel injection system problem, faulty lambda (oxygen) sensor or catalytic converter. Try an injector cleaning treatment, and check the vehicle's ECU for fault codes.

HC emissions

☐ The MOT tester has access to HC limits for all vehicles. The HC level is measured at 'fast idle' (2500 to 3000 rpm). The following limits are given as a general guide:

At 'fast idle' – Less then 200 ppm

☐ Excessive HC emissions are typically caused by oil being burnt (worn engine), or by a blocked crankcase ventilation system ('breather'). If the engine oil is old and thin, an oil change may help. If the engine is running badly, check the vehicle's ECU for fault codes.

Diesel models

☐ The only emission test for diesel engines is measuring exhaust smoke density, using a calibrated smoke meter. The test involves accelerating the engine at least 3 times to its maximum unloaded speed.

Note: *On engines with a timing belt, it is VITAL that the belt is in good condition before the test is carried out.*

☐ With the engine warmed up, it is first purged by running at around 2500 rpm for 20 seconds. A governor check is then carried out, by slowly accelerating the engine to its maximum speed. After this, the smoke meter is connected, and the engine is accelerated quickly to maximum speed three times. If the smoke density is less than the limits given below, the vehicle will pass:

Non-turbo vehicles: 2.5m-1
Turbocharged vehicles: 3.0m-1

☐ If excess smoke is produced, try fitting a new air cleaner element, or using an injector cleaning treatment. If the engine is running badly, where applicable, check the vehicle's ECU for fault codes. Also check the vehicle's EGR system, where applicable. At high mileages, the injectors may require professional attention.

Engine

- ☐ Engine fails to rotate when attempting to start
- ☐ Engine rotates, but will not start
- ☐ Engine difficult to start when cold
- ☐ Engine difficult to start when hot
- ☐ Starter motor noisy or excessively-rough in engagement
- ☐ Engine starts, but stops immediately
- ☐ Engine idles erratically
- ☐ Engine misfires at idle speed
- ☐ Engine misfires throughout the driving speed range
- ☐ Engine hesitates on acceleration
- ☐ Engine stalls
- ☐ Engine lacks power
- ☐ Engine backfires
- ☐ Oil pressure warning light illuminated with engine running
- ☐ Engine runs-on after switching off
- ☐ Engine noises

Cooling system

- ☐ Overheating
- ☐ Overcooling
- ☐ External coolant leakage
- ☐ Internal coolant leakage
- ☐ Corrosion

Fuel and exhaust systems

- ☐ Excessive fuel consumption
- ☐ Fuel leakage and/or fuel odour
- ☐ Excessive noise or fumes from exhaust system

Clutch

- ☐ Pedal travels to floor - no pressure or very little resistance
- ☐ Clutch fails to disengage (unable to select gears)
- ☐ Clutch slips (engine speed increases, with no increase in vehicle speed)
- ☐ Judder as clutch is engaged
- ☐ Noise when depressing or releasing clutch pedal

Manual transmission

- ☐ Noisy in neutral with engine running
- ☐ Noisy in one particular gear
- ☐ Difficulty engaging gears
- ☐ Jumps out of gear
- ☐ Vibration
- ☐ Lubricant leaks

Automatic transmission

- ☐ Fluid leakage
- ☐ General gear selection problems
- ☐ Transmission will not downshift (kickdown) with accelerator pedal fully depressed
- ☐ Engine will not start in any gear, or starts in gears other than Park or Neutral
- ☐ Transmission slips, shifts roughly, is noisy, or has no drive in forward or reverse gears

Driveshafts

- ☐ Vibration when accelerating or decelerating
- ☐ Clicking or knocking noise on turns (at slow speed on full-lock)

Braking system

- ☐ Vehicle pulls to one side under braking
- ☐ Noise (grinding or high-pitched squeal) when brakes applied
- ☐ Excessive brake pedal travel
- ☐ Brake pedal feels spongy when depressed
- ☐ Excessive brake pedal effort required to stop vehicle
- ☐ Judder felt through brake pedal or steering wheel when braking
- ☐ Pedal pulsates when braking hard
- ☐ Brakes binding
- ☐ Rear wheels locking under normal braking

Steering and suspension

- ☐ Vehicle pulls to one side
- ☐ Wheel wobble and vibration
- ☐ Excessive pitching and/or rolling around corners, or during braking
- ☐ Wandering or general instability
- ☐ Excessively-stiff steering
- ☐ Excessive play in steering
- ☐ Lack of power assistance
- ☐ Tyre wear excessive

Electrical system

- ☐ Battery will not hold a charge for more than a few days
- ☐ Ignition/no-charge warning light stays on with engine running
- ☐ Ignition/no-charge warning light fails to come on
- ☐ Lights inoperative
- ☐ Instrument readings inaccurate or erratic
- ☐ Horn inoperative, or unsatisfactory in operation
- ☐ Windscreen/tailgate wipers inoperative, or unsatisfactory in operation
- ☐ Windscreen washers inoperative, or unsatisfactory in operation
- ☐ Electric windows inoperative, or unsatisfactory in operation
- ☐ Central locking inoperative, or unsatisfactory in operation

Introduction

The vehicle owner who does his or her own maintenance according to the recommended service schedules should not have to use this section of the manual very often. Modern component reliability is such that, provided those items subject to wear or deterioration are inspected or renewed at the specified intervals, sudden failure is comparatively rare. Faults do not usually just happen as a result of sudden failure, but develop over a period of time. Major mechanical failures in particular are usually preceded by characteristic symptoms over hundreds or even thousands of miles. Those components which do occasionally fail without warning are often small and easily carried in the vehicle.

With any fault-finding, the first step is to decide where to begin investigations. Sometimes this is obvious, but on other occasions, a little detective work will be necessary. The owner who makes half a dozen haphazard adjustments or replacements may be successful in curing a fault (or its symptoms), but will be none the wiser if the fault recurs, and ultimately may have spent more time and money than was necessary. A calm and logical approach will be found to be more satisfactory in the long run. Always take into account any warning signs or abnormalities that may have been noticed in the period preceding the fault - power loss, high or low gauge readings,

unusual smells, etc - and remember that failure of components such as fuses or spark plugs may only be pointers to some underlying fault.

The pages which follow provide an easy-reference guide to the more common problems which may occur during the operation of the vehicle. These problems and their possible causes are grouped under headings denoting various components or systems, such as Engine, Cooling system, etc. The Chapter and/or Section which deals with the problem is also shown in brackets. Whatever the fault, certain basic principles apply. These are as follows:

Verify the fault. This is simply a matter of

being sure that you know what the symptoms are before starting work. This is particularly important if you are investigating a fault for someone else, who may not have described it very accurately.

Don't overlook the obvious. For example, if the vehicle won't start, is there fuel in the tank? (Don't take anyone else's word on this particular point, and don't trust the fuel gauge either!) If an electrical fault is indicated, look for loose or broken wires before digging out the test gear.

Cure the disease, not the symptom. Substituting a flat battery with a fully-charged one will get you off the hard shoulder, but if the underlying cause is not attended to, the new battery will go the same way. Similarly, changing oil-fouled spark plugs for a new set will get you moving again, but remember that the reason for the fouling (if it wasn't simply an incorrect grade of plug) will have to be established and corrected.

Don't take anything for granted. Particularly, don't forget that a new component may itself be defective (especially if its been rattling around in the boot for months), and don't leave components out of a fault diagnosis sequence just because they are new or recently-fitted. When you do finally diagnose a difficult fault, you'll probably realise that all the evidence was there from the start.

Engine

Engine fails to rotate when attempting to start

- [ ] Battery terminal connections loose or corroded (see *Weekly checks*).
- [ ] Battery discharged or faulty (Chapter 5A).
- [ ] Broken, loose or disconnected wiring in the starting circuit (Chapter 5A).
- [ ] Defective starter solenoid or switch (Chapter 5A).
- [ ] Defective starter motor (Chapter 5A).
- [ ] Starter pinion or flywheel/driveplate ring gear teeth loose or broken (Chapter 2 and 5A).
- [ ] Engine earth strap broken or disconnected (Chapter 5A).

Engine rotates, but will not start

- [ ] Fuel tank empty.
- [ ] Battery discharged (engine rotates slowly) (Chapter 5A).
- [ ] Battery terminal connections loose or corroded (see *Weekly checks*).
- [ ] Ignition components damp or damaged - petrol models (Chapters 1A and 5B).
- [ ] Broken, loose or disconnected wiring in the ignition circuit - petrol models (Chapters 1A and 5B).
- [ ] Worn, faulty or incorrectly-gapped spark plugs - petrol models (Chapter 1A).
- [ ] Preheating system faulty - diesel models (Chapter 5C).
- [ ] Fuel injection system fault - petrol models (Chapter 4A).
- [ ] Stop solenoid faulty - diesel models (Chapter 4B).
- [ ] Air in fuel system - diesel models (Chapter 4B).
- [ ] Major mechanical failure (eg timing belt) (Chapter 2).

Engine difficult to start when cold

- [ ] Battery discharged (Chapter 5A).
- [ ] Battery terminal connections loose or corroded (see *Weekly checks*).
- [ ] Worn, faulty or incorrectly-gapped spark plugs - petrol models (Chapter 1A).
- [ ] Preheating system faulty - diesel models (Chapter 5C).
- [ ] Fuel injection system fault - petrol models (Chapter 4A).
- [ ] Other ignition system fault - petrol models (Chapters 1A and 5B).
- [ ] Low cylinder compressions (Chapter 2).

Engine difficult to start when hot

- [ ] Air filter element dirty or clogged (Chapter 1).
- [ ] Fuel injection system fault - petrol models (Chapter 4A).
- [ ] Low cylinder compressions (Chapter 2).

Starter motor noisy or excessively-rough in engagement

- [ ] Starter pinion or flywheel ring gear teeth loose or broken (Chapter 2 and 5A).
- [ ] Starter motor mounting bolts loose or missing (Chapter 5A).
- [ ] Starter motor internal components worn or damaged (Chapter 5A).

Engine starts, but stops immediately

- [ ] Loose or faulty electrical connections in the ignition circuit - petrol models (Chapters 1A and 5B).
- [ ] Vacuum leak at the throttle body or inlet manifold - petrol models (Chapter 4A).
- [ ] Blocked injector/fuel injection system fault - petrol models (Chapter 4A).

Engine idles erratically

- [ ] Air filter element clogged (Chapter 1).
- [ ] Vacuum leak at the throttle body, inlet manifold or associated hoses - petrol models (Chapter 4A).
- [ ] Worn, faulty or incorrectly-gapped spark plugs - petrol models (Chapter 1A).
- [ ] Uneven or low cylinder compressions (Chapter 2).
- [ ] Camshaft lobes worn (Chapter 2).
- [ ] Timing belt incorrectly fitted (Chapter 2).
- [ ] Blocked injector/fuel injection system fault - petrol models (Chapter 4A).
- [ ] Faulty injector(s) - diesel models (Chapter 4B).

Engine misfires at idle speed

- [ ] Worn, faulty or incorrectly-gapped spark plugs - petrol models (Chapter 1A).
- [ ] Faulty spark plug HT leads - petrol models (Chapter 1A).
- [ ] Vacuum leak at the throttle body, inlet manifold or associated hoses - petrol models (Chapter 4A).
- [ ] Blocked injector/fuel injection system fault - petrol models (Chapter 4A).
- [ ] Faulty injector(s) - diesel models (Chapter 4B).
- [ ] Uneven or low cylinder compressions (Chapter 2).
- [ ] Disconnected, leaking, or perished crankcase ventilation hoses (Chapter 4C).

Engine misfires throughout the driving speed range

- [ ] Fuel filter choked (Chapter 1).
- [ ] Fuel pump faulty, or delivery pressure low - petrol models (Chapter 4A).
- [ ] Fuel tank vent blocked, or fuel pipes restricted (Chapter 4).
- [ ] Vacuum leak at the throttle body, inlet manifold or associated hoses - petrol models (Chapter 4A).
- [ ] Worn, faulty or incorrectly-gapped spark plugs - petrol models (Chapter 1A).
- [ ] Faulty spark plug HT leads - petrol models (Chapter 1A).
- [ ] Faulty injector(s) - diesel models (Chapter 4B).
- [ ] Faulty ignition coil - petrol models (Chapter 5B).
- [ ] Uneven or low cylinder compressions (Chapter 2).
- [ ] Blocked injector/fuel injection system fault - petrol models (Chapter 4A).

Engine (continued)

Engine hesitates on acceleration

- ☐ Worn, faulty or incorrectly-gapped spark plugs - petrol models (Chapter 1A).
- ☐ Vacuum leak at the throttle body, inlet manifold or associated hoses - petrol models (Chapter 4A).
- ☐ Blocked injector/fuel injection system fault - petrol models (Chapter 4A).
- ☐ Faulty injector(s) - diesel models (Chapter 4B).

Engine stalls

- ☐ Vacuum leak at the throttle body, inlet manifold or associated hoses - petrol models (Chapter 4A).
- ☐ Fuel filter choked (Chapter 1).
- ☐ Fuel pump faulty, or delivery pressure low - petrol models (Chapter 4A).
- ☐ Fuel tank vent blocked, or fuel pipes restricted (Chapter 4).
- ☐ Blocked injector/fuel injection system fault - petrol models (Chapter 4A).
- ☐ Faulty injector(s) - diesel models (Chapter 4B).

Engine lacks power

- ☐ Timing belt incorrectly fitted or tensioned (Chapter 2).
- ☐ Fuel filter choked (Chapter 1).
- ☐ Fuel pump faulty, or delivery pressure low - petrol models (Chapter 4A).
- ☐ Uneven or low cylinder compressions (Chapter 2).
- ☐ Worn, faulty or incorrectly-gapped spark plugs - petrol models (Chapter 1A).
- ☐ Vacuum leak at the throttle body, inlet manifold or associated hoses - petrol models (Chapter 4A).
- ☐ Blocked injector/fuel injection system fault - petrol models (Chapter 4A).
- ☐ Faulty injector(s) - diesel models (Chapter 4B).
- ☐ Injection pump timing incorrect - diesel models (Chapter 4B).
- ☐ Brakes binding (Chapters 1 and 9).
- ☐ Clutch slipping (Chapter 6).

Engine backfires

- ☐ Timing belt incorrectly fitted or tensioned (Chapter 2).
- ☐ Vacuum leak at the throttle body, inlet manifold or associated hoses - petrol models (Chapter 4A).
- ☐ Blocked injector/fuel injection system fault - petrol models (Chapter 4A).

Oil pressure warning light illuminated with engine running

- ☐ Low oil level, or incorrect oil grade (*Weekly checks*).
- ☐ Faulty oil pressure sensor (Chapter 2).
- ☐ Worn engine bearings and/or oil pump (Chapter 2).
- ☐ High engine operating temperature (Chapter 3).
- ☐ Oil pressure relief valve defective (Chapter 2).
- ☐ Oil pick-up strainer clogged (Chapter 2).

Engine runs-on after switching off

- ☐ Excessive carbon build-up in engine (Chapter 2).
- ☐ High engine operating temperature (Chapter 3).
- ☐ Fuel injection system fault - petrol models (Chapter 4A).
- ☐ Faulty stop solenoid - diesel models (Chapter 4B).

Engine noises

Pre-ignition (pinking) or knocking during acceleration or under load

- ☐ Ignition system fault - petrol models (Chapters 1A and 5B).
- ☐ Incorrect grade of spark plug - petrol models (Chapter 1A).
- ☐ Incorrect grade of fuel (Chapter 4).
- ☐ Vacuum leak at the throttle body, inlet manifold or associated hoses - petrol models (Chapter 4A).
- ☐ Excessive carbon build-up in engine (Chapter 2).
- ☐ Blocked injector/fuel injection system fault - petrol models (Chapter 4A).

Whistling or wheezing noises

- ☐ Leaking inlet manifold or throttle body gasket - petrol models (Chapter 4A).
- ☐ Leaking exhaust manifold gasket or pipe-to-manifold joint (Chapter 4).
- ☐ Leaking vacuum hose (Chapters 4 and 9).
- ☐ Blowing cylinder head gasket (Chapter 2).

Tapping or rattling noises

- ☐ Worn valve gear or camshaft (Chapter 2).
- ☐ Ancillary component fault (coolant pump, alternator, etc) (Chapters 3, 5, etc).

Knocking or thumping noises

- ☐ Worn big-end bearings (regular heavy knocking, perhaps less under load) (Chapter 2).
- ☐ Worn main bearings (rumbling and knocking, perhaps worsening under load) (Chapter 2).
- ☐ Piston slap (most noticeable when cold) (Chapter 2).
- ☐ Ancillary component fault (coolant pump, alternator, etc) (Chapters 3, 5, etc).

Cooling system

Overheating

- ☐ Insufficient coolant in system (*Weekly checks*).
- ☐ Thermostat faulty (Chapter 3).
- ☐ Radiator core blocked, or grille restricted (Chapter 3).
- ☐ Electric cooling fan or thermostatic switch faulty (Chapter 3).
- ☐ Inaccurate temperature gauge sender unit (Chapter 3).
- ☐ Airlock in cooling system.
- ☐ Expansion tank pressure cap faulty (Chapter 3).

Overcooling

- ☐ Thermostat faulty (Chapter 3).
- ☐ Inaccurate temperature gauge sender unit (Chapter 3).

External coolant leakage

- ☐ Deteriorated or damaged hoses or hose clips (Chapter 1).

- ☐ Radiator core or heater matrix leaking (Chapter 3).
- ☐ Pressure cap faulty (Chapter 3).
- ☐ Coolant pump internal seal leaking (Chapter 3).
- ☐ Coolant pump-to-housing seal leaking (Chapter 3).
- ☐ Boiling due to overheating (Chapter 3).
- ☐ Core plug leaking (Chapter 2).

Internal coolant leakage

- ☐ Leaking cylinder head gasket (Chapter 2).
- ☐ Cracked cylinder head or cylinder block (Chapter 2).

Corrosion

- ☐ Infrequent draining and flushing (Chapter 1).
- ☐ Incorrect coolant mixture or inappropriate coolant type (see *Weekly checks*).

Fuel and exhaust systems

Excessive fuel consumption

☐ Air filter element dirty or clogged (Chapter 1).
☐ Fuel injection system fault - petrol models (Chapter 4A).
☐ Faulty injector(s) - diesel models (Chapter 4B).
☐ Ignition system fault - petrol models (Chapters 1A and 5B).
☐ Tyres under-inflated (see *Weekly checks*).

Fuel leakage and/or fuel odour

☐ Damaged fuel tank, pipes or connections (Chapter 4).

Excessive noise or fumes from exhaust system

☐ Leaking exhaust system or manifold joints (Chapters 1 and 4).
☐ Leaking, corroded or damaged silencers or pipe (Chapters 1 and 4).
☐ Broken mountings causing body or suspension contact (Chapter 1).

Clutch

Pedal travels to floor - no pressure or very little resistance

☐ Faulty master or slave cylinder (Chapter 6).
☐ Faulty hydraulic release system (Chapter 6).
☐ Broken clutch release bearing or arm (Chapter 6).
☐ Broken diaphragm spring in clutch pressure plate (Chapter 6).

Clutch fails to disengage (unable to select gears)

☐ Faulty master or slave cylinder (Chapter 6).
☐ Faulty hydraulic release system (Chapter 6).
☐ Clutch disc sticking on gearbox input shaft splines (Chapter 6).
☐ Clutch disc sticking to flywheel or pressure plate (Chapter 6).
☐ Faulty pressure plate assembly (Chapter 6).
☐ Clutch release mechanism worn or incorrectly assembled (Chapter 6).

Clutch slips (engine speed increases, with no increase in vehicle speed)

☐ Faulty hydraulic release system (Chapter 6).

☐ Clutch disc linings excessively worn (Chapter 6).
☐ Clutch disc linings contaminated with oil or grease (Chapter 6).
☐ Faulty pressure plate or weak diaphragm spring (Chapter 6).

Judder as clutch is engaged

☐ Clutch disc linings contaminated with oil or grease (Chapter 6).
☐ Clutch disc linings excessively worn (Chapter 6).
☐ Faulty or distorted pressure plate or diaphragm spring (Chapter 6).
☐ Worn or loose engine or gearbox mountings (Chapter 2).
☐ Clutch disc hub or gearbox input shaft splines worn (Chapter 6).

Noise when depressing or releasing clutch pedal

☐ Worn clutch release bearing (Chapter 6).
☐ Worn or dry clutch pedal pivot (Chapter 6).
☐ Faulty pressure plate assembly (Chapter 6).
☐ Pressure plate diaphragm spring broken (Chapter 6).
☐ Broken clutch friction plate cushioning springs (Chapter 6).

Manual transmission

Noisy in neutral with engine running

☐ Input shaft bearings worn (noise apparent with clutch pedal released, but not when depressed) (Chapter 7A).*
☐ Clutch release bearing worn (noise apparent with clutch pedal depressed, possibly less when released) (Chapter 6).

Noisy in one particular gear

☐ Worn, damaged or chipped gear teeth (Chapter 7A).*

Difficulty engaging gears

☐ Clutch fault (Chapter 6).
☐ Worn or damaged gear linkage (Chapter 7A).
☐ Worn synchroniser units (Chapter 7A).*

Jumps out of gear

☐ Worn or damaged gear linkage (Chapter 7A).

☐ Worn synchroniser units (Chapter 7A).*
☐ Worn selector forks (Chapter 7A).*

Vibration

☐ Lack of oil (Chapter 1).
☐ Worn bearings (Chapter 7A).*

Lubricant leaks

☐ Leaking oil seal (Chapter 7A).
☐ Leaking housing joint (Chapter 7A).*
☐ Leaking input shaft oil seal (Chapter 7A).*

Although the corrective action necessary to remedy the symptoms described is beyond the scope of the home mechanic, the above information should be helpful in isolating the cause of the condition, so that the owner can communicate clearly with a professional mechanic.

Automatic transmission

Note: *Due to the complexity of the automatic transmission, it is difficult for the home mechanic to properly diagnose and service this unit. For problems other than the following, the vehicle should be taken to a dealer service department or automatic transmission specialist. Do not be too hasty in removing the transmission if a fault is suspected, as most of the testing is carried out with the unit still fitted.*

Fluid leakage

☐ Automatic transmission fluid is usually dark in colour. Fluid leaks should not be confused with engine oil, which can easily be blown onto the transmission by airflow.

☐ To determine the source of a leak, first remove all built-up dirt and grime from the transmission housing and surrounding areas using a degreasing agent, or by steam-cleaning. Drive the vehicle at low speed, so airflow will not blow the leak far from its source. Raise and support the vehicle, and determine where the leak is coming from.

General gear selection problems

☐ Chapter 7B deals with checking and adjusting the selector cable on automatic transmissions. The following are common problems which may be caused by a poorly-adjusted cable:
a) *Engine starting in gears other than Park or Neutral.*
b) *Indicator panel indicating a gear other than the one actually being used.*
c) *Vehicle moves when in Park or Neutral.*
d) *Poor gear shift quality or erratic gear changes.*
☐ Refer to Chapter 7B for the selector cable adjustment procedure.

Transmission will not downshift (kickdown) with accelerator pedal fully depressed

☐ Low transmission fluid level (Chapter 1).
☐ Incorrect selector cable adjustment (Chapter 7B).

Engine will not start in any gear, or starts in gears other than Park or Neutral

☐ Incorrect selector cable adjustment (Chapter 7B).

Transmission slips, shifts roughly, is noisy, or has no drive in forward or reverse gears

☐ There are many probable causes for the above problems, but unless there is a very obvious reason (such as a loose or corroded wiring plug connection on or near the transmission), the car should be taken to a franchise dealer for the fault to be diagnosed. The transmission control unit incorporates a self-diagnosis facility, and any fault codes can quickly be read and interpreted by a dealer with the proper diagnostic equipment.

Driveshafts

Vibration when accelerating or decelerating

☐ Worn inner constant velocity joint (Chapter 8).
☐ Bent or distorted driveshaft (Chapter 8).

Clicking or knocking noise on turns (at slow speed on full-lock)

☐ Worn outer constant velocity joint (Chapter 8).
☐ Lack of constant velocity joint lubricant, possibly due to damaged gaiter (Chapter 8).

Braking system

Note: *Before assuming that a brake problem exists, make sure that the tyres are in good condition and correctly inflated, that the front wheel alignment is correct, and that the vehicle is not loaded with weight in an unequal manner. Apart from checking the condition of all pipe and hose connections, any faults occurring on the anti-lock braking system should be referred to a Audi/VAG dealer for diagnosis.*

Vehicle pulls to one side under braking

☐ Worn, defective, damaged or contaminated front or rear brake pads/shoes on one side (Chapters 1 and 9).
☐ Seized or partially-seized front or rear brake caliper/wheel cylinder piston (Chapter 9).
☐ A mixture of brake pad/shoe lining materials fitted between sides (Chapter 9).
☐ Brake caliper or rear brake backplate mounting bolts loose (Chapter 9).
☐ Worn or damaged steering or suspension components (Chapters 1 and 10).

Noise (grinding or high-pitched squeal) when brakes applied

☐ Brake pad/shoe friction lining material worn down to metal backing (Chapters 1 and 9).
☐ Excessive corrosion of brake disc or drum - may be apparent after the vehicle has been standing for some time (Chapters 1 and 9).
☐ Foreign object (stone chipping, etc) trapped between brake disc and shield (Chapters 1 and 9).

Excessive brake pedal travel

☐ Faulty rear drum brake self-adjust mechanism (Chapter 9).
☐ Faulty master cylinder (Chapter 9).
☐ Air in hydraulic system (Chapter 9).
☐ Faulty vacuum servo unit (Chapter 9).
☐ Faulty vacuum pump, where fitted (Chapter 9).

Brake pedal feels spongy when depressed

☐ Air in hydraulic system (Chapter 9).
☐ Deteriorated flexible rubber brake hoses (Chapters 1 and 9).
☐ Master cylinder mountings loose (Chapter 9).
☐ Faulty master cylinder (Chapter 9).

Excessive brake pedal effort required to stop vehicle

☐ Faulty vacuum servo unit (Chapter 9).
☐ Disconnected, damaged or insecure brake servo vacuum hose (Chapters 1 and 9).
☐ Faulty vacuum pump, where fitted (Chapter 9).
☐ Primary or secondary hydraulic circuit failure (Chapter 9).
☐ Seized brake caliper or wheel cylinder piston(s) (Chapter 9).
☐ Brake pads/shoes incorrectly fitted (Chapter 9).
☐ Incorrect grade of brake pads/shoes fitted (Chapter 9).
☐ Brake pads/shoe linings contaminated (Chapter 9).

Braking system (continued)

Judder felt through brake pedal or steering wheel when braking

- ☐ Excessive run-out or distortion of brake disc(s) or drum(s) (Chapter 9).
- ☐ Brake pad/shoe linings worn (Chapters 1 and 9).
- ☐ Brake caliper or rear brake backplate mounting bolts loose (Chapter 9).
- ☐ Wear in suspension or steering components or mountings (Chapters 1 and 10).

Pedal pulsates when braking hard

- ☐ Normal feature of ABS - no fault

Brakes binding

- ☐ Seized brake caliper/wheel cylinder piston(s) (Chapter 9).
- ☐ Incorrectly-adjusted handbrake mechanism (Chapter 9).
- ☐ Faulty master cylinder (Chapter 9).

Rear wheels locking under normal braking

- ☐ Rear brake pad/shoe linings contaminated (Chapters 1 and 9).
- ☐ Rear brake discs/drums warped (Chapters 1 and 9).

Steering and suspension

Note: *Before diagnosing suspension or steering faults, be sure that the trouble is not due to incorrect tyre pressures, mixtures of tyre types, or binding brakes.*

Vehicle pulls to one side

- ☐ Defective tyre (see *Weekly checks*).
- ☐ Excessive wear in suspension or steering components (Chapters 1 and 10).
- ☐ Incorrect front wheel alignment (Chapter 10).
- ☐ Accident damage to steering or suspension components (Chapters 1 and 10).

Wheel wobble and vibration

- ☐ Front roadwheels out of balance (vibration felt mainly through the steering wheel) (Chapter 10).
- ☐ Rear roadwheels out of balance (vibration felt throughout the vehicle) (Chapter 10).
- ☐ Roadwheels damaged or distorted (Chapter 10).
- ☐ Faulty or damaged tyre (*Weekly checks*).
- ☐ Worn steering or suspension joints, bushes or components (Chapters 1 and 10).
- ☐ Wheel bolts loose (Chapter 1 and 10).

Excessive pitching and/or rolling around corners, or during braking

- ☐ Defective shock absorbers (Chapters 1 and 10).
- ☐ Broken or weak coil spring and/or suspension component (Chapters 1 and 10).
- ☐ Worn or damaged anti-roll bar or mountings (Chapter 10).

Wandering or general instability

- ☐ Incorrect front wheel alignment (Chapter 10).
- ☐ Worn steering or suspension joints, bushes or components (Chapters 1 and 10).
- ☐ Roadwheels out of balance (Chapter 10).
- ☐ Faulty or damaged tyre (*Weekly checks*).
- ☐ Wheel bolts loose (Chapter 10).
- ☐ Defective shock absorbers (Chapters 1 and 10).

Excessively-stiff steering

- ☐ Seized track rod end balljoint or suspension balljoint (Chapters 1 and 10).

- ☐ Broken or incorrectly adjusted auxiliary drivebelt (Chapter 1).
- ☐ Incorrect front wheel alignment (Chapter 10).
- ☐ Steering gear damaged (Chapter 10).

Excessive play in steering

- ☐ Worn steering column universal joint(s) (Chapter 10).
- ☐ Worn steering track rod end balljoints (Chapters 1 and 10).
- ☐ Worn steering gear (Chapter 10).
- ☐ Worn steering or suspension joints, bushes or components (Chapters 1 and 10).

Lack of power assistance

- ☐ Broken or incorrectly-adjusted auxiliary drivebelt (Chapter 1).
- ☐ Incorrect power steering fluid level (*Weekly checks*).
- ☐ Restriction in power steering fluid hoses (Chapter 10).
- ☐ Faulty power steering pump (Chapter 10).
- ☐ Faulty steering gear (Chapter 10).

Tyre wear excessive

Tyres worn on inside or outside edges

- ☐ Incorrect camber or castor angles (Chapter 10).
- ☐ Worn steering or suspension joints, bushes or components (Chapters 1 and 10).
- ☐ Excessively-hard cornering.
- ☐ Accident damage.

Tyre treads exhibit feathered edges

- ☐ Incorrect toe setting (Chapter 10).

Tyres worn in centre of tread

- ☐ Tyres over-inflated (*Weekly checks*).

Tyres worn on inside and outside edges

- ☐ Tyres under-inflated (*Weekly checks*).
- ☐ Worn shock absorbers (Chapter 10).

Tyres worn unevenly

- ☐ Tyres/wheels out of balance (*Weekly checks*).
- ☐ Excessive wheel or tyre run-out (Chapter 10).
- ☐ Worn shock absorbers (Chapters 1 and 10).
- ☐ Faulty tyre (*Weekly checks*).

Electrical system

Note: *For problems associated with the starting system, refer to the faults listed under Engine earlier in this Section.*

Battery will not hold a charge for more than a few days

- ☐ Battery defective internally (Chapter 5A).
- ☐ Battery electrolyte level low - where applicable (*Weekly checks*).

- ☐ Battery terminal connections loose or corroded (*Weekly checks*).
- ☐ Auxiliary drivebelt worn - or incorrectly adjusted, where applicable (Chapter 1).
- ☐ Alternator not charging at correct output (Chapter 5A).
- ☐ Alternator or voltage regulator faulty (Chapter 5A).
- ☐ Short-circuit causing continual battery drain (Chapters 5 and 12).

Electrical system (continued)

Ignition/no-charge warning light stays on with engine running

- ☐ Auxiliary drivebelt broken, worn, or incorrectly adjusted (Chapter 1).
- ☐ Internal fault in alternator or voltage regulator (Chapter 5A).
- ☐ Broken, disconnected, or loose wiring in charging circuit (Chapter 5A).

Ignition/no-charge warning light fails to come on

- ☐ Warning light bulb blown (Chapter 12).
- ☐ Broken, disconnected, or loose wiring in warning light circuit (Chapter 12).
- ☐ Alternator faulty (Chapter 5A).

Lights inoperative

- ☐ Bulb blown (Chapter 12).
- ☐ Corrosion of bulb or bulbholder contacts (Chapter 12).
- ☐ Blown fuse (Chapter 12).
- ☐ Faulty relay (Chapter 12).
- ☐ Broken, loose, or disconnected wiring (Chapter 12).
- ☐ Faulty switch (Chapter 12).

Instrument readings inaccurate or erratic

Instrument readings increase with engine speed

- ☐ Faulty voltage regulator (Chapter 12).

Fuel or temperature gauges give no reading

- ☐ Faulty gauge sender unit (Chapters 3 and 4).
- ☐ Wiring open-circuit (Chapter 12).
- ☐ Faulty gauge (Chapter 12).

Fuel or temperature gauges give continuous maximum reading

- ☐ Faulty gauge sender unit (Chapters 3 and 4).
- ☐ Wiring short-circuit (Chapter 12).
- ☐ Faulty gauge (Chapter 12).

Horn inoperative, or unsatisfactory in operation

Horn operates all the time

- ☐ Horn contacts permanently bridged or horn push stuck down (Chapter 12).

Horn fails to operate

- ☐ Blown fuse (Chapter 12).
- ☐ Cable or cable connections loose, broken or disconnected (Chapter 12).
- ☐ Faulty horn (Chapter 12).

Horn emits intermittent or unsatisfactory sound

- ☐ Cable connections loose (Chapter 12).
- ☐ Horn mountings loose (Chapter 12).
- ☐ Faulty horn (Chapter 12).

Windscreen/tailgate wipers inoperative, or unsatisfactory in operation

Wipers fail to operate, or operate very slowly

- ☐ Wiper blades stuck to screen, or linkage seized or binding (*Weekly checks* and Chapter 12).
- ☐ Blown fuse (Chapter 12).
- ☐ Cable or cable connections loose, broken or disconnected (Chapter 12).
- ☐ Faulty relay (Chapter 12).
- ☐ Faulty wiper motor (Chapter 12).

Wiper blades sweep over too large or too small an area of the glass

- ☐ Wiper arms incorrectly positioned on spindles (Chapter 12).
- ☐ Excessive wear of wiper linkage (Chapter 12).

- ☐ Wiper motor or linkage mountings loose or insecure (Chapter 12).

Wiper blades fail to clean the glass effectively

- ☐ Wiper blade rubbers worn or perished (*Weekly checks*).
- ☐ Wiper arm tension springs broken, or arm pivots seized (Chapter 12).
- ☐ Insufficient windscreen washer additive to adequately remove road film (*Weekly checks*).

Windscreen washers inoperative, or unsatisfactory in operation

One or more washer jets inoperative

- ☐ Blocked washer jet (Chapter 12).
- ☐ Disconnected, kinked or restricted fluid hose (Chapter 12).
- ☐ Insufficient fluid in washer reservoir (*Weekly checks*).

Washer pump fails to operate

- ☐ Broken or disconnected wiring or connections (Chapter 12).
- ☐ Blown fuse (Chapter 12).
- ☐ Faulty washer switch (Chapter 12).
- ☐ Faulty washer pump (Chapter 12).

Washer pump runs for some time before fluid is emitted from jets

- ☐ Faulty one-way valve in fluid supply hose (Chapter 12).

Electric windows inoperative, or unsatisfactory in operation

Window glass will only move in one direction

- ☐ Faulty switch (Chapter 12).

Window glass slow to move

- ☐ Regulator seized or damaged, or in need of lubrication (Chapter 11).
- ☐ Door internal components or trim fouling regulator (Chapter 11).
- ☐ Faulty motor (Chapter 11).

Window glass fails to move

- ☐ Blown fuse (Chapter 12).
- ☐ Faulty relay (Chapter 12).
- ☐ Broken or disconnected wiring or connections (Chapter 12).
- ☐ Faulty motor (Chapter 12).

Central locking system inoperative, or unsatisfactory in operation

Complete system failure

- ☐ Blown fuse (Chapter 12).
- ☐ Faulty relay (Chapter 12).
- ☐ Broken or disconnected wiring or connections (Chapter 12).
- ☐ Faulty vacuum pump (Chapter 11).

Latch locks but will not unlock, or unlocks but will not lock

- ☐ Faulty switch (Chapter 12).
- ☐ Broken or disconnected latch operating rods or levers (Chapter 11).
- ☐ Faulty relay (Chapter 12).
- ☐ Faulty vacuum pump (Chapter 11).

One lock fails to operate

- ☐ Broken or disconnected wiring or connections (Chapter 12).
- ☐ Faulty motor (Chapter 11).
- ☐ Broken, binding or disconnected lock operating rods or levers (Chapter 11).
- ☐ Fault in door lock (Chapter 11).

A

ABS (Anti-lock brake system) A system, usually electronically controlled, that senses incipient wheel lockup during braking and relieves hydraulic pressure at wheels that are about to skid.

Air bag An inflatable bag hidden in the steering wheel (driver's side) or the dash or glovebox (passenger side). In a head-on collision, the bags inflate, preventing the driver and front passenger from being thrown forward into the steering wheel or windscreen.

Air cleaner A metal or plastic housing, containing a filter element, which removes dust and dirt from the air being drawn into the engine.

Air filter element The actual filter in an air cleaner system, usually manufactured from pleated paper and requiring renewal at regular intervals.

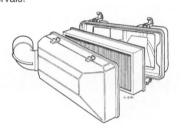
Air filter

Allen key A hexagonal wrench which fits into a recessed hexagonal hole.

Alligator clip A long-nosed spring-loaded metal clip with meshing teeth. Used to make temporary electrical connections.

Alternator A component in the electrical system which converts mechanical energy from a drivebelt into electrical energy to charge the battery and to operate the starting system, ignition system and electrical accessories.

Ampere (amp) A unit of measurement for the flow of electric current. One amp is the amount of current produced by one volt acting through a resistance of one ohm.

Anaerobic sealer A substance used to prevent bolts and screws from loosening. Anaerobic means that it does not require oxygen for activation. The Loctite brand is widely used.

Antifreeze A substance (usually ethylene glycol) mixed with water, and added to a vehicle's cooling system, to prevent freezing of the coolant in winter. Antifreeze also contains chemicals to inhibit corrosion and the formation of rust and other deposits that would tend to clog the radiator and coolant passages and reduce cooling efficiency.

Anti-seize compound A coating that reduces the risk of seizing on fasteners that are subjected to high temperatures, such as exhaust manifold bolts and nuts.

Asbestos A natural fibrous mineral with great heat resistance, commonly used in the composition of brake friction materials.

Asbestos is a health hazard and the dust created by brake systems should never be inhaled or ingested.

Axle A shaft on which a wheel revolves, or which revolves with a wheel. Also, a solid beam that connects the two wheels at one end of the vehicle. An axle which also transmits power to the wheels is known as a live axle.

Axleshaft A single rotating shaft, on either side of the differential, which delivers power from the final drive assembly to the drive wheels. Also called a driveshaft or a halfshaft.

B

Ball bearing An anti-friction bearing consisting of a hardened inner and outer race with hardened steel balls between two races.

Bearing The curved surface on a shaft or in a bore, or the part assembled into either, that permits relative motion between them with minimum wear and friction.

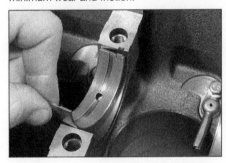
Bearing

Big-end bearing The bearing in the end of the connecting rod that's attached to the crankshaft.

Bleed nipple A valve on a brake wheel cylinder, caliper or other hydraulic component that is opened to purge the hydraulic system of air. Also called a bleed screw.

Brake bleeding Procedure for removing air from lines of a hydraulic brake system.

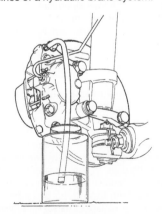
Brake bleeding

Brake disc The component of a disc brake that rotates with the wheels.

Brake drum The component of a drum brake that rotates with the wheels.

Brake linings The friction material which contacts the brake disc or drum to retard the vehicle's speed. The linings are bonded or riveted to the brake pads or shoes.

Brake pads The replaceable friction pads that pinch the brake disc when the brakes are applied. Brake pads consist of a friction material bonded or riveted to a rigid backing plate.

Brake shoe The crescent-shaped carrier to which the brake linings are mounted and which forces the lining against the rotating drum during braking.

Braking systems For more information on braking systems, consult the *Haynes Automotive Brake Manual*.

Breaker bar A long socket wrench handle providing greater leverage.

Bulkhead The insulated partition between the engine and the passenger compartment.

C

Caliper The non-rotating part of a disc-brake assembly that straddles the disc and carries the brake pads. The caliper also contains the hydraulic components that cause the pads to pinch the disc when the brakes are applied. A caliper is also a measuring tool that can be set to measure inside or outside dimensions of an object.

Camshaft A rotating shaft on which a series of cam lobes operate the valve mechanisms. The camshaft may be driven by gears, by sprockets and chain or by sprockets and a belt.

Canister A container in an evaporative emission control system; contains activated charcoal granules to trap vapours from the fuel system.

Canister

Carburettor A device which mixes fuel with air in the proper proportions to provide a desired power output from a spark ignition internal combustion engine.

Castellated Resembling the parapets along the top of a castle wall. For example, a castellated balljoint stud nut.

Castor In wheel alignment, the backward or forward tilt of the steering axis. Castor is positive when the steering axis is inclined rearward at the top.

Catalytic converter A silencer-like device in the exhaust system which converts certain pollutants in the exhaust gases into less harmful substances.

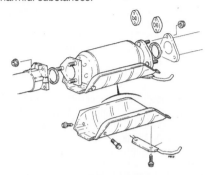

Catalytic converter

Circlip A ring-shaped clip used to prevent endwise movement of cylindrical parts and shafts. An internal circlip is installed in a groove in a housing; an external circlip fits into a groove on the outside of a cylindrical piece such as a shaft.

Clearance The amount of space between two parts. For example, between a piston and a cylinder, between a bearing and a journal, etc.

Coil spring A spiral of elastic steel found in various sizes throughout a vehicle, for example as a springing medium in the suspension and in the valve train.

Compression Reduction in volume, and increase in pressure and temperature, of a gas, caused by squeezing it into a smaller space.

Compression ratio The relationship between cylinder volume when the piston is at top dead centre and cylinder volume when the piston is at bottom dead centre.

Constant velocity (CV) joint A type of universal joint that cancels out vibrations caused by driving power being transmitted through an angle.

Core plug A disc or cup-shaped metal device inserted in a hole in a casting through which core was removed when the casting was formed. Also known as a freeze plug or expansion plug.

Crankcase The lower part of the engine block in which the crankshaft rotates.

Crankshaft The main rotating member, or shaft, running the length of the crankcase, with offset "throws" to which the connecting rods are attached.

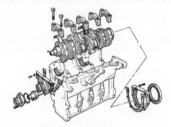

Crankshaft assembly

Crocodile clip See Alligator clip

D

Diagnostic code Code numbers obtained by accessing the diagnostic mode of an engine management computer. This code can be used to determine the area in the system where a malfunction may be located.

Disc brake A brake design incorporating a rotating disc onto which brake pads are squeezed. The resulting friction converts the energy of a moving vehicle into heat.

Double-overhead cam (DOHC) An engine that uses two overhead camshafts, usually one for the intake valves and one for the exhaust valves.

Drivebelt(s) The belt(s) used to drive accessories such as the alternator, water pump, power steering pump, air conditioning compressor, etc. off the crankshaft pulley.

Accessory drivebelts

Driveshaft Any shaft used to transmit motion. Commonly used when referring to the axleshafts on a front wheel drive vehicle.

Drum brake A type of brake using a drum-shaped metal cylinder attached to the inner surface of the wheel. When the brake pedal is pressed, curved brake shoes with friction linings press against the inside of the drum to slow or stop the vehicle.

E

EGR valve A valve used to introduce exhaust gases into the intake air stream.

Electronic control unit (ECU) A computer which controls (for instance) ignition and fuel injection systems, or an anti-lock braking system. For more information refer to the *Haynes Automotive Electrical and Electronic Systems Manual.*

Electronic Fuel Injection (EFI) A computer controlled fuel system that distributes fuel through an injector located in each intake port of the engine.

Emergency brake A braking system, independent of the main hydraulic system, that can be used to slow or stop the vehicle if the primary brakes fail, or to hold the vehicle stationary even though the brake pedal isn't depressed. It usually consists of a hand lever that actuates either front or rear brakes mechanically through a series of cables and linkages. Also known as a handbrake or parking brake.

Endfloat The amount of lengthwise movement between two parts. As applied to a crankshaft, the distance that the crankshaft can move forward and back in the cylinder block.

Engine management system (EMS) A computer controlled system which manages the fuel injection and the ignition systems in an integrated fashion.

Exhaust manifold A part with several passages through which exhaust gases leave the engine combustion chambers and enter the exhaust pipe.

F

Fan clutch A viscous (fluid) drive coupling device which permits variable engine fan speeds in relation to engine speeds.

Feeler blade A thin strip or blade of hardened steel, ground to an exact thickness, used to check or measure clearances between parts.

Feeler blade

Firing order The order in which the engine cylinders fire, or deliver their power strokes, beginning with the number one cylinder.

Flywheel A heavy spinning wheel in which energy is absorbed and stored by means of momentum. On cars, the flywheel is attached to the crankshaft to smooth out firing impulses.

Free play The amount of travel before any action takes place. The "looseness" in a linkage, or an assembly of parts, between the initial application of force and actual movement. For example, the distance the brake pedal moves before the pistons in the master cylinder are actuated.

Fuse An electrical device which protects a circuit against accidental overload. The typical fuse contains a soft piece of metal which is calibrated to melt at a predetermined current flow (expressed as amps) and break the circuit.

Fusible link A circuit protection device consisting of a conductor surrounded by heat-resistant insulation. The conductor is smaller than the wire it protects, so it acts as the weakest link in the circuit. Unlike a blown fuse, a failed fusible link must frequently be cut from the wire for replacement.

G

Gap The distance the spark must travel in jumping from the centre electrode to the side electrode in a spark plug. Also refers to the spacing between the points in a contact breaker assembly in a conventional points-type ignition, or to the distance between the reluctor or rotor and the pickup coil in an electronic ignition.

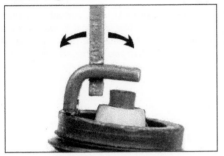

Adjusting spark plug gap

Gasket Any thin, soft material - usually cork, cardboard, asbestos or soft metal - installed between two metal surfaces to ensure a good seal. For instance, the cylinder head gasket seals the joint between the block and the cylinder head.

Gasket

Gauge An instrument panel display used to monitor engine conditions. A gauge with a movable pointer on a dial or a fixed scale is an analogue gauge. A gauge with a numerical readout is called a digital gauge.

H

Halfshaft A rotating shaft that transmits power from the final drive unit to a drive wheel, usually when referring to a live rear axle.

Harmonic balancer A device designed to reduce torsion or twisting vibration in the crankshaft. May be incorporated in the crankshaft pulley. Also known as a vibration damper.

Hone An abrasive tool for correcting small irregularities or differences in diameter in an engine cylinder, brake cylinder, etc.

Hydraulic tappet A tappet that utilises hydraulic pressure from the engine's lubrication system to maintain zero clearance (constant contact with both camshaft and valve stem). Automatically adjusts to variation in valve stem length. Hydraulic tappets also reduce valve noise.

I

Ignition timing The moment at which the spark plug fires, usually expressed in the number of crankshaft degrees before the piston reaches the top of its stroke.

Inlet manifold A tube or housing with passages through which flows the air-fuel mixture (carburettor vehicles and vehicles with throttle body injection) or air only (port fuel-injected vehicles) to the port openings in the cylinder head.

J

Jump start Starting the engine of a vehicle with a discharged or weak battery by attaching jump leads from the weak battery to a charged or helper battery.

L

Load Sensing Proportioning Valve (LSPV) A brake hydraulic system control valve that works like a proportioning valve, but also takes into consideration the amount of weight carried by the rear axle.

Locknut A nut used to lock an adjustment nut, or other threaded component, in place. For example, a locknut is employed to keep the adjusting nut on the rocker arm in position.

Lockwasher A form of washer designed to prevent an attaching nut from working loose.

M

MacPherson strut A type of front suspension system devised by Earle MacPherson at Ford of England. In its original form, a simple lateral link with the anti-roll bar creates the lower control arm. A long strut - an integral coil spring and shock absorber - is mounted between the body and the steering knuckle. Many modern so-called MacPherson strut systems use a conventional lower A-arm and don't rely on the anti-roll bar for location.

Multimeter An electrical test instrument with the capability to measure voltage, current and resistance.

N

NOx Oxides of Nitrogen. A common toxic pollutant emitted by petrol and diesel engines at higher temperatures.

O

Ohm The unit of electrical resistance. One volt applied to a resistance of one ohm will produce a current of one amp.

Ohmmeter An instrument for measuring electrical resistance.

O-ring A type of sealing ring made of a special rubber-like material; in use, the O-ring is compressed into a groove to provide the sealing action.

Overhead cam (ohc) engine An engine with the camshaft(s) located on top of the cylinder head(s).

Overhead valve (ohv) engine An engine with the valves located in the cylinder head, but with the camshaft located in the engine block.

Oxygen sensor A device installed in the engine exhaust manifold, which senses the oxygen content in the exhaust and converts this information into an electric current. Also called a Lambda sensor.

P

Phillips screw A type of screw head having a cross instead of a slot for a corresponding type of screwdriver.

Plastigage A thin strip of plastic thread, available in different sizes, used for measuring clearances. For example, a strip of Plastigage is laid across a bearing journal. The parts are assembled and dismantled; the width of the crushed strip indicates the clearance between journal and bearing.

Plastigage

Propeller shaft The long hollow tube with universal joints at both ends that carries power from the transmission to the differential on front-engined rear wheel drive vehicles.

Proportioning valve A hydraulic control valve which limits the amount of pressure to the rear brakes during panic stops to prevent wheel lock-up.

R

Rack-and-pinion steering A steering system with a pinion gear on the end of the steering shaft that mates with a rack (think of a geared wheel opened up and laid flat). When the steering wheel is turned, the pinion turns, moving the rack to the left or right. This movement is transmitted through the track rods to the steering arms at the wheels.

Radiator A liquid-to-air heat transfer device designed to reduce the temperature of the coolant in an internal combustion engine cooling system.

Refrigerant Any substance used as a heat transfer agent in an air-conditioning system. R-12 has been the principle refrigerant for many years; recently, however, manufacturers have begun using R-134a, a non-CFC substance that is considered less harmful to the ozone in the upper atmosphere.

Rocker arm A lever arm that rocks on a shaft or pivots on a stud. In an overhead valve engine, the rocker arm converts the upward movement of the pushrod into a downward movement to open a valve.

Rotor In a distributor, the rotating device inside the cap that connects the centre electrode and the outer terminals as it turns, distributing the high voltage from the coil secondary winding to the proper spark plug. Also, that part of an alternator which rotates inside the stator. Also, the rotating assembly of a turbocharger, including the compressor wheel, shaft and turbine wheel.

Runout The amount of wobble (in-and-out movement) of a gear or wheel as it's rotated. The amount a shaft rotates "out-of-true." The out-of-round condition of a rotating part.

S

Sealant A liquid or paste used to prevent leakage at a joint. Sometimes used in conjunction with a gasket.

Sealed beam lamp An older headlight design which integrates the reflector, lens and filaments into a hermetically-sealed one-piece unit. When a filament burns out or the lens cracks, the entire unit is simply replaced.

Serpentine drivebelt A single, long, wide accessory drivebelt that's used on some newer vehicles to drive all the accessories, instead of a series of smaller, shorter belts. Serpentine drivebelts are usually tensioned by an automatic tensioner.

Serpentine drivebelt

Shim Thin spacer, commonly used to adjust the clearance or relative positions between two parts. For example, shims inserted into or under bucket tappets control valve clearances. Clearance is adjusted by changing the thickness of the shim.

Slide hammer A special puller that screws into or hooks onto a component such as a shaft or bearing; a heavy sliding handle on the shaft bottoms against the end of the shaft to knock the component free.

Sprocket A tooth or projection on the periphery of a wheel, shaped to engage with a chain or drivebelt. Commonly used to refer to the sprocket wheel itself.

Starter inhibitor switch On vehicles with an automatic transmission, a switch that prevents starting if the vehicle is not in Neutral or Park.

Strut See MacPherson strut.

T

Tappet A cylindrical component which transmits motion from the cam to the valve stem, either directly or via a pushrod and rocker arm. Also called a cam follower.

Thermostat A heat-controlled valve that regulates the flow of coolant between the cylinder block and the radiator, so maintaining optimum engine operating temperature. A thermostat is also used in some air cleaners in which the temperature is regulated.

Thrust bearing The bearing in the clutch assembly that is moved in to the release levers by clutch pedal action to disengage the clutch. Also referred to as a release bearing.

Timing belt A toothed belt which drives the camshaft. Serious engine damage may result if it breaks in service.

Timing chain A chain which drives the camshaft.

Toe-in The amount the front wheels are closer together at the front than at the rear. On rear wheel drive vehicles, a slight amount of toe-in is usually specified to keep the front wheels running parallel on the road by offsetting other forces that tend to spread the wheels apart.

Toe-out The amount the front wheels are closer together at the rear than at the front. On front wheel drive vehicles, a slight amount of toe-out is usually specified.

Tools For full information on choosing and using tools, refer to the *Haynes Automotive Tools Manual.*

Tracer A stripe of a second colour applied to a wire insulator to distinguish that wire from another one with the same colour insulator.

Tune-up A process of accurate and careful adjustments and parts replacement to obtain the best possible engine performance.

Turbocharger A centrifugal device, driven by exhaust gases, that pressurises the intake air. Normally used to increase the power output from a given engine displacement, but can also be used primarily to reduce exhaust emissions (as on VW's "Umwelt" Diesel engine).

U

Universal joint or U-joint A double-pivoted connection for transmitting power from a driving to a driven shaft through an angle. A U-joint consists of two Y-shaped yokes and a cross-shaped member called the spider.

V

Valve A device through which the flow of liquid, gas, vacuum, or loose material in bulk may be started, stopped, or regulated by a movable part that opens, shuts, or partially obstructs one or more ports or passageways. A valve is also the movable part of such a device.

Valve clearance The clearance between the valve tip (the end of the valve stem) and the rocker arm or tappet. The valve clearance is measured when the valve is closed.

Vernier caliper A precision measuring instrument that measures inside and outside dimensions. Not quite as accurate as a micrometer, but more convenient.

Viscosity The thickness of a liquid or its resistance to flow.

Volt A unit for expressing electrical "pressure" in a circuit. One volt that will produce a current of one ampere through a resistance of one ohm.

W

Welding Various processes used to join metal items by heating the areas to be joined to a molten state and fusing them together. For more information refer to the *Haynes Automotive Welding Manual.*

Wiring diagram A drawing portraying the components and wires in a vehicle's electrical system, using standardised symbols. For more information refer to the *Haynes Automotive Electrical and Electronic Systems Manual.*

Note: *References throughout thos index are in the form* **"Chapter number"** • **"Page number"**